W9-DAT-934

THE PAPERS OF ALEXANDER HAMILTON

Alexander Hamilton, 1792. Oil portrait by John Trumbull.

THE PAPERS OF

Alexander Hamilton

VOLUME III: 1782–1786

HAROLD C. SYRETT, EDITOR

JACOB E. COOKE, ASSOCIATE EDITOR

COLUMBIA UNIVERSITY PRESS

NEW YORK AND LONDON, 1962

Frontispiece: Courtesy the Metropolitan Museum of Art,
gift of Henry G. Marquand, 1881

PREFACE

THIS EDITION of Alexander Hamilton's papers contains letters and other documents written by Hamilton, letters to Hamilton, and some documents (commissions, certificates, etc.) that directly concern Hamilton but were written neither by him nor to him. All letters and other documents have been printed in chronological order. Hamilton's legal papers will be published under the editorial direction of Professor Julius Goebel, Jr., of the School of Law, Columbia University.

Many letters and documents have been calendared. Such calendared items include routine letters and documents by Hamilton, routine letters to Hamilton, some of the letters or documents written by Hamilton for someone else, letters or documents which have not been found but which are known to have existed, letters or documents which have been erroneously attributed to Hamilton, and letters to or by Hamilton that deal exclusively with his legal practice.

The notes in these volumes are designed to provide information concerning the nature and location of each document, to identify Hamilton's correspondents and the individuals mentioned in the text, to explain events or ideas referred to in the text, and to point out textual variations or mistakes. Occasional departures from these standards can be attributed to a variety of reasons. In many cases the desired information has been supplied in an earlier note and can be found through the use of the index. Notes were not added when in the opinion of the editors the material in the text was either self-explanatory or common knowledge. The editors, moreover, did not think it desirable or necessary to provide full annotation for Hamilton's "Cash Book" and Hamilton's legal correspondence. Finally, the editors on some occasions were unable to find the desired information, and on other occasions the editors were remiss.

GUIDE TO EDITORIAL APPARATUS

I. SYMBOLS USED TO DESCRIBE MANUSCRIPTS

AD	Autograph Document
ADS	Autograph Document Signed
ADf	Autograph Draft
ADfS	Autograph Draft Signed
AL	Autograph Letter
ALS	Autograph Letter Signed
D	Document
DS	Document Signed
Df	Draft
DfS	Draft Signed
LS	Letter Signed
LC	Letter Book Copy
[S]	[S] is used with other symbols (AD[S], ADf[S], AL[S], D[S], Df[S], L[S]) to indicate that the signature on the document has been cropped or clipped.

II. MONETARY SYMBOLS AND ABBREVIATIONS

bf	Banco florin
V	Ecu
f	Florin
₶	Livre Tournois
medes	Maravedis (also md and mde)
d.	Penny or denier
ps	Piece of eight

£	Pound sterling or livre
Ry	Real
rs vn	Reals de vellon
rdr	Rix daller
s	Shilling, sou or sol (also expressed as /)
sti	Stiver

III. SHORT TITLES AND ABBREVIATIONS

Arch. des Aff. Etr., Corr. Pol., Etats-Unis
Transcripts or photostats from the French Foreign Office deposited in the Library of Congress.

Bemis, *The Diplomacy of the American Revolution*
Samuel F. Bemis, *The Diplomacy of the American Revolution* (New York, 1935).

Brant, *Madison*
Irving Brant, *James Madison* (Indianapolis, 1948–1961).

Burnett, *Letters*
Edmund C. Burnett, ed., *Letters of Members of the Continental Congress* (Washington, 1921–1938).

East, *Business Enterprise in the American Revolutionary Era*
Robert A. East, *Business Enterprise in the American Revolutionary Era* (New York, 1938).

Freeman, *Washington*
Douglas Southall Freeman, *George Washington* (New York, 1948–1954).

Gottschalk, *Letters of Lafayette to Washington*
Louis B. Gottschalk, ed., *The Letters of Lafayette to Washington, 1777–1779* (New York, 1944).

GW
John C. Fitzpatrick, *The Writings of George Washington* (Washington, 1931–1944).

Hamilton, *History*
John C. Hamilton, *Life of Alexander Hamilton, a History of the Republic of the United States of America* (Boston, 1879).

Hamilton, *Intimate Life*
Allan McLane Hamilton, *The Intimate Life of Alexander Hamilton* (New York, 1910).

Hamilton, *Life*
John C. Hamilton, *The Life of Alexander Hamilton* (New York, 1840).

Hawks, *The Official and Other Papers of Alexander Hamilton*	Francis L. Hawks, ed., *The Official and Other Papers of the Late Major Alexander Hamilton* (New York, 1842).
HCLW	Henry Cabot Lodge, ed., *The Works of Alexander Hamilton* (New York, 1904).
Heads of Families . . . 1790	*Heads of Families at the First Census of the United States Taken in the Year 1790, New York* (Washington, 1908).
JCC	*Journals of the Continental Congress, 1774–1789* (Washington, 1904–1937).
JCH Transcripts	John C. Hamilton Transcripts. These transcripts are owned by Mr. William H. Swan, Hampton Bays, New York, and have been placed on loan in the Columbia University Libraries.
JCHW	John C. Hamilton, ed., *The Works of Alexander Hamilton* (New York, 1851).
Laws of Massachusetts, 1786–1787	*Acts and Laws of the Commonwealth of Massachusetts, 1786–87* (Boston, 1893).
Laws of the State of New York, I	*Laws of the State of New York Passed at the Sessions of the Legislature Held in the Years 1777, 1778, 1779, 1780, 1781, 1782, 1783 and 1784 Inclusive, being the First Seven Sessions* (Albany, 1886).
Laws of the State of New York, II	*Laws of the State of New York Passed at the Sessions of the Legislature Held in the Years 1785, 1786, 1787 and 1788 Inclusive, being the Eighth, Ninth, Tenth, and Eleventh Sessions* (Albany, 1886).
Mitchell, *Hamilton*	Broadus Mitchell, *Alexander Hamilton, Youth to Maturity, 1775–1788* (New York, 1957).
Nevins, *History of the Bank of New York*	Allan Nevins, *History of the Bank of New York and Trust Company* (New York, 1934).

New Hampshire State Papers, VIII — Nathaniel Bouton, ed., *Documents and Records Relating to the State of New Hampshire* (Concord, 1874).

New York Assembly *Journal* — *Journal of the Assembly of the State of New York* (Publisher and place vary, 1782–1786).

New York Directory for 1786 — *New York Directory for 1786* (facsimile, New York, 1889).

New York Directory for 1790 — *The New York Directory and Register for the Year 1790* (New York, printed by Hodge, Allen, & Campbell, 1790).

New York Senate *Journal* — *Journal of the Senate of the State of New York* (Publisher and place vary, 1782–1786).

Platt, "Jeremiah Wadsworth" — John D. R. Platt, "Jeremiah Wadsworth: Federalist Entrepreneur" (Unpublished Ph.D. Dissertation, Columbia University, 1955).

PRO: F.O., or PRO: C.O. — Transcripts or photostats from the Public Records Office of Great Britain deposited in the Library of Congress.

Public Papers of George Clinton — *Public Papers of George Clinton* (New York and Albany, 1900).

Ramsing, "Alexander Hamilton," *Personalhistorisk tidsskrift* — Holger Utke Ramsing, "Alexander Hamilton og hans mødrene Slaegt. Tidsbilleder fra Dansk Vestindiens barndom," *Personalhistorisk tidsskrift,* 24 cm., 10 Raekke, 6 bd. (Copenhagen, 1939).

Robertson, *The Life of Miranda* — William S. Robertson, *The Life of Miranda* (Chapel Hill, 1929).

Schuyler, *Institution of the Society of the Cincinnati* — John Schuyler, *Institution of the Society of the Cincinnati, Formed by the Officers of the American Army of the Revolution, 1783* (New York, 1886).

Stokes, *Iconography of Manhattan* — I. N. Phelps Stokes, *The Iconography of Manhattan Island* (New York, 1926).

Walton, *Records of Vermont* — E. P. Walton, ed., *Records of the Governor and Council of the State of Vermont* (Montpelier, 1875).

Wharton, *Revolutionary Diplomatic Correspondence*   Francis Wharton, ed., *The Revolutionary Diplomatic Correspondence of the United States* (Washington, 1889).

IV. INDECIPHERABLE WORDS

Words or parts of words which could not be deciphered because of the illegibility of the writing or the mutilation of the manuscript have been indicated as follows:

1. ⟨– – – – –⟩ indicates illegible words with the number of dashes indicating the estimated number of illegible words.
2. Words or letters in broken brackets indicate a guess as to what the words or letters in question may be. If the source of the words or letters within the broken brackets is known, it has been given in a note.

V. CROSSED-OUT MATERIAL IN MANUSCRIPTS

Words or sentences crossed out by a writer in a manuscript have been handled in one of the three following ways:

1. They have been ignored, and the document or letter has been printed in its final version.
2. Crossed-out words and insertions for the crossed-out words have been described in the notes.
3. When the significance of a manuscript seems to warrant it, the crossed-out words have been retained, and the document has been printed as it was written.

VI. TEXTUAL CHANGES AND INSERTIONS

The following changes or insertions have been made in the letters and documents printed in these volumes:

1. Words or letters written above the line of print (for example, 9th) have been made even with the line of print (9th).
2. Punctuation and capitalization have been changed in those

instances where it seemed necessary to make clear the sense of the writer. A special effort has been made to eliminate the dash, which was such a popular eighteenth-century device.

3. When the place or date, or both, of a letter or document does not appear at the head of that letter or document, it has been inserted in the text in brackets. If either the place or date at the head of a letter or document is incomplete, the necessary additional material has been added in the text in brackets. For all but the best known localities or places, the name of the colony, state, or territory has been added in brackets at the head of a document or letter.

4. In calendared documents, place and date have been uniformly written out in full without the use of brackets. Thus "N. York, Octr. 8, '99" becomes "New York, October 8, 1799." If, however, substantive material is added to the place or date in a calendared document, such material is placed in brackets. Thus "Oxford, Jan. 6" becomes "Oxford [Massachusetts] January 6 [1788]."

5. When a writer made an unintentional slip comparable to a typographical error, one of the four following devices has been used:

a. It has been allowed to stand as written.

b. It has been corrected by inserting either one or more letters in brackets.

c. It has been corrected without indicating the change.

d. It has been explained in a note.

1 7 8 2

From James McHenry [1]

Baltimore 31st Jany. 1782

I reckon, my dear sir, among the contrasted events which have diversified my life, to have been made the confidant of the author of Publius,[2] and as a Senator of Maryland to have been present at Mr Chase's defence in our house of delegates against charges contained in your pieces.[3] I send you the proceedings which have been published and letters which have been passed between Major Giles and myself upon this occasion.[4] After you have considered the whole you will say what more I am to do. I withhold my opinion in this case in order that you may determine without the suspicion of a biass.

I have the honor   James McHenry

ALS, William L. Clements Library of the University of Michigan.

1. McHenry was elected to the Maryland Senate in September, 1781, and attended the session of the legislature which met in January, 1782.

2. The three "Publius" letters written by H were dated October 19, 26, and November 16, 1778. In them H had charged that Samuel Chase, then a delegate to the Continental Congress from Maryland, had, in anticipation of the arrival of the French fleet in America, used secret congressional information to corner the market on flour.

3. In January, 1782, John Cadwalader, a brigadier general of the Pennsylvania Militia who had moved to Maryland where he was elected a member of the House of Delegates, moved that as Chase had betrayed the public trust his appointment as a delegate to the Continental Congress be revoked. After evidence had been heard both for and against Chase, the House of Delegates, on January 16, 1782, exonerated him.

4. Major Edward Giles, first an aide-de-camp to Brigadier General Daniel Morgan and then to Major General William Smallwood, wrote McHenry that the evidence produced before the Maryland legislature had proved Chase innocent and urged McHenry to persuade the author of the "Publius" essays to retract his charges.

The proceedings to which McHenry referred were those of the Maryland House of Delegates. Both the proceedings and letters enclosed by McHenry are in the William L. Clements Library of the University of Michigan.

Receipt to Jacob Cuyler [1]

Albany, February 5, 1782. On behalf of Philip Schuyler, acknowledges receipt of twenty pounds and six shillings from Jacob Cuyler.

ADS, Mount Vernon Ladies' Association, Mount Vernon, Virginia.
   1. Jacob Cuyler, who represented Albany County in the New York legislature in 1777, was engaged during the Revolution in supplying the American army.

From Robert Morris [1]

Philadelphia, February 12, 1782. Sends the several receivers an "Advertisement respecting the Receivers of Continental Taxes," which states: "And whereas it is not only necessary that some precise mode be adopted for managing the public Business in this respect,[2] but also that the same be publickly known, so that all Persons concerned therein may have due notice thereof I have therefore established the following rules in that Behalf, for the Receivers who have been or shall be by me appointed."

LC, Robert Morris Papers, Library of Congress.
   1. H was not appointed receiver of continental taxes for New York until sometime between June 17 and July 2. On July 2, Morris, Superintendent of Finance, sent H his instructions which included a copy of this circular (Morris to H, July 2, 1782). H in turn sent this circular to Thomas Tillotson who replaced H as receiver in November, 1782 (see the second of two letters H wrote Tillotson on November 10, 1782).
   2. I.e., collecting the state quota.

To James McHenry [1]

[Albany, February 26, 1782]

Sir,

I am much obliged to you for the papers you transmitted me on the subject of Mr. C––e.[2] Nothing gives me greater pleasure on all occasions, than to see suspected and injured innocence vindicated, nor would any person more chearfully retract an ill-founded accusation, on conviction of its error, than myself. You know the motives and the grounds of my charges against Mr. C––e, at a period fertile in practices as pernicious, as base. You know that *I can have no* personal enmity to him, and that considerations of public good alone dictated my attack upon his conduct and character, influenced by a persuasion produced by the strongest authorities, that he was acting a part inconsistent with patriotism, or honor. You are not less convinced, that if the evidence of his innocence ballanced in my mind that of his guilt, I could not refuse it to my own feelings, to make him the most explicit and complete retribution. But hitherto, it is impossible, that this can be the case. My witnesses, one of them is intirely out of my reach, the other too remote to enable me to have yet known, what he may have to oppose to the late transactions in Mr. C--e's favour. The informations of both were too positive, their characters are too respectable to permit me lightly to relinquish the impressions of their testimony. I have too often seen public assemblies acquit guilt from prepossession, party spirit, want of formality or certainty (though there has been the greatest probability) in the evidence to allow myself to regard the determination of your's as conclusive. I respect however the decision of such a body too much not to be induced by it to *doubt* and *examine*. This I shall do and govern myself by the result.

As to the discovery of my name demanded with such preposterous vehemence, by a volunteer in the dispute, I conceive myself under no obligation to make it; especially to a person uninterested in the matter. I have esteemed Major [3] character; and am sorry for his sake that he has so indelicately entered the lists; and made himself, not only the champion of Mr. Ch--e's innocence in the present case, but of his virtues in general, certainly at best equivocal in spite of the Major's panygerics. He should have recollected, that by an alliance with his family, he did not ally himself with his principles; and that he degrades Mr. Ch--e, as well as commits himself by unnecessarily taking up the glove for him. I attribute it however to an imprudent generosity of temper, and forbear any strictures, that may wound him. You Sir, who are acquainted with me must be convinced that an apprehension of his, or any man's resentment is a motive incapable of operating upon me or having the least share either in the concealment of my name or in the moderate return I make to his invectives. I have the honor to &c.

Feby. 26 82

ADf, Hamilton Papers, Library of Congress.
1. This letter was crossed out, probably by J. C. Hamilton. It is incorrectly endorsed, probably by J. C. Hamilton, July 26, 1782. It probably was sent with a letter which H wrote McHenry on March 8, 1782.
2. Samuel Chase. See McHenry to H, January 31, 1782.
3. Major Edward Giles. The name was obliterated either by H or by someone else at a later date.

To George Washington

[Philadelphia, March 1, 1782]

Sir

I need not observe to yr Excellency that, Respect for the opinion of Congress will not permit me to be indifferent to the impressions they may receive of my conduct. On this principle, though I do not think the subject of the inclosed letter [1] of sufficient importance to request an official communication of it, yet I should be happy it might in some way be known to the members of that honorable body. Should they hereafter learn that though retained on the list of their officers I am not in the execution of the duties of my station, I wish them to be sensible that it is not a diminution of zeal which induces me voluntarily to withdraw my services, but that I only refrain from intruding them when circumstances seem to have made them either not necessary or not desired, and that I shall not receive emoluments without performing the conditions to which they were annexed. I also wish them to be apprised upon what footing my future continuance in the army is placed that they may judge how far it is expedient to permit it. I therefore take the liberty to request the favour of your Excellency to impart the knowlege of my situation in such manner as you think most convenient.[2]

I have the honor to be   With perfect respect   Yr. Excellency's Most Obed & humb.

ADf, Hamilton Papers, Library of Congress. In *JCHW*, I, 273–74, this letter is dated 1782.
1. The enclosure was H's letter to Washington of March 1, 1782, which follows this letter. Presumably the first letter of March 1 was a private one, and the second was public or official. As there is only a draft of the private letter, it is not certain that H sent it.
2. For information on H's army status, see the notes to his second letter to Washington on this date.

To George Washington

[Philadelphia, March 1, 1782]

Sir,

Your Excellency will, I am persuaded, readily admit the force of this sentiment, that though it is the duty of a good citizen to devote his services to the public, when it has occasion for them, he cannot with propriety, or delicacy to himself, obtrude them, when it either has, or appears to have none. The difficuties I experienced last campaign in obtaining a command will not suffer me to make any further application on that head.[1]

As I have many reasons to consider my being employed hereafter in a precarious light, the bare possibility of rendering an equivalent will not justify to my scruples the receiving any future emoluments from my commission. I therefore renounce from this time all claim to the compensations attached to my military station during the war or after it.[2] But I have motives which will not permit me to resolve on a total resignation.[3] I sincerely hope a prosperous train of affairs may continue to make it no inconvenience to decline the services of persons, whose zeal, in worse times, was found not altogether useless; but as the most promising appearances are often reversed by unforeseen disasters, and as unfortunate events may again make the same zeal of some value, I am unwilling to put it out of my power to renew my exertions in the common cause, in the line, in which I have hitherto acted. I shall accordingly retain my rank while I am permitted to do it, and take this opportunity to declare, that I shall be at all times ready to obey the call of the public, in any capacity civil, or military (consistent with what I owe to myself) in which there may be a prospect of my contributing to the final attainment of the object for which I embarked in the service.[4]

I have the honor to be   very Respectfully, Yr. Excellency's   Most Obedient servant   A Hamilton

Philadelphia
March 1   1782
His Excly General Washington

ALS, George Washington Papers, Library of Congress; ADf, Hamilton Papers, Library of Congress. The draft differs from the receiver's copy in minor particulars.

1. See H to Washington, April 27, 1781, Washington to H, April 27, 1781, H to Washington, May 2, 1781, and "General Orders," July 31, 1781.

2. According to a congressional resolve of December 31, 1781, officers who, like H, did not belong to the line of any state nor to any separate corps of the Army, were entitled to the same emoluments as other retiring officers.

3. H had been retained in service. On January 19, 1782, Benjamin Lincoln, Secretary at War, sent the President of the Continental Congress a list of officers to be retained in service under the terms of a congressional resolve of December 31, 1781. Among the officers on the list was "Lt. Colo. Hamilton." He was included, Lincoln explained, because of his "superior abilities & knowledge."

4. H's letter was forwarded by Washington to Lincoln who did not communicate it to Congress until March 13, 1783. Lincoln's letter, containing an extract from H's letter to Washington, was referred to a committee of Congress. The *Journals* of the Congress do not indicate what action the committee took (*JCC*, XXIV, 183).

Cash Book [1]

[March 1, 1782–1791] [2]

1)

Dr.   Pierre Van Cortlandt [3]   Cr

		£	
1784 Feby	To this sum due for the Clerkship of his son P. V. Cortlandt commenced	150	

AD, Hamilton Papers, Library of Congress.

1. H's "Cash Book" chiefly relates to his legal practice. Because it contains also his personal accounts and because the entries on his law practice serve as a guide to his professional life in the seventeen-eighties, it is included in these volumes.

H's entries have not been thoroughly annotated. An attempt has been made, however, to identify each individual with whom H had an account, but the individuals named in the various accounts have not been identified. Nor have the receipts which appear at the end of the cash book been annotated; many of the names mentioned in these receipts are identified in notes to the Cash Book proper, and many others are of persons too obscure to be found readily in any available source and, if found, too unimportant to warrant identification.

To facilitate cross references which H made and to indicate the accounts which appeared on the same page, the original pagination of the cash book has been retained. The page on which each account appears is placed above and to the left of the first account on that page.

2. The earliest entry in the cash book was March 1, 1782; the latest was in 1791. The book has been assigned, therefore, the first and terminal dates.

3. Van Cortlandt was the first lieutenant governor of New York, an office to which he was periodically re-elected for eighteen years.

Jacob LeRoy & Sons [4]

Dr.			Cr.	
1784	To this sum due for the Clerkship of his son Jas. LeRoy commenced this day	150	this sum given up as Mr. LeRoy did not continue his Clerkship	150
May	To opinion given in the case of Kelly & Lot	1.10.0		
	further advice & consuls	3.	Ballance due A Hamilton	12. 8
	Opinion on Question respecting renouncing Administration in favour of Mr I Labanel	1.10.0		
	Costs in the cause of Egb. Benson Administrator &c. v. Laffers	6.18		
		162.18.0		
1785 ug 4	Ballance of Acco. rendered this day	£ 12.18	By Cash	£ 12. 8
1786 eby 6.	To advice at different times consultations &c in the affairs of Broome & Plat	10.	1786 Decr. 5 Received Cash	£ 10

Abraham Ten Brook [5]

Dr.			Cr.	
1784 ebru	To this sum due for the Clerkship of his son Dirk Ten Brook commenced this day	150	1784 Oct. 11 By Cash	150

Isaac Sears [6]

Dr.			Cr.	
1783	To advice &c. in the affair of Mr. Soderstrom	3. 4	1784 1786 By Cash	£ 3. 4

4. The firm of Jacob Le Roy and Sons, merchants, was located at 31 Maiden Lane in New York City.

5. Abraham Ten Broeck (Brock) had been prominent in New York politics from 1761 when he entered the Provincial Assembly. From 1781 to 1794 he was judge of the Court of Common Pleas of Albany County. His son, Dirck, became an influential Albany lawyer and a member of the New York Assembly.

6. Sears, an ardent champion of American freedom during the pre-Revolutionary years and the Revolution, resumed his general mercantile business in New York City at the conclusion of the war in partnership with Pascal N. Smith.

Dr.   **Cr**

	To advice to M[ess]rs. Smith & Sears concerning attachment of Soderstroms effects. Quare		Aug 26	By Cash	7.10	
	To opinion concerning bills of Exchange ⟨in-⟩ dorsed by Sears & Smith	1.10	Aug. 26.	This day settled all accounts of Sears & Smith & Isaac Sears		
Aug 30	Retainer in a cause expected to be commenced by Soderstrom against Sears & Smith and advice therein at different times	6.			10.14	
		£ 10.14			£ 10.14	

3)

Dr.   Daniel Parker [7]   **Cr.**

1783 Decr.	To appearance for Capt Smith at his instance before the council	£ 6.8	1784 March 11	Received	£ 6.8

Dr.   Philip Van Renselaaer [8]   **Cr.**

1784	To this sum paid you by Mr. Robinson on my account		By rent of your house for months

3a)

Dr.   Manor of Renselaarwyck or Stephen Van Rensselaer [9]   **Cr.**

1783 Sept. 29	To an opinion given the executors this day	£ 3. 4	
1785	drawing a memorial to the Legislature	1.10	

7. Parker, a resident of Watertown, Massachusetts, was an army contractor during the American Revolution.

8. Van Rensselaer, a resident of Albany, had been commissary of public stores for the Northern Department during the Revolution.

9. Stephen Van Rensselaer was the eighth patroon of "Rensselaerswyck." On June 6, 1783, he married Margaret (or Margarita) Schuyler, daughter of Philip Schuyler.

Dr.   Cr.

pril	drawing act of Legis-lature Notice &c.	3. 4		By Cash of Leonard Gansevoort I believe	£ 200
ne 16	paid for exemplifica-tion of act	1.12	June	By ditto paid Mrs. Hamilton	100
86					
arch 16	drawing a bill to con-firm agreement made with other devisers &c.	3. 4			
ov 23	To paid Bill Hair dresser for yr. acct.	0.12			
87					
ctober	paid Francis J'ans for sundries ℔ acct.	4. 6.4			
ov 8	paid McClean & Co. for advertising notice upon application to Legisl:	4.10			
eby. 9	paid Morgan Lewis upon yr. Note	323. 5.6			

a)

Dr.   Alexander McCauley [10]   Cr.

84					
eby. 26.	To advice respecting two Mortgages	£ 3. 4		Received	£ 3. 4
786			1786		
ay	To this sum discounted upon your order upon Gardner Wilson & Co	384.10.4	May 20	By this sum liquidated with Assignees of Heart	768. 5.9
	To a note in my hands from Assignees of Heart payable first August next	384. 2.10	Aug 1	By this sum received of Assignees of Heart for amt. of Note per debit side	384. 2.10
	To paid for Reg. Mort-gage drawing assign-ment articles of Ag. & Counterpart postage for letters	4	☞	Inquire about the amount of Note to Gardner Wilson & Co. discounted	
	To this sum for my trouble in negotiating the matter	10			
ug. 1	To this sum lost on weighing the money in the bank	0. 9.11			
4	To this sum paid ye				

10. Macauley, a New York merchant and ship owner, was engaged in foreign trade, principally with the West Indies.

Dr.   Cr

draft in fav William Gillies & Co	132. 7.3	
Ballance carried to Fol 47	286.12.3	
	£1152. 8.7	1152. 8.7

Dr.   John Laurence [11]   Cr

1784	To this sum paid him in full ⅌ Receipt	settled	1784	By this sum bor- rowed of him for which he has my note	
1786	To this sum lent you	£100	1787 May	By this sum received upon your note dis- counted at the bank	99

4)
Dr.   The United States   Cr

1782 March 1	To ballance of Ac- count as per certificate dated this day bearing interest at six per Cent from the 4th of the same month.	£1128		By this sum received of Mr. Morris (being so much left in my hands out of taxes received about £80	

5)
Dr.   John Carter alias Church [12]   Cr

			1783	By this sum borrowed at Philadelphia	48.
1784 June 19	To this sum paid Cornelia De Peyster in part of the pur- chase money of a lot		1784	By this sum received of the bank on his ac- count by the hands of John Chaloner £1320 P. Cy.	1408

11. Laurence practiced law in New York City.

12. John B. Church, upon his arrival in the United States during the Revolution, had assumed the name of John Carter. From the numerous contracts he
made for supplying the American army and particularly from the contract
which he and Jeremiah Wadsworth secured for supplying the French forces
in America, Church acquired a fortune. While in the United States, he married
Angelica Schuyler, older sister of H's wife, Elizabeth. When Church returned
to England after the Revolution, he left the management of his American business affairs to H.

	in broadway	596
25	To ditto ditto	240. 4
Aug 25	This sum paid Ths. Smith on account of Mrs. De Peyster	500
October 13	Cash paid Mrs. De Peyster the ballance of the purchase money of the lot in broadway with interest	1502.10.8
☞	To John Chaloner for this sum remaining in his hands to be carried to your Credit	834. 8
		3673. 2.8
	Ballance due J Church	715. 4.5

June 18	By this sum received of the bank being for a bill of Exchange sent me on his account by John Chaloner drawn on James and Alex Stewart & discountd	597.12
J 24	By this sum received on a draft of James Bowne on John Delafield 373 dolls.	149. 4
	By this sum received of William Bowne for Js. Bownes draft on him	30.
Aug 16	By this sum received of Capt Geddes for Thomas Irvins draft on him	25. 0.5
	By this sum received for a draft sent me by Mr. Chaloner on James Buchanon & Co.	400
	By this sum received of Rand. son & Stewarts for bill sent by Mr. Chaloner	300
	By my draft on J Chaloner in favour of Daniel McCormick	382.16
Oct 13 1784	By my draft on J Chaloner for	1000
1785 June 1	Amots. of Interest on sums had for my own use to this day	57. 1
		4398. 7.1

		4388. 7.1

Aug 3d	To Cash paid you	£57.10
1785 Feby 1	To cash remitted by the Roebuck Packet paid freight of ditto	782.10.8 8
April 8	To cash paid Constable Rucker & Co. for a bill of Exchange remitted ⅌ Packet for £400 Sterling	753.15.6
June 9	To this sum remitted by Tankerville Packet	1057.17.8

1785 June 1	Ballance brought down	715. 4.5
July 7	By this sum recd. of Wm. Floyed	57.10
		772.14.5
1786 Jany	By this sum received by the hands of Jeremiah Wadsworth for your last half yry. div:	720
	By this sum received	

Dr.   Cr.

July 8	To this sum remitted by Carteret Packet & freight paid here	1000		of Bank of N York	72
			March 9	By this sum received of Isaac Moses & Co	1217.11.7
	To ballance carried forward to Fol 46	2355.11.11	May 3	By dividend N Y B	72.
			June 8	By amt. of Stock passed to my Credit	2400
			☞	By this sum received on 2 dividend of I. Moses & Co.	760.19.9
		£6015. 5.9			6015. 5.9

6)

Dr.   John Chaloner [13]   Cr.

1784	Pensylvania Currency		1784	Pensylvania Curr	
Feby. 26	To this sum received of the bank of NA by my order for a half years dividend on J. Carters dividend	£1320	Octr. 24	By my draft in favour of Jno. Mayly	46.17.6
			1784 Jany 7	By this sum paid for repairing my carriage	3.10
			Jany 13	By this sum paid for postage	2.6
			Feby 5.	By my draft in favour of Mr. Vickar	187.10
			10	By do. in favr. Mr N. Hoffman	114.16. 5
			12	postage of letters	3.10
			13	paid Philip Thompson on my account	34.13.9
				Cash pd. postage of a letter	1
					387.15
				Ballance due as per account received 28th Feby. 1784	932. 5
					1320
1784 Feby 28	To ballance of Accot. received this day	£932.5	1784 April	By my draft in favour of Haym Solomon	150
				By J Church for this sum to be carried to his credit	782. 5
1786 Nov 17	To ballance of J B Churchs last half yearly dividend	400		By Cash	400

13. Chaloner was a Philadelphia merchant who handled the Philadelphia business affairs of John B. Church. The business which H transacted with Chaloner was on behalf of Church.

7)
Dr.   Jeremiah Wadsworth [14]   Cr.

| 1786 Sept. 26. | To Cash paid N Hubbard per his receipt in bundle Receipts indorsed on my Note | £ 130— | 1782 | By this sum borrowed of him for which he has my note of hand Interest thereon to Sepr. 26. 86 | £ 106.13.4 23. 6.8 £ 130— |

8)
Dr.   Hercules Mulligan [15]   Cr.

1784	Cash To Cash paid Mr. Mulligan 20 Guineas	12.16 37. 6.8	1784 April	By amount of his account rendered this day	82.15
Aug 27	Cash	32.12.4			
October 13	Cash by a Check on the bank	30.			
1785	Cash lent	10			

9)
Dr.   State of New York—Contra   Cr.

| 1784 | To this sum lost in 76 by the desertion from the company; by which stoppage became impossible as ℔ Memorandum book No. 3 | 65.10 | 1784 | By ballance of account for sundries furnished my company of Artillery which was to have been deducted out of their pay | |
| | To this sum paid Mr. Thompson *Taylor* by Mr Chaloner on my accot for making Cloaths for the said company | 34.13.9 | | | |

14. Wadsworth, a merchant of Hartford, Connecticut, was a wartime partner of John B. Church.

15. Mulligan was a New York City merchant and tailor. His narrative of the life of H is in the Hamilton Papers, Library of Congress.

Dr.   Cr.

1785				
March 9	To ballance of Alsop Hunt and James Hunts account for leather Breeches supplied the company ꝑ Rects.	6. 8.7		
1786				
Sepr. 26	To amount of my ex- pences to Baltimore as Commissioner	76.18	By Cash	£ 76.18
Jany.	Advanced door keeper of the Assembly for wood.	20		
	To amount of expences to & at Philadelphia I believed paid			
	To amount of Acct. NY v Massachusetts	112		
	To my wages as dele- gate from 21st February when I commenced with Gansevort to 5th May when he left the City			
	Deduct omissions from May 26 when sworn in with Yates to 14 June when went to Convention from 30 July when returned to Congress to Oct 2d when removed			
	From October 4th. when attended at New House to 16 when closed for want of Congress			

10)

Dr.   James Rivington [16]   Cr.

1784			1784		
May 1	To Cash paid this day	£ 186.13.4	March 1	By amount of sun- dries as ꝑ account	£ 322.7.4
	To appearance as Council on two indict- ments	12.16			
1785			Feby 20	By sundries ꝑ acct. rendered this day	62.1
Feby 23	To Cash	100.		settled ꝑ Rect. in full	
Aug	To ditto	80.			

16. Rivington, a printer and bookseller, had edited *The Royal Gazette* during the British occupation of New York City. When the Americans re- gained the city, in 1783, he was forced to cease publication of his paper but remained in New York as a bookseller and tobacconist at No. 1 Queen Street.

1)
Dr.   Bank of New York   Cr.

1784 May 1	To this sum paid Mr. Maxwell in part of a house purchased on account of the bank	£150	1784 Aug. 16	By this sum paid to my order	£40	
	To this sum paid the Cashier being balance of subscription first moi.	150	25	Check in favour of Thomas Smith	500	
	To this sum received of James Buchanon & Co. for a bill of Exchange	400	27	Check in favour of James Barkley	84. 8	
Aug 15	To Received of Randall son & Stewards	300	27	Check in favour of Mr. Mulligan	32. 8	
Sepr. 2	received of Daniel McCormick	382.16		do Mr. Clapper	525.18	
do 13	To Cash	525.18		Check in favour of Fred. Jay	96	
25	To ditto	181.14.	Oct. 13	By Check in favr. Mr. Mulligan	30	
Oct 13	To Cash. 400 dolls.	160	ditto	By draft in favour Mrs. DePeyster	1502. 8	
	To Check from Solomon & Mordecai	1000	Nov. 7	ditto in favour of James Barkeley	50.	
				do. in fav of Pierre v. Cortlandt	40.	
		Dollars			Dollars	
Aug 6	To ballance due me this day To Cash	625 Dollars		By Check in favour of Wm. Backhouse	1250	
1787 Aug 31	To Cash for ballance due me this day	850 68/96				

12)
Dr.   John Marston & Brother [17]   Cr.

1784 June 1	To drawing a bond and Mortgage from v. Elseworth	£3. 4	June 23	By Cash received of Elseworth	£3.4
1785 Feby.	To opinion given this day respecting a conveyance to be made by Millner	1.10			

17. John Marston and Brother probably were sons of Thomas Marston, New York merchant.

Dr.   **Cr**

	To consultation with Doctr. Johnson and opinion thereon respecting his fathers will	3. 4	
1786 Feby 23	drawing power lease & release	4.	
Jun 29	drawing Notice on Mortg. & three copies fol 10	1.17.6	
1788 Octr.	To paid Samuel Loudon for advertising sale of mortgaged premisses	10.	November 13 88 Account rendered
		£ 20.11.6	

13)

Dr.   Paschal Smith [18]   **Cr.**

1784 July 16	To advice concerning ing the will of John Aspinwall	£ 1.10	1785 Jany 21	Received Cash	£ 23
S	Drawing notice on a Mortgage and advice concerning Wm. Smiths estate	2. 6			
S	opinion concerning Nuncupative will of Wm. Smith	1.10			
S	Drawing 6 leases & releases for father & brothers estate at £ 3.4 each	19. 4			
		23			
1785 March 19	Advice concerning a policy of Insurance of Aspinwalls	1.10			
Aug 9	drawing a release from Henry Smith to him as Administrator of his fathers estate	2.	November Account rendered due £ 16.12 By Cash		16.12

18. Smith was a partner in the firm of Sears and Smith. Overburdened with debt, Isaac Sears, in 1785, assigned his interest in the assets of the firm to Smith and sailed for China, where he died.

Dr.   Cr.

1786
Feby. 6   Draft of a law for
            Trustees of Aspinwall   3. 4
May 10   Opinion concerning do.   1.10
            advice &c in affair be-
            tween Executors of
            Aspinwall & Franks   3. 4
1788
            Advice concerning
            Part: concerns of Sears
            & Smith & concerning
            house erected on Mr.
            Smiths Lot   3. 4
            Costs in suit as Ads to
            Wm. Smith v Buffet   0.10
                                       ─────
                                       39.12

1788
Nov 17   To advice concerning
            a bond of Phil v Horne
            power of Atty &c.   0.10

14)
Dr.   William Duer [19]   Cr.

| 1784 Aug 14 | To cash lent 4 half Johs. 47 Guineas sent him by Mr. Ten Broeck amt. as ℔ his note to | £ 100 | 1786 May | By Cash | £ 100 |
| 1786 Aug 5. | To Cash lent. 223 dolls. | 89.4 | 1786 Nov. 1 | By Cash | £ 89.4 |

15)
Dr.   House Expences   Cr.

1784
Aug 15th   To this sum de-
            livered Mrs. Hamilton   18.13.4

19. Duer had been engaged in large-scale contracts for supplying the Revolutionary Army. After the War he was perhaps the best known New York speculator.

16)

Dr.   James Barkely [20]   Cr.

1784						
Aug. 24	To Cash paid poor tax laid on the house	3.15			By sundries as per account	70.16
	To Cash in full	67. 1				
		£ 70.16				
Novem 7	To Cash as ⅌ Receipt in Receipt book	50.		Nov 1—	By 1 Qrs. Rent due this day	50
				May 1:	By 2 quarters rent	100
1785						
January 8	To Cash paid house tax for poor	18. 9				
June 17	To Cash paid J R Meyer upon an order from J Barkely accepted	100				
	To Cash as per Check on the Bank for 211 Dollars Dated 30 Aug. 84 omitted qr. the Account	84. 8				
1786						
July 13	To Cash pd. J R Meyers pursuant to award	126. 0.10				
	Amt. of your order in favour of Richard Platt dated 22 Sepr 85 omitted	239. 7				
	Ditto dated 27 Sep. 85 omitted	60.13				

17)

Dr.   Leonard Cutting [21]   Cr.

1784			1785
Nov	To Cash lent	£ 20	March 10. Your half of 16/ re-

20. James Barclay was an auctioneer at 14 Hanover Square, New York City.
21. This may have been Leonard Cutting, an Episcopal clergyman, who was a Loyalist during the Revolution. Although he remained in the United States after the war, little is known of his subsequent life. There is also a possibility that it may have been Leonard M. Cutting, attorney at law, who opened his notary public and conveyancing office at 71 King Street, New York City, in 1786.

Dr.   Cr.

<table>
<tr><td>1785
April</td><td>To ditto</td><td>42.11.6</td><td></td><td>ceived of J Mellores
for drawing releases</td><td>0. 8</td></tr>
<tr><td>July 7</td><td>To ditto received by
him</td><td>4.17.3</td><td></td><td></td><td></td></tr>
<tr><td>Nov. 14</td><td>To paid for a Cask
of Porter</td><td>6. 6</td><td></td><td></td><td></td></tr>
<tr><td>1786</td><td>this sum advanced you</td><td>8.</td><td></td><td></td><td></td></tr>
<tr><td>March 22</td><td>Cash advanced you</td><td>16.</td><td></td><td></td><td></td></tr>
</table>

18)

Dr.   Philip Schuyler [22]   Cr.

<table>
<tr><td>1784</td><td>To paid Fred: Jay's
accot</td><td>22.11.6</td><td>April 14</td><td>By cash received of
Israel Underhill for
rent</td><td>£ 14</td></tr>
<tr><td></td><td>To paid Philandr
Brasier for carpeting</td><td>21.</td><td></td><td></td><td></td></tr>
<tr><td></td><td>To paid Guion &
Carty for sugar &c</td><td>23.10.3</td><td></td><td></td><td></td></tr>
<tr><td>1785
Jan 17</td><td>To paid H mulligans
acct.</td><td>21.19.10</td><td></td><td></td><td></td></tr>
<tr><td>Feby. 23</td><td>To James Rivington
for a set silver salts
charged to me</td><td>11. 4</td><td></td><td></td><td></td></tr>
<tr><td>March 5</td><td>To Cash lent Johnny</td><td>3. 5.6</td><td></td><td></td><td></td></tr>
<tr><td>17</td><td>ditto ℔ Sums Book</td><td>8.16</td><td></td><td></td><td></td></tr>
<tr><td>June 6</td><td>To Cash paid John
Rounsawell for a horse
he had of him</td><td>7.12</td><td></td><td></td><td></td></tr>
<tr><td>June 7</td><td>To Cash paid J
Minshutts draft on you
in fav of Alex Leckie</td><td>19.14.4½</td><td></td><td></td><td></td></tr>
<tr><td></td><td>To paid Js. Bell Hair
dresser to John Schuy-
ler paid April 16</td><td>4. 5.4</td><td></td><td></td><td></td></tr>
<tr><td>July 20</td><td>To paid Timothy
Wood for Boots &c
furnished to John ℔
Rect.</td><td>3. 8</td><td></td><td></td><td></td></tr>
<tr><td>Aug 30</td><td>To paid Nichols.
Hoffman for 5 barrels
of cider had Nov. 16,
84</td><td>5</td><td></td><td></td><td></td></tr>
<tr><td></td><td>To paid Ritson &
Bayard per accot. &
Receipt omitted</td><td>9. 8.2</td><td></td><td></td><td></td></tr>
<tr><td>Oct 1</td><td>To paid Walter
Becker for a Hat for
Philip</td><td>2</td><td></td><td></td><td></td></tr>
</table>

22. H's father-in-law.

Dr.   **Cr.**

Decr.	To paid Vanderbilt his accot. for shoes furnished himself & son	3.17
1786		
Jany 4	To paid for book for Phillip	1.
27	To paid Chs. Robertson for John & Philip	4.10.10
Jany 31	To deliverd Phillip for wood at College	13. 6
May 22	paid Barnes & Livingston for some China had sometime since	1.12
	Cash advanced Mrs. Schuyler	.16
June 16	gave Philip to purchase Livy's Ritteston	2.
	paid his Tutor for private Tuition (James Hardie)	1.17.4
	To paid a Gardiner his expences to Albany Oct 29 past	1. 0.0
Augt. 3	To Cash pd. Rot. Harpur for Copy of Poll lists	10. 0.0
26	To Cash advanced Philip to pay for Euclids elements	0.18.8
	To paid Remsen for deed to Skidmore	2.16
	To advanced Philip	£3
	To this sum advanced Phillip by Mr De Heart to purchase a Geo: book	0.14.6

19)

Dr.   Robert Watts [23]   **Cr.**

1784					
	To draft of deeds to Mr. Stephen Schuyler for Mr. Kennedy & wife pd. Mr. Popham	3.4	Decr. 12.	By Cash	£3.4

23. Watts, listed in *The New York Directory and Register for the Year 1790* (New York, 1790), as living on Great Dock Street, was a director of the Bank of New York.

•r. Corporation of Albany **Cr.**

•86		
)ctober	To my services Retainer attendance on hearing &c. in a cause before the Commissioners of the land office	15.	

o)

)r. Malachi Treat [24] **Cr.**

			1785		
784	To a negro wench Peggy sold him	£90		By his account for care and medicines of the wench	10
				By this sum received of Mr. Lowe	70

)r. Leonard Laurence [25] **Cr.**

			1785		
785	To Cash paid this day	£24.0.7	Aug	By this sum received of John Hunt	24.0.7
uly					

21)

Dr. George Harris [26] **Cr.**

			1785		
1785	To Cash paid ℔ Rect.	£25.18.4	June 17	By this sum received of Mary Harris Executrix of Js. Harris	32.15.9
July 23					
Decr. 3	To ditto	6. 7.5			
		£32.15.9	Decr. 23.	By Cash received in full for bond against Thomas & Fowler	£34. 2.7
April 8	To Cash by a Check upon the bank	£34. 2.7			
1786	To amt. of Costs in your suit agt. John			By John Ths. Sheriff per amt. of judgment against Treadwell received by him but	

24. Treat was a New York physician whose office was at 18 Little Queen Street.

25. Leonard Lawrence of Queens County, New York, had been a Loyalist during the Revolution.

26. In H's legal papers there are several bonds belonging to George Harris, but no information on him has been found.

Dr.   Cr

Hawkins	10.13.9	not paid	153. 7.2
To do. in yr. suit agt.		I presume *this has*	
S. Treadwell	9.10.3	*been settled*	
		Aug 28. 1797	

Dr.   Augustus V Cortlandt [27]   Cr

1785		1785	
July 22d.	Cash paid ℔ Receipt £383.18.7	June 6	By this sum received
			of Nicholas Jones £383.18.7
1786			
	To draft of two deeds		
	for Executors of		
	Chambers one to		
	Crommelin the other		
	to Laurence £6. 8		Received £6. 8

22)

Dr.   Aaron Burr [28]   Cr

1785		
	To one half the Tavern	
	expence of a reference	
	between Ducher &	
	Vacher paid Simmons 1.15.3	

Dr.   Johannes Hardenbergh [29]   Cr.

1785		1785	
June 25	To Cash paid Sec-	Sep 1.	By Cash received £46.1.3
	retary for extracts of		
	records 1.1.3		
July	To 9 days absence to		
	try your cause at £5		
	per day 45		

Dr.   Havens [30]   Cr.

1788		
Nov 20.	To opinion in writing	
	on two cases stated £3.4	

27. Van Cortlandt, a New York landowner, had been city clerk under the King's commission in the seventeen-fifties.

28. Burr was at this time practicing law in New York. H, as this entry reveals, was occasionally associated with him in law practice.

29. Johannes Hardenbergh of Ulster County, New York, had been a deputy to New York's first Provincial Congress.

30. As Havens was a common name in New York, it is not possible without a first name, to determine the Havens for whom H wrote an opinion.

3)
Dr.   John P. Waldrom [31]   Cr.

1785 | Retainers in suits against ten persons at £1.10 each | 15 | |

Dr.   Frederick Jay [32]   Cr.

1785 July 26. | To drawing an assignment pursuant to a writ for a waterlot | £5 | |

4)
Dr.   James Price [33]   Cr.

1785 July 28 | To advice concerning several matters | £3. 4 | 1785 | By Cash received as a fee 15 Guineas | £28 |
| To extra retainers in three Defendant causes 3 Guineas | 5.12 | | | |

5)
Dr.   John Hewlet [34]   Cr.

1784 July 21 | To advice concerning a will of Townshend | £1.17.4 | |

1786 Feby. 1. | Opinion on case with Birdsall | 1.10 | |

6)
Dr.   George Powers [35]   Cr.

1785 Jany 5 | drawing notice of sale of mortgaged premises | £1.10 | By Cash received | £1.10 |

31. Waldrom was a farmer in Harlem.
32. Jay, brother of John Jay, was an auctioneer at 11 Queen Street (*The New York Directory for 1786*, 35).
33. The census for 1790 lists three persons named James Price in Albany County (*Heads of Families . . . 1790, New York* [Washington, 1908], 14, 32, 37).
34. Hewlett, a resident of Queens County, New York, had been a Loyalist during the Revolution.
35. Powers purchased Fraunces Tavern in New York City in 1785.

27)
Dr.   Robert Bonne [36]   Cr

1784			
	drawing a petition &c. respecting rents due to persons for houses within the British lines	£ 1.10	

28)
Dr.   Assignees of John DeWindt Junr. [37]   Cr

1785			
	drawing a petition and bill to be passed into a law	£ 3	
May 6	Advice	1.10	
June 17	Advice and drawing notice to Creds.	2.	

29)
Dr.   Phillip Kissick [38]   Cr.

1785			1785		
June	To advice concerning a mortgage	£ 3. 0	Nov 29	By Cash	£ 11.10
Aug 5	Amount of Costs in suit of J. Leake ℔ acct. rendered	3.11			
	ditto in suit of V Kuren & Braisser	3. 9.3			

30)
Dr.   Nicholas Lowe [39]   Cr.

1785			
	drawing an Assignment from Soderstrom to you	£ 2	

36. Probably Robert Bowne whose retail store was at 39 Queen Street, New York City.

37. DeWindt lived on Maiden Lane in New York City.

38. This is probably the same Philip Kuysick who in 1782 announced his intention of going to England and offered for sale his tavern in New York City.

39. Nicholas Low, a member of an important Colonial merchant family, continued his commercial activities during and after the war. He was the largest stockholder in the Bank of New York.

Dr.   Cr.

Decr. 11.   Advice concerning a
            power of Attorney to
            Laurin   1.10
            Advice concerning Is-
            raels affair   1.10
            advice & appearance in
            Admiralty cause

31)
Dr.   Goadsby [40]   Cr.

1785
            To opinion concerning   By Cash received in full   £7.18
            attachmt.   £1.10
            To appearance as
            Council before the
            Assembly   6. 8   _____

Dr.   Effingham Laurence [41]   Cr.

1787
Aug 22   To advice concerning
         Bernes affair, inspec-
         tion of deeds &c.   3.4

32)
Dr.   John Murray [42]   Cr.

1785
         Advice concerning an
         offer of Paris to pay in
         certificates   £1.10
Nov. 30 Advice concerning the
         propriety of suing a
         person in whose hands
         goods were attached   1.10

1786
Aug 5   Appearance at Quarter
         session in the affair of
         the Coppias   1.10

1788
May 4.   Opinion concerning
         Lord Hollands estate   2.

40. Thomas Goadsby, according to the papers in H's legal file, was a New
York City merchant.
41. Effingham Lawrence, located at 227 Queen Street, New York City,
was druggist and apothecary to the New York Medical Society.
42. Murray, a member of the New York Chamber of Commerce, was one
of the city's most influential merchants.

33)
Dr.   Isaac Moses & Moses Meyers [43]   Cr

1785		
Aug 2.	Advice concerning a Brigantine conveyed to Mr. Ludlow	1.10

34)
Dr.   Trustees of Isaac Moses [44]   Cr

1786					
Nov. 25	for drawing assignment £ 10. actually paid for engrossing do	1.	May 17	By cash received of Henry	£ 15. 9.
	Drawing release of Dower	2.			
	actually paid for engrossing it	0. 8			
1786	paid for Copy of Assignment for Trustees in Holland	0.13.4			
March 9	paid Remsen for four deeds of the real estate of Isaac Moses per his account settled this day	12.16.			
	paid for a second copy of Assignment & notary for certifying				
July	To Cash paid Moses Meyers	15. 9.			
1788					
October	To paid Sam Loudon for advertising notice to Creditors	1.18			
	paid Do. for advertising sale of houses & lots	2.14			

35)
Dr.   Samuel Fraunces [45]   Cr.

1786			1785		
	To Cash paid Judah	£ 24.12	Decr. 18	By Cash received of Executors of Gifford	24.12
March 12.	To Cash lent	1.17.4			

43. Moses and Myers were New York City merchants who engaged extensively in foreign trade.

44. The bankruptcy of Isaac Moses in 1786 was the subject of correspondence between Jeremiah Wadsworth and H in 1785. See H to Wadsworth, April 7, 1785.

45. Fraunces was the proprietor of a well-known tavern in New York City.

r.   Laurance and Morris [46]   Cr.

86
ny 6.   To this sum lent   £200.   By your note for 200 discounted
arch 24. To my fee for trying   at bank–Dis   198.14.4
        your cause Majorel   5.

5)
r.   Gaspard Joseph Amand Ducher [47]   Cr.

86			1786		
ay 10	paid postage of a letter under cover to me to Mr. Sabatier De Catres	£0.12.0	Jany 4	by this sum borrowed of him for which he has my bond	£600
ne 3d.	paid postage	1.2			
	settled & paid	0.13.2	87 Sepr 24	By interest on ditto to the fourth of May 1788	98
					698

For this sum he has
two bonds which are
duplicates of each
other of this date
payable the 4th of
May Qr. what year

r.   John Cortlandt Schuyler [48]   Cr.

86
ny 28   To this sum paid Kelly
        upon his Note   £70. 2
ug 30   To paid Mr. Harpur
        for copy of records   0.16
March   To paid E Basset amt.
        of Jud agt. you   100. 3. 5

87
uly 28 Interest on the first &
        last sum to this day at
        7 ℔ Ct   9.17.10
                             £180.19. 3
                  cash   9
        for which sum I have
        his bond and mortgage £181

46. The firm of Thomas Lawrence and Jacob Morris, merchants, was located
at 83 Broadway, New York City.
47. Ducher was appointed vice-consul at Portsmouth, New Hampshire, in
1786 and was transferred to Wilmington, North Carolina, in 1787. He returned to France late in 1789 or early in 1790.
48. Schuyler was a nephew of Philip Schuyler.

37)

Dr.   The Agents of the Proprietors of Waway [49]   Cr

1786		
March 22d	To Account for advice & services rendered this day attending a month at Chester and divers attendance at New York	£150

Dr.   Dirk Tenbroeck [50]   Cr

1786			1786		
March 22.	To Cash lent	£16.16	March 26.	By Cash	£16.16

38)

Dr.   Baron de Polnitz [51]   Cr

1786					
May 29.	To Cash paid a Plumber for work done to the house in the outward per Rect. Peter Newman	£9. 4.3		By error	£ 6
				By Cash in full	231.16.4
July 28	To the sum advanced his daughter Wilhelmina for her maintenance	50.			
Aug. 26	To ditto ditto	18.			
Febr. 7	To Cash paid Abigail Beach for board of his sons ℈ Rect. Js. Akins	13			
19	To Cash paid Miss W Polnitz	20			
Nov 16	To Cash paid Musick Master	4.10			
21	To Cash paid Abigail Beach for boarding				

49. This bill was for a case in which H represented the proprietors of the Waywayanda land patent.

50. Dirck Ten Broeck, a lawyer of Albany, often represented Albany County in the New York Assembly.

51. Friedrich Charles Hans Bruno, Baron von Poellnitz was the proprietor of a widely publicized experimental farm in Manhattan. It consisted of twenty-two and one-half acres of land situated on Broadway between 8th and 10th Streets.

r.   **Cr.**

	your two sons ℔ J Akins Rec	13
ecr. 4	To Cash paid Miss Polnitz	16
13	To cash paid Mrs. Seton for 1 Quarters board due the 4th instant	10
87 ny.	To do. paid do. 1 Quarters board due 4th March	20
bru 2	to paid Abigail Beach for board of two sons to Jany 29	14
16	To paid Mrs. Seton for the ensuing quarters board of Miss Polnitz	15
arch 4	To paid do. for To cash paid Miss Polnitz the 18 of January omitted	8
22	To paid F. Childs for advertising your house	1. 4
arch 27	To cash paid taxes of house	9.11.8
pril 3	To cash paid Miss Polnitz	8
	Interest on ditto	

))

r.   **Rodman Field** [52]   **Cr.**

85 ug 16	To advice at different times concerning a deed of gift	£3.

r.   **Robert Lenox** [53]   **Cr.**

85 ug. 18	To advice concerning a certain Note	£1.10

52. According to papers in H's legal file, Field was from Bergen County, New Jersey.

53. Lenox had traded with the British during the war and remained in New York as a merchant at the war's end.

Dr.

Decr. 12.   To advice in writing
            concerning bill of Ex-
            change of Millers
            & Co.   3. 4

40)

Dr.   Henry A. Williams [54]   C

1785
Aug 18   For drawing adver-
          tisement of a sale
          upon a Mortgage of
          Skencks   £ 1.10
  [24   To Cash pd. S.
          Loudon for advertising
          the same for sale   .12
          To Ditto for Contg.
          Ditto 39 times (as
          per his acct.
          rendered)   7.16] [55]

Dr.   John Delafield [56]   Cᵣ

1785   Memo: I am not cer-
Aug 26.   To Cash paid S Jones   tain but this is paid.
          at your Request   1.17.4   Mr. Delafield can
          To advice concerning   ascertain it.
          Hardits Affair   1.17.4
          drawing general release 0.10

41)

Dr.   Stephen Delancey [57]   Cᵣ

1785
Aug 30   To Cash paid Mr.
          Harpur for searching
          for Original deed in
          his cause against
          Delavan   0. 4.6
          To dead charge on the
          circuit in West

54. Nothing is known concerning Williams beyond the fact that on March
31, 1798, he asked H's help in avoiding debtor's prison.
   55. Bracketed material is not in the writing of H.
   56. Delafield arrived in New York from England in 1783. He was a broker
in securities.
   57. De Lancey was the grandson of Stephen De Lancey, founder of the
family in the United States.

Dr. Cr.

Chester to try your
cause being a critical
cause & having
succeeded 20.

Dr. Shaw—Physician [58] Cr.

1785
ug 30 | To advice concerning Eagles bond | 1.10

2)
Dr. Kilian Van Rensselaar [59] Cr.

1785
Apr. 23. | To Cash lent | £4.10 | By Cash | £4.10

Dr. Family of Hoffmans [60] Cr.

1785
Octr 12 | To attendance on the trial of Jacob Moore Adsm R R Livingston at the Camp | 75.0.0 |

1786
To attendance on hearing before the Arbitrators	75.
Attendance on different consultations	25.
	175

1786 | By Cash received | £100
| By ballance believed to have been satisfied | 75
| | 175

3)
Dr. David R. Floyed [61] Cr.

1785
Octr. 29 | drawing a bill to be passed into a law re-

58. The New York directories for this period list no "Shaw" who was a "physician" in New York City.

59. Killian K. Van Rensselaer (1763–1845) in the seventeen-eighties practiced law in Albany.

60. H had represented the Hoffmans in a trespass suit which was instituted against them by the Livingstons.

61. David Richard Floyd was the son of Richard Floyd, wealthy New Yorker who adhered to the Crown during the Revolution and whose estate was confiscated. David R. Floyd, pursuant to the will of his grandfather, Judge David Jones, later changed his name to Jones.

Dr.

        specting an estate in
which he is a
Remainder man   3.4

Dr.	Haydock & Warr [62]			C
1785 Nov. 15	advice concerning dispute with Thomas Franklin	1.10	1786 Nov. 23 By Cash	£6.10
1786 March 12	advice at two different times concerning duties of a vessel drawing Petition to Legislature concerning do	3. 2.		

44)

Dr.	Egbert Benson [63]			C
1785 Nov. 14	To this sum received by him of the Trustees of Esopus as a Retainer	5.	1786 By Cash	£5.
1786 Ap 29	To paid Childs for publishing a Notice in Chan: cause of G. Schuler in which he is solicitor	2.8		

Dr.	John Lansing [64]			Cr
1785 Nov. 14.	To this sum received by him of Trustees of Schenectady as a Retainer	£5	July By Cash	5.

62. Haydock and Warr were merchants at 49 Queen Street.
63. Benson, attorney general of New York State, was a delegate to the Annapolis Convention in 1786 with H.
64. John Lansing, Jr., was a lawyer of Albany.

)
r.   Executors of H. Franklin [65]   Cr.

85
ecr 1-9 | To advice concerning Continental money deposited with Testator drawing power of Atty. to sell lands | 1.10 .16 | Charged in cause with Slingerland | 2.6 |

r.   Mathew Vischer [66]   Cr.

85
er. 15. | To opinion on a case stated by him on a Patent to Cortland van Ness and others | 3.4 | | |

6)
r.   John B. Church [67]   Cr.

786			1786		
ug. 4	To this sum ⅌ *Portlands* Packet	2000		By ballance brought forward	2355.11.11
epr. 1.	To paid John Delafield for premium of Insurance	61.10	July 31	By Cash received of Jerem: Wadsworth say 3500 ditto of Nath Shalor 3000	2600
	To this sum delivered Mr. De Heart to be shipped N. B. Shipped by the Antelope Packet	800	Oct. 7	By Dominick Lynch for purchase money of half the lot due Aug 1	1050
Decr. 6	To 2 bills of Exchange each for 100 £ Stg drawn by Wm. Backhouse & Co. remitted per Packet	376.19.9		By Walter Livingston for ditto do.	1050
Decr. 13	To 1 ditto drawn by ditto for Stg. 300 1 ditto drawn by J C. Schuyler 20		Nov 17	By Cash received from Philad. in part of your last dividend	316. 4. 3
	£ Stg 320	6 ⅌ Ct 603. 0.5⅓		By John Chaloner for ball. due deducting ½ ⅌ Ct. commission & postage amounting together	

65. Mary Franklin, James Mott, and William Ryckman were the executors of the estate of Henry Franklin.
66. Matthew Visscher was an Albany lawyer who was clerk of the city and county.
67. See note 12.

Dr.

	shipped ⅌ Betsey Capt Watson		
1787			
Feby. 7	To Cash ⅌ Duke of Cumberland Packet	679. 1.4	
April 4	To Cash ⅌ the Speedy Packet including freight	500	
	To bill of exchange Wm. Backhouse & Co. for £250 Sterling	471. 2.3	
July 25	bill of Exchange drawn by ditto for 800 £ Stg premium 7½ ⅌ Ct first sent ⅌ Ship Lord Middleton Capt Hey-hill	1528.17.9	
		7020.11.6	
August 1	bill of Exchange of Francis Upton for 40 £ Sterling a 7 ⅌ Ct. prem.	76. 1.9	
	ditto of Baron Poelnitz on Messr. Drummonds for 100 £ Stg at 7 ⅌ Ct.	190. 4.6	
Sepr 5	bill drawn by Wm. Backhouse & Co. for 800 Stg. a 8 ⅌ Ct.	1536.	
1788	paid Delafield premium of insurance ⅌ Antelope Packet	12.	
Feby. 18	To bill of Exchange of Wm. Backhouse & Co. for 400 Stg.	771.11.1	
March 20	To ditto for 200 do	385.15.7	
July 31	Bill of Hamilton on Hamilton for £ 50 Stg.	96	
Aug. 6	To this sum ⅌ Roebuck Packet including freight	1040.	
Sepr 2.	To bill of Will Backhouse & Co. for £400 Stg	778.13.4	
	To this sum paid for executing a commission in yr. suit v Fitsimmons	6.13.2	

C

	to £3.10.6		400
1787			
Feby 1	By your proportion of purchase money of Ships St. Anne and two brothers	200	
	By your Jany dividend	675	
		875	
	deduct J Chaloners Coms ⅌ act.	13. 7.6	
	Pen Curry	861.12.6	919. 1. 4
March 16	By Cash of J. Wadsworth	400	
	By ditto of N Shalor	400	
	By ditto of N Shalor	400	
			9890.17. 6
	Interest on ballance due first June 1785 to June 1. 1787		100. 2. 7
	on £715.4.5		9991. 0. 1
87			
July 25	Account transmitted this day ballance exclusive of value of lot 870.7.7.		
	Ballance brought down		870. 7. 7
Aug. 17	By your last half yearly divid. of bank stock	720.	
	By this sum receivd of J Chaloner	140	
Nov	By this sum received of R Troupe on account of Cuyler & Gans	200	
Qr			
1788			
	purchase money of lot	2100	
Augt. 4	By this sum received of J Wadsworth	1200	
Quaere?	By dividend of January omitted		
Aug 20	By dividend of July	1800 Dolls	
	Deduct loss on weight & expences of Messenger	23	
		1777.	710.16
	Ballance carried to 78		

t. 17 | To this sum pd. D Phoenix Quit rent of your lot prior to sale | 3. 4.1½

Alexander Macaulay   Cr.

			1786		
g 26	To your draft in favour of Col Jameison accepted this day vide bundle Receipts	100		By Ballance brought from fol 4	286.18.3
	To Costs Adsm Jacob Sarley	5. 1.6		By Cash received of Dan Ludlow for his brother Robert	163. 9
vr. 3	To Cash paid his Atty Nath Gardner	50			450. 7.3
	To Costs of suit v R Ludlow	10.17.9			
18	To cash paid your draft in favour of Messrs William Gillies & Co	133. 6.8			
	To Costs of suit Adsm Wardrop	21.12.3			
y 5	To Cash pd. Thos. Goadsby	120.			
	paid Reg Mortgage omitted	10.			
	paid postage at different times	8.6			
		441.16.8			
	Ballance due A. Macaulay	8.10.7			
		450. 7.3			

ıuary 9th. 1788. settled the above account this day ballance due me as above to be passed my Credit in new account   Alexr. Macaulay [68]

Dominick Lynch [69]   Cr.

			1787		
36			Aug 1	Cash	1050
ctr. 7	To one half a lot in broad way of J Barker Church sold you payable in nine months	1050			

68. This receipt is in H's writing and is signed by Macaulay.
69. Lynch, an Englishman, had settled in New York City in 1784 or 1785. He probably was a partner in the counting house of Lynch and Stoughton at 41 Little Dock Street.

48)

Dr.		Charles Crommelin [70]			(

1786					
Sepr. 29	To Cash pd. Cary Lud-low	£ 200	Buy my bond for (say 1500)	£ 1500	
Oct 19	To Cash paid ditto	200			
87					
July 7	To ditto paid ditto settled	100			

Dr.		Walter Livingston [71]			(

1786					
Oct. 7	To one half the lot of J Barker Church sold you payable in Nine months	1050.	Oct 13	By Cash (including Int. deducted for prompt payment) By Ballance due for which I have a note payable in 9 Mo:	570 480
					£ 1050
Oct. 13	To your Note of this date pay nine months	480.		By Cash	480

49)

Dr.		Samuel Broome [72]			(

1786			1786		
Oct 1	To this sum due for fee with your son as Clerk	150.	Oct. 12	By Cash received of N Miller Esqr By Note of	40.13.7 119. 6.5
1786					
Oct 1	This day Mr. S. Broome Junior entered this office as Clerk & This 1st of May absented himself to return 1789				

70. A member of the Crommelin family which had established a large trading company with branches in New York and Holland, and the Amsterdam banking house of Crommelin and Zoon. The founder of these firms, Daniel Crommelin, had died in New York in 1768.

71. Livingston practiced law in New York City.

72. Broome, a merchant of New York City before the Revolution, had moved to New Haven, Connecticut, in October, 1775.

r. Custom House Cr.

86 ct. 19	To Cash paid Mr. Marshall	£0.4	86 Octr. 19.	By duties on 4 small boxes with Caps and medicine ⅌ different vessels	0.4	

o)

r. Richard Varrick [73] Cr.

86 ctr. 31.	To Cash lent as ⅌ his note of this date	£40	1786	By Cash received	£40

r. The Minister of Spain [74] Cr.

86 Nov 2	To Cash paid Samuel Jones	£ 3. 4	Decr. 20	By Cash	£ 137.9.8
22	To Cash paid Mr. Winter ⅌ Agree	60.			
Decr. 6	To Cash pd H. Deputy Sheriff Hardenbrook	4. 1			
	To amount of Goal keepers fees assumed by me	29.14			
	To advice and services as Council	37. 6.8			
		£134.05.8			
	To Cash for Judge Morris	3. 4			
		137.09.8			

ı)

Dr. Daniel Ludlow [75] Cr.

785 Decr. 27.	To opinion in writing concerning affairs of Samuel & Moses Meyers for Assignees in Holland	3.4		By Cash	3.4

73. Varick was a lawyer and recorder of the City of New York.
74. Diego de Gardoqui.
75. Ludlow, a member of the New York Chamber of Commerce, was at
this time in partnership with Edward Goold.

Dr.	David Henly [76]			Cr

1785
Decr. 27   drawing a deed of con-
           veyance from Town-
           shend   3. 4
           ditto release of dower   1.16

Dr.	Abijah Hammond [77]			Cr

1788
Nov. 20   To opinion respecting
           a bargain with B Liv-
           ingston   1.17.4

52)

Dr.	Cuyler & Gansewort [78]			Cr

1785
Decr. 27   To advice concerning
           a bill of Exchange   £ 1.10
May 1   To paid Postage of bill
           in Chancery &c.   4.19.4

Dr.	Peter Stuyvesant [79]			Cr

1786
Jany. 19   To advice concerning
           a title to be given by
           Mr. Rivington   1.10

53)

Dr.	Balthazer DeHeart [80]			Cr

1785   To costs in a suit   1787
          against assumed by you   Sepr 3d.   By Cash received   £ 28

76. Henley was a resident of Massachusetts who became involved in a dispute between H and the Reverend Doctor William Gordon in 1779.

77. Hammond was a wealthy New York investor.

78. Jacob Cuyler and Leonard Gansevoort were Albany merchants.

79. Stuyvesant, descendant of the famous colonial governor, owned extensive property on Manhattan Island.

80. Balthazar De Haert was H's law partner.

r.   Cr.

86
y. 10 | To paid for a load of | | | By Cash at different times heretofore omitted | 17.8.10 |
Coals sent you	0.14		By Cash in Jersey money	6.
To Cash paid Rivington for Parcht.	8.	Sepr. 21	By Cash	9.
		Nov. 2.	By Cash for Costs in Skinners suit	9.0. 9
		9	By Cash Brailsford v Wooldrige	19.2. 3
		1788		
		May 28	By Cash Latting Carpenter v Nathaniel Quinbey	34.4. 7
		Novem 17	Costs in suit of Leake v Delancey & Kelly	11.

Dr.   John Stevenson [81]   Cr.

786
any 10. | To Cash paid Secretary for papers relative to Your brothers claim of land | 1.12 | |

4)
Dr.   John Hewlet [82]   Cr.

786
eby 1. | To opinion on a case between Birdsall and him sent by Youngs | 1.10 | By John Hewlet Feb 25 | 1.10 |
| | | ——— |

Dr.   Isaac Youngs [83]   Cr.

786
eby. 1 | To opinion concerning a fine | 1.10 | Nov 23. | By Cash | £ 1.10 |
| To advice at different times concerning arbitration | 3. 4 | | | ——— |
| drawing release | 4 | | |

81. Stevenson was a merchant of Albany.
82. See note 34.
83. Youngs, a resident of Huntington, Long Island, had been ordered by the British army during its control of New York City to seize horses and wagons for the King's troops. In a suit in which he later was sued for recovery of some of the seized property, he was represented by H.

55)

Dr.	Charles Smith [84]		C
1786 Feby. 2	drawing two deeds of conveyance	£6. 8	1786 Decr. 5 By Cash £8.8
6	opinion concerning his conduct as Executor	1.10	
	drawing directions for an Inventory	10	
		£8. 8	

Dr.	Isaac Moses [85]		C.
1786 Feby 15	drawing a Petition to Legislature	1.10	1787 Aug 2 By Cash £126
Feby 1	purchase money of house sold you with Interest from this day	1800.	6 By Cash 250
1787 Feby 1	Interest to this day	126	1788 Feby. 1 By ditto 117.5 ditto 100 June 9 ditto 100 567.5
1788 Feby 1	Interest to this day on 1550		Nov 25 ditto by hand of Mr. Broom 80

56)

Dr.	Messieurs Douglass (Randal Son & Stewart) [86]		C
1786 Feby 23.	To advice concerning affairs of Leary & Co consultation with Chancellor &c.	5.	By Cash in full £6.10
May 23	advice concerning a demand against F. Lewis	1.10	

84. Probably Charles Smith who in 1796 edited *The Monthly Military Repository.*
85. See notes 43 and 44.
86. Randall Son and Stewarts was a firm of merchants in New York City.

Dr. **Pearsall Thomas** [87] Cr.

1786				
March 6.	To drawing Petition & 3 affidavits on the confiscation Act attending Judgt.	3. 4	Nov 23. By Cash	£4
	drawing assignment from Ham. Cockle	0.16		
	To amt. of Costs in yr. suit v. Js. Jarvis	18. 7.9		

57)
Dr. **Samuel Franklin** [88] Cr.

March 6	drawing Petition to Judge & affid. on confiscation act attendance &c	2.
30	drawing Mortgage from Hoghland for your Partner Wm. Robinson	3. 4
Aug 26	paid Judge Morris for Certificate of debt due from St. Croix	0.16

Dr. **Gilbert v Cortlandt** [89] Cr.

1786		
March 28	To Cash lent	£ 12

58)
Dr. **John J. Skidmore** [90] Cr.

1786		
March 30	paid Mr. Remsen for drawing Mortgage to P. Schuyler	2.16

87. Thomas Pearsall and Son was a firm of merchants in New York City.
88. Franklin was listed in *The New York Directory for 1786* as "merchant, 183 Q[ueen] street."
89. Gilbert Van Cortlandt was probably the son of Pierre Van Cortlandt, the first lieutenant governor of New York State.
90. Skidmore was a farmer and resident of the township of Jamaica, Queens County, New York.

Dr.   Moses Hazen [91]   C

| 1786 April 1. | for drawing a special Indemnifying bond to sureties | 1. | | |

59)
Dr.   Joseph Strong [92]   C

| 1786 April 5 | To Cash lent | £20 | 1787 Octr. 24 By Cash | £20 |

Dr.   Executors of Cooper [93]   Cr

| 1786 April 24 | To my fee for arguing a demurrer on the citation act (Popham) | 10 | | |

60)
Dr.   Egbert Benson [94]   Cr

| 1786 April 29. | To paid Childs for publishing a Notice in a Chancery cause for General Schuyler in which he is solicitor | 2.8 | By Egbert Benson 44 | £2.8 |

Dr.   Morgan Lewis [95]   Cr.

| 1786 April 29 | To ballance due on settlement for Chan. fees. | 0.17.6 | | |

91. Hazen, a Revolutionary War general, had settled at the end of the war in Vermont where he owned land.

92. Strong at one time must have studied law in H's office. On August 11, 1786, Strong, writing to H from Cooperstown, New York, spoke of Balthazar De Haert, "your late partner in business while I was under your tuition."

93. Presumably the executors of Myles Cooper, Anglican churchman and president of King's College, who, remaining loyal to the King, had returned in 1775 to England where he died in 1785.

94. See note 63.

95. Lewis practiced law in New York City.

(1)

Dr.	Cornelius P. Lowe [96]		Cr.
786	drawing Petition to Legislature	1.10	
May 10	drawing mortgage to Constable	3. 4	
	Indorsement for further security	.16	

Dr.	Henry & McClellan [97]		Cr.
786	drawing Memorial to Congress respecting canadian affairs	1.10	
May 11.	Opinion on citation act	1.10	

(62)

Dr.	Alexander Hosack [98]		Cr.	
1786 July 15.	Trial fee at Nisi prius as Council with Thomas Smith	5.	Nov 23 By Cash	£5

Dr.	Samuel Bard [99]		Cr.
1786 July	To Council fee in a trial of a cause for your Father against Weisner assumed by you	5	By amount of your account
Oct 6	Advice in an expected land cause	3.4	

96. Cornelius P. Low was a New York City merchant. H's legal papers show that Low engaged in trade with St. Croix in the West Indies.

97. For a discussion of the memorial of Robert Henry, Robert McClallen, and Robert Henry, Jr., Albany merchants, see JCC, XXX, 205–07.

98. Hosack was listed in The New York Directory for 1786 as a woolen and linen draper.

99. Bard was a physician and a professor of natural philosophy and astronomy at Columbia College.

Dr.	Robert L. Hooper [100]			C
1786 July 15	Retainer in your cause v. Conolly council fee on trial at Nisi prius	1.10 5		

63)

Dr.	William Rowlet [101]			C
1786 July 15	Council fee at Nisi prius in your cause against Sarly and Barnwall	5.	By Cash	£5

Dr.	William Nielson [102]			Cr
1786 July 15.	To Council fee at N.P. in your cause with the Blairs	5	Nov 23. By Cash	£5

Dr.	Sarley & Barnewall [103]			Cr
1786 July 15.	Council fee at Nisi prius on Trial of your cause with Hay	5.	Nov 22d. By Cash	£5.

64)

Dr.	Peter R. Livingston & Cary Ludlow [104]			Cr.
1786 July 15.	Retainer in an Ejectment cause Trial fee (in Non suit)	£5 1.10		

100. Robert Lettis Hooper of Pennsylvania was a wartime contractor who engaged in extensive land speculations in the 1780s.

101. Rowlet was a merchant of New York City.

102. Neilson, a merchant located at 40 Dock Street in New York City, offered "freight and passage to Newry and Cork" and to sell "the times of a few good servants" (*The New York Directory for 1786*, 88).

103. The firm of Sarly and Barnewell, merchants, conducted business at 193 Water Street in New York City.

104. Probably Peter R. Livingston of Livingston Manor. Cary (Carey) Ludlow had gone to England at the outbreak of the Revolution and returned to New York in 1784. His Loyalist sympathies apparently did not diminish his wealth, for in 1792 he completed one of New York's finest mansions.

Dr. Executors of Desbross [105] Cr.

86	fee for arguing successfully a Question on citation act	10	1786 Nov 23 By Cash	£10

Dr. Executors of James v Cortlandt [106] Cr.

786	Fee for arguing successfully a Question on citation act	10	

5)
Dr. Executors of John v Cortlandt [107] Cr.

786 Aug 26	paid Judge Morris for acknowleging 6 deeds executed by him	2.14	

Dr. Cornelius Ray [108] Cr.

786 Aug 30	Advice concerning Brandy left with you by Mr. Price Quare if not paid	1.10	R.
789 Feb. 20	Advice concerning your uncle's will power by Mr. De Haert	1.10	

105. Elias Desbrosses, one of the founders of the New York Chamber of Commerce and its president during 1771–72, remained loyal to the King during the Revolution. He died in New York on March 26, 1778.

106. Colonel James Van Cortlandt, brother of Augustus Van Cortlandt, died in 1781.

107. John Van Cortlandt sold at his store at 17 Broadway, New York City, refined sugar "manufactured in his sugar house near the North River." He died on July 1, 1786.

108. Ray, a prominent New York businessman, was later a director of the Bank of New York and president of the New York branch of the Bank of the United States.

Dr.   Isaac Gouverneur [109]   C

1787		
Aug 23	To perusing sundry papers & giving a written opinion in your affair with Pray of Georgia	3.4
	To advice and other services in your affair with Assignees of Bend	3.4

66)
Dr.   James Thompson [110]   C

1786		
Sep 26	Cash lent	2.10
Nov 13	ditto	4.
1788		
Oct	ditto at Albany	4. 5

Dr.   Jesse Hunt [111]   C

1786		
	overpayment in Sheriffs Bill Harris v. Hawkins (twice Charged)	0.18
	Delancey v Browns do	3

67)
Dr.   Minister of the United Netherlands [112]   C

1786			1787		
Decr. 18	To Cash paid Postage of letter & rules to Charles town in the case of the Sloop		Sep 28	By Cash	£ 49.10.11

109. During the Revolution Isaac Gouverneur had acted as agent in Curaçao for William Bingham, the Philadelphia merchant. Gouverneur's business activities were continued in New York after the war.

110. Thompson was a merchant of New York City and the father-in-law of Elbridge Gerry of Massachusetts.

111. Hunt had been sheriff of Westchester County, New York.

112. Pieter J. Van Berckel.

r. Cr.

Chester	3. 5. 7	
[To drawing the Petition of Appeal fo. 831 at 1/6 ℔ f 68	2. 6. 6	
Engrossing Ditto	1. 3. 3	
To Abrm. Lott's Acct for translating the Affidavits into english	4. 0. 0	
paid Postage of Letter from Charlestown with Affidavits of service enclosed	0. 5. 3	
Register's Account paid	15. 1. 4	
Expences of C. C. Pinkney of Charles Town in proving notices on the Court there	3. 9. 0	
To my fav for Arguing Motion for Rule to shew Cause and for Argug against the Cause Shewn Attendance on the Court drg. Affidt. &c.	20. 0. 0	
	£49.10.11] [113]	

Shedden Patrick & Co.[114]

r. Cr.

787	To advice concerning vessell attached in New Jersey, consultations with Mr. Smith perusal of papers &c.	3.4	
	To amount of Costs in the suit of Roxburgh Adsm Seaman vide Reg. No. 2 fol 76	2.3.3	

113. Bracketed material is not in the writing of H.
114. The firm of Shedden Patrick and Company, merchants, was located at 206 Water Street, New York City.

68)

Dr.   Thomas & Richard Lee [115]   C

Curren[c]

17 June	To me two setts of bills of Wm. *Turner*	
23d July	Backhouse & Co remitted £ 200 Stg	
Aug 1	To 1 sett drawn by Jay remitted by Packet £ 100 Stg	
	To 1 sett drawn by Barnewall on Barnewall 300 do	
	Commissions on ditto at ℔ Ct	
	Commissions on £ 200 Sterling remitted by Johnson & Ogden at ditto	
Sepr. 3	To draft of Wm Backhouse & Co. for 110 £ Stg at 10 ℔ Ct. premium	
Nov 6	To two setts of bills each for £ 50 Stg one drawn by Chollet in favour of Low the other by Lowe in favour of Johnson & Ogden	
Feby 19	To bill of Wm. Backhouse & Co. remitted ℔ packet £ 100 Stg.	
do	To bill of ditto for £ 150 Stg recd. of Johnson & Ogden	
May 4	To bill recd. of J & Ogden remitted by Packet £ 100	
June 4	To bill ℔ packet £ 80 Stg C Remsen & Co	
Aug 4	To bill ℔ packet £ 80 Stg Wm Backhouse & Co	

	By this sum received of John Turner in bills of Exchange £ 200 Sterling	
	ditto of Smith & Wycoff in ditto £ 100 Stg	
	ditto of Sarley & Barnewall in ditto £ 300	
Aug 31	By Cash received of John Murray on account of Ramsay & Co.	214.19
	By Comfort Sands for Potash received by him	37. 7.6
Nov 7	By two setts of bills recd. of Johnson & Ogden £ 100 Stg	
1788		
Feby	By this sum reced of J Turner £ 100 Sterling	
Feby 19	By this sum received of Messrs J & Ogden in bills £ 150 Stg	
May 4	By bill of exchange of J & Ogden £ 100 Stg.	
June 4	By bill of Johnson & Ogden £ 80 Stg	
Aug 4	By ditto £ 80	
	By Cash received of Sarley and Barnewell £ 320 Curry	paper Curr bil[l]
Sep 2	Ditto £ 160	12½ ℔ C
Nov 4	By sett of bills of Johnson & Ogden £ 80 Stg	
Sep 27	By this sum received	

115. For several generations it was a tradition in the famous Lee family of Virginia that one son enter business in England. Although heir to the Lee estate in Virginia, Richard Lee III (grandson of the first Lee to settle in Virginia) had become a merchant in London. The firm of Thomas and Richard Lee and Son, whose New York transactions H was handling, presumably was owned by descendants of this Richard Lee.

r.

ug 9 To bill of Wm. Back- house & Co remitted ℈ Montgomery (Bunyan) £ 150 Stg 12½ ℈ C p. 4 To bill of Do. remitted ℈ Packet for £ 80 Stg dated 3d. Sepr. NB. Johnson & Ogden delivered me the second & third of a set for 80 Stg. the first of which they inform was re- mitted by them ovr. To bill of Wm Seton & Co remitted ℈ Packet £ 80 Stg 89 ny 9 Bill of ditto remitted ℈ packet for £ 80 ditto of Wm. Backhouse £ 80 Sterling ly 23 Bill of J & A MacComb 80 Stg	of Smith & Wycoff 315 Ds. Bill received of John- son & Ogden Sepr 3, 1788 amd. drawn by Wm. Backhouse £ 80 Stg 1789 Jany 7 Bill for Johnson & Ogden drawn by Wm. Seton & Co. 80 £ Stg

)

r.   Pascal N. Smith [116] Surviving Partner of Sears & Smith   **Cr.**

ug. 3 To opinion concerning the estate of Isaac Sears	1.10	vide Viner Title Money
Opinion concerning Partnership Concern	1.10	
Settled 13 Novr		

r.   Arthur St. Clair [117]   **Cr.**

89 pril 25 To discount on your note of this day in- dorsed by me for your accom., in lieu of a Warrant for which provision was not yet made. Drs. Cents Drs. 11. 66	

116. See note 18.
117. St. Clair was appointed governor of the Northwest Territory in 1787.

Dr. McCartney [118] C

| 1789 Oct 13 | This sum advanced him to procure certain articles for Mrs. Ham | 120 Drs. | By amt. of Articles procured | |

71) [119]

Dr. Executors of DeWit [120] C

| 1786 July | Trial of cause in Eject-ment at Circuit | £ 10 | By Cash | £ 3.4 |

Dr. Henry Shute [121] C

| ditto | Council fee for trial of your cause at circuit court | 5 | | |

Dr. John H. Sleight [122] C

| | council fee for trial of your cause with Hoghteling | 5 | Aug 18 | By Cash | £ 10 |
| ditto | council fee for trial of your cause with | 5 | | | |

Dr. Robert Morris [123] C

| 1787 Aug. | To Cash lent (dld. G: Morris Check on the bank of Philadelphia for | 522.8 | By Cash received of Mr. Constable | 522.8 |

118. William Macarty, a Pennsylvania merchant, who had gone bankrupt and had received a general discharge from his creditors, established a business in L'Orient, France, in 1784.

119. Page 70 in H's cash book is blank except for the heading "cash account."

120. Probably the DeWitt family of Ulster County, New York.

121. A Henry Shute mentioned in the following newspaper notice: "For sale, a farm on the Bloomingdale road, near the Glass House, for particulars enquire of Henry Shute . . ." (*The New York Directory for 1786*, 100).

122. Sleight was a partner in the firm of Sleight and Van Wyck, the dissolution of which was announced in the New York press on April 17, 1786.

123. Morris was the foremost merchant of America at this time. The transaction recorded here presumably was made while H was in attendance at the Constitutional Convention in Philadelphia.

Dr. Samuel Van Wyck [124] Cr.

1787			
Aug 30	To council fee attending Circuit in your cause with M Willet on trying the cause absent three days (travelling expences &c.	10.	

Dr. Frederick William De Steuben [125] Cr.

1787						
Sep 24	To paid the bank for a note indorsed for him	£200		By Cash received on your account of S V Rensselaer Esqr	£215	
1788			July	By ditto of ditto	100	
April	To Cash lent	60		Ballance Due A H carried to Page 73	346	
June 5	To this sum pd. my note to B Walker by way of loan to him	60				
1789						
March	To cash in specie £16 ditto paper ditto specie 50 66	40 66				
April 14	To Cash 8	5				
July	To Cash £50					
25	ditto 20					
Aug	ditto 20					
Sepr.	ditto 20	110				
Oct 6	paid Wm Constable for you	100				
Oct 26	cash pd. Lopez	20			661	
		661				

Dr. Jacob Remsen [126] Cr.

1787					
Novr.	Cash paid on account order of Mr. Lewis Ogden	£12 8		By Lewis Ogden unpaid	£8
Oct	To Cash	4			

124. Samuel Van Wyck was a New York attorney. With William Van Wyck of Dutchess County, he speculated in land in New York State.

125. For more than a decade H helped Baron von Steuben, inspector general of the Army during the Revolution, in von Steuben's repeated attempts to secure funds to meet his financial obligations.

126. Remsen was a resident of Queens County, New York, who during the American Revolution had been a Loyalist.

73)

Dr.   Land Account   C

1787	To paid Hammond for certificates to pay for lands on the River St. Laurence purchased in Company with Alexander Macombe & others	81. 4.10	
July 17	paid Delafield	36. 3	
Oct. 17	To paid Delafield for ditto. ℔ acct. and receipt of this date	315.19. 3	
	To paid Richard Platt for lands on the Ohio		

Dr.   Frederick William De Steuben [127]   C

1790	To Ballance from Page 72	346	
June 8. 90	Cash paid your draft of this date in favour of B Walker	200	
April 5	This sum paid B Walker for you ℔ Receipt	100	
	To cash paid Leonard Cutting at different times		

74)

Dr.   John J Van Rensselaer [128]   C

1787 Nov 5.	To Cash paid your draft on me in favour of Mr. Stevenson	80	
	To my fees in attending in Albany at the trial of five ejectment causes	60	
1788 January 10	To cash paid your draft in favour of Isaac Webbers	27	
		167	

127. See note 125.
128. John J. Van Rensselaer, cousin of Stephen, the patroon of "Rensselaerswyck."

Thomas Bibby [129]

r.   Cr.

87 c. 4	To Cash	£ 100	By Cash of	£ 40
	To this sum subscribed by you for Mrs. Camp- bell	10	By ditto of Mrs. Miller on accot. of Laurence By ditto of N Bayard By ditto of Wooldrige	55 950.9.1 90
		£ 110		1145.9.1
	Ballance due T Bibby	1035.9.1		
		£ 1145.9.1		

Received March 22d. 1788 of
Alexander Hamilton the above
sum of one thousand & thirty five
pounds nine shilling and one
penny.

T: Bibby [130]

Samuel Loudon [131]

)r.   Cr.

,87	To Cash lent ℔ your note of this date	£ 100	Feby	By Cash	£ 80
				Sundries	38.2
				Cash	4.5
,788 an 19	To Cash paid on Printers account	20		settled October 22d. 1788	122.7
	Interest	2.7		℔ Ret. in Rect. book	
		122.7			

William Grayson [132]

)r.   Cr.

,8[8]	To Cash paid E Blake per order	£ 3	
,ug.	to ditto ℔ do	3	
)r. 8	To ditto do	3	
	vide Rect. for £ 12 due Nov 23		
,789 eby. 28	To ditto ℔ do	£ 2	
	ditto	1	

129. Captain Thomas Bibby was located at 10 Smith Street, New York City, in 1786. (*The New York Directory for 1786,* 80.)

130. The receipt is in the writing of H and signed by Bibby.

131. Loudon was the editor of *The New-York Packet, and the American Advertiser.*

132. Probably the William Grayson of Virginia who had served with H as a member of the 1778 commission for the exchange of prisoners. Grayson served in the Continental Congress and the Constitutional Convention, and was elected to the United States Senate in 1789.

Dr.   Cr

May 27	do. in full to May 23 ꝑ Receipt	3
Sep 19	Cash paid do	3
Der. 8	Cash paid ditto	3

76)
Dr.   Edward Livingston [133]   Cr

| 1788 Sep. 2. | To Cash paid your Clerk on acct. ꝑ Ret. wood Adsm Hallet | £14 |

Dr.   Thorne [134]   Cr

| 1788 Sep. 3. | To my circuit fee in Queens in the suit be- tween his father & Cornel | £15 |

77)
Dr.   Henry K Van Rensselaer [135]   Cr

1787 Decr. 10	Cash lent your son To paid your order in favour of your son KHVR	3.12 15.
1788 Jany. 10	To paid A Brinkerhoff upon your sons order (ꝑ yr order for 25)	12.18.4
Oct 6	To paid for Chocolate furnished your son	12. 1.4

Dr.   David Galbreath [136]   Cr

| Octr. 8 | Opinion concerning certain public certifi- cates assigned by Ben- jamin Eyre. Inquiry at the Treasury &c. | £3.4 | By Cash | £3.4 |

133. Livingston practiced law in New York City where he had been admitted to the bar in 1785.
134. Probably a member of the Thorne family of Queens County, New York,
the members of which had adhered to the King during the Revolution.
135. Van Rensselaer (1743–1816) was a resident of Albany.
136. Galbreath was a member of the St. Andrew's Society of the State of
New York.

Barak Snethen [137]

Dr.   Cr.

1788 Oct 10th	To Cash paid A Burr Esquire in full of your suit of J Loyed v B Snethen	25	By Cash	£31
	To your Costs in sd. suit			

(8)

John B. Church [138]

Dr.   Cr.

Date	Dr. item	Dr. amt	Date	Cr. item	Cr. amt	Cr. amt
1788	To paid S. Loudon for advertising sale of lot in Broadway	1. 8	1789	Ballance brought from 46		
1789 January	To bill of Wm. Backhouse for £150 Sterling		Jany 20	By Cash of J Chaloner by the hands of J Lupton 440 Ds.	176	
	To bill of Cornelius Ray for 200 Stg.		21	ditto. of ditto by draft on And Craigie 106 Ds 64/96	42.13.4	
March	To Cash advanced on account of Mrs. Churchs lodgings	30.		Cash your last half yearly divid say 1800 Ds £720 Deduct exp. of Messenger 6.5.4	713.14.8	
May	To Cash paid Mrs. Church 500 Dollars				Dollars	
15	ditto by Mrs. Hamilton 200 do.		July 14	By Your yearly dividend 1540 paid Js. Cochran expence as Messenger 17½ loss on weight 7	24½	
21	ditto by Js. Cochran 200 do.					
	To paid Van Allen for a pr. horses for ditto	70				
	ditto for hay & oats ⅌ account	3. 9.8		Ds. 1515½	£606. 4	
23	paid J & P Mark for Pyrmont water ⅌ Rt. bundle	9. 2	1790 Aug 13	By this sum recd of J Wadsworth 4000 Ds	1600	
June	paid De Chosle ⅌ Mrs. Churchs order (Valet De Chamb) 11½ Guineas or 54 dollars	21.12				
June 29	To Cash by J Cochran 100 dollars	40	1791 March	By this sum received of R Troupe on account of Jacob		
July 3	Cash paid Abm. Brower Taylor	5.18.6½				

137. Snethen was a wealthy farmer and miller of French Pond, Long Island.
138. See note 12.

Dr. C:

July 14	Cash paid Mrs. Church in Guineas 238 Dollars or	95.4		Cuyler 500 Dollars omissions	300
July 16	paid Coachman for board	4.4		By this sum believed to have been received	
	paid do. for Bran for Horses	1.6	April	of J Wadsworth October 1. 1789 Quare?	1600
Sepr.	paid Mrs. Church paper paid ditto specie			draft of George Meade for 300 £ Stg	
Oct. 7	To a sett bills ♉ packet Wm. Cons[table] & Co. 130.9 a 4½ premium	242. 6.9		at 171 P. Curr.	
8	1 Do. Le Roy & Bayard 400 £ Sg. a 4½ premium				
	paid duty on articles ♉ Montgomery for Mrs. Church by way of deposit which was not settled because quantity unascertained	3.18			
1790 April 10	Draft of Jacob Le Roy & Son of this day for 4600 Guilders				
Oct 2.	Cash paid B. Livingston Esqr to go to Phil to transact the sale of your Bank Stock	140.			
1791	1 set of bills by Js. Tilghman for 200 Stg 1 ditto 512.3				

79)

Dr. Isaac Rosevelt [139] Cr

1788 Nov 20	To opinion on a will consisting of four questions and answers	£ 5.0.0	

Dr. Messrs. Pintards [140] Cr

1788 Nov 28	draft of argument in controversy with Mr. Shedden	£ 3.4	

139. Roosevelt, president of the Bank of New York from 1786 to 1791, was an import merchant.

140. Members of the Pintard family were New York merchants.

Dr.   Jonathan Nesbit & Co.[141]   Cr.

| 89 ly 11 | To Cash paid your Atty. David H Conyngham ℔ Rect. bundle Rects Your Costs in Chancery suit | 202.13.4 | 1789 | By Cash received on the Comp with Stewart & Totten | £239.6.7 |

)

Dr.   Marinus Willet [142]   Cr.

| | My Costs received by you of Layborteaux Ditto in suit of Ray v Abiel | £1.12 | | |

Dr.   Cuyler [143]   Cr.

89	To Cash paid Mrs. Dabborey	£30		
	To ditto Mr. Barkeley concerning Chan	11.15		
ly 4	Cash paid yourself	3. 4		
8	Cash paid do	20.		
ug	Cash 2 Guineas	3.17.4		
	ditto	10.		
ct	Cash	4		

Dr.   John Adams [144]   Cr.

| 789 ily 20 | To fee for your son commencing his Clerk- ship this day | | Remitted |

141. Jonathan Nesbitt had established a mercantile house in L'Orient, France, under the patronage of Robert Morris. He later had returned to the United States and established his firm in Philadelphia.

142. Willett, New York merchant and influential supporter of Governor George Clinton, was sheriff of New York City.

143. Probably Jacob Cuyler, merchant of Albany.

144. For information on the clerkship of John Adams's son, Charles, see John Adams to H, July 21, 1789.

Dr.   Stephen J. Schuyler [145]   C

1789 Nov 25	To this sum paid Robert Watts on account of his Bond to Ar. Kennedy & Jon Mallet Qr. where I received this money from Mr. Schuyler or not	200		

Dr.   George Mitchell [146]   C

1790 April 12	Cash pd. your draft in favour of James Haydock 15 Ds.	£6	By a barrel of Hams

Dr.   John Fenno [147]   C

		Dollars	
1790 Oct 19	To Cash lent	100	
1791 Jany 8	To Cash lent	100	

Dr.   William Duer [148]   C

		Dollars	
1791 Jany 12	To Cash paid Boulogne on your acct.	60.	

Dr.   Benjamin Workman [149]   C

1791 Jany 19	To Cash lent	Dollars	40

145. Brother of Philip Schuyler, H's father-in-law. (At this point H ceased to number the pages of his cash book.)

146. Mitchell was the husband of H's cousin, Ann Venton Mitchell (see Hugh Knox to H, October 27, 1783).

147. Fenno was editor of the *Gazette of the United States*.

148. See note 19.

149. Workman was a mathematics teacher in Philadelphia.

Dr.   Doctor J. Tillary [150]   Cr.

		Dollars	
1790			
October 19	To Cash lent	200	

Statement of Property belong to Mrs Elizabeth Hamilton [151]

Saratoga Patent—Lot No 4.			
Farm No 3	Lot No 10	containing	140 acres
Farm Do	part of do		140 acres
Farm No 5	Do		140 acres
Farm Do	Do		
Farm No 7	Do		90 acres
Farm Do	Do	Do	52 acres 2 Roods
Farm Do	Do	Do	81 Acres
Farm Do	Do	Do	124 acres 2 Roods
Farm Do	Do	Do	116 acres 3 Roods
Part of Farm C	Lot No 11	Do	40 acres
a Part of Farm No 5 called Layton about			40 acres

Statement of lands lying in lot No 4 Saratoga Patent [152]

Farm No 3 of Lot No 10 containing 141 acres	
Part of do	140 acres
Farm No 4 Do	140 acres
Farm	

Memoranda

Qr If not 300 Dollars due from J Blair

Angelica Church [153]   Dr.

Monies paid to Yourself

1789			
May	Cash dld you myself	500 Dollars	£ 200
15	ditto by Mrs. Hamilton	200 do	80
21	ditto by Js. Cochran	200 do	80
June 29	ditto by ditto	100 ditto	40
July 16	ditto dld myself	50 Guineas	95.4
Aug 21	ditto do		53
Sep. 19	ditto by Mrs. Hamilton	150 Ds	60
Oct. 5	ditto by do	200 do	80
			£ 688.4

150. James Tillery, a physician, was also a leading Federalist politician.

151. This statement is not in the writing of H.

152. This statement is not in the writing of H.

153. H's sister-in-law and the wife of John B. Church, whose American business affairs H often handled.

For You

May		paid Van Allen ℔ Horses	£70
		paid for Hay & oats	3. 9.8
	23	paid J & P Mark Pyrmont Water	9. 2.
June		paid your valet De Chambre ℔ order	21.12
July	3	paid Ab. Brower Taylor	25.18.6
	16	paid your Coachman for his board	4. 4
		ditto for bran &c	4. 6
		paid deposit at Custom House for articles ℔ Montgomery not ascertained	3.18
Aug	12	paid coachman for amt. of several small accounts for horses & carriage & self	14.10.9
		Paid Charles & James Warner for Coach hire &c	60. 6
		Paid Mrs. Cuyler for your lodgings from May 10 to Oct 7. 21 weeks	162.

☞ She deducts three weeks for time they were occupied by Mrs. Morris & charges three weeks at only 4 pounds the other part of the time at ten paid do. a gratuity by your desire   10.

		Advances by Mrs. Hamilton ℔ Memo	24.4.1	410.1

£ 1098.15

	1	Amount from the other side		£ 1098.15
October	28	Cash ℔ order Dld Sweney	100 Ds	40.
Oct	31	Cash ℔ order Dld Johnson	150	60

Oct 31. 89 Dld   1198.15

Nov.	2	Cash paid for passages of yourself & servant 370 Dollars & 66 Cents or		148. 5
	4	This sum advanced to take with you 200 Dollars		80
	10	paid account of your last landlady for rooms & some damage done by your servants in removing		23. 9

1450. 9

Bank Book on this
day stands thus   This sum for which I drew a Check on the Bank as ℔ Check &

200		Charge in my bank book 240 Dollars examine Bank book.	
370.66		November 4	
240			96.

	This sum omitted October 12. 1789 as ℔ Check 300 Dollars	120.
	This sum paid your former Music Master	40

1706. 9

Deduct

July 3	overcharge in Browers Acct.	£	1. 0

1705. 9

Dr.   City of New York

1788
To this sum paid <−> McClean Printer at different times
To paid an execution against Capt <−> on account of Rockets expended in the procession
To paid a draft on Richard Platt in favour of <−> Arnold to enable him to come forward to Congress

r.   Cash

ly 25	To Daniel Honan for this sum received of James Carter	£ 29.1.11

Officers' fees in different stages of the suit

Seal		£ 0. 2.3
filing writ and return		1
Entering appearance		1
Filing warrant of Atty		1
Crier & bell ringer		1.6
		0. 6.9
Judges fee	0.10.0	
Entering writ to bring in body	0. 1.6	
Entering writ to plead	0. 1.6	0.13.
Filing declaration	0. 1.6	
Entering discontinuance	1.6	0. 3.
Sheriffs fees		0.10.6

r.   Cash Account [154]   Cr.

85 pril	3	To this sum received of Executors of Swain Adsm Service	£ 6.16 SC [155]	April	3	By this sum due to Officers of the Court	1.13.3
	5	To this sum received in the suit of J Cortlant v Greene	4.18 SC		5	By this sum due to officers of the Court	1. 0.3
.ay		To this sum received of John Hunt at the suit of Leonard Laurence	4. 4.6 SC			By this sum due to officers of the Court	1. 0.9
ne	7	To this sum received in the suit of Harris v Mary Harris &c	3.19. SC	June	7	By this sum due to Officers of the Court	1. 0.3
	11	To this sum received of R Mc–Williams in his suit against Nicholls	2. 4.6 SC		do.	By this sum paid for 2 Registers SC & MC	2. 0.0
	13	To this sum received of Varin Adsm James Taylor	3.19. SC		11	By this sum due to officers of the Court	4.9
		To this sum re-			13	By this sum due to officers of the Court	1.6
						By this sum due to officers of the Court MC	
					14	By this sum due to officers of the Court MC	
				July	7	By this sum due to officers of MC (cause being tried)	
						By this sum due to do (do)	
					8	By this sum due to do (Narr filed)	

154. Bracketed material in H's cash account is not in his writing.
155. Supreme Court.

Dr.   C

		ceived of Ander-son Adsm Lowndes	1.10	MC [156]
	14	To this sum re-ceived of Ter-rason v.	1.15.9	MC
July	7.	To this sum re-ceived of Medcaf Eden Adsm Rut-gers	3.14.8	MC
	8.	To this sum re-ceived of Shrup Adsm. Thorne	3.	MC
Aug	4	To this sum re-ceived of J Le Roy in the suit of Ben-son Adm v Laffers	6. 8	SC
Sep	22	To this sum re-ceived of Wilson Adsm Robt & George Service	22.	
Nov	2	To this sum re-ceived of Lowe v Majorel & Mirandi	4. 3.9	
	27	To this sum re-ceived in two causes of Shannon Dunlap & others Vs. Archibald Gamble	18.18.	
Dec	2	To this sum re-ceived of Execu-tors of S Ketchum in two suits Adsm the Loyeds ℔ Register	35. 1.2	
	16	To this sum re-ceived of Gilbert Hogg v Thompson & Adsm Thomp-son	7.10	
	17	To this sum recd of Executors of Gifford Adsm Fraunces	25. 9.6	
	23	this sum recd for Harris Vs. Thomas & Fowler	1.10	
	27	This sum Recd of Dellois vs. Henry & Murray	2. 4.6	
1786 Jany	6	This sum received		

156. Mayor's Court.

		of Sheriff for Costs in the suit of Tremain & Stout v Carman.	11. 4.3
	9	To this sum received in suit of Curson & Gouverneur Adsm Cherry	10.12.6
		ditto Byrne Dorsten & Co. Adsm Cherry	7. 7.6
	29	ditto of Smith Adsm Hewlet	
br.	14	Received of Oakley Adsm Garrineau in part	10.
arch	7	Received of Johannes Ditzmas v. Mary H Holland Eject.	5. 3.3
	22	Received of Campbell Adsm Peckwood	11.
ay	1	Received of Miller and others v. Johnson and others	7. 2.3
		Received of Executors of Antje Covenhoven v. Bogarts	7.11.6
		[17th April 1786 Baxter & Hunt Executors of Palmer vs Benjm Palmer Reced. by Cutting four pounds. in part of costs	4. 0.0

Archibald   Costs
Blair vs.   in these
Strong &   causes
Norton   are paid
Same vs.   by Blair &
Grenon   Guin &
De Mi-   Carthy by
randa   *parcels* at
Same vs   *different*
Guin &   *times*
Carthy   amounting
Same vs   in the
Same   whole
Same vs   to   £36.15.0
Vander-   *Recd. by*
locht   *Cutting*]
Same vs
Same

Dr.

	24	Received of Lewis Mary Adsm Henry Nash	5.19.9
	31	Received of Wad- dington in *suit* of E Rutgers	9.11.3
June	19	Received at suit of Executors of Chambers vs Her- rick	9.
		Received at suit of Executors of Do v Wentworth	8. 7.9
	29	do of Willets Adsm. Loyed	18. 7.9

Dr.   SPC Cash Account

1786		Amount of debit brought forward		Amount of Credit brought forward
Aug	26	Sears v Hepburne	18. 4.9	
		Sears Adsm Ex- ecutors of Chapman —Blackbourne	3. 1.3	
		Maxwell vs. Franklin	18.10.	
Oct	19	Price vs. Haywood	2.12.6	
		Do. v. Bonfield & Haywood	2.16.6	
		Do. v. Haywood & Bindon	3.	
		Price & Haywood Adsm Perry	9.10.9	
		do . . Adsm Le Moyne	9.10.9	
		do . . adsm Beuthelier	9.16.	
		do . . Adsm Arnold	9.11.3	
		do . . Adsm Thompson	9.10.9	
		Do . . Adsm Findlay & Gregory	9.10.9	
		Do . . Adsm Du Calvet	9. 1.3	
		Do . . Adsm Cazeau	8.14.9	
		do . . Adsm Jordan	4. 8.9	
Oct	31	Terbush v. Bostwick	8.18.3	
		Mary Bowne v Ex of Thomas Thorne	8.16.6	
Oct	16	Benj Smith Adsm David Hawkins	5	
Nov	21	Nixon v Mordecai	19.12.6	
	23	Nielson v Mordecai	23. 7.3	
		Executors of Wickham v. Mesier & Van Voorhies	26. 9	

Cr.

:.

Red: Wm. Geyer vs.
Otis &c   2.16.4
cr.   5.   Hewlet v Montfort
Certiorari   10.

7
y.   11   Executors of Neilson
v. Ex. of Middleton   8. 1.6

Cash Account
D H & H [157]   Cr.

.

6
g.   26   Sears and Smith vs.
William Campbell
reced by AH   2 1.6

7
y   Cash received of Wm.
Nielson for draft of
deed &c   4.3
  4   William Bull Adsm
Charles White   1.

57. These initials refer to Balthazar De Haert and H.

Cash Account

Dr.   M C   C

1785						
July	20	Received of Thompson Adsm Tucker	£1. 9	July	20	Due officers of the Court
	22	Received of Underhill Adsm. Quackenboss	4. 1.6		22	Due officers of the Court
		[Mayors court	Recd:			
Feby	18	Frederick Jay vs. Eliahim Ford. Recd. of Eliahim Ford	1. 4.0			
May	11	Joseph Lepine vs. Jas. Griffiths. Recd of Mr Quesnay part Costs	1. 6.0			
July	4	Wm Lowry vs. Gerard H Stoddeford. Recd costs of Mr. Bard	by 4.17.3			
	8	Jacob Greene & al Vs. Henry Johnson } Recd cost of Parson	Cut- 2. 7.6			
		The same vs the same				
	23	Robt McWilliams vs. Jas. Keating. Recd Costs	3. 2.0			
	25	Daniel Homan vs. Jas. Carter. Recd Costs	ting 3.12.0]			
Aug	5	Thomas Arden vs Hugh McDole do	3.			
[Septr	2	Judn. Moses & Joseph Moses vs Henry Murphy & Ship ⟨–⟩ Recd Costs by Cutting	11. 4.6			
	19	Holmes & al vs. Brebner & Browne. Recd Costs by Cutting	13. 6.0]			
Octr.	20	Received of Verrien Adsm Executors of Dewit	4. 1.6			
	26	Received of Howard Adsm Duryee	3. 1.9			

r.

	27	Received of Joseph Crane Adsm J Shaw	1.10	
ov	1	Jn Aspinwall Assignee vs Nathan C Webb & Robert Smith] by Cutting	[1. 5.0]	
ov	29	Received of Kissick Adsm V Kurren & Baisser & Adsm Leake	7. 0.3	
ov	1	Recd of Zadock Reeve	1.12.0	Re-
	4	Recd of same in part of Costs	5. 0.0	ceived
	12	Recd of Rush v Murray	1. 7.0	
	30	Retainer from Jas Boyd	1.17.4	by
cr	13	Burdys vs Harrison	1. 8.0	
	20	Haight ads. Greenwood	1.19.0	Cut-
	23	Lefferts ads Vandevoort	12.19.0	
36				
y	5	Recd. of Mr. Connolly Costs on two Bail bond Suits ads Duboys & Co.	10. 5.0 / 10. 5.0	ting
	10	Morewood vs Dodd & Thompson Recd Costs by Cutting	2.11.0]	
	29	Springall v Whitewood & Co.	2.	
eb	26	McWilliams Adm Wright. Costs Recd. By Cutting	5. 0.0	
	27	Stanton Ads Keating Costs Recd by Cutting	5. 3.3	
rch	4	De Witt Ads. Callahan. Costs Recd by Cutting	5.12.0	
ril	7	Exrs. of Lupardas v Ruten Costs Recd by Cutting	6.12.6]	
r.	8	John Ireland Adsm Post	11. 4.6	
	[11	Strait ads Sickles Recd by Cutting	3. 2.0]	
y	22	Laffan & Amory Adsm Murray	3.11.	

To Lieutenant Colonel John Laurens

[*Philadelphia, March 2, 1782.* In July 1782, Laurens wrote to Hamilton: "I am indebted to you, my dear Hamilton, for two letters; the first from Albany, as masterly a piece of cynicism as ever was penned: the other from Philadelphia, dated the 2d March." *Letter of March 2 not found.*]

To James McHenry

[*Philadelphia, March 8, 1782.* "Dr. Mac. I write the above [1] in a form which being copied I wish to appear before the personages concerned. . . . Whatever may be my general opinion of Mr. Chase, if I find good reason to think him innocent in the present case I shall with great pleasure declare it. You know my informants." [2] *Letter not found.*]

ALS, sold at Parke-Bernet Galleries, October 30–31, 1944, Lot 62.
    1. The catalogue description states there accompanied this letter "an AL relating to" it. The autograph letter accompanying it was doubtless a copy of H's letter of February 26, 1782, to McHenry.
    2. Extract taken from catalogue of Parke-Bernet Galleries.

To Major Nicholas Fish [1]

[Albany, March, 1782] [2]

Dr. Fish

I am sorry that for want of a person to send them with, I have been obliged to detain your horses till now. The articles I shall want from Duychinks [3] are:

    four pint decanters if to be had, if not two Quart do.
    a dozen wine glasses
    two ale-glasses to hold about a pint each, if not to be had,
    two tumblers.

You will oblige me by procuring these articles as soon as possible, having them carefully packed up in a small box and forwarded to Major Kearse.[4] I shall also thank you to speak to him in your way to Camp about forwarding them as soon as they arrive by water; beg his particular care. I shall not be able to give a friend a glass of wine 'till these arrive, for they are not to be had here. Let me know what they cost by the first opportunity.

Adieu my   Dr friend   Yrs. A Hamilton

Perhaps you may meet with some friend coming directly up whose Portmanteau may not be too much crowded to receive them.

Send my horses by return of the bearer, unless they should be in too bad plight to travel. In this case, be so good as to put them out where they will be taken care of, and at the same time will not cost much for keeping.

ALS, Nicholas Fish Papers, Library of Congress.

1. Fish was a major in the Second Regiment of New York and, according to the address on the envelope, was at Poughkeepsie, New York.

2. This letter is undated. The endorsement reads "recd. April 1st. 82." It probably was written early in the last week of March.

3. G. Duychink was a merchant whose "medicine store" was at 13 Water Street (*The New York Directory for 1786, 27*).

4. H is presumably referring to John Keese, a major in the quartermaster general's department.

To Richard Kidder Meade [1]

Philadelphia March 1782

An half hour since brought me the pleasure of your letter of December last.[2] It went to Albany and came from thence to this place. I heartily felicitate you on the birth of your daughter. I can well conceive your happiness upon that occasion, by that which I feel in a similar one.[3]

Indeed the sensations of a tender father of the child, of a beloved mother can only be conceived by those who have experienced them.

Your heart, my Meade, is peculiarly formed for enjoyments of this kind, you have every right to be a happy husband, a happy father, you have every prospect of being so. I hope your felicity may never be interrupted.

You cannot imagine how entirely domestic I am growing. I lose all taste for the pursuits of ambition, I sigh for nothing but the company of my wife and my baby. The ties of duty alone or imagined duty keep me from renouncing public life altogether. It is however probable I may not be any longer actively engaged in it.

I have explained to you the difficulties which I met with in obtaining a command last campaign. I thought it incompatible with the delicacy due to myself to make any application this campaign. I have expressed this Sentiment in a letter to the General and retaining my rank only, have relinquished the emoluments of my commission, declaring myself notwithstanding ready at all times to obey the calls of the Public.[4] I do not expect to hear any of these unless the State of our Affairs, should change for the worse and lest by any unforeseen accident that should happen, I choose to keep myself in a situation again to contribute my aid. This prevents a total resignation.

You were right in supposing I neglected to prepare what I promised you at Philadelphia. The truth is, I was in such a hurry to get home that I could think of nothing else. As I set out tomorrow morning for Albany, I cannot from this place send you the matter you wish.

Imagine my Dear Friend what pleasure it *must* give Eliza & myself to know that Mrs. Meade [5] interests herself in us, without a personal acquaintance we have been long attached to her. My visit at Mr. Fitzhughs [6] confirmed my partiality. Betsy is so fond of your family that she proposes to form a match between her Boy & your girl provided you will engage to make the latter as amiable as her mother.

Truly My Dear Meade, I often regret that fortune has cast our residence at such a distance from each other. It would be a serious addition to my happiness if we lived where I could see you every day but fate has determined it otherwise. I am a little hurried & can only request in addition that you will present me most affectionately to Mrs. Meade & believe me to be with the warmest & most unalterable friendship   Yrs   A Hamilton

JCH Transcripts.
    1. Meade, who had been appointed an aide-de-camp to General Washington a few days after H had assumed his duties at Washington's Headquarters, had returned to his home in Virginia in October, 1780. In 1782 Meade was living in the valley of Virginia, where he had purchased land.
    2. Letter not found.

3. H's first child, Philip, was born on January 22, 1782.

4. See the two letters H wrote to George Washington on March 1, 1782.

5. H refers to Meade's second wife who was Mary Fitzhugh Grymes Randolph, daughter of Benjamin Grymes and the widow of William Randolph of "Chatsworth."

6. Presumably H had visited William Fitzhugh, of Fairfax County, Virginia, while Fitzhugh was serving in the Continental Congress in 1779. H was occasionally in Philadelphia during that year and could then have met Fitzhugh. Fitzhugh was Mrs. Meade's uncle.

From Marquis de Lafayette [1]

Paris April the 12th 1782

Dear Hamilton

However Silent You May please to Be, I will Nevertheless Remind You of a friend who loves You tenderly and who By His Attachment Desires a Great share in Your Affection. This letter, My dear Sir, Will Be delivered or sent By Count de Segur, an intimate friend of Mine, A Man of Wit and of Abilities, and whose Society You will Certainly Be pleased With.[2] I Warmly Recommend Him to You, and Hope He Will meet from You with more than Civilities. Now let us talk politics.

The old Ministry Have Retired and Lord North was not Sorry at the Opportunity. The New Ministers are not Much our friends, they are not friend to each other, they Have some Honest Men with little Sense, and some Sensible Men without Honesty. They are forced to New Measures not only By Circumstances But Also By the dispositions they Have formerly Announced.[3]

Entre nous seuls 81 [4] [The British Ministry] Gave a hint to 82 [the French Ministers]. But it Would not do without 54 [America]. Now the reverse will probably Be done. After which Arrangements will take place in a few Months and I wish you was here not so much 205 [secretary to Doctor Francklin] as to the Commission. However I would like 205 [5] to be 125 [Minister to the French Court]. If you are 153 [Member of Congress] and if Some thing is Said to you then I wish you May Be Employed in the Answer. 5 [French ships] without 9 [Spanish ships] (and 4 [Dutch] is nothing) Will not I fear give 40 [Charles Town]. That is a Cause of delay and the 7 [Spaniards] thinks much more of 8 [West Indies]. But I Hope for 26 [Carolina] and 22 [Georgia] in 18 [September]. 84 [The King of

France] Has Answered about 47 [peace] as You and I and every Good American May Wish.

In the Present Situation of affairs I thought My presence was more Useful to the cause in this part of the World than it Could Be on the other Side of the Atlantic. I wish to Have Some Matters Well Arranged Before I Go and then I Hope to Set Sails towards My friends in America.

Be pleased, My Dear friend, to Present My Best Respects to Your lady! My Compliments wait on Gnl Schuyler and all the family. Adieu, dear Hamilton, with the Most Sincere Attachment I am for Ever Your devoted Affectionate friend   Lafayette

ALS, Hamilton Papers, Library of Congress.
1. Lafayette had returned to France in December, 1781.
2. Louis-Phillipe, Comte de Segur, whose father was the uncle and friend of Lafayette, came to America in 1782 to replace the Vicomte de Noailles as colonel *en second*, Regiment Soissonnais.
3. Lord North was forced to resign on March 20, 1782. George III offered the government to William Petty, Marquis of Lansdowne, Earl of Shelburne, who, lacking a substantial party following, refused to accept the office. The King was then forced to accept a government headed by Charles Watson-Wentworth, Marquis of Rockingham. Under the Rockingham Ministry, Shelburne's nominal position was that of Secretary of State for the Southern Department. Charles James Fox received the secretaryship of the Northern Department.
4. The numbers refer to a cypher which Lafayette used. The bracketed words following the cypher are taken from the manuscript where they appear above the numbers in the writing of H.
5. H did not decode this number. The same number, in the preceding sentence, was translated to mean "secretary to Doctor Franklin."

From Robert Morris [1]

Office of Finance [Philadelphia] 15th. April 1782

Sir,

As several of the Legislatures have passed the Laws for levying Money in their respective states in Order to pay their Quota's of the eight Million of Dollars required by Congress for the service of the United States this present year,[2] without noticing that part of the Act of Congress of the second of November last which recommends "the passing of Acts directing the Collectors to pay the same to the Commissioner of the Loan Office or such other Person as shall be appointed by the Superintendant of Finance to receive the same

within the State &ca." [3] It hath become necessary to pass my Warrant on the executive or Treasurer of the State of   [4] Wherein
you are appointed to receive the Taxes payable to the United States,
for the first Quarterly Payment which fell due the first day of this
Month, and accordingly you will herein find my Warrant of this
date in your Favor for   [5] Dollars you will learn whether the
Payment is to be made by Order of the executive Authority or by
the State Treasurer and apply accordingly. It is not probable that
this Warrant will be discharged at one Payment and should that be
the Case you are to receive the Money or bank Notes from time
to time in such Sums as you can obtain, granting a Receipt for every
Sum you receive specifying the day on which the Payment is made
and endorse a Copy thereof on the back of the Warrant, so that
when the whole is discharged you may deliver up the said Warrant
then taking back your several loose Receipts. And as I find all the
States have been more backward in passing their Tax Bills than
was expected when my general Instructions [6] of the twelfth of
February last to the several Receivers were published, I desire that
you will commence your Monthly Publications of the Sums you receive on the first day of June next and it is also my Direction that
you publish on that day and on the first day of every succeeding
Month the Amount of what you have received during the preceeding Month or if no Payment is made that you declare in one of the
Newspapers published in the state that you have not during that
Month received any money for the use of the United States. Let
your Publications be made in Terms that will make known the
Facts without giving Offence; and I must request that you will constantly solicit such Payments as will give them a good face. Indeed
I must suppose that the State in which you reside will be anxious
on this Subject as their Reputation is so materially connected therewith.

I have found great Use and the United States have derived great
benefit from certain Notes or Orders which I have drawn on Mr.
John Swanwick [7] of this City payable at Sight to the Bearer, a Num-
ber of these Notes are now in Circulation they are struck on a
Copper plate, Numbered Letter'd, signed and directed in my own
Hand writing, they are for twenty fifty or eighty Dollars. These
Notes you are to receive as Money or if you receive Money ex-

change it for them in the same Manner as already directed with respect to Bank Notes. I shall address you from time to time as Occasion may require but being much employed you will continue to write to me such things as you may judge I ought to be informed of without expecting regular Answers to your Letters. I desire also that you will Cause all the Newspapers published in your State as also Political Pamphlets or Publications to be sent to me regularly by the Post.

I am Sir   your most obedient and humble Servant   RM

[ENCLOSURE]⁸

Warrant to Alexander Hamilton
to Receive Money as Continental Receiver
for the State of New York

[Philadelphia, April 15, 1782]

Whereas Alexander Hamilton esquire in conformity with an Act of the United States in Congress assembled passed the 2d of November 1781, hath been duly appointed by Commission under my Hand and Seal, Receiver of the continental Taxes within the State of New York. And whereas it is doubtful whether a Receiver of the continental Taxes hath yet been recognized by the Legislature of that State, In order to obviate Difficulties that might arise on that Account I do hereby especially authorize and empower the said Alexander Hamilton Esqr. to make Application to and receive from the executive Authority of the said State, the Treasurer or such other Person or Persons as are, or may be appointed and enabled to pay unto the Superintendant of the Finances, or his order for the Use of the United States the first quarterly Payment of the Quota of the said State in eight million of Dollars Specie required by Congress for the Service of this present Year, and upon the Receipt of the whole or any Part of the said first quarterly Payment which became due to the United States on the first Day of this present Month in the Sum of ninety three thousand, three hundred and ninety nine and one half Dollars Specie to give his Receipts or Discharges which shall be equally valid against the United States as if given by me. Given under my Hand and Seal of the Treasury at the Office of Finance in the City of Philadelphia this fifteenth Day of April 1782.

Robt. Morris

LC, Robert Morris Papers, Library of Congress.

1. H was not appointed receiver of continental taxes for New York until sometime between June 17 and July 2. On July 2, Morris sent H his instructions which included a copy of this circular (Morris to H, July 2, 1782). H in turn sent this to Thomas Tillotson when Tillotson was appointed to replace H in November, 1782. See the second of two letters H wrote to Tillotson, November 10, 1782. For information on the appointment of receivers of continental taxes see Morris to H, May 2, 1782, note 1.

2. See resolution of Congress of October 30, 1781 (*JCC*, XXI, 1087–88).

3. See resolutions of Congress of November 2, 1781 (*JCC*, XXI, 1089–92).

4. Space left blank in MS.

5. Space left blank in MS.

6. See Morris to H, February 12, 1782.

7. John Swanwick was a former clerk in Robert Morris's counting house. Known as both the "Treasurer to the Superintendent of Finance" and "Cashier of the Office of Finance," Swanwick held a position for which Congress had made no provision but which was solely the creation of the Superintendent of Finance.

8. DS, MS Division, New York Public Library. Although this warrant is dated April 15, 1782, it was not sent to H until July 2, 1782 (Morris to H, July 2, 1782).

From Robert Morris

[*Philadelphia, April 15, 1782.* On November 10, 1782, Hamilton sent to Thomas Tillotson, his successor as receiver of continental taxes for the State of New York, a list of papers "relative to the office of Receiver of Taxes." Item number three on that list was described as "farther instructions from the Superintendant to Alexander Hamilton dated as above." The preceding letter was dated April 15, 1782. *Second letter of April 15, 1782, not found.*]

The Continentalist No. V [1]

[Fishkill, New York, April 18, 1782]

The vesting Congress with the power of regulating trade ought to have been a principal object of the confederation for a variety

The New-York Packet, and the American Advertiser, April 18, 1782; ADf, Hamilton Papers, Library of Congress; ADf, Mrs. John C. Hamilton, Elmsford, New York. Both drafts are incomplete. The one in the Library of Congress appears to be a portion of the final draft, while the other is probably a portion of a first draft.

1. This essay was preceded in the newspaper by the following paragraph:

"*The succeeding numbers of the Continentalist were written last fall, but accidentally got out of the possession of the writer. He has lately recovered them, and he gives them to the public more to finish the development of his plan, than from any hope that the temper of the times will adopt his ideas.*"

The other issues of "The Continentalist" were dated July 12, 19, August 9, 30, 1781, and July 4, 1782.

of reasons. It is as necessary for the purposes of commerce as of revenue. There are some, who maintain, that trade will regulate itself, and is not to be benefitted by the encouragements, or restraints of government. Such persons will imagine, that there is no need of a common directing power. This is one of those wild speculative paradoxes, which have grown into credit among us, contrary to the uniform practice and sense of the most enlightened nations. Contradicted by the numerous institutions and laws, that exist every where for the benefit of trade, by the pains taken to cultivate particular branches and to discourage others, by the known advantages derived from those measures, and by the palpable evils that would attend their discontinuance—it must be rejected by every man acquainted with commercial history. Commerce, like other things, has its fixed principles, according to which it must be regulated; if these are understood and observed, it will be promoted by the attention of government, if unknown, or violated, it will be injured—but it is the same with every other part of administration.

To preserve the ballance of trade in favour of a nation ought to be a leading aim of its policy. The avarice of individuals may frequently find its account in pursuing channels of traffic prejudicial to that ballance, to which the government may be able to oppose effectual impediments. There may, on the other hand, be a possibility of opening new sources, which, though accompanied with great difficulties in the commencement, would in the event amply reward the trouble and expence of bringing them to perfection. The undertaking may often exceed the influence and capitals of individuals; and may require no small assistance, as well from the revenue, as from the authority of the state.

The contrary opinion, which has grown into a degree of vogue among us, has originated in the injudicious attempts made at different times to effect a REGULATION of PRICES. It became a cant phrase among the opposers of these attempts, that TRADE MUST REGULATE ITSELF; by which at first was only meant that it had its fundamental laws, agreeable to which its general operations must be directed; and that any violent attempts in opposition to these would commonly miscarry. In this sense the maxim was reasonable; but it has since been extended to militate against all interference by the sovereign; an extreme as little reconcileable with experience, or common sense, as the practice it was first framed to discredit.

The reasonings of a very ingenious and sensible writer,* by being misapprehended, have contributed to this mistake. The scope of his argument is not, as by some supposed, that trade will hold a certain invariable course independent on the aid, protection, care or concern of government; but that it will, in the main, depend upon the comparative industry moral and physical advantages of nations; and that though, for a while, from extraordinary causes, there may be a wrong ballance against one of them, this will work its own cure, and things will ultimately return to their proper level. His object was to combat that excessive jealousy on this head, which has been productive of so many unnecessary wars, and with which the British nation is particularly interested; but it was no part of his design to insinuate that the regulating hand of government was either useless, or hurtful. The nature of a government, its spirit, maxims and laws, with respect to trade, are among those constant moral causes, which influence its general results, and when it has by accident taken a wrong direction, assist in bringing it back to its natural course. This is every where admitted by all writers upon the subject; nor is there one who has asserted a contrary doctrine.

Trade may be said to have taken its rise in England under the auspices of Elizabeth; and its rapid progress there is in a great measure to be ascribed to the fostering care of government in that and succeeding reigns.

From a different spirit in the government, with superior advantages, France was much later in commercial improvements, nor would her trade have been at this time in so prosperous a condition had it not been for the abilities and indefatigable endeavours of the great COLBERT. He laid the foundation of the French commerce, and taught the way to his successors to enlarge and improve it. The establishment of the woolen manufacture, in a kingdom, where nature seemed to have denied the means, is one among many proofs, how much may be effected in favour of commerce by the attention and patronage of a wise administration. The number of useful

---

* Hume. Essay Jealousy of Trade.[2]
2. David Hume's essay "Of the Jealousy of Trade" first appeared in his Essays and Treatises on Several Subjects . . . a New Edition (London and Edinburgh, 1758).

edicts passed by Louis the 14th, and since his time, in spite of frequent interruptions from the jealous enmity of Great Britain, has advanced that of France to a degree which has excited the envy and astonishment of its neighbours.

The Dutch, who may justly be allowed a pre-eminence in the knowledge of trade, have ever made it an essential object of state. Their commercial regulations are more rigid and numerous, than those of any other country; and it is by a judicious and unremitted vigilance of government, that they have been able to extend their traffic to a degree so much beyond their natural and comparitive advantages.

Perhaps it may be thought, that the power of regulation will be left placed in the governments of the several states, and that a general superintendence is unnecessary. If the states had distinct interests, were unconnected with each other, their own governments would then be the proper and could be the only depositaries of such a power; but as they are parts of a whole with a common interest in trade, as in other things, there ought to be a common direction in that as in all other matters. It is easy to conceive, that many cases may occur, in which it would be beneficial to all the states to encourage, or suppress a particular branch of trade, while it would be detrimental to either to attempt it without the concurrence of the rest, and where the experiment would probably be left untried for fear of a want of that concurrence.

No mode can be so convenient as a source of revenue to the United States. It is agreed that imposts on trade, when not immoderate, or improperly laid, is one of the most eligible species of taxation. They fall in a great measure upon articles not of absolute necessity, and being partly transferred to the price of the commodity, are so far imperceptibly paid by the consumer. It is therefore that mode which may be exercised by the fœderal government with least exception or disgust. Congress can easily possess all the information necessary to impose the duties with judgment, and the collection can without difficulty be made by their own officers.

They can have no temptation to abuse this power, because the motive of revenue will check its own extremes. Experience has shown that moderate duties are more productive than high ones. When they are low, a nation can trade abroad on better terms—

its imports and exports will be larger—the duties will be regularly paid, and arising on a greater quantity of commodities, will yield more in the aggregate, than when they are so high as to operate either as a prohibition, or as an inducement to evade them by illicit practices.

It is difficult to assign any good reason why Congress should be more liable to abuse the powers with which they are intrusted than the state-assemblies. [The frequency of the election of the members is a full security against a dangerous ambition, and the rotation established by the confederation makes it impossible for any state, by continuing the same men, who may put themselves at the head of a prevailing faction, to maintain for any length of time an undue influence in the national councils. It is to be presumed, that Congress will be in general better composed for abilities, and as well for integrity as any assembly on the continent.

But to take away any temptation from a cabal to load particular articles, which are the principal objects of commerce to particular states, with a too great proportion of duties, to ease the others in the general distributions of expence; let all the duties whether for regulation or revenue, raised in each state, be creditted to that state, and let it in like manner be charged for all the bounties paid within itself for the encouragement of agriculture, manufactures, or trade. This expedient will remove the temptation; for as the quotas of the respective states are to be determined by a standard of land, agreeable to the ³ article of the confederation, each will have so much the less to contribute otherwise as it pays more on its commerce.

An objection has been made in a late instance to this principle. It has been urged, that as the consumer pays the duty, those states which are not equally well situated for foreign commerce, and which consume a great part of the imports of their neighbours, will become contributors to a part of their taxes. This objection is rather specious, than solid.

The maxim, that the consumer pays the duty has been admitted in theory with too little reserve; frequently contradicted in practice. It is true, the merchant will be unwilling to let the duty be

---

3. The blank space appears in the original. The reference is to the eighth article of the Articles of Confederation which provided that requisitions should be apportioned among the several states on the basis of the value of lands and improvements in each.

a deduction from his profits, if the state of the market will permit him to incorporate it with the price of his commodity. But this is often not practicable. It turns upon the quantity of goods at market in proportion to the demand. When the latter exceeds the former, and the competition is among the buyers, the merchant can easily increase his price and make his customers pay the duty. When the reverse is the case, and the competition is among the sellers, he must then content himself with smaller profits, and lose the value of the duty or at least of a part of it. Where a nation has a flourishing and well settled trade this more commonly happens than may be imagined, and it will, many times, be found that the duty is divided between the merchant and the consumer.

Besides this consideration, which greatly diminishes the force of the objection, there is another which intirely destroys it. There is strong reciprocal influence between the prices of all commodities in a state, by which they, sooner or later, attain a pretty exact ballance and proportion to each other. If the immediate productions of the soil rise, the manufacturer will have more for his manufacture, the merchant for his goods; and the same will happen with whatever class the increase of price begins. If duties are laid upon the imports in one state, by which the prices of foreign articles are raised, the products of land and labour within that state will take a proportionable rise; and if a part of those articles are consumed in a neighbouring state, it will have the same influence there as at home. The importing state must allow an advanced price upon the commodities, which it receives in exchange from its neighbor in a ratio to the increased price of the article it sells. To know then which is the gainer or loser, we must examine how the general ballance of trade stands between them. If the importing state takes more of the commodities of its neighbour, than it gives in exchange, that will be the loser by the reciprocal augmentation of prices— it will be the gainer, if it takes less—and neither will gain, or lose, if the barter is carried on upon equal terms. The ballance of trade, and consequently the gain, or loss, in this respect will be governed more by the relative industry and frugality of the parties, than by their relative advantages for foreign commerce.

Between separate nations, this reasoning will not apply with full force, because a multitude of local and extraneous circumstances may counteract the principal; but from the intimate connections of these states, the similitude of governments, situations, customs, manners—political and commercial causes will have nearly the same operation in the intercourse between the states, as in that between the different parts of the same state. If this should be controverted, the objection drawn from] [4] the hypothesis of the consumer paying the duty must fall at the same time: For as far as this is true it is as much confined in its application to a state within itself, as the doctrine of a reciprocal proportion of prices.

General principles in subjects of this nature ought always to be advanced with caution; in an experimental analysis there are found such a number of exceptions as tend to render them very doubtful; and in questions which affect the existence and collective happiness of these states, all nice and abstract distinctions should give way to plainer interests and to more obvious and simple rules of conduct.

But the objection which has been urged ought to have no weight on another account. Which are the states, that have not sufficient advantages for foreign commerce, and that will not in time be their own carriers? Connecticut and Jersey are the least maritime of the whole; yet the sound which washes the coast of Connecticut has an easy outlet to the ocean, affords a number of harbours and bays, very commodious for trading vessels. New-London may be a receptacle for merchantmen of almost any burthen; and the fine rivers with which the state is intersected, by facilitating the transportation of commodities to and from every part, are extremely favorable both to its domestic and foreign trade. Jersey, by way of Amboy has a shorter communication with the ocean, than the city of New-York. Princes bay, which may serve as an out port to it, will admit and shelter in winter and summer vessels of any size. Egg-harbour on its southern coast is not to be despised. The Delaware may be made as subservient to its commerce as to that of Pennsylvania, Gloucester, Burlington, and Trenton, being all conveniently situated on that river. The United Provinces with inferior advantages of position to either of these states, have for centuries held the first rank among commercial nations.

The want of large trading cities has been sometimes objected as

4. The material that appears in brackets is the same as the draft in the Hamilton Papers, Library of Congress.

an obstacle to the commerce of these states; but this is a temporary deficiency that will repair itself with the encrease of population and riches. The reason that the states in question have hitherto carried on little foreign trade, is that they have found it equally beneficial to purchase the commodities imported by their neighbours. If the imposts on trade should work an inconvenience to them, it will soon cease by making it their interest to trade abroad.

It is too much characteristic of our national temper to be ingenious in finding out and magnifying the minutest disadvantages, and to reject measures of evident utility even of necessity to avoid trivial and sometimes imaginary evils. We seem not to reflect, that in human society, there is scarcely any plan, however salutary to the whole and to every part, by the share, each has in the common prosperity, but in one way, or another, and under particular circumstances, will operate more to the benefit of some parts, than of others. Unless we can overcome this narrow disposition and learn to estimate measures, by their general tendency, we shall never be a great or a happy people, if we remain a people at all.

Suspension of the Rule Requiring Lawyers to Serve a Three-Year Clerkship in Favor of Alexander Hamilton

[Albany, April 26, 1782]

Whereas by a former rule of this Court, a Clerkship of three years at least was among other things made a necessary prerequisite to the admission of an attorney to practice in this Court.[1] And Whereas by a rule of this Court made on the eighteenth day of January last that part of the said rule which required a Clerkship of three years was suspended until the last day of April Term in favor of such young Gentlemen who had directed their studies to the profession of the Law, but upon the breaking out of the present War had entered into the Army in defence of their country, and Whereas Mr. Alexander Hamilton has in Court declared that he had previous to the war directed his Studies to the profession of the Law and upon the breaking out of the present war entered into the Army in defence of his Country, that his Situation in the Army and his services to his

Country were such as had prevented him from pursuing the Study of Law, and that being unprepared for an examination, he prayed of the Court that the said rule as to his admission to practice may be further suspended until October term next.

Thereupon Ordered that that part of the said Rule which requires a Clerkship of three years be farther suspended as to the said Alexander Hamilton until October Term next.

MS, "Minutes of the Supreme Court of New York, July 31, 1781, to November 1, 1783," 153, Hall of Records, New York City.

1. At its April term in 1778, the New York Supreme Court provided that "no person shall be admitted to practice as an Attorney of this Court unless he shall previously have served as a Clerk to an Attorney of this Court for at least three years and shall on an Examination as to his qualifications be found of Sufficient Ability and Competent learning to practice as an Attorney of this Court and produce a Certificate of his Moral Character" ("Minutes of the Supreme Court of New York, 1775–1781," 177).

Army Agreement Certified by Alexander Hamilton

[Albany] April 30, 1782. Certifies a contract made by Philip Schuyler, on behalf of the United States, and William Duer, contractor for the posts "north of Poughkeepsie in the State of New-York," for supplying the Army with meat.

Copy, RG 93, Miscellaneous Records, National Archives.

To Vicomte de Noailles [1]

[April–June, 1782]

Esteem for your talents and acquirements, is a sentiment which from my earliest acquaintance with you, my dear viscount, I have shared in common with all those who have the happiness of knowing you; but a better knowledge of your character has given it in my eyes a more intrinsic merit, and has attached me to you by a friendship founded upon qualities as rare as they are estimable.

Hamilton, Life, II, 3–6. In JCHW, I, 314–17 and HCLW, IX, 296–300, this letter is dated 1782.

1. Louis-Marie, Vicomte de Noailles, after serving with distinction at Yorktown had returned to France on December 25, 1781.

Averse as I am to professions, I cannot forbear indulging this declaration, to express to you the pleasure I feel at receiving, after an inexplicable delay, the letter you were so obliging as to write me before your departure from Boston.[2] It was of that kind which is always produced by those attentions of friends we value, which, not being invited by circumstances nor necessitated by the forms of society, bespeak the warmth of the heart; at least, my partiality for you makes me fond of viewing it in this light, and I cherish the opinion.

I was chagrined to find that you left us with an intention not to return. Though I should be happy if, by a removal of the war, this country should cease to be a proper theatre for your exertions, yet if it continues to be so, I hope you will find sufficient motives to change your resolution. Wherever you are, you will be useful and distinguished; but the ardent desire I have of meeting you again, makes me wish America may be your destination. I would willingly do it in France, as you invite me to do; but the prospect of this is remote. I must make a more solid establishment here before I can conveniently go abroad. There is no country I have a greater curiosity to see, or which I am persuaded would be so interesting to me, as yours. I should be happy to renew and improve the valuable acquaintances from thence which this war has given me an opportunity of making; and though I would not flatter myself with deriving any advantage from it, I am persuaded it is there I should meet with the greatest number of those you describe, who, &c.: but considerations of primary importance will oblige me to submit to the mortification of deferring my visit.

In the mean time, I should be too much the gainer by a communication with you, not gladly to embrace the offer you so politely make for writing to each other.

The period since you left us has been too barren of events to enable me to impart any thing worth attention. The enemy continues in possession of Charleston and Savannah, and leaves us master of the rest of the country.[3] It is said the assemblies of the two invaded

2. Letter not found. Noailles probably wrote to H sometime between December 10 and 25, 1781. He arrived in Boston on December 10, 1781, and sailed with Lafayette and other French officers on December 25, 1781, on the *Alliance.*

3. Savannah was evacuated by the British in July, 1782; Charleston was abandoned in December, 1782.

states are about meeting to restore the administration of government. This will be a step to strengthening the hands of General Greene [4] and counteracting the future intrigues of the enemy. Many are sanguine in believing that all the southern posts will be evacuated, and that a fleet of transports is actually gone to bring the garrisons away; for my part, I have doubts upon the subject. My politics are, that while the present ministry can maintain their seats and procure supplies, they will prosecute the war on the mere chance of events; and that while this is the plan, they will not evacuate posts so essential as points of departure, from whence, on any favourable turn of affairs, to renew their attack on our most vulnerable side; nor would they relinquish objects that would be so useful to them, should the worst happen in a final negotiation. Clinton,[5] it is said, is cutting a canal across New-York island, through the low ground about a mile and a half from the city.[6] This will be an additional obstacle; but if we have otherwise the necessary means to operate, it will not be an insurmountable one. I do not hear that he is constructing any other new works of consequence. To you who are so thoroughly acquainted with the military posture of things in this country, I need not say that the activity of the next campaign must absolutely depend on effectual succours from France. I am convinced we shall have a powerful advocate in you. La Fayette, we know, will bring the whole house with him if he can.

There has been no material change in our internal situation since you left us. The capital successes we have had, have served rather to increase the hopes than the exertions of the particular states. But in one respect we are in a mending way. Our financier [7] has hitherto conducted himself with great ability, has acquired an entire personal confidence, revived in some measure the public credit, and is conciliating fast the support of the moneyed men.

4. Major General Nathanael Greene.
5. Sir Henry Clinton.
6. On March 3, 1782, Major General William Heath recorded that "the enemy at New York were now contemplating means for their own defence against the next campaign, and it was determined to open a canal and strong lines from the Hudson to the East River, at some distance from the city. The canal was to be deep and wide; 2000 men were employed on the works on one day. . . . These preparations were a defensive shield for the time of approaching negotiation, for, from the debates and speeches in the British Parliament, the olive-branch was evidently putting forth its buds" (William Abbatt, ed., *Memoirs of Major General William Heath* [New York, 1901], 305).
7. Robert Morris.

His operations have hitherto hinged chiefly on the seasonable aids from your country; but he is urging the establishment of permanent funds among ourselves; and though, from the nature and temper of our governments, his applications will meet with a dilatory compliance, it is to be hoped they will by degrees succeed. The institution of a bank has been very serviceable to him. The commercial interest, finding great advantages in it, and anticipating much greater, is disposed to promote the plan; and nothing but moderate funds, permanently pledged for the security of lenders, is wanting to make it an engine of the most extensive and solid utility.

By the last advices, there is reason to believe the delinquent states will shortly comply with the requisition of congress for a duty on our imports.[8] This will be a great resource to Mr. Morris, but it will not alone be sufficient.

Upon the whole, however, if the war continues another year, it will be necessary that congress should again recur to the generosity of France for pecuniary assistance. The plans of the financier cannot be so matured as to enable us by any possibility to dispense with this; and if he should fail for want of support, we must replunge into that confusion and distress which had like to have proved fatal to us, and out of which we are slowly emerging. The cure in a relapse would be infinitely more difficult than ever.

I have given you an uninteresting but a faithful sketch of our situation. You may expect from time to time to receive from me the progress of our affairs, and I know you will overpay me.

8. H is referring to the congressional proposal of February 3, 1781, that the states grant the government of the Confederation the authority to levy an impost on all imports (*JCC*, XIX, 112). By the early summer of 1782 all the states except Maryland, Georgia, and Rhode Island had acceded to the request. Maryland gave its assent in July, 1782.

From Robert Morris[1]

Office of Finance
Philda. May 2d. 1782

Sir

Mr. Charles Stewart late Commissary general of Issues has informed me ⟨that⟩ you are disposed to quit the military line for the purpose of ⟨en⟩tering into civil life. He at the same time induced me to believe ⟨that⟩ you would accept of the Office of Receiver of the continental taxes ⟨for⟩ the state of New York. The intention of this letter is to offer you that ⟨app⟩ointment. The duties of the Office will appear in a great degree from the publications made by me on this subject. In addition it will be necessary that you correspond with me frequently and give accurate accounts of whatever may be passing in your State which it may be necessary for this Office to be acquainted with. But this and other things of that sort will be more fully communicated after you shall have signifyed your acceptance of the Office. For the trouble of executing it I shall allow you one fourth pr Cent on the monies you receive. The amount of the quota called for from New York for the current year is as you know three hundred and seventy three thousand, five hundred and ninety eight Dollars. I shall be glad to know your determination as soon as possible. I make to you no professions of my confidence and esteem because I hope ⟨they⟩ are unnecessary, but if they are, my wish that you would accept the Offer I make is the Strongest evidence I can give of them.

I pray you Sir to believe me very respectfully Your most Obedi⟨ent⟩ and Humble ⟨Servant⟩   Robt. Morris

LS, Hamilton Papers, Library of Congress.
1. In February, 1781, after more than five years of control of continental finances by committees of Congress, the Treasury Department was reorganized and placed under an individual department head. Robert Morris was appointed the first Superintendent of Finance.

On October 30, 1781, Congress called upon the states to furnish the treasury of the United States eight million dollars in specie to meet expenses for 1782. On November 2, 1781, in a resolution assigning the proportionate sum to be paid by each state, it was resolved that state quotas should be paid to the commissioners of the loan offices in the respective states or "such other person as shall be appointed by the superintendant of finance, to receive the same within the State . . ." (JCC, XXI, 1091). It was also provided that taxes levied for the United States should be distinguished from those levied for the states.

Morris decided to appoint a receiver of continental taxes in each state rather than to use the commissioners of the loan offices. The duties of the receivers were defined by Morris in a number of circular letters in which he stressed, among other things, receiving bank notes or specie in payment of taxes and the importance of the use of newspapers to publicize delinquencies in the payment of taxes. The receivers were to receive percentages varying from one-eighth to one-half percent of the revenue collected.

To Robert Morris

[*Albany, May 4, 1782.* On May 20, 1782, Morris wrote to Hamilton: "I have received your Letter of the fourth Instant." *Letter not found.*]

From James Duane

Man. Liv.[1] [New York] 5 May 1782

Dear Sir

I am much pleased to find that you have set yourself Seriously to the Study of the Law. You are welcome to the use of any of my books of which you will inform Mr Lansing. I know that I can depend upon your care of them.[2]

Whether I shall see Albany, or Philadelphia first remains undecided tho' I feel myself oblig'd by your friendly wishes to see me.[3] A seperation from my Family is extremely irksome. If I submit to it for the next Six months it will be with much more Reluctance than I shoud find in returning to private Life & the ⟨Intrigues⟩ of my profession.

Present my respectful Compliments to the General & every branch of the Family, and believe that I am with great Regard   Dr Sir Your affec & Obed Serv   Jas Duane

Colonel Hamilton

ALS, Hamilton Papers, Library of Congress.
  1. Manor Livingston. In 1759, Duane married Mary Livingston, daughter of Robert Livingston, "third lord" of Livingston Manor. Duane was staying at his father-in-law's home at this time.
  2. After his return to Albany in the fall of 1781, H began his studies in preparation for the bar. John Lansing, Jr., later mayor of Albany and chancellor of the state, was practicing law in Albany at this time.
  3. Duane, a delegate from New York to the Continental Congress, had left Philadelphia in October, 1781. He returned in June, 1782.

From Robert Morris [1]

Philadelphia, May 15, 1782. Sends a circular to the "Receivers of Taxes Eastward of Hudsons River" instructing them on the manner of transmitting notes, bank notes, and Morris notes to the Office of Finance in Philadelphia. Appoints John Brown of Philadelphia "Messenger by whom you are from Time to Time to transmit the Bank Notes which you may receive."

LC, Robert Morris Papers, Library of Congress.

1. H was not appointed receiver of continental taxes for New York until sometime between June 17 and July 2. On July 2, Morris sent H his instructions which included a copy of this circular (Morris to H, July 2, 1782). H in turn sent the circular to Thomas Tillotson when Tillotson was appointed to replace H in November, 1782. See H to Tillotson, November 10, 1782.

For information on the duties of the receivers of continental taxes, see Morris to H, April 15, 1782.

To Robert Morris

Albany May 18. 17⟨82⟩

Sir

I had this day the honor of receiving your letter of the 2d. instant and am much obliged by the mark of your confidence, which it contains; and to Col Stewart for his friendly intentions upon the occasion.[1]

My military situation has indeed become [2] so negative that I have no motive to continue in it; and if my services could be of importance to the public in any civil line I should chearfully obey its command. But the plan which I have marked out to myself is the profession of the law; and I am now engaged in a course of studies for that purpose. Time is so precious to me that I could not put myself in the way of any interruptions unless for an object of consequence to the public or to myself. The present is not of this nature. Such are the circumstances of this state, the benefit arising from the office you propose would not during the war exceed yearly one hundred pounds; for unfortunately, I am persuaded it will not pay annually into the Continental treasury above forty thousand pounds; and on a peace establishment this will not be for sometime to come much more than doubled. You will perceive Sir that an engagement of this kind does not correspond with my views and does not afford a sufficient inducement to relinquish them.

I am not the less sensible to the obliging motives which dictated the offer, and it will be an additional one to that respect and esteem with which I have the honor to be very truly Sir   Yr. most Obed & humble servant

ADf, Hamilton Papers, Library of Congress.
  1. Colonel Charles Stewart had suggested to Morris that H might accept the office of receiver of taxes. See Morris to H, May 2, 1782.
  2. H here wrote and crossed out the words "contrary to myself."

From Robert Morris

Office of Finance [Philadelphia] 20 May 1782

Sir,

I have received your Letter of the fourth Instant [1] and am very much obliged by the Attention shewn to the Subject of it. Your Sentiments on the Occasion I entirely approve and indeed before this reaches you you will probably have seen that the Letter [2] has been republished in one of the Philadelphia Papers. I should readily consent to the Publication of many others which I have written on the same Subject and am fearless of any Injury they can do us abroad. Foreigners are already acquainted with our Circumstances and so are our Enemy. The People are kept in Ignorance of their true Interests by those Men who having little Objects of their own in View are regardless of the general Cause.

I am Sir   your most obedient and humble servant   RM.

LC, Robert Morris Papers, Library of Congress.
  1. Letter not found.
  2. The letter that Morris is referring to was a circular to the governors of the several states which Morris had written on October 19, 1781 (Robert Morris Papers, Library of Congress). A copy of this circular had been printed in Rivington's *Royal Gazette* on April 13, 1782, under the incorrect date of October 15, 1781. The letter, as Morris states, was republished in *The Freeman's Journal or The North American Intelligencer* on May 1, 1782, under the incorrect date of October 15, 1781.

From Robert Morris

Office of Finance [Philadelphia] 4th. June 1782

Sir

I have received your favor of the eighteenth of May. I am much obliged by the friendly Sentiments you express for me which be assured I shall retain a gratefull Sense of. I see with you that the Office I had the Pleasure of Offering will not be equal to what your own Abilities will gain in the Profession of the Law but I did intend that the whole Sum should have been paid altho the whole quota of the Taxes had not been collected by the state,[1] consequently the object is greater than you supposed and the business might probably be effected without more attention than you could spare from your Studies, if so, I should still be happy in your acceptance and will leave the Matter open untill I have an Opportunity of hearing from you upon the Subject.

I pray you to believe that I am with unfained Esteem   Your Most Obedient Servant   Robt. Morris

Colo Alexr. Hamilton at Albany

LS, Hamilton Papers, Library of Congress.
   1. For the remuneration initially offered H, see Morris to H, May 2, 1782.

To Major General Henry Knox [1]

[Albany, June 7, 1782]

Dr. General

We are told here that there is a British officer coming on from Cornwallis's army to be executed by way of retaliation for the murder of Capt Huddy.[2] As this appears to me clearly to be an ill-timed proceeding, and if persisted in will be derogatory to the national character I cannot forbear communicating to you my ideas upon the subject. A sacrifice of this sort is intirely repugnant to the genius of the age we live in and is without example in modern history nor can it fail to be considered in Europe as wanton and unnecessary. It appears that the enemy (from necessity I grant but the operation is the same) have changed their system and adopted a more humane one; and therefore the only justifying motive of retaliation, the preventing a repetition of cruelty, ceases. But if this were not the case, so solemn and deliberate a sacrifice of the innocent for the guilty must be condemned on the present received notions of humanity, and encourage an opinion that we are in a certain degree in a state of barbarism. Our affairs are now in a prosperous train, and so vigorous, I would rather say so violent a measure would want the plea of necessity. It would argue meanness in us that at this late stage of the war, in the midst of success, we should suddenly depart from that temper with which we have all along borne with as great and more frequent provocations. The death of André could not have been dispensed with; but it must still be viewed at a distance as an act of *rigid justice;* if we wreak our resentment on an innocent person, it will be suspected that we are too fond of executions. I am persuaded it will have an influence peculiarly unfavourable to the General's character.

If it is seriously believed that in this advanced state of affairs retaliation is necessary let another mode be chose. Let under actors be employed and let the authority by which it is done be wrapt in obscurity and doubt. Let us endeavour to make it fall upon those who have had a direct or indirect share in the guilt. Let not the Commander in Chief considered as the first and most respectable character among us come forward in person and be the avowed author of an act at which every humane feeling revolts. Let us at least have as much address as the enemy, and, if we must have victims, appoint some obscure agents to perform the ceremony, and bear the odium which must always attend even justice itself when directed by extreme severity.

For my own part my Dear Sir I think a business of this complexion intirely out of season. The time for it, if there ever was one, is past.

But it is said the Commander in Chief has pledged himself for it and cannot recede. Inconsistency in this case would be better than consistency. But pretexts may be found and will be readily admitted in favour of humanity. Carelton[3] will in all probability do something like apology and concession. He will give assurances of preventing everything of the kind in future. Let the General appear to be satisfied with these assurances. The steps Carleton is said to have taken to suppress the refugee incursions will give the better color to lenity.

I address myself to you upon this occasion because I know your liberality and your influence with the General. If you are of my opinion I am sure you will employ it—if it should not be too late. I would not think a letter necessary, but I know how apt men are to be actuated by the circumstances which immediately surround them and to be led into an approbation of measures which in another situation they would disapprove. Mrs. Hamilton joins me in compliments to Mrs. Knox; believe me to be very truly & Affecty Dr. Sir   Yr. Obed ser   A Hamilton

Albany June 7 82

ALS, Massachusetts Historical Society, Boston.
    1. Knox was a commissioner for the exchange of prisoners.
    2. Captain Joshua Huddy, New Jersey State Artillery, had been captured by a group of Loyalists, or refugees, and taken to New York. He was accused of the murder of Philip White, a refugee, and on April 12, 1782, was hanged by refugees who were commanded by Captain Richard Lippincott of the Associated Loyalists, British Provincial Troops. When the murder came to the attention of Washington, he requested the opinion of the general and field officers of the Army on whether retaliation was "justifiable and expedient." The officers agreed that it was, but they suggested that Sir Henry Clinton, the British commander in America, be first asked to turn over Captain Lippincott, or those responsible for the murder, to the American army. If Clinton refused, Washington was determined to retaliate by hanging a British prisoner of equal rank. On May 3, he directed Brigadier General Moses Hazen to designate by lot a British captain to be hanged. On May 27, Hazen informed Washington that "the unfortunate Lot had fallen on the Honourable Capt. Charles Asgill, of the Guards; a young Gentleman seventeen Years of Age." On June 4, Washington informed Colonel Elias Dayton that Asgill had arrived in Philadelphia on his way to the "Jersey Line, the place assigned for his execution." See GW, XXIV, 136-39, 144-47, 217-21, 226-27, 231-32, 241-44, 262-64, 305-08.
    3. Sir Guy Carleton succeeded Sir Henry Clinton as commander in chief in America in February, 1782. He arrived in New York City on May 5, 1782.

To Robert Morris

[Albany, June 17, 1782]

Sir,

The letter, which you did me the honor to write me of the 4th. instant came to my hands too late to permit me to answer it by the return of the same post. The explanation you give of your intention in your late offer makes it an object that will fully compensate for the time it will deduct from my other occupations. In accepting it I have only one scruple, arising from a doubt whether the service I can render in the present state of things will be an equivalent for the compensation. The whole system (if it may be so called) of taxation in this state is radically vicious, burthensome to the people and unproductive to government. As the matter now stands there seems to be little for a Continental Receiver to do. The whole business appears to be thrown into the hands of the County treasurers, nor do I find that there is any appropriation made of any part of the taxes collected to Continental purposes, or any provision to authorise payment to the officer you appoint. This however must be made. There is only one way in which I can imagine a prospect of being materially useful that is in seconding your applications to the State. In popular assemblies much may sometimes be brought about by personal discussions, by entering into details and combating objections as they rise. If it should at any time be thought adviseable by you to empower me to act in this capacity, I shall be happy to do every thing that depends on me to effectuate your views. I flatter myself, to you Sir, I need not profess that I suggest this not from a desire to augment the importance of office but to advance the public interest.

It is of primary moment to me as soon as possible to take my station in the law, and on this consideration I am pressing to qualify myself for admission the next term which will be the latter end of July. After this if you should think an interview with me necessary I will wait upon you in Philadelphia. In the mean time I shall be happy to receive your instructions, and shall direct my attention more particularly to acquiring whatever information may be useful to my future operations. I have read your publications at different times; but as I have not the papers containing them in my possession, it will be necessary that their contents should be comprized in your instructions. A meeting of the Legislature is summoned early in the next month at which, if I previously receive your orders, it may be possible to put matters in train.

I am truly indebted to you Sir, for the disposition you have manifested upon this occasion; and I shall only add an assurance of my endeavours to justify your confidence and prove to you the sincerity of that respectful attachment with which I am Sir   Yr most Obed serv   AH

Albany June 17. 1782

ADfS, Hamilton Papers, Library of Congress.

To Comfort Sands

[Albany, June 23, 1782]

Sir,

Mr. Morris having lately offered me the appointment of Receiver of Continental taxes for this state, I wish to collect as much and as accurate information as possible of the situation of its money-concerns. It will be among other things of great importance that I should form an idea of the money brought into the state and carried out of it; and with a view to this I take the liberty to request you will furnish me with an estimate of what you have reason to think you will lay out in this state in the course of a year in the transactions of your contract business.[1] Mr. Duer has been so obliging as to promise me a sketch of his disbursements in this quarter;[2] and has informed me that you are principally charged with what relates to the supplies of the main army as well as West Point; and will therefore be best able to enlighten me on that head. The calculation may not admit of absolute precision; but if it comes near the truth it will answer. It would be useful that you could distinguish as nearly as possible what part will be in specie, what in bank and in other notes. As this is a matter that can be attended with no inconvenience to any person and will be conducive to the public utility, I flatter myself you will favour me with a speedy communication.

I am with ⟨esteem⟩   Sir   Yr. most Obed serv   A Hamilton

Albany June 23 1782
Comfort Sands Esqr.

ALS, Hamilton Papers, Library of Congress. In *JCHW*, I, 282, this letter is dated June 22, 1782.

1. Soon after his appointment as Superintendent of Finance in February, 1781, Robert Morris sought to improve the manner of supplying the Continental Army by introducing a system of private contract. In December, 1781, he entered into agreements with Comfort Sands and Company for supplying West Point and with Sands, Livingston and Company of New York for supplying "the Moving Army." The two major stockholders in the latter company were Comfort Sands and Walter Livingston. For a discussion of these companies and their contracts, see East, *Business Enterprise in the American Revolutionary Era*, 118, 124-25.

2. Early in 1782, soon after Robert Morris established the contract system
for supplying the American army, William Duer became a principal contractor. At first, with his base in Albany, he was engaged in supplying the Army
posts north of Poughkeepsie, New York. Later in 1782, he secured another
contract to supply the Army in New York and New Jersey.

From Marquis de Lafayette

Paris June the 29th 1782

My dear Hamilton

How it Happens that I still am in Paris, I Hardly Can Myself Conceive [1] and What is More Surprising, there are two frigates Going,
Neither of Which Will Carry Your friend to America. Don't think
However, dear Hamilton, I Am So Much Alterd as to Be Kept
Here By pleasure or private Affairs. But in the present Circumstances the American Ministers Have insisted Upon My Remaining
some time longer at this Court Where they Say I May Render Myself More Useful to our Cause than I Can possibly Be in America
during an Inactive Campaign. My Return However is only deferd
for a few weeks, and after some Answers Have Arrived from England, Which I think will discover the views of, But Not Yet Produce
a Reconciliation With Great Britain, I intend embarking for Philadelphia where I Hope to land in the first days of September.

This stroke of Count de Grasse Has Greatly deranged My
schemes.[2] I Hoped for 40 [Charles Town] [3] and perhaps for Better
than that—But Nothing Untill 6 [Jamaica] was done.[4] 40 [Chs.
Town] I much expected. 9 [The Spaniards] don't like 54 [Amer-
ica]. We must previously Have 40 [Chs. Town], and then to put
them in good Humour do some thing about 8 [West Indies]. Both
of which are not yet done, and after that I Hope—But at all events
this Campaign will Be Very inactive, I think. However they are
going to take Gibraltar, and Will Gather So Many Means of doing
of it, that it is Said they will Succeed.[5] After this trial, the forces
of the House of Bourbon will Be distributed with a Better scale.
46 [Negotiations] is Going, and 47 [Peace] expected, But not, I
think, immediately.

You have a good Chance, and I Believe You Have time to Be one
of the 125 [Commissioners]. Jefferson does not Come.[6] Mr Laurens,
I am told, intends to Return Home, and I Cannot Conceive, (entre

nous) what He is About.[7] Mr Adams thinks His presence is Wanting in Holland.[8] I thought I Had Better Give You these intelligences.

Not a Word from You, Since we parted in Virginia, But I am a Good Natured Man and Will not Get tired to speak to a deaf Man. My Best Respects to Your Amiable lady—to Mrs Carter,[9] Mrs Schuyler,[10] Miss Peggy.[11] My affectionate Compliments to your old father in law.

Adieu, Most affectionately Your forever   devoted friend

Lafayette

ALS, Hamilton Papers, Library of Congress.

1. On April 12, 1782, Lafayette had written H of his intention to come to America in the near future.

2. Lafayette probably referred to Admiral Sir George Rodney's decisive victory over the French fleet, commanded by François Joseph Paul, Comte de Grasse, in the West Indies on April 12, 1782.

3. The British were still in possession of Charleston. Lafayette apparently had hoped that the French fleet would convoy troops there.
The decoding of the cypher on the manuscript is written above the numerals in H's writing.

4. In November, 1782, after the defeat of Charles, Earl Cornwallis at Yorktown, De Grasse had sailed for the West Indies to attack British possessions, among them Jamaica.

5. Soon after Spain entered the war in 1779, France and Spain had laid seige to Gibraltar. Lafayette probably referred to plans for a more vigorous effort.

6. Thomas Jefferson had been appointed one of the Peace Commissioners on June 15, 1781; he resigned on October 8, 1781, and was reappointed on November 12, 1782.

7. Henry Laurens, Minister Designate to the Netherlands, was captured by the British in 1780 and imprisoned in the Tower of London. On the last day of 1781 he was released, ostensibly on bail but actually in anticipation of his exchange for Lord Cornwallis. Lord Shelburne, in the spring of 1782, sent Laurens to the Hague to confer with John Adams. According to reports Shelburne had received, Adams was reported to have said that the American Ministers were free to negotiate for peace independently of France. On June 15, 1781, Laurens had been appointed as one of the American Peace Commissioners.

8. Adams, because of negotiations he was conducting in Holland for a loan and treaty, did not arrive in Paris until October, 1782.

9. Angelica Church, H's sister-in-law and wife of John B. Church (John Carter).

10. Mrs. Philip Schuyler, H's mother-in-law.

11. Margaret (Margarita) Schuyler, H's sister-in-law.

From Robert Morris

Office of Finance [Philadelphia] 2 July 1782

Sir,

I yesterday received your Letter of the seventeenth of June and am very happy to find you have determined to accept the office I had the Pleasure of offering to you. I enclose the commission, Instructions &ca. together with a Bond for Performance of the Duties which I must request you to fill up, execute with some sufficient Surety and transmit.[1] The complaint you make of the System of taxation, in New York might I beleive very justly be extended, for tho' it may be more defective in some than in others it is I fear very far from perfect in any. I had already heard that no part of the Taxes were appropriated to continental Purposes, but I expect that the Legislature will when they meet make such appropriations as well as lay new and I hope Productive Taxes for the purposes of Paying what may remain of their quotas. It gives me a singular pleasure to find that you have yourself pointed out one of the principal objects of your appointment.[2] You will find that it is specified in the Enclosure of the fifteenth of April.[3] I do not conceive that any interview will be necessary, tho' I shall always be happy to see you when your Leisure and convenience will admit. In the mean time I must request you to exert your talents in forwarding with your Legislature the Views of Congress.[4] Your former situation in the Army, the present situation of that very army, your connections in the state, your perfect knowledge of men and measures, and the abilities which heaven has blessed you with will give you, a fine opportunity to forward the public service by convincing the Legislature of the necessity of copious supplies, and by convincing all who have claims on the Justice of Congress that those claims exist only by that hard Necessity which arises from the Negligence of the States. When to this you shall super add the conviction that what remains of the War being only a War of Finance solid arrangements of Finance must necessarily terminate favorably not only to our Hopes, but even to Our Wishes, then Sir the Governments will be disposed to lay and the people to bear those Burthens which ⟨are⟩ necessary, and then the Utility of your office, and of the Officer ⟨wil⟩l be as manifest to other's as at present to me.

I am with perfect Respect Your most obedient & Humble Servant   Robt Morris

Alexander Hamilton Esquire
Receiver of Taxes for New York

LS, Hamilton Papers, Library of Congress.
1. The commission has not been found. The bond was returned to Morris. See H to Morris, July 22, 1782. The instructions probably included: Morris to H, February 12, 1782; Morris to H, April 15, 1782, and the enclosed warrant of the same date; and Morris to H, May 15, 1782.
2. H had written Morris on June 17, 1782, that the most important aspect of his job would be to urge the state legislature to accept Morris's recommendations.
3. The enclosure was presumably the letter of April 15, 1782, referred to in note 1.
4. The meeting of the New York legislature was scheduled for July, 1782.

The Continentalist No. VI [1]

[Fishkill, New York, July 4, 1782]

Let us see what will be the consequences of not authorising the Fœderal Government to regulate the trade of these states.

Besides the want of revenue and of power, besides the immediate risk to our independence, the danger of all the future evils of a precarious union, besides the deficiency of a wholesome concert and provident superintendence to advance the general prosperity of trade, the direct consequence will be, that the landed interest and the labouring poor will in the first place fall a sacrifice to the trading interest, and the whole eventually to a bad system of policy, made necessary by the want of such regulating power.

Each state will be afraid to impose duties on its commerce, lest the other states, not doing the same, should enjoy greater advantages than itself; by being able to afford native commodities cheaper abroad, and foreign commodities cheaper at home.

A part of the evils resulting from this would be: A loss to the revenue of those moderate duties, which, without being injurious

The New-York Packet. And the American Advertiser, July 4, 1782.
1. This is the sixth and final essay entitled "The Continentalist." The preceding five are dated July 12, 19, August 9, 30, 1781, and April 18, 1782.

to commerce, are allowed to be the most agreeable species of taxes to the people.

Articles of foreign luxury while they would contribute nothing to the income of the state, being less dear by an exemption from duties, would have a more extensive consumption.

Many branches of trade hurtful to the common interest would be continued for want of proper checks and discouragements.

As revenues must be found to satisfy the public exigencies in peace and in war, too great a proportion of taxes will fall directly upon land and upon the necessaries of life, the produce of that land.

The influence of these evils will be, to render landed property fluctuating and less valuable, to oppress the poor by raising the prices of necessaries, to injure commerce by encouraging the consumption of foreign luxuries, by encreasing the value of labor, by lessening the quantity of home productions, enhancing their prices at foreign markets, of course, obstructing their sale and enabling other nations to supplant us.

Particular caution ought at present to be observed in this country, not to burthen the soil itself and its productions, with heavy impositions; because the quantity of unimproved land will invite the husbandmen to abandon old settlements for new, and the disproportion of our population for some time to come, will necessarily make labor dear, to reduce which, and not to increase it, ought to be a capital object of our policy.

Easy duties therefore on commerce, especially on imports, ought to lighten the burthens, which will unavoidably fall upon land. Though it may be said, that on the principle of a reciprocal influence of prices, whereon the taxes are laid in the first instance, they will in the end be borne by all classes; yet it is of the greatest importance that no one should sink under the immediate pressure. The great art is to distribute the public burthens well and not suffer them, either first, or last, to fall too heavily upon parts of the community; else distress and disorder must ensue. A shock given to any part of the political machine vibrates through the whole.

As a sufficient revenue could not be raised from trade to answer the public purposes, other articles have been proposed.

A moderate land and poll tax, being of easy and unexpensive collection, and leaving nothing to discretion, are the simplest and best, that could be devised.

It is to be feared, the avarice of many of the landholders will be opposed to a perpetual tax upon land, however moderate. They will ignorantly hope to shift the burthens of the national expence from themselves to others; a disposition as iniquitous as it is fruitless. The public necessities must be satisfied; this can only be done by the contributions of the whole society. Particular classes are neither able nor will be willing to pay for the protection and security of the others; and where so selfish a spirit discovers itself in any member, the rest of the community will unite to compel it to do its duty.

Indeed many theorists in political œconomy have held, that all taxes, wherever they originate fall ultimately upon land; and have therefore been of opinion, that it would be best to draw the whole revenue of the state immediately from that source, to avoid the expence of a more diversified collection, and the accumulations which will be heaped in their several stages upon the primitive sums advanced in those taxes, which are imposed on our trade.* But though it has been demonstrated, that this theory has been carried to an extreme, impracticable in fact, yet it is evident, in tracing the matter, that a large part of all taxes, however remotely laid, will by an insensible circulation, come at last to settle upon land; the source of most of the materials employed of commerce.

It appears from calculation made by the ablest masters of political arithmetic, about sixty years ago, that the yearly product of all the lands in England amounted to £42,000,000 sterling, and the whole annual consumption, at that period, of foreign as well as domestic commodities, did not exceed £49,000,000, and the surplus of the exportation above the importation [2] £2,000,000; on which sums, must arise all the revenues in whatever shape which go into the treasury. It is easy to infer from this, how large a part of them must directly, or indirectly be derived from land.[3]

* The merchant it is said will have an advance on the duty he pays, the shop keeper a further advance &c.

2. In the newspaper version the phrase was written "exportation above the exportation."

3. H's information was taken from Postlethwayt, *The Universal Dictionary of Trade and Commerce*. (For full title see *The Papers of Alexander Hamilton*, I, 142, note 35.) See the section on "Postleth waits on Funds" in H's "Pay Book of the State Company of Artillery," 1777 (*ibid.*, 385).

Nothing can be more mistaken, than the collision and rivalship, which almost always subsist between the landed and trading interests, for the truth is they are so inseparably interwoven, that one cannot be injured, without injury, nor benefitted, without benefit to the other. Oppress trade, lands sink in value, make it flourish, their value rises, incumber husbandry, trade declines, encourage agriculture, commerce revives. The progress of this mutual reaction might easily be delineated, but it is too obvious to every man, who turns his thoughts, however superficially, upon the subject, to require it. It is only to be regretted that it is too often lost sight of, when the seductions of some immediate advantage or exemption tempt us to sacrifice the future to the present.

But perhaps the class is more numerous than those, who not unwilling to bear their share of public burthens, are yet averse to the idea of perpetuity, as if there ever would arrive a period, when the state would cease to want revenues and taxes become unnecessary. It is of importance to unmask this delusion and open the eyes of the people to the truth. It is paying too great a tribute to the idol of popularity to flatter so injurious and so visionary an expectation. The error is too gross to be tolerated any where, but in the cottage of the peasant; should we meet with it in the senate house, we must lament the ignorance or despise the hypocrisy, on which it is ingrafted. Expence is in the present state of things entailed upon all governments. Though if we continue united, we shall be hereafter less exposed to wars by land,[4] than most other countries; yet while we have powerful neighbours on either extremity, and our frontier is embraced by savages, whose alliance they may without difficulty command, we cannot, in prudence, dispense with the usual precautions for our interior security. As a commercial people, maritime power must be a primary object of our attention, and a navy cannot be created or maintained without ample revenues. The nature of our popular constitutions requires a numerous magistracy, for whom competent provision must be made; or we may be certain our affairs will always be committed to improper hands; and experience will teach us, that no government costs so much as a bad one.

4. In the newspaper version the word "band" was used. In *JCHW*, II, 197, this is changed to "land."

We may preach till we are tired of the theme, the necessity of disinterestedness in republics, without making a single proselyte. The virtuous declaimer will neither persuade himself nor any other person to be content with a double mess of porridge,* instead of a reasonable stipend for his services. We might as soon reconcile ourselves to the Spartan community of goods and wives, to their iron coin, their long beards, or their black broth. There is a total dissimulation in the circumstances, as well as the manners, of society among us; and it is as ridiculous to seek for models in the simple ages of Greece and Rome, as it would be to go in quest of them among the Hottentots and Laplanders.[6]

The public, for the different purposes, that have been mentioned, must always have large demands upon its constituents, and the only question is whether these shall be satisfied by annual grants perpetually renewed—by a perpetual grant once for all or by a compound of permanent and occasional supplies. The last is the wisest course. The Fœderal Government should neither be independent nor too much dependent. It should neither be raised above responsibility or controul, nor should it want the means of maintaining its own weight, authority, dignity and credit. To this end permanent funds are indispensable, but they ought to be of such a nature and so moderate in their amount, as never to be inconvenient. Extraordinary supplies can be the objects of extraordinary grants; and in this salutary medium will consist our true wisdom.

It would seem as if no mode of taxation could be relished but that worst of all modes which now prevails, by assessment. Every proposal for a specific tax is sure to meet with opposition. It has been objected to a poll tax, at a fixed rate, that it will be unequal, as the rich will pay no more than the poor. In the form under which it has been offered in these papers, the poor properly speaking are not comprehended, though it is true that beyond the exclusion of

* It was a custom with the Lacedaemonians[5] when any new Senator was elected, to present him at their public tables with a double allowance as a mark of distinction.

5. In the newspaper this word is "Lacydemonians."
6. H's information was taken from *Plutarch's Lives*. See his notes from Plutarch in "Pay Book of the State Company of Artillery," 1777. In the newspaper version the last word of this paragraph is "Lapoons." In *JCHW*, II, 198, it is "Laplanders."

the indigent the tax has no reference to the proportion of property; but it should be remembered that it is impossible to devise any specific tax, that will operate equally on the whole community. It must be the province of the legislature to hold the scales with a judicious hand and ballance one by another. The rich must be made to pay for their luxuries; which is the only proper way of taxing their superior wealth.

Do we imagine that our assessments opperate equally? Nothing can be more contrary to the fact. Wherever a discretionary power is lodged in any set of men over the property of their neighbours, they will abuse it. Their passions, prejudices, partialities, dislikes, will have the principal lead in measuring the abilities of those over whom their power extends; and assessors will ever be a set of petty tyrants, too unskilful, if honest, to be possessed of so delicate a trust, and too seldom honest to give them the excuse of want of skill. The genius of liberty reprobates every thing arbitrary or discretionary in taxation. It exacts that every man by a definite and general rule should know what proportion of his property the state demands. Whatever liberty we may boast in theory, it cannot exist in fact, while assessments continue. The admission of them among us is a new proof, how often human conduct reconciles the most glaring opposites; in the present case the most vicious practice of despotic governments, with the freest constitutions and the greatest love of liberty.

The establishment of permanent funds would not only answer the public purposes infinitely better than temporary supplies; but it would be the most effectual way of easing the people. With this basis for procuring credit, the amount of present taxes might be greatly diminished. Large sums of money might be borrowed abroad at a low interest, and introduced into the country to defray the current expences and pay the public debts; which would not only lessen the demand for immediate supplies, but would throw more money into circulation, and furnish the people with greater means of paying the taxes. Though it be a just rule, that we ought not to run in debt to avoid present expence, so far as our faculties extend; yet the propriety of doing it cannot be disputed when it is apparent, that these are incompetent to the public necessities. Efforts beyond our abilities can only tend to individual distress and national disappointment.

The product of the three forgoing articles [7] will be as little as can be required to enable Congress to pay their debts, and restore order into their finances. In addition to these—

The disposal of the unlocated lands will hereafter be a valuable source of revenue, and an immediate one of credit. As it may be liable to the same condition with the duties on trade, that is the product of the sales within each state, to be creditted to that state, and as the rights of jurisdiction are not infringed, it seems to be susceptible of no reasonable objection.

Mines in every country constitute a branch of the revenue. In this where nature has so richly impregnated the bowels of the earth, they may in time become a valuable one; and as they require the care and attention of government to bring them to perfection, this care and a share in the profits of it, will very properly devolve upon Congress. All the precious metals should absolutely be the property of the Fœderal Government, and with respect to the others, it should have a discretionary power of reserving in the nature of a tax, such part as it may judge not inconsistent with the encouragement due to so important an object. This is rather a future than a present resource.

The reason of allowing Congress to appoint its own officers of the customs, collectors of taxes, and military officers of every rank, is to create in the interior of each state a mass of influence in favour of the Fœderal Government. The great danger has been shown to be, that it will not have power enough to defend itself and preserve the union, not that it will ever become formidable to the general liberty. A mere regard to the interests of the confederacy will never be a principle sufficiently active to curb the ambition and intrigues of different members. Force cannot effect it: A contest of arms will seldom be between the common sovereign and a single refractory member; but between distinct combinations of the several parts against each other. A sympathy of situations will be apt to produce associates to the disobedient. The application of force is always disagreeable, the issue uncertain. It will be wise to obviate the necessity of it, by interesting such a number of individuals in each state in

7. H presumably was referring to the three means of raising a revenue (i.e., imports, land, and poll taxes) which he suggested in paragraphs 10, 11, and 12 of this essay.

support of the Fœderal Government, as will be counterpoised to the ambition of others; and will make it difficult for them to unite the people in opposition to the just and necessary measures of the union.

There is something noble and magnificent in the perspective of a great Fœderal Republic, closely linked in the pursuit of a common interest, tranquil and prosperous at home, respectable abroad; but there is something proportionably diminutive and contemptible in the prospect of a number of petty states, with the appearance only of union, jarring, jealous and perverse, without any determined direction, fluctuating and unhappy at home, weak and insignificant by their dissentions, in the eyes of other nations. Happy America! if those, to whom thou hast intrusted the guardianship of thy infancy, know how to provide for thy future repose; but miserable and undone, if their negligence or ignorance permits the spirit of discord to erect her banners on the ruins of thy tranquillity!

From Comfort Sands and Company [1]

Fishkill [New York] July 8th, 1782

Sir

We was Hond. with your favor of the 23 Ult but two or three days ago, it is impossible for us to give you an exact account of the Money laid out in this State. Flour is almost the only Article purchased in it. Sometimes a little Beef. In the Course of the year we may purchase 15,000 Barrels of Flour, which will Amt. to about 60.000 Dolrs., the greatest part of which we draw Bills for, and is paid in Phila. Very few Bank Notes is Circulated by us, as the Farmers will not take them, and the Traders we give our own Drafts to which Answer our purposes better. The bulk of the Money we have brought on here has gone to the Eastern States for Beef Cattle, this they can furnish better than this State & all our Contracts for Beef is with Gentlemen from the State of Massachusetts. Any further information that you may want from us, we shall with pleasure give you—and Remain with great Respect   Your most Obedt Servts.   Comfort Sands & Co.

Col Alex. Hamilton

ALS, Hamilton Papers, Library of Congress.
1. Comfort Sands and Company had contracted with Robert Morris, Super-intendent of Finance, to supply West Point with provisions. See H to Sands, June 23, 1782. The information in this letter was used by H in a report to Morris of August 13, 1782.

From Robert Morris

Office of Finance [Philadelphia] 12 July 1782.

Sir,

I inclose you the Copy of my circular Letter to the several States of the twenty fifth of July 1781.[1] The Answers I have received have been very few and very short of the Objects so that I have not been able to Act as I wished for want of necessary Information.[2] I must beg you to take the most speedy and effectual Means in your Power to enable me to form a proper Judgment on such of the Subjects referred to as the actual State of Things renders it important to know.

I am Sir   your most obedient and humble Servant   RM

LC, Robert Morris Papers, Library of Congress.
1. In a circular letter addressed to the governors of the several states on July 25, 1781, Morris discussed the accounts outstanding between the states and the Continental government. The accounts were based on the books of the Treasury of the United States which had been so carelessly kept that Morris had to request each state to supply him with the amount of money, supply, transportation, and other services furnished the Confederation. Morris also requested copies of the laws of each state relating to the collection of taxes and information on the execution of such laws. In addition, he wished to know the amount and character of paper currencies still circulating as well as "what Monies are in your Treasury and what Sums you expect to have there, as also the Times by which they must probably be brought in." Morris explained that he intended to settle all outstanding accounts with the states in an equitable manner (Robert Morris Papers, Library of Congress).
2. The governors of the states apparently considered the information re-quested by Morris unwarranted by the duties of his office. The answers of those who replied were "evasive and unsatisfactory." See Ellis P. Oberholtzer, *Robert Morris* (New York, 1903), 123.

To Robert Morris

Albany July 13th. 1782

Sir

I have this moment received your letter of the 2d. instant and as the post will set out on its return in half an hour I have little more than time to acknowlege the receipt of it.

I shall tomorrow morning commence a journey to Poughkepsie, where the Legislature are assembled;[1] and I will endeavour by every step in my power to second your views; though I am sorry to add without very sanguine expectations. I think it probable the Legislature will do something; but whatever momentary effort they may make 'till the intire change of their present system very little will be done. To effect this, mountains of prejudice and particular interest are to be levelled. For my own part, considering the late serious misfortune to our ally,[2] the spirit of reformation of wisdom and of unanimity, which seems to have succeeded to that of blunder, perverseness, and dissention in the British government;[3] and the universal reluctance of these states to do what is right, I cannot help viewing our situation as critical; and I feel it the duty of every citizen to exert his faculties to the utmost to support the measures, especially those solid arrangements of finance, on which our safety depends.

I will by the next post forward you the Bond executed with proper sureties.[4]

It is not in the spirit of compliment but of sincerity I assure that the opinion I entertain of him who presides in the department was not one of the smallest motives to my acceptance of the office; nor will that esteem and confidence which make me now sensibly feel the obliging expressions of your letter fail to have a great share in influencing my future exertions.

I have the honor to be with perfect esteem & respect Sir,   Yr Most Obed Servant   A Hamilton

ALS, Hamilton Papers, Library of Congress.

1. A proclamation issued on June 11, 1782, by Governor George Clinton called on the legislature of New York to convene at Poughkeepsie on July 3, 1782.

2. H probably referred to the decisive naval victory of the English over the French fleet in the West Indies on April 12, 1782.

3. Lord North had been forced to resign on March 20, 1782. The new ministry was nominally headed by Rockingham, but Shelburne and Charles James Fox were the dominant figures. H must have been unaware of the personal jealousy and rivalry which characterized the relationship of Shelburne and Fox.

4. On July 2, Morris had sent H a bond for the performance of duties as receiver of continental taxes in New York. H returned the bond to Morris on July 22, 1782.

To George Clinton

Poughkepsie [New York] July 16. 1782

Sir.

I have the honor to inclose Your Excellency the copy of a warrant [1] from The Honorable Robert Morris Esqr. Superintendant of the Finances of the United States; by which you will perceive that agreeable to the resolution of Congress of the 2d. of November last, he has appointed me Receiver of the Continental Taxes for this state. I am therefore to request that the Legislature will be pleased to vest in me the authority required by that resolution.

It is a part of my duty to explain to the Legislature from time to time the views of the Superintendant of Finance in persuance of the orders of Congress that they may be the better enabled to judge of the measures most proper to be adopted for an effectual cooperation. For this purpose I pray Your Excellency to impart my request, that I may have the honor of a conference with a Committee of the two houses, at such time and place as they may find convenient.[2]

I have the honor to be   With perfect respect & esteem   Yr. Excellency's Most Obed Ser   Alex Hamilton

His Excellency Governor Clinton

ADfS, Hamilton Papers, Library of Congress; ALS, the Reverend David H. Coblentz, Clover, South Carolina.

1. "Warrant to Alexander Hamilton to Receive Money as Continental Receiver for the State of New York," enclosure in Morris to H, April 15, 1782.

2. On July 16, 1782, Clinton transmitted H's letter with its enclosure to the New York Senate. A committee of the Senate composed of Ephraim Paine, William Floyd, and Isaac Roosevelt, was appointed to confer with H on the subject of his letter and directed to report the result of the conference to the Senate. In the afternoon of the same day the letter was transmitted by the Senate to the Assembly. The letter was referred to a committee consisting of Robert Harpur, John Lansing, Jr., Ezra L'Hommedieu, William Malcom, Nathaniel Tom, Henry Williams, Thomas Thomas, John Stagg, Cornelius Humphrey, Zephariah Batchelor, and Joseph McCracken. Neither the journal of the Senate nor that of the Assembly, however, contains references to a report of the committees (New York Senate *Journal*, 1782, 84; New York Assembly *Journal*, 1782, 112).

From Robert Morris

Office of Finance [Philadelphia] 19th. July 1782.

Sir,

I have found it necessary to draw Bills on Mr. Swanwick in favor of different People and payable at various Periods.[1] These are Bills of Exchange in the common Form and must be negotiated by Indorsements. You will always receive them in like Manner with my other Notes or Bank Notes and remit them which you can do without cutting them as they will be paid only to the Indorsee.

I am Sir your most obedient Servant RM.

LC, Robert Morris Papers, Library of Congress.
    1. In the absence of other currency, Morris supplemented the notes of the Bank of North America with his own notes. Issued in anticipation of the future collections of taxes in the states, they usually were drawn to the order of John Swanwick. See Morris to H, April 15, 1782.

Resolution of the New York Legislature Calling for a Convention of the States to Revise and Amend the Articles of Confederation [1]

[Poughkeepsie, New York, July 20, 1782] [2]

The Senate again resolved itself into a Committee of the Whole, to take into Consideration the State of the Nation; and after some considerable Time spent therein, the President resumed the Chair,

New York Senate *Journal*, 1782, 89–90.
    1. J. C. Hamilton stated that the text of the resolution which he printed was "abridged from the original draft" and that the original was "from the pen of Hamilton" (Hamilton, *History*, II, 295–97). Most scholars have followed his lead in attributing the resolutions to H. See *HCLW*, I, 291; Mitchell, *Hamilton*, 266.
    The resolutions were submitted to the Senate through Abraham Ten Broeck by the committee of the whole. Because Philip Schuyler, H's father-in-law and close political ally, was a member of the committee of the whole and because H was in Poughkeepsie at the time the resolutions were prepared, it is generally assumed H must have been the author of the resolutions. There is no conclusive evidence, however, that he wrote them or that he advised the person who did write them.
    2. The resolutions were adopted by the Senate on this date, and on July 21 they were unanimously approved by the Assembly.

and Mr. Ten Broeck from the said Committee, delivered in a Report; which he read in his Place, and delivered in at the Table, where it was again read, considered by Paragraphs, and agreed to. Whereupon the Senate came into the following Resolutions, viz.

Resolved, That it appears to this Legislature; after full and solemn Consideration of the several Matters communicated by the Honorable the Committee of Congress, relative to the present Posture of our Affairs, foreign and domestic, and contained in a Letter from the Secretary for foreign Affairs respecting the Former, as well as of the Representations from Time to Time made by the Superintendent of the Finances of the United States, relative to his particular Department—That the Situation of these States is in a peculiar Manner critical, and affords the strongest Reason to apprehend from a Continuance of the present Constitution of the Continental Government; a Subversion of public Credit; and Consequences highly dangerous to the Safety and Independence of these States.

Resolved, That while this Legislature are convinced by the beforementioned Communications, that notwithstanding the generous Intentions of an Ally from whom we have experienced, and doubtless shall still experience all possible Support; Exigencies may arise to prevent our receiving pecuniary Succours hereafter, in any Degree proportioned to our Necessities—They are also convinced from Facts within their own Knowledge, that the Provisions made by the respective States for carrying on the War, are not only inadequate to the End, but must continue to be so, while there is an Adherence to the Principles which now direct the Operation of public Measures.

Resolved, That it is also the Opinion of this Legislature, that the present Plan instituted by Congress for the Administration of their Finances, is founded in Wisdom and sound Policy—That the salutary Effects of it, have already been felt in an extensive Degree; and that after so many violent Shocks sustained by the public Credit, a Failure in this System, for Want of the Support which the States are able to give, would be productive of Evils too pernicious to be hazarded.

Resolved, That it appears to this Legislature, that the present British Ministry, with a Disposition not less hostile than that of their Predecessors, taught by Experience to avoid their Errors, and assuming the Appearance of Moderation, are pursuing a Scheme cal-

culated to conciliate in Europe, and seduce in America—That the
œcomical Arrangements they appear to be adopting, are adopted to
enlarging the Credit of their Government, and multiplying its Resources, at the same Time that they serve to confirm the Prepossessions and Confidence of the People; and that the Plan of a
defensive War on this Continent, while they direct all their Attention and Resources to the Augmentation of their Navy, is that
which may be productive of Consequences ultimately dangerous to
the United States.

Resolved, That it is the Opinion of this Legislature, that the
present System of these States, exposes the common Cause to a
precarious Issue, and leaves us at the Mercy of Events over which
we have no Influence; a Conduct extremely unwise in any Nation,
and at all Times, and to a Change of which we are impelled at this
Juncture, by Reasons of peculiar and irresistable Weight; and that
it is the natural Tendency of the Weakness and Disorders in our
national Measures, to spread Diffidence and Distrust among the People, and prepare their Minds to receive the Impressions the Enemy
wish to make.

Resolved, That the general State of European Affairs, as far as
they have come to the Knowledge of this Legislature, affords in their
Opinion, reasonable Ground of Confidence, and assures us, that with
judicious vigorous Exertion on our Part, we may rely on the final
Attainment of our Object; but far from justifying Indifference and
Security, calls upon us by every Motive of Honor, good Faith and
Patriotism, without Delay, to unite in some System more effectual,
for producing Energy, Harmony and Consistency of Measures, than
that which now exists, and more capable of putting the common
Cause out of the Reach of Contingencies.

Resolved, That in the Opinion of this Legislature, the radical
Source of most of our Embarrassments, is the Want of sufficient
Power in Congress, to effectuate that ready and perfect Co-operation
of the different States, on which their immediate Safety and future
Happiness depend—That Experience has demonstrated the Confederation to be defective in several essential Points, particularly in
not vesting the fœderal Government either with a Power of providing Revenue for itself, or with ascertained and productive Funds,
secured by a Saction so solemn and general, as would inspire the

fullest Confidence in them, and make them a substantial Basis of Credit—That these Defects ought to be without Loss of Time repaired, the Powers of Congress extended, a solid Security established for the Payment of Debts already inured, and competent Means provided for future Credit, and for supplying the current Demands of the War.

Resolved, That it appears evidently to this Legislature, that the annual Income of these States, admitting the best Means were adopted for drawing out their Resources, would fall far short of the annual Expenditure; and that there would be a large Deficiency to be supplied on the Credit of these States; which, if it should be inconvenient for those Powers to afford, on whose Friendship we justly rely, must be sought for from Individuals, to engage whom to lend, satisfactory Securities must be pledged for the punctual Payment of Interest, and the final Redemption of the Principal.

Resolved, That it appears to this Legislature, that the aforegoing important Ends, can never be attained by partial Deliberations of the States, separately; but that it is essential to the common Welfare, that there should be as soon as possible a Conference of the Whole on the Subject; and that it would be adviseable for this Purpose, to propose to Congress to recommend, and to each State to adopt the Measure of assembling a general Convention of the States, specially authorised to revise and amend the Confederation, reserving a Right to the respective Legislatures, to ratify their Determinations.

Ordered, That Mr. Paine[3] carry a Copy of the aforegoing Resolutions, to the Honorable the House of Assembly, and request their Concurrence thereto.[4]

3. Ephraim Paine was a member of the New York Senate from the middle district.

4. Governor George Clinton enclosed the concurrent resolutions in a letter of August 4 to the Continental Congress. They were referred on August 15, 1782, to a "Grand Committee" (*JCC*, XXIII, 470, note 2), and on April 28, 1783, they were recommitted to a committee consisting of Oliver Ellsworth, Daniel Carroll, James Wilson, Nathaniel Gorham, and H. On July 23, 1783, the committee was renewed and Clinton's letter referred to H, Richard Peters, James McHenry, Ralph Izard, and James Duane. On July 30, 1783, H, who left the Continental Congress at that time, was replaced by Samuel Huntington (*JCC*, XXIV, 285, note 2). The committee reported on September 2, 1783, that consideration of the New York legislature's resolution be postponed until the states replied to the congressional resolution of April 18, 1783, calling for congressional authority to levy an impost (*JCC*, XXV, 523).

From Robert Morris

Office of Finance [Philadelphia] July 22nd. 1782

Sir

I have received your letter dated at Albany the 13th, Instant, as I can have no doubt but that your Efforts will be applyed to promote the Public Interests, I hope the Journey you propose to Poughkepsie may prove every way agreable to your Wishes.

I am Sir   Your Most Obedient Servt.   Robt Morris

Alexander Hamilton Esqr.

LS, Hamilton Papers, Library of Congress.

To Robert Morris

Poughkepsie [New York] July 22d. 1782

Sir

Agreeable to my letter to you from Albany [1] I came to this place and had an interview with a Committee of the Legislature in which I urged the several matters contained in your instructions.[2] I strongly represented the necessity of solid arrangements of Finance, and, by way of argument, pointed out all the defects of the present system. I found every man convinced that something was wrong, but few that were willing to recognise the mischief when defined and consent to the proper remedy. The quantum of taxes already imposed is so great as to make it useless to impose any others to a considerable amount. A bill has however passed both houses payable in specie, bank notes or your notes for Eighteen thousand pounds.[3] It is at present appropriated to your order, but I doubt whether some subsequent arrangement will not take place for a different appropriation. The Commander in Chief has applied for a quantity of forage, which the legislature is devising the means of furnishing and I fear it will finish by diverting the Eighteen thousand pounds to that purpose.[4] I have hitherto been able to prevent this, but as it is of indispensable importance to me to leave this place immediately to prepare for an examination for which I have pledged myself the ensuing term, which is at hand;[5] it is possible after I have left it, contrary ideas will prevail. Efforts have been made to introduce a species of negotiable certificates which I have strenuously opposed. It has not yet taken place; but I am not clear how the matter will terminate.

Should the bill for the Eighteen thousand pounds go out in its present form I cannot hope that it will produce in the treasury above half the sum; such are the vices of our present mode of collection.

A bill has also passed the Assembly for collecting arrearages of taxes, payable in specie, bank notes, your notes, old Continental emissions at One hundred and twenty eight for one and a species of certificates issued by the state for the purchase of horses. This is now before the Senate. The arrearages are very large.[6]

Both houses have unanimously passed a set of resolutions to be transmitted to Congress and the several states proposing a Co[n]vention of the states to enlarge the powers of Congress and vest them with funds.[7] I think this a very eligible step though I doubt of the concurrence of the other states; but I am certain without it, they never will be brought to cooperate in any reasonable or effectual plan. Urge reforms or exertions and the answer constantly is what avails it for one state to make them without the concert of the others? It is in vain to expose the futility of this reasoning; it is founded on all those passions which have the strongest influence on the human mind.

The Legislature have also appointed at my instance a Committee to devise in the recess a more effectual system of taxation and to communicate with me on this subject.[8] A good deal will depend on the success of this attempt. Convinced of the absurdity of multiplying taxes in the present mode, where in effect the payment is voluntary, and the money received exhausted in the collection, I have laboured chiefly to instil the necessity of a change in the plan, and though not so rapidly as the exigency of public affairs requires, truth seems to be making some progress.

There is no other appropriation to the use of Congress than of the Eighteen Thousand pounds.

I shall as soon as possible give you a full and just view of the situation and temper of this state. This cannot be 'till after my intended examination; that over I shall lay myself out in every way that can promote your views and the public good.

I am informed you have an appointment to make of a Commissioner of accounts for this state. Permit me to suggest the expediency of choosing a citizen of the state, a man who to the qualifications requisite for the execution of this office adds an influence in its affairs.[9] I need not particularise the reasons of this suggestion; in my next I will also take the liberty to mention some characters.

I omitted mentioning that The two houses have also passed a bill authorising Congress to adjust the quotas of the states on equitable principles, agreeable to your recommendation.[10]

I have the honor to be with sincere attachment and respect Sir yr Most Obed Servant

I enclose you the bond executed jointly with General Schuyler.

ADf, Hamilton Papers, Library of Congress. In *JCHW*, I, 287, this letter is misdated May 22, 1782.

1. See H to Morris, July 13, 1782.

2. A committee of the Senate and a committee of the Assembly were appointed on July 16 to confer with H. See H to George Clinton, July 16, 1782.

3. A bill entitled "An Act for raising the Sum of £18,000 by Tax" was passed by the legislature on July 21, with the amended title, "An Act for levying a Tax within this State." The Council of Revision approved the bill on July 22, 1782 (New York Assembly *Journal*, 1782, 118, 123).

4. On July 15, Governor Clinton submitted to the legislature a letter from the Commander in Chief, dated July 11, "on the Necessity of providing . . . an immediate Supply of Forage . . ." (New York Assembly *Journal*, 1782, 110).

5. H planned to qualify for admission to the bar at the October term of the Supreme Court of Judicature to be held in Albany. See "Admission as Counsel before the New York Supreme Court," October 26, 1782.

6. The bill entitled "An Act to compel the Payment of the Arrearages of Taxes" was amended by the Senate; the amendments were accepted by the Assembly, and on July 24, the act was passed (New York Assembly *Journal*, 1782, 127).

7. See "Resolution of the New York Legislature Calling for a Convention of the States to Revise and Amend the Articles of Confederation," July 20, 1782.

8. On July 21, the Assembly resolved "That a joint Committee of both Houses of the Legislature be appointed, to report at their next Meeting, a System for establishing such Funds within this State, as may be best calculated to answer the purposes of this State, and the United States; and for the more effectual Collection of Taxes within this State" (New York Assembly *Journal*, 1782, 117). The Senate concurred, and a subsequent resolution of the legislature recommended that all state officials furnish the committee with such documents as it might require (New York Assembly *Journal*, 1782, 128). The journals do not show that the committee was authorized to communicate with H.

9. On February 20, 1782, Congress resolved that a commissioner be appointed in each state to settle "all accounts between the United States and each particular State" (*JCC*, XXII, 84). On November 21, 1782, Morris wrote to Governor Clinton: "I now do myself the Honor to nominate Colo. Henry Sherburne for Commissioner to settle the Accounts between the State of New York and the United States" (Robert Morris Papers, Library of Congress).

10. In a circular letter addressed to the "Governors of the Several States," of July 25, 1781 (Robert Morris Papers, Library of Congress), Morris had expressed the hope that proper principles might be established for liquidating the accounts of the states with the Union on equitable principles. Consonant with Morris's wish the New York legislature, on July 22, 1782, approved "An Act to authorize the United States in Congress assembled, to adjust the Proportions of this State, towards the Expences of the War, in a Mode different from that prescribed by the Articles of Confederation" (New York Assembly *Journal*, 1782, 123).

Appointment as Delegate to the Continental Congress

Poughkeepsie, New York, July 22, 1782. On this date the New York legislature passed the following resolution: "*Resolved,* That the Honorable James Duane, William Floyd, John Morin Scott, Ezra L'Hommedieu and Alexander Hamilton, Esquires, be, and are hereby declared duly nominated and appointed Delegates, to represent this State in the United States in Congress assembled, for one Year, from the first Monday in November next ensuing." [1]

New York Senate *Journal*, 1782, 91.

1. On July 22, the Senate nominated a delegation consisting of James Duane, William Floyd, Philip Schuyler, John Morin Scott, and Ezra L'Hommedieu. Although the Assembly nominated four of the same men, it substituted H for Schuyler. At a joint meeting of the two houses a ballot was taken and H was nominated (New York Senate *Journal*, 1782, 91). H's credentials were dated October 25, 1782.

From Major General Henry Knox

New Windsor [New York] 24 July 1782

I have been waiting my dear Hamilton, for a Crisis in the case of the intended retaliation for the murder of Huddy before I answer'd your favor of the 7th of last month.[1] But it has yet to have arrived. A Captain of Cornwallis's Army was brought up to the Jersey line by a mistake of General Hazens in lieu of an unconditional prisoner as a subject for execution.[2] As this person is of considerable family it was thought proper to let his importance have all the influence possible, to obtain the delivery or the execution of the guilty person in New York. Fortunately for this a Captain of the 57 Regt has since been taken without any terms who probably will be the unhappy sufferer. Sir Guy Carleton in a late letter to the General says "the trial of Lippincot is finished and he shall soon forward the proceedings with some other documents" by which a conclusion may be fairly drawn that the Court martial have not found him guilty.[3] From some conversations which I have had with the General on the subject he appears to think that it is impossible for him to recede from his first determinations, but that he shall not put [it] into execution untill every other method has been tried in vain.

As soon as he receives the proceedings from Genl Carelton he will probably repeat the demand he made to Genl Clinton that the guilty be punished before the innocent. After this possibly something may turn up to procrastinate the matter still further. You cannot but know that this affair has created much ill blood between the tories and regular troops in New York and this rancour seems to increase as the matter is protracted, and their fears alarmed. Therefore to agitate it with[out] coming to the ultimate point is in our favor.

My sentiments on frequent executions at this or any other period are very similar to yours. I am persuaded that after reflexions will convince dispasionate and enlightened minds that executions have been too frequent, under the color of the Laws of the different states and they will hereafter be recited to sully the purity of our cause. In the present case, I am pretty well convinced that, the representations, and the light in which the murder of Huddy has been received on both sides the lines will prevent a repetition of the crime and so far render retaliation unnecessary. But yet it will be difficult for the General circumstanced as he is with his own declarations, the resolution of Congress on the subject and the expectations of the people, to find reasons to justify him to the publick for a total suspension of the matter. If it can be done consistently he will be happy, not [to] be obliged to have recourse to a measure, the execution of which must cost him great pain.

We have no news. The General has not yet returned from Philadelphia where he has been to make some plans with Count de Rochambeau.[4] However The affair [in] the West Indies is so important as to affect American operations.[5] I am afraid we shall only be able this ⟨year beginning⟩ to eat Beef and drink Whiskey.

My dear Sir—with compliments to Mrs Hamilton   Your affectionate & Obt Servant   H. Knox

Colonel Hamilton

ADfS, Massachusetts Historical Society, Boston.
1. The case of Captain Joshua Huddy is explained in H to Knox, June 7, 1782, note 2.
2. In retaliation for the murder of Huddy, Washington had directed Brigadier General Moses Hazen to select by lot an unconditional prisoner, one who had no claim to protection. Captain Charles Asgill, the officer selected, was covered by the terms of Lord Cornwallis's capitulation which prescribed specific treatment of officers. Asgill was released by an act of Congress of November 7, 1782 (JCC, XXIII, 715).
3. Captain Richard Lippincott had commanded the group of refugees who hanged Huddy. As Knox anticipated, Lippincott was acquitted of murder.
4. Washington and Jean Baptiste Donatien de Vimeur, Comte de Rochambeau, met in Philadelphia to discuss military plans and operations in the event of the anticipated arrival of a French fleet under Louis Philippe de Rigaud, Marquis de Vaudreuil.
5. Knox referred to the naval victory of the British on April 12, 1782, in the West Indies.

To Robert Morris

[*Albany, July 27, 1782.* On August 28, 1782, Morris wrote to Hamilton: "I have duly received your several Favors of the Twenty second & twenty Seventh of July, and tenth and thirteenth of August." *Letter of July 27 not found.*]

To Gerard Bancker [1]

[Albany, July 31, 1782]

Sir

I inclose you a copy of a warrant [2] to me from The Superintendant of Finance on the Treasury of this State for the sum due the 1st day of April last as the first quarte[r]ly payment of the quota of the present year.[3] I shall be obliged to you to inform me what appropriations have been made by the Legislature of the State on this account; and I am at the same time to request the payment of such monies as may now be in your hands for this purpose; as well as that you will take the most speedy and effectual measures so far as you are authorised to urge the collection of those taxes which have been imposed by the Legislature for the use of *The United States.*

I am with great consideration Sir   Yr. most Obed serv

A Hamilton

Albany July 31st. 1782
E Banker Esq. Treasurer of the State

ALS, Hamilton Papers, Library of Congress.
  1. Bancker, a merchant, had succeeded Peter Livingston as treasurer of the State of New York, a post which he retained until his death in 1798.
  2. "Warrant to Alexander Hamilton to Receive Money as Continental Receiver for the State of New York," enclosure in Robert Morris to H, April 15, 1782.
  3. On November 2, 1781, the Continental Congress estimated the revenue required for 1782 at eight million dollars and apportioned the sum among the states by quotas according to population. New York's quota was set at $373,598. Quarterly requisitions were to be made for the amount due from each state (*JCC*, XXI, 1089–91).

From Lieutenant Colonel John Laurens [1]

[South Carolina, July, 1782]

I am indebted to you, my dear Hamilton, for two letters; the first from Albany,[2] as masterly a piece of cynicism as ever was penned, the other from Philadelphia, dated the 2d March;[3] in both, you mention a design of retiring, which makes me exceedingly unhappy. I would not wish to have you for a moment withdrawn from the public service; at the same time, my friendship for you, and knowlege of your value to the United States, make me most ardently desire, that you should fill only the first offices of the Republic. I was flattered with an account of your being elected a delegate from N. York,[4] and am much mortified not to hear it confirmed by yourself. I must confess to you, that, at the present state of the War, I shd. prefer your going into Congress, and from thence, becoming a Minister plenipotentiary for peace, to your remaining in the Army, where the dull System of seniority and the Tableau would prevent you from having the important commands to which you are entitled;

but at any rate I wd. not have you renounce your rank in the Army, unless you entered the career abovementioned. Your private affairs cannot require such immediate and close attention; you speak like a pater familias [5] surrounded with a numerous progeny.

I had, in fact, resumed the black project,[6] as you were informed, and urged the matter very strenuously, both to our privy council and legislative body; but I was out-voted, having only reason on my side, and being opposed by a triple-headed monster that shed the baneful influence of Avarice, prejudice, and pusillanimity in all our Assemblies. It was some consolation to me, however, to find that philosophy and truth had made some little progress since my last effort, as I obtained twice as many suffrages as before.[7]

AL, Hamilton Papers, Library of Congress. This letter is dated 1781 in *JCHW*, I, 214–15.

1. Early in September, 1781, Laurens had returned from France where he had served as envoy extraordinary. He immediately re-entered the Army, serving until January, 1782. He was a member of the "Jacksonborough legislature" which convened on January 18 and adjourned on February 26, 1782. Seeking to play a more active part in the Revolution, Laurens then returned to active duty in the Army.

2. Letter not found.

3. Letter not found.

4. H was elected to the Continental Congress on July 22, 1782.

5. H's first child, Philip, was born on January 22, 1782.

6. This is a reference to Laurens's plan to enlist slaves to fight against the British. On May 19, 1782, Laurens wrote to Washington that this plan had been again defeated (George Washington Papers, Library of Congress).

7. The remaining page or pages of this letter are missing. It is possible that the fragment, Laurens to H, July, 1782, is the concluding paragraph of this letter.

From Lieutenant Colonel John Laurens

[*South Carolina, July, 1782.*[1] The printed extract of a letter Laurens wrote to Hamilton reads as follows: "The enemy's system was perfectly defensive, and rendered the campaign insipid. Many of our sanguine citizens have flattered themselves with the idea of a prompt evacuation of Charleston. I wish the garrison would either withdraw or fight us. Adieu, my dear friend; while circumstances place so great a distance between us, I entreat you not to withdraw the *consolation* of your letters. You know the unalterable sentiments of your affectionate Laurens." *Letter not found.*]

Hamilton, *History*, II, 299–300.

1. It is not possible to date this letter precisely. J. C. Hamilton gives the letter no date but states only that "Hamilton replied on the fifteenth of August." It is possible that this is the concluding paragraph of the preceding letter.

Admission as Attorney before the New York Supreme Court

[*Albany*] *July, 1782.* In July, 1782, Hamilton was admitted to practice as an attorney before the Supreme Court of the State of New York.

MS "Roll of Attornies of . . . Supreme Court of . . . New York, 1754–95," Hall of Records, New York City.

From Richard Kidder Meade

[*August 1, 1782.* On August 27, 1782, Hamilton wrote to Meade: "I thank you my dear Meade for your letter of the first of this month." *Letter not found.*]

To The New-York Packet

[Albany, August 1, 1782]

THE SUBSCRIBER has received nothing on account of the quota of this state for the present year. Published agreeable to the instructions of the Superintendant of Finance.[1]

> Alexander Hamilton
> Receiver of Continental Taxes
> for the State of New-York

Albany, August 1, 1782

The New-York Packet, and the American Advertiser, August 22, 1782.

1. Robert Morris, Superintendent of Finance, had instructed the several receivers of continental taxes to make use of newspapers to advertise delinquencies in the payment of taxes (Morris to H, April 15, 1782).

To George Clinton

Albany Aug. 3d. 1782

Sir

I have lately received a letter from the Superintendant of Finance inclosing a copy of a circular letter from him to the several states dated 25th of July 81 in which he requests information upon the following important points: [1]

"What supplies of every kind money provisions forage transportation &c. have been furnished by this State to the United States since the 18th. of March 1780."

"The amount of the money in the treasury, the sums expected to be there, the times they will probably be brought in, the appropriations."

"The amount of the different paper currencies in the state, the probable increase or decrease of each and the respective rates of depreciation."

"The acts passed since the 18th. of March 1780 for raising taxes, furnishing supplies &c, the manner they have been executed, the time necessary for them to operate, the consequences of their operation, the policy [2] of the state relative to laying assessing levying and collecting taxes."

In his letter which is *circular* to the Receivers he says the answers he has received to these inquiries are few and short of the object and he therefore *urges* me to take the "most speedy and effectual means in my power to enable him to form a proper judgment on such of the subjects referred to as the actual state of things renders it important to know."

In compliance with this I request the favour of your Excellency to inform me what steps have been taken on the several heads of which the above is an abstract and what progress has been made in the business, particularly with respect to the 1st article. I shall also be much obliged to you to direct Mr. Holt [3] to furnish me without delay with the acts mentioned in the inclosed list.[4]

Your Excellency must have been too sensible of the necessity of enabling the Director of the Finance of the United States to form a just judgment of the true state of our affairs to have omitted any measure in your power to procure the fullest information on the several matters submitted to you and I am persuaded the business is in such a train that little will be left for me to do.

I entreat you will do me the honor to let me hear from you as soon as possible on the subject. With perfect respect I am Your Excellency's Most Obed servant A Hamilton

It would promote the public business if you would be so good as to direct Mr. Banker to supply me with such information as I might call upon him for.[5] He is very obliging but without some authority for the purpose there is a delicacy in calling upon him.

Note. I wrote at the same time to Mr. Holt Printer for the State [6] desiring him to forward me the copies of the acts abovementioned and telling him that, if the Governor did not make satisfaction, I would do it. These acts were all those relative to Finance & Supply from March 18th. 1780 to this time.

His Excellency Governor Clinton

ADfS, Hamilton Papers, Library of Congress.
1. See Robert Morris to H, July 12, 1782. Morris's letter of July 25, 1781, was addressed to the governors of the states.
2. In MS, "police."
3. John Holt, a supporter of the Patriot cause before and during the American Revolution and publisher of *The New-York Journal, and the General Advertiser,* had been appointed in January, 1782, to print the laws of New York State.
4. The list of acts is printed as an enclosure to H's letter in the *Public Papers of George Clinton,* VIII, 25–26.
5. Gerard Bancker, treasurer of the State of New York.
6. Letter not found.

To Udny Hay [1]

Albany Aug. 3d. 1782

Dr. Sir

Mr. Morris, some time since, in a circular letter to the states,[2] among other things, requested to have an account of all the money, provisions, transportation, &c., furnished by this state to the United States, since the 18th. of March, 1780.

I have been very happy to hear, that this business has been intrusted to your hands, for I am sure, feeling its importance, you will give it all the dispatch in your power.

I have written to the Governor on the subject,[3] but lest other occupations should delay his attention to it I must request you to inform me precisely what part of the matter has been intrusted to your management, and what progress you have been able to make.

I shall also thank you to send me the amount of any certificates or paper money in any shape, which, through your office, have passed into circulation, distinguishing the different species.[4]

You will do me a favour by letting me hear from you as soon as possible.[5]

I am with sincere esteem   Your Obedient servant   A Hamilton

I must still trouble you with an additional request which is that you let me know as exactly as possible the gross product of each supply-bill in your department in specie value and the amount of all expences on each. This I want with a view to the subjects we have been speaking of.   AH

ADfS, Hamilton Papers, Library of Congress.
    1. A duplicate of this letter was sent on August 18, 1782 (see endorsement on H to Hay, September 7, 1782), and a triplicate was enclosed in H's letter to Hay on September 7, 1782.
    Hay was commissioned state agent on June 29, 1780. On that date Governor George Clinton wrote to him: "About an Hour since the Council of Appointment made you agent for this State to supply the Quota of Provisions &c. to be furnished by this State for the use of the Army" (*Public Papers of George Clinton*, V, 892).
    2. Robert Morris to the Governors of the Several States, July 25, 1781 (Robert Morris Papers, Library of Congress).
    3. See H to Clinton, August 3, 1782.
    4. The New York Provincial Congress and its successors had authorized issues of paper money. In addition to the regular issues of paper, state agents had been authorized to pay for provisions with special promissory notes.
    5. Hay did not answer H's request. See H to Hay, September 7, 1782.

To Robert Morris

[*Albany, August 3, 1782.* On the back of a letter which Robert Morris wrote to H on July 22, 1782, H wrote: "Ansd. Aug 3d." *Letter not found.*]

From Gerard Bancker

[*August 5, 1782.* The last item on the "List of Papers delivered by Alexander Hamilton to Thomas Tillotson Esquire relative to the office of Receiver of Taxes for the state of New York," November 10, 1782, was described as a "letter from Mr. Banker state Treasurer dated August 5th. 1782 informing of what was to be expected from the state." *Letter not found.*]

To the County Treasurers of the State of New York

Circular   Albany Aug. 5th. 1782

Sir

It will be of great utility to the state and is essential to the execution of my instructions from the Superintendant of Finance, that I should be able to ascertain as speedily as possible, the expense attending the collection of taxes within this state. In order to this I shall be much obliged to you to send me without delay an account of what you have received in your county since the beginning of the year 80 to this time, as well for the taxes laid for county purposes as for those imposed by the legislature, and of the expences of every kind attending the collection; those of the supervisors assessors the allowance to the collectors and to yourself.[1]

When I assure you I want this information for an important purpose I doubt not you will forward it to me as speedily as it can be prepared and with as much accuracy as circumstances will permit; by doing which you will serve the public & oblige Sir   Your most Obed ser

A Hamilton
Receiver of C T
for the State of N.Y.[2]

ADfS, Hamilton Papers, Library of Congress.
  1. Late in 1779, the New York legislature established a county quota system for raising money through taxation. Supervisors in each county apportioned the quota among the various wards; assessors determined the amount to be paid by each individual; and collectors were charged with the responsibility

of collecting the taxes and transferring the money to the county treasurers. For a detailed discussion of the duties of these state and local finance officers, see H to Robert Morris, August 13, 1782.

2. The endorsement, in the writing of H, reads as follows: "Circular letter to County Treasurers. Col. R. Hoffman, Dutchess, Christopher Tappen, Ulster, Thomas Moffat, Orange, Abijah Gilbert, W. Chester. Augt. 5. 1782."

To Robert Morris

[*Albany, August 10, 1782.* On August 28, 1782, Morris wrote to Hamilton: "I have duly received your several Favors of the Twenty second & twenty Seventh of July, and tenth and thirteenth of August." *Letter of August 10 not found.*]

From James McHenry

Baltimore 11th. Augt. 1782

If you are not in the humor to read a long letter do, prithee, give this to the child to play with and go on with your amusement of rocking the cradle. To be serious, my dear Hamilton, I have been thinking of late upon my own situation, and this had led me as often to think of yours. Some men, I observe, are so born and tempered that it is not till after long bustling and battling it in the world (and some scarcely then) that they come to learn a little prudence. Much I begin to suspect that you and I want a great deal of this quality to bring us on a level with our neighbours and to carry us chearfully through life. Have we not both of us continued long enough in the service of the public? Should not I exercise my profession or some profitable business, and should not you, putting of[f] the politician, exert yourself *only* to acquire a profession? I find that to be dependent on a father is irksome, because I feel that it is in my power to be independent by my own endeavours. I see that the good things of this world are all to be purchased with money, and that the man who has money may be whatever he pleases.

Hamilton, there are two lawyers in this Town, one of which has served the public in the General Assembly for three years with reputation, and to the neglect of his practice. The other has done nothing but attend to his profession, by which he has acquired a handsome competency. Now the people have taken it into their heads to displace the lawyer who has served them till he is become poor, in order to put in his stead the lawyer who has served himself and become rich. Let me add to this anecdote, a bon mot of our friend Fleury's.[1] Talking to me the other day, you are a Senator said he, pray what is your salary.[2] I told him it might perhaps defray about two thirds of ones expences, while attending the Senate, and that we were only paid during our attendance, provided one was unmarried and lived frugally. Then, said he, I pity Maryland, for her Senate must be composed chiefly of rich fools. What is the moral of all this, my dear friend, but that it is high time for you and I to set about, in good earnest, doing something for ourselves.

I hear you are chosen a delegate to Congress; will you forgive me for saying that I would rather have heard that you had not been chosen. If you accept of the office, there is a stop to any further studying of the law, which I am desirous you should finish, because a few years practice at the bar, would make you independent, and do you more substantial good than all the fugitive honors of Congress. This would put it in your power to obtain them and to hold them, with more certainty, should you still be inclined to risque in a troubled sea. The moment you cease to be a candidate for public places, the people will lament your loss, and wait with impatience till they can persuade a man of your abilities to serve them. In the mean time you will be doing justice to your family. Besides, you know that there is nothing at present to be had worthy your acceptance. The negotiators for peace have been long since appointed. The great departments of Government are all filled up. Our foreign ministers sit firm in their seats. It is not to be expected that any new ministers will be created before a peace. And when this comes, be assured, long residence and large possessions in this country will preclude superior merit.

I wish therefore, my dear friend, that I could prevail upon you

ALS, Hamilton Papers, Library of Congress.

1. François Louis Teisseydre, Marquis de Fleury, after a trip to France in 1779, joined the army of Comte de Rochambeau in 1780, and was present at the Battle of Yorktown.

2. McHenry had been elected to the Maryland Senate in September, 1781, and had attended the legislative session of January, 1782.

to avoid a disappointment and a loss which I think I foresee. For should you go to Congress, you will lose another year of time that is become more precious than ever, and retire perhaps in disgust, to renue your studies, and to those domestic endearments which you will regret to have forsaken. How would it vex me to learn that you had exclaimed in the stile of an English cardinal—If I had but served my family as faithfully as I have the public, my affairs would have been to-day in a very different order.

It appears to me, Hamilton, to be no longer either necessary or a duty, for you and I, to go on to sacrifice the small remnant of time that is left us. We have already immolated largely on the alter of liberty. At present our Country neither wants our services in the field or the cabinet; so that it is incumbent upon us to be useful in another line. By pushing your studies to a conclusion, you at once perfect your happiness. But I wander, nor recollect whilst my own life runs on in idleness and small follies, that I stand in most need of this advice which I am presuming to offer. You have a wife and an increasing offspring to urge you forward, but I am without either —without your incitements to begin a reform, or your perseverance to succeed. Write me than what you are doing—what you have done,—and what you intend to do, that I may endeavour to follow your example. And be full, for I really intend to be wise, and you shall be my Apollo.

I have been a second time on the point of gaining immortality— by a fever. It seized me a little after the arrival of the French troops here,[3] and has only permitted me to come abroad a few days since. Mrs. Carter and Miss Peggy [4] are with us, and of course you will think I have been often with them. But I must tell you something of your relations. Mr. Carter [5] is the mere man of business, and I am informed has riches enough, with common management, to make

3. Early in July, 1782, Rochambeau began to march his army from its encampment at Williamsburg, Virginia, toward New York. En route the troops were given a month's rest at Baltimore.

4. Angelica Schuyler, oldest daughter of Philip Schuyler, married John Barker Church who assumed the alias of John Carter during the American Revolution.

Margarita (or Margaret) Schuyler, H's sister-in-law, was the third daughter of Philip Schuyler.

5. John B. Church, in association with Jeremiah Wadsworth, had a contract for supplying the French forces in America, a fact which explains the presence of the Church family in Baltimore (see note 3).

the longest life very comfortable. Mrs. Carter is a fine woman. She charms in all companies. No one has seen her, of either sex, who has not been pleased with her, and she has pleased every one, chiefly by means of those qualities which make you the husband of her Sister. Peggy, though, perhaps a finer woman, is not generally thought so. Her own sex are apprehensive that she considers them, poor things, as Swifts Vanessa did; and they in return do not scruple to be displeased. In short, Peggy, to be admired as she ought, has only to please the men less and the ladies more. Tell her so. I am sure her good sense will soon place her in her proper station.

My dear Hamilton adieu. Remember a man who lives in this world without being satisfied with it. Who strives to seem happy among a people who cannot inspire happiness, but who thinks it unbecoming the dignity of man to leave his post merely because it does not please him. I am melancholly you perceive. This plaugy fever has torn me to pieces, and my mind yet shares in the weakness of my body. But I will recover spirits as I recover strength. In the mean while do not fail to write me. Again my friend and philosopher adieu—   James McHenry

I wrote you between my fevers on the affair of Chase, which letter I inclosed to Secretary Trumbul. Has it been received? It contained what you asked for.[6]

6. McHenry wrote to H on January 31, 1782, concerning H's attacks on Samuel Chase under the pseudonym of "Publius." H replied on February 26. In neither letter, however, is there any mention of a request by H. It is possible that the request was made in an unfound letter which H wrote to McHenry on March 8, 1782.

Secretary Trumbull presumably was Jonathan Trumbull, Jr., who succeeded Robert Hanson Harrison as secretary to General Washington in June, 1781. Trumbull was the son of the governor of Connecticut.

From George Clinton

Poughkeepsie [New York] Augt. 13th. 1782

Sir

I have received your Letter of the 3d. Instant. I am not authorized to direct the Printer to deliver any of the Laws except a certain number of Setts which are by Law directed for particular Purposes.

I have however mentioned your Desire to the Gentlemen of the Committee appointed to superintend the printing and distribution of them and requested them to furnish you with a Sett which I doubt not will be complied with.

Some short time before the appointment of a Superintendant of Finance I transmitted to Congress the most perfect Information I was able to collect of many of the Matters mentioned in your Letter [1] and it was my Intention from time to time to have continued these communications to Mr. Morris: but our Laws remaining so long unprinted, the dispersed Situation of the different public Officers and the Difficulty from this Circumstance as well as the want of authority in some instances to command the necessary Returns, rendered it a Business, if not impracticable, requiring more time and attention than the indispensable Duties of my Office afforded Leizure to bestow. I shall however be happy to give you every Aid in my Power to facilitate it. The Laws with the Returns which have lately been made by the different public Officers and may be found on the Files of the Legislature and in the Treasurers Office, will answer most of the Questions stated. The answers to the others appear to me to depend in some measure on matter of Opinion and, as the operation of our Laws is often obstructed and the intended Consequences defeated by unforeseen Events arising from our embarrassed Situation, they cannot be given with any great Degree of precision.

You will readily perceive Sir that the Treasurer from the nature of his Office is not, except in Cases provided for by Law, subject to my controul. I am persuaded however that he as well as the Clerks of the Legislature will readily give you every Information and Assistance consistent with the Duties of their respective Offices. [2]

I am with great Respect & Esteem　Sir Your most Obedient Servant　　　　　　　　　　　　　　　　Geo. Clinton

Colo. Alexr. Hamilton

LS, Hamilton Papers, Library of Congress.
　1. See Clinton to the President of Congress, February 5, 1781 (Papers of the Continental Congress, National Archives).
　2. On the envelope of this letter H made the following notations: "history of New York of England since the Revolution to the last peace—Entales history of the late war." Presumably H wished books on the history of New

York and of England to aid in the preparation of reports on the finances of New York.

Following these notations the following names appeared:

Judge
Jno. Herring   Orange
Joseph Gagerce   Kingston
Ths. Moffat at Goshen

In 1780, Joseph Gasherie, John Haring, and Thomas Moffat were appointed "Auditors to Liquidate the Accounts of the Troops" (James A. Roberts, *New York in the Revolution* [Albany, 1904], II, 22).

To Robert Morris [1]

Albany Augt. 13th. 1782

Sir,

I promised you in former letters to give you a full view of the situation and temper of this state: I now sit down to execute that task.

You have already in your possession a pretty just picture of the 1st [2] drawn by the Legislature in   [3] perhaps too highly coloured in some places, but in the main true. It is the opinion of the most sensible men, with whom I converse, who are best acquainted with the circumstances of the state, and who are not disposed to exaggerate its distresses as an excuse for inactivity, that its faculties for revenue are diminished at least two thirds.

It will not be difficult to conceive this, when we consider, that five out of the fourteen counties of which the state was composed, including the capital, are in the hands of the enemy—that two and

ALS, Hamilton Papers, Library of Congress.

1. The version of this letter printed in *JCHW*, I, 293, and *HCLW*, IX, 269 is incomplete. Except for a draft (Hamilton Papers, Library of Congress) of the last few paragraphs of the letter, H retained no copy of it. The receiver's copy remained in the possession of the descendants of Robert Morris who refused to allow publication of the sections dealing with New York politicians. For a history of the letter see *The Magazine of History*, XXIII (July–December, 1916), 158–69. The letter was sold in January, 1917, by S. V. Henkels in Philadelphia. It was presumably purchased by Allan McLane Hamilton, H's grandson, for it now is with the miscellaneous documents in the Hamilton papers which he gave to the Library of Congress.

2. I.e., a full view of the situation of the state, to which H referred in the first paragraph of his letter. All other published versions of this letter have either omitted the word "1st" or transcribed it as "list" or "lott."

3. In the blank space left by H he probably intended later to insert the date of Governor George Clinton's letter to Congress of February 5, 1781. See Clinton to H, August 13, 1782, note 1.

part of a third have revolted—two others have been desolated, the greater part, by the ravages of the enemy and of our own troops—and the remaining four have more or less suffered partial injuries from the same causes. Adding the fragments of some to repair the losses of others, the efficient property, strength and force of the state will consist in little more than four counties.

In the distribution of taxes before the war the city of New York used to be rated at one third of the whole; but this was too high, owing probably to the prevalency of the country interest; its proper proportion I should judge to have been about one fourth; which serves further to illustrate the probable decrease of the state.

Our population indeed is not diminished in the same degree, as many of the inhabitants of the dismembered and ruined counties, who have left their habitations, are dispersed through those which remain; and it would seem that the labor of the additional hands ought to increase the culture and value of these; but there are many deductions to be made from this apparent advantage—the numbers that have recruited the British army—[4] those that have been furnished to ours—the emigrations to Vermont and to the neighbouring states, less harrassed by the war, and affording better encouragements to industry; both which have been considerable. Besides these circumstances, many of the fugitive families are a burthen for their subsistence upon the state. The fact is labor is much dearer than before the war.

This state has certainly made in the course of the war great exertions, and upon many occasions of the most exhausting kind. This has sometimes happened from want of judgment, at others from necessity. When the army, as has too often been the case, has been threatened with some fatal calamity, for want of provisions, forage, the means of transportation &c, in consequence of pressing applications from the Commander in Chief, the Legislature has been obliged to have recourse to extraordinary expedients to answer the present emergency, which have both distressed and disgusted the people. There is no doubt that with a prudent and systematic administration the state might have rendered more benefit to the common cause, with less inconvenience to itself, than by all its forced efforts; but here as every where else we have wanted experience and knowl-

4. I.e., the number recruited by the British army.

ege. And indeed had this not been the case, every thing every where has been so radically wrong, that it was difficult, if not impossible, for any one state to be right.

The exposed situation of the frontier and the frequent calls upon the inhabitants for personal service on each extremity, by interfering with industry, have contributed to impoverish the state and fatigue the people.

Deprived of foreign trade, our internal traffic is carried on upon the most disadvantageous terms. It divides itself into three branches; with the city of New York, with Jersey and Pensylvania, and with New England.

That with New York consists chiefly of luxuries on one part and returns of specie on the other. I imagine we have taken goods from that place to the annual amount of near £30.000. The Legislature have passed a severe law to prevent this intercourse; but what will laws avail against the ingenuity and intrepidity of avarice?

From Jersey and Pensylvania we take about thirty thousand pounds more and we pay almost intirely in cash.

From Massachusettes and other parts of New England we purchase to the amount of about £50.000, principally in tea and salt. We sell to these states to the value of about £30.000. The articles of tea and salt alone cost this state the annual sum of sixty thousand pounds.

The immense land transportation of which the chief part is carried on by the subjects of other states is a vast incumbrance upon our trade.

The principal article we have to throw in the opposite scale is the expenditures of the army. Mr. Sands [5] informs me that the contractors for the main army and West point lay out in this state at the rate of about 60.000 dollars a year: Mr. Duer,[6] for these northern posts about Thirty thousand: If the Quarter Master general expends as much more in his department, the whole will amount to about 180.000 dolls. I speak of what is paid for in specie or such paper as answers the purposes of specie.

5. Comfort Sands had contracted with the Superintendent of Finance to supply Army officers in the district of West Point.
6. William Duer supplied the Army posts north of Poughkeepsie, New York, with rations.

These calculations cannot absolutely be relied on because the data are necessarily uncertain; but they are the result of the best information I can obtain; and if near the truth, prove that the general ballance of trade is against us; a plain symptom of which is an *extreme* and *universal* scarcity of money.

The situation of the state, with respect to its internal government is not more pleasing. Here we find the general disease which infects all our constitutions, an excess of popularity. There is no *order* that has a will of its own. The inquiry constantly is what will *please* not what will *benefit* the people. In such a government there can be nothing but temporary expedient, fickleness and folly.

But the point of view in which this subject will be interesting to you is that which relates to our finances. I gave you in a former letter a sketch of our plan of taxation; but I will now be more particular.[7]

The general principle of it is an assessment, according to *circumstances and abilities collectively considered.*

The ostensible reason for adopting this vague basis was a desire of equality: It was pretended, that this could not be obtained so well by any fixed tariff of taxable property, as by leaving it to the discretion of persons chosen by the people themselves, to determine the ability of each citizen. But perhaps the true reason was a desire to discriminate between the *whigs* and *tories*. This chimerical attempt at perfect equality has resulted in total inequality; or rather this narrow disposition to overburthen a particular class of citizens (living under the protection of the government) has been retorted upon the contrivers or their friends, wherever that class has been numerous enough to preponderate in the election of the officers who were to execute the law. The exterior figure a man makes, the decency or meaness of his manner of living, the personal friendships, or dislikes of the assessors have much more share in determining what individuals shall pay, than the proportion of property.

The Legislature first *assesses*, or quotas the several counties. Here the evil begins. The members cabal and intrigue to throw the burthen off their respective constituents. Address and influence, more than

7. In a letter dated July 22, 1782, H informed Morris of the financial measures enacted by the New York legislature at its July session.

considerations of real ability prevail. A great deal of time is lost and a great deal of expence incurred before the juggle is ended and the necessary compromises made.

The Supervisors, of whom there are upon an average sixteen in each county, meet at the notification of the County-clerk, and assign their proportions to the sub-divisions of the county; and in the distribution play over the same game, which was played in the Legislature.

The Assessors assembled on a like notification, according to their fancies, determine the proportion of each individual; a list of which being made out and signed by the Supervisors is a warrant to the collectors. There are near an hundred upon average in each County.

The allowance to these officers has been various; it is now six shillings a day besides expences: in some cases they have been limited to a particular time for executing the business; but in general it is left to their discretion, and the greater part of them are not in a hurry to complete it, as they have a compensation for their trouble, and live better at the public charge than they are accustomed to do at their own. The consequence is not only delay but a heavy expence.

It now remains for the collectors to collect the tax, and it is the duty of the supervisors to see that they do it. Both these offices, as well as that of the assessors, are elective; and of course there is little disposition to risk the displeasure of those who elect. They have no motive of interest to stimulate them to their duty, equivalent to the inconvenience of performing it. The collector is intitled to the trifling compensation of sometimes four—sometimes six pence out of each pound he collects, and is liable to the trifling penalty of twenty or five and twenty pounds for neglect of duty. The supervisors have no interest at all in the collection; and it will on this account appear not extraordinary, that with continual delinquencies in the collector⟨s⟩ there has never been a single prosecution.

As I observed on a former occasion, if the collector happens to be a zealous man and lives in a zealous neighbourhood the taxes are collected; if either of these requisites is wanting the collection languishes or intirely fails.

When the taxes are collected, they are paid to the County treasurer; an officer chosen by the Supervisors. The collectors are responsible to him also; but as he is allowed only one fourth or one half per Cent, he has no sufficient inducement to incur the odium of compelling them to do their duty.

The County Treasurer pays what he receives into the state Treasurer who has an annual salary of £300; and has nothing to do but to receive and pay out according to the appropriations of the legislature.

Nothwithstanding the obvious defects of this system, notwithstanding experience has shown it to be iniquitous and ineffectual and that all attempts to amend it without totally changing it are fruitless, notwithstanding the⟨re⟩ is a pretty general discontent from the inequality of the taxes, still ancient habits, ignorance, the spirit of the times, the opportunity afforded to some popular characters of skreening themselves by intriguing with the assessors, have hitherto proved an over-match for common sense and common justice as well as the manifest advantage of the State and of the United States.

The temper of the state, which I shall now describe, may be considered under two heads, that of the rulers and that of the people.

The rulers are generally zealous in the common cause, though their zeal is often misdirected. They are jealous of their own power; but yet as this state is the immediate theatre of the war their apprehensions of danger and an opinion that they are obliged to do more than their neighbours make them very willing to part with power in favour of the Fœderal Government. This last opinion and an idea added to it, that they have no credit for their past exertions has put them out of humour and indisposed many of them for future exertions. I have heard several assert, that in the present situation of this state, nothing more ought to be expected, than that it maintain its own government, and keep up its quota of troops. This sentiment however is as yet confined to a few, but it is too palatable not to make proselytes.

There is no man in the government who has a decided influence in it. The present governor [8] has declined in popularity, partly from a defect of qualifications for his station and partly from causes that do him honor—the vigorous execution of some necessary laws that bore hard upon the people, and severity of discipline among the militia. He is, I believe, a man of integrity and passes with his par-

8. George Clinton.

ticular friends for a statesman; it is certain that without being destitute of understanding, his passions are much warmer, than his judgment is enlightened. The preservation of his place is an object to
his private fortune as well as to his ambition; and we are not to be
surprised, if instead of taking a lead in measures that contradict a
prevailing prejudice, however he may be convinced of their utility,
he either flatters it or temporises; especially when a new election
approaches.

The next character of a most uniform influence is General Schuyler.[9] He has more weight in the Legislature than the Governor; but
not so much as not to be exposed to the mortification of seeing important measures patronised by him frequently miscarry. Your
knowlege of him and my connection prevent my enlarging. I shall
only add that he hazards his popularity in support of what you wish
and what the public safety demands.

I omitted speaking of the Lt. Governor in this place; I shall only
say he is an honest man, without pretensions.[10] I shall be silent on
the subject of the Chancellor [11] and of Mr. Duane; [12] because I could
not give you any additional light into their characters.

Mr. Scot [13] you also know. He has his little objects and his little
party. Nature gave him genius; but *habit* has impaired it. He never
had judgment; he now has scarcely plausibility; his influence is just
extensive enough to embarrass measures he does not like; and his
only aim seems to be by violent professions of popular principles
to acquire a popularity which has hitherto coyly eluded his persuit.

9. Philip Schuyler, H's father-in-law, had entered the New York Senate in
September, 1780.
10. In 1777, Pierre Van Cortlandt was elected the first lieutenant governor
of New York. He retained that post until 1795.
11. Robert R. Livingston was appointed chancellor of New York in May,
1777; and although he served as a delegate to the Continental Congress for several terms and, from August, 1781, to August, 1783, as Secretary for Foreign
Affairs, he retained the chancellorship until 1801.
12. James Duane who for ten continuous years, 1774–84, served as one of
the New York delegates to the Continental Congress was also from 1782 to 1786
a member of the New York Senate. As he had served on many important
congressional committees devoted to economic affairs, he was of course well
known to Morris.
13. The popularity of John Morin Scott, a man of wealth and social prom-
inence, made him a serious contender for the governorship of the state against
George Clinton in 1777. Scott was a member of the New York Senate from
1777 to 1782, secretary of state of New York from 1778 to 1784, and a member
of the Continental Congress from 1779 to 1784.

His views as a statesman are warped; his principles as a man are said to be not the purest.

In the senate Judge Platt,[14] Judge Paine [15] and Mr. Yates [16] have each their share of influence.

The first is a man of plain sense, thoroughly acquainted with agriculture. He intends to do well whenever he can hit upon what is right.

The second is a man of strong natural parts and as strong prejudices; his zeal is fiery, his obstinacy unconquerable. He is as primitive in his notions, as in his appearance. Without education, he wants more knowlege, or more tractableness.

The third is a man whose ignorance and perverseness are only surpassed by his pertinacity and conceit. He hates all high-flyers, which is the appellation he gives to men of genius. He has the merit of being always the first man at the Legislature. The people have been a long time in the *habit* of choosing him in different offices; and to the title of prescription, he adds that of being a preacher to their taste. He *assures* them, they are too poor to pay taxes. He is a staunch whig, that deserves to be pensioned by the British Ministry. He is commissioner of the loan office in this state.

In the assembly the leading members are, Mr. Malcolm,[17] Mr. Laurance,[18] Mr. Lansing,[19] Judge Tredwell [20] and Mr. Humphreys.[21]

14. Zephaniah Platt represented the middle district in the New York Senate from 1777 to 1784. He represented the state in the Continental Congress from 1784 to 1787.

15. Ephraim Paine was a senator from the middle district. He served in the New York Senate from 1780 to 1781, and from 1782 to 1786.

16. Abraham Yates, Jr. of Albany, one of George Clinton's most important political lieutenants, served in the New York Senate from 1777 to 1791.

17. William Malcom, a colonel of the New York Levies, was a representative in the Assembly for the sixth, seventh, ninth, and tenth sessions.

18. John Laurence of New York City had served as judge advocate general in the Revolution and was a member of the New York Assembly during the sixth and eighth sessions. He served two terms in the Continental Congress (1785 and 1786).

19. John Lansing, Jr. of Albany County later became chief justice of the Supreme Court of New York and chancellor of the state. With the exception of the time during 1784 and 1785 when he served as a member of the Continental Congress, Lansing was a member of the New York Assembly from 1780 to 1788.

20. Thomas Tredwell of Suffolk County was a member of the Assembly from 1777 to 1784 and judge of the Court of Probates from 1778 to 1787.

21. Cornelius Humphrey represented Dutchess County in the New York Assembly from 1781 to 1786.

Malcolm has a variety of abilities: he is industrious and expert in business; he wants not resource and is pretty right on the subjects of the day; but he is too fond of popularity and too apt to think every scheme bad, that is not his own. He is closely linked with Scot, because he can govern him: A man of warm passions, he can controul all but his vanity, which often stands in the way of his interest. He is accused of duplicity and insincerity. He has it in his power to support or perplex measures, as he may incline, and it will be politic to make it his interest to incline to what is right. It was on this principle I proposed him for a certain office.[22]

Laurence is a man of good sense and good intentions—has just views of public affairs—is active and accurate in business. He is from conviction an advocate for strengthening the Fœderal government and for reforming the vices of our interior administration.

Lansing is a good young fellow and a good practitioner of the law; but his friends mistook his talents when they made him a statesman. He thinks two pence an ounce upon plate a *monstrous tax*. The county of Albany is not of my opinion concerning him.

Tredwell [23] is esteemed a sensible and an honest man.

Mr. Humphreys has his admirers, because he is pretty remarkable for *blunder* and vociferation. He said the last session in the assembly that it was very inconvenient for the country members to be detained at that season, that for his own part no motive would induce him to stay, but *to sacrifice* the interest of his country.

In the council of revision,[24] which is composed of the Governor, Chancellor and the three Judges; Mr. Morris [25] the chief Justice is a well meaning man. Judge Yates [26] is upright and respectable in his profession. Hobart [27] is solemn and sententious. He thinks rightly

22. H probably had recommended Malcom for the office of receiver.

23. In MS, "Treaddle."

24. Provision had been made for a Council of Revision in the state constitution of 1777. Rather than give the governor the veto power, the council, composed of the governor, the chancellor, and the justices of the Supreme Court, was to review all bills passed by the legislature. A two-thirds vote of each house could override a veto by the council.

25. Richard Morris, a judge of the Vice-Admiralty Court having jurisdiction over New York, Connecticut, and New Jersey from 1762 until his resignation in 1775, was appointed in 1779 to succeed John Jay as chief justice of the New York Supreme Court.

26. Robert Yates was appointed a justice of the New York Supreme Court in May, 1777.

27. John Sloss Hobart, appointed a New York Supreme Court justice in May, 1777, held that office until 1798.

in the main as to the imperfections of our present system, both general and particular and the proper remedy; but he has a prodigious propensity to a *convulsion;* and he augurs many fine things from a second *bankruptcy* and a total derangement of our affairs. "Then (says he) and not 'till then *Order* will rise out of confusion."

I have now touched upon the principal *public* characters among us; there are others who have their little circles of influence; some of whom deserve more others much less. I have contented myself with outlines, because Mr. G Morris will be able to give you much more satisfactory portraits. What I have done is only in compliance with your request.

The rulers of this state are attached to the alliance, as are the whigs generally.

They have also great confidence in you personally; but pretty general exception has been taken to a certain letter of yours written I believe in the winter or spring.[28] The idea imbibed is, that it contains a reflection upon them for their past exertions. I have on every account combatted this impression, which could not fail to have an ill effect, and I mention it to you with freedom, because it is essential you should know the temper of the states respecting yourself.

As to the people, in the early periods of the war, near one half of them were avowedly more attached to Great Britain than to their liberty; but the energy of the government has subdued all opposition. The state by different means has been purged of a large part of its malcontents; but there still remains I dare say a third whose secret wishes are on the side of the enemy; the remainder sigh for peace, murmur at taxes, clamour at their rulers, change one incapable man for another more incapable; and I fear if left to themselves would, too many of them, be willing to purchase peace at any price, not from inclination to great Britain, or disaffection to independence, but from mere supineness and avarice. The speculation of evils from the claims of Great Britain gives way to the pressure of inconveniences actually felt; and we required the event which has

28. On August 28, 1782, Morris wrote to H that the letter in question must have been his letter of December 11, 1781, to Governor George Clinton. Commenting on resolutions of the New York legislature which described the difficulties of raising a revenue and the previous exertions of the state, Morris insisted that the state was able to pay its share of the public expense and was critical of the large bounties the state had given for enlistment in the Army. The bounties, Morris wrote, were "fully equal to the Pay and Rations of so many Men for six Months" (Robert Morris Papers, Library of Congress).

lately happened, the recognition of our independence by the Dutch [29] to give a new spring to the public hopes and the public passions. This has had a good effect. And if the Legislature can be brought to adopt a wise plan for its finances, we may put the people in better humour, and give a more regular and durable movement to the machine. The people of this state as far as my observation goes, have as much firmness in their make and as much submissiveness to government as those of any part of the Union.

It remains for me to give you an explicit opinion of what it is practicable for this state to do. Even with a judicious plan of taxation I do not think the state can afford or the people will bear to pay more than seventy, or eighty thousand pounds a year. In its intire and flourishing state according to my mode of calculating it could not have exceeded two hundred and thirty or forty thousand pounds; and reduced as it is with the wheels of circulation so exceedingly clogged for want of commerce and a sufficient medium more than I have said cannot be expected. Passed experience will not authorise a more flattering conclusion.

Out of this is to be deducted the expence of the interior administration and the money necessary for the ⟨levies⟩ of men. The first amounts to about £15.000—as you will perceive by the inclosed state[ment], but I suppose the Legislature would choose to retain £20.000. The money hitherto yearly expended in recruits has amounted to between twenty and thirty thousand pounds; but on a proper plan ten thousand might suffice. There would then remain forty thousand pounds for your department.

But this is on the supposition of a change of system; for with the present I doubt there being paid into the Continental treasury one third of that sum. I am endeavouring to collect materials for greater certainty upon this subject. But the business of supplies has been so diversified, lodged in such a variety of independent hands and so carelessly transacted that it is hardly possible to get any tolerable idea of the gross and nett product.

With the help of these materials I shall strive to convince the Committee when they meet that a change of measures is essential; if they

29. On December 29, 1780, Congress appointed John Adams Minister to the United Provinces, and on August 16, 1781, it commissioned him Minister Plenipotentiary to the United Provinces. On April 22, 1782, Adams was recognized as minister plenipotentiary by the United Provinces.

enter cordially into right views we may succeed; but I confess I fear more than I hope.[30]

I have taken every step in my power to procure the information you have desired in your letter of July 81. The most material part of it, an account of the supplies furnished since march 80 has been committed to Col Hay. I have written to him in pressing terms to accelerate the preparation.[31]

You will perceive Sir, I have neither flattered the state nor encouraged high expectations. I thought it my duty to exhibit things as they are not as they ought to be. I shall be sorry, if it give an ill-opinion of the state for want of equal candor in the representations of others; for however disagreeable the reflection, I have too much reason to believe that the true picture of other states would be in proportion to their circumstances equally unpromising. All my inquiries and all that appears induces this opinion. I intend this letter *in confidence to yourself* and therefore I indorse it *private.*

Before I conclude I will say a word on a point that possibly you could wish to be informed about. The contract up this way is executed generously to the satisfaction of the officers and soldiers, which is the more meritorious in the Contractor as in all probability it will be to him a losing undertaking.[32]

I have the honor to be with sentiments of unfeigned esteem   Sir Your most Obedient & humble servant   A Hamilton

The Honble The Superintendant of Finance

[ENCLOSURE] [33]

Expences of our internal Government

To the Governor . . . . . for salary	£	1600
To the Chancellor . . . . . . do		400
To the Secretary of State & Clerks about		300
To the Attorney General . . . by estimation . .		100

30. H is referring to a joint committee of both houses appointed to report on a system for establishing funds. See H to Morris, July 22, 1782.

31. Morris's letter was dated July 25, 1781. See Morris to H, July 12, 1782. H's letter to Udny Hay, state agent for New York, was dated August 3, 1782.

32. William Duer had contracted with Morris to supply the Army posts north of Poughkeepsie.

33. AD, Hamilton Papers, Library of Congress.

To the Chief Justice . . . . salary	400
Puisne Justices each 350 £ do	700
for travelling expences by estimation 40 days . .	100
in the year at 12/ per day each	
Auditor	300
Aide De Camp to the Governor Lt. Col Pay & rations	360
Occasional do. at the same rate	
Delegates to Congress 34/ pr day while attending and 6	
days going and coming abt	1500
Treasurer . . . . . Salary	300
Members of Legislature 8/ per day, upon an average [--]	
members for 88 days ⟨including coming &c.⟩	1936
two Clerks of do. each 20/ a day for 72 days	144
time actually together	
two Door Keepers each 10/ pr day . . . do . . .	72
Printer for printing laws &c. about	300
Incidental expences	
	————
	8412
To the poor annually about 500	
	6588
To the Indians do 600	
⟨charges⟩ of Militia expresses occasional officers & other	
occasional demands allowd	6088	3500
	———— ————
	15884
Regtr	say	£ 12000
	————
	£ 15000 [34]

Transmitted a copy of the above to Mr. Morris
Aug. 1782

34. There is an error in this column for the figures in it do not total £ 15,000.

To Lieutenant Colonel John Laurens [1]

[Albany, August 15, 1782]

I received with great Pleasure, My Dear Laurens, the letter which you wrote me in　　　　last.[2]

Your wishes in one respect are gratified; this state has pretty unanimously delegated me to Congress. My time of service commences in November.[3] It is not probable it will result in what you mention.[4] I hope it is too late. We have great reason to flatter ourselves peace on our own terms is upon the carpet. The making it is in good hands. It is said your father is exchanged for Cornwallis and gone to Paris to meet the other commissioners and that Grenville on the part of England has made a second trip there, in the last instance, vested with Plenipotentiary powers.[5]

I fear there may be obstacles but I hope they may be surmounted.

Peace made, My Dear friend, a new scene opens. The object then will be to make our independence a blessing. To do this we must secure our *union* on solid foundations; an herculean task and to effect which mountains of prejudice must be levelled!

It requires all the virtue and all the abilities of the Country. Quit your sword my friend, put on the *toga*, come to Congress. We know each others sentiments, our views are the same: we have fought side by side to make America free, let us hand in hand struggle to make her happy.

Remember me to General Greene with all the warmth of a sincere attachment.[6]

Yrs for ever   A Hamilton

Albany Aug. 15. 1782
Col Laurens

ALS, Pierpont Morgan Library, New York City.

1. Laurens, after participating in the Yorktown campaign, returned to South Carolina where he joined in the irregular warfare which continued there. On August 27, 1782, he was killed in a skirmish with a British foraging expedition. It is, of course, doubtful that H's letter reached him.

2. See Laurens to H, July, 1782. Date left blank by H.

3. H was appointed a delegate to the Continental Congress on July 22, 1782, his one-year term to commence in November, 1782.

4. Laurens had written to H in July, 1782, "I shd. prefer your going into Congress, and from thence, becoming a Minister plenipotentiary for peace. . . ."

5. Benjamin Franklin, American Minister to France, in June, 1782, approved the exchange of Henry Laurens and Lord Cornwallis, reserving to Congress the right to disavow his act. Laurens had not gone to Paris to join the American Peace Commissioners, as H states, but had gone to southern France to visit relatives.

In the spring of 1782, Charles James Fox, who as Secretary of Northern Department was charged with the conduct of foreign affairs in the Rockingham

Ministry, sent Thomas Grenville to France to treat with Franklin and Vergennes. Grenville, however, had not made a second trip to Paris, for, upon Rockingham's death on July 1, 1782, Lord Shelburne became Prime Minister. Fox resigned, and the peace negotiations were carried on by Richard Oswald who earlier had represented Shelburne in Paris.

6. Major General Nathanael Greene commanded the American forces in the South.

From William Duer [1]

Albany August 16th. 1782

Sir,

You wish to be informed what, I conceive, will be the Amount of the Monies necessary for defraying the Charges of the Northern Contract, from the first of April to the last day of December; and what Proportion of that Sum will be Expended within the State.

Unless a Considerable Reinforcement of Troops should be ordered into this Quarter (of which at present there does not appear a great Probability) I do not imagine the Monthly Issue of Rations during the Term of the Contract will average more than Sixty Six thousand: This at the Contract Price amounts for the Space of nine Months to . . . . Dollrs. 52,717½

Of this Sum according to the best Estimate I can form, . 23,760

will be remitted to the Eastern States for the Proportion of Beef, Salt, and Liquor Imported thence; which leaves, . 28,957½

Ballance of Expenditures within this State.

I am, Sir   Your Obed: Hble Servt   Wm. Duer

Colo. Alexr. Hamilton
Receiver of the Continental Taxes
State of New York

ALS, Hamilton Papers, Library of Congress.

1. Duer had contracted to supply the levies in northern New York and on the frontier. In a letter to Comfort Sands on June 23, 1782, H wrote that Duer had promised to send him a statement of money expended in the northern part of the state.

To Robert Benson [1]

Albany Aug. 18. 1782

Sir

In obedience to Mr. Morris's instructions I lately wrote to His Excellency The Governor requesting information on a variety of matters, which it is of great importance to the Financier and to the public to know.[2] The Governor in his answer [3] tells me that the returns lately made by different public officers and on the files of the Legislature will answer most of the questions stated by me.

The principal ones were concerning—

"The supplies of every kind, money provisions forage transportation &c., which have been furnished by this state to the United States since the 18th. of March 1780.

The amount of the different paper Currencies in the state and the respective rates of depreciation."

You will materially serve the public and personally oblige me by letting me have copies of those returns as speedily as possible. Without these data The Superintendant of Finance, far from being able to liquidate the accounts between the United States and this state, an essential object to both, will be able to form no idea of the comparitive extent of the compliances of the respective states with the requisitions of Congress; consequently he will neither know how to proportion future demands, nor how to regulate any reasonable scheme of finance.

I trust the Governor will have anticipated my request as you are on the spot with him, as he is no doubt convinced that this is a business of importance to the public in general and to this state in particular and as he assures me of his disposition to give me every aid in his power.

If these returns should be on the files of the Assembly and not of the senate, you will do me a particular favour by communicating this letter to Mr. McKesson [4] to whom I make the same request.

I am   with very great esteem &c.

AL, Hamilton Papers, Library of Congress.
   1. Benson was clerk of the New York Senate. H wrote to Benson again on September 7, 1782, and enclosed a duplicate of this letter. Both a signed draft

of the letter of August 18 and a draft of the letter of September 7 are in the Hamilton Papers, Library of Congress. In the printed version of the letter in the *Public Papers of George Clinton*, VIII, 31–32, a sentence is added after the closing which reads: "I beg the copies may be certified."
  2. See H to George Clinton, August 3, 1782.
  3. See George Clinton to H, August 13, 1782.
  4. John McKesson was clerk of the Assembly of the State of New York.

From Colonel Timothy Pickering

New Windsor [New York] Augt. 20. 1782

Dr. Sir,

I have some bills of exchange drawn by Mr. Morris on John Swanwick,[1] which I am authorized to exchange with the Receivers of the Continental taxes in any of the states eastward of Pensylvania. Mr. Morris informed me that he had advised the receivers of this measure, & directed their taking up the bills whenever they were in cash. By taxes or by loan I expect this state will shortly furnish you with money: I am indebted to the subjects of it by many special engagements, which I am anxious to fulfil. You will therefore greatly oblige me by giving me from time to time information of the money you shall receive, and in order to secure the earliest supply, I would lodge, if you please, some of the bills in your hands. Bank notes or Mr. Morris's notes will be useful to me, tho' not so beneficial as cash.

  I am, dear sir,   with respect & esteem   Yr. most obedt. servt.

Tim: Pickering QMG

Colo. Alexr. Hamilton

ALS, Hamilton Papers, Library of Congress; LC, RG 93, Letters of Col. T. Pickering, National Archives.
  1. See Robert Morris to H, July 19, 1782.

To George Clinton [1]

Albany [August] 25. 1782

Sir

By advices from Philadelphia I find that the present is a period rather critical on the subject of money and concenters a variety of demands which it is not easy to satisfy. It becomes therefore of importance to the Financier to avail himself of every immediate resource.

This induces me to request you will be so good as [to] inform me, whether there is any near prospect of obtaining the loan directed to be applied to Continental use; [2] also whether any measures can be taken to accelerate the collection of the late tax imposed for the same use.[3]

I would willingly write to the County treasurers myself, but unauthorised as I am I could expect no good effect from it.

I have the honor to be with perfect respect   Yr. Excellency's Obed serv   AH

ADfS, Hamilton Papers, Library of Congress.
  1. The endorsement in H's handwriting on this letter reads, "To Governor Clinton, August 25. 1782, Duplicate Septr. 7, 82."
  2. H was referring to a section of "AN ACT for levying a tax within this State," which was passed by the New York legislature on July 22, 1782 (Laws of the State of New York, I, 505–08). This section provided for a loan of ten thousand pounds which could be used to "pay such sum or sums to the commissioner of the loan office of this State, or to the superintendent of the finances of the United States, or to such person as he shall appoint to receive the same, as part of the quota assigned to this State for the present year."
  3. H referred to "AN ACT for levying a tax within this State," which was passed by the legislature on July 22, 1782. See note 2. H had written to Robert Morris on July 22, 1782, that the tax "is at present appropriated to your order, but I doubt whether some subsequent arrangement will not take place for a different appropriation."

To Robert Morris

Albany Aug. 25. 82

Sir

This letter serves only to transmit the two last papers: [1] I wish the measures I have taken to satisfy you on the points you desire to be informed of,[2] had been attended with so much success as to enable me now to transmit the result. But I find a singular confusion in the accounts kept by the public officers from whom I must necessarily derive my information, and a singular dilatoriness in complying with my applications, partly from indolence and partly from jealousy of the office.

I hope by the next post to transmit you information on some particulars.

I have the honor to be   Sir   Your most Obed serv   A Hamilton

ALS, Hamilton Papers, Library of Congress.
1. Presumably New York newspapers which H regularly sent to Morris.
2. The reference is presumably to the questions asked in Morris's circular letter of July 25, 1781, which was enclosed in a letter Morris wrote to H on July 12, 1782.

To Richard Kidder Meade

Albany Augt 27th. 1782

I thank you my dear Meade for your letter of the first of this month[1] which you will perceive has travelled much faster than has been usual with our letters. Our correspondence hitherto has been unfortunate, nor in fact can either of us compliment himself on his punctuality but you were right in concluding that however indolence or accident may interrupt our intercourse, nothing will interrupt our friendship. Mine for you is built on the solid basis of a full conviction that you deserve it and that it is reciprocal and it is the more firmly fixed because you have few competitors. Experience is a continued comment on the worthlessness of the human race and the few exceptions we find have the greater right to be valued in proportion as they are rare. I know few men estimable, fewer amiable & when I meet with one of the last description it is not in my power to withhold my affection.

You reproach me with not having said enough about our little stranger.[2] When I wrote last I was not sufficiently acquainted with him to give you his character. I may now assure you that your daughter when she sees him will not consult you about the choice or will only do it in respect to the rules of decorum. He is truly a very fine young gentleman, the most agreable in his conversation and manners of any I ever knew—nor less remarkable for his intelligence and sweetness of temper. You are not to imagine by my beginning with his mental qualifications that he is defective in personal. It is agreed on all hands, that he is handsome, his features are good, his eye is not only sprightly and expressive but it is full of benignity. His attitude in sitting is by connoisseurs esteemed graceful and he has a method of waving his hand that announces the future orator. He stands however rather awkwardly and his legs have not all the delicate slimness of his fathers. It is feared He may never excel as much in dancing which is probably the only accomplishment in which he will not be a model. If he has any fault in manners, he laughs too much. He has now passed his Seventh Month.

I am glad to find your prospect of being settled approaches. I am sure you will realize all the happiness you promise yourself with your amiable partner. I wish Fortune had not cast our lots at such a distance, Mrs. Meade you, Betsy & myself would make a most affectionate & most happy *partie* quarré.

As to myself I shall sit down in New York when it opens & the period we are told approaches. No man looks forward to a Peace with more pleasure than I do, though no man would sacrifice less to it than myself, If I were not convinced the people sigh for peace. I have been studying the Law for some months and have lately been licenced as an attorney.[3] I wish to prepare myself by October for Examination as a Counsellor but some public avocations may possibly prevent me.

I had almost forgotten to tell you, that I have been pretty unanimously elected by the legislature of this state, a member of Congress to begin to serve in November.[4] I do not hope to reform the State although I shall endeavour to do all the good I can.

Suffer Betsey & me to present our love to Mrs. Meade; she has a sisterly affection for you. My respects if you please to Mr. & Mrs. Fitzhugh.[5]

God Bless you   A Hamilton

JCH Transcripts.

1. Letter not found.

2. H's first son, Philip, had been born on January 22, 1782.

3. See "Admission as Attorney before the New York Supreme Court," July, 1782; see also, "Admission as Counsel before the New York Supreme Court," October 26, 1782.

4. On July 22, 1782, H was elected a delegate from New York to the Continental Congress.

5. H is referring to Mr. and Mrs. William Fitzhugh, the uncle and aunt of Meade's wife, the former Mary Fitzhugh Grymes Randolph. Benjamin Grymes, Mrs. Meade's father, had married William Fitzhugh's sister, Elizabeth.

From Robert Morris

Office of Finance [Philadelphia] 28th, August 1782

Sir,

I have duly received your several Favors of the Twenty second & twenty Seventh of July, and tenth and thirteenth of August.[1] My not answering them is owing to Causes which you will easily conceive; because you will easily conceive the Multiplicity of Objects to which I must turn my Attention. I am very sorry to learn that you can no longer continue in the Office of Receiver.[2] It would have given me great Pleasure that you should have done so, because I am sure that you would have rendered very signal Services to the public Cause: This you will now do in another Line more important, as it is more extensive; and the Justness of your Sentiments on public Affairs induce my warm Wish that you may find a Place in Congress so agreeable as that you may be induced to continue in it.

I should readily have complied with your Wish as to a Successor,[3] but there are many Reasons which have called my Attention to and fixed my Choice upon Doctor Tillotson.[4] We will converse on this Subject when we meet. I am however very far from being unmindful of your Recommendations; and altho I cannot name the Citizen of any State to settle the Accounts of that particular State consistently with the general Line of Conduct I have laid down for myself; yet I shall do in other Respects what is in my Power. I have not hitherto been able to fix on a proper Commissioner for the State of New York.[5] The Office is vacant for New Hampshire & Rhode Island. I enclose you a Copy of the Ordinance on the Subject, that

AL, Hamilton Papers, Library of Congress; LC, Robert Morris Papers, Library of Congress.

1. The letters of July 27 and August 10 have not been found.
2. H must have resigned in either the letter of July 27 or of August 10, 1782. His resignation is not mentioned in his letters to Morris of July 22 or August 13, 1782.
3. See H to Morris, August 13, 1782, note 22.
4. Thomas Tillotson, a native of Maryland, settled in New York after the American Revolution. During the war he served first as a lieutenant in the Maryland Militia and from 1780 until the end of the war as physician and surgeon general of the Northern Department of the Army.
5. The office was commissioner of accounts. On July 22 H wrote to Morris: "I am informed you have an appointment to make of a Commissioner of Ac-

you may know the Powers, Duties and Emoluments;[6] and I have to request that you offer these Places to Colo. Malcolm and Mr. Lawrence.[7] You will make the first offer including the Choice as your own Judgement may direct. Should the Gentlemen, or either of them accept, you will be so Kind as to give me early Notice. I will then immediately recommend them to the States respectively and on receiving their Approbation, the proper Instructions &c can be expedited.

I am sorry to learn that any Letter of mine should have given Offence, but I conclude that this Effect must follow from many Parts of my Writings and Conduct, because the steady Pursuit of what appears to be the true Line of Duty will necessarily cross the various oblique Views of Interest & Opinion. To offend is sometimes a Fault, always a Misfortune. The Letter in Question is, I suppose, under the date of the Eleventh of December, of which I inclose you a Copy.[8] Let me at the same time assure you that in all your excellent Letter of the thirteenth Instant, I must esteem the Clause now in question because it contains that useful Information which is least common. I will make no Apologies for the Letter to any one because Apologies are rarely useful, and where the Intention has been good, they are to candid Minds unnecessary. Possessed of the Facts, you can guard against Misrepresentation; and I have ever found that to be the most hostile Weapon which either my personal or political Enemies have been able to wield against me.

I have not *even yet* seen the Resolutions of your Legislature relative to an Extension of the Powers of Congress.[9] I had supposed

counts for this state. Permit me to suggest the expediency of choosing a citizen of the state. . . . I need not particularise the reasons of this suggestion; in my next I will also take the liberty to mention some characters." In his letter of July 27, or that of August 10, neither of which has been found, H probably named those he considered qualified. The office was not filled until November 21, 1782, when Morris nominated Henry Sherburne.

6. Although the enclosures have not been found, Morris was probably referring to the congressional resolve of February 20, 1782, which describes "the Powers, Duties and Emoluments," of the commissioner of accounts (*JCC*, XXII, 84–86).

7. William Malcom was a representative in the New York Assembly. Morris is referring to John Laurence of New York City. See H to Morris, August 13, 1782, notes 17 and 18.

8. See H to Morris, August 13, 1782, note 28.

9. See "Resolution of the New York Legislature Calling for a Convention of the States to Revise and Amend the Articles of Confederation," July 20, 1782.

the same Reason for them which you have expressed.[10] Indeed Power is generally such a darling Object with weak Minds that they must feel extreme Reluctance to bid it farewell; neither do I believe that any Thing will induce a general Consent to part with it, but a perfect Sense of absolute Necessity. This may arise from two Sources, the one of Reason and the other of Feeling; the former more safe and more uncertain; the latter always severe and often dangerous. It is, my dear Sir, in Circumstances like this, that a patriot Mind, seeking the great good of the Whole on enlightened Principles, can best be distinguished from those vulgar Souls whose narrow Opticks can see but the little Circle of selfish Concerns. Unhappily such Souls are but too common, and but too often fill the Seats of Dignity and Authority. A firm, wise, manly System of federal Government is what I once wished, what I now Hope, what I dare not expect, but what I will not despair of.

Your Description of the Mode of Collecting Taxes, contains an Epitome of the Follies which prevail from One End of the Continent to the Other.[11] There is no End to the Absurdity of human Nature. Mankind seem to delight in Contrast & Paradox; for surely Nothing else could sanctify (during a Contest on the precise Point of being taxed by our own Consent) the arbitrary Police which on this Subject almost universally prevails. God grant you Success in your Views to amend it. Your Ideas on the Subject are perfectly correspondent to my own. As to your Doubt on the Mode of collecting it, I would wish to obviate it by the Observation that the farther off we can remove the Appointment of Collectors from popular Influence, the more effectual will be their Operations, and the more they conform to the Views of Congress the more effectually will they enable that Body to provide for general Defence. In political Life, the Creature will generally pay some Deference to ⟨the Creator. The⟩ [12] having a double Set of Officers is indeed an Evil, but a good Thing is not always to be rejected because of that necessary Portion of Evil which in the Course of Things must be attached to it. Neither is this a necessary Evil, for with a proper federal Gov-

10. See H's discussion of the resolutions in his letter to Morris of July 22, 1782.

11. See H to Morris, August 13, 1782.

12. All material in broken brackets is taken from the letter book copy in the Robert Morris Papers, Library of Congress.

ernment, Army, Navy & Revenue the civil Administration might well be provided for by a Stamp Act, Roads by Turnpikes, and Navigation by Tolls.

The Account you give of the State is by no Means flattering, and the more true it appears, the more Concern it gives me. The Loan I hope will be compleated; and I wish the *whole* Amount of the Tax may be collected.[13] The forage Plan I have disagreed to, and inclose for your Information the Copy of my Letter on that Subject to the Quarter Master General.[14] I believe your State is exhausted, but perhaps even you consider it as being more so than it is. The Certificates which now form an useless load will (if the United States adopt, and the several States agree to a Plan now before Congress) become valuable Property: This will afford great Relief.[15] The Scarcity of Money also may be immediately relieved, if the Love of popular favor would so far give Way to the Love of public Good as to inforce plentiful Taxation. The Necessity of having Money will always produce Money. The Desire of having it produces, you see, so much as is necessary to gratify the Desire of enjoying foreign Luxuries. Turn the Stream which now flows in the Channels of Commerce to those of Revenue, and the Business is compleated. Unfortunately for us this is an Operation which requires Fortitude, Perseverance, Virtue, and which cannot be effected by the weak or wicked Minds, who have only partial, private or interested Views.

When I consider the Exertions which the Country you possess

13. For information on the loan and the tax see H to George Clinton, August 25, 1782.

14. George Washington, in a letter to Governor George Clinton dated July 11, 1782, requested that the New York legislature provide aid in supplying the Army with forage "untill the Financier shall be enabled to take more effectual measures for the purpose" (George Washington Papers, Library of Congress). Clinton submitted Washington's letter to the legislature which in its July session provided that a quantity of forage should be furnished. Morris's letter to Colonel Timothy Pickering, dated August 5, 1782, is in the Robert Morris Papers, Library of Congress.

15. Morris is referring to the various certificates which along with the foreign debt constituted the public debt of the United States. They were loan office certificates and certificates issued for various goods and services.

On July 29, 1782, Morris had submitted to Congress a report on the public credit which he hoped would lead to adoption of a system for funding the public debt. His report is printed in *JCC*, XXII, 429–46. For an extended discussion of it, see Clarence L. Ver Steeg, *Robert Morris, Revolutionary Financier* (Philadelphia, 1954).

has already made under striking Disadvantages and with astonishing Prodigality of national wealth by pernicious Modes of applying it, I persuade myself that regular consistent Efforts would produce much ⟨more than you suppose.⟩

For your accurate, clear and comprehensive Descriptions of general and particular Characters, Sentiments and Opinions, accept my sincere Thanks and warm Approbation. They do equal Justice to your Talents both for Observation & Description.

Mr. Duer's Attention to the Business of his Contract is very pleasing to me and honorable to himself. I am sorry that he should loose by it, but to avoid this as much ⟨as possible I am determined to support him by liberal Advances so soon as it shall be in my Power to do it.[16]

I pray you to believe me   very sincerely   your Friend and Servant   RM.⟩

16. By the summer of 1782 army contractors, among whom was William Duer, were insisting that Morris meet his obligations by providing them with funds.

From Robert Morris [1]

Office of Finance [Philadelphia] 29. Augt. 1782.

Sir,

I have for certain Reasons thought it expedient to issue no more Orders on Mr. Swanwick *payable at Sight* but destroy them as they are brought in.[2] And as the larger Bills of Exchange mentioned in my Letter of the nineteenth of July last tho an excellent Mode of general Remittance will not by Reason of the Greatness of the Sums answer the Ends intended by the States in making my Notes receivable in Taxes, I have thought it alike useful to the Public and convenient to the People to issue Notes in the following Form. At sixty Days from the Date pay on Account of the United States   Dollars to   [3] or Bearer. These Notes are signed by me directed to Mr. Swanwick and are for Sums of one hundred, fifty, thirty and twenty Dollars each of them have in the Body of the Bill in Water Marks. *United States* and the Bills of one hundred Dollars have a Water Mark 1. & those of fifty 2. those of thirty 3 and those of twenty 4. You will receive them as Cash and when you have Cash you will give it for them in like Manner as for Bank Notes and that without any Regard whether they have any Time still to run or whether the sixty Days are expired.

I am Sir   your most obedient Servant   RM

LC, Robert Morris Papers, Library of Congress.
  1. This was a circular letter sent by Morris to the continental receivers in the various states.
  2. For the "orders on Mr. Swanwick," see Morris to H, April 15, 1782.
  3. Spaces left blank in MS.

To Robert Morris

[Albany, August 31, 1782]

Sir

I send you herewith all the acts of the Legislature of this state since the Government has been organized; on the margin of which I have numbered all the acts relative to the matters you mention in your letter of July 81 to the states agreeable to the within list.[1] I inclose you the papers of the last week.[2]

The indolence of some and the repugnancy of others make every trifle lag so much in the execution that I am not able at this time to give you any further information. I wish to hear from you on the subjects of my former letters previous to the meeting of the Committee the 15th. of the ensuing month.[3]

I have the honor to be very truly   Sir   Your most Obed serv.

A H

Albany Aug. 31st 1782
To The Honbe. Super. of Finance

ADfS, Hamilton Papers, Library of Congress.
  1. In the Hamilton Papers, Library of Congress, there are two documents either or both of which H may have enclosed in this letter to Morris. One is entitled "An Account of Taxes ordered to be raised, and of the Monies that have been paid into the Treasury of this State, in consequence thereof, since the Commencement of the present War." It is dated May 10, 1781, and is certified as an extract from the treasury books by Gerard Bancker, treasurer of the state. The second document, which is without a title, is a list of New York tax laws from March 6, 1780, through July 22, 1782, and a statement of the amount of money raised under each. This document is dated August 1, 1782. Neither of the documents has in the margin the numbers to which H refers in his letter, but he may have added the numbers on the copy he sent Morris.
  2. Presumably New York newspapers which H sent regularly to Morris.

3. The committee had been appointed by the New York legislature in July to report on means of raising funds within the state and of improving the collection of taxes. See H to Morris, July 22, 1782, note 8.

To The New-York Packet [1]

[Albany, September 1, 1782]

The Subscriber has received nothing for the month of August, on account of the quota of this state for the present year. Published agreeable to the instructions of the Superintendant of Finance.

Alexander Hamilton
Receiver of Continental Taxes
for the State of New York

Albany, September 1, 1782

The New-York Packet. And the American Advertiser, September 5, 1782.
1. H wrote the same letter to the *Packet* on August 1, 1782.

From George Clinton

Poughkeepsie [New York] Septr. 2nd. 1782

Sir

I am favored with your Letter of the 25th. Ulto. previous to which with a view of accelerating the collection of the last Tax I had prepared & have since dispatched a circular Letter to the several County Treasurers urging them & the other Officers concerned to a prompt execution of their Duty or that in Case of Neglect the Penalty of the Law will without favor be put into Execution.

I have not received Information from all the Counties but in this and some others I know the Business is in good Train and am led to hope that the Taxes will be speedily collected & paid in.

My Agents employed to procure Monies on loan had sometime since transmitted me a small Sum but not sufficient to answer the Orders of the Legislature in favor of the Delegates and some other public matters. As the Channel through which this money is procured is subject to interruption & disappointment I cannot at present inform you of any Sum to be depended on; but I expect soon to see

or hear from the Gentlemen & you may rest assured of being informed of the Result without delay.

I am with great Respect   & Esteem Sir   Your most Obedt. Servt.

Geo. Clinton

Colo. Hamilton

LS, Hamilton Papers, Library of Congress.

From Robert Morris

Office of Finance [Philadelphia] 6th. September 1782.

Sir.

I have received your Favor dated at Albany on the 25th. of last
Month, with the Enclosures. I am much obliged by your attention
in the Business you allude to,[1] and knowing that your abilities and
Zeal to promote the public Good are equal to the most arduous
Undertakings I have no doubt but your Endeavours will be success-
ful.

I am Sir   Your most obedient Servant   Robt Morris

Alexr. Hamilton Esqr.
Albany.

LS, Hamilton Papers, Library of Congress.
    1. H had written of his efforts to secure information on the financial situation
in New York State.

To Robert Benson [1]

[Albany, September 7, 1782]

Dr. Sir

Not having had the pleasure of hearing from you in answer to my
letter of the 18th. of Augt. I now send you a duplicate.

I wish at least to be able to let Morris know what prospect I have
of fulfilling his views and I therefore shall be indebted to you to let
me hear from you on the subject by the first opportunity.

I am Sir   Your most Obed   A Hamilton
Albany Sepr. 7. 82

ALS, Hamilton Papers, Library of Congress.
  1. A draft of this letter appears at the end of the letter H wrote to Benson on August 18. The envelope of the receiver's copy is addressed "Robert Benson, Esquire clerk of the Senate, Poughkeepsie," and is endorsed by Benson: "Colo. Hamiltons Letter abt. Returns of specific Supplies &c &c &c &c." A copy of the letter is also in the Hamilton Papers, Library of Congress.

To the County Treasurers of the State of New York

Albany Sepr. 7. 1782

Sir

The fifteenth of this month is the period fixed for the payment of the tax imposed at the last meeting of the legislature for the use of The United States.[1] The public exigencies and the reputation of the state require that every exertion should be made to collect this tax with punctuality and dispatch; and it is therefore my duty to urge you that you employ the powers vested in you, and all your personal influence to induce the collectors to expedite the collection with all the zeal and vigor in their power. While the other states are all doing something, as a citizen of this I shall feel a sensible mortification in being obliged to continue publishg to the others that this state pays nothing in support of the war as I have been under a necessity of doing the two last months. Besides this and other still more weighty considerations a regard to the ⟨subjects of the State itself⟩[2] demands every exertion ⟨in our power. They have parted⟩ with their property on the public faith and it is impossible for the public to fulfil its engagement⟨s⟩ to individuals unless it is enabled to do it by the equal and just contributions of the community at large.

I am Sir   Your most Obed serv   A H

ADfS, Hamilton Papers, Library of Congress.
  1. For a discussion of the tax law passed by the New York legislature at its July, 1782, session, see H to Robert Morris, July 22, 1782.
  2. Material in broken brackets is taken from *JCHW*, I, 304.

To Udny Hay [1]

Albany September 7. 1782

Persuaded my Dear Sir of your punctuality, of your disposition to oblige me and to promote public business, I am at a loss to explain to my self the reason of your silence on the letter of which the fore-going is a triplicate.[2]

I hope the ill state of your health has not been the cause of it.

The Governor informed me that returns on the files of the Legis-lature would answer most of the inquiries in my letter to him, of which the matter I have requested your Assistance upon make a part. In consequence of this I have entreated Mr. Benson to furnish me with Copies of those returns.

Probably if you were to see him the business might be made the easier to both. Mr. Morris is so pressing to me that I am really anxious to comply with his wishes. Besides I conceive the honor of the State is concerned in it, for while we insist (justly upon our past) exertions if we withhold the testimonies of what we have done, it may be con-cluded that they will not bear examination.

I am Dear Sir   Very truely Your obedient   A Hamilton

The certificates alluded to on the other side are such as have been made receivable in taxes.[3]

Copy, Hamilton Papers, Library of Congress.
1. This copy appeared on the back of the autograph letter H wrote to Udny Hay on August 3, 1782. Another copy is in the Hamilton Papers, Library of Congress.
2. H is referring to his letter of August 3, 1782, to Hay.
3. See H to Hay, August 3, 1782.

To Robert Morris

Albany Septemr. 7. 1782

Sir,

I have had the inclosed ready for some time; but in hopes of re-ceiving the returns of the certificates mentioned in memorandum B I delayed sending the present sketch. Having even received no answers from some of the parties who live at a distance from me, I suspect they have done their business in so disorderly a manner (to say nothing worse of it) that they are at a loss how to render the accounts; and I have therefore concluded not to detain any longer what I had procured.[1]

I do not take the step mentioned in memorandum A because I doubted its propriety: It might raise expectations about the old money which possibly it may not enter into your plans to raise; and besides this by knowing what has been called in in each state (which from the sketch I send you will appear as to this) you can determine the ballance of emissions remaining out, except what may have worn out and been accidentally destroyed. If you desire this step to be taken I will obey your commands.

I have said nothing of the rates of depreciation because I imagine your letter written in July 80 had referrence to the rates at which the money was then actually circulating; and the circulation has now totally ceased.[2] The laws I sent you by the last post will inform you of the rates fixed at different periods by the legislature: forty; seventy five and lastly one hundred and twenty eight.[3]

I am obliged to infer there is a studied backwardness in the officers of the state who ought to give me the information you require respect⟨ing⟩ the supplies of different kinds which have been furnished to the use of The United States. Indeed I find on inquiry that their joint information will not be so full as to satisfy your intentions; and that this cannot be done, 'till you have appointed a commissioner of accounts authorised to enter into all the details aided by some legislative arrangement, which may be obtained the next session.

I have the honor to be   With the greatest respect & esteem   Sir
Your most Obed serv   AH

ADfS, Hamilton Papers, Library of Congress.
    1. During August, H had written various state officials—the governor, state agent, treasurer, and clerk of the Senate—requesting information on the finances of New York State.
    2. Morris to the Governors of the Several States, July 25, 1781 (Robert Morris Papers, Library of Congress). In this letter Morris requested the governors of the states to send him, among other information, the amount of paper currency in each state and the estimated rate of depreciation.
    3. See H to Morris, August 31, 1782. In the second of the two enclosures mentioned in note 1 to that letter there appears opposite a statement of the amount of money brought into the treasury from taxes, the words "75 for one." The other rates of depreciation may have been included in the copy of the New York laws which H sent to Morris.

To Colonel Timothy Pickering

Albany Septr. 7. 1782

Dear Sir

I this day received your letter of the 20th. of August.

Mr. Morris has advised me of the Bills you desired and directed my purchasing them together with his notes and the bank notes with what money shall come in to my hands on public account.[1]

They are now beginning to collect the tax imposed for the use of the United States though I can as yet form no judgment with what success or expedition.[2] I shall with pleasure give you the information you ask, but I would rather wish to be excused from anticipation by previous deposits in my hands; as this will in some measure pledge me to give a preference to the bills deposited and may here after expose me to a charge of partiality. There has been several applications to me for a similar anticipation which I have avoided, reserving to my self the power of paying the bills as they shall be presented and in proportion to the nearness or remoteness of the periods of payments.

You may however depend that I shall be happy to assist your department and will keep in view your present request.

I hope towards the latter end of the month I shall receive some thing considerable on the late tax.

I am D Sir very truly   your obedient Servant   A Hamilton

Copy, Hamilton Papers, Library of Congress.
    1. See Pickering to H, August 20, 1782, and Robert Morris to H, August 29, 1782.
    2. On July 22, 1782, the New York legislature had passed a law for raising £18,000 in specie to be appropriated to the use of the United States.

From Robert Benson

Poughkeepsie [New York] Septr. 10th, 1782.

Sir, In consequence of the Request in your Letter of the 18th ulto. I have with great chearfulness searched the Senate Papers for the Returns you allude to. Inclosed are all I find in my Possession. What Papers Mr. McKesson [1] may have relative to this subject I know not, but I dare say he will on your Application give you every Information in his Power. He is now in Albany and has the Returns of the State of the Taxes made last Winter by the several County Treasurers.

I also enclose you the last Sheet of the Laws which Mr. Holt says is wanted to compleat the Sett he sometime since sent you by the Govr's. Orders.[2]

Colo. Hay's[3] absence during the late Meeting of the Legislature & his Indisposition since, has prevented his making any Returns to them or the Gov'r. for the present Year.

As the enclosed Papers are official & entrusted to our Care, I must request you, Sir, when you have done with them to return them to me or Mr. McKesson. I am &c.

Colo. Hamilton

Public Papers of George Clinton, VIII, 32–33.
1. John McKesson was clerk of the Assembly of the New York legislature.
2. John Holt was the printer for the State of New York.
3. Udny Hay was state agent of New York.

From Robert Morris [1]

Office of Finance [Philadelphia] 12. Septem. 1782

Sir,

Enclosed you will find Copies of my Letters of the twenty-ninth and thirtieth of July to Congress.[2] I know not what Determinations they may come to on these Subjects but I transmit the Letters that you may be possessed of the Matter, fully obviate Misrepresentations, and inculcate at proper Opportunities those Principles of national Integrity which are essential to our Safety.

I am Sir with Esteem   your most obedient Servt.   RM

P.S. You will also find enclosed Acts of Congress of the fourth and tenth Instant.[3]

LC, Robert Morris Papers, Library of Congress.
1. This was sent as a circular letter to the receivers of continental taxes in the various states.
2. On July 29, 1782, Morris submitted to the President of Congress a report on the public credit in which he recommended measures for funding the debt and stressed the necessity of adequate, permanent funds for the United States. The letter is printed in *JCC,* XXII, 429–46.
   On July 30, 1782, Morris again wrote to Congress enclosing the "Estimates for the Service of the Year 1783" (Robert Morris Papers, Library of Congress).
3. On September 4, 1782, several laws dealing with finance were passed by Congress. It was resolved that the states be requisitioned for $1,200,000; recommended that the several states impose a land tax, a poll tax, and a tax on spirituous liquors for the payment of the debts of the United States; and recommended that the states comply with the congressional request for authority

to impose a duty of five percent on imports. On September 10, the quota of $1,200,000 imposed on September 4 was apportioned among the several states (*JCC*, XXIII, 545–47, 564–71).

To Robert Morris

Albany Sepr. 14th 1782

Sir,

I have the honor to acknowlege the receipt of your letter of the 29th. of August; the contents of which shall be executed.

I have just received by the post accounts of the specific supplies furnished by this state; copies of which I shall prepare to be transmitted to you by the next post, as I am to return the Originals, which are for the inspection of the legislature.[1] I hope to add to these accounts of the money supplied.

I have written to you a number of letters since my journey to Poughkepsie; of which as they contain some things of a confidential nature, I am not without anxiety to learn the safe arrival. I should also have been happy to have received your instructions against the meeting of the Committee, which is to take place to morrow.[2] As they will have other business, if I hear from you by the next post it will not be too late. I am at a loss to know whether I ought to press the establishment of *permanent funds* or not; though unless I receive your instructions following my own apprehensions of what are probably your views, I shall dwell upon this article.

I have the honor to be   With perfect respect   Sir   Your most Obed serv   A H

I enclose you a copy of a letter from the Governor of the 2d instant by which you will see his hopes; ⟨mine⟩ are not so good.[3] In this ⟨vicinity,⟩ [4] always delinquent, little is doing.

ADfS, Hamilton Papers, Library of Congress.
1. H probably enclosed the papers sent to him by Robert Benson on September 10, 1782.
2. The committee, established by the legislature during the July session, was a joint committee that was charged with devising a system for establishing funds within the state and a system for the more effective collection of taxes. See H to Morris, July 22, 1782, note 9.
3. See George Clinton to H, September 2, 1782.
4. Material in broken brackets is from *JCHW*, I, 306–07.

From Robert Morris

Office of Finance [Philadelphia] 17. Sepr. 1782

Sir,

I received by the Post your Favor of the seventh Instant. I have always suspected that the disorderly Manner of doing Business in many Parts of this Continent has enabled People to commit Frauds or what is the same thing as to the Public Loss covered their Ignorance Indolence and Extravagance. It is only by probing these Matters to the Bottom that the Extent of the Evil can be discovered and I shall be very happy that the Legislature step in with their Authority to the Aid of my Efforts. The Commissioner for settling the Accounts of your State shall be appointed as soon as a proper Person offers which no one has yet done. You have formed a proper Conception as to what were my Views in enquiring into the Rates of Depreciation which are now of but little Consequence indeed of none unless to know what Degree of real Taxation may be necessary to absorp the Remainder of that useless Paper Mass which has so long burthened all our Movements.

I am by no Means surprized at the Backwardness which you meet with from public Officers in rendering an Account of Supplies furnished to the Public. The several States and many of their public Officers have so long been in the Habit of boasting superior Exertions that what was at first Assumption has advanced along the Road of Belief to perfect Conviction. And the Delusion is now kept up by the Darkness in which it is inveloped. It is not impossible that somewhat both of Interest and Importance is concerned in leading the Public Officers to keep up the Mistery.

I am Sir   your most obedient and humble Servant   RM.

LC, Robert Morris Papers, Library of Congress.

To Robert Morris

Albany Sepr. 21st 1782

Sir,

The hurry in which I wrote to you by the last post, prevented my examining particularly the papers which I informed you I had received.[1] On a more careful inspection of them, I found them not so complete as I had hoped. There is a general state[ment] of specific supplies; but the returns referred to in that [statement] for the particulars were by some mistake omitted. I have written for them, but they have not yet arrived; when they do I shall lose no time in forwarding them.

I observe there is nothing respecting transportation;[2] and there is a part of the supplies for the period before Col Hay came into office,[3] which is estimated on a scale of proportion too vague a method to be satisfactory. I have urged him to send me an account of the transportation and to collect as speedily as possible official returns of the supplies above mentioned.

There is a practice obtaining which appears to me to contravene your views. The Contractors I am informed have gotten into a method of carrying your bills immediately to the collectors and drawing the specie out of their hands; by which means the paper never goes into circulation at all; but passes so to speak immediately out of one hand of the public into the other. The people therefore can never be familiarized to the paper nor can it ever obtain a general currency.

If the specie were to come into the Receivers and the Contractors were left under a necessity of exerting their influence to induce the inhabitants to take your notes to be afterwards redeemed by the Receivers agreeable to your plan, this would gradually accustom the people to place confidence in the notes; and though the circulation at first should be momentary it might come to be more permanent.

I am in doubt whether on the mere speculation of an evil without your instructions I ought to take any step to prevent this practice. For should I forbid the exchange, it might possibly cause a suspicion that there was a preference of the paper to the specie which might injure its credit.

I have thought of a method to prevent without forbidding it in direct terms. This was to require each collector to return the names of the persons from whom he received taxes, and in different columns specify the kind of money, whether specie your Notes or bank Notes in which the tax was paid, giving the inhabitants receipts accordingly and paying in the money in the same species in which it was received. This would cover the object.

I have tried to prevail upon the County treasurer of this place to instruct the collectors accordingly; but the great aim of all these people is to avoid trouble; and he affected to consider the matter as an Herculean labour. Nor will it be done without a legislative injunction

A method of this kind would tend much to check fraud in the collectors, and would have many good consequences.

I thought it my duty at any rate to apprise you of the pra[c]tice, that if my apprehensions are right it may not be continued without controul. I have reason to believe it is very extensive—by no means confined to this state.

Permit me to make one more observation. Your notes though in Credit with the Merchants by way of remittance do not enter far into ordinary circulation, and this principally on account of their size; which even makes them inconvenient for paying taxes.[4] The taxes of very few amount to twenty dollars a single tax; and though the farmers might combine to sell their produce for the notes to pay the taxes jointly; yet this is not always convenient & will seldom be practiced. If the Notes were in considerable part of five eight or ten dollars, their circulation would be far more general, the merchants would even in their retail operations give specie in exchange for ballances; which few of them care to do or can do with the larger notes; though they are willing to take them for their goods.[5]

ADf, Hamilton Papers, Library of Congress.

1. See H to Morris, September 14, 1782.

2. H had requested that he be furnished information on "the supplies of every kind, money provisions forage transportation &c." See H to Robert Benson, August 18, 1782.

3. Udny Hay was appointed state agent on June 29, 1780. H had requested information on supplies furnished the United States since March 18, 1780.

4. Morris's personal notes issued in anticipation of the collection of taxes were for the sums of twenty, fifty, and one hundred dollars.

5. Page or pages of the MS may be missing. A J. C. Hamilton transcript of this letter, however, ends at the same place and is followed by H's signature, indicating that the MS may be complete.

From Sands, Livingston and Company [1]

Fishkill [New York] Septemr. 25th. 1782

Sir,

Mr. Morris for want of Specie, has put into our hands his Bills on John Swanwick in order to exchange for the Specie as it is Collected in the States eastward of New Jersey. The Bills are made payable at different Periods; some Jany, some Feby & so on; he has engaged us that they shall be exchanged for Specie in any Collectors hands; & that he had wrote all his receivers on that Subject. His view ⟨in⟩ making them payable sometime hence was to prevent their returning speedily to him. Mr Hoofman the Treasurer of this County [2] has made some difficulty about exchanging them. We promised to write you, & the State Treasurer on that head; & we wish you to declare in some public manner your approbation of the Notes being exchanged; as it will relieve us in our present distress, & answer the purpose Mr. Morris expected.

We are   Sir,   your most obedt. & very hbl Servt.

Sands Livingston & Co

Alexr. Hamilton Esqr

ALS, Hamilton Papers, Library of Congress.
1. See Robert Morris to H, April 15, July 19, and August 29, 1782, for a discussion of the bills mentioned here. For information on Sands, Livingston and Company, see letters to and from Comfort Sands, dated June 23, July 8, 1782.
2. This was probably Colonel R. Hoffman, treasurer of Dutchess County (see endorsement on H to the County Treasurers of the State of New York, August 5, 1782).

To Robert Morris

[Albany, September 28, 1782] [1]

Sir

I have been honord this week with your letters of the 28 August 6th. 12th and 17th instant with their inclosures.

It gives me the most real pleasure to find that my past communications have meet your approbation; and I feel a particular satisfaction in the friendly confidence which your letters manifest.

I am persuaded that substanial reasons have determined your choice in a particular instance to Doctor Tillotson; and I am flattered by the attention you have Obligingly paid to my recommendations of Col. Malcolm and Lawrence.[2] Those Gentlemen are now here: they make you the warmest acknowlegements for your offer, but decline leaving the State; which indeed is not compatible with the present prospects of either of them.

I am glad to have had an oppertunity of perusing your letter to this state at which so much exception has been taken;[3] because it has confirmed me in what I presumed, that there has been much unjustifiable ill humour upon the occasion. I will make use of the knowledge I have to combat misrepresentation.

Yours of the 29th of July to Congress is full of principles and arguments as luminous as they are conclusive. Tis to be lamented that they have not had more weight than we are to infer from the momentary expedient adopted by the resolutions of the 4 and 10th:[4] which will alone not be satisfactory to the public Creditors; and I fear will only tend to embarrass your present opperations without answering the end in view.[5] The more I see the more I find reason for those who love this country to weep over its blindness.

The committee on the subject of Taxation[6] are met; some have their plans and they must protect their own children however mishapen; others have none but are determined to find fault with all. I expect little, but I shall promote any thing though imperfect that will mend our situation. With sentiments of the greatest respect and esteem I have the honour to be　Sir　Your most obedient and humble servant　　　　　　　　　　　　　　　A Hamilton

The public Creditors in this quarter have had a meeting and appointed a Committee to devise measures; the Committee will report petitions to Congress & the Legislature and an address to the public creditors in other parts of the State to appoint persons to meet in convention to unite in some Common measure. I believe they will also propose a general convention of all the creditors in the different States.[7]

Copy, Hamilton Papers, Library of Congress.
1. The endorsement gives the date as September 28.
2. Morris had indicated that he intended to appoint Thomas Tillotson re-

ceiver of continental taxes for New York and had offered to appoint William Malcom and John Laurence loan commissioners for New Hampshire and Rhode Island (Morris to H, August 28, 1782).

3. H is referring to a letter of December 11, 1781, from Morris to Governor George Clinton which had angered Clinton and the New York legislature. See H to Morris, August 13, 1782.

4. See Morris to H, September 12, 1782, note 3.

5. See Morris to H, September 12, 1782.

6. The committee had been appointed by the July session of the New York legislature to recommend financial measures for adoption by the legislature. See H to Morris, July 22, 1782, note 8.

7. Perhaps encouraged by the concerted action of public creditors in Philadelphia who, at a public meeting in June, 1782, had urged Congress to grant them immediate relief, a meeting of public creditors was held at Albany. General Philip Schuyler, H's father-in-law, presided at the Albany meeting. See "To the Public Creditors of the State of New York," September 30, 1782.

To Sands, Livingston and Company

[*Albany, September 29, 1782.* On the back of the letter that Sands, Livingston and Company wrote to Hamilton on September 25, 1782, Hamilton wrote: "Ansd. 29th." *Letter not found.*]

To the Public Creditors of the State of New York [1]

[Albany, September 30, 1782]

The appellation by which we have chosen to address you, indicates at once the broad and equitable basis upon which we wish to unite the influence and efforts of those who are Creditors to the Public, to obtain that justice, which the necessities of many, and the rights of all demand.

Whatever distinctions may characterize the different classes of Creditors, either of the United States, or of this State; whatever may be their different degrees of merit as patriots, or their comparative

The New-York Packet. And the American Advertiser, October 24, 1782.

1. On September 25, 1782, many public creditors, both of the State of New York and of the United States, met in Albany. Philip Schuyler, H's father-in-law, was chairman of the meeting. It was resolved on the first day of the meeting that a committee be appointed to prepare and report an "Address to the Public Creditors in the State of New York." The purpose of the meeting was to promote a convention of public creditors in New York and, if possible, a convention of public creditors in all the states.

In Hamilton, *History,* II, 309-14, it is implied, though not explicitly stated, claims upon the gratitude or generosity of their country; in one circumstance they all agree—they have an equal claim upon the justice and plighted faith of the Public.

Alarmed by the successive violations of public engagements, and by that recent and distressing one, the with-holding the interest hitherto paid by Bills on France, upon the monies loaned previous to 1st of March, 1778; [2] the public Creditors in this City have thought it necessary to follow the example of those of the City of Philadelphia: [3] and to convene and consult upon the measures proper to be taken for their own security.

They will not dwell upon the measure alluded to, further than to observe, that its weight is most oppressively felt by those whose zeal in the cause and confidence in their country have been most conspicuous: who in times of danger have demonstrated their concern for the common safety by voluntary deposits, in some instances, of the whole; in others, of a large part of their fortunes in the public funds; and who now, many of them at least, feel themselves reduced from affluence to indigence; from circumstances of ease and plenty to penury and unaffected distress.

They cannot but add, that there are others not less meritorious, who have perhaps experienced even a worse fate: those who having made subsequent Loans, have long since seen the payment of interest

---

that the address was written by H. Other writers (see, for example, Mitchell, *Hamilton*, 273–74) have attributed the address to him. H was in Albany at the time of the meeting and may either have aided Philip Schuyler in its composition or drafted it himself. On September 28, 1782, H informed Robert Morris of the meeting of the convention, and on October 9 he told the Superintendent that he soon hoped to send him "a copy of the address (of) the public creditors in this town to the rest of that denomination (in) this state. It inculcates the ideas, which ought to prevail." The absence of conclusive evidence, however, precludes the definite establishment of H's authorship.

2. The "recent and distressing" violation of public credit presumably was a congressional resolution of September 9, 1782. On that date Congress instructed the Superintendent of Finance "to stop the drawing any more bills, for the interest due upon Loan office certificates on France, and that each Loan officer remit to the Superintendent of Finance all such bills as may be now upon hand" (*JCC*, XXIII, 554–55).

3. A meeting of the public creditors in Philadelphia, held in June, 1782, had appointed a committee to draw up and circulate throughout the other states an address entitled "To the Citizens of America, *who are Creditors of the United States.*" The Philadelphia address, dated August 26, 1782, had been read at the meeting of the New York creditors.

cease; and those, who, when the distresses of the army have had no resource but in the patriotism of individuals, have cheerfully parted with the fruits of their industry, scarcely reserving a sufficiency for the subsistence of their own families, without any compensation since, besides the consciousness of having been the benefactors of their country.

We entertain not so injurious an idea as to imagine, that levity or a contempt of the obligations of national faith, or of the dictates of policy, have influenced those infringements of the public engagements, which have too often happened. We have been sensible of the necessity which has in some cases produced them; but we apprehend it to have resulted, not from the want of ability or means, but from the want of a proper system for the beneficial application of them. And we conceive it our duty to acquiesce in that necessity only so far as there appears to be an unavoidable sacrifice to the urgent calls of particular conjunctures, followed by effectual endeavours to prevent a continuance or return of the same necessity, or to make satisfaction in some other way.

Few States have been without their vicissitudes, in which the strict obligations of good faith, have been obliged to bend to momentary necessities: but the example of all wise and happy ones, combine with reason and justice to establish this truth, that no time ought to be lost in providing the means of repairing those breaches, and making compensation to the sufferers.

Unfortunately for us and for every citizen of the United States (for the calamity directly or in its consequences, is general) the same policy has been too long delayed in this country; the only expedient in our power for effecting the object being still unattempted.

We need no arguments to convince us, that it is not possible for these States, by any exertions they can make, to pay off at once the principal of the public debts, and furnish the supplies for the current demands of the war, and for the support of civil government. We even think it as manifest as experience and calculation can make it, that our abilities fall greatly short even of the two latter objects. This in an infant country will not surprise those who know, that nations the most opulent, and in all the vigour of maturity, are compelled to have recourse to large loans in time of war, to satisfy the public exigencies.

The quota of the present year has been fixed at eight millions of dollars, which we are to consider as the sum requisite for the annual expenditure; and those accustomed to computation of such a nature will be convinced, that to make this sum suffice, requires œconomy and good management. Have we a prospect of raising one third of this sum within the States? Those who have attended to the publications of the receipts on continental account, will easily answer the question for themselves. If this must be in the negative, the enquiry then becomes, What means have we to supply the deficiency?

Admit that there are defects in the system of taxation in almost every State; and that more judgment and equality in the manner of laying them, more energy and œconomy in the collection, would be more productive to the revenue, and less burthensome to the people: still we cannot imagine that the reformation of these defects would augment the product of the taxes in any proportion to the deficiency.

It is plain therefore, that the principal part of the balance must be procured upon credit; nor is it less plain, that this must chiefly be from *individuals*, at home and abroad. We are assured that the situation of our Allies will not permit them to make us governmental loans in any proportion to our wants; and without this assurance, we might have inferred it, from a consideration of the immense land and naval establishments which they are obliged to support in the prosecution of the war on their own part.

It may be asked, if such are the necessities of the public, how are they to spare any part of their funds for the payment of old debts? The answer is easy; those necessities can only be supplied by a sound and healthy state of public credit; and there is only one way to effect the restoration of this credit—the putting the old debts in a course of redemption, or at least securing the punctual payment of the interest by substantial funds, permanently pledged for that purpose.

It cannot be expected that individuals in this country will hereafter lend to the public, unless they perceive a disposition to do justice to its creditors. If, without providing for those who have already risked their fortunes, securities should be held out to invite future creditors, a suspicion of their faithful application would deter every prudent man. There must be a good opinion of public faith, before there can be a confidence in public securities; and this opinion can only be created by unequivocal demonstrations of a disposition to justice, nor will any thing amount to a proof of this, short of the measure on which we insist.

In common life no credit would be given to any man who departed from these principles; and the same rule is not less applicable to nations.

If individuals among ourselves would not have the necessary confidence, it were chimerical to expect it from foreigners; such of them as having been already adventurers in our funds, are holders of public certificates, would have little encouragement to adventure further.

No presumptions of the speedy termination of the war will invalidate the force of these reflections: not only the grounds of them are vague and uncertain: and it would be the extremity of folly to abandon an indispensable resource for continuing the war, because there is a possibility of its being ended; but the fullest assurance of the event would not take away this irresistible argument, that public justice, and its inseparable companion public credit, are alike essential to the prosperity of a nation in peace and in war.

We scruple not to assert, that these States might with ease to themselves, provide the means requisite to fund the debts already incurred, and to procure further loans: a moderate sum would be sufficient. It is an expedient which we conceive besides calculated to lighten the burthens of the people, and to increase their ability to bear them. The more we can procure on credit, the less we need exhaust ourselves in immediate taxation; and the public creditors themselves will be enabled to bear a large share of the future burthen, which will of course diminish the contributions of others. We might expatiate on the influence of public credit over private industry, and on its tendency in that way to multiply the riches of the community; and we might add, that the wheels of circulation and commerce, now clogged by the want of an adequate medium, would derive new motion and vivacity from the increase of that medium, by rendering the public securities a valuable negociable property.

We have indulged in these reflections to shew that patriotism, not less than necessity, interest and safety, prompt us to an emphatical appeal to the justice and honour of our country.

What will be the condition of individuals, if a disregard to the sanctity of public obligations should become the spirit of public councils? We indeed should be the immediate victims; but who can answer when his turn might come? It it true those who are not already embarked may avoid hereafter becoming volunteers in their own ruin: but can they guard against the pressing calls of necessity, enforced by legislative coertions? Should we see a renewal of the distresses of the army for want of subsistence, must not the inhabitants of this State again feel the weight of compulsory laws; and unless justice be done to the present creditors, what hope can they have of recompence? What, in short, will be the security of private property, if the powers of government may be employed to take it from us, and no provision be afterwards made to render satisfaction?

A purity of faith has ever been the more peculiar attribute of Republics, the very being of which, depends on virtue in all, and a sacred regard to justice in those to whom the administration of affairs is entrusted. A contrary disposition in these States would be as novel as pernicious; and we flatter ourselves we never shall suffer such a stigma to be fixed upon our national character, especially on our first emerging into political existence.

We have now explained to you fully, the views by which we are actuated in this address. It remains, in pursuance of the resolution we have formed, to invite you to appoint in each county, members to represent you in a Convention, to meet at Poughkeepsie, the 19th day of November next,[4] to unite their applications to Congress and to the Legislature of this State, for a redress of the grievances under which the Public Creditors in general labour.[5]

4. There is no evidence that the proposed convention was ever held.
5. Following the introduction of the address to the public creditors the Albany meeting adopted two resolves. They read as follows:
"*Resolved unanimously*, That the Chairman sign and transmit printed copies of the above address to gentlemen in other counties of this State, and request them to convene the Public Creditors in their respective counties, to take the same into consideration. That the Chairman transmit to the Committee of Philadelphia, a copy of the above address, and to suggest whether a General Con-

vention composed of deputies from the Public Creditors in each State, might not tend to public advantage.

"*Resolved unanimously*, That Philip Schuyler, Abraham Ten Broeck, Leonard Gansevoort, John N. Bleecker, Robert M'Clallen, and Lucas Van Vegthen, Esquires, be a Committee to receive communications, and to correspond with other Committees which are or may be appointed in this or any of the United States, and that they are authorised to call a Meeting of the Public Creditors in this City and county, whenever it shall appear to them, or the majority of them, to be necessary." (*The New-York Packet. And the American Advertiser,* October 24, 1782.)

To The New-York Packet [1]

[Albany, October 1, 1782]

THE SUBSCRIBER has received nothing on account of the quota of this State for the present year.

Alexander Hamilton
Receiver of Continental Taxes

Albany, October 1, 1782

The New-York Packet. And the American Advertiser, October 17, 1782. The same letter, under the same date, was republished in *The New-York Packet* of October 24, 1782.

1. For similar letters to *The New-York Packet,* see August 1 and September 1, 1782.

From Robert Morris

Office of Finance [Philadelphia] 5th October 1782

Sir,

I have now before me your Letters of the fourteenth and twenty first of last Month. I am sorry to find that you are less sanguine in your pecuniary Expectations than the Governor appears to be, for I have always found that the worst forebodings on this Subject are the truest. You will find at the Bottom of this Letter a List of all those which I have hitherto received from you. I think they have all been already acknowledged, but lest they should not, you will see in One Moment by the List whether any have miscarried.[1]

I am not surprized to find that the Contractors apply with their Paper in the first Instance to the Receiver and Collectors: This I expected, because much of that Paper is not fit for other Purposes. Some of it however which is payable to the Bearer is calculated for circulation, which you observe is not so general as otherwise it might have been; by Reason of the Largeness of the Sums expressed in the Notes. Mr. Duer's [2] Letters contain the same Sentiment.

In issuing this Paper one principal View was to facilitate the Payment of Taxes by obviating the too general (tho unjust) Complaint of the Want of a circulating Medium. In substituting Paper to Specie the first Obstacle to be encountered was the total Diffidence which had arisen from the late Profusion of it. Had a considerable Quantity been thrown into the Hands of that Class of the People whose Ideas on the Subject of Money are more the Offspring of Habit than of Reason, it must have depreciated. That this Apprehension was just is clear from this Fact, that the Paper I first issued, and the Bank Paper which came out after it, did depreciate from ten to fifteen per Cent in the Eastern States not withstanding all the Precautions which were used. If I had not taken immediate Measures to create a Demand for it on the Spot, and to stop Issues to that Quarter it's Credit would have been totally lost for a Time, and not easily restored; besides that, the Quantities which were pouring in from thence would have done Mischief here. Confidence is a Plant of very slow Growth, and our political Situation is not too favorable to it. I am therefore very unwilling to hazard the Germ of a Credit which will in its greater Maturity become very useful. If my Notes circulate only among mercantile People, I do not regret it, but rather wish that the Circulation may for the present be confined to them and to the wealthier Members of other Professions. It is Nothing but the greater Convenience which will induce People to prefer any Kind of Paper to the precious Metals, and this Convenience is principally felt in large Sums. Whenever the Shop Keepers in general discover that my Paper will answer as a Remittance to the principal Ports, and will be readily exchanged by the Receivers, they will as readily exchange it for other People. When the People in general find that the Shop Keepers receive it freely, they will begin to look after it, and not before: For you must know that whatever fine plausible Speeches may be made on this Subject, the Farmers will not give full Credit to Money merely because it will pay Taxes, for that is an Object they are not very

violently devoted to; but that Money which goes freely at the
Store and the Tavern, will be sought after as greedily as those
Things which the Store and the Tavern contain. Still, however, your
Objection remains good, that the Traffickings in which the greater
Part of the Community engage do not require Sums so large as
Twenty Dollars. This I shall readily acknowledge; but you will observe that there is infinitely less Danger that large Notes, which go
only thro the Hands of intelligent People, will be counterfeited than
small ones, which come to the Possession of illiterate Men. When
public Credit is firmly established, the little Shocks it receives from
the Counterfeitors of Paper Money do not lead to material Consequences; but in the present ticklish State of Things there is just
Ground of Apprehension. Besides this, the Value of Paper will
depend much upon the Interchanges of it for Specie, and these will
not take place when there is a Circulation of small Paper. Lastly, I
have to observe, that until more Reliance can be placed on the
Revenues required, I dare not issue any very considerable Amount
of this Paper, lest I should be run upon for more than I could
answer, and as the Circulation of what I dare issue by increasing
the general Mass, enables People (so far as it goes) more easily to
get hold of other Money, it consequently produces in its Degree
that Object of facilitating Taxation which I had in View.

I am, Sir,   Your most obedient & Humbl Servant   Robt Morris

Alexander Hamilton Esquire
Receiver for New York.

LS, Hamilton Papers, Library of Congress.
    1. The list is neither in the Hamilton Papers nor in the Robert Morris Official
Letter Book, Robert Morris Papers, Library of Congress.
    2. William Duer.

From Robert Morris [1]

Office of Finance [Philadelphia] 5 Octo: 1782

Sir

I enclose you the Copy of an Act of the first Instant [2] with the
Copy of my Circular Letter to the Governors inclosing it. [3] You will
consider this Act as an Additional Evidence of the firm Determina-

tion of our Sovereign to persevere in those Systems which they have adopted. I recommend this Act to your serious and vigilant Attention in all its Parts. It is a mighty fashionable Thing to declaim on the Virtue and sufferings of the Army and it is a very common Thing for these very Declaimers to evade by one Artifice or another the Payment of those Taxes which alone can remove every Source of Complaint. Now Sir it is a matter of perfect Indifference by what Subterfuge this Evasion is effected whether by voting against Taxes or what is more usual agreeing to them in the first Instance but taking Care in the second to provide no competent Means to compel a Collection which cunning Device leaves the Army at last as a Kind of Pensionary upon the voluntary Contributions of good Whigs and suffers those of a different Complection to skulk and skreen themselves entirely from the Weight and Inconvenience. I am far from desiring to involve in general and indiscriminate Censure all the Advocates for wrong Measures. I know that much of it may be attributed to an Ignorance which exists both from the Want of proper Means and Materials of Instruction and from the Defect of Experience. But the Evil exists and you must labor assiduo[u]sly for the Remedy.

I am Sir your most obedient and humble Servant   RM

LS, Robert Morris Papers, Library of Congress.
    1. This was sent as a circular letter to the receivers of continental taxes in the several states.
    2. The congressional resolutions of October 1 were the result of a representation of the New Jersey legislature which stated that other states had made partial payments to the soldiers of their own lines and that unless Congress took measures to assure equal justice to the troops of New Jersey the legislature would apply a part of the taxes appropriated to the use of the United States to pay the state's soldiers. The resolutions stated that Congress had adopted "every means in their power" to pay the troops and had consistently discouraged partial payments by the states; that no money advanced by the states to the Army should be considered as advanced by the United States; and "That the several states be required to make speedy payment of the respective quotas into the public treasury, that Congress may be thereby enabled to pay the officers and soldiers of the American army the amount of their pay for the present year" (*JCC*, XXIII, 631).
    3. Morris's circular to the governors of the states was also dated October 5. He enclosed the congressional resolutions of October 1 and stated that it was not his duty "to ask for our Officers and Soldiers any Reward but merely the Means to do them Justice" (Robert Morris Papers, Library of Congress).

To Robert Morris

[Albany, October 5, 1782]

In my last I informed you that the Committee [1] appointed by the Legislature on the subject of taxation were together. In spite of my efforts, they have parted without doing any thing decisive. They have indeed agreed upon several matters and those of importance but they have not reduced them to the form of a report, which in fact leave every thing afloat to be governed by the impressions of the moment when the legislature meet.

The points agreed upon are these—that there shall be an actual valuation of land and a tax of so much in the pound. The great diversity in the qualities of land would not suffer them to listen to an estimated valuation ⟨or⟩ to a tax by the quantity agreeable to the idea in your late report to Congress. That there shall be also a tariff of all personal property to be ⟨also⟩ taxed at so much in the pound— that ⟨th⟩ere shall be a specific tax on carriages clocks watches & other similar articles of luxury—that money at usury shall be taxed at a fixed rate in the pound excluding that which is loand to the public—that houses in all towns shall be taxed at a certain proportion of the annual rent—that there shall be a poll tax on all single men from fifteen upwards and that the Collection of the taxes should be advertised to the lowest bidder at a fixed rate ℔ Cent bearing all subordinate expences.

Among other things which were rejected I pressed hard for an excise on distilled liquors; but all that could be carried on these articles was a license on taverns.

The Commitee were pretty generally of opinion that the system of funding for payment of old debts & for procuring further credit was wise & indispensable but a majority thought it would be unwise in one state to contribute in this way alone.

Nothing was decided on the quantum of taxes which the state was ⟨able⟩ to pay; those who went furthest ⟨would⟩ not exceed 70000 £ of which fifty for ⟨the⟩ use of the United states.

I send you My Cash Account, which is for what has been received in this County. We have not heard from the others.

I &c

Albany Octr. 5. 1782

ADf, Hamilton Papers, Library of Congress.

1. On July 21, 1782, a joint committee of the New York legislature was appointed to report to the next session of the legislature "a System for establishing such Funds within this State, as may be best calculated to answer the Purposes of this State, and the United States; and for the more effectual Collection of Taxes within this State" (New York Assembly *Journal*, 1782, 117). The committee met on September 15 and adjourned early in October. H was in attendance and probably suggested ideas to be incorporated in a plan of taxation.

To Robert Morris

[Albany, October 9, 1782]

Sir,

I wrote you a hasty letter by the last post which arrived late and set out very soon after its arrival.

Since that I have received two thousand dollars all in your bills on Mr. Swanwick in favour of Messrs. Sands & Co.[1] One half the sum is in bills payable in February ⟨next⟩ exchanged by them for specie with one of the County treasurers. I am sensible there is an inconvenience in this in different ways; but it appears by your letter of the 19th. of July that you mean to have those bills received upon the same footing with your [notes] and the bank-notes, without regard to the time they have to run. I have however induced the treasu⟨rer⟩ to write in a manner that I hope will discourage like exchanges in future, without giving any unfavourable impression. Besides the inconvenience from this practice which I mentioned in a former letter, there is another which I am persuaded will result. People will get into a way of discounting your bills & notes with the treasurers and collectors to the injury of their Credit.

Probably you are apprised of a fact which however I think it my duty to mention; it is that the bank notes pass pretty currently as Cash with a manifest preference to your Notes.

I have not yet received the other papers relative to the account of supplies I have sent you.

I hope to be able to inclose you a copy of the address ⟨of⟩ the public creditors in this town to the rest of that denomination ⟨in⟩ this state. It inculcates the ideas, which ought to prevail.[2]

I have not yet heard of your Messenger, Mr. Brown. I presume his circuit is regulated by ⟨y⟩our occasional direction.[3]

I have the honor to be &c

Albany Oct. 9. 1782

ADf, Hamilton Papers, Library of Congress.
   1. See Morris to H, April 15, 1782.
   2. For information on the address of the public creditors, see H to Morris, September 28, 1782. See also address "To the Public Creditors of the State of New York," September 30, 1782.
   3. John Brown of Philadelphia was often employed by Morris. On May 15, 1782, the Superintendent of Finance informed the receivers of the taxes in the states "Eastward of Hudsons River" that he had "appointed Mr. Brown to be the Messenger by whom you are from Time to Time to transmit the Bank Notes which you may receive" (Morris to H, May 15, 1782).

To Major General Nathanael Greene [1]

[Albany, October 12, 1782]

Dr General

It is an age since I have either written to you or received a line from you; yet I persuade myself you have not been the less convinced of my affectionate attachment and warm participation in all those events which have given you that place in your countrys esteem and approbation which I have know⟨n⟩ you to deserve while your enemies and rivals were most active in sullying your reputation.[2]

You will perhaps learn before this reaches you that I have been appointed a member of Congress. I expect to go to Philadelphia in the ensuing month, where I shall be happy to correspond with you with our ancient confidence and I shall entreat you not to confine your observations to military subjects but to take in the whole scope of national concerns. I am sure your ideas will be useful to me and to the public.

I feel the deepest affliction at the news we have just received of the loss of our dear and ⟨inesti⟩mable friend Laurens.[3] His career of virtue is at an end. How strangely are human affairs conducted, that so many excellent qualities could not ensure a more happy fate? The world will feel the loss of a man who has left few like him behind, and America of a citizen whose heart realized that patriotism of which others only talk. I feel the loss of a friend I truly and most tenderly loved, and one of a very small number.

I take the liberty to inclose you a letter to Mr. Kane [4] Executor to the estate of Mr. Lavine [5] a half brother of mine who died some time since in South Carolina. Capt Roberts,[6] if you should not be acquainted with him, can inform you who he is. I shall be much obliged to you to have my letter carefully forwarded.

Mrs. Hamilton sends her particular compliments to Mrs Greene & yourself; to the former please to join mine.

I am Dr. Sir, truly Yr. friend & ser   A Hamilton

Albany October 12. 1782
General Greene

ALS, Hamilton Papers, Library of Congress; copy, Hamilton Papers, Library of Congress.
  1. Greene was at this time in command of the Southern army.
  2. In 1780 Greene, then quartermaster general of the Army, had been accused of failing to detect peculation among officers in his department.
  3. On August 27, 1782, John Laurens, while leading a party of American soldiers in a skirmish against the British, was killed.
  4. Letter not found. Mr. Kane may have been John Kean, a prominent South Carolinian who later became cashier of the Bank of the United States in Philadelphia.
  5. Peter Lavien, H's half-brother, was the only son of Johann Michael Lavien and Rachel Fawcett Lavien, H's mother. As Rachael and her children by James Hamilton had been disinherited by the terms of a divorce decree in 1759, Peter Lavien was the sole heir of his father.
  6. Presumably Richard Brooke Roberts, who had been a captain of a South Carolina state artillery regiment during the Revolution.

To Robert Morris

[*Albany, October 12, 1782.* On October 23, 1782, Morris wrote to Hamilton: "I have received your favors of the 9th. and 12th. Instant." *Letter of October 12 not found.*]

From William Duer

[*Albany, October 15, 1782.* On October 15, 1782, Hamilton wrote to Duer: "In answer to your letter of this date." *Letter not found.*]

To William Duer

[Albany, October 15, 1782]

Sir

In answer to your letter of this date,[1] I am sorry to inform you, that I have not in my hands at this time more than Eighty dollars in specie which I informed you I would reserve for you in addition to the one hundred and sixty dollars, which I have already exchanged for your use.[2]

I wish I had a prospect of complying with what you mention to be Mr. Morris's[3] expectation, but I should deceive you to give you encouragement on this head. Notwithstanding repeated letters to the County Treasurers, I have no certain accounts of their receipts. The few who have brought in any money have paid it almost wholly in Mr. Morris's notes and bills; for a great part of which it appears specie has been exchanged by the County treasurers; and this practice which may probably continue gives me little hope of any considerable supply of specie hereafter on the present tax.

The whole amount of Notes which have hitherto come into my hands payable to Messrs. William Duer & Co. is Two hundred & fifty dollars; which added to One hundred & sixty dollars in notes payable to the bearer at sight gives the whole of the paper money issued in your department which has been received by me on account of taxes.

I am Sir   Your most Obedt servant   A Hamilton

Albany October 15th. 1782

Wm. Duer Esqr.

ALS, Columbia University Libraries.
  1. Letter not found.
  2. Duer was contractor for supplying the levies in northern New York and on the frontier. For an account of money estimated by Duer as necessary to fulfill his contract see Duer to H, August 16, 1782.
  3. Robert Morris.

From Robert Morris [1]

Office of Finance [Philadelphia] 15 Octo: 1782.

Sir,

On perusing the Advertizement enclosed herewith [2] you will see the Propriety of its having a general Circulation throughout the United States. I therefore request you will cause it to be published in the several News Papers that are printed in your State.

I am Sir   Your most obedient & humble Servant   RM.

LC, Robert Morris Papers, Library of Congress.
1. This was sent as a circular letter to the receivers of continental taxes in the various states.
2. The enclosure was a notice dated October 17, 1782, from the Office of Finance "to all persons who may incline to Contract for the Supply of Rations, that the seven following Contracts will be entered into for the Year 1783" (*The Freeman's Journal: or, the North-American Intelligencer*, October 16, 1782).

From Robert Morris

Office of Finance [Philadelphia] 16 Octo: 1782.

Sir,

I am indebted for two of your Favors, one of which is without date,[1] the other of the fifth Instant enclosing the Account of your Receipts to that Time. I am sorry the Propositions I made did not suit Colo. Malcolm and Mr. Lawrence.[2] I am pleased that you approve the Plans for restoring public Credit and wish they had been adopted, as I conceive the substituting a mere temporary Expedient is dangerous. I am happy to find that the public Creditors are organizing themselves, their Numbers and Influence joined to the Justness of their Cause must prevail if they persevere. The Proceedings of the Committee on Taxation are just what are to be expected on such Occasions.[3]

The Establishment of solid Systems require Time and Industry and the Bulk of Mankind are so attached to their particular Interests, that they are seldom persuaded to extend their Efforts in favor of general Regulations, untill Experience convinces them of their Necessity. I hope the People of America will feel that Conviction before it be too late.

and remain   Sir, your most obedient and humble Servant   RM.

LC, Robert Morris Papers, Library of Congress.
  1. The letter without date was probably that of September 28, 1782.
  2. William Malcom and John Laurence. See H to Morris, September 28, 1782, note 2.
  3. See H to Morris, October 5, 1782, note 1.

To Robert Morris

[*Albany, October 19, 1782.* On October 28, 1782, Morris wrote to Hamilton: "I have received your Favor dated at Albany on the 19th Instant with the Enclosures." *Letter not found.*]

From Robert Morris

Office of Finance [Philadelphia] 23rd. October 1782

Sir

I have received your favors of the 9th. and 12th.[1] Instant with the account of your Receipts to the latter Date.

As the purposes for which Mr Brown[2] is employed will not admit of his passing through Albany, I shall consider of some arrangement for making Remittances from thence; of which you shall be seasonably Informed. Your Letter for General Green[3] shall be forwarded. I shall soon have Occasion to write you Respecting the appointment of Doctor Tillotson and his acceptance[4] which I am prevented, by much business, from doing by this Post.

I am Sir   Your most Obedient & most humble Servant

Robt Morris

Alexander Hamilton Esqr.
Receiver for the State of New York.

LS, Hamilton Papers, Library of Congress.
  1. H's letter of October 12, in which he enclosed a letter for Major General Nathanael Greene, has not been found.
  2. John Brown. See H to Morris, October 9, 1782, note 3.
  3. See H to Greene, October 12, 1782.
  4. Thomas Tillotson. See Morris to H, August 28, 1782, note 4.

Commission as Delegate to the Continental Congress [1]

[Poughkeepsie, New York, October 25, 1782] [2]

State of New York.

The People of the State of New York by the Grace of God free & Independent: To all whom these presents shall come send Greeting. Know Ye that we having inspected the records remaining in the Secretary's Office of our said State do find there a certain Commission in the words following to wit "The people of the State of New York by the Grace of God free & independent: To all to whom these presents shall come send Greeting, Whereas our Senate & assembly have on the twenty second day of July in this present year nominated & appointed the honorable James Duane,[3] William Floyd,[4] John Morin Scott,[5] Ezra L'Hommedieu [6] and Alexander Hamilton Esquires Delegates to represent our said State in the United States of America in Congress Assembled for one year from the first Monday in November next. Now therefore know Ye that in pursuance of the said nomination & appointment we have by these presents commissioned the said James Duane, William Floyd, John Morin Scott, Ezra L'Hommedieu and Alexander Hamilton Esquires, with full power & authority to them the said James Duane, William Floyd, John Morin Scott, Ezra L'Hommedieu, & Alexander Hamilton to represent our said State in the said Congress accordingly: In Testimony whereof we have caused these our letters to be made patent and the great seal of our said State to be hereunto affixed: Witness our trusty and well beloved George Clinton Esquire—Governor of the said State General and Commander in Chief of all the Militia & Admiral of the Navy of the same. Given at Poughkeepsie the said twenty second day of July in the year of our Lord One thousand seven hundred and Eighty two and of our Independence the seventh." All which we have caused to be exemplified by these presents. In Testimony whereof we have caused these our Letters to be made patent & the Great Seal of our said State to be hereunto afixed. Witness our Trusty & well beloved George Clinton Esquire Governor of our said State General and Commander in Chief of all the Militia and Admiral of the Navy of the same at Poughkeepsie the twenty fifth day of October in the Year of our Lord 1782, and of our Independence the seventh.

Geo Clinton

Passed the Secretary's Office
25th Octr 1782 Rob. Harpur D Secy

D, Papers of the Continental Congress, National Archives.
1. On July 22, 1782, the New York Senate nominated James Duane, William Floyd, John Morin Scott, Ezra L'Hommedieu, and Philip Schuyler to represent New York in the Continental Congress. On the same day the Assembly nominated four of the same men but named H instead of Schuyler. At a joint meeting of the two houses of the legislature, a ballot was taken to decide between them, and H was elected. (New York Senate *Journal*, 1782, 91).
2. H's commission, certified by the deputy secretary of state on October 25, 1782, appointed him a delegate as of the first Monday in November, which was the 4th. Although James Duane, Ezra L'Hommedieu, and John Morin Scott, all of whom had been members of Congress during the preceding year, were in attendance earlier, H did not attend until November 25.
3. Duane frequently had represented New York in the Continental Congress. In 1782, he was a member of the state Senate.
4. Floyd was a member of the Continental Congress from 1774 to 1777. He was elected again in 1778 and served until 1783.
5. Scott, the secretary of state of New York from 1778 until his death in 1784, was first elected to the Continental Congress in 1779.
6. L'Hommedieu had represented New York in the Continental Congress since October, 1779. He subsequently served in the New York Senate.

Admission as Counsel before the New York Supreme Court [1]

[*Albany*] *October 26, 1782.* An entry in the "Minutes of the Supreme Court" on this date reads: "Alexander Hamilton Esquire having on Examination been found of sufficient Ability and Competent learning to practise as Counsel in this Court Ordered that he be admitted accordingly."

MS "Minutes of the Supreme Court of New York, July 31, 1781, to November 1, 1783," 289, Hall of Records, New York City.
1. H already had been admitted to practice as an attorney before the Supreme Court. See "Admission as Attorney before the New York Supreme Court," July, 1782.

To Robert Morris

[Albany, October 26, 1782]

Sir

I am honored with your letters of the 5th. 15th and 16th instant.

The detail you have been pleased to enter into in that of the 5th exhibits very cogent reasons for confining yourself to pretty large denominations of notes. Some of them had occurred to me others had not; but I thought it my Duty to state to you the operations which that circumstance had, as in the midst of the variety and extent of the objects, which occupy your attention you may not have so good opportunities of se⟨eing⟩ [1] the effect of your plans in detail. While I acknowlege that your observations have corrected my ideas upon the subject and showed me that there would be danger in generally lessening the denominations of the paper issued, I should be uncandid not to add that it still appears to me, there would be a preponderance of advantages in having a *part* of a smaller amount. I shall not trouble you at present with any further reasons for this opinion.

I have immediately on the receipt of your ⟨letter⟩ taken measures for the publication of your adver⟨tisement⟩ in the newspapers of this state.

You will perceive by the inclosed account, that since my last, I have received five and twenty hundred dollars.[2] This was procured in part of the loan I mentioned to you. It was chiefly paid to me in specie and I have exchanged it with Colo. Pickering [3] and Mr. Duer [4] for your notes; the latter had twelve hundred dollars. Taxes [5] coll⟨ect⟩ slowly, but I must shortly receive two or three hundred pounds more, of which Mr. Duer will have the principal benefit, as it appears by your letter to him, that you hoped he might receive three thousand Dollars from me.[6]

As I may shortly set out for philadelphia I wish to surrender to Mr. Tillot⟨son⟩ [7] as soon as you think proper the office in wich he is to succeed. I have the honor to be with sincere respect & esteem

Sir   Your Most Obed servant   Alx Hamilton

Albany October 26 1782

Copy, Hamilton Papers, Library of Congress. The endorsement is in the writing of H.

1. Material in broken brackets is taken from *JCHW*, I, 319.

2. H's receipt for the sum mentioned reads as follows: "Received October 22d, 1782 from Gerard Banker Treasurer, Two thousand five hundred dollars in specie pursuant to the within written Warrant" (ADS, MS Division, New York Public Library).

3. Colonel Timothy Pickering.

4. William Duer.

5. See H to George Clinton, August 25, 1782, note 2.

6. Duer needed money to pay for the supplies he had procured as contractor for the posts north of Poughkeepsie, New York (Morris to Duer, October 2, 1782, Robert Morris Papers, Library of Congress). H probably had expressed the hope that Duer might receive the $3,000 from Morris in the unfound letter which H wrote to Duer on October 15, 1782.

7. Thomas Tillotson.

From Robert Morris

Office of Finance [Philadelphia] 28th October 1782

Sir,

I have received your Favor dated at Albany on the 19th Instant with the Enclosures.[1] What you say of your Prospect with Respect to the Receipt of Money for Taxes, is as you may easily suppose very unpleasing. I hope it will soon assume a different Appearance. Unless Something more be done by the States, many very dangerous as well as disagreable Consequences are to be apprehended.

With sincere Esteem   I am Sir   Your most obedient Servant

Robt Morris

Alexander Hamilton Esquire
Receiver for the State of New York.

LS, Hamilton Papers, Library of Congress.
1. Letter not found.

To Marquis de Lafayette

[Albany, November 3, 1782]

Since we parted My Dear Marquis at York Town I have received three letters from you one written on your way to Boston, two from France. I acknowlege that I have written to you only once,[1] but the reason has been that I have been taught dayly to expect your return. This I should not have done from my own calculations; for I saw no prospect but of an inactive campaign, and you had much better be intriguing for your hobby horse at Paris than loitering away your time here. Yet they seemed to be convinced at Head Quarters that you were certainly coming out; and by your letters it appears to have been your own expectation. I imagine you have relinquished it by this time.

I have been employed for the last ten months in rocking the cradle and studying the art of fleecing my neighbours. I am now a Grave Counsellor at law, and shall soon be a grand member of Congress. The Legislature at their last session took it into their heads to name me pretty unanimously one of their delegates. I am going to throw away a few months more in public life and then I retire a simple citizen and good paterfamilias. I set out for Philadelphia in a few days. You see the disposition I am in. You are condemned to run the race of ambition all your life. I am already tired of the career and dare to leave it.

But you would not give a pin for my letter unless politics or war made a part of it. You tell me they are employed in building *a peace;* And other accounts say it is nearly finished; I hope the work may meet with no interruptions: it is necessary for America; especially if your army is taken from us as we are told will soon be the case. That was an essential *point d'appui;* Though money was the *primum mobile* of our finances, which must now lose the little activity lately given them, our trade is prodigiously cramped. These states are in no humour for continuing exertions; if the war lasts, it must be carried on by external succours. I make no apology for the inertness of this country. I detest it; but since it exists I am sorry to see other resources diminish.

Your Ministers ought to know best what they are doing; but if the war goes on and the removal of the army does not prove an unwise measure I renounce all future pretensions to judgment. I think however the circumstances of the enemy oblige them to peace.

We have been hoping that they would abandon their posts in these states; it no doubt was once in contemplation, but latter appearances are rather ambiguous. I begin to suspect that if Peace is not made New York & Charles Town, the former at least will still be held.

There is no probability that I shall be one of the Commissioners for peace. It is a thing I do not desire myself and which I imagine other people will not desire.

Our army is now in excellent order but small.

The temper we are in respecting the alliance you will see from public acts. There never was a time of greater unanimity on that point.

I wish I durst enter into a greater detour with you but our cypher is not fit for it and I fear to trust it in another shape.

Is there anything you wish on this side the water? You know the warmth & sincerity of my attachment. Command me.

I have not been so happy as to see Mr. De Segur.[2] The title of your friend would have been a title to every thing in my power to manifest.

Adieu

General & Mrs. Schuyler & Mrs. Hamilton all join warmly in the most affectionate remembrances to you. As to myself I am in truth yours pour *la vie*

AH

I wrote a long letter to the Viscount De Noailles whom I also love.[3] Has he received it? Is the worthy Gouvion well? [4] has he succeeded? how is it with our friend Gimat? [5] how is it with General Du Portail,[6] all those men are men of merit & interest my best wishes.

Poor Laurens; he has fallen a sacrifice to his ardor in a trifling skirmish in South Carolina. You know how truly I loved him and will judge how much I regret him.

I will write you again soon after my arrival at Philadelphia

Albany November 3d. 1782

ADfS, Hamilton Papers, Library of Congress.

1. The two letters Lafayette wrote to H from Paris are dated April 12 and June 29, 1782. The letter written by Lafayette while on his way to Boston has not been found. The letter from H to Lafayette has not been found.

2. Lafayette wrote to H on April 12, 1782, that his letter would be delivered by the Count de Segur to whom he hoped H would show "more than civilities." De Segur came to America in 1782 to replace the Vicomte de Noailles. See Lafayette to H, April 12, 1782, note 2.

3. See H to Noailles, April–June, 1782.

4. Lieutenant Colonel Jean Baptiste Gouvion, a Frenchman who served with the Continental forces as an engineer.

5. Jean Joseph Sourbader de Gimat had served as aide-de-camp to Lafayette with the rank of lieutenant colonel.

6. Louis Le Bèque Du Portail had commanded the Corps of Engineers and Sappers and Miners during the Revolution. He had been promoted to the rank of major general on November 16, 1781.

To The New-York Packet [1]

[Albany, November 9, 1782]

THE SUBSCRIBER has received on account of the quota of this State for the present year, since the last of September to this day, Six Thousand Four Hundred and Thirty Four Dollars and Ten Pence.   Alex. Hamilton,
                                                                 Receiver
Albany, Nov. 9, 1782.

The New-York Packet. And the General Advertiser, November 21, 1782.
1. The same letter, under the same date, was republished in *The New-York Packet* of November 28. H wrote similar letters to *The New-York Packet* on August 1, September 1, and October 1, 1782.

Receipts for Monies Received from the Treasurer of the State of New York [1]

[*Albany, November 9, 1782.*] Gives to Gerard Bancker, treasurer of the State of New York, five receipts, the first dated October 2, 1782, the last dated November 9, 1782, for money received on behalf of the Superintendent of Finance. The receipts totaled $6,434 and "10 pence."

ADS, MS Division, New York Public Library.
1. These receipts were endorsed on the back of "Warrant to Alexander Hamilton to Receive Money as Continental Receiver for the State of New York," April 15, 1782. In a circular letter to the receivers of the same date, Robert Morris had instructed them "to endorse a Copy" of the receipts for every sum received "on the back of the Warrant so that when the whole is discharged you may deliver up the said Warrant then taking back your several loose Receipts" (Morris to H, April 15, 1782).
The same document contains receipts from Thomas Tillotson, who succeeded H as receiver. Tillotson's receipts were dated from December 2, 1782, to June 9, 1784.

To Thomas Tillotson [1]

[Albany, November 10, 1782]

Thomas Tillotson Esquire having been appointed by The Superintendant of Finance to succeed me in the Office of the Receiver of The Continental Taxes within this State I do hereby assign to him the foregoing warrant to do whatsoever in virtue thereof I the underwritten am authorised to do.

Alex Hamilton
late Receiver

Albany November 10th. 1782

ADS, MS Division, New York Public Library.
1. The letter in which H submitted his resignation to Robert Morris has not been found. On September 5, 1782, Morris wrote to Thomas Tillotson: "Colo. Hamilton having resigned the Office of Receiver for your State I take the Liberty to make you an Offer of it. Colo. Hamilton will be able and willing to give you every necessary Information as to the Duties and Emoluments of that Office. I shall be happy to hear from you as soon as may be convenient" (Robert Morris Papers, Library of Congress). H's resignation probably was effective October 31, for his appointment as delegate to the Continental Congress was effective November 4. The Robert Morris Papers do not, however, reveal the exact date of H's resignation.
    This assignment of warrant was added by H to the "Warrant to Alexander Hamilton to Receive Money as Continental Receiver for the State of New York," April 15, 1782. See enclosure in Morris to H, April 15, 1782.

To Thomas Tillotson

Albany November 10th. 1782

Sir

I herewith deliver you No. 1 to 12 all the letters and instructions from the Superintendant of Finance, which will be requisite for your government in the conduct of the office to which you are appointed, together with a letter from the Treasurer of the State No. 13 informing of what measures have been taken by the state for complying with the requisitions of Congress for the present year.

The money I have hitherto received you will find indorsed on the Superintendants warrant of the 15th. of April 1782 for the first quarterly payment.[1]

ALS, MS Division, New York Public Library.
1. See "Receipts for Monies Received from the Treasurer of the State of New York," November 9, 1782.

It is incumbent upon me to explain to you how far I have advanced in forwarding the business committed to the Receivers by the Superintendants letters of the   of July 1782.[2] I have transmitted the best accounts to be obtained of the money paid by this state for Continental use since the 18th. of March 1780—a general state of the specific supplies since the same period (which refers to several inventories of particulars which were not sent me, but which I am promised by Mr. McKesson,[3] and which it will be proper for you to procure and transmit)—a sketch of paper money issued in this state—the amount of the paper money both Continental and state called in and destroyed to this time. I apprehend it will be proper for you from time to time to get from the Treasurer the subsequent sums called out of circulation and communicate the same to the Superintendant.

I believe in doing what I now mention you will do all that is possible towards satisfying the inquiries in the letter of the 25th. of July 1781 to the Governor.[4]

As to the article of transportation furnished the business has been transacted in so irregular and diversified a manner, that nothing can be ascertained on that head, 'till the Commissioner of Accounts appears to make a general liquidation with the public officers and individuals.

I believe experience will demonstrate that however tax laws are heaped upon each other they will continue to be very little productive while the present system for laying and collecting them continues. I have endeavoured to inculcate the necessity of a change and at their last session induced the legislature to appoint a Committee for that purpose. How far they answered the end you will gather from the inclosed copy of my letter to Mr. Morris of the 5th of last month. I suppose the question will be again agitated at the next meeting of the legislature; if you can procure a determination in favour of the views which seemed to prevail with the Committee,

2. The reference is to Robert Morris's circular of July 12, 1782, in which he enclosed a copy of his letter of July 25, 1781, directed to the governors of the states and calling for detailed information on the state of finances in the respective states (Robert Morris Papers, Library of Congress). Space left blank in MS.
    3. John McKesson, clerk of the Assembly of New York.
    4. Robert Morris to the Governors of the Several States, July 25, 1781 (Robert Morris Papers, Library of Congress).

you will in my apprehension accomplish an object of great importance to the public.

With great consideration and esteem I am Sir   Your most Obed servant   Alex Hamilton

Thomas Tillotson Esqr.
Receiver

[ENCLOSURE] [5]

List of Papers Delivered to Thomas Tillotson

[Albany, November 10, 1782]

List of Papers delivered by Alexander Hamilton to Thomas Tillotson Esquire relative to the office of Receiver of Taxes for the state of New York.

No. 1   General instructions from the Superintendant of Finance to the Receivers dated February 12th. 1782

2   Letter from do. to Alexander Hamilton inclosing warrant on the Treasury for the amount of the 1st quarterly payment of the Quota of this state, with the receipts indorsed thereon to the 5th. of November inclusive letter dated April 15th. 1782

3   farther instructions from the Superintendant to Alexander Hamilton dated as above.[6]

4   farther instructions dated May 15th 1782

5. Circular letter from the Superintendant to the Receivers dated July 12th. 1782 containing one to the respective states dated 25th. of July 1781.

6. do. do. dated 19th of July 1782

7. do. do. . . . dated August 29th. 1782

8. Copy of a letter from the Superintendant to His Excellency the Governor dated December 11th 1781 [7]

9   do. of do. to the Qr. Master General respecting forage dated Augt. 5. 1782 [8]

5. AD, Hamilton Papers, Library of Congress.
6. Only one letter of April 15, 1782, to H from Morris has been found.
7. See Morris to the Governor of the State of New York, December 11, 1781 (Robert Morris Papers, Library of Congress).
8. See Morris to H, August 28, 1782, note 15.

10– from the Superintendant to the Receivers dated 12th. of September 1782 with sundry inclosures referred to therein.

11 Two circular letters from do. to do. inclosing a set of resolution of Congress of the 1st of October 82, the letters dated the 5th.

12 Circular letter from do. to do.[9]

13 letter from Mr Banker state Treasurer dated August 5th. 1782 informing of what was to be expected from the state.[10]

> Tho: Tillotson
> Receiver for New-York [11]

9. Since this item is undated it is impossible to identify it.
10. Letter not found.
11. The words, "Tho: Tillotson Receiver for New-York" are not in H's handwriting.

To Elizabeth Hamilton

Fish Kill [New York] 18th. Novr 1782

I am just arrived My Love at this place and shall cross Kings ferry tomorrow. I am much pleased with the horses; they are both free and gentle; and I think you will learn to have confidence in them. I am perfectly well, and as happy as I can be when absent from you. Remember your promise; don't fail to write me by every post. I shall be miserable if I do not hear once a week from you and my precious infant. You both grow dearer to me every day. I would give the world for a kiss from either of you.

Adieu My precious charmer Yr tender   A H

Send my sword by your father.

ALS, Mr. George T. Bowdoin, New York City.

Continental Congress
Remarks on the Exchange of Charles, Earl Cornwallis [1]

[Philadelphia, November 25, 1782]

Col: Hamilton who warmly & cogently espoused the ratification,[2] as an additional argument mentioned, that some intimations had been given by Col: Laurens [3] of the army with the privity of Genl. Washington, to Cornwallis previous to his capitulation, that he might be exchanged for his father, then in the Tower.

"Notes of Debates in the Continental Congress, MS, James Madison Papers, Library of Congress.

1. The only record of H's participation in the debates in the Continental Congress is James Madison's notes. All of the remarks by H which Madison recorded have been printed in these volumes with the following three exceptions: 1. Brief expressions of agreement with reports or motions; 2. Remarks which taken out of the context of Madison's record would be meaningless; and 3. Statesments which only repeat, without explanation, ideas which were fully expressed in motions or reports which H formally submitted to Congress. Madison's notes are printed in Gaillard Hunt (ed.), *The Writings of James Madison* (New York, 1902), I, 250–484, and JCC, XXIII, 843–75 and XXV, 845–974.

2. The ratification concerned the proposed release of Charles, Earl Cornwallis, in exchange for the discharge of Henry Laurens, former President of Congress, who had been captured by the British in 1780 while on his way to the Netherlands to negotiate a loan and a treaty of amity and commerce with the Dutch. In April, 1782, Laurens was exchanged for Cornwallis, then on parole in London. Benjamin Franklin assumed the responsibility for setting Cornwallis free until "the pleasure of Congress should be known." Some members of Congress refused to ratify Franklin's action, both because of the treatment Laurens had received while imprisoned in the Tower of London, and because of Earl Cornwallis's "cruel and barbarous" conduct while in America. Congress, on November 25, was debating a motion that the ratification of Cornwallis's discharge be refused. See debates on November 22 and 25, 1782, "Notes of Debates in the Continental Congress," MS, James Madison Papers, Library of Congress, and JCC, XXIII, 753.

3. John Laurens, son of Henry Laurens, took part in the Battle of Yorktown and, as captain general of prisoners, had held Cornwallis as a prisoner.

Continental Congress
Remarks on the Redemption of Continental Currency

[Philadelphia, November 26, 1782]

That Congress sd. renew their call on the States to execute the Acts of the 18th. of M. 1780 and leave it to the States to level the money by negotiations among themselves. This was Mr. Hamilton's idea. . . .[1] One consideration suggested by Mr. Hamilton in its [2] favor was that it would multiply the advocates for federal funds for discharging the public debts, and tend to cement the Union.

"Notes of Debates in the Continental Congress," MS, James Madison Papers, Library of Congress.

1. On March 18, 1780, Congress devaluated continental currency by ruling that it should be redeemed at one-fortieth of its face value (*JCC*, XVI, 262–67). A request of New Hampshire and Massachusetts that they be credited for currency redeemed before March 18 in excess of their quota was discussed by a committee composed of a member from each state on November 26, 1782. The committee agreed that states which had redeemed a surplus of currency should be given credit for it by an increased apportionment on other states ("Notes of Debates in the Continental Congress," MS, James Madison Papers, Library of Congress).

2. A proposal by Thomas FitzSimons of Pennsylvania for redeeming the public debt. He proposed ". . . that the Commissioners appointed to traverse the U. S., for the purpose of settling accounts should be empowered to take up all the outstanding old money and issue certificates in place of it, in specie value, according to a rule to be given them by Congress. The amount of the certificates to be apportioned on the States as part of the public debt. The same rule to determine the credit for redemptions by the States." "Notes of Debates in the Continental Congress," MS, James Madison Papers, Library of Congress.

Colonel John Lamb to Alexander Hamilton and William Floyd [1]

Newburgh [*New York*] *December 2, 1782.* Asks to be promoted to rank of brigadier general. Requests "the friendly interposition" of Hamilton and Floyd to prevent the promotion of Colonel John Crane.[2]

ALS, Hamilton Papers, Library of Congress.

1. Before the Revolution Lamb had been a prosperous wine merchant in New York City. In July, 1775, he was commissioned captain of an artillery company and later was with the army of Major General Richard Montgomery during the invasion of Canada. He was wounded and captured during the assault on Quebec but was released on parole a few months later. In January, 1777, he was exchanged, and during the same month he was appointed colonel of the Second Continental Artillery.

2. Crane, a resident of Massachusetts, was appointed a colonel of the Third Continental Artillery in January, 1777. On October 5, 1779, a board of general officers, which had been appointed to determine which of the officers was the senior colonel of the Continental Artillery, decided in favor of Crane.

Continental Congress
Report on Subsistence for the Army
in Lieu of Rations [1]

[Philadelphia] December 3, 1782

The Committee [2] to whom was referred the letter from the Superintendant of Finance and the Secretary at War respecting the subsistence of the army for the ensuing year[3] pray leave to report in favour of the following resolutions

Resolved that after the last day of december Inst, in lieu of the rations hitherto allowed to the officers of the army including those for servants they shall be allowed subsistance money at the rate of four dollars per month for each ration, provided that where circumstances in any case shall not permit the payment of such subsistence money, they shall draw their rations as heretofore.

Resolved, that after the forementioned period, in lieu of the pay and rations allowed to the officers of the Hospital department (including rations for servants) they shall be intitled to the following monthly pay and subsistence, provided in like manner that where the said subsistence money shall not be paid, they shall be intitled to draw an equivalent number of rations at the rate of four dollars for each ration per month

To the Director	102 dollars pay		60 dollars subsistence
Dy Director & Physician each	100 do.	do.	48 do.	do.
Surgeons	90 do.	do.	40	
Apothecary & Purveyor each	9⟨2⟩ do.	do.	⟨32⟩ do.	do.
Dy Apothecary & Purveyor each	59 do.	do.	16 do.	do.
Mates	42 dollars pay		12 do.	subsistence
Stewards	31 do.		8 do.	do.
Ward Masters	21 do.		8 do.	do.

AD, Papers of the Continental Congress, National Archives.

1. Unless otherwise indicated, the date ascribed to reports or motions made by H in the Continental Congress is the date they were read in Congress. If the date a document was read cannot be determined, the date on which it was passed is given. When the date is stated on the endorsement, it is printed at the top of the document without brackets. If it is taken from another source or is inferred from the contents of the document, it is bracketed. If not in the writing of H, the reports of committees of which he was a member are neither printed nor calendared.

Motions by H that a vote be taken, that a report or motion be referred to a committee, or that a minor change be made in a report have not been printed. Such motions are in *JCC*, XXIV, 35, 41, 115, 149, 222. Motions seconded by H are not printed unless the motion which he seconded is in his writing.

2. The committee consisted of H, Richard Peters of Pennsylvania, and Samuel Osgood of Massachusetts.

3. The letter dated November 22, 1782, signed jointly by Robert Morris, Superintendent of Finance, and Benjamin Lincoln, Secretary at War, is in the Papers of the Continental Congress, National Archives.

Continental Congress
Motion on Appointment of Committee to Confer
with Legislature of Pennsylvania [1]

[Philadelphia, December 4, 1782]

On motion of Mr. (Alexander) Hamilton, seconded by Mr. (David) Howell,[2]

Resolved, That a committee be appointed to confer with a committee of the legislature of Pensylvania, relative to the subjects of their late memorial to Congress.[3]

JCC, XXIII, 761.

1. The members appointed to the committee were H, John Rutledge of South Carolina, and James Madison.
2. Howell was a delegate from Rhode Island.
3. The Assembly of Pennsylvania had informed Congress that a part of the requisition levied by Congress was to be appropriated to the Pennsylvania creditors of the United States. The committee of Congress met with a committee from the Pennsylvania legislature and persuaded its members to abandon their plan. For minutes of the conference, see Madison's "Notes of Debates in the Continental Congress," MS, James Madison Papers, Library of Congress.

The committee wrote to Frederick A. Muhlenberg, the speaker of the Pennsylvania Assembly, on December 4, presumably recommending a conference.

Committee of Continental Congress
to Frederick A. Muhlenberg [1]

[*Philadelphia, December 4, 1783. Letter not found.*]

LS, in writing of H, sold at the Anderson Galleries, April 14, 1919.
1. The committee consisted of H, John Rutledge, and James Madison.

Continental Congress
Report on a Letter from Captain John Paul Jones

[*Philadelphia, December 4, 1782.*] Report of a committee, consisting of Samuel Osgood, James Madison, and Hamilton on a request of Captain John Paul Jones [1] for permission to serve on a campaign with the Marquis de Vaudreuil.[2] The committee reported that, "Congress having a high sense of the merit and services of Capt Jones," the permission be granted.

D, in writing of James Madison, with interlineations by H, Papers of the Continental Congress, National Archives.

1. John Paul Jones, a native of Scotland, was in the American colonies at the outbreak of the Revolution, having shortly before left England to avoid facing charges against him. In December, 1775, he was given a commission in the Continental Navy and during the Revolution became, as is well known, the naval hero of the war. His fame in France was as great as in the American colonies. In February, 1781, Congress expressed its "high sense of the distinguished bravery and military conduct" of Jones and in June elected him to command the *America*, the largest ship in the Continental Navy, then being built at Portsmouth, New Hampshire. After he had supervised the construction of the *America*, it was presented to the French. Jones requested permission to join the Marquis de Vaudreuil for the purpose of gaining experience in the management of fleets.

2. Louis Philippe de Rigaud, Marquis de Vaudreuil, had a long and distinguished career in the French navy. He had served with Comte de Grasse at the battle of the Saintes in April, 1782, and in August of the same year had been promoted to the rank of lieutenant general. In December, 1782, Vaudreuil was commander of a French fleet which was at Boston.

Continental Congress
Report on the Memorials of Chevalier de Cambray-Digby and Captain Jacques Schreiber

[Philadelphia] December 4, 1782

The Committee[1] to whom were referred the memorials of Lt Col Cambray & Capt Schreiber beg leave to report[2]

That although they consider the situation of foreigners in the service of this country, remote from any resources which they may have in their own, and destitute of any competent provision here, as involving a peculiar hardship and requiring if possible some discrimination in their favour, yet in the present embarrassed state of the public finances, they cannot advise any measure for their relief which may derange the general plans of the Superintendant of Finance, and they therefore recommend that the matter may be left to his discretion to act therein as he may conceive most proper.

AD, Papers of the Continental Congress, National Archives.

1. The committee consisted of H, Richard Peters, and Samuel Osgood.

2. Louis Antoine Jean Baptiste, Chevalier de Cambray-Digby, was commissioned a lieutenant colonel in the Corps of Engineers in June, 1778. Captain

Jacques Schreiber, who first served in the artillery, was made a captain in the Corps of Engineers in March, 1780. Both Cambray and Schreiber had been taken prisoner at Charleston, South Carolina, in 1780, and exchanged in 1781.

A letter from Schreiber of November 22, 1782, requesting arrears of pay due him, had been referred to the Superintendent of Finance. The Superintendent reported to Congress on November 25, 1782, that he had declined to furnish the money because he considered "it of the utmost importance to delay such payment until the State of the Treasury will admit of equal sums being granted to every officer in the Service." On November 27, this report was referred to a committee (*JCC*, XXIII, 757).

A letter from Cambray dated November 25, requesting back pay, was referred to the same committee on November 27.

Continental Congress
Motion on Vermont [1]

[Philadelphia] December 5, 1782

Whereas it appears to Congress by authentic documents that the people inhabiting the district of Country on the West-side of Connecticut River commonly called the New Hampshire Grants, and claiming to be an independent state, in contempt of the authority of Congress and in direct violation of their resolutions of the 24th. of September 1779 and of the 2d. of June 1780,[2] did, in the month of September last, proceed to exercise jurisdiction over the persons and properties of sundry inhabitants of the said district professing themseves to be subjects of and to owe allegiance to the State of New York; by means whereof divers of them have been condemned to banishment, not to return on pain of death and confiscation of estate, and others have been fined in large sums and otherwise deprived of property. Therefore

Resolved that the said acts and proceedings of the said people, being highly derogatory to the authority of the United States *and dangerous to the confederacy, require the immediate and decided interposition of Congress* for the protection and relief of such as have suffered by them, and for preserving peace in the said district, until a decision shall be had of the controversy relative to the jurisdiction of the same.

Resolved that the people inhabiting the said district claiming to be independent; be and they are hereby required without delay to make full and ample restitution to Timothy Church, Charles Phelps, Henry Evans, William Shattuck and such others as have been condemned to banishment and confiscation of Estate or have otherwise been deprived of property since the first day of September last for the damages they have sustained by the acts and proceedings aforesaid; and that they be not molested in their persons or properties on their return to their habitations in the said district.[3]

Resolved, that the United States will take effectual measures to enforce a compliance with the aforesaid resolutions in case the same shall be disobeyed by the people of the said district.

Resolved that no persons holding commissions under the state of New York, or under the people of the said district claiming to be independent exercise any authority over the persons and properties of any inhabitants in the said district, contrary to the forementioned resolutions of the 24th. of September 1779 and the 2d. of June 1780.

Resolved that a copy of the foregoing resolutions be transmitted to Thomas Chittendon Esquire of Bennington [4] in the district aforesaid to be communicated to the people thereof.[5]

AD, Papers of the Continental Congress, National Archives.

1. The motion was introduced by Thomas McKean of Delaware, and seconded by H.

2. Vermont (the New Hampshire Grants) was formed from lands claimed by New York, New Hampshire, and Massachusetts. Before the Revolution, New York successfully asserted its claim and governed the area. For several years settlers in the New Hampshire Grants had objected to policies of the New York officials and Assembly. In January, 1777, independence was proclaimed, and in July of the same year a convention adopted a constitution for the new state. Vermont then requested permission to join the union. Congress was disposed to ignore the request, but the relentless pressure of New York forced some decision. On September 24, 1779, a resolution passed Congress recommending that the disputant states empower it to settle all boundary and land disputes (JCC, XV, 1096–97). None of the states involved in the controversy was willing to give Congress the power, and during the next years the question of Vermont's independence and the claims of New York and New Hampshire were frequently debated; but no decisive action was taken. On June 2, 1780, Congress resolved that the people in the New Hampshire Grants "are strictly required to forbear and abstain from all acts of authority" over inhabitants of the area; it also resolved that when representatives from nine states were present in Congress that Congress would "proceed to hear and examine into and finally determine the disputes between the three States of New Hampshire, Massachusetts Bay and New York . . . and the people of the district aforesaid" (JCC, XVII, 482–84). In the fall of 1782, New York again tried to obtain a favorable decision, but a committee report of October 17 expressed only a wish for a peaceful settlement. The subject was brought up intermittently between that time and December 5.

3. These men, who were New Yorkers living in Vermont, endeavored to support the authority of New York. According to a petition sent on February 24, 1786, to Governor George Clinton and the New York legislature, the "law-

less usurpers of Vermont drove them from their homes, confiscated their estates, and banished them" (E. B. O'Callaghan, ed., *The Documentary History of the State of New-York* [Albany, 1851], IV, 1014–15). In a report on a letter from Governor Clinton and petitions from Charles Phelps, William Shattuck, and Henry Evans, a committee of Congress had proposed on November 14 that it be recommended to the officials of Vermont "to make full and ample satisfaction to Charles Phelps, William Shattuck, and Henry Evans, and to all others in a similar predicament, for the damages which they have sustained in person and property, in consequence of the measures taken against them in the said district" (*JCC*, XXIII, 724). Congress rejected the committee's proposal.

4. Chittenden was the governor of Vermont. Having moved from Connecticut and taken up residence in the disputed region in 1774, Chittenden soon played an important part in the establishment of the new state; he was president of the council of safety, helped draw up the constitution of Vermont, and, in March, 1778, was elected its first governor.

5. After debate on a motion to strike out the clause which empowered the United States to "take effectual measures to enforce a compliance with the aforesaid resolutions," the motion was passed without amendment.

Continental Congress
Motion on Payment of Interest on the Domestic Debt and on Sending a Deputation to Rhode Island

[Philadelphia] December 6, 1782

That the Superintendant of Finance be & he is hereby directed to represent to the Legislatures of the several States the indispensible Necessity for their complying with the requisitions of Congress for raising 1,200,000 dollars for paying a years Interest of the Domestick Debt of the U.S.[1] & 2 Millions towards defraying the Expences of the Estimate for the ensuing year[2] & the Inconveniences, Embarrassments & Injuries to the publick Service which will arise from the States Individually making Appropriations[3] of any part of the sd. 2 Millions of dollars or of any other Monies required by the U.S. in Congress assembled;[4] assuring them withall that Congress are determined to make the fullest justice to the public Creditors an invariable object of their ⟨counsels⟩ and exertions.[5]

Resolved that a deputation consisting of   [6] be sent to the State of Rhode Island[7] for the purpose of making a full & just representation of the public affairs of the U.S. and of urging the absolute necessity of a compliance with the Resolution of Congress of the 3d day of feby 1781 respecting the duty on imports & prizes[8] as a measure essential to the safety and reputation of these states.[9]

D, in the writings of H, John Rutledge, and James Madison, Papers of the Continental Congress, National Archives.

1. On September 4, 1782, Congress resolved to call on the states for $1,200,000 "as absolutely and immediately necessary" for payment of the interest on the public debt (*JCC*, XXIII, 545).

2. On October 16, 1782, Congress acted to raise a part of the money which the Superintendent of Finance, Robert Morris, had estimated as required for the year 1783. Of the total of six million dollars needed for the year, Congress asked the states to raise immediately two million (*JCC*, XXIII, 660).

3. The part of the motion asking the states not to appropriate the money requested by Congress resulted from a conference between a committee of Congress and a committee of the Pennsylvania legislature ("Motion on Appointment of Committee to Confer with Legislature of Pennsylvania," December 4, 1782, note 3). It was feared that the Pennsylvania legislature at its next session might again appropriate money to satisfy the claims of its citizens against the United States rather than to meet the congressional requisition. According to James Madison, many members assumed that the only way to forestall such state action was to provide a permanent fund for discharging the public debt ("Notes of Debates in the Continental Congress," MS, James Madison Papers, Library of Congress).

4. The preceding portion of the manuscript is in the writing of John Rutledge. The remainder is in the writing of H except for a few words by Madison.

5. At the request of David Howell of Rhode Island, the first part of the motion was voted on separately. It was agreed to unanimously.

6. Space left blank in MS.

7. All the states except Rhode Island and Georgia had passed laws granting Congress the impost requested in the congressional resolve of February 3, 1781 (*JCC*, XIX, 112). As Georgia was in the possession of the British and infrequently represented in Congress, her assent was not important. The assent of Rhode Island, however, was indispensable to the success of the plan. Repeated requests by Congress that Rhode Island agree to the impost, led to repeated refusals. Early in November, Congress learned unofficially that the lower house of the Rhode Island legislature had rejected the impost.

James Madison recorded that the resolution to send a deputation to Rhode Island was added because it was believed "that a renewal of the call on R. Island for the impost ought to accompany the motion; that such a combination of these plans would mutually give efficacy to them, since R. Island would be solicitous to prevent separate appropriations, & the other States would be soothed with the hope of the Impost" ("Notes of Debates in the Continental Congress," MS, James Madison Papers, Library of Congress).

8. "3d," "feby 1781," "& prizes" were inserted by Madison.

9. After considerable debate on the propriety of sending a deputation to Rhode Island, the motion was resolved in the affirmative, and a deputation of three members was appointed (*JCC*, XXIII, 771–72). The deputation left for Rhode Island on December 22. Before it had traveled far, news was received that Virginia had repealed its act of accession to the impost and that Maryland possibly would do the same.

Alexander Hamilton and William Floyd
to George Clinton

Philadelphia, Decr. 9th, 1782.

Sir,

Inclosed we have the honor to transmit Your Excellency sundry resolutions of Congress of the 5th instant;[1] by which you will judge of the present temper of that body, respecting the affairs of the grants. We cannot, however, absolutely rely upon the execution of the coercive part of them if the matter should require an exertion of force. Many who at a distance adopt very decisive ideas, might shrink from a measure replete with consequences at least delicate, if not dangerous. The principal advantage we promise ourselves from these resolutions is, that they will give a complexion to the future deliberations on the subject and may induce Congress the more readily to adopt some moderate medium. It, therefore, becomes the policy of the State to facilitate as much as lies in its power this object, by doing everything (if anything remains undone) that may tend to conciliate the inhabitants of the Grants, and to take away all motives of opposition from the private interests of individuals on the other States. It is to be recollected in particular that a considerable part of the army is interested in grants of land to a large extent under the usurped government of Vermont. Much will depend upon their disposition in the progress of the business, and it is, therefore, of primary importance that they should be secured at all events. We apprehend there should be a confirmation of their titles unfettered by any condition whatsoever; if any are annexed by the acts of last Winter relative to that subject (which we do not find among our papers) we take the liberty to suggest that they will be worthy the future consideration of the legislature.[2] We enlarge the less on these topics as we are persuaded the wisdom of the State will distinguish and pursue the true line of policy upon this occasion, and will clearly perceive the propriety of moderation.

Congress have resolved to send a deputation of three members to the State of Rhode Island to urge their compliance with the requisition of the five per Cent duty as a measure essential to the safety and reputation of these states.[3] The members chosen are Mr. Mifflin, Mr. Nash and Mr. Osgood.[4]

We have the honor to be With perfect respect, Yr Excellency's Most Obedt. Hum. Serv.

Wm Floyd
Alex Hamilton

His Excellency George Clinton, Esqr.

Public Papers of George Clinton VIII, 56–57.
1. The enclosure is printed in the *Public Papers of George Clinton,* VIII, 57–58. The resolutions enclosed were those of December 5, 1782, in which Congress forbade Vermont to exercise jurisdiction over citizens of New York.
2. An act of the New York legislature, passed on April 14, 1782, had confirmed all grants of lands made by the "government under the name, stile or title of the government of the State of Vermont." This confirmation of title included, of course, the lands granted by Vermont to the Army over which H expressed concern. See *Laws of the State of New York,* I, 486–88.
3. See "Motion on Payment of Interest on the Domestic Debt and on Sending a Deputation to Rhode Island," December 6, 1782.
4. Thomas Mifflin of Pennsylvania, Abner Nash of North Carolina, and Samuel Osgood of Massachusetts.

Continental Congress
To William Greene [1]

Philadelphia [December 11, 1782] [2]

Sir

Congress are equally affected and alarmed by the information they have received that the Legislature of your state at their last meeting have refused their concurrence in the establishment of a duty on imports.[3] They consider this measure as so indispensable to the prosecution of the war, that a sense of duty and regard to the common safety compel them to renew their efforts to engage a compliance with it; and in this view they have determined to send a deputation of three of their members to your state, as expressed in the inclosed resolution.[4] The Gentlemen they have appointed will be able to lay before you a full and just representation of the public affairs, from which they flatter themselves will result a conviction of the propriety of their solicitude upon the present occasion. Convinced by past experience of the zeal and patriotism of the state of Rhode Island, they cannot doubt that It will yield to those urgent considerations which flow from a knowlege of our true situation.

They will only briefly observe that the increasing discontents of the army, the loud clamours of the public creditors, and the extreme disproportion between the current supplies and the demands of the public service are so many invincible arguments for the fund recommended by [5] Congress. They feel themselves unable to devise any other, that will be more efficacious, less exceptionable or more generally agreeable; and if this is rejected they anticipate calamities of a most menacing nature, with this consolation however, that they have faithfully discharged their trust, and that the mischiefs which may follow cannot be attributed to them.

A principal object of the proposed fund is to procure loans abroad. If no security can be held out to lenders, the success of these must necessarily be very limited. The last accounts on the subject were not flattering; and when intelligence shall arrive in Europe that the state of Rhode Island has disagreed to the only fund, which has yet been devised there is every reason to apprehend it will have a fatal influence on their future progress. Deprived of this resource, our affairs must in all probability rapidly hasten to a dangerous crisis, and these states be involved in greater embarrassments than they have yet experienced, and from which it may be much more difficult to emerge.

Congress will only add a request to Your Excellency that if the Legislature should not be sitting, it may be called together as speedily as possible to enable the Gentlemen whom they have deputed to perform the purpose of their mission.[6]

ADf, Papers of the Continental Congress, National Archives.
    1. The draft is prefaced by the following statement: "The Committee appointed to prepare a letter to the state of Rhode Island report the following for the consideration of Congress." It probably was prepared for the signature of Elias Boudinot, President of Congress. The resolution reported by the committee, which consisted of H, James Madison, and Thomas FitzSimons, stated that the letter "be sent to the governor of Rhode Island and Providence Plantations, with the deputation appointed to proceed to that State" (*JCC*, XXIII, 783).
    Greene was the governor of Rhode Island from 1778 to 1786.
    2. The date is that of the introduction of the report in Congress.
    3. For information on Rhode Island's refusal to accede to Congress's demand for the authority to impose impost duties, see "Motion on Payment of Interest on the Domestic Debt and on Sending a Deputation to Rhode Island," December 6, 1782.

4. The enclosed resolution was that of December 6. The deputation was composed of Thomas Mifflin, Abner Nash, and Samuel Osgood.

5. The preceding "the" and the words "recommended by" are not in the writing of H.

6. At the bottom of the page H wrote the words "His Excellency" without the name of an addressee.

Continental Congress
Remarks on the Hiring Out of British Prisoners

[Philadelphia, December 11, 1782]

The Secy. at War was authorized to permit the British prisoners to hire themselves out on condition of a bond from the Hirers for their return. The measure was not opposed, but was acquiesced in by some, only as conformable to antecedent principles established by Congress on this subject. Col. Hamilton in particular gave this explanation.[1]

"Notes of Debates in the Continental Congress," MS, James Madison Papers, Library of Congress.

1. H's explanation was of the following resolution:

"*Resolved*, That the Secretary at War be empowered to permit any British prisoner of war to hire himself as a labourer, provided the person who employs him shall give sufficient security for his appearance when called for, in a penal bond of one hundred pounds current money of Pensylvania, and that he pays to the Superintendant of Finance four dollars monthly for the hire of such prisoner while retained in his service." (*JCC*, XXIII, 785.)

The resolution was adopted by Congress on December 11, the date of H's remarks.

To John Laurence [1]

[Philadelphia, December 12, 1782] [2]

I was equally sorry My Dear friend that you were absent when I called at your house: I should have been happy to have seen you to converse on many things.

You seem to wish a further explanation of the reasons which prevented the success of my application on a certain head.[3] They were purely what I conjectured—a desire to conciliate a certain Gentleman on the spot and gain his influence in some matters of importance; but this I mention in confidence.

There is nothing I can recommend to your attention at your next meeting, so interesting as your system of taxation.[4] In all probability the war will not end here and to carry it on we require absolutely more solid arrangements of finance, besides you ought to adopt them with a view to your own internal prosperity and to your future security as a state.

I should also be glad to see a good establishment for your militia adopted, something like that of Swisserland. God grant the union may last, but it is too frail now to be relied on, and we ought to be prepared for the worst. I inclose you a few outlines on the subject. Show them to our friend Malcolm,[5] and under the character of Adjutant General or Inspector or whatever else you please, put the execution in his hands.

The affairs of Vermont will engage your attention;[6] be moderate by all means. You will see our ideas in a late letter[7] to the Governor. They certainly will have a good effect if adopted. Meet New Hampshire on compromising grounds. I wish the two states would appoint commissioners and make a division; if a slice were given to Massachusettes it would be good policy and silence all opposition. A measure of this nature will meet the general support of Congress. I believe something will be recommended with a view to it, so soon as we have a fuller representation.

I am Your war⟨– – –⟩   Affe⟨– – – –⟩   AH

Novemr. 12th.

ALS, New-York Historical Society, New York City.

1. This letter was found among the Alexander McDougall Papers. Although it is unaddressed, the contents indicate that it was sent to John Laurence and not to McDougall. The recipient had to be a member of the New York legislature, which Laurence was at this time. McDougall was not elected until 1784. That the letter was found in the McDougall papers probably is explained by the fact that Laurence had married McDougall's daughter.

2. H dated this letter November 12. He apparently made a mistake for the last paragraph indicates that at the time it was written he was in Congress. Since he did not present his credentials to Congress until November 25, 1782, this letter could not have been written on November 12. H probably meant to write December 12.

3. H was probably referring to his suggestion to Robert Morris that William Malcom be appointed as his successor as receiver of continental taxes. See H to Morris, August 13, 1782, note 22.

4. Laurence had been elected in 1782 to attend the sixth session of the New York Assembly which met in Poughkeepsie from July 11 to 25, 1782, and at Kingston from January 27 to March 23, 1783.

5. Malcom was a member of the New York Assembly.
6. See "Motion on Vermont," December 5, 1782.
7. H and William Floyd to George Clinton, December 9, 1782.

Continental Congress
Report on Power of Secretary at War to
Discharge Soldiers

[Philadelphia] December 13, 1782

The Committee[1] on the letter from Col Stewart[2] to the Secretary at War report the following resolution:

Reso[l]ved that the Secretary at War have a power of discharging soldiers from the army of The United States similar to that given to the Commander in Chief.[3]

AD, Papers of the Continental Congress, National Archives.
  1. The committee consisted of H, James Madison, and Samuel Osgood.
  2. Walter Stewart, a colonel of the Second Pennsylvania Regiment, had served as aide-de-camp to Major General Horatio Gates. Stewart's letter, according to the endorsement on this report, was dated December 11.
  3. The endorsement states that the action on the report was postponed and "the letter of Col Stewart refd to Secy at War to take order."

Continental Congress
Report on a Letter from the Speaker of the
Rhode Island Assembly

[Philadelphia] December 16, 1782

The Committee[1] to whom was referred the letter from The Honorable William Bradford[2] Esquire speaker of the lower house of Assembly of the state of Rhode Island containing under three heads the reasons of that state for refusing their compliance with the recommendation of Congress for a duty on imports and prize goods,[3] after having maturely considered the same beg leave to report.

ADf, Papers of the Continental Congress, National Archives.
  1. The committee consisted of H, James Madison, and Thomas FitzSimons.
  2. A printed version of Bradford's letter is in JCC, XXIII, 788–89.
  3. The congressional recommendation, dated February 3, 1781 (JCC, XIX, 112), requested that the several states give Congress the power to levy, after May 1, 1781, a duty of five percent ad valorem on all imports and the same duty on all prizes condemned in state Admirality Courts, the proceeds to be appropriated to the discharge of the national debt.

That your Committee flatter themselves the State on a reconsideration of the objections they have offered, with a candid attention to the arguments which stand in opposition to them, will be induced to retract their dissent, convinced that the measure is supported on the most solid grounds of equal justice, policy and general utility. The following observations contrasted with each head of the objections successively will furnish a satisfactory answer to the whole.

First objection

"That the proposed duty would be unequal in its operation, bearing hardest upon the most commercial states, and so would press peculiarly hard upon *that* state, which draws its chief support from Commerce."

The most common experience joined to the concurrent opinions of the ablest commercial and political observers have established, beyond controversy, this general principle, "That every duty on imports is incorporated with the price of the commodity and ultimately paid by the consumer; with a profit on the duty itself, as a compensation to the Merchant for the advance of his money."

The Merchant considers the duty demanded by the state on the imported article in the same light with freight or any similar charge, and adding it to the original cost, calculates his profit on the aggregate sum. It may happen, that at particular conjunctures where the markets are overstocked and there is a competition among the sellers, this may not be practicable, but in the general course of trade the demand for consumption preponderates, and the Merchant can with ease indemnify himself and even obtain a profit on the advance. As a consumer he pays his share of the duty, but it is no further a burthen upon him.

The consequence of the principle laid down is that every class of the community bears its share of the duty in proportion to its consumption; which last is regulated by the comparative wealth of the respective classes in conjunction with their habits of expence or frugality. The rich and luxurious pay in proportion to their riches and luxury, the poor and parsimonious in proportion to their poverty and parsimony.

A chief excellence of this mode of revenue is, that it preserves a just measure to the abilities of individuals, promotes frugality and taxes extravagance.

The same reasoning in our situation applies to the intercourse between two states. If one imports and the other does not, the latter must be supplied by the former. The duty being transferred to the price of the commodity is no more a charge on the importing state for what is consumed in the other, than it is a charge on the Merchant for what is consumed by the farmer or artificer. Either state will only feel the burthen in a ratio to its consumption, and this will be in a ratio to its population and wealth. What happens between the different classes of the same community internally happens between the two states; and as the Merchant in the first case, so far from losing the duty himself has a profit on the money he advances for that purpose, so the importing state which in the second case is the Merchant with respect to the other is not only reimbursed by the non-importing state but has a like benefit on the duty advanced.

It is therefore the reverse of a just position that the duty proposed will bear hardest on the most commercial states. It will, if any thing, have a contrary effect, though not in a sufficient degree to justify an objection on the part of the non importing states; for it is as reasonable they should allow an advance on the duty paid as on the first cost, freight or any incidental charge. They have also other advantages in the measure fully equivalent to this disadvantage. Over-nice and minute calculations in matters of this nature are inconsistent with national measures, and in the imperfect state of human affairs would stagnate all the operations of government. Absolute equality is not to be attained; to aim at it is pursuing a shadow at the expence of the substance, and in the event we should find ourselves wider of the mark, than if in the first instance we were content to approach it with moderation.

Second objection

"That the recommendation proposes to introduce into that and the other states, officers unknown and unaccountable to them, and so is against the constitution of the state"

It is not to be presumed that the constitution of any state could mean to define and fix the precise numbers and descriptions of all officers to be permitted in the state, excluding the creation of any new ones, whatever might be the necessity derived from that variety of circumstances, incidental to all political institutions. The Legislature must always have a discretionary power of appointing officers, not expressly known to the constitution, and this power will include that of authorising the Fœderal government to make the appointments in cases where the general welfare may require it. The denial of this would prove too much; to wit, that the power given by the confederation to Congress to appoint all officers in the post-office was illegal and unconstitutional.

The doctrine advanced by Rhode Island would perhaps prove also that the Fœderal government ought to have the appointment of no internal officers whatever, a position that would defeat all the provisions of the Confederation and all the purposes of the union. The truth is that no Fœderal constitution can exist without powers, that in their exercise affect the internal police of the component members. It is equally true that no government can exist without a right to appoint officers for those purposes which proceed from and concenter in itself; and therefore the confederation has expressly declared that Congress shall have authority to appoint all such "civil officers as may be necessary for managing the general affairs of The United States under their direction." All that can be required is that the Fœderal government confine its appointments to such as it is empowered to make by the original act of union, or by the subsequent consent of the parties. Unless there should be express words of exclusion in the constitution of a state, there can be no reason to doubt, that it is within the compass of legislative discretion to communicate that authority.

The propriety of doing it upon the present occasion is founded on substantial reasons.

The measure proposed is a measure of necessity. Repeated experiments have shown that the revenue to be raised within these states is altogether inadequate to the public wants. The deficiency can only be supplied by loans. Our applications to the foreign powers on whose friendship we depend have had a success far short of our necessities. The next resource is to borrow from individuals. These will neither be actuated by generosity nor reasons of state. 'Tis to their interest alone we must appeal. To conciliate this we must not only stipulate a proper compensation for what they lend, but we must give security for the performance. We must pledge an ascertained fund, simple and productive in its nature, general in its prin-

ciple and at the disposal of a single will. There can be little confidence in a security under the constant revisal of thirteen different
deliberatives. It must once for all be defined and established on the
faith of the states solemnly pledged to each other and not revocable
by either without a breach of the general compact.

'Tis by such expedients that nations, whose resources are understood, whose reputations and governments are erected on the foundation of ages, are enabled to obtain a solid and extensive credit.
Would it be reasonable in us to hope for more easy terms who have
so recently assumed our rank among the nations? Is it not to be
expected, that individuals will be cautious in lending their money to
a people in our circumstances, and that they will at least require
the best security we can give?

We have an enemy vigilant, intriguing, well acquainted with
our defects and embarrassments. We may expect that he will make
every effort to instill diffidences into individuals, and in the present
posture of our internal affairs he will have too plausible ground on
which to tread. Our necessities have obliged us to embrace measures
with respect to our public credit, calculated to inspire distrust. The
prepossessions on this article must naturally be against us, and it
is therefore indispensable we should endeavour to remove them, by
such means as will be the most obvious and striking.

It was with these views Congress determined on a general fund;
and the one they have recommended must upon a thorough examination appear to have fewer inconveniences than any other.

It has been remarked as an essential part of the plan, that the
fund should depend on a single will. This will not be the case unless
the collection as well as the appropriation is under the controul
of The United States; for it is evident, that after the duty is agreed
upon it may in a great measure be defeated by an ineffectual mode
of levying it. The United States have a common interest in an
uniform and equally energetic collection; and not only policy but
justice to all the parts of the Union designates the utility of lodging
the power of making it where the interest is common. Without this
it might in reality operate as a very *unequal tax.*

Third objection

"That by granting to Congress a power to collect monies from
the commerce of these states indefinitely as to time and quantity

and for the expenditure of which they are not to be accountable
to the states, they would become independent of their constituents,
and so the proposed impost is repugnant to the liberty of the United
States"

Admitting the principle of this objection to be true, still it ought
to have no weight in the present case because there is no analogy
between the principle and the fact.

First, the fund proposed is sufficiently definite as to time because
it is only coextensive with the existence of the debt contracted and
to be contracted in the course of the war. Congress are persuaded
that it is as remote from the intention of their constituents to perpetuate that debt as to extinguish it at once by a faithless neglect of
providing the means to fulfil the public engagements. Their ability
to discharge it in a moderate time can as little be doubted as their
inclination, and the moment that debt ceases the duty so far as respects the present provision ceases with it.[4]

The resolution recommending the duty specifies the object of it
to be the[5] discharge of the Principal & Interest of the Debts already
contracted or which may be contracted on the faith of the united
States for supporting the present war.

Secondly.

The rate per Cent is fixed, and it is not at the option of the United
States to increase it. Though the product will vary according to
the variations in trade, yet as there is this limitation of the rate, it
cannot be properly said to be indefinite as to quantity.

By the confederation Congress have an absolute discretion in
determining the quantum of revenue requisite for the national expenditure. When this is done nothing remains for the states separately but the mode of raising. No state can dispute the obligation
to pay the sum demanded without a breach of the confederation,
and when the money comes into the treasury, the appropriation is
the exclusive province of the Fœderal government. This provision
of the confederation (without which it would be an empty form)
comprehends in it, the principle in its fullest latitude, which the

4. H at this point wrote and then deleted the following paragraph:
"Independent of other provisions for discharging the public debt, the
revenue from this duty in the future progress of our trade will afford a surplus
beyond the appropriations for interest, which from the express condition of
the grant must be applied as a sinking fund to pay off the principal, and by
which the supposition of perpetuity is destroyed."
5. The remainder of this paragraph is not in H's writing.

objection under consideration treats as repugnant to the liberty of the United States; to wit an indefinite power of prescribing the quantity of money to be raised and of appropriating it when raised.

If it be said that the states individually having the collection in their own hands may refuse a compliance with exorbitant demands, the confederation will answer that this is a point of which they have no constitutional liberty to judge. Such a refusal would be an exertion of power not of right, and the same power which could disregard a requisition made on the authority of the confederation might at any time arrest the collection of the duty.

The same kind of responsibility which exists with respect to the expenditure of the money furnished in the forms hitherto practiced would be equally applicable to the revenue from the imports.

The truth is the security intended to the general liberty in the confederation consists in the frequent election and in the rotation of the members of Congress, by which there is a constant and an effectual check upon them. This is the security which the people in every state enjoy against the usurpations of their internal governments; and it is the true source of security in a representative republic. The government so constituted ought to have the means necessary to answer the end of its institution. By weakening its hands too much it may be rendered incapable of providing for the interior harmony or the exterior defence of the state.

The measure in question if not within the letter is within the spirit of the confederation. Congress by that are empowered to borrow money for the use of the United States, and by implication to concert the means necessary to accomplish the end. But without insisting upon this argument, if the confederation has not made proper provision for the exigencies of the state, it will be at all times the duty of Congress to suggest further provisions; and when their proposals are submitted to the unanimous consent of the States, they can never be charged with exceeding the bounds of their trust. Such a consent is the basis and sanction of the confederation, which expressly in the 13th. article empowers Congress to agree to and propose such additional provisions.

The remarks hitherto made have had referrence principally to the future prosecution of the war. There still remains an interesting light in which the subject ought to be viewed.

The United States have already contracted a debt in Europe and in this country for which their faith is pledged. The capital of this debt can only be discharged by degrees; but a fund for this purpose and for paying the interest annually on every principle of policy and justice ought to be provided. The omission will be the deepest ingratitude and cruelty to a large number of meritorious individuals, who in the most critical periods of the war have adventured their fortunes in support of our independence. It would stamp the national character with indelible disgrace.

An annual provision for the purpose will be too precarious. If its continuance and application were certain it would not afford complete relief. With many the regular payment of interest by occasional grants would suffice; but with many more it would not. These want the use of the principal itself; and they have a right to it: but since it is not in our power to pay off the principal, the next expedient is to fund the debt and render the evidences of it negotiable.

Besides the advantage to individuals from this arrangement, the active stock of the nation would be increased by the whole amount of the domestic debt, and of course the abilities of the community to contribute to the public wants. The national credit would revive and stand hereafter on a secure basis.

This was another object of the proposed duty.

If it be conceded that a similar fund is necessary it can hardly be disputed that the one recommended is the most eligible. It has been already shown that it affects all parts of the community in proportion to their consumption; and has therefore the best pretensions to equality. It is the most agreeable tax to the people that can be imposed, because it is paid insensibly and seems to be voluntary.

It may perhaps be imagined that it is unfavourable to commerce; but the contrary can easily be demonstrated. It has been seen that it does not diminish the profit of the Merchant and of course can be no diminution of his inducements to trade. It is too moderate in its amount to discourage the consumption of imported goods, and cannot on that account abrige the extent of importations. If it even had this effect it would be an advantage to Commerce by lessening the proportion of our imports to our exports [6] and inclining the ballance in favour of this country.

The principal thing to be consulted for the advancement of com-

6. In MS, H by mistake wrote "exports to our imports."

merce is to promote exports. All impediments to these either by way of prohibition or by increasing the prices of native commodities, descreasing by that mean their sale and consumption at foreign markets are injurious. Duties on exports have this operation. For the same reason taxes on possessions and the articles of our own growth or manufacture, whether in the form of a land tax excise or any other are more hurtful to trade than import duties. The tendency of all such taxes is to increase the prices of those articles which are the objects of exportation and to enable others to undersell us abroad. The farmer if he pays a heavy land tax must endeavour to get more for the products of his farm: the mechanic and labourer if they find the necessaries of life grow dearer by an excise must endeavour to exact higher wages; and these causes will produce an increase of prices within and operate against foreign commerce.

It is not however to be inferred that the whole revenue ought to be drawn from imports: All extremes are to be rejected. The chief thing to be attended to is that the weight of the taxes fall not too heavily in the first instance upon particular parts of the community. A judicious distribution to all kinds of taxable property is a first principle in taxation. The tendency of these observations is only to show that taxes on possessions, on articles of our own growth and manufacture are more prejudicial to trade than duties on imports.

The observations which conclude the letter on which these remarks are made naturally lead to reflect⟨ions⟩ that deserve the serious attention of every member of the union.[7] There is a happy mean between too much confidence and excessive jealousy in which the health and prosperity of a state consist. Either extreme is a dangerous vice; the first is a temptation to men in power to arrogate

7. The observations to which H refers are in the last two paragraphs of Bradford's letter and read as follows:

"This State may be justly ranked among the foremost in the common cause, having furnished in support of it as many men, and as much money, in proportion to its abilities, as any State in the union, and much more than most of them, and it is still disposed to continue its exertions; but it will raise and collect its quota of public taxes in such a way as shall be judged most proper.

"And it is hoped, that when its resolutions are founded on the great principles of liberty and a general interest, it will not be thought to suspect the public virtue of the present Congress, by withholding from them or their servants, a power of which their successors might make a dangerous use." (*JCC*, XXIII, 788–89.)

more than they have a right to—the latter enervates government, prevents system in the administration defeats the most salutary measures; breeds confusion in the state, disgusts and discontents among the people and may eventually prove as fatal to liberty as the opposite temper.

It is certainly pernicious to leave any government in a situation of responsibility, disproportioned to its power.

The conduct of the war is intrusted to Congress and the public expectation turned upon them without any competent means at their command to satisfy the important trust. After the most full and solemn deliberation under a collective view of all the public difficulties, they recommend a measure, which appears to them the corner stone of the public safety: They see this measure suspended for near two years—partially complied with by some of the states, rejected by one of them and in danger on that account to be frustrated; the public embarrassments every day increasing, the dissatisfaction of the army growing more serious, the other creditors of the public clamouring for justice, both irritated by the delay of measures for their present relief or future security, the hopes of our enemies encouraged to protract the war, the zeal of our friends depressed by an appearance of remissness and want of exertion on our part, Congress harrassed, the national character suffering and the national safety at the mercy of events.

This state of things cannot but be extremely painful to Congress and appear to your Committee to make it their duty to be urgent to obviate the evils with which it is pregnant.

Resolved that Congress agree to the said Report [8]

Whereas it is essential to justice and to the preservation of public credit that whenever a nation is obliged by the exigencies of public affairs to contract a debt, proper funds should be established not only for paying the annual value or interest of the same but for discharging the principal within a reasonable period, by which a nation may avoid the evils of an excessive accumulation of debt—Therefore

Resolved, that whenever the Neat product of any funds recommended by Congress and granted by the states for funding the debt

8. This sentence is not in H's writing. At this point H deleted the following: "Your Committee observing that the apprehension of perpe[t]uity in the duration of the fund recommended has great share in the opposition with which it meets, take the liberty to propose the following resolutions as tending effectually to remove all apprehension on that head."

already contracted or for procuring future loans for the support of the war shall exceed the sum requisite for paying the interest of the whole amount of the national debt which these states may owe at the termination of the present war, the surplus of such grants shall form a sinking fund to be inviolably appropriated to the payment of the principal of the said debt and shall on no account be diverted to any other purpose. And[9] in Order that the several States may have proper information of the state of their finance it is further resolved that as soon as the publick debt can be liquidated each State be annually furnished with the amount thereof & the interest thereon and also of the proceeds and disposition of the sd. funds for the redemption thereof.

Resolved that the faith of the United States be pledged for the observance of the foregoing resolution, and that if any state shall think it necessary to make it a condition of their grants the same will be[10] considered by Congress as consistent with their Resolution of the 3d Febry 1781.

9. This sentence is in the writing of Thomas FitzSimons.

10. The words following "be" are not in the writing of H. In *JCHW*, II, 212-13, the last three paragraphs of this report are printed as a separate resolution dated December 16, 1782, and entitled "Sinking Fund." The date in the last paragraph is printed in error as "23d February 1781."

"The answer to the objections of Rho: Island," James Madison recorded, "passed without opposition, 8 States being present, of which Rho: Isd. was one" ("Notes of Debates in the Continental Congress," MS, James Madison Papers, Library of Congress).

Continental Congress
Motion on the Promotion of Brigadiers

[Philadelphia, December 16-19, 1782][1]

That the Secretary at War report to Congress on friday next the number of additional promotion of Brigadiers requisite to the service of the ensuing Campaign; and the names and dates of Commissions of such Cols & Lt Cols Command[an]ts as stand next in order of promotion; and that Congress then proceed to the election of the necessary Brigadiers.[2]

AD, Papers of the Continental Congress, National Archives.

1. In the *Journals* of the Congress this undated motion is printed in a note to the proceedings of October 14, 1782 (*JCC*, XXIII, 652). As H was not

then a delegate to the Congress, it must have been made later. On December 22, the Secretary at War wrote to Congress: "I omitted to report on the motion respecting the appointments of Brigadiers, before I left Philadelphia" (*JCC*, XXIII, 836). The motion to which he referred was probably the one printed above. As it directed the Secretary at War to "report to Congress on friday next," and as the Secretary's letter was dated, Sunday, December 22, the motion must have been made between Monday, December 16 and Thursday, December 19.

2. See "Report on Brigadier Generals James Clinton and Edward Hand," December 31, 1782.

Continental Congress
Report on the Deputation to Rhode Island

[Philadelphia, December 17, 1782]

That the deputation appointed to go to the state of Rhode Island to Urge the Necessity of a Compliance with the recommendation of Congress for laying an impost of 5 ⅌ Ct. delay their journey till the further order of Congress [1]

The Committee to whom was referred the foregoing motion beg leave to report it as their opinion that the deputation ought to proceed as soon as possible.[2]

D, in the writings of H and Abraham Clark, Papers of the Continental Congress, National Archives.

1. This paragraph is in the writing of Abraham Clark of New Jersey.
2. H's motion of December 6 that a deputation be sent to Rhode Island was passed by the Congress on the same day. When the letter to accompany the deputation was reported to the Congress on December 11 (see the letter to William Greene, December 11, 1782), David Howell, delegate from Rhode Island, made a motion that the resolution authorizing the deputation be repealed. On the day following, December 12, a substitute motion, delaying the departure of the deputation, was passed. The latter motion was referred to H, James Madison, and Thomas FitzSimons (*JCC*, XXIII, 788–90). Congress agreed to the committee's report (*ibid.*).

Continental Congress
Motion Censuring David Howell

[Philadelphia, December 17, 1782] [1]

Mr. Howel having avowed himself the author of the letter [2] respecting foreign loans and other matters as published in the Boston Gazette of Nov 10 1782 [3] mentioned in the report of the Committee thereupon,[4] It is the sense of this house that the said letter contains a misrepresentation of facts of a tendency injurious to the public affairs *and a disclosure of an important foreign transaction requiring secrecy* [5] and that therefore the said letter is highly unjustifiable.[6]

AD, Papers of the Continental Congress, National Archives.

1. The motion is undated. It is printed under the date of December 17 in *JCC*, XXIII, 812.

2. This letter was dated October 16, 1782.

3. The date is not in the writing of H.

4. Howell, delegate from Rhode Island, had written that the negotiations for a loan which John Adams was conducting with the Dutch were proceeding satisfactorily, that the credit of the United States was such that "they have of late failed in no application for foreign loans," and that Sweden had made a secret proposal to enter into a treaty with the United States (*JCC*, XXIII, 791–92). Howell's letter was brought to the attention of Congress on December 6 and referred to a committee which reported on December 12 that "the Secretary for foreign affairs be instructed to write to the executive of Rhode Island, requesting them to enquire through what channel the above communication was made, or who is the supposed author of the extract referred to, and report accordingly" (*ibid.*, 792). H's motion was made after Daniel Carroll, delegate from Maryland, had moved "That the Secretary of Foreign Affairs be discharged from the instructions given him on the 12 instant" (*ibid.*, 812). Carroll's motion was not approved by the Congress until the next day. H, according to James Madison, was unwilling that the matter be settled without a reference to Howell's authorship of the publication ("Notes of Debates in the Continental Congress," MS, James Madison Papers, Library of Congress).

5. H refers to Howell's disclosure of the overtures made by the Court of Sweden for a treaty with the United States.

6. H's motion was postponed for consideration until the following day, December 18.

To George Clinton

⟨Philadelphia, December 18, 1782.⟩

⟨Dear Sir:⟩

I shall very shortly be out of cash, and shall therefore be much obliged to you to forward to me the State allowance. It will answer as well in Mr. Morris' notes as in Specie provided the notes have not more than a fortnight or so to run. It will be better if they are due. ⟨A disappointment in this will greatly embarrass me, and from what your Excellency said, I take it for granted it cannot happen.⟩ Nothing new, except a pretty probable account of the evacuation of Charles Town.

⟨I have the honor to be, with great esteem, Your most obedient servant.⟩ [1]

ALS, sold at Anderson Galleries, January 21, 1904, Lot 234.
    1. The text is taken from the extract printed in the catalogue of the Anderson Galleries. The material in broken brackets is taken from James A. Hamilton, *Reminiscences of James A. Hamilton* (New York, 1879), 7.

To Elizabeth Hamilton

[Philadelphia, December 18, 1782]

I thank you my beloved for your precious letter by the post. It is full of that tender love which I hope will characterise us both to our latest hour. For my own part I may say, there never was a husband who could vie with yours in fidelity and affection.

I begin to be insupportably anxious to see you again. I hope this pleasure may not be long delayed. I wish you to take advantage of the first good snow that promises to carry you through, to get as far as Mr. Cortland's at Persepenni.[1] Take the advice of your friends about the route. It will depend upon the state of the River. If you can come by Kings ferry, I think it will be best.

Should your Cash fall short and you have not yet otherwise disposed of it, you may keep for your own use what you would receive from Mr. Taylor.[2]

When you are in the Jerseys write me of your arrival and I will come for you. Write me indeed when you will set out. I do not know whom you will get to travel with you. I am loth that you should make so long a journey alone.

For God's sake take care of my child on the journey. I am very apprehensive on his account.

God bless my lovely Betsey and send her soon to me. I delay sending your habit, because you can better get it made here.

Adieu My love   AH

Philadelphia
18th Decemr.

At Poughkepsie you will probably receive some money from Governor Clinton for me and can use what you may want of it.

You may also borrow if you find it necessary from Mr. Barry [3] or any other having connections here and draw upon me.

You will have occasion for Martinique [4] on the road. If you come by Kings ferry and have occasion to make a stage [5]

ALS, The Andre deCoppet Collection, Princeton University Library.

1. H is probably referring to Parsipanny, New Jersey, and to one of the many descendents of Stephen Van Cortlandt who lived in that area.

2. Presumably John Tayler, an Albany merchant, who had been a member of the New York legislature and later became lieutenant governor of New York.

3. "Mr. Barry" may have been Thomas Barry, an Albany merchant.

4. "Martinique" may have been the name of a slave, or it may, as Mrs. Dorothy Bobbé of New York City has suggested, have been a reference to rum which in 1782 was being imported from the French West Indies, particularly Martinique.

5. The letter is incomplete.

Continental Congress
Motion on Instructions to be Given the Secretary for Foreign Affairs

[Philadelphia, December 18, 1782]

On motion of Mr Carroll seconded by Mr Ramsay
Resolved That the Secy for foreign affairs be discharged from the instruction given him on the 12 instant [1]
Mr. Howel delegate from the State of R Island having acknowleged himself the author of the extract of the letter quoted in the report of the Committee of that day.[2]

D, in the writings of Charles Thomson and H, Papers of the Continental Congress, National Archives.

1. This first portion of the manuscript is in the writing of Charles Thomson. On December 12, 1782, the Secretary for Foreign Affairs had been instructed to correspond with the executive of Rhode Island on the identity of the author of an article which had revealed information Congress had designated secret. See *JCC*, XXIII, 792.

2. For a summary of Howell's letter see "Motion Censuring David Howell," December 17, 1782, note 4. In the left hand margin, opposite the part in H's writing, is written: "Hamilton [and William] Blount [of North Carolina] to add." The *Journals* of the Congress indicate only that the motion was made by Daniel Carroll and seconded by David Ramsay of South Carolina (*JCC*, XXII, 812).

Continental Congress
Remarks on the Censure of David Howell [1]

[Philadelphia, December 18, 1782]

The day was chiefly spent on the case of Mr. Howel; whose behaviour . . . led to a determined opposition to him, those who were most inclined to spare his reputation. If the affair could have been closed without an insertion of his name on the Journal, He seemed willing to withdraw his protest; but the impropriety which appeared to some, & particularly to Mr. Hamilton, in suppressing the name of the author of a piece wch. Congress had so emphatically reprobated, when the author was found to be a member of Congress, prevented a relaxation as to the yeas & nays.

"Notes of Debates in the Continental Congress," MS, James Madison Papers, Library of Congress.
  1. For an explanation of the move to censure Howell, see "Motion Censuring David Howell," December 17, 1782, and "Motion on Instructions to be Given the Secretary of Foreign Affairs," December 18, 1782.

Continental Congress
Motion that a Committee be Appointed on a Motion by David Howell

[Philadelphia, December 18, 1782]

Congress having in respect to the articles of Confederation admitted on their journals an entry of a motion made by Mr Howell Seconded by Mr Arnold [1] *highly derogatory to the honor & dignity of* the United States in Congress Assembled; [2]

Resolved that a Committee be appointed to report such measures as it will be proper for Congress to take thereupon. [3]

D, in the writings of Daniel Carroll and H, Papers of the Continental Congress, National Archives.
  1. To Carroll's motion of December 18, Howell offered a substitute motion, seconded by Jonathan Arnold of Rhode Island. In this motion, Howell defended his publication of information on congressional transactions for foreign loans by asserting the right of a delegate to communicate to his constituents any information he might consider proper. Howell's motion was defeated. See *JCC*, XXIII, 814–16.

2. Except for the words "derogatory to," which H inserted, this paragraph is in the writing of Carroll.

3. A motion by Jonathan Arnold, that the words "highly derogatory to the honor and dignity of the United States in Congress assembled" be struck out, was defeated (*JCC*, XXIII, 818). John Taylor Gilman of New Hampshire, H, and James Madison were chosen for the committee recommended in H's motion (*JCC*, XXIII, 819). On December 20 this committee issued a report, in the writing of Madison, which stated:

"*Resolved*, That the said motion, with the preceding resolutions of Congress, to which it refers, be transmitted by the Secretary for foreign affairs to the executive authority of the State of Rhode Island, with an authenticated state of the several applications for foreign loans, and the result thereof." (*JCC*, XXIII, 822.)

Continental Congress
Motion that Requisitions on the States
Be Revised [1]

[Philadelphia, December 20, 1782]

That the Committee appointed to consider and report what further or different provision may be made for discharging the interest that is or may be due on loan office certificates & other liquidated debts of the United states be also directed to revise the requisitions for the service of the preceding and present year and to report whether the same ought to be continued or altered.[2]

AD, Papers of the Continental Congress.

1. This motion is not printed in the *Journals* of the Congress. A notation on the back of the document reads "February 1783." It was probably made, however, on December 20, 1782. On that date, James Madison in his "Notes of Debates in the Continental Congress," recorded that "A motion was made by Mr. Hamilton for revising the requisitions of the preceding and present years, in order to reduce them more within the faculties of the States" (MS, James Madison Papers, Library of Congress). In *JCHW*, II, 223, this motion is dated "December, 1782."

2. The motion, according to Madison, met "with little patronage" and was withdrawn ("Notes of Debates in the Continental Congress," MS, James Madison Papers, Library of Congress).

From George Clinton

Poughkeepsie [New York] Decr. 29th. 1782

Dear Sir

Before I was honored by your Letter of the 18th. Instant I had received a Line from Colo. Floyd on the same Subject. As my answer

to his is forwarded by the present Conveyance I beg leave to refer
you to it for Information.[1] I hope it may prove satisfactory and I
flatter myself no further Disappointment can take Place. Should I
however be mistaken you have only to advise me of it & I will immediately forward the Cash.

Phelps [2] who was delayed on the Road by the late heavy fall of
Snow waited on me a few Days since & delivered me your official
Dispatches of the 9th Instant. Considering the Disposition heretofore
discovered by Congress on the Subject of our Controversy with the
Grants, their Resolutions which you enclosed me, tho' short of
what we are justly entitled to, exceed my Expectations & I am not
without Hope, if properly improved, may be the Mean of leading
to a just and favorable Issue. The Idea of many of the Military being
interested in the Independency of Vermont in consequence of their
having taken Grants of Lands under them I believe is without
foundation. There was a Period when the Disposition of Congress,
founded on political Expedience, appeared so favorable to the
Independence of that District, as to have induced some Gentlemen
of the Army to apply to the usurped Government for Grants: But
when it was discovered that they were intriguing with the common
Enemy, the more respectable Characters withdrew their Applications
and relinquished all kind of Connections with them and even those
who did not go so far I immagine conceive themselves as perfectly
secure under our late Acts. If however this should not be the Case
any Difficulty which may be apprehended from it may be easily
obviated; as I am persuaded the Legislature are disposed to every
liberal Act that may consist with the Honor of the State and tend
to facilitate a Settlement of the Dispute. There was a Time, not long
since, when Congress had only to have spoken decisively on the
Subject and they would have been obeyed; nor do I believe the
Time is yet past if they could be convinced that Congress were in
earnest. But if force is necessary to carry their Decision into execution the longer it is delayed the more force it will require. The Misfortune is, tho' I believe there are but few States that favor their
Independence, some members, of those who do, take great Pains
to encourage the Revolters in their Opposition by secret assurances
that Congress will not direct any coercive Measures against them,

and I am not without my Fears that this Conduct will in some Measure defeat the present Resolutions.

I am with great Respect & Esteem Dear Sir Your most Obedt. Servt.   Geo: Clinton

The Honble
Alexander Hamilton Esqr.[3]

LS, Hamilton Papers, Library of Congress.
1. Clinton's letter to William Floyd has not been found. Presumably Clinton wrote of an arrangement for providing H and Floyd with money, for on December 7, 1782, Floyd wrote to Clinton asking for money (Burnett, *Letters,* VI, 557), and on February 18, 1783, Floyd wrote to the governor: "two hundred pounds which your Excellency forwarded me . . . is expended" (*Public Papers of George Clinton,* VIII, 75–76).
2. Charles Phelps had gone to Philadelphia in October, 1782, to testify before a committee of Congress on the confiscation of his property in Vermont by the officials of that state.
3. On the back of the last page of this letter H wrote the following:
"Not to suppose that those who made the confederation did not consider various plans.
states do not pay tax because we do not proceed according to confederation
Exists in every state
plan not bad because in every state
go according to confederation
Did you not require in vain a duty on imposts
All public creditors ruined
Ought to try"
These were ideas which he probably used in the course of the debate on one of the various plans which were proposed in Congress during January, 1783, for raising a permanent revenue for the United States. The fragmentary nature of this outline, however, makes it impossible to determine the specific proposal to which these statements refer.

Continental Congress
Report on the Claim of Baron von Steuben [1]

[Philadelphia] December 30, 1782

The Committee[2] to whom was referred the letter from Major General The Baron De Steuben[3] having conferred with him thereupon, submit to the consideration of Congress the following facts, resulting from the communications made to them supported by the testimonials of the Commander in Chief and many other principal officers of the army:

First. That the Baron De Steuben was in Europe possessed of respectable military rank and different posts of honor and emolument, which he relinquished to come to America and offer his services, at a critical period of the war, and without any previous stipulations.

Secondly. That on his arrival here he actually engaged in the army in a very disinterested manner and without compensations similar to those which had been made to several other foreign officers.

Thirdly. That under singular difficulties and embarrassments, in the department in which he has been employed he has rendered very important and substantial services by introducing into the army a regular formation and exact discipline and by establishing a spirit of order and œconomy in the interior administration of the Regiments, which besides other advantages, have been productive of immense savings to The United States.

That in the commands in which he has been employed he has upon all occasions conducted himself like *an experienced and brave* officer.

Your Committee are therefore of opinion that the sacrifices and services of the Baron De Steuben justly entitle him to the distinguished notice of Congress, and to a generous compensation whenever the situation of public affairs will permit.

Your Committee further report that the Baron De Steuben has considerable arrearages of pay due to him from these states on a liquidated account, and that having exhausted his resources in past expences, it is now indispensable that a sum of money should be paid to him for his present support and to enable him to take the field another campaign, and propose that the sum of two thousand four hundred dollars be paid to him for that purpose and charged to his account aforesaid.[4] Your Committee observing that from the nature of the department, in which The Baron De Steuben is employed, he is under the necessity of making frequent journies, by which he incurs an additional expence and is often deprived of the allowance of forage to which he is entitled, propose

That he be allowed *three hundred* dollars per Month in lieu of his extra pay, and of subsistence and forage for himself and family (including waggon as well as saddle horses), and that these allowances hereafter cease.[5]

ADf, Papers of the Continental Congress, National Archives.

1. H's draft differs in minor particulars from the report published in the *Journals* of the Continental Congress. See *JCC*, XXIII, 833–34.

2. The letter of Frederick William Augustus Henry, Baron von Steuben, was read in Congress on December 10 and referred to H, Abraham Clark of New Jersey, and Ezekiel Cornell of Rhode Island. The committee which reported consisted of H, Clark, and Daniel Carroll.

3. Von Steuben's letter, addressed to Elias Boudinot and dated December 5, 1782, is in the Papers of the Continental Congress, National Archives.

The acceptance, early in 1778, by Congress of von Steuben's services in the American army was accompanied by an unwritten financial agreement. According to von Steuben, Congress promised 1. that his expenses, while on duty in the Continental Army, would be paid by the government; 2. that if he contributed effectively to the success of the patriot cause he would be reimbursed both the cost of his trip to America and the income with interest which he would have received had he remained in Germany; 3. that at the successful conclusion of the war he would receive an income for the rest of his life. Since the pending peace treaty would establish American independence, von Steuben requested congressional fulfillment of what he believed to be the terms of the agreement. In addition, the Baron's pay and expenses were in arrears.

In his letter of December 5, von Steuben recounted his services to the American cause and requested Congress to grant him the emoluments to which he considered himself entitled.

4. At this point there appears in the *Journals* the following sentence: "Whereupon, *Resolved*, That the foregoing proposal of the committee be referred to the Superintendant of finance to take order" (*JCC*, XXIII, 834).

5. Von Steuben's claim, although he repeatedly petitioned Congress during the remaining six years of government under the Articles of Confederation, was not settled by the Continental Congress. In 1789, just before the expiration of the Congress, Charles Thomson, its secretary, wrote the following as an introduction to the papers Congress had on file relating to Baron von Steuben: "These papers were collected from different files by Comee. on meml. of Baron Steuben. The report not being acted on they are preserved together in case it should again be brought into view by the future government" (Papers of the Continental Congress, National Archives).

Continental Congress
Report on the Suspension of Acts Relating to State Militia

[Philadelphia] December 31, 1782

The Committee [1] to whom was referred the letter of the 24th. instant from the Secretary at War with the inclosure from the Commander in Chief [2] *report that* [3] *it will be expedient to suspend* the operation of the resolution of the   [4] so far as relates to the lines of New Hampshire Rhode Island & New Jersey be suspended [5] till the first day of March next [6] and also as to the Pennsylvania Line so far as to retain in Service only the Officers necessary to the Compleating of three Regiments.

AD, Papers of the Continental Congress, National Archives.
    1. The committee consisted of Thomas FitzSimons, James Madison, and H.
    2. The report from the Secretary at War, Benjamin Lincoln, is in the Papers of the Continental Congress, National Archives. On December 24, 1782, George Washington informed Lincoln that the two regiments of New Jersey and New Hampshire and the regiment of Rhode Island should remain "entire Corps untill the States to which they respectively belonged should . . . determine whether they would recruit these Corps to the number required by Congress or not." Washington's letter is printed in *GW*, XXV, 460–61.
    3. A different version of the first part of the report is published in the *Journals* of the Continental Congress. It reads: "On the report of a committee . . . to whom were referred letters of the 22 and 24 from the Secretary at War: Resolved, That . . ." (*JCC*, XXIII, 837).
    4. H left a blank space at this point in the MS. The date given in the published report is "7th of August last" (*JCC*, XXIII, 837).
    On August 7, 1782, Congress had requested Army officers to retire voluntarily in accordance with a program to go into effect on January 1, 1783 (*JCC*, XXII, 451–55).
    5. The words "be suspended" are not in the handwriting of H.
    6. The remainder of the sentence is not in the handwriting of H.

Continental Congress
Report on Brigadier Generals James Clinton and Edward Hand

[Philadelphia] December 31, 1782

The Committee[1] to whom was referred the letter from the Secretary at War of the 22 instant[2] report that it will be adviseable to promote B General Clinton to the rank of Major General and to continue Brigadier General Hand in the office of Adjutant General.[3]

AD, Papers of the Continental Congress, National Archives.
    1. The committee was composed of Thomas FitzSimons, James Madison, and H.
    2. The Secretary at War's letter, dated December 22, 1782, in which he discussed the appointment of brigadier generals, the promotion of Clinton, and the reappointment of Hand, is printed in *JCC*, XXIII, 836.
    3. The endorsement reads: "Brigr Genl Hand Continud in the Office of Adjt Genl. Decr. 31st. 1782. The rest recommitted."

To Elizabeth Hamilton

[1782]

Engrossed by our own immediate concerns, I omitted telling you of a disagreeable piece of intelligence I have received from a gentleman of Georgia. He tells me of the death of my brother Levine.[1] You know the circumstances that abate my distress, yet my heart acknowledges the rights of a brother. He dies rich, but has disposed of the bulk of his fortune to strangers. I am told he has left me a legacy. I did not inquire how much. When you have occasion for money you can draw upon Messrs. Stewart & ⟨Totten⟩,[2] Philadelphia. They owe me upwards of an hundred pounds.

Hamilton, *Intimate Life*, 4.
1. Peter Lavien, H's half-brother. See H to Major General Nathanael Greene, October 12, 1782.
2. The firm of Stewart and Totten was located in Philadelphia. Although the firm is listed on the tax rolls for 1782 in the *Pennsylvania Archives* (3rd ser. XVI, 295, 521), no information is given concerning the firm's activities. The proprietors were Robert Totten, and either James Stewart (*ibid.*, XVI, 286) or Alexander Stewart (*ibid.*, XVI, 295).

1 7 8 3

To George Clinton

Sir,

As the Legislature will shortly meet I take the liberty to mention to Your Excellency, that it appears to me of Great importance, they should take up the affair of Vermont on the idea of a *compromise* with Massachusetts and New Hampshire and propose to those States a meeting of Commissioners for that purpose.[1] I have little hope that we shall ever be able to engage Congress to act with decision upon the matter or that our State will ever recover any part of the revolted territory but upon a plan that will interest the two States I have mentioned, or at least one of them. If you agree with Massachusetts and New Hampshire, or with one of them, the agreement will I think meet with support here.

A peace may shortly take place; this makes it of great importance to our pretensions that the affair should be speedily determined.

I have the honor to be yr. Excellencys Most Obed. & hm. Serv.

A. Hamilton.

Walton, *Records of Vermont*, III, 288–89.

1. See "Motion on Vermont," December 5, 1782, H and William Floyd to Clinton, December 9, 1782, and H to John Laurence, December 12, 1782.

Continental Congress Resolution on the Services of Comte de Rochambeau [1]

[Philadelphia, January 1, 1783]

That the President make the acknowlegements of Congress in a particular manner to His Excellency The Count De Rochambeau and signify to him the high sense they entertain of the distinguished talents displayed by him with so much advantage to these states in the most important conjunctures as well as of the strict and exemplary discipline which have been uniformly conspicuous in the troops under his command and which have deservedly acquired the admiration and Esteem of the citizens of these states by whom his signal services and the delicate attention at all times paid to their private rights will ever be held in affectionate remembrance.

AD, Papers of the Continental Congress, National Archives.
1. Jean Baptiste Donatien de Vimeur, Comte de Rochambeau, and the French troops under his command left the United States on December 29, 1782. On receipt of a letter from the Secretary for Foreign Affairs informing Congress of the departure of the French army and the intention of the French King "to direct them to return whenever an object should offer, in which they might effectually co-operate with the troops of the United States," a resolution was introduced expressing appreciation for the French contribution to American victory. H's resolution concerning Rochambeau comprised the last paragraph of the congressional resolution thanking the French (see *JCC*, XXIV, 1–2).

Continental Congress
Report on the Promotion of Colonels

[Philadelphia] January 7, 1783

The Committee to whom was recommitted the letter of the 22d. of December from the Secretary at War submit the following resolution: [1]

Resolved that Cols John Greaton and Rufus Putnam of the Massachusettes line [and] Col Elias Dayton of the Jersey line be promoted to the rank of Brigadier Generals,[2] agreeably to the resolution of Congress of the 12 Decr 1782.[3]

AD, Papers of the Continental Congress, National Archives.
1. In the *Journals* of the Congress the following paragraph precedes the first sentence of the draft: "On the report of a committee, consisting of Mr. (Thomas) Fitzismmons, Mr. (James) Madison, and Mr. (Alexander) Hamilton, to whom was referred a report from the Secretary at War: . . ." (*JCC*, XXIV, 38).
The letter from the Secretary at War is printed in *JCC*, XXIII, 836.
2. The remaining words of this sentence are not in the writing of H.
3. The congressional resolve of December 12, 1782, provides that "whensoever it shall be deemed necessary for the command of troops in service, to appoint brigadiers in any state or states, where the number of troops in the field are sufficient to form one or more brigades, the brigadiers shall be ap-

pointed from the senior colonels or lieutenant colonels commandant in the lines of such states . . ." (*JCC*, XXIII, 790–91).

The report, according to the endorsement, was "Acted on Jany. 7th, 1783."

To Elizabeth Hamilton

[Philadelphia, January 8, 1783]

⟨The post my⟩ angel has met with some interruption (I suppose by the river being impassable) which deprives me of the pleasure of hearing from you. I am inexpressibly anxious to learn you have began your journey. I write this for fear of the worst, but I should be miserable if I thought it would find you at Albany. If by any misapprehension you should still be there I entreat you lose not a moment in coming to me. I have borne your absence with patience 'till abo⟨ut⟩ a week since, but the period we fixed for our reunion being come I can no longer reconcile my self ⟨to it.⟩ Every hour in the day I feel a severe pang on this account and half my nights are sleepless. Come my charmer and relieve me. Bring my darling boy to my bosom.

Adieu Heaven bless you & speedily restore you to yr. fond husband   A H

Jany 8 1783

ALS, Mr. George T. Bowdoin, New York City.

Continental Congress
Remarks on the Valuation of Lands

[Philadelphia, January 8, 1783]

On the report [1] for valuing the land conformably to the rule laid down in the fœderal articles, the delegates from Connecticut contended for postponing the subject during the war, alledging the impediments arising from the possession of N. Y., &c. by the enemy; but apprehending (as was supposed) that the flourishing state of Connecticut compared with the Southern States, would render a valuation at this crisis unfavorable to the former. Others, particularly Mr. Hamilton and Mr. Madison, were of opinion that the rule of the confederation [2] was a chimerical one since if the intervention of the individual states were employed their interests would give a biass to their judgments, or that at least suspicions of such biass wd prevail; and without their intervention, it could not be executed but at an expense, delay & uncertainty which were inadmissible; that it would perhaps be therefore preferable to represent these difficulties to the States & recommend an exchange of this rule of dividing the public burdens for one more simple easy & equal.

"Notes of Debates in the Continental Congress," MS, James Madison Papers, Library of Congress.

1. James Madison recorded on November 20, 1782, that a committee was appointed to consider the best mode "of obtaining a valuation of the land within the several States, as the Article of Confederation directs" ("Notes of Debates in the Continental Congress," MS, James Madison Papers, Library of Congress). The report of this committee, which is not given in the *Journals* of the Congress, was referred to a grand committee consisting of a member from each state. The debate printed above was in this committee.

The report of the committee, which required the states to evaluate their lands and submit to Congress the valuations, is printed in the *Journals* under date of February 17, 1783 (*JCC*, XXIV, 133–37). See "Motion on Evaluation of State Lands for Carrying into Effect Article 8 of the Articles of Confederation," February 6, 1783. For the different versions of the report considered by Congress, see H to George Clinton, February 24, 1783.

2. The reference is to Article 8 of the Articles of Confederation which provided that expenses of the Confederation should be defrayed from funds supplied by the several states. The quota of each was to be based on the value of lands within the state.

Continental Congress
Report on the Quartermaster Department

[Philadelphia] January 9, 1783

The Committee[1] to whom was referred the letter from the Qr. Mr. General of the 4th. of December [2] last have conferred with him find that there are several omissions in the plan adopted by Congress the 23d. of October last for regulating the Qr. Mrs. department [3] and are of opinion that some of the salaries of particular officers therein are reduced too low.

They therefore recommend that the resolutions of the aforesaid 23d. of October be repealed that the following plan [4] be substituted in their place.

AD, Papers of the Continental Congress, National Archives.
  1. The committee consisted of Thomas Mifflin, Samuel Osgood, and H.
  2. This letter, which was written by Colonel Timothy Pickering and is in his handwriting, is in the Papers of the Continental Congress, National Archives.
  3. The plan of October 23, 1782, is printed in *JCC*, XXIII, 682–86.
  4. In *JCHW*, II, 225, the plan is attributed to H; but the undated plan, which is in the Papers of the Continental Congress, National Archives, is in the writing of Pickering.
  According to the endorsement of the report, it was "Read Jany 9. 1783" and on January 13, "Referred to the Secy. at War to report. Thursday next assigned for the consideration." There is no record in the *Journals* that it was considered then or subsequently.

To George Clinton

Philda. [January 12] 1783 [1]

Sir,

I am honored with your excellency's letter of the 29th. Decr. I have received an order from Col. Hay on Mr. Sands, which I have no doubt will shortly be paid.[2] I have felt no inconvenience from not having the money sooner.

Since my last to you, we have received no further accounts from Europe, so that we remain in the same uncertainty with respect to the negotiations for peace. Wether it will take place or not, is a problem of difficult solution. The duplicity and unsteadiness for which Lord Shelburne [3] is remarkable will not justify any confidence in his intentions; and the variety of interests to be conciliated in a treaty of peace, with the best intentions on all sides must render it a work of difficulty. I suspect, too, the Spaniards and Dutch will have large demands.

We have now here a deputation from the army, and feel a mortification of a total disability to comply with their just expectations.[4] If, however, the matter is taken up in a proper manner, I think their application may be turned to a good account. Every day proves more & more the insufficiency of the confederation. The proselytes to this opinion are increasing fast, and many of the most sensible men acknowledge the wisdom of the measure recommended by your legislature at their last sitting.[5] Various circumstances conspire at this time to incline to the adoption of it, and I am not without hope it may ere long take place. But I am far from being sanguine.

We are deliberating on some mode for carrying that article of the confederation into execution, which respects the valuation of lands to ascertain the quotas of the several states. None has yet been proposed, that appears to me eligible. I confess I dislike the principle altogether, but we are tied down by the Confederation.

The affairs of the grants have been no further touched since the resolutions transmitted to you.[6] It is a business in which nobody cares to act with decision. As intimated before, I must doubt the perseverance of Congress, if military coercion should become necessary. I am clear the only chance the legislature have for recovering any part of the revolted territory is by a compromise with N. Hampshire, and this compromise must originate between the states themselves. I hope the legislature will revise the late act for confirming the possessions of those who hold lands in that country.[7] I am certain there are doubts upon the subject, and it were much to be wished such doubts did not exist. The present dissatisfaction of the army is much opposed to any experiment of force in a service where scruples of interest or prejudice may operate.

I am, &c.   A. Hamilton

Sparks Transcripts, Harvard College Library.
    1. Sparks incorrectly dated this letter July 12, 1783.
    2. Colonel Udny Hay was state agent of New York. Among his many duties was to serve as paymaster of the state. Comfort Sands, formerly the auditor general of New York, was in 1783 contractor for supplying the Army officers in the district of West Point.
    3. Following Rockingham's death on July 1, 1782, Shelburne had become British Prime Minister.
    4. The Army deputation consisted of Major General Alexander McDougall and Colonels Matthias Ogden and John Brooks. On January 6, 1783, these officers presented to Congress a memorial on behalf of the Army.
    5. In July, 1782, the Senate and Assembly of New York adopted concurrent resolutions which attributed American difficulties in the prosecution of the war to defects in the Articles of Confederation. These resolutions further recommended a "Convention of the States . . . specially authorized to revise and amend the Confederation." See "Resolution of the New York Legislature Calling for a Convention of the States to Revise and Amend the Articles of Confederation," July 20, 1782.
    6. In their letter to George Clinton of December 9, 1782, H and William Floyd enclosed the congressional resolutions on Vermont dated December 5, 1782.
    7. For information on the legislation confirming land grants made by Vermont, see H and Floyd to Clinton, December 9, 1782.

Continental Congress
Report on a Motion of the Rhode Island Delegate
on the Communication of Information to His State

[Philadelphia] January 13, 1783 [1]

The Committee to whom was referred the motion of Mr. Arnold and those subsequent thereupon [2] report that in their opinion it would be improper for Congress to concur in the object of that motion, as with respect to a part of the extracts specified relating merely to the general growing political importance of these states, the injunction of secrecy being taken off, any member who inclines to communicate them to his state may take copies of them [and more Especially as Mr. Howel [3] was furnished with compleat Copies of Letters from which particular detached sentences are now requested]; [4] and with respect to such extracts as relate to the subject of foreign loans, they are already within the purview of the resolution of the [20 Decr.] last directing the secretary for foreign affairs to transmit to the state of Rhode Island an authenticated state of the applications for foreign loans and the result; that the same observation applies to that part of the motion which relates generally to the transmission of the letters from our foreign ministers on the subject of loans not under the injunction of secrecy, with this additional consideration that such of those letters as would in fact throw light upon the subject comprehend many delicate transactions which it is the duty of Congress at the present juncture to conceal.

The Committee are not withstanding of opinion that to obviate misrepresentation it will be adviseable to transmit to the executive of the state of Rhode Island a copy of Mr. Arnolds motion and the proceedings thereupon, with a request that precautions may be taken to prevent their appearing in the public prints. [5]

AD, Papers of the Continental Congress, National Archives.

1. According to the endorsement, this report was delivered on January 13, 1783. It is printed in the *Journals* under January 14, the date on which it was passed (*JCC*, XXIV, 45–46).

2. On December 3, 1782, Jonathan Arnold of Rhode Island moved that the Secretary for Foreign Affairs be directed to send to the governor of Rhode Island copies of extracts of certain letters received from Europe. See *JCC*, XXIV, 32–34. Arnold's purpose was to show that the United States would have

no trouble in securing foreign loans. After several proposals for amending Arnold's motion had been made, H moved that the original motion and motions to amend it be referred to a committee. H's motion was adopted; and a committee, consisting of H, John Taylor Gilman, and Oliver Ellsworth, was appointed.

3. See "Motion Censuring David Howell," December 7, 1782, note 4.

4. The bracketed words are not in the writing of H.

5. The endorsement states that after this report was read on January 13 it was rejected by a vote of 4 ayes to 5 noes. But on January 14, "on motion of Mr Arnold second[ed] by Mr. [John] Collins [of Rhode Island] who were yesterday both in the negative this report was reconsidered. And being amended passed." In *JCC*, XXIV, 46, it is stated that Congress agreed to the report, but no amendments are given.

Continental Congress
Report on Army Memorial

[Philadelphia] January 22, 1783 [1]

The Grand Committee having considered the contents of the Memorial presented by the army [2] find that they comprehend five different articles.

1st.   Present pay

2dly.   A settlement of accounts of the arrearages of pay and security for what is due.

3dly.   A commutation of the half pay allowed by different resolutions of Congress for an equivalent in gross.

4thly. A settlement of the accounts of deficiences of rations and compensation.

5thly. A settlement of the accounts of deficiencies of Cloathing and compensation.

[Resolved] [3] as to the first that the Superintendant of Finance be directed conformable to the measures already taken for that purpose [4] as soon as the state of the public finances will permit to make such payment and in such manner as he shall think proper 'till the further order of Congress.

[Resolved] With respect to the second article so far as relates to the settlement of accounts [That the several States be called upon to compleat without delay the Settlements with their respective Lines of the Army up to the first day of August 1780 [5] and] that the Superintendant of Finance be directed to take such measures as shall appear to him most proper for effecting the settlement from that Period.

As to what relates to the providing of security for what shall be found due on such settlement:

[Resolved] that the troops of the United States in common with all the creditors of the same have an undoubted right to expect such security; and that Congress will make every effort in their power to obtain from the respective states substantial funds adequate to the object of funding the whole debt of the United States and will enter upon an immediate and full consideration of the nature of such funds and the most likely mode of obtaining them.

With respect to the 3d article, [resolved that it be left] to the option of all officers entitled to half pay either to preserve their claim to that provision as it now stands by the several resolutions upon that subject, or to accept in lieu thereof   6 years full pay to be paid to them in one year after the conclusion of the war in money, or placed upon good funded security bearing an annual interest of six per Cent; provided that the allowance to widows and orphans of such officers as have died or been killed or may die or be killed in the service during the war shall remain as established by the resolution of the   .7

With respect to the 4th and fifth articles the Committee beg leave to delay their report until they have obtained more precise information than they now possess upon the subject.8

AD, Papers of the Continental Congress, National Archives.

1. The endorsement reads: "Report of grand Comee delivered Jany 22. 1783, read, to be considered 23. 23 debated; postponed till 24." The report is printed in *JCC*, XXIV, 93–96, under date of January 25, 1782.

2. On January 6, 1783, Major General Alexander McDougall and Colonels Matthias Ogden and John Brooks, on behalf of the Army, presented a memorial to Congress for overdue pay and other claims. A committee was appointed to meet the Army deputation, and on January 13 the meeting took place. As a result of the conference, H, James Madison, and John Rutledge were made a subcommittee to report, after consulting with the Superintendent of Finance, on the Army memorial.

3. The bracketed words in this document are not in H's writing.

4. The phrase "conformable to the measures already taken for that purpose," according to Madison, was "meant to shew that the payment to the army did not originate in the Memol . . ." ("Notes of Debates in the Continental Congress," MS, James Madison Papers, Library of Congress).

5. The report originally stated "to the 31 December 1780." A motion to substitute "the first day of August" for "the thirty-first day of December" was passed in the affirmative.

For an explanation of the importance of this change in dates, see "Notes of Debates in the Continental Congress," MS, James Madison Papers, Library of Congress. For a challenge to the accuracy of Madison's account of H's part in the controversy, see Hamilton, *History*, II, 358.

6. H here wrote "at the conclusion of the war six years full pay," but crossed it out. The printed report (*JCC*, XXIV, 95) reads: "or to accept in lieu ~~six~~ years full pay. . . ." According to James Madison, "a motion was made by Mr. Hamilton, to fill the blank with 'six' . . . in conformity to tables of Dr. Price, estimating the officers on the average of good lives" ("Notes of Debates in the Continental Congress," MS, James Madison Papers, Library of Congress).

7. H at this point left a blank space. The same blank space appears in the report as printed in *JCC*, XXIV, 95. The resolutions providing pensions for widows and orphans were passed August 17, 1779 (*JCC*, XIV, 973–74) and August 24, 1780 (*JCC*, XVII, 773).

8. The first part of the report was adopted on January 25, but the last two paragraphs, according to the endorsement, were referred to "Mr. [Samuel] Osgood, Mr. [Thomas] Fitzsimmons, Mr. [John Lewis] Gervais [of South Carolina], Mr. [Alexander] Hamilton and Mr. [James] Wilson [of Pennsylvania]."

Continental Congress
Remarks on Raising Funds for the United States

[Philadelphia, January 27, 1783]

Mr. Hamilton went extensively into the subject;[1] the sum of it was as follows: he observed that funds considered as permanent sources of revenue were of two kinds: 1st. Such as wd. extend generally & uniformly throughout the U.S., & wd. be collected under the authority of Congs. 2dly., such as might be established separately within each State, & might consist of any objects which were chosen by the States, and which might be collected either under the authority of the States or of Congs. Funds of the 1st. kind he contended were preferable; as being 1st., more simple, the difficulties attending the mode of fixing the quotas laid down in the Confederation rendering it extremely complicated & in a manner insuperable; 2d, as being more certain; since the States according to the secd. plan wd. probably retain the collection of the revenue and a vicious system of collection prevailed generally throughout the U.S. a system by which the collectors were chosen by the people & made their offices more subservient to their popularity than to the public revenue; 3d. & as being more œconomical since the collection would be effected with fewer officers under the management of Congress, than under that of the States.

"Notes of Debates in the Continental Congress," MS, James Madison Papers, Library of Congress.

1. I.e., the manner of raising adequate and permanent funds for the Confederation.

Consistent with the "Report on the Army Memorial" of January 25, 1783, Congress on the same day resolved "to take into consideration the means of obtaining from the several states substantial funds, for funding the whole debt of the United States" (*JCC*, XXIV, 95). The problem was debated for several days. On January 27, after making some observations on the necessity of permanent and substantial funds for the Confederation, James Wilson recommended that it be resolved "That it is the opinion of Congress that complete justice cannot be done to the Creditors of the United States, nor the restoration of public credit be effected, nor the fuuture exigences of the war provided for, but by the establishment of *general* funds to be collected by Congress." Nathaniel Gorham of Massachusetts proposed that the latter part of Wilson's motion be amended to read "establishment of permanent and adequate funds to operate generally throughout the U. States" ("Notes of Debates in the Continental Congress," MS, James Madison Papers, Library of Congress). H's remarks followed Gorham's proposal.

Continental Congress
Remarks on the Collection of Funds by Officers of the United States

[Philadelphia, January 28, 1783]

Mr. Hamilton, in reply to Mr. Elseworth [1] dwelt long on the inefficacy of State funds.[2] He supposed too that greater obstacles would arise to the execution of the plan than to that of a general revenue. As an additional reason for the latter to be collected by officers under the appointment of Congress, he signified that as the energy of the fœderal Govt. was evidently short of the degree necessary for pervading & uniting the States it was expedient to introduce the influence of officers deriving their emoluments from & consequently interested in supporting the power of Congress.[3]

"Notes of Debates in the Continental Congress," MS, James Madison Papers, Library of Congress.

1. Oliver Ellsworth had proposed that the national debt be discharged by congressional requisitions on permanent funds raised by the states.

2. The debate of January 27, 1783, on establishing adequate permanent funds for the United States was continued on the next day. Ellsworth had objected to a proposition made by James Madison that Congress establish "permanent

& adequate funds to operate generally throughout the U. States" and that it be considered whether the funds should "be collected under the authority of Congress" ("Notes of Debates in the Continental Congress," MS, James Madison Papers, Library of Congress).

3. Madison wrote the following note concerning H's last statement:

"This remark was imprudent & injurious to the cause wch. it was meant to serve. This influence was the very source of jealousy which rendered the States averse to a revenue under the collection as well as appropriation of Congress. All the members of Congress who concurred in any degree with the States in this jealousy smiled at the disclosure. Mr. [Theodorick] Bland [of Virginia] and still more Mr. [Arthur] L[ee of Virginia] who were of this number took notice in private conversation that Mr. Hamilton had let out the secret." ("Notes of Debates in the Continental Congress," MS, James Madison Papers, Library of Congress.)

Continental Congress
Remarks on Plans for Paying the Public Debt

[Philadelphia, January 29, 1783]

Mr. Hamilton disliked every plan that made but partial provision for the public debts;[1] as an inconsistent & dishonorable departure from the declaration made by Congs. on that subject. He said the domestic Creditors would take the alarm at any distinctions unfavorable to their claims;[2] that they would withhold their influence from any such measures recommended by Congress; and that it must be principally from their influence on their respective legislatures that success could be expected to any application from Congs. for a general revenue.

"Notes of Debates in the Continental Congress," MS, James Madison Papers, Library of Congress.

1. Following a two-day debate on the necessity of establishing permanent funds for the United States (see the two preceding documents), John Rutledge on January 29, 1783, moved "That Congress be resolved into a committee of the whole, to consider of the most effectual means of restoring and supporting public credit . . ." (JCC, XXIV, 97). From that date until February 21, Congress intermittently resolved itself into a committee of the whole to consider ways of creating a permanent fund for the United States.

2. H is referring to a proposal by John Rutledge that Congress impose a five percent impost to continue twenty-five years for the exclusive purpose of paying the interest and principal on the money borrowed by the United States in Europe ("Notes of Debates in the Continental Congress," MS, James Madison Papers, Library of Congress).

Notes on a Plan for Providing for the Debts of the United States [1]

[Philadelphia, January–April, 1783]

Debts to be funded probably consist of

	Dollars		
Foreign debt	6000.000—	a 4 ₩ Ct —	240000
Army debt for pay—6000.000			
Commutation of			
half pay 4000.000	10000.000—	a 6 ₩ Ct . .	600000
Domestic liquidated debt	12000.000—	a do —	720000
Unliquidated debt suppose	12000.000—	a do —	720.000
	40000 000		2280 000
			1560.000

to form an aggregate fund for the army debt foreign debt & domestic liqui- dated debt

Duty on Imports at 5 ₩ Ct ad valorem supposing the amount of imports to be 18000.000		900.000
Salt duty at ⅛ of a dollar ₩ bushel estimating consumption at 1000.000		125.000—
do. on Wine ⁶⁄₁₀ ₩ Gall—Cons:	1000.000 . . .	66.666⅔
Rum &c. — ³⁄₁₀ do. .	1500.000 . . .	50.000—
Tea fine— ⁶⁄₁₀ ₩ ld. .	200.000 . . .	13.333⅔
Bohea— ³⁄₁₀ ₩ do. .	700.000 . . .	23.333⅓
Sugar . ⅔ of a doll per civ. . .	75.000 Civ. .	50.000
		1228.333
deduct for charge of collection } smuggling &c. . . . . }		61.416⅔
	Nett	1166 917
Land tax on Mr. Morris' plan		480.000
		1646.917

For the unliquidated debt a tax on houses on one of the two following plans. For every house half a dollar & for every window above six to Eighteen the additional sum of ⅓ of a dollar ₩ Window & for every window above Eighteen to thirty ⅙ of a dollar, for every window above Thirty ¼ of a dollar ₩ window.

The preceding mode would be most simple & definite and in the view of revenue preferable but in point of equality it would not be as eligible as the following.

Every dwelling house to pay the general rate of half a dollar ₩ house and the particular rate of 2½ ₩ Cent on the excess of the rent above twenty dollars ₩ annum.

When the house is rented the calculation should be made on the actual rent when in the occupancy of the owner on an appraised rent—the appraisement to be made once in seven years by Commissioners under oath.

In towns the lot and its appurtenances to be comprehended with the house—in the country the outhouses orchard & garden & these to be excluded from the land tax.

According to the idea of land quotas—the land & house taxes must be credited to the respective states.

The whole of these revenues to be collected under the authority of Congress.

ADf, James Madison Papers, Library of Congress.

1. The exact purpose for which H prepared these notes cannot be determined. They were presumably intended to be incorporated in a plan which he proposed to submit to the Continental Congress for redeeming the debt of the United States. From January to April, 1783, H was a member of several committees appointed to suggest means for providing for the continental debt. Although these notes bear little resemblance to the plan drafted by James Madison and adopted by the Continental Congress on April 18, 1783, they probably were suggested to the committee which recommended that plan to the Continental Congress. This presumption is strengthened by the fact that they are in the James Madison Papers, Library of Congress.

Continental Congress
First Motion on Evaluation of State Lands for Carrying into Effect Article 8 of the Articles of Confederation

[Philadelphia, February 6, 1783] [1]

Resolved, That in order to enable Congress to form an eventual plan towards carrying into execution the 8th. article of confederation the several States be required to pass laws for forming or dividing their respective states into such districts as they judge most convenient for procuring an accurate valuation of the lands and of the buildings and improvements thereon, & to appoint Commissioners in each district to return to them the quantity of land in such district, the quantity surveyed, the quantity in actual occupation, the general quality of the land, the number and kind of buildings, the average rate at which lands under improvement and lands unimproved are usually sold in such district; and also an account of the males between 16 & 60, distinguishing the whites from the blacks, within such district, and that the executive of each state transmit such returns to Congress on or before the 1st of January 1784.[2]

AD, Papers of the Continental Congress, National Archives.

1. The motion is undated. It is printed in a note in *JCC*, XXIV, 114, under date of February 6, 1783.

2. The constant but unsuccessful attempt of Congress to secure funds led to a demand that the states be ordered to comply with Article 8 of the Articles of Confederation which stipulated that Confederation expenses should be ap-

portioned among the states on the basis of land values (see "Remarks on the Valuation of Lands," January 8, 1783). On January 13, 1783, a grand committee, of which H was a member, was appointed to report on the most effectual way of estimating the land values in the various states. In a debate on the subject on January 31, H said that he ". . . wished the valuation to be taken up in order that its impracticability & futility might become manifest" ("Notes of Debates in the Continental Congress," MS, James Madison Papers, Library of Congress). On February 6, the committee recommended that the states pass laws providing for an evaluation of their lands and that the valuations be transmitted to Congress by January 1, 1784, so that requisitions "as shall be agreeable to the Articles of Confederation" might be made upon the states (*JCC*, XXIV, 113).

H's motion differed from the committee report in that it recommended the valuations be used not as the basis for imposition of an immediate requisition but to enable Congress to form an eventual plan.

For the changes in the report before its adoption on February 17, 1783, see H to George Clinton, February 24, 1783.

Continental Congress
Second Motion on Evaluation of State Lands for Carrying into Effect Article 8 of the Articles of Confederation [1]

[Philadelphia] February 6, 1783

Whereas the carrying into execution the 8th article of the confederation relative to a valuation of land for ascertaining the quotas of each state towards the general expence in a manner consistent with justice to all the members of the Union and with such accuracy as the importance of the subject demands will necessarily be attended with very considerable expence to which the present state of the public finances is inadequate; and whereas in a matter so fundamental in the Confederation, it is essential to the harmony and welfare of the United States that the said article should be carried into effect with great care circumspection and impartiality, and a short delay will be much less pernicious than a defective execution.

Therefore Resolved that Congress are under a necessity of deferring the attempt to a period when the situation of the finances of the United States will admit of the necessary expence for effecting the object with as much precision and equity as possible, and that they will then proceed to such valuation by Commissioners appointed by them and acting under their authority, upon principles uniform throughout the United States.

Resolved that when this valuation is complete Congress will finally adjust the accounts of the United States with the states separately agreeable to that standard making equitable abatements to such states as have been more immediate sufferers by the war; and in the mean time will adhere in the temporary adjustment of those accounts to the proportions established from time to time by the several requisitions of Congress.

Resolved, for the information of Congress in forming an eventual plan that those states which have already made valuations of their lands respectively be requested to transmit to Congress the amount of such valuations with an explanation of the principles on which they have been made.[2]

AD, Papers of the Continental Congress, National Archives.

1. This was the second of two motions on this date relating to the manner of carrying into effect Article 8 of the Articles of Confederation. For an explanation of the committee report for which these motions were offered as a substitute see note 2 to the preceding document.

In the *Journals* the paragraph preceding the motion reads: "A motion was made by Mr. (Alexander) Hamilton, seconded by Mr. (Thomas) Fitzsimmons, to postpone the resolution before the house and to take into consideration the following motion" (*JCC*, XXIV, 114).

2. H's motion was defeated, and the resolution for which his motion was intended as a substitute "was debated and revised and on February 11 referred to another committee" (*JCC*, XXIV, 114).

Continental Congress
Report on the Memorial of Francis Cazeau [1]

[Philadelphia] February 6, 1783

The Committee [2] to whom was referred the Memorial from Mr. De Cazeau report:

That it appears by Mr. Cazeaus representation that he was possessed of large property in Canada; that he took an early and decided part in favour of the American revolution; rendered services to our army in that Country by supplies of provisions & otherwise which were productive of immediate loss to him and attempted to render still greater services in which he was unsuccessful; that his conduct and principles drew upon him the resentment of the British government which operated in the sequestration of all his property, in the imprisonment of himself and son and in other outrages, that he made his escape from prison, and after encountering many dangers and hardships, has arrived among us, destitute of every thing to throw himself upon the justice and generosity of Congress

That it appears by other respectable testimony that Mr. Cazeau was a man of influence and property in Canada and has been ruined by his attachment to the American cause.

The Committee however are upon the whole of opinion, that as it is impossible now to judge of the eventual circumstances of Mr. Cazeau or of the precise extent of his services and sacrifices, Congress ought at present to take up the General consideration of his case but that policy and justice require as far as the situation of public affairs will permit some relief to his distress, they therefore advise that the Superintendant of Finance be directed to advance him One thousand dollars on acct.

AD, Papers of the Continental Congress, National Archives.

1. Francis Cazeau was a Montreal merchant, who, according to his memorial, sold provisions to the American troops in 1775 and 1777. He argued that the money paid him had depreciated in value and that because he had assisted the Americans he had been imprisoned by Canadian officials. He asked Congress to compensate him for his losses.

2. The endorsement states that the report was "referred to the Superint. of finance to take Order." The Superintendent did not immediately comply with the congressional resolution. On March 18, 1784, Cazeau's memorial was again the subject of a congressional resolution which awarded him part of the compensation for which he asked. The report, however, was not acted on by the Superintendent of Finance (*JCC*, XXVII, 398, 410). On April 30, 1784, Cadwalader Morris wrote to Edward Hand that "Poor Cazeau is very much distressed at the hesitation of the Comptroller and Treasurer to comply with the Resolution of Congress on his Memorial . . ." (Burnett, *Letters*, VII, 508).

Continental Congress
Motion on the Establishment of Permanent Funds

[Philadelphia, February 12, 1783] [1]

That it is the Opinion of Congress that complete justice cannot be done to the Creditors of the United States nor the restoration of public Credit be effected; nor the future exigencies of the war provided for, but by the establishment of [permanent & adequate funds to operate generally throughout the united States, to be collected by Congress].[2]

AD, Papers of the Continental Congress, National Archives.

1. H's motion is undated. Although not submitted to Congress, H's motion probably was intended for introduction on February 12, the date on which James Madison (see note 2) made a similar motion.

2. The bracketed material is not in the writing of H. It was substituted for the following phrase, in the writing of H: "of general funds to be collected by Congress and appropriated by Congress." This phrase was crossed out.

On February 12, Congress considered a proposition, in the writing of James Madison, reported by a committee of the whole. It reads:

"That it is the opinion of Congress that the establishment of permanent and adequate funds on taxes or duties, which shall operate generally and on the whole in just proportion throughout the United States, ~~and to be collected under the authority of the U.S. in Congress assembled~~ are indispensably necessary towards doing complete justice to the public creditors, for restoring public credit, and for providing for the future exigencies of the war." (*JCC*, XXIV, 126-27.)

For an account of the debate on this proposition in the committee of the whole, see Madison's "Notes of Debates in the Continental Congress," MS, James Madison Papers, Library of Congress.

H's motion was not submitted to Congress, for the rejection of Madison's similar proposal that taxes be collected by Congress made it apparent that it would be rejected.

To George Washington

[Philadelphia, February 13, 1783] [1]

Sir

Flattering myself that your knowlege of me will induce you to receive the observations I mak⟨e⟩ [2] as dictated by a regard to the public good, I take the liber⟨ty⟩ to suggest to you my ideas on some matters of delicacy and importance. I view the present juncture as a very interesting one. I need not observe how far the temper and situation of the army make it so. The stat⟨e⟩ of our finances was perhaps never more critical. I am under injunctions which will not permit me to disclo⟨se⟩ some facts that would at once demonstrate this posi⟨tion,⟩ but I think it probable you will be possessed of the⟨m⟩ through another channel. It is however certain that there has scarcely been a period of the revolution which called more for wisdom and decision in Congress. Unf⟨or⟩tunately for us we are a body not governed by reason ⟨or⟩ foresight but by circumstances. It is probable we shall ⟨not⟩ take the proper measures, and if we do not a few ⟨months⟩ may open an embarrassing scene. This will be the ⟨case⟩ whether we have peace or a continuance of the war.

If the war continues it would seem th⟨at⟩ the army must in June subsist itself *to defend the* ⟨country;⟩ if peace should take place it *will* subsist itself to pr⟨ocure⟩ *justice to itself.* It appears to be a prevailing opini⟨on in⟩ the army that the disposition to recompence their s⟨ervices⟩ will cease with the necessity for them, and that if they ⟨once⟩ lay down their arms, they will part with the means of ob⟨taining⟩ [3] justice. It is to be lamented that appearances aff⟨ord⟩ too much ground for their distrust.

It becomes a serious inquiry what will be the true line of policy. The claims of the army urged with moderation, but with firmness, may operate on those weak minds which are influenced by their apprehensions more than their judgments; so as to produce a concurrence in the measures which the exigencies of affairs demand. They may add weight to the applications of Congress to the several states. So far an useful turn may be given to them. But the difficulty will be to keep a *complaining* and *suffering army* within the bounds of moderation.

This Your Excellency's influence must effect. In order to it, it will be adviseable not to discountenance their endeavours to procure redress, but rather by the intervention of confidential and prudent persons, *to take the direction of them.* This however must not appear: it is of moment to the public tranquillity that Your Excellency should preserve the confidence of the army without losing that of the people. This will enable you in case of extremity to guide the torrent, and bring order perhaps even good, out of confusion. 'Tis a part that requires address; but 'tis one which your own situation as well as the welfare of the community points out.

I will not conceal from Your Excellency a truth which it is necessary you should know. An idea is propagated in the army that delicacy carried to an extreme prevents your espousing its interests with sufficient warmth. The falsehood of this opinion no one can be better acquainted with than myself; but it is not the less mischievous for being false. Its tendency is to impair that influence, which you may exert with advantage, should any commotions unhappily ensue, to moderate the pretensions of the army and make their conduct correspond with their duty.

The great *desideratum* at present is the establishment of general funds, which alone can do justice to the Creditors of the United

States (of whom the army forms the most meritorious class), restore public credit and supply the future wants of government. This is the object of all men of sense; in this the influence of the army, properly directed, may cooperate.

The intimations I have thrown out will suffice to give Your Excellency a proper conception of my sentiments. You will judge of their reasonableness or fallacy; but I persuade myself you will do justice to my motives.

I have the honor to be With great respect   Your Excellencys Most Obedt servt.   Alex Hamilton

General Knox has the confidence of the army & is a man of sense. I think he may be safely made use of. Situated as I am Your Excellency will feel the confidential nature of these observations.

Philadelphia
Feby. 13th, 1783
His Excellency General Washington

ALS, George Washington Papers, Library of Congress; ADf, MS Division, New York Public Library. H made minor changes in wording when he copied the receiver's copy from the draft.
    1. H endorsed the draft "Feby 13th 1783." The receiver's copy in the Hamilton Papers was first dated "Feb 13th." A "7," probably in the writing of J. C. Hamilton, is written over the number "13." Washington endorsed the receiver's copy "Feby 1783." *JCHW*, I, 327, and *HCLW*, IX, 310, dated this letter February 7.
    2. Material in broken brackets is taken from the draft.
    3. In the draft the word "obtaining" is crossed out and "securing" substituted. It is evident, however, from the letters which are still visible that the word "obtaining" is used in the finished copy.

To George Clinton

Philadelphia, Feb'y 14th, 1783.

Sir,

In a letter which I wrote lately to General Schuyler,[1] I informed him of the import of the answer from Vermont, and what had been done with it in Congress.[2] The Committee to whom it was referred have not yet reported; but I have little expectation of decision.

Congress have been for some time employed on matters of the 1st. importance, devising a plan for carrying the 8th. Article of the

Confederation into execution, and for funding all the debts of the United States. General principles with respect to the 1st. object have been agreed upon, and are referred to a Committee to be digested into form. The plan is crude, and will be opposed in its last stage, but perhaps it will be adopted by a majority. With respect to funds we have made little progress, and from the turn of the debates, I have not sanguine hopes of proper measures. Whenever any thing has been matured it will be communicated to the State.

I congratulate your Excellency on the strong prospect of peace which the late speech of the British King [3] affords. I hope the conclusion of the war may not be the prelude of civil commotions of a more dangerous tendency. It is to be suspected the Army will not disband, till solid arrangements are made for doing it justice; and I fear these arrangements will not be made.

In this position of things it will be wise in the State of New York to consider what conduct will be most consistent with its safety and interest. I wish the Legislature would set apart a tract of territory, and make a liberal allowance to every officer and soldier of the Army at large who will become a citizen of the State. A step of this kind would not only be politic in the present posture of affairs, but would embrace important future consequences. It is the first wish of my heart that the Union may last; but feeble as the links are, what prudent man would rely upon it? Should a disunion take place, any person who will cast his eye upon the map will see how essential it is to our State to provide for its own security. I believe a large part of the Army would incline to sit down among us, and then all we shall have to do will be to govern well.

These are loose but important ideas. I wish they may occur with their full weight to those who have it in their power to turn them to account. At present I mean them merely for your Excellency's consideration.

I have the honor to be Yr. Excellency's most obedt. servt.

A. Hamilton

This letter by mistake has been delayed.

Sparks Transcripts, Harvard College Library.
1. H's letter to Philip Schuyler has not been found.
2. On December 5, 1782, after years of fruitless debate, Congress adopted a resolution denouncing the action of Vermont "as highly derogatory to the authority of the United States" and ordering that complete restitution should

be made to those whose property Vermont officials had seized. The United States, according to the resolution, would "take effectual measures to enforce a compliance" with its orders. See "Motion on Vermont," December 5, 1782. On February 4, 1783, Governor Thomas Chittenden replied that Vermont would not accept the orders of Congress.

3. The speech was George III's opening speech to the third session of the Fifteenth Parliament on December 5, 1782. Concerning peace with the American colonies the King said:

". . . I have pointed all my views and measures, as well in Europe as in North America, to an entire and cordial reconciliation with those colonies.

"Finding it indispensable to the attainment of this object, I did not hesitate to go the full length of the powers vested in me, and offered to declare them free and independent states, by an article to be inserted in the treaty of peace. Provisional articles are agreed upon, to take effect whenever terms of peace shall be finally settled with the court of France." (*The Parliamentary History of England* [London, 1814], XXIII, 206.)

From James Duane [1]

Newburgh [New York] 17th February 1783

Dear Sir

I am now on a Visit to the General from ⟨Kingston,⟩ [2] where the Legislature is convened. The British King's ⟨speech to⟩ his Parliament [3] and his Secretary's Letters to the Lord ⟨Mayor⟩ of London, [4] which we had the pleasure of meeting here afford us the fairest prospect of a speedy Peace. I have but one anxiety remaining and that respects a better Establishment of our General Government on a Basis that will secure the permanent Union of the States, and a punctual Payment of the publick Debts. I do not think our Legislature will be averse to a reasonable System. The Assembly have agreed to the Requisitions of Congress and to press for the Arrears of Taxes, and a Joint Committee of both Houses have taken Measures to compel the immediate production of the Accounts of all who have been intrusted with publick money. This last step became so necessary that I found no difficulty in getting it adopted. I woud even hazard an attempt to introduce an Intendant if I had proper Materials: but I am disappointed in not receiving the Maryland plan [5] which was promised me by Mr Wright and Mr Hemsley. [6] If possible I still wish you would forward their Act on this Subject and for the Collection of Taxes. The Example of a State may be adopted, when any Plan of my own might be rejected. There is such Confusion in the present Administration of our State Finances, and the Weight of our Debts is so burthensome, that a Remedy must be provided; and I apprehend the production of the publick accounts before alluded to will furnish us with sufficient Arguments to prove its necessity.

We act in want of the Report ⟨and of the⟩ Evidence and arguments in support of our territor⟨ial ri⟩ghts.[7] If as you proposed you have taken the trouble to copy it be so obliging as to transmit your Copy. Should your Leisure not have been sufficient for the undertaking be pleased to get it transcribed and forwarded. It is a Collection of great Importance to the State and if it should be lost I do not know who would submit to the Labour of a second Effort.

General Schuyler was sent for a week ago to pay the last duties to your Grandfather.[8] He wrote me the 10th. that there was no hopes of his surviving many days; but I learn that he was still living four days ago without the least prospect of Recovery.

From your known punctuality I take it for granted that you have written to me agreeably to your promise and that your Letters have miscarried. Any Communication while the Legislature are convened woud be peculiarly acceptable and probably useful.

Be pleased to present any respectful Compliments to Col. Floyd [9] to Mrs. Hamilton and Mr. and Mrs. Carter [10] and to the Gentlemen of our Family &c.

With the utmost Regard I remain Dear Sir   Your Affectionate & most Obedient humble Servant   Jas. Duane

Col. Alexander Hamilton

ALS, Hamilton Papers, Library of Congress.
  1. Duane was at this time a member of the New York Senate which was meeting at Kingston, New York.
  2. Material in broken brackets is taken from *JCHW*, I, 329–31.
  3. See H to George Clinton, February 14, 1783, note 3.
  4. On November 23, 1782, letters were sent by the Secretary of State (presumably the Secretary of State for Foreign Affairs, Thomas Robinson, Lord Grantham) to the Lord Mayor of London and the governors of the Bank of England "acquainting them, for the information of the public, and to prevent the mischiefs arising from speculations in the funds, that the negotiations carrying on at Paris were brought so far to a point, as to promise a decisive conclusion, either for peace or war, before the meeting of the parliament, which on that account was to be prorogued to the 5th of December" (*The Annual Register for the Year 1783* [London, 1784], 138).
  5. In November, 1781, Maryland had established the office of intendant of revenue. This is probably what Duane means by the "Maryland plan."
  6. Turbutt Wright served as a Maryland delegate to the Continental Congress until late in 1782; William Hemsley was a Maryland delegate in 1782

and 1783. Duane had been a New York representative in Congress from June to November, 1782.

7. Duane is probably referring to H's "Motion on Vermont" of December 5, 1782 and to the evidence H presumably collected for a refutation of Vermont's claim of jurisdiction over citizens of New York.

8. Colonel John Van Rensselaer, the father of Mrs. Philip Schuyler.

9. William Floyd, like H, was a New York State delegate to the Continental Congress.

10. Angelica Schuyler, H's sister-in-law, was married to John B. Church who used the pseudonym John Carter during the Revolution.

Continental Congress
Motion on Abatements for States in
Possession of the Enemy

[Philadelphia] February 17, 1783

Whereas it is in the opinion of Congress essential to those principles of justice & liberality which ought to govern the intercourse between these states that equitable abatements shall be made in favour of such states, parts of which have been for different periods in the course of the war in possession of the enemy, in the application of the rule prescribed by the confederation and on which the foregoing resolutions have been founded [1]—and whereas Congress impressed with this conviction did on the 20th. day of February last [2] recommend to the respective states to authorise and empower Congress in the final settlement of the proportions to be borne by each state of the general expences of the war from the commencement thereof until the first day of January 1782 except the monies loaned to the United States for the security and discharge of the principal and interest of which Congress rely on a compliance with their requisition of the 3d. day of Feby. 1781 [3] to assume and adopt such principles as from the particular circumstances of the several states at different periods may appear just & equitable, without being wholly confined to the rule laid in the 8th. article of the confederation in cases where the same cannot be applied [4] without manifest injustice. And Whereas some of the states have not yet complied with the said recommendation—

Therefore Resolved that the several states be earnestly requested without delay to pass laws conformable to the spirit of the aforesaid recommendation extending the period to the conclusion of the present war. [5]

AD, Papers of the Continental Congress, National Archives.

1. H is referring to resolutions on the evaluation of state lands to serve as a basis for congressional requisitions under Article 8 of the Articles of Confederation. See "First Motion on Evaluation of State Lands for Carrying into Effect Article 8 of the Articles of Confederation," February 6, 1783 note 2. The resolutions, introduced by Eliphalet Dyer, a delegate from Connecticut, and adopted on February 17, provided that each state submit to Congress before March 1, 1784, an account of the quantity of land, number of buildings, and number of inhabitants within its borders. A committee of Congress was then to estimate the value of the lands and submit its estimates to the states for approval or rejection.

2. February 20, 1782. See JCC, XXII, 83–86.

3. See JCC, XIX, 110–13.

4. The words "be applied" are not in the writing of H.

5. H's motion, according to the endorsement, was referred to Arthur Lee of Virginia, Eliphalet Dyer of Connecticut, and Samuel Holten of Massachusetts. On February 26, 1783, according to the Journals, it was "read and consideration postponed" (JCC, XXIV, 152). H and William Floyd informed Governor George Clinton in a letter dated March 5, 1783, that the report of this committee was "unfavourable." Another motion, different in wording but the same in content, was introduced by H on March 4.

Continental Congress
Motion that Debates on the Establishment of Funds Be Public

[Philadelphia] February 18, 1783

Whereas it is the desire of Congress that the motives of their deliberations and measures (as far as they can be disclosed consistently with the public safety) should be fully known to their constituents:

Therefore Resolved that when the establishment of funds for paying the principal & interest of the public debts shall be under the consideration of this house the doors thereof shall be open.[1]

AD, Papers of the Continental Congress, National Archives. In HCLW, I, 303, this is dated 1783.

1. On February 18, 1783, Congress again resolved itself into a committee of the whole to discuss the raising of general funds. According to Madison, H's motion, seconded by James Wilson, was prompted by the Pennsylvania delegates who

". . . said privately that they had brought themselves into a critical situation by dissuading their Constituents from separate provision for Creditors of U. S. within Pena. hoping that Congs. wd. adopt a general provision, & they wished their Constituents to see the prospect themselves & to witness the conduct of their Delegates. Perhaps the true reason was that, it was expected the presence of public creditors numerous & weighty in Philada. wd. have an in-

fluence & that it wd. be well for the public to come more fully to the knowledge of the public finances." ("Notes of Debates in the Continental Congress,"
MS, James Madison Papers, Library of Congress.)

On the following day, February 19, H's motion was defeated, only Pennsylvania voting for it ("Notes of Debates in the Continental Congress," MS,
James Madison Papers, Library of Congress).

Continental Congress
Motion and Remarks Against Limiting
the Duration of the Proposed Impost

[Philadelphia, February 19, 1783]

A motion was made by Mr. Hamilton seconded by Mr. Bland to
postpone the clause of the report made by the Come. of the whole,
for altering the Impost, viz. the clause limiting its duration to 25
years,[1] in order to substitute a proposition declaring it to be inexpedient to limit the period of its duration; first because it ought
to be commensurate to the duration of the debt, 2dly. because it was
improper in the present stage of the business, and all the limitation
of which it wd. admit had been defined in the Resolutions of
, 1782.[2]

Mr. Hamilton said in support of his motion that it was in vain
to attempt to gain the concurrence of the States by removing the
objections publickly assigned by them against the Impost, that these
were the ostensible & not the true objections; that the true objection
on the part of R.I. was the interference of the impost with the
opportunity afforded by their situation of levying contributions on
Cont., &c which recd. foreign supplies through the ports of R.I.;
that the true objection on the part of Va. was her having little share
in the debts due from the U.S. to which the impost would be applied;
that a removal of the avowed objections would not therefore, remove the obstructions whilst it would admit on the part of Congs.
that their first recommendation went beyond the absolute exigences
of the public; that Congs. having taken a proper ground at first,
ought to maintain it till time should convince the States of the
propriety of the measure.

"Notes of Debates in the Continental Congress," MS, James Madison Papers,
Library of Congress.

1. Since January 29 (see "Remarks on Plans for Paying the Public Debt,"

January 29, 1783, note 1), a committee of the whole had considered means of raising permanent funds for the United States. In addition to resolutions calling on the states to provide an evaluation of lands as a basis of congressional requisitions, other sources of revenue had been discussed. H's remarks refer to the proposal that Congress request authority to levy an impost of five percent for not more than twenty-five years (*JCC*, XXIV, 128).

2. The resolutions, the date of which Madison left blank, were probably those of December 16, 1782. On that date Congress in a letter to William Bradford, speaker of the Assembly of Rhode Island, answered the objections Rhode Island had made to Congress's request for authority to levy impost duties. At the end of the letter, which was in the writing of H, several resolutions limiting Congress's use of continental funds were appended. See "Report on a Letter from the Speaker of the Rhode Island Assembly," December 16, 1782.

Continental Congress
Remarks on Appropriating the Impost Exclusively to the Army

[Philadelphia, February 19, 1783]

Mr. Hamilton opposed the motion [1] strenuously, declared that as a friend to the army as well as to the other Creditors & to the public at large he could never assent to such a partial dispensation of Justice; that the different States being differently attached to different branches of the public debt would never concur in establishg. a fund wch. was not extended to every branch; that it was impolitic to divide the interests of the civil & military Creditors, whose joint efforts in the States would be necessary to prevail on them to adopt a general revenue.

"Notes of Debates in the Continental Congress," MS, James Madison Papers, Library of Congress.

1. John Rutledge had made a motion that the impost should be used exclusively for the Army. This was a renewal of a proposal which he had made in the committee of the whole on February 18.

Continental Congress
Report on a Letter from the Commander in Chief

[Philadelphia] February 20, 1783

The Committee [1] to whom were referred the letter from The Commander in Chief [2] with its inclosures submit the following resolution

Resolved that The Commander in Chief be informed that Congress always happy to receive his sentiments either on the political or military affairs of these states the utility of which they have upon so many occasions experienced have paid all the attention to his letter of the 30th. of Jany which the importance of it demands.

That should the war continue another campaign every motive of policy and œconomy would operate in favour of the enterprise suggested, but that such are the present situation and prospects of these states that it would be inexpedient at this time to determine upon the plan or to enter upon the expensive preparations which it would require.

That the official accounts received by Congress corresponding with other intelligence afford appearances of an approaching peace.

Resolved that the Secretary for foreign affairs be directed to make a confidential communication to the Commander in Chief of the state of the negotiations for peace when the last advices were received.[3]

AD, Papers of the Continental Congress, National Archives.

1. The committee consisted of H, Richard Peters, Theodorick Bland, John Rutledge, and Thomas Mifflin.

2. On January 30, 1783, George Washington wrote to the President of Congress that the Army should be prepared for the possible continuation of the war, and recommended that Congress provide adequate supplies for the quarter-master's department. Although he stated that he had no desire to increase the Army "in the smallest degree beyond what the exigence of the Circumstances may appear to demand," he suggested that if the peace negotiations failed, it would be wise "to attempt by one great and decisive effort to expel the Enemy from the remaining part of their possessions in the United States" (*GW*, XXVI, 82–86).

3. The endorsement states that the resolution was passed on the day it was delivered, February 20, 1783.

Continental Congress
Remarks on the Revenue and the
Situation of the Army

[Philadelphia, February 20, 1783]

The conversation [1] turned on the subject of revenue under the consideration of Congress, and on the situation of the army. The conversation on the first subject ended in a general concurrence (Mr. Hamilton excepted) in the impossibility of adding to the impost on trade any taxes that wd. operate equally throughout the States, or be adopted by them. On the second subject Mr. Hamilton & Mr. Peters who had the best knowledge of the temper, transactions & views of the army, informed the company that it was certain that the army had secretly determined not to lay down their arms until due provision & a satisfactory prospect should be afforded on the subject of their pay; that there was reason to expect that a public declaration to this effect would soon be made; that plans had been agitated if not formed for subsisting themselves after such declaration; that as a proof of their earnestness on this subject the Comander was already become extremely unpopular among almost all ranks from his known dislike to every unlawful proceeding, that this unpopularity was daily increasing & industriously promoted by many leading characters; that his choice of unfit & indiscreet persons into his family was the pretext and with some a real motive; but the substantial one a desire to displace him from the respect & confidence of the army in order to substitute Genl.   [2] as the conductor of their efforts to obtain justice. Mr. Hamilton said that he knew Genl. Washington intimately and perfectly, that his extreme reserve, mixed sometimes with a degree of asperity of temper both of which were said to have increased of late, had contributed to the decline of his popularity; but that his virtue his patriotism & his firmness would it might be depended upon never yield to any dishonorable or disloyal plans into which he might be called; that he would sooner suffer himself to be cut into pieces; that he, (Mr. Hamilton) knowing this to be his true character wished him to be the conductor of the army in their plans for redress, in order that they might be moderated & directed to proper objects, & exclude some other leader who might foment and misguide their councils; that with this view he had taken the liberty to write to the Genl. on this subject and to recommend such a policy to him.[3]

"Notes of Debates in the Continental Congress," MS, James Madison Papers, Library of Congress.

1. The conversation recorded by Madison took place on the evening of February 20 at the home of Thomas FitzSimons between FitzSimons, Nathaniel Gorham, Richard Peters, Daniel Carroll, James Madison, and H. ("Notes of Debates in the Continental Congress," MS, James Madison Papers, Library of Congress.)

2. The name was crossed out and is illegible.

3. See H to George Washington, February 13, 1783.

Continental Congress
Remarks on the Utility of Permanent Funds

[Philadelphia, February 21, 1783]

Mr. Hamilton enlarged on the general utility of permanent funds to the fœderal interests of this Country, & pointed out the difference between the nature of the Constitution of the British Executive, & that of the U.S. in answer to Mr. Lee's reasoning from the case of Ship money.[1]

"Notes of Debates in the Continental Congress," MS, James Madison Papers, Library of Congress.
1. Congress on February 21 discussed the subject of general funds for the Confederation. Arthur Lee said: ". . . it was an established truth that the purse ought not to be put into the same hands with the Sword; that like arguments had been used in favor of Ship money in the reign of Charles I it being then represented as essential to the support of the Govt., that the Executive should be assured of the means of fulfilling its engagements for the public service" ("Notes of Debates in the Continental Congress," MS, James Madison Papers, Library of Congress).

To Samuel Hodgdon [1]

[Philadelphia, February 22, 1783]

Sir

The bearer Abby Mot[2] is a soldiers widow in great distress who wants to go to her friends in the Jerseys but has not the means. If you could find her a place in some public waggon going that way, you would do an act of charity. I am Sir   Yr. Obed ser.

A Hamilton

Philadelphia
Feby. 22. 1783 [3]

Mr. Hodgdon
Assistant Qr. Mr.

ALS, Buffalo and Erie County Public Library, Buffalo, New York.
1. Hodgdon was commissary general of military stores.
2. In 1789 H paid Abby Mott's funeral expenses. See "Receipt from John Murray," August 15, 1789.
3. This date could possibly read February 22, 1782.

Memorial of Philip Thompson

[*Philadelphia, February 22, 1783*. On the last page of a memorial of Philip Thompson to the Supreme Executive Council of Pennsylvania Hamilton and Major General Alexander McDougall made endorsements. The paragraph by Hamilton reads: "I certify that the Memorialist was an active and zealous whig in the early periods of the contest and I have reason to believe the above representation is true. A. Hamilton." [1] *Document not found.*]

ADS, sold at City Book Auction, October 18, 1941, Lot 183.
  1. Extract taken from City Book Auction catalogue.

From George Clinton

(Confidential)   Kingston [New York] 24th. Feby. 1783.

Sir

I have been honored by your Letter of the 12th. January. You may remember that in July last, I submitted to the Consideration of our Legislature certain Resolutions of the Assembly of New Hampshire making Overtures for an Amicable settlement of a Boundary Line between the two States, which were read & Committed but as the Session was Short and devoted principally to the particular Business for which they were convened no Determination was had on the Subject.[1] I had some reason to expect a Consideration of these Resolutions would have taken Place at the present Meeting. This induced me to defer answering your Letter until I could inform you of the Result. I cannot however discover any Disposition to take up this Business. It seems to be the prevailing Opinion that as Congress has engaged to make a final Decision of the Controversey respecting the District called the Grants, a partial Compromise of the Matter would be improper as any Measures for the purpose might alienate the Affections of our most Zealous Subjects in that Quarter and be attended with other Dangerous consequences. Besides Doubts exist whether the Legislature have Authority by any Act of theirs to consent to such a Dismemberment of the State as would probably be insisted upon on a Compromise with New Hampshire. I am nevertheless still persuaded should Congress determine the Summit of the Mountains [2] to be the Boundary between the two States, this State (whatever our Sentiments might be of the Equity of the Decision) would for the sake of Peace submit to it, and there cannot be a Doubt but that New Hampshire would be perfectly satisfied with the Jurisdiction of so Extensive and Valuable a Territory. I take it for granted that whatever may be the Decision equitable Measures will be adopted for securing the Property of Individuals.

I congratulate you most sincerely on the promising Prospects of Peace. I pray nothing may prevent the Desireable Event soon taking place. Our Friends from the City and Long Island anxiously wait for the Moment in which they may Return to their Homes. The Expectations of all are so much raised as to obstruct Public Business not a little. Please to offer my best Respects to Mrs. Hamilton & believe me, With great Respect & Esteem Sir Your Most Obedt. Servt. Geo: Clinton

P.S. It is with great Concern I mention that since writing the above I am informed of the Death of your Relation Colo. John Van Renselaer [3] He departed this Life on Fryday last. Genl. Schuyler who was sent for when his Recovery was dispaired of, is to set out from Albany on his Return to this place on Wednesday next.

G C

LS, Hamilton Papers, Library of Congress.
1. The resolution is printed in *New Hampshire State Papers*, VIII, 943–44. On July 15, 1782, Governor Clinton submitted to the New York legislature a letter from Meschech Weare, the president of New Hampshire, of July 2, 1782, enclosing certain resolutions of that state of June 21 (New York Assembly *Journal*, 1782, 110). Weare wrote to Clinton that an agreement between New York and New Hampshire might settle the Vermont question and asked Clinton to "take the mind of your Legislature Respecting the Matter" (*New Hampshire State Papers*, X, 490–91). As is intimated later in Clinton's letter to H, the legislative resolution enclosed by Weare probably revived the proposal to divide Vermont between the two states, using the Green Mountains as a line of division.
2. Presumably the Green Mountains.
3. Colonel John Van Rensselaer was the father-in-law of Philip Schuyler.

To George Clinton

Philadelphia February 24th. [-27] 1783

Sir,

In my letter of the 14th. I informed Your Excellency that Congress were employed in devising a plan for carrying the 8th article of the confederation into execution. This business is at length brought to a conclusion. I inclose for the information of the Legislature the proceedings upon it in different stages, by which they will see the part I have acted.[1] But as I was ultimately left in a small minority, I think it my duty to explain the motives upon which my opposition to the general sense of the house was founded.

I am of opinion, that the article of the confederation itself was ill-judged. In the first place I do not believe there is any general representative of the wealth of a nation, the criterion of its ability to pay taxes. There are only two that can be thought of *land* and *numbers*.

The revenues of the United Provinces (general and particular) were computed before the present war to more than half as much as those of Great Britain. The extent of their territory is not one fourth part as great, their population less than a third. The comparison is still more striking between those Provinces and the Swiss-Cantons in both of which extent of territory and population are nearly the same, and yet the revenues of the former are five times as large as those of the latter, nor could any efforts of taxation bring

ALS, Hamilton Papers, Library of Congress; Df, Hamilton Papers, Library of Congress. The receiver's copy is incorrectly endorsed, "Letter from Delegates in Congress."

1. The enclosure, but not H's letter, is printed in *Public Papers of George Clinton*, VIII, 66–72, under the title "For the Adjustment of the National Debt" with no identification of the person from whom Clinton received it.

The congressional resolution dated February 17, 1783, for carrying into effect Article 8 of the Articles of Confederation provided that the legislatures of the several states should "take such measures as shall be most effectual for obtaining a just and accurate account of the quantity of land in such State, granted to or surveyed for any person the number of buildings thereon distinguishing dwelling houses from other buildings, and the number of its inhabitants distinguishing white from black" (*JCC*, XXIV, 133–34). The results were to be transmitted to Congress by March 1, 1784. See the first and second "Motion on Evaluation of State Lands for Carrying into Effect Article 8 of the Articles of Confederation," February 6, 1783.

them to any thing like a level. In both cases the advantages for agriculture are superior in those countries which afford least revenue in proportion. I have selected these examples, because they are most familiar, but who ever will extend the comparison between the different nations of the world, will perceive that the position I have laid down is supported by universal experience.

The truth is the ability of a country to pay taxes depends on infinite combinations of physical and moral causes, which can never be accommodated to any general rule, climate, soil, productions, advantages for navigation, government, genius of the people, progress of arts and industry, and an endless variety of circumstances. The diversities are sufficiently great in these states to make an infinite difference in their relative wealth—the proportion of which can never be found by any common measure whatever.

The only possible way then of making them contribute to the general expence in an equal proportion to their means is by general taxes imposed under Continental authority. In this mode there would no doubt be inequalities and for a considerable time material ones; but experience and the constant operation of a general interest which by the very collision of particular interests must in the main prevail in a Continental deliberative would at length correct those inequalities, and ballance one tax that should bear hard upon one state by another that should have a proportional weight in others. This idea however was not at the period of framing the confederation, and is not yet agreeable to the spirit of the times. To futurity we must leave the discovery how far this spirit is wise or foolish. One thing only is now certain that Congress having the discretionary power of determining the quantum of money to be paid into the general treasury towards defraying the common expences, have in effect the constitutional power of general taxation. The restraints upon the exercise of this power amount to the perpetuating a rule for fixing the proportions which must of necessity produce inequality, and by refusing the fœderal government a power of specific taxation and of collection, without substituting any other adequate means of coertion do in fact leave the compliance with Continental requisitions to the good will of the respective states. Inequality is inherent in the theory of the confederation, and in the practice that inequality must increase in proportion to the honesty or dishonesty of the component parts. This vice will either in its consequences reform the fœderal constitution or dissolve it.

If a general standard must be fixed numbers were preferable to land. Modes might be devised, to ascertain the former with tolerable precision, but I am persuaded the experiment will prove that the value of all the land in each state cannot be ascertained with any thing like exactness. Both these measures have the common disadvantage, of being no equal representative of the wealth of the people; but one is much more simple definite and certain than the other.

I have indulged myself in these remarks to show that I have little expectation of success from any mode of carrying the article in question into execution upon equitable principles. I owe it however to myself to declare that my opposition did not arise from this source. The confederation has pointed out this mode, and though I would heartily join in a representation of the difficulties (of which every man of sense must be sensible on examination) that occur in the execution of the plan to induce the states to consent to a change, yet as this was not the disposition of a Majority of Congress, I would have assented to any mode of attempting it which was not either obviously mischievous or impracticable.

The first plan proposed as Your Excellency will see was an actual valuation of each state by itself. This was evidently making the interested party judge in his own cause.[2] Those who have seen the operation of this principle between the counties in the same state and the districts in the same county cannot doubt a moment that the valuations on this plan would have been altogether unequal and unjust. Without supposing more liberality in one state than in another the degree of care, judgment and method employed in the execution would alone make extreme differences in the results.

This mode had also the further inconvenience of awakening all the jealousies of the several states against each other. Each would suspect that its neighbour had favoured itself, whether the partiality appeared or not. It would be impossible to silence these distrusts and to make the states sit down satisfied with the justice of each

2. The first plan was introduced in Congress on February 6, 1783. It provided that each state should be divided into districts for the evaluation "of all lands in such States Granted to or surveyed for any person and of the buildings and improvements thereon" (JCC, XXIV, 113). The evaluation was to be made by commissioners appointed by the state.

other. Every new requisition for money would be a new signal for discussion and clamour, and the seeds of disunion already sown too thick would be not a little multiplied.

To guard against these evils the plan proposes a revision by Congress; [3] but it is easy to be seen that such a power could not be exercised. Should any states return defective valuations, it would be difficult to find sufficient evidence to determine them such—to alter would not be admissible, for Congress could have no data, which could be presumed equivalent to those which must have governed the judgment of Commissioners under oath on an actual view of the premises. To do either this, or to reject would be an impeachment of the honor of the states which it is not probable there would be decision enough to hazard, and which if done could not fail to excite serious disgusts. There is a wide difference between a single state exercising such a power over its own counties and a confederated government exercising it over sovereign states, which compose the confederacy. It might also happen that too many states would be interested in the defective valuations to leave a sufficient number willing either to alter or to reject.

These considerations prevailed to prevent the plan being adopted by a Majority.

The last plan may be less mischievous than the first, but it appears to me altogether ineffectual: The mere quantity of land granted and surveyed with the general species of buildings upon them can certainly be no criteria to determine their value.[4] The plan does not even distinguish the improved from the unimproved land; the qualities of soil, or degrees of improvement; the qualities of the houses and other buildings are intirely omitted. These it seems are to be judged of by the commissioners to be appointed by each state; but I am unable to conceive how any commissioner can form the least

3. The first plan provided that the evaluation made by the states should be submitted to Congress "in order that Congress may examine such estimates, and if they shall be approved of by them . . . proceed to make such requisitions upon the respective states as shall be agreeable to the Articles of Confederation" (*JCC*, XXIV, 113).

4. The specific provision of the last plan to which H refers in this and the following sentences was the requirement that each legislature make an "accurate account of the quantity of land in such State, granted to or surveyed for any person, the number of buildings thereon, distinguishing dwelling houses from other buildings, and the number of its inhabitants distinguishing white from black" (*JCC*, XXIV, 133–34).

estimate of these circumstances with respect even to his own state, much less with respect to other states, which would be necessary to establish a just relative value. If even there was a distinction of improved from unimproved land, by supposing an intrinsic value in the land and adopting general rates something nearer the truth might be attained; but it must now be all conjecture and uncertainty.

The numbers of inhabitants distinguishing white from black are called for. This is not only totally foreign to the confederation but can answer no reasonable purpose. It has been said that the proportion of members may guide and correct the estimates; an assertion purely verbal. A judgment must first be formed of the value of the lands upon some principles. If this should be altered by the proportion of numbers, it is plain numbers would be substituted to land.

Another objection to the plan is, that it lets in the particular interests of the states to operate in the returns of the quantities of land, number of buildings and number of inhabitants. But the principle of this objection applies less forcibly here than against the former plan.

Whoever will consider the plain import of the 8th. article of the confederation must be convinced that it intended an *actual* and *specific* valuation of land buildings and improvements, not a mere general estimate according to the present plan. While we insist therefore upon adhering to the confederation, we should do it in reality, not barely in appearance.

Many of those who voted for this scheme had as bad an opinion of it as myself; but they were induced to accede to it, by a persuasion that some plan for the purpose was expected by the states, and that none better in the present circumstances of the country could be fallen upon.

A leading rule which I have laid down for the direction of my conduct is this—that while I would have a just deference for the expectations of the states, I would never consent to amuse them by attempts, which must either fail in the execution or be productive of evil. I would rather incur the negative inconveniences of delay than the positive mischief of injudicious expedients. A contrary conduct serves to destroy confidence in the government, the greatest misfortune that can befal a nation. There should in my opinion be a character of wisdom and efficiency in all the measures of the fœderal council, the opposite of a spirit of temporising concession.

I would have sufficient reliance on the judgments of the several states to hope that good reasons for not attempting a thing would be more satisfactory to them than precipitate and fruitless attempts. My idea is that taking it for granted the states will expect an experiment on the principles of the confederation the best plan will be to make it by Commissioners appointed by Congress and acting under their authority. Congress might in the first instance appoint three or more of the principal characters in each state for probity and abilities, with a power to nominate other commissioners under them in each subdivision of the state. General principles might be laid down for the government of their conduct by which uniformity in the manner of conducting the business would obtain. Sanctions of such solemnity might be prescribed and such notoriety given to every part of the transaction, that the commissioners could neither be careless nor partial without a sacrifice of reputation.

To carry this plan however into effect with sufficient care and accuracy would be a work both of time and expence; and unfortunately we are so pressed to find money for calls of immediate necessity that we could not at present undertake a measure, which would require so large a sum.

To me it appears evident that every part of a business, which is of so important and universal concern should be transacted on uniform principles and under the direction of that body which has a common interest.

In general I regard the present moment probably the dawn of peace as peculiarly critical; and the measures which it shall produce as of great importance to the future welfare of these states. I am therefore scrupulous[ly] cautious of assenting to plans which appear to me founded on false principles.

Your Excellency will observe that the valuation of the lands is to be the standard for adjusting the accounts for past supplies, between the United States and the particular states. This if adhered to without allowance for the circumstances of those states which have been more immediately the theatre of the war, will charge our state for the *past* according to its *future ability*, when in an intire condition; if the valuation should be finally made after we regain possession of the parts of the state now in the power of the enemy.

I have therefore introduced a motion for repeating the call in a more earnest manner upon the states to vest Congress with a power of making equitable abatements, agreeable to the spirit of the resolution of the 20th. of February last which few of the states have complied with. This motion has been committed.[5] I know not what will be its fate.

Nothwithstanding the opposition I have given, now the matter has been decided in Congress, I hope the state will chearfully comply with what is required. Unless each state is governed by this principle, there is an end of the union. Every state will no doubt have a right in this case to accompany its compliance with such remarks as it may think proper. I have the honor to be Yr. Excellency's Most Obedient servant   Alx Hamilton

P.S.   After the plan was agreed upon, it was committed to be put into form, and when reported instead of Commissioners an alteration was carried for making the estimate by a Grand Committee.[6]

Feby. 27

Mr. Morris has signified to Congress his resolution to resign by the first of June if adequate funds are not by that time provided.[7] This will be a severe stroke to our affairs. No man fit for the office will be willing to supply his place for the very reasons he resigns.

Tis happy for us we have reason to expect a peace; I am sorry that by different accounts it appears not to have been concluded late in December.

5. H's motion was made on February 17, 1783. See "Motion on Abatements for States in Possession of the Enemy."
6. In the report which Congress first adopted it was provided that commissioners appointed by each state and approved by Congress should evaluate the lands in the several states. The final version of the report provided that a grand committee appointed by Congress, consisting of one member from each state, should make the evaluation.
7. On January 24, 1783, Robert Morris wrote to Congress that he intended to resign at the end of May. This letter was placed under a ban of secrecy which was not removed until February 26, 1783 (JCC, XXIV, 92, note 1; and 151).

George Clinton to Alexander Hamilton and William Floyd

Kingston [New York] 25th. Feby. 1783.

Gentm.

From the Affidavits which I now do myself the Honor to Inclose You [1] and which I must request you to lay before Congress it appears that the Usurped Government on the New Hampshire Grants so far from yielding Obedience to the Resolutions of Congress of the 5th. December [2] last have repeated their Outrages on the well affected Subjects of this State.

The distressed situation of our fellow Citizens in that District, the Preservation of the Public Peace and the Faith and Dignity of Congress require their immediate and effectual Interposition.

I also transmit a Printed Remonstrance [3] of which Copies have been sent by the Leaders of the Defection to some of the Principal Officers of the Army to be distributed among the Soldiery with a View doubtless improperly to influence them should it be requisite to employ the Military to carry the Resolutions of Congress into Execution.

There can be no doubt but that these People are induced to perseverence in their Opposition from a Belief that Congress never will decide the Controversy relative to the Jurisdiction and will never have Recourse to coercive Means to enforce their Determination, and I am therefore perswaded that Tranquility and good Order cannot be restored to that part of the Country unless by an Adjudication of Congress in the Question of Jurisdiction.

Several Circumstances in my Opinion conspire to render the present the most proper Moment and I am convinced (should any be necessary) a small regular Military Force will be sufficient to compel a Submission.

The Legislature are now sitting and exceedingly Anxious to be informed of the Issue of a Business in which the State is so deeply interested and this anxiety is increased by the Consideration that consistent with the Recommendations of Congress it would be improper in the State to attempt to relieve the Sufferers.

Major Shattuck one of the Deponents goes to Philadelphia expressly to convey this Distatch and to him I must refer you for more particular Information.[4]

I have the Honor to be with great Respect   Gentm.   Your Most Obedt. Servt.   Geo: Clinton

the Honorable the Delagates for the State of New York

LS, Papers of the Continental Congress, National Archives.
    1. The enclosures consist of a deposition by William Lee stating that he had heard it declared that there was a conspiracy of Vermonters to deny the authority of the United States and join the British; a deposition by Charles Phelps reporting the refusal of Vermonters to obey the congressional resolve of December 5, 1782, which had ordered the officials of Vermont to make restitution to those deprived of property; a sworn statement by Jonathan Kittredge that he had heard several men from Vermont denounce the Continental Congress and drink the health of King George III; and a declaration by Thomas Frink that he had heard people of the New Hampshire Grants express their determination to ignore the resolves of Congress. These enclosures to Clinton's letter are in the Papers of the Continental Congress, National Archives.
    2. See "Motion on Vermont," December 5, 1782.
    3. The remonstrance which Clinton enclosed was probably that of January 9, 1783, which was addressed to the President of Congress and signed by Thomas Chittenden, governor of Vermont (Walton, *Records of Vermont*, III, 254–62).
    4. For information on Major William Shattuck, see "Motion on Vermont," December 5, 1782, note 3.

From Brigadier General John Cadwalader

Philada: 2d: March 1783

As General Reed's Remarks on a late publication relating to a Conversation I had with him at Bristol in the year 1776, require an answer;[1] I shall be much obliged if you will endeavour to recollect whether I did not at some period of the war mention the said Conversation to you, in confidence & beg you will be particular with respect to time, place, & any other Circumstances which you may remember.

The obvious necessity of my address to you upon the present occasion, will, I hope, render any apology unnecessary. I am dear Sir with great respect & esteem your most O & very hble Servt.

John Cadwalader

ADfS, Historical Society of Pennsylvania, Philadelphia.

1. In September, 1782, an article in *The* [Philadelphia] *Independent Gazetteer; or The Chronicle of Freedom* stated that Joseph Reed in December, 1776, had told Cadwalader that he was considering the abandonment of the American cause and the acceptance of British protection. Reed immediately wrote Cadwalader, his bitter rival in Pennsylvania politics, and asked for an explanation. In reply Cadwalader maintained that such a conversation had taken place. For his defense Reed collected letters and sworn statements denying the charge, and in January, 1783, he published them, together with his defense, in a pamphlet entitled: *Remarks on a Late Publication in the Independent Gazetteer, with a Short Address to the People of Pennsylvania on the Many Libels and Slanders Which Have Lately Appeared Against the Author* (Philadelphia, 1783). After Reed's pamphlet appeared, Cadwalader began preparing his reply.

From George Washington

Newburgh [New York] 4th. Mar: 1783

Dear Sir,

I have received your favor of February   [1] & thank you for the information & observations it has conveyed to me. I shall always think myself obliged by a free communication of sentiments, & have often thought (but suppose I thought wrong as it did not accord with the practice of Congress) that the public interest might be benefitted, if the Commander in Chief of the Army was let more into the political & pecuniary state of our affairs than he is. Enterprises, & the adoption of Military & other arrangements that might be exceedingly proper in some circumstances, would be altogether improper in others. It follows then by fair deduction, that where there is a want of information there must be chance medley; & a man may be upon the brink of a precipice before he is aware of his danger—when a little foreknowledge might enable him to avoid it. But this by the by. The hint contained in your letter, and the knowledge I have derived from the public Gazettes respecting the nonpayment of Taxes contain all the information I have received of the danger that stares us in the face, on acct. of our funds, and so far was I from conceiving that our finances were in so deplorable a state, *at this time*, that I had imbibed ideas from some source or another, that with the prospect of a loan from Holland we should be able to rub along.

To you, who have seen the danger, to which the Army has been exposed, to a political dissolution for want of subsistence, & the unhappy spirit of licentiousness which it imbibed by becoming in one or two instances its own proveditors, no observations are necessary to evince the fatal tendency of such a measure; but I shall give it as my opinion, that it would at this day be productive of Civil commotions & end in blood. Unhappy situation this! God forbid we should be involved in it.

The predicament in which I stand as Citizen & Soldier, is as critical and delicate as can well be conceived. It has been the subject of many contemplative hours. The sufferings of a complaining army on one hand, and the inability of Congress and tardiness of the States on the other, are the forebodings of evil; & may be productive of events which are more to be depricated than prevented; but I am not without hope, if there is such a disposition shewn as prudence & policy dictates, to do justice, your apprehensions, in case of Peace, are greater than there is cause for. In this however I may be mistaken, if those ideas, which you have been informed are propagated in the Army, should be extensive; the source of which may be easily traced; as the old leven,[2] *it is said*, for I have no proof of it, is again beginning to work, under the mask of the most perfect dissimulation & apparent cordiallity.

Be these things as they may, I shall pursue the same steady line of conduct which has governed me hitherto; fully convinced that the sensible, and discerning part of the army, cannot be unacquainted (although I never took pains to inform them) of the services I have rendered it, on more occasions than one. This, and pursuing the suggestions of your letter, which I am happy to find conincides with my own practice for several months past, & which was the means of directing the business of the Army into the Channel it now is, leaves me under no *great* apprehension of its exceeding the bounds of reason & moderation, nothwithstanding the prevailing sentiment in the Army is, that the prospect of compensation for past Services will terminate with the War.

The just claims of the Army ought, and it is to be hoped will, have their weight with every sensible Legislature in the Union,[3] if Congress point to their demands; shew (if the case is so) the reasonableness of them, and the impracticability of complying ⟨with them⟩[4] without their aid. In any other point of view it would, in my opinion, be impolitic to introduce the Army on the Tapis; lest it should excite jealousy, and bring on its concomitants. The States cannot, surely, be so devoid of common sense, common honesty, & common policy as to refuse their aid on a full, clear, & candid representation of facts from Congress; more especially if these should be enforced by members of their own body; who might demonstrate what the inevitable consequences of failure must lead to.

In my opinion it is a matter worthy of consideration how far an Adjournment of Congress for a few months is advisable. The Delegates in that case, if they are in unison themselves respecting the great defects of their [5] Constitution may represent them fully & boldly to their Constituents. To me, who ⟨know⟩ nothing of the business which is before Congress, nor of the arcanum, it appears that such a measure would tend to promote the public weal; for it is clearly my opinion, unless Congress have powers competent to all *general* purposes, that the distresses we have encountered, the expences we have incurred, and the blood we have spilt in the course of an Eight years war, will avail us nothing.

The contents of your letter is known only to myself and your prudence will direct what should be done with this. With great esteem and regard   I am Dr Sir   Yr. Most Obedt. Servt

Go: Washington

ALS, Hamilton Papers, Library of Congress; Df, George Washington Papers, Library of Congress.
1. H's letter was dated February 13, 1783. Space left blank in MS.
2. Washington probably was referring to Major General Horatio Gates. "The context," according to Douglas S. Freeman, "scarcely affords ground for doubt of his meaning" (Freeman, *Washington*, V, 429, note 17).
3. In draft, "United States."
4. Material in broken brackets, which was omitted from the receiver's copy, has been taken from the draft.
5. In draft, "our."

Continental Congress
Motion on Abatements for States in
Possession of the Enemy

[Philadelphia] March 4, 1783

Whereas in the opinion of Congress it is essential to those principles of justice and liberality which ought to govern the intercourse between these states that in the final adjustment of accounts for the supplies or contributions of the states respectively towards the common expences in the course of the war equitable allowances should be made in favour of those states parts of which have been at different periods in possession of the enemy—And Whereas the *strict* application of the rule prescribed by the 8th. article of the confederation as declared by the resolution of the 17th. of February [1] would operate greatly to the prejudice of such states, and to the calamities of war add an undue proportion of the public burthen

Resolved That Congress will in the application of the said rule make such abatements in favour of the said states, as from a full consideration of circumstances, shall appear to them just and equitable for the time the said parts of the said states may have been in possession of the enemy.[2]

AD, Papers of the Continental Congress, National Archives. A similar motion had been made by H on February 17, 1783.

1. The congressional resolution of February 17 required each state to make an evaluation of its lands and to ascertain the number of its inhabitants. The results were to be used as a basis for apportioning the sums required by the Confederation. For a discussion of the resolution, see H to George Clinton, February 24, 1783.

2. A motion was made by Abraham Clark to postpone consideration of the motion. After Clark's motion was defeated, Congress voted and rejected H's motion (*JCC*, XXIV, 162–63). "The motion of Mr. Hamilton on the Journal relative to the abatement of the quotas of distressed States was rejected," James Madison recorded, "partly because the principle was disapproved by some, and partly because it was thought improper to be separated from other objects to be recommended to the States. The latter motive produced the motion for postponing which was lost" ("Notes of Debates in the Continental Congress," MS, James Madison Papers, Library of Congress).

Alexander Hamilton and William Floyd to George Clinton

[Philadelphia, March 5, 1783] [1]

Sir

Mr. Hamilton having transmitted Your Excellency the late proceedings of Congress for carrying the 8th. article of the confederation into execution, by which the legislature will see the part we acted in this affair.[2] They will not be at a loss for our motives; and we hope will not disapprove them. Our opposition to the first plan [3] proposed was founded principally on this consideration that it left the interested party judge in his own cause, might have produced great injustice and inequality, and would in all probability have excited great jealousies between the respective states. We dissented from the second plan chiefly because we did not perceive that it afforded sufficient data to make the valuations upon and because it applied the 8th. article of the confederation in such a manner as would have produced great injustice to the state of New York and others in similar circumstances by charging us with our proportion of the past contributions of the states according to our future ability when the valuation shall be made.

After this plan was resolved upon, we introduced a motion [4] to call a second time upon the different states to vest Congress with a power of making equitable abatements agreeable to the resolution of the [20th Feby 1781.] [5]

This was committed, and an unfavourable report made, which together with the original motion [6] was postponed.

We renewed the motions in a something different form, which has been negatived by a large majority. We have the honor to inclose the motion and the votes upon it.[7] Different motives operated in the dismission. Many were opposed to the principle and others wished to postpone 'till this matter with many others could be taken up on a general plan.

We have the honor to be &c &c

Your Excellency's letter by Mr. Shattuck [8] has been read in Congress & with the papers accompanying it committed to the same Committee which has before them the remonstrance from [Chittenden].[9] We need not assure you that we shall pay all the attention in our power to a matter so interesting to the state, which however we are obliged to see posponed to the consideration of funds for restoring the credit of the United States, which now occupies the first attention of Congress.

[We have the honour to be &c. &c.

His Excellency Governor Clinton] [10]

Df, in the writing of H, New-York Historical Society, New York City.
1. The draft is undated. The receiver's copy, printed in the *Public Papers of George Clinton*, VIII, 83–85, is dated March 5.

2. See H to George Clinton, February 24, 1783.

3. The plans debated by Congress for carrying into effect Article 8 of the Articles of Confederation are discussed at length in H to Clinton, February 24, 1783.

4. See "Motion on Abatements for States in Possession of the Enemy," February 17, 1783.

5. Bracketed words are not in H's writing. The resolution referred to was actually that of February 20, 1782, rather than 1781 (See *JCC*, XXII, 83–86).

6. The original motion was made on February 6, 1783 ("Motion on Evaluation of State Lands for Carrying into Effect Article 8 of the Articles of Confederation"). The motion of February 17 was referred to a committee consisting of Arthur Lee, Eliphalet Dyer, and Samuel Holten. According to the *JCC*, XXIV, 138, note 1, the committee reported on February 26, and its report was acted upon on March 3. The *Journals* on March 3 do not, however, refer to this report. On March 4, as stated in the next paragraph of their letter, H and Floyd introduced a similar motion which was defeated.

7. The enclosure is printed in the *Public Papers of George Clinton*, VIII, 82–83.

8. William Shattuck was an adherent of New York State living in Vermont. His property had been seized by Vermont.

9. The bracketed word is not in the writing of H. See Clinton to H and Floyd, February 25, 1783. Clinton's letter was referred to a committee consisting of Daniel Carroll, Nathaniel Gorham, Arthur Lee, John Taylor Gilman, and Oliver Wolcott, Sr. The committee was renewed on April 28, and on May 26 it reported that Congress should first determine whether Vermont should be admitted into the Confederation and then consider the action to be taken on Clinton's letter and the affidavits accompanying it (*JCC*, XXIV, 164, note 1; 367).

This remonstrance was from Governor Thomas Chittenden of Vermont (Walton, *Records of Vermont*, III, 254–62). On February 11, 1783, General George Washington sent to the President of Congress "Printed copies of 'A remonstrance of the Council of the State of Vermont, against the Resolutions of Congress of the 5th. of December last'" (*GW*, XXVI, 119). Washington's letter and the enclosure were referred to the committee, described in the preceding paragraph. On March 4 Clinton's letter of February 25, 1783 was also referred to that committee (*JCC*, XXIV, 138).

10. The bracketed material is not in the writing of H.

To George Washington

[Philadelphia, March 5, 1783] [1]

Sir

I had the honor of writing to your Excellency lately on a very confidential subjec⟨t⟩ [2] and shall be anxious to know as soon as c⟨on⟩venient whether the letter got safe to han⟨d⟩. [3] The bearer Shattuck [4] thinks he can poin⟨t⟩ out the means of apprehending Wells & Knowle⟨ton⟩ the two persons whom Your Excellency was authorised to have taken into custody. [5] I hav⟨e⟩ desired him to call upon you to disclose th⟨e⟩ plan. I will not trouble Your Excellency w⟨ith⟩ any observation on the importance of getting hold of those persons. The surmise that Mr. Arnold a member of Congress gave intellige⟨nce⟩ to them of the design to take them mak⟨es⟩ it peculiarly important. I have the hon⟨or to be

    Your Excellency's most ob't serv't   A. Hamilton.

To His Excellency General Washington⟩

AL, Hamilton Papers, Library of Congress.

  1. The letter is endorsed "From Alexander Hamilton, Esq., 5th March 1783."

  2. Material in broken brackets is taken from *JCHW*, I, 342.

  3. H probably referred to his letter to Washington of February 13, 1783.

  4. William Shattuck's claim for property seized by Vermont had been validated by a report of Congress ("Motion on Vermont," December 5, 1782). He had carried George Clinton's letter of February 25, 1783, to the New York delegates in Congress.

  5. Samuel Wells, pre-Revolutionary member of the New York Assembly from a part of the New Hampshire Grants and a staunch supporter of New York's claim to the area claimed by Vermont, became a Loyalist after the outbreak of the American Revolution. Luke Knoulton (also spelled "Knowlton"), who had come to Vermont from Massachusetts, also supported the British.

On November 27, 1782, a committee of Congress recommended that Washington be empowered to apprehend Knoulton and Wells on suspicion of their having corresponded with the enemy (*JCC*, XXIII, 756). On January 20, 1783, Washington forwarded to Congress a report of the officer sent to apprehend them. The report stated that the two men had received a letter from Jonathan Arnold, delegate in Congress from Rhode Island, "which informed them that affairs in Congress were unfavorable to them & wd. have them look out for themselves" ("Notes of Debates in the Continental Congress," MS, James Madison Papers, Library of Congress).

Continental Congress
Remarks on Robert Morris

[Philadelphia, March 5, 1783]

This motion [1] produced . . . lengthy & warm debates. Mr. Lee [2] & Mr. Bland on one side disparaging the Administration of Mr. Morris, and throwing oblique censure on his character. . . . On the other side Mr. Wilson & Mr. Hamilton went into a copious defence & Panegyric of Mr. Morris, the ruin in which his resignation if it sd. take effect wd. involve public credit and all the operations dependent on it; and the decency altho' firmness of his letters.

"Notes of Debates in the Continental Congress," MS, James Madison Papers, Library of Congress.

1. A motion had been made by Theodorick Bland that a "committee be appointed to devise the most proper means of arranging the Department of Finance" (*JJC*, XXIV, 165).

On January 24, 1783, Robert Morris wrote to Congress that unless adequate measures for securing revenue were adopted before the end of May, he would resign the office of Superintendent of Finance. Congress, disturbed by the possible repercussions of Morris's resignation, ordered his letter kept secret. On February 26, Morris asked that the injunction of secrecy be removed; when Congress complied, he published his letter (*JCC*, XXIV, 92, note 1; and 151).

On March 5, a committee which had been appointed to consider his resignation reported that no immediate action was necessary. Bland's motion was occasioned by the committee report (*JCC*, XXIV, 165).

2. Arthur Lee of Virginia.

Continental Congress
Report on the Memorials of Pelatiah Webster and William Judd

[Philadelphia] March 6, 1783

The Committee to whom was committed the report of the Grand Committee on the memorial of Pelatiah Webster & William Judd in behalf of the deranged officers of the lines of Massachusettes & Connecticut [1] submit the following resolution:

That the accounts of the officers who have retired on half pay at different periods of the war [or their representatives] [2] be settled on the same principles with the accounts of the army as contained in the resolution of the [25] of Jany last.

The Committee advise that the parts of their memorial relating to an advance of money be referred to the Superintendant of Finance to take order. [3]

AD, Papers of the Continental Congress, National Archives.

1. On January 7, 1783, Pelatiah Webster, pamphleteer and merchant, and William Judd of the Connecticut Militia sent Congress a petition on behalf of the Connecticut line. On January 8, Webster sent a similar petition on behalf of the Massachusetts line. On January 8, both petitions were referred to a grand committee which reported on February 27 (*JCC*, XXIV, 43). The report was recommitted on the same day to a committee consisting of Richard Peters, H, and Eliphalet Dyer (*JCC*, XXIV, 154).

2. The bracketed material is not in the writing of H.

3. The endorsement states that the report was read on March 5 and negatived on March 6.

Continental Congress
Motion that the Duties Imposed by the United States be Coexistent with the Public Debt

[Philadelphia, March 11, 1783]

A motion was made by Mr. Hamilton and Mr. Wilson to strike out the limitation of 25 years and to make the revenue co-existent with the debts.[1]

"Notes of Debates in the Continental Congress," MS, James Madison Papers, Library of Congress.

1. On March 6, 1783, Congress took up a committee report on the means of restoring the public credit and securing from the several states adequate funds for funding the debt of the United States. The report recommended that the states give Congress power to levy a five percent duty on imports, the same duty on all prizes condemned in the court of admiralty, and specific duties on various enumerated articles. The duties were to be imposed for no longer than twenty-five years (See *JCC*, XXIV, 170–73). H had made the same motion in a committee of the whole on February 19. The motion, according to Madison, was lost.

Continental Congress
Motion on the Appointment of Collectors

[Philadelphia, March 11, 1783]

A motion was made by Mr. Hamilton & Mr. Wilson to strike out the clauses relative to the appointment of Collectors,[1] and to provide that the Collectors shd. be inhabitants of the States within which they sd. collect should be nominated by Congs. and appointed by the States, and in case such nomination should not be accepted or rejected within   [2] days it should stand good.

"Notes of Debates in the Continental Congress," MS, James Madison Papers, Library of Congress.

1. This motion referred to the committee report described in the notes to the preceding motion. The clauses of the report, to which this motion refers, read as follows:

". . . provided, that the collectors of the said duties shall be appointed by the states within which their offices are to be respectively exercised; but, when so appointed, shall be amenable to and removable by the United States in Congress assembled alone, and in case any State shall not make such appointment within   after notice given for that purpose, the appointment may then be made by the United States in Congress assembled." (*JCC*, XXIV, 171.) H's motion was lost by a vote of 5 ayes and 6 nays.

2. Space left blank in MS.

From George Washington

Newburgh [New York] 12th. Mar. 1783.

Dear Sir,

When I wrote to you last we were in a state of tranquility, but after the arrival of a certain Gentleman,[1] who shall be nameless at present, from Philadelphia, a storm very suddenly arose with unfavourable prognostics; which tho' diverted for a moment is not yet blown over, nor is it in my power to point to the issue.

The Papers which I send officially to Congress,[2] will supercede the necessity of my remarking on the tendency of them. The notification and address,[3] both appeared at the same instant, on the day preceding the intended meeting. The first of these I got hold of the same afternoon; the other, not till next morning.[4]

There is something very misterious in this business. It appears, reports have been propagated in Philadelphia, that dangerous combinations were forming in the Army; and this at a time when there was not a syllable of the kind in agitation in Camp. It also appears, that upon the arrival in Camp of the Gentleman above alluded to such sentiments as these were immediately circulated: That it was universally expected the army would not disband untill they had obtained justice; That the public creditors looked up to them for Redress of their own grievances, wd afford them every aid, and even join them in the Field if necessary; That some mem⟨bers⟩ of Congress wished the measure might take effect, in order to compel the public, particularly the delinquent States, to do justice; with many other suggestions of a similar nature.

From this, and a variety of other considerations, it is firmly believed, by *some*, the scheme was not only planned but also digested and matured in Philadelphia;[5] but in my opinion shall be suspended till I have a better ground to found one on. The matter was managed with great art; for as soon as the Minds of the Officers were thought to be prepared for the transaction, the anonymous invitations and address to the Officers were put in circulation, through every state line in the army. I was obliged therefore, in order to arrest on the spot, the foot that stood wavering on a tremendous precipice; to prevent the Officers from being taken by surprize while the passions were all inflamed, and to rescue them from plunging themselves into a gulph of Civil horror from which there might be no receding, to issue the order of the 11th.[6] This was done upon the principle that it is easier to divert from a wrong, and point to a right path, than it is to recall the hasty and fatal steps which have been already taken.

It is commonly supposed if the Officers had met agreeably to the anonymous summons, with their feelings all alive, Resolutions might have been formed the consequences of which may be more easily conceived than described. Now they will have leizure to view the matter more calmly, and will act more seriously. It is to be hoped they will be induced to adopt more rational measures, and wait a while longer for a settlement of their accts., the postponing of which, appears to be the most plausible and almost the only article of which designing men can make an improper use, by insinuating (which they really do) that it is done with design that Peace may take place and prevent any adjustment of accts. which say they would inevitably be the case if the war was to cease tomorrow. Or supposing the best, you would have to dance attendance at public Offices at great distances perhaps, and equally great expences to obtain a settlement, which would be highly injurious, nay ruinous to you. This is their language.

Let me beseech you therefore, my good Sir, to urge this matter earnestly, and without further delay. The situation of these Gentlemen [7] I do verily believe, is distressing beyond description. It is affirmed to me, that a large part of them have no better prospect before them than a Goal, if they are turned loose without liquidation of accts. and an assurance of that justice to which they are so worthily entitled. To prevail on the Delegates of those States through whose means these difficulties occur, it may, in my opinion, with propriety be suggested to them, if any disastrous consequences should follow, by reason of their delinquency, that they must be answerable to God & their Country for the ineffable horrors which may be occasioned thereby.

I am Dear Sir Yr. Most Obedt. Serv

P.S. I have received your letter of the 5th. & have put that matter in train which was mentioned in it.   GW

I am this instant informed, that a second address to the Officers, distinguished No. 2, is thrown into circulation.[8] The Contents, evidently prove that the Author is in, or near Camp; and that the following words, erased in the second page of this Letter, ought not to have met with this treatment. viz: "By others, that it is the illegitimate offspring of a person in the army." [9]

AL[S], Hamilton Papers, Library of Congress; Df, George Washington Papers, Library of Congress.

1. Colonel Walter Stewart, who had been in Philadelphia, was ordered on active duty as inspector. When he reached Washington's headquarters at Newburgh, he reported to his friends that Congress planned to dissolve the Army in the near future and argued that the army officers should demand that Congress fulfill the promises it had made to them.

2. In a letter to the President of Congress, dated March 12, Washington enclosed three papers: 1. a proposal that a meeting of the general and field officers be held on March 11; 2. An address to the officers of the Army; 3. Washington's general orders of March 11, 1783. Washington's letter is printed in *GW*, XXVI, 211–12. All three enclosures are printed in *JCC*, XXIV, 294–98.

3. The address, which circulated at Washington's main camp near Newburgh, advised the officers of the Army to "suspect the man who would advise to more moderation and longer forbearance." Written by Major John Armstrong, the address also attacked Congress for not having fulfilled its obligations to the Army.

The "notification" was a written call for a meeting on March 11 of general and field officers to make a "last remonstrance." The officers were advised that if Congress should fail to act on the remonstrance the Army would be justified in defying that body.

4. Washington received the notification and address on March 10.

5. At this point Washington crossed out the following phrase: "By others, that it is the illegitimate offspring of a person in our camp."

6. In answer to the anonymous address of March 10, Washington in his general orders of March 11 denounced "such disorderly proceedings" and requested all general and field officers to assemble on March 15 "to devise what further measures ought to be adopted as most rational and best calculated to attain the just and important object in view" (*GW*, XXVI, 208).

7. In MS, "gentleman."

8. The second address, more moderate than the first, was dated March 12. Also written by Armstrong, it argued that Washington's call for a meeting proved that he "sanctified" the claims of the officers. This is printed in *JCC*, XXIV, 298–99.

9. See note 5.

To Brigadier General John Cadwalader

[Philadelphia, March 14, 1783]

Dear Sir

Though disagreeable to appear in any manner in a personal dispute, yet I cannot in justice to you refuse to comply with the request contained in your note.[1] I have delayed answering it to endeavour to recollect with more precision the time place and circumstances of the conversation to which you allude. I cannot however remember with certainty more than this, that sometime in the campaign of seventy seven, at Head Quarters, in this state, you mentioned to Col Harrison,[2] Col Tilghman,[3] myself and I believe some other Gentlemen of General Washington's family, in a confidential way, that at some period in seventy six, I think after the American army had crossed the Delaware in its retreat, Mr. Reed[4] had spoken to you in terms of great despondency respecting the American affairs and had intimated that he thought it time for Gentlemen to take care of themselves and that it was unwise any longer to follow the fortunes of a ruined cause, or something of a similar import. It runs in my mind that the expressions you declared to have been made use of by Mr. Reed were that he thought he ought no longer to "risk his life and fortune with the shattered remains of a broken army"; but it is the part of candour to observe that I am not able to distinguish with certainty whether the recollection I have of these words arises from the strong impression made by your declaration at the time, or from having heard them more than once repeated within a year past.

I am Dr Sir with great eseem Your Obedt ser   A Hamilton

Philadelphia
March 14. 1783

ALS, Historical Society of Pennsylvania, Philadelphia.
1. See Cadwalader to H, March 2, 1783.
2. Lieutenant Colonel Robert Hanson Harrison.
3. Lieutenant Colonel Tench Tilghman.
4. Joseph Reed. See Cadwalader to H, March 2, 1783, note 1.

Alexander Hamilton and William Floyd
to George Clinton

Philadelphia [March 17, 1783] [1]

Sir,

We have the honor to inclose Your Excellency the provisional articles agreed upon between the United States and Great Britain, which are upon the whole as advantageous as could have been expected.[2] Whether the negotiations terminate in a general peace or not, important and it is to be hoped, useful consequences will flow from what has been done. The acknowlegement of our independence by Great Britain will facilitate connections and intercourse between these states and the powers of Europe in general. With respect to the probability of a peace we can only observe that the interest of every party calls for it, but that the state of the negotiations when the last advices left France makes the event not a little doubtful.

One thing however may be inferred with tolerable certainty, which is that whether there is peace or war New York will ere long be evacuated.

We have the honor to be With perfect respect   Your Excellency's Most Obed Sevts.

His Excellency Governor Clinton

Df, in writing of H, New-York Historical Society, New York City.
1. H mistakenly dated this draft February 17, 1783, but on the endorsement he correctly gave the date as March 17.
2. The provisional peace treaty between the United States and Great Britain had been signed on November 30, 1782. On March 12, 1783, Captain Joshua Barney arrived in the United States with dispatches from the American Peace Commissioners and with the provisional treaty.

To George Washington

Philadelphia, March 17. 1783

Sir,

I am duely honored with Your Excellency's letter of the 4th. and 12th. instant. It is much to be regretted though not to be wondered at, that steps of so inflammatory a tendency have been taken in the army. Your Excellency has in my opinion acted wisely. The best way is ever not to attempt to stem a torrent but to divert it.

I am happy to find You coincide in opinion with me on the conduct proper to be observed by yourself. I am persuaded more and more it is that which is most consistent with your own reputation and the public safety.

Our affairs wear a most serious aspect as well foreign as domestic. Before this gets to hand Your Excellency will probably have seen the provisional articles between Great Britain and these states.[1] It might at first appearance be concluded that these will be the prelude to a general peace; but there are strong reasons to doubt the truth of such a conclusion. Obstacles may arise from different quarters, from the demands of Spain & Holl⟨and⟩, from the hope in France of greater acquisitions in the East, and perhaps still more probab⟨ly⟩ from the insincerity and duplicity of Lord Shelburn⟨e⟩, whose politics founded in the peculiarity of his situa⟨tion⟩, as well as in the character of the man ⟨may⟩ well be suspected of insidiousness. I am really appr⟨ehensive⟩ if peace does not take place, that the negotiation⟨s⟩ will tend to sow distrusts among the allies and wea⟨ken⟩ the force of the common league. We have I fear men ⟨among⟩ us and men in trust who have a hankering afte⟨r⟩ British connection. We have others whose confidence in France savours of credulity. The intrigues of the former and the incautiousness of the latter may be both, though in different degrees, injurious to the American interests; and make it difficult for prudent men to steer a proper course. There are delicate circumstances with respect to the late foreign transactions which I am not at liberty to reveal; but which joined to our internal weaknesses, disorders, follies & prejudices make this country stand upon precarious ground.

Some use perhaps may be made of these ideas to induce moderation in the army. An opinion that their country does not stand upon a secure footing will operate upon the patriotism of the officers against hazarding any domestic commotions.

When I make these observations I cannot forbear adding that if no excesses take place I shall not be sorry that ill-humours have appeared. I shall not regret importunity, if temperate, from the army.

There are good intentions in the Majority of Congress; but there is not sufficient wisdom or decision. There are dangerous prejudices in the particular states opposed to those measures which alone can give stability & prosperity to the Union. There is a fatal opposition to Continental views. Necessity alone can work a reform. But how apply it and how keep it within salutary bounds? [2]

I fear we have been contending for a shadow.

The affair of accounts I considered as having been put on a satisfactory footing. The particular states have been required to settle 'till the first of August 80 and the Superintendant of Finance has been directed to take measures for settling since that period. I shall immediately see him on the subject.

We have had Eight states and a half in favour of a commutation of the half pay for an average of ten years purchase, that is five years full pay instead of half pay for life, which on a calculation of annuities is nearly an equivalent. I hope this will now shortly take place.

We have made considerable progress in a plan to be recommended to the several states for funding all the public debts including those of the army; which is certainly the only way to restore public credit and enable us to continue the war, by borrowing abroad, if it should be necessary to continue it.

I omitted mentioning to Your Excellency that from European intelligence, there is great reason to believe at all events, peace or War, New York will be evacuated in the Spring. It will be a pity if any domestic disturbances should change the plans of the British Court.

I have the honor to be With the greatest respect   Yr Excellency's Most Obed se⟨rvant⟩

P.S Your Excellency mentions that it has been surmised the plan in agitation was formed in Philadelphia; that combinations have been talked of between the public creditors and the army; and that members of Congress had incouraged the idea. This is partly true. I have myself urged in Congress the propriety of uniting the influence of the public creditors, & the army as a part of them, to prevail upon the states to enter into their views. I have expressed the same sentiments out of doors. Several other members of Congress have done the same.[3] The meaning however of all this was simply that Congress should adopt such a plan as would embrace the relief of all the public creditors including the army; in order that the personal influence of some, the connections of others, and a sense of justice to the army as well as the apprehension of ill consequences might form a mass of influence in each state in favour of the measures of Congress. In this view, as I mentioned to Your Excellency in a former letter, I thought the discontents of the army might be turned to a good account. I am still of opinion that their earnest, but respectful applications for redress will have a good effect.

As to any combination of *Force* it would only be productive of the horrors of a civil war, might end in the ruin of the Country & would certainly end in the ruin of the army.

ADf, Hamilton Papers, Library of Congress.
1. On March 12 Congress received the official text of the provisional articles of peace which had been signed in Paris on November 30, 1782.
2. This sentence appears in the draft as follows: "But how ~~is this what~~ necessity ~~to be produced~~, how ~~is it to be~~ applyed it and how k~~ep~~t it within salutary bounds?"
3. This sentence appears in the draft as follows: "~~Many~~ several ~~of the most sensible~~ members of Congress ~~but~~ have done the same."

To Philip Schuyler

[*Philadelphia, March 18, 1783.* On May 4, 1783, Schuyler wrote to Hamilton: "Your several favors of the 18th & 25th March and 2d. ult. were delivered me." *Letter of March 18 not found.*]

Continental Congress
Report on the Memorial of Thomas Wiggins

[*Philadelphia*] *March 18, 1783.* A memorial of Thomas Wiggins, a Canadian merchant and Indian trader near Detroit during the American Revolution, was read in Congress on February 4, 1783, and referred to a committee consisting of Hamilton, Richard Peters, and Samuel Osgood. Wiggins, whose aid to the American cause had occasioned imprisonment and the seizure of his property by the British, requested relief from Congress that he might "have time to form a new plan of life." The committee report, appearing on the endorsement of the memorial, requested that the quartermaster general provide employment for the memorialist.

AD, Papers of the Continental Congress, National Archives.

Christopher Tappen to Alexander Hamilton and William Floyd [1]

Kingston [New York] March 19, 1783. States that the Corporation of Kingston desires to become the seat of the Continental Congress and discusses the advantages it affords as well as the privileges the town is willing to extend. Encloses a letter from Governor George Clinton [2] to Congress transmitting a joint resolution of the New York legislature and an act of the Corporation of Kingston proposing that Congress make Kingston its permanent residence.

ALS, Hamilton Papers, Library of Congress.
    1. Christopher Tappen was the clerk of the trustees of the Corporation of Kingston.
    2. According to the *Journals*, Clinton's letter was received on April 4, 1783, and referred to a committee (*JCC*, XXIV, 229, note 2).

Continental Congress
Remarks on the Provisional Peace Treaty [1]

[Philadelphia, March 19, 1783]

Mr. Hamilton urged the propriety of proceeding with coolness and circumspection. He thought it proper in order to form a right judgment of the conduct of our Ministers, that the views of the French & British Courts should be examined. He admitted it as not improbable that it had been the policy of France to procrastinate the definite acknowledgmt. of our Independence on the part of G B in order to keep us more knit to herself & untill her own interests could be negotiated. The arguments hower, urged by our Ministers on this subject, although strong, were not conclusive; as it was not certain, that this policy & not a desire of excluding obstacles to peace, had produced ye. opposition of the French Court to our demands. Caution & vigilance he thought were justified by the appearance & that alone. But compare this policy with that of G B, survey the past cruelty & present duplicity of her councils, behold her watching every occasion & trying every project for dissolving the honorable ties which bind the U.S. to their ally, & then say on which side our resentments & jealousies ought to lie. With respect to the instructions submitting our Ministers to the advice of France,[2] he had disapproved it uniformly since it had come to his knowledge, but he had always judged it improper to repeal it. He disapproved highly of the conduct of our Ministers in not shewing the preliminary articles to our Ally before they signed them, and still more so of their agreeing to the separate article. This conduct gave an advantage to the Enemy which they would not fail to improve for the purpose of inspiring France with indignation & distrust of the U.S. He did not apprehend (with Mr. Mercer) any danger of a coalition between F & G B against America,[3] but foresaw the destruction of mutual Confidence between F & the U.S., which wd. be likely to ensue, & the danger which would result from it in case the war should be continued. He observed that Spain was an unwise nation, her policy narrow & jealous, her King old her Court divided & the heir apparent notoriously attached to G B. From these circumstances he inferred an apprehension that when Spain sd. come to know the part taken by America with respect to her, a separate treaty of peace might be resorted to. He thought a middle course best with respect to our Ministers; that they ought to be commended in general; but that the communication of the separate article ought to take place. He observed that our Ministers were divided as to the policy of the Ct of France, but that they all were agreed in the necessity of being on the watch against G B. He apprehended that if the ministers were to be recalled or reprehended, that they would be disgusted & head & foment parties in this Country. He observed particularly with respect to Mr. Jay that altho' he was a man of profound sagacity & pure integrity, yet he was of a suspicious temper, & that this trait might explain the extraordinary jealousies which he professed. He finally proposed that the Ministers sd. be commended and the separate article communicated.[4]

"Notes of Debates in the Continental Congress," MS, James Madison Papers, Library of Congress.

1. The provisional peace treaty between the United States and Great Britain, signed on November 30, 1782, reached Congress on March 12, 1783. Although pleased with most of its provisions, Congress was disturbed that the peace commissioners, in violation of their instructions to make no peace without the knowledge and concurrence of the French, had concealed their negotiations with the British from the French ministry until the treaty had been signed.

On March 18, 1783, Congress received a letter from the Secretary for Foreign Affairs, Robert R. Livingston, concerning the peace treaty's secret article relating to West Florida. This article provided that, if at the conclusion of the war Great Britain should be in possession of West Florida, "the line of north boundary between the said province and the United States shall be a line drawn from the mouth of the river Yassous, where it unites with the Mississippi, due east to the river Apalachicola" (*Secret Journals of the Acts and Proceedings of Congress* [Boston, 1821], III, 338). The Secretary for Foreign Affairs stated that Congress was reduced to the alternative "either of dishonoring themselves by becoming a party to the concealment, or of wounding the feelings & destroying the influence of our Ministers by disclosing the article to the French Court" ("Notes of Debates in the Continental Congress," MS, James Madison Papers, Library of Congress). The Secretary proposed that he be authorized to communicate the article relating to West Florida to the French Minister; that the American Ministers in France be instructed to agree that the boundaries of West Florida, as established in the provisional articles, be allowed to the country to which West Florida might be given in the final peace treaty; and that the preliminary articles between the United States and Great Britain should not take effect until peace had been signed between Great Britain and France. Livingston's letter provoked a long debate.

2. The Treaty of Alliance between the United States and France, signed in 1778, had stipulated that neither country should make peace without the concurrence of the other. During the peace negotiations Congress repeatedly had reminded the American commissioners of this treaty obligation to France and warned them against separate negotiations.

3. John Francis Mercer, delegate from Virginia, had predicted that if Congress approved the secret article of the treaty relating to West Florida, France might form an alliance with Great Britain for "our destruction and for a division of the spoils" ("Notes of Debates in the Continental Congress," MS, James Madison Papers, Library of Congress).

4. Madison recorded that the motion contained in the last sentence of H's remarks was seconded by Samuel Osgood on the ground that it was preferable to the propositions of the Secretary for Foreign Affairs. (See note 1). Osgood, however, recommended that H's motion not be accepted, but that it be referred to a committee.

Continental Congress
Motion on the Provisional Peace Treaty [1]

[Philadelphia] March 19, 1783

Resolved that as Congress are desirous of manifesting at all times the most perfect confidence in their ally, the Secretary for foreign affairs be directed to Communicate to the Minister P. from the Court of France to these states the separate [2] article of the provisional treaty between The United States and His Britannic Majesty and that he inform the Commissioners from these states for making peace of the reasons for that communication, repeating to them the desire of Congress that they will upon all occasions maintain perfect harmony and confidence with an ally, to whose generous assistance the United States are so signally indebted.

Resolved that Congress entertain a high sense of the services of their Commissioners in their steady attention to the dignity and essential interests of the United States, and in obtaining from the Court of Great Britain articles so favourable and so important to those interests.[3]

AD, Papers of the Continental Congress, National Archives.
   1. For an explanation of the context in which this motion was made, see note 1 of the preceding document.
   2. "Separate" is not in the writing of H.
   3. H's motion was rejected, and the question of what instructions should be given to the Secretary for Foreign Affairs was referred to a committee ("Notes of Debates in the Continental Congress," MS, James Madison Papers, Library of Congress).

Continental Congress
Motion on Establishment of Permanent Funds [1]

[Philadelphia] March 21, 1783

Whereas Congress did on the 12 day of February last resolve— "that it is the opinion of Congress that the establishment of permanent and adequate funds on taxes or duties which shall operate generally and on the whole in just proportions, throughout the United States are indispensably necessary towards doing complete justice to the public creditors for restoring public credit and for providing for the future exigencies of the war."

And Whereas it is the duty of Congress on whose faith the public debts have been contracted for the common safety to make every effort in their power for the effectual attainment of objects so essential to the honor and welfare of the United States, relying on the wisdom and justice of their constituents for a compliance with their recommendations.[2]

Therefore Resolved, that it be earnestly recommended to the several states, without delay to pass laws for the establishment of the following funds, to be vested in the United States, and to be collected and appropriated by their authority; provided that the officers for the collection of the said funds shall be inhabitants of each state respectively in which they reside, and being nominated by Congress shall be approved and appointed by such state accountable to and removeable by Congress; and provided that if, after any nomination being reported to the state, the same is not approved or rejected at the next meeting of the legislature, the person or persons so nominated shall be deemed to be duly appointed [3]-viz.[4]

A duty of 5 ⅌ Cent ad valorem at the time and place of importation upon all goods wares and merchandizes for foreign growth and manufactures, which may be imported into any of the said states from any foreign port Island or plantation, except arms ammunition cloathing and other articles imported on account of the United States or any of them, and except wool cards, cotton cards and wire for making them; and also except the articles hereafter enumerated, the duty on which shall be regulated according to the specified rates thereunto annexed.[5]

here insert the articles enumerated in the other report [6]

Also a duty of 5 ⅌ Cent ad valorem on all prizes and prize goods condemned in the court of Admiralty of any of these states as lawful prize.

A land tax at the rate of   [7] Ninetieths of a dollar for every hundreds acres of located and surveyed land.

A house-tax at the general rate of half a dollar for each dwelling house (cottages excepted) and at the additional rate of 2½ ⅌ Cent on whatever sum the rent of the said house may exceed twenty dollars—to be calculated on the actual rent when the house is rented—and when in the occupancy of the owner on an appraised rent by Commissioners under oath appointed by the state once in   [8] years—the lot and its appurtenances in towns and in the Country the outhouses garden and orchard to be comprehended with the dwelling house.[9]

The duties on imports to pass to the general benefit of The United

States, without credit for the proceeds to any particular states—but the product of the land and house taxes to be credited to each state in which it shall arise.[10]

The said funds to continue 'till the principal of the debt due by the United States at the termination of the present war shall be finally discharged.[11]

Resolved that an estimate be transmitted to each state of the amount of the public debt as far as the same can now be ascertained, and that Congress will inviolably adhere to their resolutions of the 16th. day of December last,[12] respecting the appropriation of any funds which might be granted, and the annual transmission of the state of the public debt, and the proceeds and dispositions of the said funds by which all doubts and apprehensions respecting the perpetuity of the public debt may be effectually removed.[13]

AD, Papers of the Continental Congress, National Archives. On the endorsement this motion is dated March 21, 1783. It is dated March 20, in the *Journals*.

1. From January 29, until February 21, 1783, Congress frequently resolved itself into a committee of the whole to devise ways of restoring the public credit. See notes to H's "Remarks on Plans for Paying the Public Debt" on January 29. On February 21, Daniel Carroll, reported that "the committee have taken into consideration the subject referred to them, and are of opinion, that the committee of the whole be discharged and the business referred to a special committee." Nathaniel Gorham, H, James Madison, Thomas FitzSimons, and John Rutledge were appointed. The committee reported on March 6 (see notes to H's motions of March 11). The report was considered until April 18, when it was adopted in amended form. (See *JCC*, XXIV, 256–61.)

On March 20, 1783, the committee recommended that the states give Congress the power to levy certain enumerated duties on goods imported into the United States and suggested that the states provide other revenue for discharging the debt of the United States. James Madison stated that H's motion "was meant as a testimony on his part of the insufficiency of the report of the Come as to the establishment of revenues, and as a final trial of the sense of Congs with respect to the practicability & necessity of a *general* revenue equal to the public wants" ("Notes and Debates of the Continental Congress," MS, James Madison Papers, Library of Congress).

2. H's motion placed more emphasis on the necessity for permanent funds than the committee report did. The report stated only that "it be recommended to the several states, as indispensably necessary to the restoration of public credit, and to the punctual and honorable discharge of the public debts, to invest in the United States in Congress assembled, a power to levy for the use of the United States, the following duties upon goods imported into the said states from any foreign port, island or plantation" (*JCC*, XXIV, 195).

3. The committee report had recommended that the collectors be appointed by the states "within which their offices are to be respectively exercised" and that Congress have the right of appointment only if a state failed to make an appointment (*JCC*, XXIV, 196).

4. H at this point wrote and then crossed out the following: "a duty of 5

℔ cent ad valorem upon all goods imported from any foreign country into any part of these states, the following articles excepted which shall pay a duty according to the rate hereafter specified."

5. After specifying the duties to be levied on certain enumerated products, the committee report proposed that a duty of five percent *ad valorem* be levied upon "all other goods, except arms, ammunition and cloathing, or other articles imported for the United States, . . . provided that there be allowed a bounty of ⅛th of a dollar for every quintal of dried fish exported out of these United States, and a like sum for every barrel of pickled fish, beef or pork, to be paid or allowed to the exporters thereof, at the ports from which they shall be so exported" (*JCC*, XXIV, 195–96).

6. For the articles enumerated in the committee report see *JCC*, XXIV, 195.

7. Space left blank in MS.

8. Space left blank in MS.

9. The committee report had recommended neither a land nor a house tax, but had asked that the states raise "substantial and effectual revenues, of such nature as they may respectively judge most convenient" (*JCC*, XXIV, 196).

10. The committee report recommended "That an annual account of the proceeds and application of the aforementioned revenues, shall be made out and transmitted to the several states, distinguishing the proceeds of each of the specified articles, and the amount of the whole revenue received from each State" (*JCC*, XXIV, 196–97).

11. The committee report recommended that the proposed duties should continue for only twenty-five years.

12. On December 16, 1782, Congress had resolved that, "Whereas it is essential to justice and to the preservation of public credit, that whenever a nation is obliged by the exigencies of public affairs to contract a debt, proper funds should be established, not only for paying the annual value or interest of the same, but for discharging the principal within a reasonable period, by which a nation may avoid the evils of an excessive accumulation of debt" (*JCC*, XXIII, 809).

13. At this point in the *Journals* appears the following: "That none of the preceding resolutions shall take effect, &c. (in the words of the report to the end)" (*JCC*, XXIV, 200).

At the end of this motion H wrote and then crossed out two resolves which read as follows:

"Resolved, That a Committee be appointed to prepare an ordinance agreeable to the tenor of these resolutions with such additional provisions as may be found necessary to determine in the most explicit and precise manner the nature and extent of the said funds and of the powers to be vested in the United states for the collection and appropriation thereof, and that the said ordinance be transmitted to the several states with a recommendation that the same be incorporated with their acts.

"Resolved, that in case any of the states shall refuse to concur in the plan recommended by the preceding resolutions, it will become indispensable for Congress to require of the several states in payments at short periods the sums necessary for the discharge of the principal of the public debt, in proportions agreeable to the 8th. article of the confederation."

H's motion for postponement was rejected by Congress.

Continental Congress
Report on Half Pay to the Army [1]

[Philadelphia] March 21, 1783

Whereas the officers of the several lines under the immediate command of His Excellency General Washington did, by their late memorial transmitted by their committee, represent to Congress that the half pay granted by sundry resolutions was regarded in an unfavourable light by the citizens of some of these states, who would prefer a compensation for a limited term of years, or by a sum in gross, to an establishment for life; and did on that account solicit a commutation of their half pay for an equivalent in one of the two modes above-mentioned, in order to remove all subject of dissatisfaction from the minds of their fellow citizens:

And Whereas Congress are desirous [2] as well of gratifying the reasonable expectations of the officers of the army as of removing all obj⟨ections⟩ which may exist in any part of The United States to the princi⟨ple⟩ of the half-pay establishment, for which the faith of The United States hath been pledged; persuaded that those objections can only arise from the nature of the compensation, not from an⟨y⟩ indisposition to compensate those whose services sacrifi⟨ces⟩ and sufferings have so just a title to the approbation and rewards of their country:

Therefore Resolved That such officers as are now in service and shall continue therein to the end of the war shall be intitled to receive the amount of five years full pay in money or securities on interest at six per Cent as congress shall find most convenient, instead of the half pay promised for life by the resolution of the 21 of October 1780, the said securities to be such as shall be given to other creditors of The United States, provided that it be at the option of the lines of the respective states and not of officers individually in those lines, to accept or refuse the same; and provided also that their election shall be signified to Congress through the Commander in Chief from the lines under his immediate command within two months and through the Commanding officer of the Southern army from those under his command within Six months from the date of these resolutions:

That the same commutation shall extend to the corps not belonging to the lines of particular states [& who are entitled to half pay for life as aforesd,] [3] the acceptance or refusal to be determined by corps and to be signified in the same manner and within the same time as above-mentioned:

That all officers belonging to the hospital department who are intitled to half pay [by the resolution of 17 Janry 1781] [4] may collectively agree to accept or refuse the aforesaid commutation, signifying the same through the Commander in Chief within Six months from this time:

That such officers as have retired at different periods, intitled to half pay for life may collectively in each state of which they are inhabitants accept or refuse the same, their acceptance or refusal to be signified by agents authorised for that purpose within Six months from this period:

That with respect to such retiring officers [5] the commutation if accepted by them shall be in lieu of whatever may be now due to them since the time of their retiring from service as well of what might hereafter become due; and that so soon as their acceptance shall be signified, The Superintendant of Finance be directed to take measures for the settlement of their accounts accordingly and to issue to them certificates bearing interest at six per Cent.

That all officers intitled to half pay for life not included in the preceding resolutions may also collectively agree to accept or refuse the aforesaid commu[ta]tion, signifying the same within Six months from this time.[6]

AD, Papers of the Continental Congress, National Archives. The endorsement states that the report was read on March 21, 1783. In the *Journals* it is dated March 22.

1. On January 22 a grand committee delivered a report, in the writing of H, on a memorial presented by the Army. A part of the report, including a section on the commutation of half pay for life to full pay for a certain number of years, was referred to a committee whose report was debated several times during February and March (See *JCC*, XXIV, 95–207).

The paragraph in the *Journals* which precedes these resolutions reads: "On the report of a committee, consisting of Mr. (Alexander) Hamilton, Mr. (Eliphalet) Dyer and Mr. (Gunning) Bedford [Jr.], to whom was referred a motion of Mr. (Eliphalet) Dyer, together with the memorial of the officers of the army, and the report of the committee thereon; Congress came to the following resolutions:" (*JCC*, XXIV, 207).

2. In MS, "diserous."

3. The bracketed phrase is not in the writing of H.

4. The bracketed phrase is not in the writing of H.

5. H first wrote "to the deranged officers who have retired on half pay for life," but the phrase was bracketed and the words inserted, "to such retiring officers." The word "retiring" is not in H's handwriting.

6. In H's draft this resolution appears between the paragraph ending ". . . within six months from this period" and that beginning "That with respect to such retiring officers." In the report printed in the *Journals* it was transposed and made the last resolution of the report (*JCC*, XXIV, 209).

The votes of the delegates from each state are recorded on the last page of the document. As nine states voted in the affirmative, the report was passed on March 22, 1783.

Alexander Hamilton and William Floyd to George Clinton

[Philadelphia, March 24, 1783]

Sir,

We have the happiness to inform your Excellency that yesterday arrived the Triumph a Cutter from Cadiz, with letters from the Marquis La Fayette announc⟨ing⟩ the certainty of the preliminaries of a general peace signed between all the belligerent powers the 20th. of January.[1] There are letters from the Count D'Estaing to the French Minister to the same effect, and an instruction from him to the Captain of the Cutter to advertise all British and French vessels of the event, with an order to the latter to cease hostilities.[2]

The preliminaries for America we have already had the honor of transmitting. We mean the provisional articles.

The French are reinstated in the East Indies as in 63—mutual cessions of all conquests during the war are made, except of Tobago & Senegal which remain to France—France has in substance the same share in the Fisheries as before the war.

Spain has acquired Minorca and the two Floridas.

The Dutch lose *Negapatam* to the English.[3] It only remains to provide for internal tranquillity—and by drawing the links ⟨of⟩ the Union closer to prevent those states from becoming ⟨the⟩ foot ball of European politics.

We have the honor to be With perfect respect   Your Excellency's Most Obedient servants   Wm Floyd
                                                                  A Hamilton

Philadelphia
March 24th. 1783

LS, in the writing of H, from the original in the New York State Library, Albany.

1. On March 24, 1783, the *Journals* of the Continental Congress announced receipt of "a letter, of February 5, from the Marquis de la Fayette, announcing [the signing of preliminary articles for] a general peace, and a copy of orders given by the Count D'Estaing, vice admiral of France, to the Chevalier Du Quesne, commander of the corvette *Triumph*, despatched from Cadiz the 6 of February last, for the purpose of putting a stop to all hostilities by sea" (*JCC*, XXIV, 210–11).

2. In 1778 the Count d'Estaing was appointed a vice-admiral of the French fleet and sent to America to assist the United States against Great Britain. In 1783, when peace was signed, he was in command of the combined fleet before Cadiz.

3. At this point one sentence is missing.

To George Washington

[Philadelphia, March 24, 1783]

Sir

Your Excellency will before this reaches you have received a letter from the Marquis De la Fayette informing you that the preliminaries of peace between all the belligerent powers have been concluded.[1] I congratulate your Excellency on this happy conclusion of your labours. It now only remains to make solid establishments within to perpetuate our union to prevent our being a ball in the hands of European powers bandied against each other at their pleasure—in fine to make our independence truly a blessing. This it is to be lamented will be an arduous work, for to borrow a figure from mechanics, the centrifugal is much stronger than the centripetal force in these states—the seeds of disunion much more numerous than those of union.

I will add that Your Excellency's exertions are as essential to accomplish this end as they have been to establish independence. I will upon a future occasion open myself upon this Subject.

Your conduct in the affair of the officers is highly pleasing here.[2] The measures of the army are such as I could have wished them and will add new lustre to their character as wel⟨l⟩ as strengthen the hands of Congress.

I am with great truth & respect. Yr. Excellency's Most Obed ser

A Hamilton

Philadelphia
March 24th. 1783
His Excelly General Washington

ALS, Hamilton Papers, Library of Congress.

1. Lafayette's letter announcing the signing of the preliminary articles of peace between Great Britain, France, and Spain on January 20, 1783, was sent from Cadiz on February 5 and was read in Congress on March 24.

2. H referred to the Newburgh addresses (see Washington to H, March 12, 1783) which threatened drastic action by the Army unless Congress satisfied the Army's demands. The possibility of coercion by the Army was obviated by an address by Washington to the officers on March 15 in which he expressed his confidence in Congress and counseled patience. After Washington's speech the officers adopted resolutions indicating their confidence in Congress.

Continental Congress
Remarks on the Provisional Peace Treaty

[Philadelphia, March 24, 1783] [1]

Mr. Hamilton said that whilst he despised the man who wd. enslave himself to the policy even of our Friends, he could not but lament the overweening readiness which appeared in many, to suspect every thing on that side & to throw themselves into the bosom of our enemies. He urged the necessity of vindicating our public honor by renouncing that concealment to which it was the wish of so many to make us parties.

"Notes of Debates in the Continental Congress," MS, James Madison Papers, Library of Congress.

1. On this date, as on the days preceding, Congress continued the debate begun on March 19 on the provisional peace treaty's secret article concerning West Florida. See H's "Remarks on the Provisional Peace Treaty," March 19, 1783. When on March 24 Congress learned of the signing of the preliminary articles of peace between Great Britain, France, and Spain, the problem of the separate negotiation of the treaty was no longer urgent.

To Philip Schuyler

[*Philadelphia, March 25, 1783.* On May 4, 1783, Schuyler wrote to Hamilton: "Your several favors of the 18th & 25th March and 2d. ult. were delivered me." *Letter of March 25 not found.*]

To George Washington

Phila. Mar 25th 1783

Sir

The inclosed [1] I write more in a public than in a private capacity. Here I write as a citizen zealous for the true happiness of this country, as a soldier who feels what is due to an army which has suffered everything and done much for the safety of America.

I sincerly wish *ingratitude* was not so natural to the human heart as it is. I sincerely wish there were no seeds of it in those who direct the councils of the United States. But while I urge the army to moderation, and advise Your Excellency to take the direction of their discontents, and endeavour to confine them within the bounds of duty, I cannot as an hon⟨est⟩ man conceal from you, that I am afraid their distrusts ha⟨ve⟩ too much foundation. Republican jealousy has in it a principle of hostility to an army whatever be their merits, whatever be ⟨their⟩ claims to the gratitude of the community. It acknowleges their services with unwillingness and rewards them with reluctance. I see this temper, though smothered with great care, involuntarily breaking out upon too many occasions. I often feel a mortification, which it would be impolitic to express, that sets my passions at variance with my reason. Too many I perceive, if they could do it with safety or colour, would ⟨be⟩ glad to elude the just pretensions of the army. I hope ⟨that⟩ this is not the prevailing disposition.

But supposing the Country ungrate⟨ful⟩ what can the army do? It must submit to its hard f⟨ate.⟩ To seek redress by its arms would end in its ruin. The ar⟨my⟩ would moulder by its own weight and for want of the means of keeping together. The soldiery would abandon their officers. There would be no chance of success without having recourse to means that would reverse our revolution. I make these observations not that I imagine Your Excellency can want motives to continue your influence in the path of moderation; but merely to show why I cannot myself enter into the views of coertion which some Gentlemen entertain, for I confess could force avail I should almost wish to see it employed. I have an indifferent opinion of the honesty of this country, and ill-forebodings as to its future system.

Your Excellency will perceive I have written with sensations of chagrin and will make allowance for colouring; but the general picture is too true.

God send us all more wisdom. I am with very sincere respect
Yr Excellys Obed servt   A Hamilton

Philadelphia 25th of March

ALS, George Washington Papers, Library of Congress.
  1. See the following letter: H to George Washington, March 25, 1783.

To George Washington

[Philadelphia, March 25, 1783]

Sir,

I wrote to Your Excellency a day or two ago by express.[1] Since that a Committee appointed on the communications from you have had a meeting,[2] and find themselves embarrassed. They have requested me to communicate our embarrassments to you in confidence and to ask your private opinion. The army by their resolutions express an expectation that Congress will not disband them previous to a settlement of accounts and the establishment of funds. Congress may resolve upon the first; but the general opinion is that they cannot constitutionally declare the second. They have no right by the Confederation to *demand* funds, they can only recommend; and to determine that the army shall be continued in service 'till the states grant them, would be to determine that the whole present army, shall be a standing army during peace unless the states comply with the requisitions for funds. This it is supposed would excite the alarms and jealousies of the states and increase rather than lessen the opposition to the funding scheme. It is also observed that the longer the army is kept together, the more the payment of past dues is procrastinated, the abilities of the states being exhausted for their immediate support and a new debt every day incurred. It is further suggested that there is danger in keeping the army together, in a state of inactivity, and that a separation of the several lines would facilitate the settlement of accounts, diminish present expence and avoid the danger of union; it is added that the officers of each line, being on the spott, might by their own solicitations & those of their friends, forward the adoption of funds in the different states.

A proposition will be transmitted to you by Colonel Bland in the form of a resolution to be adopted by Congress framed upon the principles of the foregoing reasoning.[3]

Another proposition is contained in the following resolution:

"That the Commander in Chief be informed it is the intention of Congress to effect the settlement of the accounts of the respective lines previous to their reduction; and that Congress are doing, and will continue to do, everything in their power towards procuring satisfactory securities for what shall be found due on such settlement." [4]

The scope of this Your Excellency will perceive without comment.

I am to request you will favour me with your sentiments on both the propostions, and in general with your ideas of what had best be done with reference to the expectation expressed by the officers; taking into view the situation of Congress.

On one side the army expect they will not be disbanded 'till accounts are settled & funds established, on the other hand, they have no constitutional power of doing any thing more than to recommend funds, and are persuaded that these will meet with mountains of prejudice in some of the states.

A considerable progress has been made in a plan for funding the public debts and it is to be hoped it will ere long go forth to the states, with every argument that can give it success.

I have the honor to be With sincere respect   Yr Excellys Most Obedt serv   A Hamilton

Philadelphia
25. of March 1783
His Excellency General Washington

ALS, George Washington Papers, Library of Congress.
     1. H to Washington, March 24, 1793.
     2. Washington's letter to the President of Congress, dated March 18, 1783, was read in Congress on March 22. In it Washington enclosed the proceedings of a grand convention of officers which had been held on March 15. The meeting was called by Washington to obviate the threat of violence which had been implied in two anonymous addresses to the Army (see Washington to H, March 12, 1783, and H to Washington, March 24, 1783). In his letter of March 18 Washington implored Congress to meet the just demands of the Army (*GW*, XXVI, 229–32). This letter, together with a letter he had addressed to Congress on March 12 which also discussed the officers' claims, was referred to Samuel Osgood, Theodorick Bland, H, Oliver Wolcott, Sr., and Richard Peters.
     3. The proposition enclosed by Theodorick Bland in his letter of March 25 to Washington reads as follows:
     "That they be further informed that Congress will Take the most speedy and effectual measures to settle the accounts of the whole Army as well for the half Pay, or commutation if accepted as for the arrearages due to them in the most ample and satisfactory manner—and will devise the best and most efficacious means of Providing funds for the discharge of the Interest and Principal found due to them on such Settlement—and assure the Army that

Congress will not direct any Line or corps to be disbanded untill they be respectively Marchd to a Rendevous within their respective States, and their accounts shall be finally settled and adjusted." (Burnett, *Letters*, VII, 106–08.)

4. This proposed resolution, like the first, was also submitted to Washington by Bland (Burnett, *Letters*, VII, 108).

Continental Congress
Report on Colonel Charles Armand

[Philadelphia] March 26, 1783

The Committee [1] to whom were referred the letters from the Commander in Chief & from Col Armand [2] submit the following resolution:

Col Armand having entered at an early period of the war into the army of The United States with the rank of Colonel, and having served with distinction in that rank, so as to acquire the particular approbation of the Commander in Chief for his intelligence zeal and bravery,

Resolved, that in consideration of the merit & services of Col Armand he be promoted to the rank of Brigadier General, retaining the command of his present corps. [3]

AD, Papers of the Continental Congress, National Archives.

1. The committee consisted of Theodorick Bland, H, and Richard Peters.

2. Charles Armand-Tuffin, Marquis de la Rouerie, had served in the Continental Army from May, 1777, to the close of the war. Washington's letter, dated March 7, 1783, is in *GW*, XXVI, 197–98. Armand's letter, dated March 13, is in the Papers of the Continental Congress, National Archives.

3. His corps was known as "Armand's Partisan Corps."

Congress accepted the recommendation of the committee report on March 26.

Although it is not included in the printed report (*JCC*, XXIV, 211–12), the following proviso, not in H's writing, appears at the bottom of the manuscript: "Provided that no Emoluments shall accrue to the several Officers afd. in their Promotions, other than those they have been heretofore entitled to."

From George Washington

Newburgh [New York] 31st. March 1783

Dear Sir,

I have duly received your favors of the 17th. & 24th. ulto. I rejoice most exceedingly that there is an end to our warfare, and that such a field is opening to our view as will, with wisdom to direct the cultivation of it, make us a great, a respectable, and happy People; but it must be improved by other means than State politics, and unreasonable jealousies & prejudices; or (it requires not the second sight to see that) we shall be instruments in the hands of our Enemies, & those European powers who may be jealous of our greatness in Union to dissolve the confederation; but to attain this, altho the way seems extremely plain, is not so easy.

My wish to see the Union of these States established upon liberal & permanent principles, & inclination to contribute my mite in pointing out the defects of the present Constitution, are equally great. All my private letters have teemed with these Sentiments, & whenever this topic has been the subject of conversation, I have endeavoured to diffuse & enforce them; but how far any further essay, by me, might be productive of the wished for end, or appear to arrogate more than belongs to me, depends so much upon popular opinion, & the temper & disposition of People, that it is not easy to decide. I shall be obliged to you however for the thoughts which you have promised me on this subject, and as soon as you can make it convenient.

No man in the United States is, or can be more deeply impressed with the necessity of a reform in our present Confederation than myself. No man perhaps has felt the bad efects of it more sensibly; for to the defects thereof, & want of Powers in Congress may justly be ascribed the prolongation of the War, & consequently the Expences occasioned by it. More than half the perplexities I have experienced in the course of my command, and almost the whole of the difficulties & distress of the Army, have there origin here; but still, the prejudices of some, the designs of others, and the mere machinery of the majority, makes address & management necessary to give weight to opinions which are to Combat the doctrine of those different classes of men, in the field of Politics.

I would have been more full on this subject but the bearer (in the clothing department) is waiting. I wish you may understand what I have written.

I am Dr Sir   Yr. Most Obedt Servt   Go: Washington

Honble. Alexr Hamilton.

The inclosed extract of a Letter to Mr Livingston,[1] I give you in confidence. I submit it to your consideration, fully persuaded that

you do not want inclination to gratify the Marquis's wishes as far
as is consistent with our National honor. GW

ALS, Hamilton Papers, Library of Congress; ADfS, George Washington Papers, Library of Congress.
1. The extract from Washington's letter of March 29, 1783, to Robert R.
Livingston, the Secretary for Foreign Affairs, is in Washington's writing and
reads as follows:
"In a Letter I received by the Cutter from the Marqs. De la Fayette dated
Cadiz 5th. of Feby is this passage.
" 'Independent of my public letter to Mr. Livingston, there is a private one
which he will also communicate, amongst the many favors I have received,
I would take it as the most flattering circumstance in my life to be sent to
England with the ratification of the American Treaty; You know it is but
an honorary Commission, that requires the attendance of a few Weeks, and
if any Sedentary Minister is sent, I should have the pleasure of introducing him;
This, my dear General is entirely Confidential.'
"From hence, I presume it is necessary for Congress to ratifie the Treaty
of Peace entered into by their Commissioners at Paris, to give it the solemnity
which is essential to such a work, and that the Marqs. wishes for the honor
of putting the last hand to this business, by being the bearer of the Ratification.
"How far it is consistant with our National character, how far motives of
policy in the present case, make for or against sending a foreigner with it,
or how far such a measure might disappoint the expectation of others, I pretend
not to determine, but if there is no impropriety or injustice in it, I should
hope that Congress would feel a pleasure in gratifying the wishes of a Man
who has been such a zealous labourer in the cause of this Country. Whether
the above paragraph was only meant to bring me acquainted with what he
had done, or that I might second his views, I know not, & therefore, notwithstanding the injunction I have offered these Sentiments." (Hamilton Papers,
Library of Congress.)
Lafayette's private letter to Livingston, also dated February 5, is in the
Hamilton Papers, Library of Congress. In *JCHW*, I, 325-27, and in Wharton,
Revolutionary Diplomatic Correspondence, VI, 240-41, H is named as the
addressee. Lafayette's manuscript letter, however, is clearly addressed to Robert
R. Livingston, for in it he recommended that H be named the American minister to sign the peace treaty.

George Clinton to Alexander Hamilton and William Floyd

Head Quarters Newburgh [New York] 1st April, 1783

Gentlemen, I have the honor to enclose for your Information &
Instruction Copies of concurrent Resolutions of the Senate and Assembly of the 27th Ulto. and am with the highest Respect and Esteem
Gentlemen, Your most obedt. Servant G. Clinton

The Honorable: The Delegates of the State of New York in
Congress, Philadelphia

[ENCLOSURE] [1]

Resolution on the Garrisoning of the Northern and Western Posts

[Kingston, New York, March 27, 1782]

Whereas upon the Conclusion of a general Peace, between the several belligerent Powers in Europe and these United States, the Posts at present occupied by the British Troops in the Northern and Western Parts of this State, will be evacuated by them, and may be seized by Savages inimical to these United States; whereby the inhabitants of the Frontiers may be exposed to great Danger and Distress;

AND WHEREAS by the sixth Article of the Confederation and Perpetual Union between the United States of America, it is declared, that no Body of Forces shall be kept up by any State in Time of Peace, except such Number only as in the Judgment of the United States in Congress assembled, shall be deemed requisite, to garrison the Forts necessary for the Defence of such State;

RESOLVED, THEREFORE, (If the Honorable the House of Assembly concur herein) That the Delegates of this State in Congress, be and they are hereby instructed to represent to the United States in Congress assembled, that this State deem it essentially necessary to make Provision to garrison the said Posts immediately, on the Evacuation thereof by the British Troops; that, therefore, the said Delegates request the United States in Congress assembled, to declare the number of Troops which they may deem necessary for such Garrisons; the said Delegates at the same Time, informing the said United States, that it is the Opinion of this Legislature, that a Body of Troops, not exceeding five Hundred Rank and File, properly officered, would be adequate for the Purpose aforesaid: That the said Delegates do further represent, that the Troops commonly called the State Troops, raised in this State by Virtue of an Act of the Legislature, passed the 20th March, 1781, and which the United States in Congress assembled, by their Act of the 2d Day of April, 1781, declared should be paid, substituted and clothed at the general Expence, being inlisted for three Years, might be beneficially employed for the Purpose aforesaid: That the said Delegates do, therefore, request, that the United States in Congress assembled will be pleased to declare, that the said Troops shall henceforth be considered as Troops in the immediate Service of this State, and not in the Pay or Service of the United States; and that in Consideration of the present impoverished Condition of this State, which renders it unable to provide immediate Subsistence for the said Troops, or Munitions of War for the said Garrisons, Congress be entreated to give Orders for issuing the necessary provisions, and Munitions of war, for maintaining the said Garrisons on Condition, that the Expence of such Provisions and Munitions, shall be charged by the United States to this State.

Public Papers of George Clinton, VIII, 108.
1. *Public Papers of George Clinton*, VIII, 108–09. This was not submitted to Congress. For H's explanation of his refusal to introduce it, see his letter to Clinton of October 3, 1783.

Continental Congress
Resolution on the Conduct of Officers of the Army

[Philadelphia, April 1, 1783] [1]

The Committee to whom were referred the letters from The Commander in Chief submit the following resolut⟨ions⟩: [2]

Resolved That Congress consider the conduct of the Commander in Chief on the occasion of some late attempts to create disturbances in the army as a new proof of his prudence and zealous attachment to the welfare of the community.

That he be informed, Congress also entertain a high sense of the patriotic sentiments expressed by the officers in their proceedings of the   [3] which evince their unshaken perseverance in those principles, that have distinguished them in every period of the war, and have so justly intitled the troops of the United States to the esteem and gratitude of their country and to the character of a patriot army.

The Committee ask leave to report further.

AD, Papers of the Continental Congress, National Archives.
1. The report is undated. According to the Committee Book of Congress (JCC, XXIV, 305–06, note 1), the committee reported on April 1, but the *Journals* contain no reference to its delivery on that date. It is printed there under date of April 29 (JCC, XXIV, 306).

2. A letter from George Washington, dated March 18, on the subject of the demands of the Army, and an earlier letter on the same subject were referred to a committee consisting of Samuel Osgood, Theodorick Bland, H, Oliver Wolcott, Sr., and Richard Peters. See the second of two letters H wrote to Washington, March 25, 1783, note 2.

3. Space left blank in MS. H is referring to the proceedings of a grand convention of officers called by Washington on March 15. The officers had expressed their confidence in the willingness of Congress to provide funds for payment of the Army.

Continental Congress
Remarks on the Calling of States Conventions

[Philadelphia, April 1, 1783]

Mr. Madison & Mr. Hamilton disapproved of these partial conventions,[1] not as absolute violations of the Confederacy, but as ultimately leading to them & in the mean time exciting pernicious jealousies; the latter observing that he wished instead of them to see a general Convention take place & that he sd. soon in pursuance of instructions from his Constituents propose to Congs. a plan for that purpose; the object wd. be to strengthen the fœderal Constitution.

"Notes of Debates in the Continental Congress," MS, James Madison Papers, Library of Congress.

1. These remarks were prompted by a suggestion of Nathaniel Gorham, delegate from Massachusetts, that the Congress should hasten the passage of a report on raising funds for the United States as "the Eastern States at the invitation of the Legislature of Massts., were with N.Y. about to form a convention for regulating matters of common concern, & that if any plan sd. be sent out by Congs. during their session, they would probably cooperate with Congs. in giving effect to it." John Francis Mercer and Theodorick Bland, delegates from Virginia, objected to the proposed convention as a dangerous precedent and were answered by the Massachusetts delegates, Samuel Osgood and Nathaniel Gorham, who defended the convention as "within the purview of the federal articles" ("Notes of Debates in the Continental Congress," MS, James Madison Papers, Library of Congress).

To Philip Schuyler

[*Philadelphia, April 2, 1783.* On May 4, 1783, Schuyler wrote to Hamilton: "Your several favors of the 18th & 25th March and 2d. ult. were delivered me." *Letter of April 2 not found.*]

From George Washington

Newburgh [New York] 4th. April 1783

Dear Sir,

The same Post which gave me your two letters of the 25th. of March, handed me one from Colo. Bland on the same point.[1]

Observing that both have been written at the desire of a Committee, of which you are both members, I have made a very full reply to their subject in my letter which is addressed to Colo. Bland; and supposing it unnecessary to enter into a complete detail to both, I must beg leave to refer you to Colo. Bland's (a sight of which I have desired him to give you) for a full explanation of my ideas & sentiments.[2]

I read your private letter of the 25th. with pain, & contemplated the picture it had drawn with astonishment & horror—but I will yet hope for the best. The idea of redress by force is too chimerical to have had a place in the imagination of any serious mind in this Army; but there is no telling what unhappy disturbances may result from distress, & distrust of Justice. And as the fears and jealousies of the Army are alive, I hope no resolution will be come to for disbanding or seperating the Lines till the Accts. are liquidated. You may rely upon it, Sir, that unhappy consequences would follow the attempt. The suspicions of the Officers are afloat, notwithstanding the resolutions which have passed on both sides; any act therefore can be construed into an attempt to seperate them before the accts. are settled will convey the most unfavourable ideas of the rectitude of Congress. Whether well or ill founded matters not, the consequences will be the same.

I will now, in strict confidence, mention a matter which may be useful for you to be informed of. It is that some men (& leading ones too) in this Army, are beginning to entertain suspicions that Congress, or some members of it, regardless of the past sufferings & present distress, maugre the justice which is due to them, & the returns which a grateful people should make to men who certainly have contributed more than any other class to the establishment of Independency, are to be made use of as mere Puppits to establish Continental funds; & that rather than not succeed in this measure, or weaken their ground, they would make a sacrafice of the Army and all its interests.

I have two reasons for mentioning this matter to you: the one is, that the Army (considering the irritable state it is in, its sufferings & composition) is a dangerous instrument to play with. The other, that every possible means consistant with their own views (which certainly are moderate) should be essayed to get it disbanded without delay. I might add a third: it is, that the Financier is suspected to be at the bottom of this scheme. If sentiments of this sort should become general their operation will be opposed to this plan; at the same time that it would encrease the present discontents. Upon the whole, disband the Army, as soon as possible; but consult the wishes of it; which really are moderate, in the mode, & perfectly compatible with the honor, dignity, and justice which is due from the Country to it.

I am with great esteem & regard   Dr Sir   Yr. Most Obedt Serv.

Go: Washington

The Honble Alexr. Hamilton

ALS, Hamilton Papers, Library of Congress; ADfS, George Washington Papers, Library of Congress.

1. For information on the letter written on March 25, 1783, by Theodorick Bland, see the second of two letters H wrote to Washington on that date.

2. Washington explained to Bland the minimum expectations of the Army. His letter, dated April 4, 1783, is printed in *GW*, XXVI, 285–91.

Continental Congress
Report on Reduction of Expenses in the War Department

[Philadelphia] April 7, 1783

The Committee [1] appointed to consider and report such eoconomical measures as may be proper and necessary beg leave to report the following.[2] Resolve [3]

That the Secretary at war in concert with the Commander in Chief be directed to consider and report to Congress as speedily as may be such measures as it will be proper to take in the present juncture for reducing the expences of The United States in the war department.[4]

AD, Papers of the Continental Congress, National Archives.

1. The committee consisted of H, Richard Peters, and Nathaniel Gorham.
2. The committee had been appointed on April 4, 1783, "to consider the means of reducing expenditures in the military department" (*JCC*, XXIV, 240, note 1).
3. This paragraph is not in the writing of H.
4. The report was passed, according to the endorsement, on April 7, 1783.

To George Washington

[Philadelphia, April 8, 1783] [1]

Sir,

I have received your Excellency's letters of the 31st of March & 4th. of April, the last to day. The one to Col Bland as member of the Committee has been read in Committee confidentially and gave great satisfaction.[2] The idea of not attempting to separate the army before the settlement of accounts corresponds with my proposition. That of endeavouring to let them have some pay had also appeared to me indispensable. The expectations of the army as represented by Your Excellency are moderation itself.[3] To morrow we confer with the Superintendant of Finance on the subject of money. There will be difficulty, but not we hope insurmountable.

I thank your Excellency for the hints you are so obliging as to give me in your private letter.[4] I do not wonder at the suspicions that have been infused, nor should I be surprised to hear that I have been pointed out as one of the persons concerned in playing the game described. But facts must speak for themselves. The Gentlemen who were here from the army; General Mc.Dougall[5] who is

ALS, George Washington Papers, Library of Congress.
1. This letter is undated. In *JCHW*, I, 355–59, it is dated April 11, 1783, and in *HCLW*, IX, 331–37, it is dated April, 1783. The last line of the first paragraph of this letter refers to a conference with Robert Morris. This conference, which was to be held the day after this letter was written, was held on April 9. The letter therefore has been dated April 8. See Morris to H, Theodorick Bland, Thomas FitzSimons, Samuel Osgood, and Richard Peters, April 14, 1783.
2. See Washington to H, April 4, 1783.
3. On April 4, Washington wrote to Theodorick Bland that the expectations of the Army were "compleat Settlement, and partial payment, *previous* to any Dispersion." The minimum partial payment acceptable to the Army, Washington explained, was three months' pay. Washington had requested Bland to communicate the contents of his letter to H (See *GW*, XXVI, 285–91).
4. The reference is to Washington's letter of April 4, 1783, to H.
5. Major General Alexander McDougall.

still here will be able to give a true account of those who have supported the just claims of the army, and of those who have endeavoured to elude them.

There are two classes of men Sir in Congress of very Different views—one attached to state, the other to Continental politics. The last have been strenuous advocates for funding the public debt upon solid securities, the former have given every opposition in their power and have only been dragged into the measures which are now near being adopted by the clamours of the army and other public creditors. The advocates for Continental funds have blended the interests of the army with other Creditors from a conviction, that no funds for partial purposes will go through those states to whose citizens the United States are largely indebted—or if they should be carried through from impressions of the moment would have the necessary stability; for the influence of those unprovided for would always militate against a provision for others, in exclusion of them. It is in vain to tell men who have parted with a large part of their property on the public faith that the services of the army are intitled to a preference. They would reason from their interest and their feelings. These would tell them that they had as great a title as any other class of the community to public justice, and that while this was denied to them, it would be unreasonable to make them bear their part of a burthen for the benefit of others. This is the way they would reason & as their influence in some of the states was considerable they would have been able to prevent any partial provision.

But the question was not merely how to do justice to the creditors, but how to restore public credit. Taxation in this Country, it was found, could not supply a sixth part of the public necessities. The loans in Europe were far short of the ballance and the prospect every day diminishing. The Court of France telling us in plain terms she could not even do as much as she had done—Individuals in Holland & every where else refusing to part with their money on the precarious tenure of the mere faith of this country, without any pledge for the payment either of principal or interest.

In this situation what was to be done? It was essential to our cause that vigorous efforts should be made to restore public credit —it was necessary to combine all the motives to this end, that could operate upon different descriptions of persons in the different states.

The necessity and discontents of the army presented themselves as a powerful engine.

But Sir these Gentlemen would be puzzled to support their insininuations by a single fact. It was indeed proposed to appropriate the intended impost on trade to the army debt and what was extraordinary by Gentlemen who had expressed their dislike to the principle of the fund. I acknowlege I was one that opposed this; for the reasons already assigned & for these additional ones—*That* was the fund on which we most counted—to obtain further loans in Europe it was necessary we should have a fund sifficient to pay the interest of what had been borrowed & what was to be borrowed. The truth was these people in this instance wanted to play off the army against the funding system.

As to Mr. Morris, I will give Your Excellency a true explanation of his conduct. He had been for some time pressing Congress to endeavour to obtain funds, and had found a great backwardness in the business. He found the taxes unproductive in the different states —he found the loans in Europe making a very slow progress—he found himself pressed on all hands for supplies; he found himself in short reduced to this alternative either of making engagements which he could not fulfill or declaring his resignation in case funds were not established by a given time. Had he followed the first course the bubble must soon have burst—he must have sacrificed his credit & his character, and public credit already in a ruinous condition would have lost its last support. He wisely judged it better to resign; this might increase the embarrassments of the moment, but the necessity of the case it was to be hoped would produce the proper measures; and he might then resume the direction of the machine with advantage and success. He also had some hope that his resignation would prove a stimulus to Congress.

He was however ill-advised in the publication of his letters of resignation.[6] This was an imprudent step and has given a handle to his personal enemies, who by playing upon the passions of others

6. On January 24, 1783, Robert Morris wrote to Congress that unless adequate measures for securing revenue were adopted by the end of May, he would resign the office of Superintendent of Finance. Congress, disturbed by the possible repercussions of Morris's resignation, ordered his letter kept secret. On February 26 Morris asked that the injunction of secrecy be removed; when Congress complied he published his letter.

have drawn some well meaning men into the cry against him. But Mr. Morris certainly deserves a great deal from his country. I believe no man in this country but himself could have kept the money-machine a going during the period he has been in office. From every thing that appears his administration has been upright as well as able.

The truth is the old leaven of Deane & Lee is at this day working against Mr. Morris.[7] He happened in that dispute to have been on the side of Deane & certain men can never forgive him. A man whom I once esteemed, and whom I will rather suppose *duped* than wicked is the second actor in this business.[8]

The matter with respect to the army which has occasioned most altercation in Congress and most dissatisfaction in the army has been the half pay. The opinions on this head have been two. One party was for referring the several lines to their states to make such commutation as they should think proper—the other for making the commutation by Congress and funding it on continental security. I was of this last opinion and so were all those who will be represented as having made use of the army as puppets. Our principal reasons were 1st by referring the lines to their respective states, those which were opposed to the half pay would have taken advantage of the officers necessities, to make the commutation far short of an equivalent. 2dly. The inequality which would have arisen in the different states when the officers came to compare (as has happened in other cases) would have been a new source of discontent. 3dly. such a reference was a continuance of the old wretched state system, by which the ties between Congress and the army have been nearly dissolved—by which the resources of the states have been diverted from the common treasury & wasted; a system which Your Excellency has often justly reprobated.

I have gone into these details to give You a just idea of the parties in Congress. I assure you upon my honor Sir I have given you a candid state of facts to the best of my judgment. The men against

7. For an explanation of the controversy between Silas Deane and Arthur Lee, see H to John Laurens, May 22, 1779, note 4. Deane and Lee each had supporters in Congress. As Robert Morris defended Deane and as Arthur Lee was a critic of Morris, the group in Congress known as the Lee faction opposed the Superintendent of Finance.

8. Probably Stephen Higginson of Massachusetts who was one of Morris's severest critics.

whom the suspicions you mention must be directed are in general the most sensible the most liberal, the most independent and the most respectable characters in our body as well as the most unequivocal friends to the army. In a word they are the men who think continentally.

I have the honor to be With sincere respect & esteem Yr. Excellcys Most Obed servt. A Hamilton

I am Chairman of a Committee for peace arrangements.[9] We shall ask Your Excellency's opinion at large on a proper military peace establishment. I will just hint to Yr. Excellency that our prejudices will make us wish to keep up as few troops as possible.

We this moment learn an officer is arrived from Sir Guy Car[l]eton with disptaches, probably official accounts of peace.[10]

9. See H to Washington, April 9, 1783.
10. See H and William Floyd to George Clinton, April 9, 1783, note 4.

Alexander Hamilton and William Floyd to George Clinton

[Philadelphia, April 9, 1783]

Sir,

We inclose Your Excellency a letter to the corporation of Kingston open for your perusal that you may be informed what is likely to be the fate of their late offer.[1]

Your letter [with the Concurrent Resolves of the Senate and Assembly] [2] on the subject of the state troops has been committed.[3] We think it improbable Congress will accede to the idea. We congratulate your Excellency on the further accounts of peace. We are just informed of the arrival of an officer from Sir Guy Careltone with dispatches to Congress.[4] Tis probable they contain official information.

With perfect respect We have the honor to be Y Excellency's Most Obed ser

Philadelphia
April 9th. 1783
His Excellency Governor Clinton

Df, in the writing of H, New-York Historical Society, New York City.
  1. See Christopher Tappen to H and Floyd, March 19, 1783.
  2. The bracketed words are not in the writing of H.
  3. Clinton's letter, addressed to the President of Congress, was enclosed in Tappen's letter of March 19 to H and Floyd. It was referred on April 4 to a committee consisting of John Rutledge, William Hemsley, and Stephen Higginson (*JCC*, XXIV, 229, note 2).
  4. On March 23, 1783, Congress received dispatches from Lafayette announcing the signing of preliminary articles of peace between Great Britain, France, and Spain. Sir Guy Carleton transmitted to Congress the official notification, and on April 15 the treaty was ratified by Congress (*JCC*, XXIV, 244–51).

To George Washington

Philadelphia
April 9th. 1783

Sir

Congress having appointed a committee consisting of Messrs. Maddison Osgood, Wilson, Elseworth [1] and myself to consider what arrangements it will be proper to adopt in the different departments with reference to a peace; I am directed by the Committee to address your Excellency on the subject of the military department.[2]

The Committee wish Your Excellency's sentiments at large on such institutions of every kind, for the interior defence of these states as may be best adapted to their circumstances and conciliate security with œconomy and with the principles of our governments. In this they will be glad you will take as great latitude as you may think necessary; and will therefore omit entering into any details.

The Committee apprehend it to be the intention of Congress to lay down a general plan to be carried into execution as circumstances will permit; and that in attending to such dispositions as the immediate situation of the Country may require, they are chiefly desirous of establishing good principles, that will have a permanently salutary operation.

I have the honor to be Yr. Excellency's Most Obedient servant

Alx Hamilton
Chairman.

His Excellency General Washington

ALS, George Washington Papers, Library of Congress; copy, Massachusetts Historical Society, Boston.
  1. James Madison, Samuel Osgood, James Wilson, and Oliver Ellsworth.
  2. Although there is no reference to its appointment in the *Journals* of the

Congress, the committee probably was appointed on April 3 or 4. Madison, in his "Notes of Debates in the Continental Congress," under the inclusive dates of April 3–6, states that

"A Come., consisting of Mr. Hamilton, Mr. Madison &   was appointd to report the proper arrangements to be taken in consequence of peace. The object was to provide a system for foreign affairs, for Indian affairs, for military and naval peace establishments; and also to carry into execution the regulation of weights & measures & other articles of the Confederation not attended to during the war. To the same Come. was referred a resolution of the Executive Council of Pa., requesting the Delegates of that State to urge Congs. to establish a general peace with the Indians." ("Notes of Debates in the Continental Congress," MS, James Madison Papers, Library of Congress.)

Robert Morris to Alexander Hamilton, Theodorick Bland, Thomas FitzSimons, Samuel Osgood, and Richard Peters

Office of Finance [Philadelphia] 14 April 1783

Gentlemen

Since the Conference I had the Honor to hold with you the ninth Instant, my Mind has been continually occupied on the important Subject to which it relates.[1] My Feelings are strongly excited by what I wish for the Public and what I apprehend both for them and for myself. The two Points which relate to my Department are the Settlement of Accounts and Advance of Pay. With respect to the first it is now going on in a satisfactory Manner and will be as speedily accomplished as can reasonably be expected. The Arrangements taken on that Subject are of such a Nature that I conceive the disbanding of the Army need not be delayed until the Settlement is compleated because the proper Officers may be kept together altho the Men be dismissed. The Amount of three Months Pay, which is stated by the General to be *indispensible*,[2] is according to the Estimates, seven hundred and fifty thousand Dollars. From what I have already Stated to Congress it will appear that Reliance for a great Part of this Sum must be on the Sales of public Property and the Taxes. Neither of these Sources can produce much immediately and from the latter there is but little Hope at all unless Something can be done to stimulate the Exertions of the States. The Receipts being regularly published spare me the Necessity of disagreeable Observations on that Topick. To supply so large a Sum as is required is utterly impracticable or indeed to obtain any very considerable Part. The most therefore which can be done is to risk a large Paper Anticipation. This is an Operation of great Delicacy and it is essential to the Success of it that my Credit should be staked for the Redemption. Do not suppose Gentlemen that this Declaration is dictated by Vanity. It becomes my Duty to mention the Truth. I had rather it had fallen from any other Person and I had [– – –] rather it did not exist. In issuing my Notes to the required Amount it would be n⟨ecessary that⟩ I should give an express Assurance of Payment: And in so doing I should ⟨be answerable⟩ personally for about half a Million when I leave this Office and depe⟨nd on the arrange⟩ments of those who come after to save me from Ruin. I am willing ⟨to risk as much⟩ for this Country as any Man in America but it cannot be expected tha⟨t I would place⟩ myself in so desperate a Situation. To render the Arrangements which ⟨the plan would⟩ require effectual in an official Point of View would be a Work of Time ⟨and the end⟩ of my official Existence is nearly arrived. Disbanding the Army in a Manner Satisfactory to them and to the Country is doubtless desirable and altho extremely difficult yet is I beleive practicable. I shall be very ready at all Times Gentlemen to give my advice and Assistance to those who may be charged with that delicate and perilous Undertaking and I would go as far to effect it myself as any reasonable Man could require. But tho I would sacrifice much of my Property yet I cannot risk my Reputation as a Man of Integrity nor expose myself to absolute Ruin.

I am Gentlemen with perfect Respect   your most obedient and humble Servant   Robt Morris

Honble. Mr. Bland ⎫
    Mr. FitzSimmons ⎪
    Mr. Hamilton ⎬ A Committee of Congress
    Mr. Osgood ⎪
    ⟨Mr.⟩ Peters ⎭

LS, Papers of the Continental Congress, National Archives.
   1. An entry in Robert Morris's Diary for April 9 reads:
"The Hon. Colo. Bland Mr. Fitzsimmons, Mr. Osgood Mr. Gorham, Mr. Hamilton, Mr. Peters a Committee of Congress came to Consult me relative to certain Propositions contained in Genl. Washington's Letter to Colo. Bland for settling the Accounts of the Army and giving them three Months Pay in

Order that they may be disbanded on Terms agreeable to themselves and useful to the Public &c. I told them that the Paymaster General is already Authorized to settle the Army Accounts and that he is now there for that Purpose—That as to three Months Pay I think the Proposition most reasonable on the Part of the Army, that it ought to be complied with, but the Question is whether the States will enable that Compliance, for that the present State of the Treasury is not sufficient to Compleat the Months pay already engaged and that the Anticipations already Amount to half a Million of Dollars which must be provided for out of the foreign Loans but finally I desired them to leave the Papers and I will consider of the Matter and see the Committee again." (Robert Morris Papers, Library of Congress.)

See also H to George Washington, March 25, April 19, 1783.

2. In a letter to Theodorick Bland, dated April 4, 1783, Washington had stated that the Army expected at least three months pay before disbanding (*GW*, XXVI, 285–91). In a letter to H on the same date, Washington referred H to his letter to Bland.

To Robert Morris

[*Philadelphia, April 15, 1783.* On April 16 Morris wrote to Hamilton: "I have been duly honored with the Receipt of your favor of the fifteenth Instant." *Letter not found.*]

To George Washington

[Philadelphia, April 15, 1783]

Sir,

There are two resolutions passed relative to the restoration of the British Prisoners and to making arrangements for the surrender of the posts in the possession of the British troops, the first of which is to be transacted by you in conjunction with the secretary of War —the latter by yourself alone.[1] I will explain to you some doubts which have arisen in Congress with regard to the true construction of the provisional treaty—which may be of use to you in transacting the business abovementioned.

The sixth article declares that there shall be no future confiscations &c. after the *ratification of the treaty in America;* and the seventh article makes the surrender of prisoners, evacuation of posts, cessation of hostilities &c. to depend on that event, to wit—the *ratification of the treaty in America.* Now the doubt is whether *the treaty* means the provisional treaty *already concluded* or the *definitive* treaty *to be concluded.* The last construction is most agreeable to the letter of the provisional articles—the former most agreeable to the usual practice of nations, for hostilities commonly cease on the ratification of the preliminary treaty. There is a great diversity of Opinion in Congress. It will be in my opinion adviseable, at the same time that we do not communicate our doubts to the British, to extract their sense of the matter from them.

This may be done by asking them at what periods they are willing to stipulate the surrender of posts, at the same time that they are asked in what manner it will be most convenient to them to receive the prisoners.

If they postpone the evacuation of the different posts to the definitive treaty we shall then be justified in doing the same with respect to prisoners. The question will then arise whether on principles of humanity œconomy and liberality we ought not to restore the prisoners at all events without delay. Much may be said on both sides. I doubt the expedience of a total restoration of prisoners 'till they are willing to fix the epochs at which they take leave of us. It will add considerably to their strength, and accidents though improbable may happen. I confess however I am not clear in my opinion.

I have the honor to be Yr. Excellency's Most Obed serv

Philadelphia   A Hamilton
April 15. 1783

The provisional or preliminary treaty is ratified by us—for the greater caution.[2]

His Excellency General Washington

ALS, George Washington Papers, Library of Congress.
1. H is referring to the second paragraph of his "Report on the Ratification of the Peace Treaty," April 15, 1783, which directed the commanders in chief of Britain and the United States to enter into "preparatory arrangements relative to the 7th article" of the treaty. The seventh article provided, among other things, that prisoners on both sides be freed. The second resolution to which H refers, also passed on April 15, reads as follows:
"*Resolved*, That the Commander in Chief be, and he is hereby instructed to make the proper arrangements with the Commander in Chief of the British forces, for receiving possession of the posts in the United States occupied by the troops of his Britannic Majesty. . . ." (*JCC*, XXIV, 242.)
2. Congressional ratification was on April 15, 1783 (*JCC*, XXIV, 242–52).

Continental Congress
Report on the Ratification of the Provisional Peace Treaty

[Philadelphia] April 15, 1783

Resolved [1] a Committee be appointed to prepare and lay before Congress a draft of a ratification of the articles entered into between the Commissioners of the United States & the commissioner of His Britannic Majesty at Paris on the 30th day of November last.

Resolved that the Commander in Chief be directed to enter into preparatory [2] arrangements relative to the 7th. article of the said treaty with the Commanders in Chief of the British land & naval forces in America; and that a Committee be appointed to prepare a letter to him on this subject.[3]

AD, Papers of the Continental Congress, National Archives.

1. In the *Journals* there is a paragraph that precedes this resolution. It reads: "Congress took into consideration the articles agreed upon at Paris, on the 30 day of November last, entitled 'Articles agreed upon by and between Richard Oswald, esq. the commissioner of his Britannic Majesty, for treating of peace with the commissioners of the United States of America, in behalf of his said Majesty on the one part, and John Adams, Benjamin Franklin, John Jay and Henry Laurens, four of the commissioners of the said states, for treating of peace with the commissioner of his said Majesty, on their behalf, on the other part; to be inserted in, and to constitute the treaty of peace proposed to be concluded between the crown of Great Britain and the said United States; but which treaty is not to be concluded until terms of a peace shall be agreed upon between Great Britain and France, and his Britannic Majesty shall be ready to conclude such treaty accordingly;' and thereupon. . . ." (*JCC*, XXIV, 241.)

During the debate on April 14, 1783, H had objected to a committee report which stated that it was not necessary for Congress to ratify the provisional peace treaty and that a discharge of prisoners of war would be "premature and unadvisable." "Mr. Hamilton," Madison recorded, "contended that Congress were bound, by the tenor of the Provl. Treaty immediately to Ratify it, and to execute the several stipulations inserted in it; particularly that relating to discharge of Prisoners." Two days later H "acknowledged that he began to view the *obligation* of the . . . Treaty in a different light and in consequence wished to vary the direction to the Commander in chief from a positive to a preparatory one . . ." ("Notes of Debates in the Continental Congress," MS, James Madison Papers, Library of Congress). Madison dates this statement April 16, but according to the *Journals* it was made on April 15.

2. H first wrote and then crossed out the word "necessary."

3. On April 16, 1783, H made a motion to delete the last part of the report which read "and that a Committee be appointed to prepare a letter to him on this subject." Congress refused to accept it (*JCC*, XXIV, 252).

George Clinton to Alexander Hamilton and William Floyd

Pokeepsie [New York] 16th April 1783

Gentlemen,

I have prevailed on the Bearer, the Attorney Genl.[1] to Repair to Philadelphia for the Express Purpose of disclosing to you certain Information of a very interesting Nature.[2] The Communications he is to make are too extensive to be the subject of a Letter & it might be improper to intrust them to Paper. I, therefore, begg Leave to refer you to Mr. Benson for the Particulars of which he is fully possessed.

Your letter of the 9th Instant inclosing one to Mr. Tappen is this Moment received.[3] The Inclosure shall be forwarded by a safe and speedy Conveyance.

I have the Honor to be, &c.   G.C.

To Wm. Floyd and Alexr. Hamilton, Esquires.
Delegates for the State of New York in Congress.

Public Papers of George Clinton, VIII, 139-40.
    1. Egbert Benson was attorney general of the State of New York.
    2. The information disclosed by Benson was doubtless an account of his interview with Sir Guy Carleton, the British commander in America (H and Floyd to Clinton, April 23, 1783). On April 8, 1783, Governor Clinton asked Benson to interview Carleton, and on April 17, Benson sent the governor a detailed report of his conversations with the British commander. Benson's mission evidently was to arrange a meeting between Carleton and Clinton to discuss plans for the evacuation of New York City by the British. Although Carleton agreed to such a meeting, Benson was convinced "that Sir Guy Carleton is not seriously disposed to enter into a Convention, and that he only intends to save appearances to negotiate and by that means to effect a Delay, but I will not hazard a Conjecture for what purpose" (*Public Papers of George Clinton*, VIII, 140-44).
    3. See Christopher Tappen to H and Floyd, March 19, 1783.

From Robert Morris

Office of Finance [Philadelphia] 16. April 1783

Sir,

I have been duly honored with the Receipt of your favor of the fifteenth Instant.[1] I accepted the Marine Agency simply with a View to save the Expence of the Department but whenever a marine is to be established a previous Point would be (in my Opinion) to nominate a Minister of Marine and let his first Work be the forming of those Plans and Systems which when adopted by Congress he would have to execute. For my own Part were my Abilities equal to this Task my Leizure would not permit the Attempt.[2]

With Respect to the Finances I am of Opinion that as we cannot increase our Revenue we must do all we can to lessen our Expenditures and that therefore we should take off every Expence not absolutely necessary as soon as possible.

On the Subject of the Coin I hope soon to make a Communication to Congress which if approved of by them will compleat that Business.

I am Sir with very sincere Esteem and Respect—your most obedient and humble Servant

RM.

LC, Robert Morris Papers, Library of Congress.
1. Letter not found. See note 2.
2. An entry in Morris's Diary for April 8 reads:
"Colo. Hamilton informed me that he is of a Committee to Consider of Peace managements and was desired by that Committee to Consult me respecting the Plan for establishing a Navy. I replyed nothing would be more agreeable to me than to Assist in that Business; but as I shall soon quit Public Office I recommended that Congress should appoint a Minister of Marine who might now form the Plans he is to execute." (Robert Morris Papers, Library of Congress.)
H's letter of April 15, 1783, which has not been found, probably discussed the appointment of a Minister of Marine.

From George Washington

Newburgh [New York] April 16th 1783

Dear Sir,

My last letter to you [1] was written in a hurry, when I was fatigued by the more public—yet confidential letter which (with several others) accompanied it; possibly, I did not on that occasion express myself (in what I intended as a hint) with so much perspicuity as I ought—possibly too, what I then dropped, might have conveyed more than I intended; for I do not, at this time, recollect the force of my expression.

My meaning however, was only to inform, that there were different sentiments in the Army as well as in Congress, respecting Continental & State Funds; some wishing to be thrown upon their respective States rather than the Continent at large, for payment & that, if an idea should prevail generally that Congress, or part of its members or Ministers, bent upon the latter, should *delay* doing them justice, or *hazard* it in pursuit of their favourite object; it might create such divisions in the Army as would weaken, rather than strengthen the hands of those who were disposed to support Continental measures—and might *tend* to defeat the end they themselves had in view by endeavouring to involve the Army.

For these reasons I said, or meant to say, the Army was a dangerous Engine to work with, as it might be made to cut both ways—and, considering the Sufferings of it, would, more than probably, throw its weight into that Scale which seemed most likely to preponderate towards its immediate relief, without looking forward (under the pressure of present wants) to future consequences with the eyes of Politicians. In this light also I meant to apply my observations to Mr. Morris, to whom, or rather to Mr. G.— M—[2] is ascribed, in a great degree, the ground work of the superstructure which was intended to be raised in the Army by the Anonymous Addresser.

That no man can be more opposed to State funds & local prejudices than myself, the whole tenor of my conduct has been one continual evidence of. No man perhaps has had better opportunities to *see* & to *feel* the pernicious tendency of the latter than I have—and I endeavor (I hope not altogether ineffectually) to inculcate them upon the Officers of the Army upon all proper occasions; but their feelings are to be attended to & soothed; and they assured that if Continental funds cannot be established, they will be recommended to their respective States for payment. Justice must be done them.

I should do injustice to report & what I believe to be the opinion of the Army were I not to inform you, that they consider you as a friend, Zealous to serve them, and one who has espoused their interests in Congress upon every proper occasion. It is to be wished, as I observed in my letter to Colo. Bland,[3] that Congress would send a Comee. to the Army with Plenipo: powers; The matters requested of me in your letter of the   [4] as Chairman of a Comee., and many other things might then be brought to a close with more dispatch & in a happier manner than it is likely they will be by an intercourse of letters at the distance of 150 miles; which takes *our* Expresses, a week *at least* to go & come. At this moment, being without any instructions from Congress, I am under great embarrassment with respect to the Soldiers for the War & shall be obliged more than probably from the necessity of the case, to exercise my own judgment without waiting for orders, as to the discharge of them. If I should adopt measures which events may approve; all will be well. If other wise, why & by what authority did you do so.

How far a *strong* recommendation from Congress to observe *All* the Articles of Peace as well as the ⁵ may imply a suspicion of good faith in the people of this Country, I pretend not to judge; but I am much mistaken if something of the kind will not be found wanting as I already perceive a disposition to Carp at, & to elude such parts of the treaty as affect their different interests altho' you do not find a man who, when pushed, will not acknowledge that upon the *whole* it is a more advantageous Peace than we could possibly have expected.

I am Dear Sir With great esteem & regard Yr. Most obedt servt   Go: Washington

Honble Alexr. Hamilton

ALS, Hamilton Papers, Library of Congress.
    1. Washington is referring to his letter of April 4, 1783, to which H replied on April 8.
    2. Gouverneur Morris.
    3. Washington's letter to Theodorick Bland, April 4, 1783, is printed in *GW*, XXVI, 285–91.
    4. H's letter was dated April 9, 1783. Space left blank in MS.
    5. Space left blank in MS.

From George Washington

Head Quarters [Newburgh, New York] 16th April 1783

Sir

I have received your letter of the 9th instant in behalf of a Committee of Congress, requestg my Sentiments upon the military Department of a Peace Establishment.

As this Discussion will involve a variety of Considerations, & these of very great Importance, The Committee will indulge me in a little Time to collect & concenter my Ideas on this Subject & they may depend on my communicating them in the best Manner I am able & at the earliest period in my power.[1]

I am &c

Colo Hamilton—in Congress

Df, in writing of Jonathan Trumbull, Jr., George Washington Papers, Library of Congress.

1. Washington submitted his plan for a peace establishment to Congress on May 2, 1783.

Continental Congress
Report on Sale of Military Equipment

[Philadelphia] April 17, 1783

The Committee [1] to whom was referred the letter from the Secretary of war of the 14th. instant [2] submit the following resolution

Resolved that immediate measures be taken for the sale of all the dragoon horses belonging to the United States and of all such articles in the several military departments as may not be necessary for the use of the army previous to its reduction or for the formation of magazines on a peace establishment.[3]

AD, Papers of the Continental Congress, National Archives.

1. The committee consisted of Samuel Osgood, Theodorick Bland, H, Oliver Wolcott, Sr., and Richard Peters.

2. The letter from the Secretary at War, Benjamin Lincoln, is printed in *JCC*, XXIV, 253–54. Lincoln, after discussing the problem of pay for the Army, recommended that horses and other articles which might be sold for cash, be sold to public creditors who would be "debited for the value of what they buy."

3. The endorsement states that the report was adopted on April 17, 1783.

Continental Congress
Report on Peace with the Indians

[Philadelphia] April 21, 1783

Report of a Committee to whom was committed the letter from His Excelly The President of the State of Pensylvania respecting a peace with the Indians.[1]

Whereas by the 9th article of the confederation The United States in Congress assembled are vested with the sole and exclusive right and power among other things "of regulating the trade and managing all affairs with the Indians not members of any of the States"—

Resolved, that the general superintendence of Indian Affairs under Congress be annexed to the department of war.

That there be a suspension of offensive hostilities against the Indian nations, and that immediate measures be taken to communicate the same to the several tribes preparatory to a final pacification.

That there be four Agents appointed for the transaction of affairs with the indians in the different districts—one for the eastern district comprehending all the tribes under the general denomination of the Penobscot Indians; one for the Northern district comprehending the six nations and the nations depending on them; one for the Western district comprehending all the tribes under the general denomination of the Western indians; one for the Southern district comprehending all the southern nations with an allowance not exceeding ^{2} dollars ℔ annum to each agent. That measures be taken to purchase articles proper for presents to the indians to the amount of ^{3} to be distributed when their deputies shall assemble for the purpose of a treaty of peace.

That in order to a speedy pacification till the commissioners aforesaid can be appointed a special Committee be appointed instructed to endeavour to engage one or more respectable inhabitants for each district acquainted with indian affairs to undertake the negotiation of an immediate peace and that the said Committee digest such further measures as it will be proper for Congress to take with reference thereto.[4]

AD, Papers of the Continental Congress, National Archives.

1. The committee, consisting of H, James Madison, Samuel Osgood, Oliver Ellsworth, and James Wilson, had been appointed on April 3 or 4 to consider arrangements necessitated by the treaty of peace. The letter from the president of Pennsylvania, John Dickinson, had been referred to the same committee. See H to Washington, April 9, 1783, note 2.

2. Space left blank in MS.

3. Space left blank in MS.

4. The endorsement to this report reads as follows: "April 21. 1783. Read. Ent[ered]. Monday 28. April assigned for the Consideration. Augt 12th. 1783 referred to Comte. on peace Arrangements." The editor of the *Journals* of the Congress states that this committee reported on September 19 (*JCC*, XXIV, 264, note 1). Acceptance of the report, however, was prevented by the objections of New England delegates. "The report," Irving Brant writes, "finally

became a part of the proceedings which led to the Western territorial plan of 1784 and the Ordinance of 1787" (Brant, *James Madison*, II, 291).

From George Washington

Newburgh [New York] 22d. April 1783.

Dear Sir;

I did not receive your letter of the 15th. till after my return from Ringwood,[1] where I had a meeting with the Secretary at War for the purpose of making arrangements for the release of our Prisoners, agreeably to the resolve of Congress of the 15th. Instt.[2]

Finding a diversity of opinion respecting the Treaty, and the line of conduct we ought to observe with the Prisoners; I requested, in precise terms, to know from Genl. Lincoln [3] (before I entered on the business) whether we were to exercise our own judgment with respect to the *time*, as well as *mode* of releasing them,—or was to be confined to the latter. Being informed that we had no option in the first, Congress wishing to be eased of the expence as soon as possible, I acted *solely* on that ground.

At the same time I scruple not to confess to you, that if this measure was not dictated by necessity, it is, in my opinion, an impolitic one; as we place ourselves in the power of the British, before the Treaty is definitive. The manner in which Peace was first announced, & the subsequent declarations of it, have led the Country & Army into a belief that it was final. The ratification of the Preliminary articles on the 3d. of February, so far confirmed this, that one consequence resulting from it is, the Soldiers for the War conceive the term of their Services has actually expired; & I believe it is not in the power of Congress or their officers, to hold them much, if any, longer, for we are obliged at this moment to increase our Guards to prev[en]t rioting, and the Insults which the Officers meet with in attempting to hold them to their duty. The proportion of these men amount to Seven Elevenths of this Army—these we shall loose at the moment the British Army will receive, by their Prisoners, an augmentation of five or 6000 Men.

It is not for me to investigate the causes, which induced this measure; nor the policy of those Letters (from authority) which gave the ton to the present sentiment—but since they have been adopted, we ought, in my opinion, to put a good face upon matters; and by a liberal conduct throughout, on our part (freed from appearances of distrust) try if we cannot excite similar dispositions on theirs: Indeed circumstances as things *now* are, I wish most fervently that all the Troops which are not retained for a Peace Establishment were to be discharged immediately—or such of them at least as do not incline to await the Settlement of their Accts. If they continue here, their claims, I can plainly perceive, will encrease; & our perplexities multiply. A Petition is this moment handed to me from the Non Comd. Officers of the Connecticut line solliciting half Pay; It is well drawn I am told, but I did not read it. I sent it back without appearing to Understand the Contents, because it did not come through the Channel of their Officers. This may be followed by others, and I mention it to shew the necessity—the absolute necessity of discharging the *Wars men* as soon as possible.

I have taken much pains to support Mr. Morris's Administration in the Army—and in proportion to its numbers I believe he had not more friends any where. But if he will neither adopt the mode which has been suggested, point out any other, nor shew cause why the first is either impracticable or impolitic [4] (I have heard he objects to it) they will certainly attribute their disappointment to a lukewarmness in him—or some design incompatable with their Interests. And here, my dear Colo. Hamilton, let me assure you, that it would not be more difficult to still the raging Billows in a tempestuous Gale, than to convince the Officers of this Army of the justice or policy of paying men in Civil Offices full wages, when *they* cannot obtain a Sixtieth part of their dues. I am not unapprised of the arguments which are made use of upon this occasion, to discriminate the cases; but they really are futile; & may be summed up in this, that tho' both are contending for the same rights, & expect equal benefits, yet, both cannot submit to the same inconveniences to obtain them; otherwise, to adopt the language of simplicity & plainness, a ration of Salt Porke with, or without Pease, as the case often is, would support the one as well as the other,—& in such a struggle as ours, wd., in my opinion, be alike honourable in both.

My anxiety to get home increases with the prospect of it, but when is it to happen? I have not heard that Congress have yet had under consideration the Lands, & other gratuities which at different periods of the War have been promised to the Army. Does not these things evince the necessity of a Committee's repairing to Camp, in order to arrange & adjust matters without spending time in a tedious exchange of Letters; Unless something of this kind is adopted, business will be delayed & expences accumulated—or the Army will break up in disorder, go home enraged, complaining of injustice— & committing enormities on the innocent Inhabitants in every direction.

I write to you unreservedly. If therefore, contrary to my apprehension, all these matters are in a proper train, & Mr. Morris has devised means to give the Army three Months pay, you will, I am persuaded excuse my precipitency and sollicitude, by ascribing it to an earnest wish to see the War happily, & honourably terminated— to my anxious desire of enjoying some repose & the necessity of my paying a little attention to my private concerns, which have suffered considerably in Eight years absence.

McHenry, expressing in a letter I have lately received from him, a wish to be appointed Official Secretary to the Court of Versailles, or London, I have by this opportunity written to Mr. Livingston, & Mr. Maddison; [5] speaking of him in warm terms; & wish him success with all my heart.

I am Dr Sir   With great esteem & regard   Yr. Most obedt Servt.
Go: Washington

Colo. Hamilton

ALS, Hamilton Papers, Library of Congress; ADfS, George Washington Papers, Library of Congress.
1. Ringwood, New Jersey.
2. See H to Washington, April 15, 1783, and "Report on the Ratification of the Provisional Peace Treaty," April 15, 1783.
3. Benjamin Lincoln was Secretary at War.
4. The "first mode" to which Washington refers probably was his proposal that the soldiers should receive at least three months' pay before disbandment. Congress, unable to raise the $750,000 which the three months' pay would require, asked the advice of Robert Morris, the Superintendent of Finance. Morris told Congress that such a sum could be acquired only through a paper anticipation of taxes for the redemption of which he would have to pledge his own credit. He said that he would assume the risk if Congress wished him to remain in office until the necessary arrangements were made and would assure him of support. The congressional assurances having been made (see "Report on Continuance in Office of the Superintendent of Finance," April 23, 1783, and "Report on Conference with the Superintendent of Finance," April 28, 1783), Morris paid the Army by giving his own notes (payable in six months) for three months' pay.

5. The letter to James Madison concerning James McHenry is printed in *GW*, XXVI, 349. Washington's letter to Madison is endorsed: "A Similar Letter was written to Mr. [Robert R.] Livingston Secretary of F: Affairs."

Continental Congress
Report on a Letter from the President
of Pennsylvania

[Philadelphia] April 22, 1783

The Committee [1] to whom was referred the letter from His Excellency The President of Pensylvania to the Delegates of that state of the 18th. instant [2] report that in their opinion it is inexpedient for Congress to come to any formal decision on the subject of that letter.

AD, Papers of the Continental Congress, National Archives.
1. The committee consisted of H, Oliver Ellsworth, and James Wilson.
2. The letter from John Dickinson, president of Pennsylvania, to the Pennsylvania delegates reads as follows:
"Gentlemen:
"By a law of this state the introduction of British goods is forbid during the war. Many respectable merchants of this city have applied to council, desiring to be informed, if British Vessels may in the present situation of affairs be admitted to Entry. We therefore earnestly wish to know the sense of Congress on this point—'whether the United States are now at Peace with Great Britain.'
"The Decision of this Question belongs to the National Council & will when clearly made, produce uniformity of proceedings throughout the States: But without it, there may be contradictory sentiments & measures among them. April 18, 1783." (Papers of the Continental Congress, National Archives.)

Continental Congress
Motion on Committee Reports

[*Philadelphia*] *April 22, 1783.* On this date Hamilton offered a motion, seconded by Hugh Williamson, which reads as follows: "That the Secretary lay before Congress on every Monday a List of all the Committees which have been apointed at any time before the preceding Week and have not reported and that such Committees shall be then calld on to state the Reasons why they have not reported."

D, in writing of Hugh Williamson, Papers of the Continental Congress, National Archives.

Continental Congress
Report on Proposal of Sir Guy Carleton [1]

[Philadelphia] April 22, 1783

The Committee on the letter of the 14th instant from His Excellency Sir Guy Carelton submit the following resolution.[2]

Whereas His Excellency Sir Guy Carleton has proposed to Congress to empower one or more persons on behalf of The United States to be present at New York and to assist such persons as shall be appointed by him to inspect and superintend all embarkations which the evacuation of that place may require and to represent to him every infraction of the letter or spirit of the 7th article of the treaty entered into between The United States and His Britannic Majesty the 30th. day of November last that redress may be immediately ordered

Therefore Resolved that three Commissioners be appointed for the purposes abovementioned.[3]

AD, Papers of the Continental Congress, National Archives.
    1. The report was read on April 22, 1783. It is printed in the *Journals* under date of April 24. Sir Guy Carleton was commander in chief of the British forces in America.
    2. The endorsement reads: "Report of a Committee on letter of 22 April from Secy for foreign Affairs & Letter of 14 from Sir Guy Carleton." The committee consisted of H, John Rutledge, and Nathaniel Gorham.
    3. On April 24, it was "*Ordered,* That the said letter from Sir Guy Carleton, be referred to the Commander in Chief, and that he take such measures for carrying into effect the several matters therein mentioned . . ." (*JCC*, XXIV, 274).

Alexander Hamilton and William Floyd to George Clinton

Philadelphia
April 2[3]d.[1] 1783

Sir,

We have the honor to inclose Your Excellency a copy of the resolutions passed on the [fifteenth Instant] relative to a ratification of the preliminary treaty—the reception of the posts in possession of the British troops and the surrender of the prisoners.[2]

We have this day received a letter from Sir Guy Carleton proposing that Congress should appoint one or more persons to assist persons appointed by him to superintend all embarkations which shall take place toward an evacuation of New York, conformable to the spirit of the 7th. article of the treaty—[which will probably be referred to the Commander in Chief.] ³

Mr. Benson has made to us the communications directed by Your Excellency; it is possible Sir Guy's reserve may have arisen from an unwillingness to enter into stipulations with a particular state.⁴ His present letter has the air of candour and good faith; but it is also possible there may be an intention of delaying the evacuation of the posts in hope of influencing our measures with respect to the British adherents.

We also communicate to your Excellency in confidence, that there is a doubt as to the true construction of the preliminary articles —to wit whether the evacuation of the posts & the other matters mentioned in the 7th. article are to take place on the ratification of the preliminary or deffinitive treaty. This doubt, however, Congress are unwilling to bring into view. The measures taken by the inclosed resolutions will bring [Genl] Careleton to an explanation—[perhaps the] ambiguity of Sir Guy's conduct [may be attributed to the Same doubt.]

We have the honor to be   With perfect respect   Your Excellency's Most Obed Serv

There is a frigate arrived from France which left Rochefort the 14th. of March. She brings little more than we have already had. It seems the dutch had not yet made their peace, but the Count De Vergennes ⁵ considers the terms last offered by England as reasonable enough; and it is therefore probable that matter will soon have been brought to a [close.] ⁶ He adds that they are about the definitive treaties, which offer no difficulty, and are only delayed by an invitation given to the two mediating powers to be parties to the business—Russia & the Empire.⁷ The matter would perhaps have been as well done without them.

[Wm. Floyd

[His Excellency Govornor Clinton]   Alexander Hamilton]

ADf, New-York Historical Society, New York City. The letter, except for the bracketed parts which probably were added by William Floyd, is in the writing of H.

1. The second number of the date is obliterated. In the *Public Papers of George Clinton*, VIII, 153, the letter is dated April 23.

2. The enclosure is printed in the *Public Papers of George Clinton*, VIII, 155.

3. See "Report on Proposal of Sir Guy Carleton," April 22, 1783.

4. For information on Egbert Benson's communication, see George Clinton to H and William Floyd, April 16, 1783. Benson, at the request of Governor Clinton, had an interview with Sir Guy Carleton on April 8, 1783, to arrange a convention for the evacuation of New York City. In the account of the interview which Benson sent to Clinton he concluded that he had not ". . . obtained from Sir Guy Carleton a determinate answer to any Question I proposed to him . . . but on the contrary there was an evidently designed Evasion & a Desire to turn the Conversation to other Subjects" (*Public Papers of George Clinton*, VIII, 144).

5. Charles Gravier, Comte de Vergennes.

6. The Anglo-French preliminaries of peace had been signed on January 20, 1783, but Great Britain and the United Provinces continued to negotiate over terms. Preliminary articles between the Dutch and the English were not made definitive until the treaty of May 20, 1784.

7. Russia and Austria were invited to serve as mediators in arranging peace between England and France. The invitation was extended, however, only after the French and English had signed preliminaries of peace on January 20, 1783.

To Philip Schuyler

[*Philadelphia, April 23, 1783.* On May 4, 1783, Schuyler wrote to Hamilton: "Your several favors of the 18th & 25th March and 2d. ult: were delivered me . . . that of the 23d April I had the pleasure to receive yesterday." *Letter of April 23 not found.*]

Continental Congress
Report on Continuance in Office of the Superintendent of Finance [1]

[*Philadelphia*] *April 23, 1783.* On this date a committee, consisting of Samuel Osgood, Theodorick Bland, Hamilton, James Madison, and Richard Peters, reported on plans to be adopted for paying and discharging the Army. It was recommended that Robert Morris, Superintendent of Finance, continue in office until funds could be procured for paying the officers and soldiers of the Army. To this report, in the writing of Samuel Osgood, Hamilton added the concluding section which recommended ". . . to Congress the propriety of appointing a Committee [2] to confer with him [3] on his continuance in office 'till proper arrangements can be carried into effect for advancing to the army three months pay at the time of its dissolution or at such short subsequent periods as will satisfy their expectations." [4]

D, in the writings of Samuel Osgood and H, Papers of the Continental Congress, National Archives.

1. On January 24, 1783, Robert Morris had informed Congress that he intended to resign as Superintendent of Finance. (See H to George Washington, April 8, 1783, note 7.) For the immediate background of the congressional resolve to continue Morris in office, see George Washington to H, April 22, 1783, note 4. See also Robert Morris to Theodorick Bland, Thomas FitzSimons, H, Samuel Osgood, and Richard Peters, April 14, 1783.

2. An entry in Morris's Diary for April 24, 1783, concerning the committee and the meeting Morris had with its members reads:

"The Honble. Mr. Osgood, Madison Peters, Hamilton and Bland Committee of Congress appointed to Confer with me as to my Continuance in Office called this morning in Consequence of Mr. G. Morris having told Mr. Osgood that he imagined I was ready for a Conference with them. I told this honorable Committee that my mind had been constantly occupied on the Subject from the Time they first called until the present Moment; That I see and feel the necessity and Propriety of dismissing the Army amongst their fellow Citizens satisfied and Contented; that I dread the Consequence of sending them into civil Life with Murmurs and Complaints in their mouths and that no Man can be better disposed than I am to satisfy the Army or more desirous of serving our Country but that my own Affairs call loudly for my Care and Attention &c. however being already engaged in this Business and willing to Oblige Congress if they think my Assistance essential I will Consent to remain in Office for the Purpose of Compleating such Payment to the Army as may be agreed on as necessary to disband them with their own Consent &c. but praying of Congress to excuse me from even this Service if they can accomplish their Views in such other Way as they may approve." (Robert Morris Papers, Library of Congress.)

3. Robert Morris.

4. The endorsement states that this report was "Referred back to the Comee. to confer with the Superintendt. of finance respecting his continuance in Office." See "Report on Conference with the Superintendent of Finance," April 28, 1783.

Continental Congress
Report on Conference with the Superintendent of Finance

[Philadelphia] April 28, 1783

[The Committee appointed to confer with the superintendant of Finance respecting his Continuance in his Office [1] have conferred with him accordingly] [2] and report that [the Substance] of the conferrence [was on the Part of Mr. Morris as follows:]

That his continuance in office was highly injurious to his private affairs and contrary to his private inclinations; but that he felt the importance of the exertions necessary to be made at the present juncture towards the reduction of the army in a manner satisfactory to them and convenient to the public; that therefore if Congress should think his services towards effecting that object of importance and should desire them, he would be ready to continue them till arrangements for that purpose could be made, and the engagements taken by him in consequence as well as those already entered into could be finally completed. That in this case he should hope for the support of Congress.[3]

[Resolved, That the Superintendant of Finance be informed that Congress are of opinion the public Service requires his Continuance in Office till Arrangements for the Reduction of the Army can be made, and the Engagements that shall be taken by him in Consequence, as well as those already entered into shall be finally completed.] [4]

D, in the writings of Elias Boudinot, Samuel Osgood, and H, Papers of the Continental Congress, National Archives; copy, signed by Charles Thomson, Robert Morris Papers, Library of Congress.
1. The resolution of April 23, 1783, the last part of which was written by H, was referred back to the committee which had reported it. The committee was composed of Samuel Osgood, Theodorick Bland, H, James Madison, and Richard Peters. Information on Morris's continuation in office is given in George Washington to H, April 22, 1783, note 4. See also "Report on Continuance in Office of the Superintendent of Finance," April 23, 1783.
2. The bracketed portions of this report are not in the writing of H.
3. For Morris's version of this conference, see "Report on Continuance in Office of the Superintendent of Finance," April 23, 1783, note 2.
On April 29, 1783, Morris made the following entry in his Diary:
"This Morning when I received the Book from the Office of the Secretary of Congress in which the Acts of Congress that respect this Department are entered every Day I perceived that the Committee which had Conferred with me respecting my Continuance in Office, after the last Day of next month had not reported the whole of the Conversation which passed and that the report as entered on the Journals of Congress mistakes the Sense of what passed on my Part, therefore I wrote a Note to the Honble. Mr. Osgood informing the Committee that they had misconstrued my Sentiments. He soon called here and upon my repeating some material parts of the Conversation he acknowleged they had been omitted. I requested him to call the Committee together again, but he said they had made their Report and are disolved but he would immediately return to Congress, have my Note to him read and move to have the Report of the Committee expunged from the Journals." (Robert Morris Papers, Library of Congress.)
Osgood successfully moved to "expunge" the second paragraph of this report from the Journals (JCC, XXIV, 311).

On May 1 Morris met again with the committee:

"The Honble. Mr. Hamilton, Mr. Fitzsimmons, Mr. Wilson Mr. Carrol Mr. Gorham and Mr. Osgood called to Confer with and Convince me of the Propriety of continuing in this Office untill the Army are disbanded and Peace Arrangements take place &c. To all their Arguments I opposed my Observations on the Conduct of Congress towards me; And I wish for nothing so much as to be releived from this cursed Scene of Drudgery and Vexation. I determined not to Continue and told them I will immediately write a Letter to that Effect to the President." (Robert Morris Papers, Library of Congress.)

It was not until May 3 according to an entry in his Diary that Morris agreed to remain in office:

"The Hon. Mr. Wilson, Colo Hamilton and Mr. Fitzsimmons came to assign Reasons why I shall not quit this Office on the last of this Month and Use many Arguments to induce me to continue until the Army are disbanded and proper Arrangements taken &c. I find all my Friends so extremely anxious on this Subject that I have considered it maturely and as Congress have pledged themselves to support me, and to enable me to fulfill all Engagements taken on Public Account, I have concluded to continue so much longer as may be necessary to disband the Army and fulfill my Engagements already taken as well as those to be made for the above Purpose." (Robert Morris Papers, Library of Congress.)

4. The report was adopted on April 28, 1783.

Continental Congress
Report on Brigadier General Moses Hazen's Regiment [1]

[*Philadelphia*] *April 29, 1783.* A committee of Thomas Mifflin, Hamilton, and Theodorick Bland, which had been appointed on April 17 "to enquire into the state of Hazen's regiment, and the propriety of promotion of officers in that corps," reported on this date.[2] The report recommended that Hazen "be intitled to the pay and emoluments of his rank from the first day of January last" and "That the corps formerly under his command be considered as then arranged on the establishment of the Regiments of the several lines and that commissions issue accordingly." [3]

AD, Papers of the Continental Congress, National Archives.

1. Hazen, of the Second Canadian Regiment, had been made a brigadier general in June, 1781. He retired on January 7, 1783.

2. The report is printed in *JCC*, XXIV, 312.

3. According to the editor of the *Journals* of the Congress, the report was "postponed April 30, 1783; decided 16 April, 1784" (*JCC*, XXIV, 312, note 1).

Continental Congress
Report on a Treaty of Commerce between the United States and Great Britain

[Philadelphia] May 1, 1783

The Commitee to whom was referred the letter from Mr. Adams of the report: [1]

That they have examined the different instructions given to our Commissioners and Ministers abroad and find that the Commissioners for making peace have an implied power to comprehend commercial stipulations in a Treaty of peace; but that there is no direct subsisting power of entering into a treaty of commerce with Great Britain distinct from the treaty of peace.

The Committee are of opinion that a special commission for that purpose ought without delay to be transmitted to the three remaining commissioners for peace Mr. Franklin Mr. Adams and Mr. Jay; and this for the following reasons:

First it is to be inferred from Mr Adams letter who as one of them is to be supposed to know their intention that the Commissioners for making peace have it not in contemplation to interweave into the treaty of peace such ample commercial stipulations as might supersede the necessity of particular treaty of commerce, otherwise it would be misplaced to urge Congress to appoint and authorise a minister for that purpose

2dly. Though it should be the intention of the said Commissioners to enter largely into commercial stipulations, yet if difficulties should intervene in that business, which might postpone too long the benefits of a definitive treaty of peace, they may judge it preferable to forego for the present such stipulations, to bring that important object to a speedy conclusion.

3dly. It is of great importance to The United states as soon as practicable to have a treaty of commerce with Great Britain, not only on account of the immediate advantages of that commerce, but from the possibility of making it the means of extending our commercial privileges with other nations; and because it is probable the impressions of the present conjuncture, may be more favourable to the views of these states than a future period.

The Committee are also of opinion that it will be expedient to authorise the Commissioners to enter into a temporary convention agreeable to Mr. Adam's idea to last for one year, to give time to mature and conclude the treaty of commerce and to instruct them at the same time to stipulate that the treaty which they may enter into shall be subject to the reversal and observations of Congress before it shall be finally concluded.[2]

On these principles The Committee submit the following resolution:

That a Commission be prepared to Messrs. Adams, Franklin & Jay, authorising them or either of them in the absence of the others, to enter into a treaty of Commerce between the United States and Great Britain, subject to the revisal of the contracting parties previous to its final conclusion; and in the mean time to enter into a commercial convention to continue in force One—year; That the secretary for foreign affairs lay before Congress without delay a plan of a treaty of commerce and instructions relative to the same to be transmitted to the said Commissioners.

AD, Papers of the Continental Congress, National Archives.

1. Space left blank in MS. The paragraph in the *Journals* which precedes this report reads: "On the report of a committee, consisting of Mr. (Alexander) Hamilton, Mr. (Oliver) Ellsworth and Mr. (John) Rutledge, to whom was referred a letter of February 5, from the honourable J. Adams" (*JCC*, XXIV, 320).

In his letter to Robert R. Livingston, Secretary for Foreign Affairs, Adams argued that there were no valid reasons for Congress to forbid a treaty of commerce with Great Britain or to refuse to acredit a minister to the Court of St. James (Wharton, *Revolutionary Diplomatic Correspondence*, VI, 242–47).

2. Adams had suggested that the American minister, whom he hoped Congress would appoint, should send any proposed treaty of commerce to Congress for approval or new instructions. Upon receipt of a treaty, Congress should transmit it to the legislatures of all the states and ask for their opinions. In the meantime, Adams recommended that the American minister be instructed "to enter into a temporary convention for regulating the present trade for a limited number of months or years, or until the treaty of commerce shall be completed" (Wharton, *Revolutionary Diplomatic Correspondence*, VI, 244)

Continental Congress ## *Report on the Corps of Invalids*

[Philadelphia] May 1, 1783

Resolved [1] that the corps of Invalids be reduced; such officers as have lost a limb or been equally disabled in service to retire on full pay for life, such officers as may not be included in this description to retire on the same principles with other officers of the army; such non commissioned officers and soldiers as being strangers in the country and having been disabled in service are incapable of providing for their own subsistence and are proper subjects for a hospital, to be received into some fixed hospital to be appropriated for the purpose and there supported during life on such provision as may be hereafter determined to be intitled in the mean time to their usual rations and cloathing—and such non commissioned officers and soldiers disabled in service, as may have homes to which they can retire, to be discharged on the principles of the resolution of the 23d. of April last.[2]

That the Secretary at War be directed to take proper measures previous to the reduction to ascertain the different classes above described.

That the officers who shall retire on full pay, may at their option collectively accept in lieu of such full pay for life the amount of
       years full pay on the terms of the resolutions of the
last.[3]

That at the reduction of this corps all the officers and men shall receive one months pay and shall share in any further payments which may be made to the other parts of the army when reduced.

AD, Papers of the Continental Congress, National Archives.
  1. The committee consisted of H, Richard Peters, and Daniel Carroll.
  2. The resolution of April 23, 1782, provided that sick or wounded soldiers who requested a discharge in preference to continuance in the Corps of Invalids be given a pension of five dollars a month (JCC, XXIV, 210).
  3. The blank spaces presumably refer to the information contained in the "Report on Half Pay to the Army," March 21, 1783.

From George Washington [1]

Newburgh [New York] 2d May 1783.

Sir

A necessary absence from Camp and several unavoidable interruptions have been the occasion of, and must be my apology for with holding the inclosed thoughts [2] on a peace establishment so long.

If they will afford any assistance, or contain any thing satisfactory, I shall think my time and labour well spent.

I have the honour to be Sir   Your Most Obt: servt G Washington

Varick Transcripts, George Washington Papers, Library of Congress.
1. This letter was sent to H in his capacity as chairman of a committee of Congress. See H to Washington, April 9, 1783, and the second of two letters Washington wrote to H on April 16.
2. The enclosure, entitled "Sentiments on a Peace Establishment" is printed in *GW*, XXVI, 374–98.

Continental Congress
Motion on Funds for Payment of the Army

[Philadelphia] May 2, 1783

Whereas it is the desire of Congress when the reduction of the army shall take place to enable the officers and soldiers to return to their respective homes with convenience and satisfaction, for which purpose it will be indispensable to advance them a part of their pay before they leave the field: [1] And Whereas at the present juncture, there are many other engagements, for which the public faith is pledged and the punctual performance of which is essential to the credit of the United States; neither of which important objects can be effected, without the vigorous exertions of the several states in the collection of taxes;

Therefore Resolved that the respective states be called upon in the most earnest manner, to make every effort in their power to forward the collection of taxes, that such a sum may without delay be paid into the common treasury as will be adequate to the public exigencies; and that Congress confidently rely, for an immediate and efficacious attention to the present requisition, upon the disposition of their constituents not only to do justice to those brave men, who have suffered and sacrificed so much in the cause of their country, and whose distresses must be extreme should they be sent from the field without the payment of a part of their well earned dues; but also to enable Congress to maintain the faith and reputation of the United States; both which are seriously concerned in relieving the necessities of a meritorious army and fulfulling the public stipulations.

Resolved that as an additional mean of accomplishing the same and a further application be immediately made to His Most Christian [Majesty] to induce him to add three millions of livres to the six millions already granted in part of the loan of 4,000,000 of dollars requested by the resolutions of   [2] and that his said Majesty be informed that Congress will consider his compliance in this instance as a new and valuable proof of his friendship, peculiarly interesting in the present conjuncture of the affairs of the United States; and will apply a part of the requisitions now subsisting upon the several states to the repayment of the said three millions.

Resolved that the Superintendant of Finance be directed to take the necessary arrangements for carrying the views of Congress into execution & that he be assured of their firm support towards fulfilling the engagements he has already taken, or may take on the public account during his continuance in office.[3]

AD, Papers of the Continental Congress, National Archives.
  1. For information on the attempts to secure money to pay the Army, see Robert Morris to H, Theodorick Bland, Thomas FitzSimons, Samuel Osgood, and Richard Peters, April 14, 1783; George Washington to H, April 22, 1783, note 4; "Report on Continuance in Office of the Superintendent of Finance," April 23, 1783; "Report on Conference with the Superintendent of Finance," April 28, 1783.
  2. Space left blank in MS. The motion printed in the *Journals* of the Congress reads: "14th day of September, 1782" (*JCC*, XXIV, 326).
  3. To minimize the risk in pledging his credit for a partial payment to the Army, Robert Morris had asked for the firm support of Congress. See references in note 1.
  The endorsement states that H's motion, seconded by James Wilson, was passed on May 2, 1783.

From Philip Schuyler [1]

Saratoga [New York] May ⟨4⟩ 1783

My Dear Sir

Your several favors of the 18th & 25th March and 2d. ult: were delivered me on the first Instant [2] by a man from Charlotte County who found them at Mr Loudons at Fish kill,[3] that of the 23d April I had the pleasure to receive yesterday.[4]

Persuaded as I have long been of the necessity of terminating the war both from the want of exertion in ourselves and the possibility

of a change in European politics I received the account of the preliminaries being signed with the sincerest satisfaction.[5] I confess I
suspected Lord Shelburnes sincerity and dreaded with you that
France and her allies would have insisted on terms that would have
thrown the Game into his hands had he negotiated only with a view
to divide, and deceive the powers opposed to Britain, and yet favorable as I concieve the terms are to us, I find many amongst us not
satisfied especially with respect to the boundary of these states, for
my part I think the partition lines more favorable to us than those
which our Commissioners had in charge to insist upon.[6]

I did not pay much attention to the terms in which the offer of
a seperate Jurisdiction within this state to Congress were couched
as I was persuaded Congress would not approve of the Situation.[7]
If that body should seriously determine on a permanent residence
in this state, and signify it to the legislature I make little doubt but
that the cession of Jurisdiction will be made agreable to their wishes,
& that at the place in question or any other, the two cities excepted.

Altho our legislature seems still inclined to confer powers on Congress Adequate to the proper discharge of the great duties of the
Soverign council of these states, yet I perceive with pain that some,
chagrined at disappointment, are already attempting to inculcate
a contrary principle, and I fear It will gain too deep a root, to be
eradicated until such confusion prevails as will make men deeply
feel the necessity of not retaining so much soveriegnty in the states
Individually.

I attempted during the last meeting to make the landed provision
you mention but found mens minds not quite ripe for it, a concurrent
resolution was however carried with few dissentments, to make a
generous allowance to our line.[8] I hope It will be a prelude to another extending to the whole Army. It would facilitate the measure
if the other lines could be induced to petition Congress for a recommendation to this state to give the bounty lands promised in 1776,[9]
and to extend the quantity, and If Congress in the recommendation
would declare that we should have credit for the Amount on the
same terms as we shall Sell to our own citizens, the request would
certainly be complied with.

The sentiment is so universal not to pardon those of the disaffected
whose estates have been confiscated, that I believe their warmest

advocates will not attempt to Introduce a bill for the purpose, but I believe that in conformity to one of the provisional articles no molestation will be given to such other Citizens of New York as have remained in the power of the enemy and whose conduct may have been equivocal or opposed.

I don't much relish the invitation given to Russia and the emperor to become parties to the treaties.[10] They may perhaps insist on stipulations being inserted which might greatly embarrass us. Suppose Shelburn should be able to Induce them to Insist on more favorable terms for the disaffected, especially as he has been pressed so hard on that Subject in the british parliment and that France should comply? What will be the consequences? Singly to prosecute the war may not be in our powers, and to restore all, burthened with debt as we are, would be severely felt.

We wait with impatience the happy moment when we shall Embrace you Betsy and my Little Grandson. Adieu we all Join in Love & best wishes

I am Dr Sir every affectionately & sincerely Yours &c. &c.

Ph: Schuyler

Colo Hamilton

I do not answer Betsys letter as I suppose she will have left Philadelphia before this.

ALS, Hamilton Papers, Library of Congress.

1. Schuyler at this time represented the western district of New York in the New York Senate.

2. Letters not found.

3. Samuel Loudon was the publisher of *The New-York Packet, and the American Advertiser.* With the arrival of the British forces in New York City in 1776, Loudon moved to Fishkill, New York, where, in addition to editing the *Packet,* he served as state printer.

4. Letter not found.

5. In March, 1783, Congress had received the official text of the provisional articles of peace between Great Britain and the United States signed in Paris, November 30, 1782; and the preliminary articles of peace between Great Britain, France, and Spain signed January 20, 1783.

6. On August 14, 1779, Congress resolved that the Americans should insist on the Mississippi River as the western boundary of the United States and the line of 31 degrees north latitude as the southern boundary on the West Florida frontier. The preliminary articles established the eastern boundary of the United States at the St. Croix River, the northern boundary at the line of 45 degrees, the western boundary at the Mississippi River, and the southern boundary at the 31st degree parallel. For a more specific description of the boundaries awarded the United States by the peace treaty, see Bemis, *The Diplomacy of the American Revolution,* 234–35.

7. Schuyler is probably referring to the offer made by the Corporation of Kingston, New York, to Congress. See Christopher Tappen to H and William Floyd, March 19, 1783.

8. On March 27, 1783, the New York legislature resolved that "the Legislature of this State are willing, not only to take upon themselves to discharge the said Engagement of Congress, so far as it relates to the Line of this State, but likewise as [to] a Gratuity to the said line" (New York Senate *Journal*, 1783, 164).

9. To encourage enlistments in the Continental Army, Congress in September, 1776, had offered bounties of money and land.

10. Schuyler is referring to the invitation given to Russia and Austria to serve as mediators in arranging peace between England and France. The invitation actually was extended only after England and France had arranged their own peace terms (Bemis, *The Diplomacy of the American Revolution*, 254).

Continental Congress
Report on Peace Arrangements for the
Department of Foreign Affairs

[Philadelphia] May 8, 1783

The Committee [1] appointed "to consider what arrangements it will be proper to make relatively to peace," submit the following report on the department of foreign affairs:

Resolved that the ordinances and resolutions heretofore passed relatively to the department of foreign affairs shall continue in force subject to the alterations and additions following:

That the Secretary for that department shall be considered as the head of the diplomatic corps of the United States, and to remove any doubts which may have existed respecting the nature of his office, it is hereby declared to be his duty from time to time to lay before Congress such plans for conducting the political and commercial intercourse of the United States with foreign nations, as may appear to him conducive to the interests of the said states.

That the said secretary be intitled to the same allowance for salary and expences as is hereafter specified for a minister at a foreign court, and that instead of two under secretaries as by the resolution of the 1st of March 1782, there be appointed under him one official secretary with the same allowance as to a secretary of embassy, the said secretary to be nominated by him & appointed by Congress.

That each minister shall be allowed Eight thousand dollars in lieu of all salary and expences; except for the postage of letters and for the purchase of public prints and papers, which shall be a charge upon the United States.

That the said minister shall be invested with consular powers, and shall accordingly be at the same time, consul general in the Country where he resides having the superintendence and controul of all vice consuls or inferior commercial agents, but shall not be at liberty to engage directly or indirectly, in any kind of trade or traffic whatsoever.

That for the more convenient management of the commercial interests of the United States, there shall be so many vice-consuls appointed to reside in foreign ports, with which the trade of the said states may be carried on, as shall from time to time be found necessary; and that the said vice-consuls shall have free liberty to trade, but no salary or other emolument, except the usual commissions on such matters as they may be authorised to transact on account of the United States, and reimbursement for contingent and reasonable expences incurred on their behalf.

That the secretary for foreign affairs prepare and lay before Congress an ordinance conformable to the foregoing principles for regulating the consular powers and privileges and the plan of a convention to be entered into with foreign nations for that purpose.

That whenever Congress shall judge it expedient to appoint an official secretary to any embassy he shall be intitled to a salary of one thousand dollars and to a place in the house and at the table of the Minister with whom he shall reside.

The Committee think it unnecessary to report concerning the rank of the Secretary for foreign affairs, relatively to other heads of the executive departments as this is an object comprehended in another report depending before Congress.[2]

AD, Papers of the Continental Congress, National Archives; copy, Papers of the Continental Congress, National Archives. In *JCHW*, II, 242–43, this report is dated April 2, 1783.

1. The committee consisted of H, James Madison, Oliver Ellsworth, James Wilson, and Samuel Holten. Except for the substitution of Holten for Samuel Osgood, the committee was the one appointed between April 3 and 6 to report on peace arrangements (H to Washington, April 9, note 2). The same committee, according to the endorsement, also was to report on "the posts on the frontiers & within the U S possessed by the british." Its report on that subject was delivered May 12.

2. The endorsement of the copy of this report, which is not in the writing of H, states that it was to be considered on May 12, 1783. In the *Journals* there is no record of subsequent consideration of the report, but James Madison in his "Notes of Debates in the Continental Congress," (MS, James Madison Papers, Library of Congress), recorded that on May 15 "The Report relating to the Dept. of For. Affairs taken up, and, after some discussion of the expediency of raising the salary of the Secy. Congress adjourned."

Continental Congress
Report on the Garrisoning of Frontier Posts by Continental Troops

[Philadelphia] May 12, 1783

The same Committee [1] submit the following report on the letter of the 3d. instant from the Commander in Chief: [2]

That the Commander in Chief be directed whenever the posts within the United states shall be evacuated pursuant to the articles of peace to *place within* the same, composed of the troops under his command [who have inlisted for three years &] [3] whose times of service may not then have expired, such garrisons as he may judge necessary; till Congress shall determine on the further arrangements proper to be made relatively to that object; and that he take such measures for transporting to the said posts artillery stores and provisions, as he may judge expedient, for which purpose the Superintendant of Finance is directed to afford all the assistance in his department which circumstances will permit.

ADf, Papers of the Continental Congress, National Archives. According to the *Journals*, another copy of this report, in the writing of Oliver Ellsworth and Elias Boudinot, is in the Papers of the Continental Congress (*JCC*, XXIV, 338, note 1). The report printed in the *Journals* differs in minor particulars from the draft by H.

1. The committee, with the substitution of Samuel Osgood for Samuel Holten, was the one which presented the "Report on Peace Arrangements for the Department of Foreign Affairs" on May 8, 1783.

2. Washington's letter, in which he asked for an explanation of the intentions of Congress respecting posts in the United States occupied by British troops, is printed in *GW*, XXVI, 398–400.

3. The bracketed words are not in the writing of H.

To George Clinton

Philadelphia
May 14 1783

Sir

The President of Congress will of course have transmitted to Your Excellency the plan lately adopted by Congress for funding the public debt.[1] This plan was framed to accommodate it to the objections of some of the states; but this spirit of accomodation will only serve to render it less efficient, without making it more palatable. The opposition of the state of Rhode Island for instance is chiefly founded upon these two considerations. The Merchants are opposed to any revenue from Trade, and the state depending almost wholly on commerce wants to have credit for the amount of the duties.

Persuaded that the plan now proposed will have little more chance of success than a better one; and that, if agreed to by all the states, it will in a great measure fail in the execution, it received my negative. My principal objections were:

1st That it does not designate the funds (except the impost) on which the whole interest is to arise; and by which (selecting the capital articles if visible property) the collection would have been easy, the fund productive and necessarily increasing with the increase of the Country.

2dly. That the duration of the fund is not coextensive with the debt but limited to twenty five years, though there is a moral certainty that in that period, the principal will not by the present provision be fairly extinguished.

3dly That the nomination and appointment of the collectors of the revenue are to reside in each state; instead of at least the nomination being in the United States, the consequence of which will be, that those states which have little interest in the fund by having a small share of the public debt due to their own citizens will take care to appoint such persons as are least likely to collect the revenue.

The evils resulting from these defects will be that in many instances the objects of the revenues will be improperly chosen and will consist of a multitude of little articles which will on experiment prove insufficient—that for want of a vigorous collection in each state, the revenue will be unproductive in many and will fall chiefly upon those states which are governed by most liberal principles; that for want of an adequate security, the evidences of the public debt will not be transferrable for anything like their value —that this not admitting an incorporation of the Creditors in the nature of banks will deprive the public of the benefit of an increased circulation, and of course will disable the people from paying the taxes for want of a sufficient medium.

I shall be happy to be mistaken in my apprehensions but the experiment must determine.

I hope our state will consent to the plan proposed; because it is her interest at all events to promote the payment of the public debt on Continental funds (independent of the general considerations of Union & propriety). I am much mistaken if the debts due from the United States to the citizens of the state of New York do not considerably exceed its proportion of the necessary funds, of course it has an immediate interest that there should be a Continental provision for them. But there are superior motives that ought to operate in every state, the obligations of national faith honor and reputation.

Individuals have been already too long sacrificed to public convenience. It will be shocking and indeed an eternal reproach to this country, if we begin the peaceable enjoyment of our independence by a violation of all the principles of honesty & true policy.

It is worthy of remark that at least four fifths of the domestic debt are due to the citizens of the states from Pensylvania inclusively Northward.

I have the honor to be   Sir   Your most Obed ser   AH

P. S.

It is particularly interesting that the state should have a representation here. Not only many matters are depending which require a full representation in Congress and there is now a thin one; but those matters are of a nature so particularly interesting to our state, that we ought not to be without a voice in them. I wish two other Gentlemen of the delegation [2] may appear as soon as possible for it would be very injurious to me to remain much longer here. Having no future view in public life, I owe it to myself without delay to enter upon the care of my private concerns in earnest.[3]

ALS, Hamilton Papers, Library of Congress.
1. The congressional resolution of April 18, 1783, passed after more than a month of deliberation and debate, repeated the request made on February 3, 1781, that the states invest Congress with the power to levy duties on imported goods. The report of April 18 listed the specific duties to be levied on certain enumerated imports and requested a duty of five percent *ad valorem* on all other goods. The proceeds from the impost were to be applied only to the discharge of the interest and principal of the debt of the United States, and its collection was limited to a twenty-five year term. The resolution is printed in *JCC*, XXIV, 257-60.
2. On July 22, 1782, the legislature of New York had nominated H, James Duane, William Floyd, John Morin Scott, and Ezra L'Hommedieu delegates to the Continental Congress for one year, beginning November 1, 1782. Only H and William Floyd had been in attendance from November to the date of this letter.
3. The version of this letter printed in the *Public Papers of George Clinton*, VIII, 179-81, concludes with the following additional sentence: "I take the liberty to inclose Y'r. Excell'y a letter to Mr. LeRoy's son for Mr. Floyd."

Robert Morris to Alexander Hamilton, Richard Peters, and Nathaniel Gorham [1]

Office of Finance [Philadelphia] 15th. May 1783

Gentlemen

In Consequence of the Conversation [2] which passed between us this Morning I shall give you the best information in my Power as

LS, Papers of the Continental Congress, National Archives.
1. On May 9, 1783, Congress appointed a committee consisting of H, Peters, and Gorham "to consider and report the means of reducing expenditures in all other Departments as well as the military." The committee was directed to confer with the Superintendent of Finance and the Secretary at War (*JCC*, XXIV, 337).
2. Morris recorded in his Diary under the date May 15 the following account of the interview:
"The Honble. Mr. Gorham and Mr. Hamilton, two Members of a Committee of Congress for conferring with the Secretary of War, The Secretary of foreign Affairs and myself relative to disbanding the Army, met with the said Ministers at this Office this Morning. I opened the Business and stated very fully the Necessity of disbanding the Army in Order to get clear of an Expence which our Resources are unequal to, and which cannot be supported many Months at any rate, but which if continued any longer, will consume the only Means now left for making a payment to the Army when disbanded. The Gentlemen of the Committee seemed perfectly satisfied of the Necessity of Disbanding the Army on Principles of Oeconomy but opposed to it on

to the State of my Department and the Resources I can command.

You have in the enclosed Paper Number one an Account of Receipts and Expenditures from the Commencement of the Year to the End of the last Month [3] by which it appears that there is an Advance on Credit to the Amount of near six hundred thousand Dollars exclusive of what may appear in Mr. Swanwicks [4] Accounts for the Month of April. A large Sum is also due on Genl. Green's Drafts and the Contractors are to be paid in this Month for the Supplies of January last. At the End of this Month therefore that Anticipation must necessarily be much increased. As will appear from the slightest Reflection after what is to be said of our Resources.

These are either foreign or domestic. As to the first I enclose the Copy of the last Letter I have received from Mr. Grand [5] and I have to add to what is contained in that Letter that the Day it was received my Drafts on him over and above those mentioned in it amounted to Three million and forty thousand two hundred and seventy eight Livres and six deniers. I have directed therefore Mr. Barclay [6] to pay over to Mr. Grand any Monies which may be in his Possession and I have directed Messrs. Willink &ca. of Amsterdam [7] to do the same after deducting what may be necessary to pay the Interest of their Loan falling due the first of June next. But as I have no Accounts how much has been borrowed since the End

---

Principles of Policy in which the Honble. Secretary of foreign Affairs joins them. The Secretary at War said little, and I related an Observation which he had made to me a few Days before in favor of disbanding the Army directly, viz: That they would not continue in the field under their present Enlistments if the War was to break out again; but that in such a Case we must begin entirely a New. The Conclusion of the Conference is that I am to State the Reasons resulting from the Situation of our Finances which induce an immediate disbanding of the Army in writing to the Committee." (Robert Morris Papers, Library of Congress.)

3. The enclosure is in the Papers of the Continental Congress, National Archives.

4. John Swanwick was an official in the office of the Superintendent of Finance.

5. Ferdinand Le Grand was a French banker who handled most of the financial operations of the United States in France during the American Revolution. Le Grand's letter is in the Papers of the Continental Congress, National Archives.

6. Thomas Barclay, American consul in France, was appointed by Congress in November, 1782, to settle its accounts in Europe.

7. The Amsterdam banking house of Jan and Wilhem Willink was employed in the financial operations of the United States in Holland.

of January and as all which had been borrowed before was disposed of I cannot determine how far they can come in Aid of Mr. Grand neither can I tell until the Receipt of his Accounts what Aid he may stand in need of. In these Circumstances I am obliged to leave about eighteen hundred thousand Livres (which remain of a Sum placed in the Hands of Messrs. Le Couteulx[8] for answering Drafts intended thro Havanna to answer any Deficiency of other Funds to pay my Drafts on Mr. Grand. These then Gentlemen are all the foreign Resources except what the french Court may advance on the late Resolutions of Congress[9] and you will see by the enclosed Translation of a Letter from the Minister of france what little Hope is to be entertained from that Quarter.[10]

Our domestic Resources are twofold first certain Goods and other Property such as Horses Waggons &ca. These latter will produce very little and the former are (by the Peace) very much reduced in Value and from the nature of the Goods themselves they are chiefly unsaleable. Very little Reliance therefore can be placed on this first Dependance. The Amount I cannot possibly ascertain for I do not yet know (and cannot until the opening of them now in Hand shall be compleated) the Kinds Quality and Situation. Some are damaged those which were deemed most Saleable have been tried at Vendue and went under the first Cost and much the greater Part will certainly not sell at a fourth of their Value.

The only Remaining Resource is in the Taxes and what they may amount to, it is impossible to tell. But you have enclosed an Account of what they yielded the four first Months of this Year[11] and you will see from thence that if all Expence had ceased on the first day of this Month the Anticipations already made would

8. I. L. and C. Le Couteulx and Company was a French banking house which aided the United States in its financial operations abroad.

9. The resolution of Congress to which Morris is referring was dated May 2, 1783, and requested the French King to add three million livres to the amount he had granted the Americans.

10. The Chevalier de La Luzerne, French Minister to the United States, had written to Morris on March 15 warning him that the French King would not lend the United States more money until Congress established substantial revenues. It was to this letter rather than to one discussing the resolution of May 2 (see note 9) that Morris is referring. La Luzerne's letter is printed in Wharton, *Revolutionary Diplomatic Correspondence*, VI, 303–05.

11. The enclosure is in the Papers of the Continental Congress, National Archives.

not have been absorped by the same Rate of Taxation in eight Months more.

Now then Gentlemen you will please to consider that if your Army is kept together they will consume as much in one Month as the Taxes will produce in two and Probably much more. To make them three Months Pay will require I suppose at least six hundred thousand Dollars and every Day they continue in the Field lessens the Practicability of sending them Home satisfied. The Anticipations of Revenue are threefold two of which appear as to their Effects in the public Accounts and one very considerable one tho it produces great Relief is not seen. It consists in the Drawing of Bills on me for the public Service by different Persons and at different Usances. I imagine that these Amount at the present Moment to one hundred thousand Dollars. The other Anticipations consist in Loans from the Bank or the issuing of my own Notes. As to the first of these it is limited in its Nature by the Capital of the Bank which being small will not admit of great Deductions and it depends much upon Circumstances whether the Bank will go to the Extent which they may go. If they find the Revenues increasing and the Expences diminishing they will; otherwise they certainly will not. As to the Notes I issue (and which form the greater Part of my Anticipations) these have also a certain Limit to exceed which would be fatal. I must not so extend that Circulation as that I shall be unable to pay them when presented for that would totally destroy their Credit and of Course their Utility.

Now Gentlemen if any Thing of this Sort should take place before the Army are disbanded you will see at once that they could be fed no longer and must of Course disband themselves. I will not dwell on the Consequences but I will draw one clear Conclusion which you have doubtless by this time anticipated viz. that unless they are disbanded immediately the Means of paying them even with Paper will be gone. And this Sentiment I have not only delivered to you but to a former Committee as well as to many individual Members of Congress.

But Gentlemen when I speak of disbanding the Army I beg to be understood as meaning to reserve a sufficient Garrison for West Point. And on this Subject I pray to be indulged in a View of our Political and military Situation as far as relates to this capital Object of my Department. And first as to our political Situation I conceive that we are at Peace. It is true that the definitive Treaty is not that we know of compleated but it is equally true that all the other beligerent Powers have been disarming for months past and I presume they are at least as well acquainted with the State of things as we are. To express Doubts of the Sincerity of Britain on this Subject is I know a fashionable but in my Opinion a very foolish Language. We have the best Evidence of their Sincerity which the Nature of Things will admit for we know they are unable to carry on the War and we see & feel that they are passing every Act and doing everything in their Power to conciliate our Affections. Expressions of Doubts as to their Sincerity if intended to foster Enmity against them will fail of the Effect and produce the direct Contrary for every Body will soon learn to consider them as unjustly suspected and their Ministers will take Care to inculcate and enforce the Sentiment.

As to our military Situation some of the Troops in the Southern States have already mutinied [12] the principal Part of them are ordered away and since the floridas are ceded to Spain it follows that those Troops which may remain in the Southern States will have to operate against the Spaniards if they operate at all. So that every Man except those under the Generals immediate Command and the little Garrison of fort Pitt are in fact disbanded to every Purpose but that of Expence.

The Prisoners are some of them going and the rest gone into New York so that in a few Days the Enemy will be able to do every Thing which they could do if the greater Part of our Army were gone Home. For they could not take West Point if it is properly Garrisoned and they could ravage the Country in spite of our Army when theirs shall be all collected.

Our Situation therefore seems to be this. We are keeping up an Army at a great Expence and very much against their Inclinations for a meer Punctilio and by that Means incapacitating ourselves from Performing what they begin to consider as a kind of Engagement taken with them. I shall detain you no longer on this Subject but

12. Morris is presumably referring to the mutiny of Colonel George Baylor's regiment in Virginia. Benjamin Harrison, governor of Virginia, informed the Virginia delegates in Congress of such a mutiny in a letter which he wrote on May 31, 1783 (Burnett, *Letters*, VII, 157).

must repeat one Observation which is that unless the far greater Part of our Expences be immediately curtailed the Object Congress had in View by their Resolutions of the second Instant [13] cannot possibly be accomplished.

I have the Honor to be Gentlemen your most obedient and humble Servant   Robt. Morris

The honorable Mr. Hamilton
           Mr. Gorham   a Committee of Congress
           Mr. Peters

13. See "Motion on Funds for Payment of the Army," May 2, 1783.

Continental Congress
Motion on Prohibition of Naval Forces on Great Lakes [1]

[Philadelphia] May 20, 1783

That the said Ministers also endeavour to stipulate that neither party shall keep any naval force on the lakes on the Northern & Western Frontier.[2]

AD, Papers of the Continental Congress, National Archives.
    1. H's motion was one of several on this date suggesting provisions to be included in the final peace treaty.
    2. The motion was referred to John Francis Mercer, Thomas FitzSimons, and Theodorick Bland (JCC, XXIV, 348).

Continental Congress
Motion on Instructions to Francis Dana [1]

[Philadelphia, May 21, 1783]

Resolved that Mr. Dana [2] be informed that the treaties lately entered into for restoring peace have caused such an alteration in the affairs of these states as to have removed the primary object of his mission to the Court of Russia, the acquisition of new supports to their independence; that though Congress approve the principles of the armed neutrality founded on the liberal basis of a maintenance of the rights of neutral nations and of the privileges of commerce; yet they are unwilling at this juncture to become a party to a confederacy [which may hereafter too far complicate the Interests of the united States with the Politics of Europe] [3] and therefore if such a progress is not yet made in this business as may make it dishonorable to recede; it is their desire that no further measures may be taken at present towards the admission of the United States into that confederacy.

[That Congress deem it inexpedient at this time to accede to the Armed nutrality if such progress is not already made in that business as to render it dishonorable] [4] provided the steps already taken do not imply an honorary engagement for the payment of that money.

That with respect to a commercial treaty with Russia, they consider the benefits of it to this country in any extensive degree as rather remote, and have therefore little present inducement to enter into it, besides a desire of cultivating the friendship of that Court and preserving a consistency with the disposition already manifested towards forming a connection therewith—and also of laying the foundation of a future intercourse when the circumstances of the two countries may be more favourable to the same. That as experience will enable both nations to form a better judgment hereafter of the principles upon which that intercourse may be most advantageously conducted, Congress would wish any treaty now formed to be of temporary duration & limited to a fixed period. That in this view unless Mr. Dana shall have already formed engagements or made proposals from which he cannot easily recede if a more indefinite or extensive nature before this reaches him, he be instructed to confine the duration of the proposed treaty of commerce to fifteen years agreeable to the term limited for a similar treaty with the Court of Sweden and to stipulate expressly that the same shall be subject to the revisal of Congress previous to its final conclusion; and that in all matters he insist upon exact reciprocity. That so soon as this object shall be accomplished, or if he discovers any repugnancy on the part of the Court of Russia to entering into a treaty with these states on liberal principles he be permitted to return. That with respect to the money mentioned in his letter of the [5] to be employed in presents to the ministers of that Court he be informed, that as by the confederation no persons holding offices under the United States are permitted to receive presents from foreign powers, so it is not consistent with the situation or policy of these states to adopt that practice in their transactions with other nations [and that he be instructed to decline paying the same unless the Steps already taken by him towards forming a Treaty or Treaties shall in his Judgmt imply an Engagemt to make such Payment.] [6]

ADf, Papers of the Continental Congress, National Archives.

1. The paragraph which precedes this motion reads:
"The committee, consisting of Mr. (James) Madison, Mr. (Nathaniel) Gorham and Mr. (Thomas) Fitzsimmons, to whom was referred a letter of 21 April, from the Secretary for foreign affairs, together with letters of 16 and 19 December, 1782, o.s., from Mr. Dana, having reported thereon, and the report being postponed, a motion was made by Mr. (Alexander) Hamilton, seconded by Mr. (James) Madison, in the words following." (*JCC*, XXIV, 348.)

The committee report is printed in *JCC*, XXIV, 267. Robert R. Livingston's letter is printed in Wharton, *Revolutionary Diplomatic Correspondence*, VI, 388; Dana's letters are in *ibid.*, 170–72.

For a discussion of the significance of this resolution in the diplomatic history of the United States, see Bemis, *The Diplomacy of the American Revolution*, 166–67.

2. Francis Dana of Massachusetts, a former member of the Continental Congress and secretary to John Adams, had been appointed American Minister to Russia on December 19, 1780. He was directed to secure an invitation to the United States to join the League of Armed Neutrality which Russia had invited European neutrals to join.

3. Bracketed words are in the writing of Elias Boudinot.

4. Bracketed words are in the writing of Oliver Ellsworth.

5. Space left blank in MS. The final version of this report, which is printed in the *Journals* following the draft, gives the dates of Dana's letters as August 25, November 10, December 19, 1782, and January 20, 1783 (*JCC*, XXIV, 351). In Wharton, *Revolutionary Diplomatic Correspondence*, V, 700–02, the letter of August 25 is dated old style August 23, new style September 5. In *ibid.*, VI, the letter of November 10 (dated old style November 7, new style November 18) is printed on pages 54–56; the letter of December 19 (dated old style December 19, new style December 30) is printed on pages 171–72; the letter of January 20 (dated old style January 20, new style January 31) is found on pages 234–35.

6. Bracketed words are in the writing of Elias Boudinot.

The motion, amended after debate, was rejected. For the final version of the motion as well as the motions for amending it, see *JCC*, XXIV, 350–54.

Continental Congress
Report on the Discharge of Noncommissioned Officers and Soldiers

[Philadelphia] May 23. 1783

The Committee consisting of Mr. Hamilton, Mr. Peters and Mr. Gorham to whom was referred a letter of the 9th. from the Superintendent of finance and Secretary at war,[1] in order to confer with them on the resolutions of the 7th. & 28th. of April and 2d Inst report [2] "that all the non commissioned officers and soldiers in the service of the United States, enlisted to serve during the war, be discharged; and that the Secretary at war and Commander in Chief take the proper measures for doing this, in a manner most convenient to the soldiery and to the inhabitants, having the men previously conducted, under proper officers, to their respective states, and that they be at the same time authorized to retain as many officers as they may judge necessary to command the men who still continue in service, permitting the others to retire.[3]

JCH Transcripts. Although this report is printed in *JCC*, XXIV, 358, it has not been found among the Papers of the Continental Congress, National Archives.

1. The letters from Robert Morris and Benjamin Lincoln are in the Papers of the Continental Congress, National Archives.

2. The resolutions of these dates were in the writing of H.

3. There was disagreement in Congress on whether the soldiers should be discharged or granted a furlough. According to Madison, H's report calling for the discharge of soldiers enlisted for the war was based on the belief "that it was called for by Economy and justified by the degree of certainty that the war would not be renewed." Those who were in favor of furloughing rather than discharging the soldiers "wished to avoid expence, and at the same time to be not wholly unprepared for the contingent failure of a definitive treaty of peace." As no compromise between the opposing ideas could be reached, "it was agreed that the whole subject should lye over" ("Notes of Debates in the Continental Congress," MS, James Madison Papers, Library of Congress).

Continental Congress
Motion that Furloughs be Granted to Noncommissioned Officers and Soldiers

[*Philadelphia, May 26, 1783.*] On this date Hamilton moved "That the Commander in Chief be instructed to grant Furlows to the non-commission'd Officers & Soldiers in the service of the U S inlisted to serve during the War, who shall be discharged as soon as the definitive Treaty of Peace is concluded." [1]

D, in writing of Hugh Williamson, Papers of the Continental Congress, National Archives.

1. A committee report, in the writing of H and dated May 23, 1783, calling for the discharge of soldiers enlisted for the war had been defeated (see "Report on the Discharge of Noncommissioned Officers and Soldiers," May 23,

1783). In the motion printed above H accepted the argument of those who had opposed the report of May 23 on the grounds that the soldiers should be granted furloughs rather than discharges.

On May 27 Robert Morris made the following entries in his Diary:

"The Honble Mr. Hamilton respecting the dismissing the Soldiers enlisted for the War by granting Furloughs which I did not approve and think they ought to be discharged.

"The Honble. Secy at War on the same business he says he will go to Camp himself on this business." (Robert Morris Papers, Library of Congress.)

Continental Congress
Motion of Protest against British Practice of Carrying off American Negroes

[*Philadelphia, May 26, 1783.*] A motion made by Hamilton on this date protested against the British seizure of Negroes belonging to citizens of the United States.[1]

JCC, XXIV, 363–64. The motion is in the writing of John Rutledge.

1. The preliminary peace treaty included an article forbidding the carrying away of slave property by evacuating British armies.

During the war approximately two thousand Negroes had sought refuge behind the British lines. Contrary to the stipulation of the peace treaty that they be returned, Sir Guy Carleton, the British commander in America, did not return them.

Continental Congress
Motion on Officers Holding Brevet Commissions

[Philadelphia, May 26, 1783] [1]

Resolved That the officers at present holding brevet commissions in the army be intitled to the pay and emoluments of the ranks which they respectively hold.

AD, Papers of the Continental Congress, National Archives.

1. The motion is undated, but it is printed in the *Journals* under date of May 26, 1783.

Continental Congress
Motion on the Evacuation of New York

[Philadelphia] May 29, 1783

Resolved that General Washington be informed in answer to his letter of the   [1] that it is the desire of Congress the evacuation

of New York and its dependencies may not be retarded by a preference to that of any other place.[2]

AD, Papers of the Continental Congress, National Archives.
  1. Space left blank in MS. On May 14, 1783, Washington wrote to the
President of Congress: "I shall wait the Instructions of Congress before I
answer Sir Guy [Carleton] respecting the Evacuation of Penobscot, in
preference to his attendg to that of N York, and will conform myself wholly
to their Wishes on that head" (GW, XXVI, 430).
  2. The endorsement states that the motion was passed on the same day that
it was made.

Continental Congress
Report on Measures to be Taken for Carrying into Effect the Provisional Peace Treaty [1]

[Philadelphia] May 30, 1783. On this date a committee, consisting
of Hamilton, Oliver Ellsworth, Ralph Izard,[2] James Madison, and
Benjamin Hawkins,[3] reported on "what further steps are proper to
be taken . . . for carrying into effect the stipulations contained in
the articles between the United States and Great Britain." The committee recommended that the states execute the articles of the treaty
providing for the recovery of debts owed English merchants, the
cessation of confiscations of Loyalist property, and the restitution
of the property already seized.

D, Papers of the Continental Congress, National Archives.
  1. As H was chairman of the committee which made the report, he was
presumably the author of it. The report, however, is not in H's writing.
  2. Izard was a delegate from South Carolina.
  3. Hawkins was a delegate from North Carolina.

Continental Congress
Motion on Appointment of Committee to Consider Allowances of Land for the Army [1]

[Philadelphia] May 30, 1783

That a Committee be appointed to consider of the best manner of
carrying into execution the engagements of the United States for
certain allowances of land to the army at the conclusion of the war.[2]

AD, Papers of the Continental Congress, National Archives.

1. In September, 1776, Congress, to encourage enlistments in the Continental Army, had offered bounties of land to all officers and soldiers who agreed to serve for the duration of the war.

2. The motion is endorsed: "grand comee., Mr [Samuel] Holten, Mr. [Jonathan] Arnold, Mr. [Oliver] Ellsworth, Mr. [Alexander] Hamilton, Mr. [Abraham] Clarke, Mr. [James] Wilson, Mr. [Gunning] Bedford [Jr.], Mr. [John Francis] Mercer, Mr. [Benjamin] Hawkins, Mr. [John] Rutledge to meet tomorrow morning at 9 oClock in the Comee. chamber." The committee reported on June 4.

To George Clinton

Philadelphia
June 1st 1783

Sir.

In my last letter [1] to Your Excellency I took occasion to mention that it was of great importance to the state, at this time to have a representation here as points in which by its present situation it is particularly interested are dayly and will be dayly agitated. It is also of importance at this moment to the United States (not only from general considerations but) because we have a very thin representation in Congress and are frequently unable to transact any of those matters which require nine states. I wish your Excellency would urge a couple of gentlemen to come on, as it becomes highly inconvenient to me to remain here and as I have staid the full time to be expected.

I observe with great regret the intemperate proceedings among the people in different parts of the state in violation of a treaty the faithful observance of which so deeply interests the United States.[2] Surely the state of New York with its capital and its frontier posts (on which its important fur-trade depends) in the hands of the British troops ought to take care that nothing is done to furnish a pretext on the other side, even for delaying much less for refusing

ADf, Hamilton Papers, Library of Congress.

1. The letter was dated May 14, 1783.

2. Article 5 of the treaty of peace, which stipulated that Congress should "earnestly recommend" to the states that they restore the rights and possessions of Loyalists who had not borne arms against their countrymen, was not popular in New York. Early in 1783 many towns adopted resolutions forbidding Loyalists to settle within their limits. In addition, the newspapers contained many letters urging the state to exclude all Loyalists.

the execution of the treaty. We may imagine that the situation of Great Britain puts her under a necessity at all events of fulfilling her engagements and cultivating the good will of this country. This is no doubt her true policy; but when we feel that passion makes us depart from the dictates of reason, when we have seen that passion has had so much influence in the conduct of the British councils in the whole course of the war—when we recollect that those who govern them are men like ourselves and alike subject to passions & resentments—when we reflect also that all the great men in England are not United in the liberal scheme of policy with respect to this Country and that in the anarchy which prevails, there is no knowing to whom the reins of government may be committed when we re-collect how little in a condition we are to enforce a compliance with-out claims—we ought certainly to be cautious in what manner we act, especially when we in particular have so much at stake, and should not openly provoke a breach of faith on the other side, by setting the example.

An important distinction is not sufficiently attended to—the 5th article is recommendatory the sixth positive.[3] There is no option on the part of the particular states as to any future confiscations pros-ecutions or injuries of any kind to person liberty or property on account of any thing done in the war. It is matter of discretion in the states whether they will comply with the recommendations con-tained in the 5th article; but no part of the 6th can be departed from by them without a direct breach of public faith and of the confedera-tion. The power of making treaties is exclusively lodged in Congress. That power includes whatever is essential to the termination of the war and to the preservation of the general safety. Indemnity to individuals in similar cases is an *usual* stipulation in treaties of peace, of which many precedents are to be produced.

Should it be said[4] that the associations of the people, without legal authority do not amount to a breach[5] of the public faith? The answer is if the government does not repress them and prevent there having effect, it is as much a breach, as a formal refusal to comply on its part. In the eye of a foreign nation, if our engagements are

3. The sixth article prohibited any future confiscations of Loyalist property.
4. In MS, "should be it be said."
5. In MS, "breath."

broken, it is of no moment whether it is for the want of good intention in the government or for want of power to restrain its subjects. Suppose a violence committed by an American vessel on the vessel of another nation upon the high seas and after complaint made, there is no redress given. Is not that a hostility against the injured nation which will justify reprisals?

But if I am not misinformed there are violations going on in forms of law. I am told that indictments continue to be brought under the former confiscation laws; a palpable infraction if true of the 6th article of the treaty to which an immediate stop ought no doubt to be put.

It has been said by some men that the operation of this treaty is suspended 'till the definitive treaty—a plain subterfuge. Whatever is clearly expressed in the provisional or preliminary treaty is as binding from the moment it is made as the definitive treaty which in fact only developes explains and fixes more precisely what may have been too generally expressed in the former. Suppose the British should now send away not only the negroes but all other property and all the public records in their possession belonging to us on the pretence above stated should we not justly accuse them with breaking faith? Is this not already done in the case of the negroes, who have been carried away, though founded upon a very different principle a doubful construction of the treaty, not a denial of its immediate operation? [6] In fine is it our interest to advance this doctrine and to countenance the position that nothing is binding 'till the definitive treaty, when there are examples of *years* intervening between the preliminary & definitive treaties?

Sir Guy Carelton in his correspondence has appeared to consider the treaty as immediately obligatory and it has been the policy which I have persued to promote the same idea.

I am not indeed apprehensive of a renewal of the war, for peace is necessary to Great Britain; I think it also most probable her disposition to conciliate this country will outweigh the resentments which a breach of our engagements is calculated to inspire. But with a treaty which has exceeded the hopes of the most sanguine

6. The treaty of peace included an article forbidding the carrying away of slave property by evacuating British armies. Contrary to this stipulation, some two thousand Negroes who had sought refuge behind the British lines were not returned.

which in the articles of boundary & the fisheries is even better than
we asked, circumstanced too as this Country is with respect to the
means of making war, I think it the height of imprudence to run any
risk. Great Britain without recommencing hostilities may evade
parts of the treaty. She may keep possession of the frontier posts,
she may obstruct the free enjoyment of the fisheries, she may be
indisposed to such extensive concessions in matters of commerce as
it is our interest to aim at; in all this she would find no opposition
from any foreign power; and we are not in a condition to oblige
her to any thing. If we imagine that France, obviously embarrassed
herself in her Finances would renew the war to oblige Great Britain
to the restoration of our frontier posts, or to a compliance with the
stipulations respecting the fisheries (especially after a manifest breach
of the treaty on our part) we speculate much at random. Observations might be made on the last article which would prove that it
is not the policy of France to support our interests there. Are we
prepared, for the mere gratification of our resentments to put those
great national objects to the hazard—to leave our western frontier
in a state of insecurity—to relinquish the fur trade and to abridge
our pretensions to the fisheries? Do we think national character so
light a thing as to be willing to sacrifice the public faith to individual
animosity?

Let the case be fairly stated: Great Britain and America two independent nations at war—The former in possession of considerable
posts and districts of territory belonging to the latter—and also of
the means of obstructing certain commercial advantages in which it
is deeply interested.

It is not uncommon in treaties of peace for the *uti possidetis* to take
place. Great Britain however in the present instance stipulates to
restore all our posts & territories in her possession. She even adds an
extent not within our original claims more than a compensation for
a small part ceded in another quarter. She agrees to readmit us to a
participation in the fisheries. What equivalent do we give for this?
Congress are to recommend the restoration of property to those who
have adhered to her, and expressly engage that no future injury shall
be done them on person liberty or property. This is the sole condition on our part where there is not an immediate reciprocity (the
recovery of debts and liberation of prisoners being mutual, the former

indeed only declaring what the rights of private faith which all civilized nations hold sacred would have dictated without it) and stands as the single equivalent for all the restitutions and concessions to be made by Great Britain. Will it be honest in us to violate this condition or will it be prudent to put it in competition with all the important matters to be performed on the other side? Will foreign nations be willing to undertake any thing with us or for us, when they find that the nature of our governments will allow no dependence to be placed upon our engagements?

I have omitted saying any thing of the impolicy of inducing by our severity a great number of useful citizens, whose situations do not make them a proper object of resentment to abandon the country to form settlements that will hereafter become our rivals animated with a hatred to us which will descend to their posterity. Nothing however can be more unwise than to contribute as we are doing to people the shores and wilderness of Nova-scotia, a colony which by its position will become a competitor with us among other things in that branch of commerce in which our navigation and navy will essentially depend. I mean the fisheries in which I have no doubt the state of New York will hereafter have a considerable share.

To your Excellency I freely deliver my sentiments because I am persuaded you cannot be a stranger to the force of these considerations. I fear not even to hazard them to the justice and good sense of those whom I have the honor to represent. I esteem it my duty to do it because the question is important to the interests of the state in its relation to the United States.

Those who consult only their passions might choose to construe what I say as too favourable to a set of men who have been the enemies of the public liberty; but those for whose esteem I am most concerned will acquit me of any personal considerations and will perceive that I only urge the cause of national honor, safety and advantage. We have assumed an independent station; we ought to feel and to act in a manner consistent with the dignity of that station.

I anxiously wish to see every prudent measure taken to prevent those combinations which will certainly disgrace us, if they do not involve us in other calamities. Whatever distinctions are judged necessary to be made in the case of those persons who have been in opposition to the common cause, let them be made by legal authority on a fair construction of the treaty, consistent with national faith and national honor.

I have the honor to be with perfect respect Yr. Excellency's Most Obed servant

Your Excellency will have been informed that Congress have instructed General Washington to garrison the frontier posts when surrendered with the three years Continental troops. This is more for the interest of the state than to have them garrisoned at its particular expence—and I should wish that permanent provision might be made on the same principle. I wait to see whether any Continental peace establishment for garrisons &c. will take place before I engage the consent of Congress to a separate provision.[7]

I cannot forbear adding a word on the subject of money. The only reliance we now have for redeeming a large anticipation on the public credit already made and making for the benefit of the army is on the taxes coming in. The collection hitherto is out of all proportion to the demand. It is of vast consequence at this juncture that every thing possible should be done to forward it. I forbear entering into details which would be very striking upon this subject. I will only say that unless there is a serious exertion in the states public credit must ere long receive another shock very disagreeable in its consequences.

His Excellency Governor Clinton

7. See Clinton to H and William Floyd, April 1, 1783, and "Report on the Garrisoning of Frontier Posts by Continental Troops," May 12, 1783.

Continental Congress
Report on Land for the Army

[Philadelphia] June 4, 1783

The Committee appointed to consider of the best manner of carrying into execution the engagements of the United States for certain allowances of land to the army at the conclusion of the war submit the following resolution: [1]

Congress having by their resolution of the [2] promised certain allowances of land to all officers, and to such soldiers of the United States engaged to serve during the war, who should continue in service to the end thereof.

Resolved that 'till provision can be made by the United States for locating and surveying to the officers and soldiers aforesaid the portions of land to which they are respectively intitled, certificates be given to them when furloughed or discharged as evidences of their claim upon the United States, specifying the name of each person, the regiment or corps to which he belongs, his rank therein, and the quantity of land to which he is in intitled—the certificates to be signed by the Pay Master General and to be in the form following: (Name and station) in the (Regiment or corps) is intitled to (insert the quantity) acres of land as a gratuity for his services during the war, agreeable to the resolutions of the day of 1783 [and that Certificates issue in like manner to the legal representatives of such officers & Soldiers as have been slain by the Enemy on producing proper proofs of the Titles.] [3]

AD, Papers of the Continental Congress, National Archives.

1. See "Motion on Appointment of Committee to Consider Allowances of Land for the Army," May 30, 1783. A grand committee of Congress was appointed on May 30 to report on H's motion. Its members were: Samuel Holten, Jonathan Arnold, Oliver Ellsworth, H, Abraham Clark, James Wilson, Gunning Bedford, Jr., John Francis Mercer, Benjamin Hawkins, and John Rutledge.

2. Spaces in this and following paragraph left blank in MS. To encourage the enlistment of soldiers "to serve during the present war," Congress on September 17, 1776, resolved that every private and noncommissioned officer who enlisted for the duration of hostilities was to receive twenty dollars and one hundred acres of land. Officers who engaged to remain in service during the war were also to receive a land bounty, the amount received depending on the rank held (*JCC*, V, 762–63).

3. The bracketed words are in the writing of Elias Boudinot.

The report, according to the *Journals* of the Congress, was read on June 4, and the decision on it was deferred. The grand committee, the membership of which changed, was discharged on October 15, 1783 (*JCC*, XXIV, 421, note 2).

Continental Congress
Motion Respecting the Secretary for Foreign Affairs

[Philadelphia] June 4, 1783

Mr. Livingston [1] having signified to Congress his desire of relinquishing the exercise of the office of foreign affairs and his intention of returning to the state of New York:

Resolved that the secretary of Congress be directed to receive the papers of the said office into his care, 'till a successor to Mr. Livingston can be appointed and that next Wednesday [2] be assigned for the election of a Secretary for the department of foreign affairs.

Resolved that the thanks of Congress be presented to Mr. Livingston for his services during his continuance in office, and that he be assured Congress entertain a high sense of the ability zeal & fidelity with which he hath discharged the important trust reposed in him.

AD, Papers of the Continental Congress, National Archives.
1. As early as December 2, 1782, Robert R. Livingston had submitted his resignation to Congress, but he was twice induced to remain in office, first until January 1, 1783, and then until May, 1783. On May 9, 1783, he informed Congress (*JCC*, XXIV, 336–37) that he would no longer remain in office.
2. The words "next Wednesday" are not in the writing of H.

From Robert R. Livingston

[Philadelphia] 5th. June 1783

Dr Sir

Mr Thompson [1] this morning requests me in persuance of the order of yesterday [2] to send the papers of this office under my seal to his office. I had supposed that it would have been the wish of Congress to continue them in the public office I have hired & to have given Mr. Thompson the direction of them. I am now perplexed to know what is to be done with the secretaries & clerks whether they are to be dismissed of course without any further notice which they will presume from every things being taken from under their care or whether they are to be continued till a successor is appointed.

The first of these cases will be very hard upon them as it is un-expected & they have made no provision for it. But at all events I should know it that I may settle their accounts which I should not do otherwise till this quarter was up.

My own accounts too will be a matter of some difficulty till I know whether Congress think it reasonable to make the allowance of the extra expence from the 2d Decr to this time & grant the com-mission which I shd otherwise have a right to charge to their ministers. Could I be satisfied that they would do me this justice which I presume to hope I would wait a few days in town after I had sent away my family till there were a sufficient number of states to pass the vote. Otherwise I must leave many accounts unsettled or borrow money to discharge them neither of which would be agreeable. If you shd find it convenient I shd. wish to speake with you on these subjects before you go into Congress.

ADf, New-York Historical Society, New York City.
1. Charles Thomson, secretary of the Continental Congress.
2. See "Motion Respecting the Secretary for Foreign Affairs," June 4, 1783.

To John Fitzgerald [1]

[Philadelphia, June 10, 1783]

Dr. Sir

The inclosed letter is for Mr. Bowman who married Mrs. Cattle.[2] I am told he is at Alexandria which make me trouble you with the letter. Should he have left that place for South Carolina, I will thank you to forward it to him.

No definitive treaty yet arrived nor any thing else of importance new. I write in Congress & have only time to add that I am   Yr. sincere & affectionate friend   A Hamilton

Philadelphia, June 10. 1783

ALS, Broadcast Music, Inc., New York City.
1. Fitzgerald, a Virginian, had served with H as aide-de-camp to General Washington.
2. Sabina Lynch Cattell, the daughter of Thomas Lynch of South Carolina, married William Cattell, who died in 1778. She later married John Bowman.

To Major General Nathanael Greene [1]

[Philadelphia, June 10, 1783]

Dr. General,

I inclose you a couple of letters from Mr. Carter [2] one for yourself, the other for Mr. Kenlock.[3] There is nothing for me to add, except that I wish you when the business shall be transacted to transmit the bond to me under cover to General Schuyler at Albany. I expect to leave this shortly for that place and to remain there 'till New York is evacuated; on which event I shall set down there seriously on the business of making my fortune. It has been hinted to me that you have some thoughts of making our state the place of your residence. You will easily believe me sincere when I express my wishes that this may be the case—and when I add that I shall consider it as a valuable acquisition to the state.

There is so little disposition either in or out of Congress to give solidity to our national system that there is no motive to a man to lose his time in the public service; who has no other view than to promote its welfare. Experience must convince us that our present establishments are Utopian before we shall be ready to part with them for better.

I write in Congress and therefore can not enlarge; but I need not assure you that no one will at all times have more pleasure in hearing from you than myself as no one is more warmly & sincerely Your friend than Dr Sir Yr. Obed serv   A Hamilton

Philadelphia

June 10. 1783

ALS, Hamilton Papers, Library of Congress.

1. Greene was at this time commander of the American forces in the Southern Department.

2. John Carter was an alias assumed by John Barker Church. (Church to H, May 18, 1781). On June 9, 1783, Church wrote to Greene that he was willing to receive a certain bond "at the legal Interest of the State calculating only simple Interest," and requested that the bond be transmitted "to my Brother in Law, Coll. Alexr. Hamilton." This letter is in the Hamilton Papers, Library of Congress.

3. Francis Kinlock, a South Carolina planter and member of the Continental Congress. The nature of Church's business transactions with Kinlock is described in a letter written by Kinlock's brother, Cleland, to H on September 20, 1785.

To George Clinton

[Philadelphia, June 11, 1783]

Sir

In two or three letters,[1] which I have had the honor of writing to Your Excellency lately, I mentioned the necessity of a representation of the state here and at the same time of my returning to my private occupations. I am obliged to inform Your Excellency that I cannot remain here above ten days longer.

I have the honor to be Yr. Excellency's Most Obed ser

Alex Hamilton

Philadelphia
June 11th. 1783

ALS, Blumhaven Library and Gallery, Philadelphia.
1. See H to Clinton, May 14 and June 1, 1783.

Continental Congress
Report on American Participation in a European Neutral Confederacy

[Philadelphia] June 12, 1783

Resolved that the Ministers Plenipotentia[r]y be instructed in case they should comprise in the definitive treaty any stipulations amounting to a recognition of the rights of neutral nations, to avoid accompanying them by any engagements which shall oblige the contracting parties to support those stipulations by arms.[1]

AD, Papers of the Continental Congress, National Archives.
1. This resolution was the last paragraph of a report delivered by a committee consisting of James Madison, Oliver Ellsworth, and H. A letter, dated March 20, 1783, from the Secretary for Foreign Affairs had been referred to the committee. The Secretary informed Congress of a Dutch proposal to the American peace commissioners that the United States either join the League of Armed Neutrality or enter into an agreement with France, Spain, and the United Provinces of the Netherlands to enforce neutral rights on the high seas. Such action on the part of the United States, the American commissioners were told, would make an express stipulation in favor of freedom of navigation unnecessary in the treaty between Great Britain and the Netherlands. The committee reported that "the true interest of these states requires that

they should be as little as possible entangled in the politics and controversies of European nations" (*JCC*, XXIV, 394). Although concluding that the United States should not join any neutral confederacy, the committee reported that it was in the interest of the nation to promote such a treaty. The report is printed in *JCC*, XXIV, 392–94.

Continental Congress
Report on a Military Peace Establishment [1]

[Philadelphia, June 18, 1783]

The Committee observe with respect to a military peace establishment, that before any plan can with propriety be adopted, it is

AD, Papers of the Continental Congress, National Archives; ADf, Hamilton Papers, Library of Congress.

1. The report submitted to Congress is longer than the draft, for the former contains additional tables of organization and discussions of other aspects of a peace establishment. In both *JCHW*, II, 253–68, and *HCLW*, VI, 463–83, the draft, dated 1783, and not the completed report, is printed.

This report is printed in the *Journals* under date of October 23 (*JCC*, XXV, 722–44). The report is preceded by the following paragraph:

"The Committee consisting of Mr (Alexander) Hamilton, Mr (James) Madison, Mr (Oliver) Ellsworth, Mr (James) Wilson and Mr (Samuel) Holten, 'appointed to take into consideration the arrangements proper to be taken in case of a general peace' observe. . . ." (*JCC*, XXV, 722.)

A note in the *Journals* which appears at the end of the report states that "according to the record in Committee Book No. 186, the committee on the peace arrangements was appointed June 12 and reported June 18" (*JCC*, XXV, 744).

As H had left Congress almost three months earlier, he obviously was no longer chairman of the committee reporting on October 23. The note in the *Journals*, quoted in the preceding paragraph and giving the date of the appointment of this committee as June 12, is incorrect. H had written Washington on April 9 of the appointment of a committee, consisting of James Madison, Samuel Osgood, James Wilson, Oliver Ellsworth, and himself, "to consider what arrangements it will be proper to adopt in the different departments with reference to a peace." The committee, with Samuel Holten replacing Osgood on May 6, reported during April and May on various plans. On May 2 Washington submitted to H, as chairman of the committee, his "Sentiments on a Peace Establishment." It was this committee, and not the one appointed on June 12, which issued the report on the military peace establishment.

The report was obviously made between May 2, the date of Washington's letter enclosing his "Sentiments on a Peace Establishment," and July 27, when H wrote to Governor George Clinton of New York: "there was a prospect of some general provision for . . . a Continental establishment. A report for this purpose is now before Congress but the thinness of representation has for some time retarded and still retards its consideration." Although there is no record in the *Journals* on June 18 of it having been considered, that date is ascribed to the report on the basis of the notation in the committee book mentioned above.

The membership of the committee, as indicated above, changed between necessary to inquire what powers exist for that purpose in the confederation.

By the 4th. clause of the 6th article it is declared that "no vessels of war shall be kept up by any state in time of peace, except such number only as shall be deemed necessary by the United States in Congress assembled, for the defence of such state or its trade; nor shall any body of forces be kept up by any state in time of peace, except such number only, as in the judgment of the United States in Congress assembled shall be deemed requisite to garrison the forts necessary for the defence of such state."

By the 5th. clause of the 9th article, The United States in Congress assembled are empowered generally (and without mention of peace or war) "to build and equip a navy, to agree upon the number of land forces, and to make requisitions from each state for its quota, in proportion to the number of white inhabitants in each state, which requisition shall be binding, and thereupon the legislature of each state, shall appoint the Regimental officers, raise the men and clothe arm and equip them in a soldier-like manner at the expence of the United States and the officers and men so cloathed armed and equipped shall march to the place appointed and within the time agreed on by the United States in Congress assembled."

By the 4th. clause of the same article the United States are empowered "to appoint all officers of the land forces except regimental officers, to appoint all officers of the naval forces, and to commission all officers whatever in the service of the United States, making rules

---

the reading of the report on June 18 and its reintroduction on October 23. A committee, consisting of Samuel Holten, James Wilson, Daniel Carroll, Samuel Huntington, and James Duane was appointed on August 7 to confer on the peace arrangements with Washington. Washington attended Congress in late August, 1783. The committee reported on September 10, 1783. That the committee was charged with submitting to Washington the report drafted by H and printed here is seen by Washington's "Observations Consequent of a Request of the Committee" (JCC, XXV, 549–51), in which he approved some parts and recommended changes in other sections of H's draft. The Journals do not reveal to what extent Congress at that time considered the subject. After the committee reported on October 23, the plans for a military peace establishment were discussed in a committee of the whole for two days. It cannot be determined whether the committee recommended any changes, for the report printed in the Journals, under date of October 23, is H's report of June 18.

The parts of the report deleted by H have not been indicated. They are given in the version of the report printed in JCC, XXV, 722–44.

for the government and regulation of the said land and naval forces and directing their operations."

It appears to the Committee that the terms of the first clause are rather restrictive on the particular states than directory to the United States, intended to prevent any state from keeping up forces land or naval without the approbation and sanction of the Union, which might endanger its tranquillity and harmony, and not to contravene the positive power vested in the United States by the subsequent clauses, or to deprive them of the right of taking such precautions as should appear to them essential to the general security. A distinction that this is to be provided for in time of war, by the forces of the Union, in time of peace, by those of each state would involve, besides other inconveniences, this capital one, that when the forces of the Union should become necessary to defend its rights and repel any attacks upon them, the United States would be obliged to *begin to create* at the very moment they would have occasion *to employ* a fleet and army. They must wait for an actual commencement of hostilities before they would be authorised to prepare for defence, to raise a single regiment or to build a single ship. When it is considered what a length of time is requisite to levy and form an army and still more to build and equip a navy, which is evidently a work of leisure and of peace requiring a gradual preparation of the means—there cannot be presumed so improvident an intention in the Confederation as that of obliging the United States to suspend all provision for the common defence 'till a declaration of war or an invasion. If this is admitted it will follow that they are at liberty to make such establishments in time of peace as they shall judge requisite to the common safety. This is a principle of so much importance in the apprehension of the Committee to the welfare of the union, that if any doubt should exist as to the true meaning of the first-mentioned clause, it will in their opinion be proper to admit such a construction as will leave the general power, vested in the United States by the other clauses, in full force; unless the states respectively or a Majority of them shall declare a different interpretation. The Committee however submit to Congress, (in conformity to that spirit of Candour and to that respect for the sense of their constituents, which ought ever to characterize their proceedings) the propriety of transmitting the plan which they may adopt to the several states to afford an opportunity of signifying their sentiments previous to its final execution.

The Committee, are of opinion, if there is a contitutional power in the United States for that purpose, that there are conclusive reasons in favour of fœderal in preference to state establishments.

First there are objects for which separate provision cannot conveniently be made; posts within certain districts, the judisdiction and property of which are not yet constitutionally ascertained—territory appertaining to the United States not within the original claim of any of the states—the navigation of the Missippi and of the lakes —the rights of the fisheries and of foreign commerce; all which belonging to the United States depending on the laws of nations and on treaty, demand the joint protection of the Union, and cannot with propriety be trusted to separate establishments.

Secondly, the fortifications proper to be established ought to be constructed with relation to each other on a general and well-digested system and their defence should be calculated on the same principles. This is equally important in the double view of safety and œconomy. If this is not done under the direction of the United States, each state following a partial and disjointed plan, it will be found that the posts will have no mutual dependence or support— that they will be improperly distributed, and more numerous than is necessary as well as less efficacious—of course more easily reduced and more expensive both in the construction and defence.

3dly. It happens, that from local circumstances particular states, if left to take care of themselves, would be in possession of the chief part of the standing forces and of the principal fortified places of the union; a circumstance inconvenient to them and to the United States—to them, because it would impose a heavy exclusive burthen in a matter the benefit of which will be immediately shared by their neighbours and ultimately by the states at large—to the United States, because it confides the care of the safety of the *whole* to a *part*, which will naturally be unwilling as well as unable to make such effectual provision at its particular expence, as the common welfare requires—because a single state from the peculiarity of its situation, will in a manner keep the keys of the United States—

because in fiine a considerable force in the hands of a few states may have an unfriendly aspect on the confidence and harmony which ought carefully to be maintained between the whole.

4thly. It is probable that a provision by the ⟨Congress⟩ of the forces necessary to be kept up will ⟨be based⟩ upon a more systematic and œconomical plan than a provision by the states separately; especially as it will be of importance as soon as the situation of affairs will permit, to establish founderies, manufactaries of arms, powder &c; by means of which the labour of a part of the troops applied to this purpose will furnish the United States with those essential articles on easy terms, and contribute to their own support.

5thly. There must be a corps of Artillery and Engineers kept on foot in time of peace, as the officers of this corps require science and long preliminary study, and cannot be formed on an emergency; and as the neglect of this institution would always oblige the United States to have recourse to foreigners in time of war for a supply of officers in this essential branch—an inconvenience which it ought to be the object of every nation to avoid. Nor indeed is it possible to dispense with the service of such a corps in time of peace, as it will be indispensable not only to have posts on the frontier; but to have fortified harbours for the reception and protection of the fleet of the United States. This corps requiring particular institutions for the instruction and formation of the officers cannot exist upon separate establishments without a great increase of expence.

6thly.[2] It appears from the annexed papers No. 1 to 4,[3] to be the concurrent opinion of the Commander in Chief, the Secretary at War, the Inspector General and the Chief Engineer, not only that some militia establishment is indispensable but that it ought in all respects to be under the authority of the United States as well for military as political reasons. The plan hereafter submitted on considerations of œconomy is less extensive than proposed by either of them.[4]

2. In MS, "7thly."
3. The papers were not filed with the report in the Papers of the Continental Congress, and no reference is given to them in the *Journals*.
4. On the last page of the draft H listed additional arguments in support of a continental peace establishment. These were entitled "Notes to be recollected." They read as follows:
"An Absurdity that Congress are empowered to build & equip a navy & yet in time of peace the states are to keep up one for their own defence.

The Committee upon these principles submit the following plan.

The Military peace establishment of the United States to consist of four regiments of infantry, and, one of Artillery incorporated in a corps of Engineers, with the denomination of the corps of Engineers.

Each Regiment of infantry to consist of two batalions, each batalion of four companies, each company of 64 rank and file, with the following, commissioned and Non commissioned officers, pay, rations and cloathing; to be however recruited to one hundred & twenty eight rank & file in time of war, preserving the proportion of corporals to privates.

"There must be a navy formed in time of peace; it ought to be proportioned to our defence & will then be all in the hands of certain states.

"Congress constituted as they are cant have time for usurpation. Usurpation in such an extensive empire requires long previous preparation &c.

"A people seldom r[e]form with moderation. Men accustomed to read of usurpations suddenly effected in small cities look upon such a thing as a work of a day.

"The weak side of democracies is danger of foreign corruption. No individual has sufficient interest in the state to be proof against the seduction.

"The want of an army lost the liberty of Athens. Vide Demosthenes."

STATE OF A REGIMENT OF INFANTRY

	Number Persons	Ranks	Including subsistence	Pay per Month in Dollars	Rations per day
A	1	Colonel		100	1
	2	Majors		70	1
	8	Captains, one to each company		50	1
B	8	First Lieutenants . . . do		25	1
	13	second Lieutenants one to each company and to furnish Regiml. staff P. Master Qr. Mr. Adjutant & two Ensigns one to each batalion		20	1
		Pay Master extra emoluments		15	. . . .
		Qr. Master . . . do		15	. . . .
		Adjutant . . . do		12	. . . .
	1	chaplain		40	1
	1	Surgeon		40	1
	1	Mate		20	1
C	2	sergeant Majors one to each batalion		8	1
	2	Qr. Mr. sergeants do		8	1
	2	Drum & fife Majors do		8	1
	32	sergeants 4 to each company		5	1
D	64	Corporals included in rank & file 8 to each company		3	1
	448	privates 56 to each company		2	1
	16	drums & fifes 2 to each company		2	1

Total 601 [5]

5. A copy of this report, which stops at this point, is in the Papers of the Continental Congress, National Archives. This copy is in the writing of Charles Thomson.

A   The pay of these three ranks is high in proportion for these reasons: It makes those ranks an object which will prove an inducement to proper characters to enter into the army and it is for the safety and honor of the community to have their army respectably officered. The number of the higher ranks being small the increase of pay does not add much to the aggregate expence and its consequences conduces to œconomy; for the hope of attaining to those ranks induces those in inferior grades to be content with small pay, and these being numerous there is a saving upon the whole.

It ought also to be observed that in the pay is included subsistence, that is the value of the extra rations heretofore allowed to officers which makes the difference not so great between the present and former pay as it at first appears.

Cloathing to NC Officers & privates										Rations Forage per day
once in two years			yearly							
cloth coats	do Jackets	do Overalls	linnen frock	do. Overalls	do. shirts	leather stocks	shoes	Hats		2 2
· ·	· ·	· ·	· ·	· ·	· ·	· ·	· ·	· ·		· · ·
· ·	· ·	· ·	· ·	· ·	· ·	· ·	· ·	· ·		
· ·	· ·	· ·	· ·	· ·	· ·	· ·	· ·	· ·		1
· ·	· ·	· ·	· ·	· ·	· ·	· ·	· ·	· ·		1
· ·	· ·	· ·	· ·	· ·	· ·	· ·	· ·	· ·		1
· ·	· ·	· ·	· ·	· ·	· ·	· ·	· ·	· ·		1
· ·	· ·	· ·	· ·	· ·	· ·	· ·	· ·	· ·		1
· ·	· ·	· ·	· ·	· ·	· ·	· ·	· ·	· ·		· ·
1	1	1	1	2	2	2	4	1		· · ·
1	1	1	1	2	2	2	4	1		· · ·
· ·	· ·	ditto	· ·	· ·	· ·	· ·	· ·		· · ·
· ·	· ·	ditto	· ·	· ·	· ·	· ·	· ·		· · ·
· ·	· ·	ditto	· ·	· ·	· ·	· ·	· ·		· · ·
· ·	· ·	ditto	· ·	· ·	· ·	· ·	· ·		· · ·
· ·	· ·	ditto	· ·	· ·	· ·	· ·	· ·		· · ·

B   The pay of the subalterns is considerably lower than formerly. Instead of Ensigns, second lieutenants are proposed, because the ensign is properly speaking the standard bearer; and one standard bearer or Engisn to each batalion is sufficient who may be taken out of the second Lts. The Regimental staff are also to be taken out of this class, because its pay is the lowest; and because the having served in these offices will better qualify officers for the superior stations. It is necessary to have an extra number of officers for these purposes because three officers to a company so large as is here proposed are not more than sufficient and none can be taken away without injury to the service; and there is besides an obvious propriety that whatever number of officers may be deemed necessary to command a company should serve in it and none be detached for any other purpose. It may be remarked here that the companies are large which will have two good effects; it will promote œconomy by having a smaller proportion of officers to a given number of men and it will render their commands more respectable.

C   It is to be desired that each batalion should be as complete in itself as possible in case of one being detached from the other; and as the batalions are large one of each of these inferior staff to a batalion will find full employment.

D   The proportion of corporals will be as 1 to 7—this will be found beneficial in several ways—the number of corporals who from the mere circumstance of being distinguished from the others, having a better opinion of themselves will of course be better soldiers and being mixed with the others will render the whole better. Every seven men also being put constantly under the direction of a particular corporal to be answerable for the good behaviour of his squad will have a happy influence on discipline and good orders.

	Number Persons	Rank	Pay ⅌ Month in Dollars	Rations per day	Clothing	Rations Forage ⅌ day	
	1	Major General Commandant	. .	. .	. . .	. . .	Vide
	1	Colonel	110.	1	. . .	2	eral
B	2	Lt. Colonels	80	1	. . .	2	
	4	Majors	75	1	. . .	2	
	16	Captains 1 to each company	60	1	. . .	1	
C	16	first Lieutenants 2 to each company	30	1	. . .	. . .	
	19	second do . . do . . . including Pay Master Qr. Mr. Adjutant . . .	25	1	. . .	. . .	
		Quarter Master extra pay &c	15	1	. . .	1	
		Pay Master . . . do	15	. .	. . .	1	
		Adjutant . . . . do	12	. .	. . .	1	
	1	Professor of Mathematics	75	1	. . .	. .	
	1	Professor of Chemistry	do	1	. . .	. .	
D	1	Professor of Natural Philosophy	do	1	. . .	. .	
	1	Professor of Civil Architecture	do	1	. . .	. .	
	1	Drawing Master	do	1	. . .	. .	
		Commissary of Military Stores	75	1		2	
	5	Deputies . . . each . .	40	1	. . .	1	
		Conductors as many as may be found necessary to be appointed out of the Non Commissioned officers with the additional pay of 2 dollars ⅌ Month					
	1	Chaplain	40	1	. . .	1	
	1	Surgeon	40	1	. . .	1	
	1	Mate	20	1	. . .	. .	
E	1	Sergeant Major	8	1			
	2	Qr. Mr. sergeant	8	1			
	1	Drum and fife Major	8	1	the same as the Infantry		
	32	sergeants 4 to each company	6	1			
	32	bombadiers do. included in rank & file	4	1			
	384	cannoniers 48 to each company	3	1			
	96	sappers & miners 12 to do	3	1			
	16	drums & fifes 2 to do	3	1			

Total   630

Corps of Artificers

Number Persons	Trades	Pay ⅌ Month Dollars	Rations per day	Clothing	Rations forage ⅌ day
	1st class				
1	Master Founder in Brass—				
1	ditto—Iron				
1	Master Armourer				
1	Master Engraver				
1	Master Cutler				
1	Master Blacksmith				
1	Master Carpenter				
1	Master Wheelright				
1	Master Mason				
1	Master Sadler				
1	Master Manufacturer of Cartrige boxes &c				
	of the second Class				
4	Founders in brass and iron				
4	Armourers				
2	Cutlers				
2	blacksmiths				
2	Carpenters				
2	Wheelrights				
2	Masons				
2	saddlers				
2	Manufacturers of Cartridge boxes &c				
	of the 3d or Ordinary Class				
4	founders in brass & iron				
20	armourers				
12	Cutlers				
30	blacksmiths				
30	Carpenters				
20	Wheelrights				
12	Masons				
6	sadlers				
6	Manufacturers of Car: Boxes &c				
2	Powder makers				
2	Turners				
2	Tinmen				
2	Brick Makers				
2	Potters				
1	Glasier				
2	Cabinet makers				
1	Lock smith				
1	Spur maker				
1	Tanner				

A[6]   The corps of Engineers to consist of one Regiment or two batalions of Artillery, each batalion consisting of four companies, each company of sixty four rank and file; and of a corps of Artificers; with the following Commissioned and non-commissioned officers, pay and other emoluments.

6. This letter, and those following, refer to explanatory material included in the last section of the report under "Remarks."

The Ration of provisions to consist of one pound of bread or flour or Rice ¾ of a pound of salt or 1 lb of fresh beef pork or fish, one gill of vinegar and half a gill of salt; each part of the ration to be estimated as follows and when not furnished to the troops in service to be paid for at the rates annexed to each

$$\frac{90}{}$$

Bread	2¼
Meat	3¼
gill of vinegar	¼
salt	¼

9⁄90 of a dollar

Officers if they prefer it to be at liberty to receive the value of the ration in money.

All the troops to be obliged to receive fish, two days in the week.

No Regiment to be allowed to draw rations for more than four women to serve as nurses in the Regimental hospitals and to receive four dollars per month in addition to a ration per day.

A weekly allowance of soap to be made at the rate of   [7] for each commissioned officer and   for each non commissioned officer or private; all persons intitled to provisions to be intitled to soap at the same rate.

The ration of forage to consist of the following articles to be estimated at the rates annexed to each.

12 lb hay	7⁄90
8 quarts of oats or other grain equivalent	5⁄90

12⁄90

When officers intitled to forage are absent from their corps on duty and cannot draw it they shall be paid for it at the rates abovementioned, which shall also be done as to any articles not furnished when with their corps.

F   The articles of Cloathing already enumerated to be furnished to the non commissioned officers soldiers and others to be estimated at the following rates; and when not furnished to be paid for accordingly; also when more than the stipulated allowance shall be furnished, there shall be a deduction from the pay at the same rates . . . . viz

7. Spaces in this paragraph left blank by H.

		Dollars
1 Coat		5
1 Jacket		$1\,^{90}\!/_{60}$
1 pr overalls		1.45
1 linnen frock		1
2 do. overalls	each 1 dollar	2
2 do. shirts	each $1\tfrac{1}{3}$ do	2.60
2 leather stocks	each $^{12}\!/_{60}$ of a dollar	24
4 pr. shoes	each 1 dollar	4
1 Hat		60

The idea of the confederation being adhered to, the number of troops to be raised must be distributed to the several states according to the proportion of their respective populations; and each must appoint Regimental officers in proportion to the number of men it furnishes; but as no state will have to furnish a complete regiment this apportionment of the officers will become extremely difficult, if not impracticable on any satisfactory footing, and the filling up vacancies as they arise will create endless perplexity. It would be much to be preferred that the states could be induced to transfer this right to Congress and indeed without it, there can never be regularity in the military system; it would also be much the best that the men should be inlisted under Continental direction, which will be a more certain and more frugal mode; for if it is to be done by the particular states, they will raise the price of the men by competition, and the United States will be obliged to pay for any mismanagement or extravagance which may happen though without their participation or controul.

The officers however to command the different corps in the first instance may with propriety be reserved out of those now in service who are willing to continue in the military line; provided that such as are retained shall not be intitled to the half pay for their services during the war.

All promotions to be made Regimentally to the rank of Major inclusively according to seniority; and from that rank upwards, in the line of the army, according to the same rule; the officers of dragoons and infantry rolling together without distinction of corps.

The promotion in the Engineers to be distinct and according to seniority in that corps.

Provided that no officer whatsoever shall consider it as a violation of his rights, if another receives an extra promotion in the corps on account of brilliant services or peculiar talents.

And in order that such extra-promotion may not depend on misrepresentation, it shall not be made but on the recommendation of the Commander of the army, accompanied by the facts and reasons upon which it is founded, and with the opinion of the officer commanding the corps in which the promotion is to be made, all which shall be reported to Congress, by the secretary at war with his opinion concerning the same.

All non commissioned officers and privates to be engaged for six years; with this condition that if a war should break out during the time, they shall be obliged to serve to the end of it.[8]

FORTIFICATIONS

The fortifications necessary to be kept up are of two kinds, land and naval; the first for internal security the last for the protection of the fleets of the United States.

As to the first kind, there are many important posts already existing, several of which it will be essential to occupy and guard 'till more permanent provision can be made on a general plan. For this Congress have already made temporary provision by their resolution of the   .[9] If the time therein limited should be likely to expire before a general system can be adopted, it can be prolonged.

The Committee are of opinion that the principles laid down by Major General Du Portail, Chief Engineer, in the memorial annexed to this report,[10] so far as they respect merely the article of fortifications are in general sound and just; and that it will be expedient for Congress, so soon as they have determined on the establishment of the corps of Engineers, to instruct the head of that corps to make a survey of the points proper to be fortified and to digest a general plan proportioned to the military establishment of the United States to be laid before Congress for their consideration.

8. At this point in the draft H added the following phrase: "women to each company."

9. Space left blank in MS.

10. See Major General Louis Le Bèque Du Portail to George Washington, May 25, 1783, ALS, George Washington Papers, Library of Congress.

ARSENALS AND MAGAZINES

The Committee are of opinion that it will be proper for Congress to keep constantly on foot Arsenals and magazines of such articles as are not of a perishable nature, in different parts of the United States equal to the complete equipment of thirty thousand men, for the field or for a seige calculated on a three years supply; and that in this view it will be proper to select the following places of deposit: Springfield in the State of Massachusettes; West Point & its dependencies, State of New York; Carlisle, State of Pensylvania; Some convenient position on James River to be reconnoitered for that purpose; [11] Cambden State of South Carolina.

All the artillery and military stores in the possession of the United States to be distributed to these deposits in equal proportions, and as soon as may be deficiencies in the proposed quantity to be made up; so that each deposit may suffice for six thousand men.

MILITARY ACADEMIES

The Committee are of opinion that the benefit of such institutions rarely compensates for the expence—that military knowlege is best acquired in service, that with respect to those branches of service which are of a more scientific nature, the professors proposed to be attached to the corps of Engineers, will produce substantially all the utility to be expected from academies—that at all events institutions of this kind can only be an object of future consideration.

FOUNDERIES AND MANUFACTORIES

The Committee are of opinion that as soon as the situation of public affairs will permit, it ought to be a serious object of our policy to be able to supply ourselves with all articles of first necessity in

11. On June 13, 1783, a committee of Congress, to which had been referred a letter from the Secretary at War, reported that "it would be most proper to erect the magazine in Virginia at a place more convenient than New London" and authorized the Secretary to select some other site in that state. In the Papers of the Continental Congress there is the following undated motion in the writing of H: "*Resolved*, That so much of the resolution of the   as relates to the establishment of a magazine at New London on James River in Virginia be repealed and that the Secretary at War be authorised to examine and fix upon such other place on that river in said State, as shall appear to him most convenient." According to the editor of the *Journals*, the motion was not acted on (*JCC*, XXIV, 395).

war, and in this view to establish founderies of cannon, manufactories of arms, powder &c.

There are two reasons which appear to them conclusive for this; the first that every country ought to endeavour to have within itself all the means essential to its own preservation, as to depend on the casualties of foreign supplies is to render its own security precarious. The second that as it will be indispensable to keep up a corps of Artillery and some other troops, the labour of a part of these bestowed upon the manufactories will enable the public to supply itself on better and cheaper terms than by importation. The Committee propose that the Secretary at war be directed to lay before Congress a plan in detail for this purpose designating the places where those founderies and manufactories can be erected with advantage—the means to be employed and the expence to be incurred in the execution.

GENERAL STAFF

The Committee are of opinion that a general staff in time of peace (except a General officer to command the troops another to command the corps of Engineers and Artillery and an Inspector General) ought to be dispensed with as all the purposes may be answered by the war department, by contracts, and by the Regimental staff.

The pay of the officers here mentioned and other emoluments to be as follows

	Pay per Month Dollars	Rations per day	Rations forage ♯ day	Dollars pay & Subsistence
General Commanding the troops	300	. . .	indefinite	
General commanding Engs				250
Inspector General				250

In time of war two Regiments to compose a Brigade and a Brigadier General to be appointed to each brigade with 200 dollars pay per Month and 5 rations of forage per day.

GENERAL HOSPITAL

A general hospital for the reception of the invalids of the army and navy will be necessary to consist for the present of the following persons:

		Pay ℔ month Dollars
1 Director to have at the same time the superintendence of the Regimental Hospitals	}	80—
1 Surgeon		50
4 Mates . . . . each		25—
1 Purveyor and Apothecary		50—
1 Steward		15—
1 Matron		8—
4 Nurses . . . each		5—

To be intitled to draw each a ration of provision per day, but to no other allowance.

The Invalids to receive one dollar ℔ month and the provisions and clothing of a common soldier during life.

Not quite exact but very near the truth	{ The total expence of this establishment as reduced in peace would amount to about . . . }	359.530
	Deduct the product of the manufactories which is estimated at	131.950
	Ballance on annual charge upon The United States . . . . } Dolls.	227.580

G   The Committee are of opinion that this expence is necessary and that the only question is whether it shall be borne by the United States or by particular states; in which last case it is probable it will be increased for want of general system. The considerations already stated leave no doubt with the Committee in what manner the question ought to be decided.

MILITIA

The Committee are also of opinion that in considering the means of national defence, Congress ought not to overlook that of a well regulated militia; that as the keeping up such a militia and proper arsenals and magazines by each state is made a part of the confederation, the attention of Congress to this object becomes a constitutional duty; that as great advantages would result from uniformity in this article in every state, and from the militia establishment being as similar as the nature of the case will admit to that of the Continental forces, it will be proper for Congress to adopt and recommend a plan for this purpose.

The Committee submit the following outlines of such a plan which if thought necessary may be digested and improved.

All the free male inhabitants in each state from 20 to fifty, except such as the laws of the state shall exempt, to be divided into two general classes; one class to consist of married the other class of single men.

Each class to be formed into corps of infantry and dragoons, organised in the same manner as proposed for the regular troops.

Those who are willing to be at the expence of equipping themselves for dragoon service to be permitted to enter into that corps, the residue to be formed into infantry. This will consult the convenience and inclinations of different classes of citizens.

Each officer of the dragoons to provide himself with a horse saddle &c. pistols and sabre, and each non commissioned officer and private with the preceding articles and these in addition, a carbine [12] and cartouch box, with twelve rounds of powder & ball for his carbine and six for each pistol.

Each officer of the infantry to have a sword and each non commissioned officer and private, a musket, bayonet & cartouch box with twelve rounds of powder and ball.

The corps of single men to be obliged to assemble for inspection and exercise once in two months by companies and once in four months regimentally; to be subject to proper penalties in case of delinquency.

The corps of married men to be obliged to assemble for the same purpose & subject to like penalties once in three months by companies and once in six months regimentally.

When the state itself is invaded, the corps of either class indifferently to be obliged to take the field for its defence, and to remain in service one year; unless sooner relieved by special order.

When another state is attacked and it is necessary to march to its succour, one half of all the corps of single men shall be obliged to take their tour of duty first and to serve for the same period—to be succeeded for a like period by one half of all the corps of married men; and then alternately.

In addition to these two classes there shall be a third under a particular denomination as fencibles, fusileers, train bands or whatever else may be thought proper, with the same organization as the infantry of the other classes but composed as follows:

12. In MS, "cabine."

Of all such of either of the two other classes inhabiting cities or incorporated towns as will voluntarily engage to serve for the term of Eight years, provided they shall not exceed the proportion of one to fifty of all the enrolled militia of the state, and provided that if a war breaks out they shall be obliged to serve three years after they take the field and to march wherever the service may require.

The conditions on the part of the public to be these: each non commissioned officer and soldier to be furnished with a musket bayonet and cartouch box, and every two years with a suit of uniform, consisting of a coat jacket and breeches of cloth; the arms and accoutrements to become his property at the end of his time of service.

These corps to be obliged to assemble Regimentally once a month, for exercise and inspection, with a power in the officer commanding each company to assemble his company once in the interval of each Regimental assembling the better to perfect them in the exercise; the non commissioned officers and privates to be intitled to $\frac{1}{12}$ of a dollar for each day of assembling.

The officers of this corps to have equality of rank with the officers of the army, and to take precedency of the officers of the militia, that is every officer of the train bands shall command every officer of the two other classes of equal grade without regard to date of commission. This preference will induce proper persons to accept commissions in the train bands, and be at the extra trouble which that service will require.

Any of the militia when in service to be intitled to the same emoluments as the regular troops—or in lieu of cloathing to the two first classes to the addition of one dollar ℔ Month of pay.

The Committee are of opinion that with a view to either of the proposed establishments, it will be proper to direct the Commander in Chief to appoint a board of officers, the Inspector General, Commandant of Artillery and Chief Engineer being members, to revise the regulations for the army of the United States, and to digest a general ordinance for the service of all the troops of the United States, and another for the service of the militia; and to transmit both with his observations to Congress for their consideration; the latter when approved to be recommended to the several states.

The expence of the Militia establishment will amount to about 60,000 dollars ℔ annum a sum which may be nearly defrayed out of the militia fines if properly managed.

The present population will afford about 8000 of the 3d. Class.

REMARKS

A.　　　Corps of Engineers.

The artillery and Engineers are united in one corps from the great analogy in the service which when the corps are separated gives rise to frequent disputes about the respective duties of each, very injurious to the service; there is a great resemblance in the preliminary studies and qualifications requisite to form the officers of both, and the Union is conducive to œconomy. There is an extra number to serve as Engineers.

B.　　　The pay of this corps is generally higher than of any other; because there is much preparatory study and labour to qualify an officer, and promotion is much less rapid.

C.　　　There are a great number of officers in proportion to the men; because artillery are chiefly in detachments & are of so much consequence in military operations that the pieces ought rarely to be trusted to non commissioned officers.

D.　　　These professors are indispensable for the instruction of the officers, the pay is considerable to induce able men to engage.

E.　　　There are fewer non Commissioned staff than in the infantry because when the corps is united fewer will answer & when divided it is so much divided, that sergeants must do their duties on the detachments.

F.　　　The allowance of cloathing is less than it has heretofore been, a suit of uniform being allowed only once in two years; but this is as much as is done in the European armies in general and is sufficient.

G.　　　The expence may be still further diminished by raising only two regiments and those full which will give the same number of men as this reduction of the 4; but the United States will by this means have too small a number of officers; and should a war take place they will be intirely at a loss to officer properly the additional forces.

It is to be remarked that in the calculation of expence in every case, there ought to be a deduction of the half pay of the officers retained in service; which ought to be considered as lowering the expence of the military establishment during the lives of the present set of officers which upon an average may be estimated at twenty five years.

This makes the difference between the expence of 4 Regiments of officers or of two much less considerable than it appears at first sight and is an additional reason for that consideration not being put in competition with the national utility of keeping them in service.

To Major William Jackson [1]

[Philadelphia, June 19, 1783]

Sir,

Information having been received, that a detachment of about Eighty mutineers are on their way from Lancaster to this place,[2] you will please to proceed to meet them and to endeavour by every prudent method to engage them to return to the post they have left. You will inform them of the orders that have been given permitting them to remain in service 'till their accounts shall have been settled, if they prefer it to being furloughed and of the allowance of pay which has been made to the army at large & in which they are to be included. You will represent to them, that their accounts cannot be settled without their officers whom they have left behind them at Lancaster. You will represent to them with coolness but energy the impropriety of such irregular proceedings, and the danger they will run by persisting in an improper conduct. You will assure them of the best intentions in Congress to do them justice; and of the absurdity of their expecting to procure it more effectually by intemperate proceedings. You will point out to them the tendency which such proceedings may have to raise the resentments of their country and to indispose it to take effectual measures for their relief. In short you will urge every consideration in your power to induce them to return; at the same time avoiding whatever may tend to irritate. If they persist in coming to town, you will give the earliest notice to us of their progress and disposition. Should they want provisions, you will assure them of a supply, if they will remain where they

are, which you are to endeavour to persuade them to do in preference to coming to town.

I am Sir   Yr. most Obed serv   A Hamilton
                                        In behalf of the Committee

Philadelphia
June 19th. 1783
Major Jackson

ALS, Papers of the Continental Congress, National Archives.
   1. Jackson was the Assistant Secretary at War.
   2. After the signing of the provisional peace treaty, Army demands for
pay and discharge were aggressively asserted. There was disagreement among
congressional delegates on whether to grant the soldiers a furlough or to discharge them. On May 26, 1783, Congress authorized an immediate furlough.
The troops, however, objected to either a furlough or discharge without pay.
Some of the soldiers ordered home refused to go.
   On June 19, Congress was informed that eighty soldiers from the Third
Pennsylvania Regiment stationed at Lancaster were marching to Philadelphia
under command of their sergeants to secure a settlement of their accounts by
Congress. It was reported to Congress that they were gaining recruits en route.
Two letters, one from Colonel Richard Butler and another from William
Henry, who was later elected a delegate to Congress from Pennsylvania, were
sent from Lancaster on June 17 to the president of the Pennsylvania Supreme
Executive Council advising him of the mutiny of the Pennsylvania troops. The
letters were read in Congress and referred to a committee consisting of H,
Richard Peters, and Oliver Ellsworth. The committee was to confer with the
Executive Council of Pennsylvania "and to take such measures as they shall
judge and find necessary" (JCC, XXIV, 405, note 1).

Continental Congress
Report on Letter from George Washington
Respecting Pay for the Army

[Philadelphia] June 19, 1783

The Committee [1] on the letter from General Washington report:

Resolved that copies of the letter from the Commander in Chief
of the 7th. instant with its inclosures [2] be transmitted to the several
states for their information and that their attention be recalled to
the resolutions of the 2d of May [3] last to facilitate the punctual payment of the notes issued to the army on account of their pay.

That the Commander in Chief be informed Congress approve the
variation made by him in the manner of furloughing the troops. [4]

AD, Papers of the Continental Congress, National Archives.

1. The committee, consisting of H, James Madison, and Theodorick Bland, was appointed on June 11 to report on a letter from Washington which was received on that date (*JCC*, XXIV, 392, note 1). Washington's letter was dated June 7, 1783, and is described in note 2.

2. On June 7, Washington wrote to the President of Congress enclosing a memorial sent to him by some officers and stating that "The Two subjects of Complaint with the Army appear to be, the Delay of the three Months pay which had been expected, and the want of a settlement of Accounts" (*GW*, XXVI, 478–79).

3. See "Motion on Funds for Payment of the Army," May 2, 1783.

4. Washington had informed Congress that he had "made some little variations respecting furloughs." He did not describe them (*GW*, XXVI, 478–79).

The report, according to the endorsement, was adopted on June 19, 1793.

Continental Congress
Report on Conference with the Supreme Executive Council of Pennsylvania on the Mutiny [1]

[Philadelphia] June 20, 1783

The Committee to whom you were referred the letters & papers communicated to Congress by the Executive council of Pensylvania, through their delegates report.

That they had a conference yesterday as directed with the Supreme Executive Council, in which in the first instance the propriety of calling out a detachment of Militia to intercept the mutineers on their march from Lancaster was proposed to the Council suggesting the danger of their being suffered with impunity to join the troops in the barracks, who a few days before had manifested a dangerous spirit by an insolent and threatening message sent to Congress in the name of a Board of serjeants and who it was apprehended would be ready to make common cause with those on their march for mutinous purposes.[2] That the Council having shown a reluctance to call out any part of the Militia expressing an opinion that they would not be willing to act till some outrage should have been committed by the troops, there appeared to the Committee no alternative but to endeavour to dissuade the mutineers from coming to town and if they failed in that attempt, to make use of expedients to prevent the troops in the barracks from joining in any excesses and to induce the detachment from Lancaster to return to that place.

That in this view & at their desire Major Jackson met the detach-

ment then on its march to the city and endeavoured to engage them
to return to the former place (urging the considerations contained
in the annexed instruction to him) [3] but the said detachment persisted in their intention of coming to this city and arrived here this
morning. That upon conferring with the Superintendent of Finance,
they find there is a probability, that the Pay Master General to
whom the settlement of the accounts of the army has been committed, and who having all the documents in his possession can alone
execute the business with propriety, will shortly arrive from the
army and will immediately enter upon a settlement with the troops
in this state; that in the mean time measures will be taken to prepare
the business for a final adjustment. That there will immediately be
sent to Lancaster a sum of money to be paid to the troops on account
of the month's pay heretofore directed to be advanced to them, the
payment of which has hitherto been delayed by particular circumstances; together with notes for three months pay intended to be
advanced to the men when furloughed. That they have desired this
information to be transmitted to the Commanding officer here and
at Lancaster, with this declaration that the corps stationed at Lancaster (including the detachment) can only be settled with or paid
at that place.

AD, Papers of the Continental Congress, National Archives. In *JCHW*, II,
276–77, this document is dated July 1, 1783.
    1. The committee appointed on June 19 (see H to Major William Jackson,
June 19, 1783) to confer with the Supreme Executive Council of Pennsylvania
on measures to be taken to deal with the mutinous troops marching from Lancaster to Philadelphia, made a verbal report on the same day; and on the following day, it submitted a written report. According to the *Journals*, the
written report was recommitted, and the committee was requested to amend
it by adding its verbal report. The final version of the report is printed in the
Journals under date of July 1 (*JCC*, XXIV, 413–16), but there are no indications that the committee, as directed, added its verbal report. The report,
which is in the writing of H and is printed above, conforms exactly to that
in the *Journals*. It was written, according to the endorsement, on June 20,
and no additions or amendments to it have been found.
    2. On June 17 Congress had received a petition from the troops stationed
in Philadelphia. "The troops in the barracks at this place," James Madison
wrote to Edmund Randolph on June 17, "emboldened by the arrival of a
furloughed regiment returning to Maryland, sent in a very mutinous remonstrance to Congress, signed by the noncommissioned officers on behalf
of the whole. It painted the hardships which they had suffered in defense of
their country and duty of their country to reward them, demanding a satisfactory answer the afternoon which it was sent in, with a threat of otherwise

taking such measures as would right themselves" (James Madison Papers, Library of Congress).

3. See H to William Jackson, June 19, 1783. A copy of the letter was attached to this report.

Continental Congress
Resolutions on Measures to be Taken in Consequence of the Pennsylvania Mutiny [1]

[Philadelphia] June 21. 1783

Resolved that the President and Supreme Executive Council of Pennsylvania be informed that the authority of the United States having been this day grossly insulted by the disorderly and menacing appearance of a body of armed soldiers about the place within which Congress were assembled, and the peace of this City being endangered by the mutinous disposition of the said troops now in the barracks, it is, in the opinion of Congress, necessary that effectual measures be immediately taken for supporting the public authority.

Resolved that the Committee,[2] on a letter from Colonel Butler, be directed to confer, without loss of time, with the Supreme Executive Council of Pennsylvania, on the practicability of carrying the preceding Resolution into effect, and that in case it shall appear to the Committee that there is not a satisfactory ground for expecting adequate & prompt exertions of this State for supporting the dignity of the federal government, the president on the advice of the Committee be authorized to summon the members of Congress to meet on Thursday next at Trenton or Princeton in New Jersey, in order that further and more effectual measures may be taken for suppressing the present revolt & maintaining the dignity & authority of the United States.

Resolved that the Secretary at war be directed to communicate to the commander in chief the state & disposition of the said troops, in order that he may take immediate measures to despatch to this City, such force as he may judge expedient for suppressing any disturbances that may ensue.

JCH Transcripts.

1. The editor of the *Journals* of the Continental Congress does not name the author of this document but states only that "the entry for this day was

made in the Journal by George Bond" (*JCC*, XXIV, 410, note 1). As H was the author of most of the congressional papers on the mutiny, J. C. Hamilton probably was correct in attributing this resolve to him. No copy in H's writing, however, has been found.

On Friday, June 20, 1783, mutinous soldiers marched into Philadelphia and took possession of the barracks where other troops were quartered (see H to William Jackson, June 19, 1783, note 2). Congress had adjourned until Monday, June 23, but indications of trouble caused the President of Congress, Elias Boudinot, to call for a session of Congress on Saturday, June 21. The delegates from only six states had assembled when several hundred troops—the Lancaster soldiers having been joined by men from the Philadelphia barracks—surrounded the State House, where in separate rooms the Congress and the Supreme Executive Council of Pennsylvania were sitting. The President of Congress wrote to George Washington on June 21:

"The mutineers sent in a paper, demanding of the President and Council to authorize them to choose their own Officers . . . in order to represent their grievances. That they should wait twenty minutes, and if nothing was then done, they would turn in an enraged Soldiery on the Council, who would do themselves Justice, and the Council must abide the consequences. . . . This was handed to the Members of the Congress by the President of the State. . . . Neither Congress, or the Council, would take any measures while they were so menaced, and matters continued thus till half past 3 O'Clock this afternoon, when the Mutineers were prevailed on, for the present, to march back to the Barracks. . . ." (Burnett, *Letters*, VII, 193–94.)

Boudinot called Congress together on the evening of June 21 and the resolution printed above was introduced and passed.

2. The letter from Colonel Richard Butler to the president of the Supreme Executive Council of Pennsylvania was referred to a committee which consisted of H, Richard Peters, and Oliver Ellsworth.

Alexander Hamilton and Oliver Ellsworth to John Dickinson

[Philadelphia, June 23, 1783]

Sir,

We have the honor to inclose for Your Excellency and the Council a copy of the resolutions [1] communicated in our conference yesterday. Having then fully entered into all the explanations which were necessary on the subject, we shall not trouble your Excellency with a recapitulation. But as the object is of a delicate and important nature, we think it our duty to request the determination of the council in writing.

We have the honor to be with perfect respect   Yr. Excellency's Most Obed servts

Philadelphia
June 23d. 1783

Df, in writing of H, Papers of the Continental Congress, National Archives.
   1. The enclosure probably was the "Resolution on Measures to be Taken in Consequence of the Pennsylvania Mutiny," June 21, 1783.
   Consistent with the congressional resolve of June 21, H and Oliver Ellsworth conferred with the Supreme Executive Council of Pennsylvania on June 22. On the following day, preceding another conference, this letter was presented to the president of the Council, John Dickinson. It is explained in, and was attached as an enclosure to, the "Report of a Committee Appointed to Confer with the Supreme Executive Council of Pennsylvania on the Mutiny," June 24, 1783.

Continental Congress
Report of a Committee Appointed to Confer with the Supreme Executive Council of Pennsylvania on the Mutiny

[Philadelphia] June 24, 1783 [1]

The Committee [2] appointed to confer with the Supreme Executive Council of Pensylvania on the practicability of taking effectual measures to support the public authority, in consequence of the disorderly and menacing appearance of a body of armed soldiers surrounding the place where Congress were assembled on Saturday the 21st instant beg leave to report:

That they had a conference the morning following with the Supreme Executive council aggreeably to the intention of Congress and having communicated their resolution on that subject informed the Council that Congress considered the proceeding on which that resolution was founded of so serious a nature as to render palliatives improper and to require that vigorous measures should be taken to put a stop to the further progress of the evil and to compel submission on the part of the offenders. That in this view they had

AD, Papers of the Continental Congress, National Archives.
   1. The conference was held, as is stated in the report, on June 22 and 23. Although the report is dated June 24, it was not presented until later. The endorsement states that it was "Delivered 30 June 1783. Read. Ent[ered]. July 1. Ordered to be entered on the Journal." It is printed in the *Journals* under date of July 1 (*JCC*, XXIV, 416–21).
   2. The committee, appointed on June 19 and given additional instructions on June 21 (see "Resolution on Measures to be Taken in Consequence of the Pennsylvania Mutiny," June 21, 1783), consisted initially of H, Oliver Ellsworth, and Richard Peters. Peters did not join the other committee members in the conference. His name, first listed on the endorsement as a member of the committee, was later crossed out.

thought it expedient to declare to the executive of the state in which they reside, the necessity of taking effectual measures for supporting the public authority. That though they had declined a specification of the measures which they would deem effectual, it was their sense that a number of the militia should be immediately called out sufficient to suppress the revolt. That Congress, unwilling to expose the United States to a repetition of the insult, had suspended their ordinary deliberations in this city 'till proper steps could be taken to provide against the possibility of it.

The Council after some conversation informed the Committee, that they would wish previous to a determination to ascertain the state and disposition of the Militia, and to consult the officers for that purpose.

The day following the Committee waited upon the Council for their final resolution, having previously presented a letter addressed to His Excellency The President of which a copy is annexed,[3] requesting the determination of the Council in writing.

The Council declined a written answer alleging, that it had been unusual on similar occasions, that they were unwilling to do anything which might appear an innovation in the manner of conducting conferences between their body and Committees of Congress; adding however that they were ready to give their answer in writing, if Congress should request it. They then proceeded to a verbal answer in substance as follows.

That the Council had a high respect for the representative sovereignty of the United States and were disposed to do every thing in their power to support its dignity. That they regretted the insult which had happened, with this additional motive of sensibility, that they had themselves had a principal share in it. That they had consulted a number of well-informed officers of the militia, and found that nothing in the present state of things was to be expected from that quarter. That the Militia of the city in general were not only ill provided for service, but disinclined to act upon the present occasion. That the Council did not believe any exertions were to be looked for from them, except in case of further outrage and actual violence to person and property. That in such case a respectable body of citizens would arm for the security of their property and

3. See H and Oliver Ellsworth to John Dickinson, June 23, 1783.

of the public peace; but it was to be doubted what measure of outrage would produce this effect; and in particular it was not to be expected merely from a repetition of the insult which had happened.

The Council observed, that they thought it their duty to communicate their expectations with candour, and passed from the subject of the practicability of vigorous measures to the policy of them. They stated that General St Clair [4] with the approbation of several members of Congress & of Council had by a declaration in writing permitted the mutineers to choose a committee of commissioned officers to represent their grievances to Council and had authorised them to expect that a conference would be allowed for that purpose. That it was said the mutineers began to be convinced of their error and were preparing submissions. That from the steps which had been taken the business seemed to be in a train of negotiation, and that it merited consideration how far it would be prudent to terminate the matter in that way, rather than employ coercive means.

The Committee remarked with respect to the scruple about giving an answer in writing, that they could not forbear differing in opinion as to its propriety. That nothing was more common than written communications between the executives of the different states, and the civil and military officers acting under the authority of the United States. That for a much stronger reason, there was a propriety in this mode of transacting business between the Council and the committee of the Body of Congress. That indeed it would be conformable to the most obvious and customary rules of proceeding, and that the importance of the present occasion made it desireable to give to every transaction the greatest precision.

With respect to the practicability of employing the militia, the Committee observed, that this was a point of which the Council was alone competent to judge. That the duty of the Committee was performed in explicitly signifying the expectations of Congress.

And with respect to the policy of coertion the Committee remarked that the measures taken by Congress clearly indicated their

4. Major General Arthur St. Clair, who was in Philadelphia at this time, was instructed by Congress to take such measures as he considered advisable to end the mutiny. James Madison recorded that it was H who proposed "that Genl St. Clair in concert with the Executive Council of [the] State should take order for terminating the mutiny" ("Notes of Debates in the Continental Congress," MS, James Madison Papers, Library of Congress).

opinion. That the excesses of the mutineers had passed those bounds within which a spirit of compromise might consist with the dignity and even the safety of government. That impunity for what had happened might encourage to more flagrant proceedings, invite others to follow the example and extend the mischief. That the passiveness of conduct observed towards the detachment which had mutinied at Lancaster and come to the city in defiance of their officers had no doubt led to the subsequent violences.[5] That these considerations had determined Congress to adopt decisive measures. That besides the application to the state in which they reside for its immediate support, they had not neglected other means of ultimately executing their purpose but had directed the Commander in Chief to march a detachment of troops towards the city. That whatever moderation it might be prudent to exercise towards the mutineers, when they were once in the power of government it was necessary in the first instance to place them in that situation. That Congress would probably continue to persue this object unless it should be superseded by unequivocal demonstrations of submission on the part of the mutineers. That they had hitherto given no satisfactory evidence of this disposition, having lately presented the officers they had chosen to represent their grievances with a formal commission in writing, enjoining them if necessary to use compulsory means for redress, and menacing them with death in case of their failing to execute their views.

Under this state of things, The Committee could not forbear suggesting to the Council that it would be expedient for them so to qualify the reception which they should think proper to give to any propositions made by the mutineers as not to create embarrassment should Congress continue to act on the principle of coertion.

The Committee finding that there was no satisfactory ground to expect prompt and adequate exertions on the part of the Executive of this state for supporting the public authority were bound by the resolution under which they acted to advice the president to summon Congress to assemble at Princeton or Trenton on Thursday the 26th. instant. Willing however to protract the departure of Congress as long as they could be justified in doing it, still hoping that further information would produce more decisive measures on the part of the

5. In MS "violencies."

Council, and desirous of seeing what complexion the intimated submission would assume, they ventured to defer advising the removal 'till the afternoon of the day following that on which the answer of the Council was given. But having then received no further communications from the Council, and having learnt from General St Clair that the submissions proposed to be offered by the mutineers, through the officers they had chosen to represent them, were not of a nature sufficiently explicit to be accepted or relied on; that they would be accompanied by new demands, to which it would be improper to listen; that the officers themselves composing the Committee had shown a mysterious reluctance to inform General St Clair of their proceedings, had refused in the first instance to do it and had afterwards only yielded to a peremptory demand on his part; The Committee could no longer think themselves at liberty to delay their advice for an Adjournment, which they this day accordingly gave; persuaded at the same time that it was necessary to impress the mutineers with a conviction that extremities would be used against them before they would be induced to resolve on a final and unreserved submission.

Philadelphia June 24th. 1783

To George Clinton

Princeton [New Jersey] June 29th. 1783

Sir,

It is proper I should inform Your Excellency that Congress have lately removed to this place. I cannot enter into a detail of the causes; but I imagine they will shortly be published for the information of the United States. You will have heared of a mutiny among the soldiers stationed in the barracks of Philadelphia, and of their having surrounded the state house where Congress was sitting. Fortunately no mischief insued. There was an insolent message sent to the Council. It was at once determined that should any propositions be made to Congress they would not take them into consideration whatever extremities might ensue, while they were surrounded by an armed force.

General St Clair with the advice of some members of Congress and of the Council permitted the mutineers to appoint some commissioned officers to represent their grievances and they were at last glad of a pretext for going away.[1]

Congress judged it proper to use coertion upon the occasion & having sent an order to the Commander in Chief for a detachment of troops, at the same time called for the assistance of the militia. The conduct of the executive of this state was to the last degree weak & disgusting. In short they pretended it was out of their power to bring out the militia, without making the experiment.

This feebleness on their part determined the removal of Congress from a place where they could receive no support; and I believe they will not easily be induced to return.

The removal and a proclamation by the President announcing to the mutineers that extremities would be persued against them have intimidated them into a submission. They have impeached two of their officers Carbury & Sullivan,[2] who immediately fled. A few others are suspected.

It is to be lamented that the offers from our state have not been upon a more acceptable plan;[3] it is probable if they had been, the scales would incline in our favour. I wish the Legislature were sitting and would enlarge them. To your Excellency I need not urge the advantages that will accrue to a state from being the residence of Congress.

I have the honor to be   Yr. Excellency's Most Obed serv

A Hamilton

ALS, MS Division, New York Public Library.
    1. For details of the Pennsylvania mutiny, see "Report of a Committee Appointed to Confer with the Supreme Executive Council of Pennsylvania on the Mutiny," June 24, 1783.
    2. Captain Henry Carbery and Lieutenant John Sullivan, after their impeachment by the mutinying soldiers, fled Philadelphia and sailed for England.
    3. Christopher Tappen to H and William Floyd, March 19, 1783.

To James Madison [1]

[Princeton, New Jersey, June 29, 1783]

Dear Sir

I am informed that among other disagreeable things said about the removal of Congress from Philadelphia it is insinuated that it was a contrivance of some members to get them out of the state of

Pensylvania into one of those to which they belonged and I am told that this insinuation has been pointed at me in particular.

Though I am persuaded that all distinterested persons will justify Congress in quitting a place where they were told they were not to expect support (for the conduct of the Council amounted to that) yet I am unwilling to be held up as having had an extraordinary agency in the measure for interested purposes when the fact is directly the reverse. As you were a witness to my conduct and opinions through the whole of the transaction, I am induced to trouble you for your testimony upon this occasion. I do not mean to make a public use of it; but through my friends to vindicate myself from the imputations I have mentioned.

I will therefore request your answers to the following questions:

Did that part of the resolutions which related to the removal of Congress originate with me or not? [2]

Did I as a member of the Committee appear to press the departure; or did I not rather manifist a strong disposition to postpone that event as long as possible, even against the general current of opinion?

I wish you to be as particular & full in your answer as your memory will permit. I think you will recollect that my idea was clearly this: that the mutiny ought not to be terminated by negotiation; that Congress were justifiable in leaving a place where they did not receive the support which they had a right to expect; but as their removal was a measure of a critical and delicate nature, might have an ill appearance in Europe, and might from events be susceptible of an unfavourable interpretation in this country, it was prudent to delay it 'till its necessity became apparent, not only 'till it was manifest there would be no change in the spirit which seemed to activate the council, but 'till it was evident complete submission was not to be expected from the troops; that to give full time for this, it would be proper to delay the departure of Congress 'till the latest period which would be compatible with the idea of meeting at Trenton or Princeton on thursday—perhaps even 'till thursday morning.

I am Sir   Yr. most Obed serv

Princeton June 29th. 178⟨3⟩

AL[S], Hamilton Papers, Library of Congress.
   1. This letter apparently was not sent. See H to Madison, July 6, 1783.

2. The congressional resolution to which H refers is that of June 21, 1783 (*JCC*, XXIV, 410).

Continental Congress
Motion that Major General Howe be Directed to March Troops to Philadelphia [1]

[Princeton, New Jersey] June 30, 1783

That Major General Howe [2] be directed to march such part of the force under his command as he shall judge necessary to the State of Pensylvania; and that the Commanding Officer in the said state be instructed to apprehend and confine all such persons, belonging to the army, as there is reason to believe instigated the late mutiny; to disarm the remainder; to take, in conjunction with the civil authority, the proper measures to discover and secure all such persons as may have been instrumental therein; & in general to make full ⟨examination⟩ into all parts of the transaction & ⟨having⟩ taken the proper steps to report to Congress.[3]

AD, Papers of the Continental Congress, National Archives.
  1. Congress met on June 30, 1783, in Princeton, in accordance with a proclamation by President of Congress Elias Boudinot, dated June 24, 1783.
  2. Major General Robert Howe was stationed at West Point. On June 25 Washington had ordered him to take command of the detachment ordered to march to Philadelphia.
  3. The motion was referred to H, Oliver Ellsworth, and Theodorick Bland.

Continental Congress
Resolution Directing Major General Howe to March Troops to Philadelphia [1]

[Princeton, New Jersey] July 1, 1783

That Major General Howe be directed to march such part of the force under his command as he shall judge necessary to the state of Pensylvania; in order that immediate measures may be taken to confine and bring to trial all such persons belonging to the army, as have been principally active in the late mutiny, to disarm the remainder and to examine fully into all the circumstances relating thereto; [2]

That in the execution of the foregoing resolution, if any matter shall arise which may concern the civil jurisdiction, or in which its aid may be necessary, application be made for the same to the Executive authority of the state.

[That the Executive of Penna. be informed of the foregoing resolutions & requested to afford their assistance whensoever the same shall be required.] ³

AD, Papers of the Continental Congress, National Archives.
    1. See motion by H, dated June 30, and referred to H, Oliver Ellsworth, and Theodorick Bland.
    2. At this point H wrote the following which was crossed out, probably by Elias Boudinot, the President of Congress:
"and in case, in the progress of the investigation, it shall appear that any persons not belonging to the army have been concerned in promoting or abetting the disorders of the soldiery, that application be made to the civil authority of the state to proceed against them as the law shall direct."
    3. Bracketed words are in the writing of Elias Boudinot.

Continental Congress
Motion that States be Requested to Send Delegates to Congress

[Princeton, New Jersey] July 2, 1783

Whereas by the Confederation the assent of nine states is requisite to the determination of matters of principal importance to the United States and the representation in Congress has for some time past generally consisted of less than that number of states in consequence whereof the public business at an interesting juncture has suffered and continues to suffer great delay and embarrassment:

Resolved that the states which are not present in Congress be informed that it is indispensable they should without loss of time send forward a delegation to Congress.¹

AD, Papers of the Continental Congress, National Archives.
    1. According to the endorsement, H's motion, which was seconded by James Madison, was passed on the same day that it was introduced.

Continental Congress
Motion that Congress Return to Philadelphia

[Princeton, New Jersey] July 2, 1783. On this date, John Francis Mercer moved that Congress adjourn and return to Philadelphia. This motion was written and seconded by Hamilton.

AD, Papers of the Continental Congress, National Archives.

To James Madison [1]

[Philadelphia, July 6, 1783]

On my arrival in this city I am more convinced than I was before of the necessity of giving a just state of facts to the public. The current runs strongly against Congress and in a great measure for want of information. When facts are explained they make an impression and incline to conclusions more favourable to us. I have no copy of the reports in my possession, which puts it out of my power to publish them: Will you procure and send me one without loss of time? Without appearing I intend to give them to the public with some additional explanations. This done with moderation will no doubt have a good effect.

The prevailing idea is that the actors in the removal of Congress were influenced by the desire of getting them out of the city, and the generality of the remainder by timidity—some say passion; few give a more favourable interpretation.

I will thank you in your letter to me to answer the following question.

What appeared to be my ideas and disposition respecting the removal of Congress? Did I appear to wish to hasten it, or did I not rather show a strong disposition to procrastinate it?

I will be obliged to you in answering this question to do it fully. I do not intend to make any public use of it, but through my friends to vindicate myself, from the insinuation I have mentioned, and withal to confute the supposition that the motive assigned did actuate the members on whom it fell to be more particularly active.

Philadelphia
July 6th. 83

AL[S], James Madison Papers, Library of Congress.
1. This letter repeats the request made in H to Madison, June 29, 1783. Madison's reply is dated October 16, 1783.

Continental Congress
Motion that the States Settle the Accounts of Officers in the Mustering Department

[Princeton, New Jersey] July 18, 1783

That it be recommended to the several states to liquidate & settle the accounts of the depreciation of the officers employed in the Mustering department on the same principles as have been observed in liquidating & settling those of other officers of the army.[1]

AD, Papers of the Continental Congress, National Archives; copy, Papers of the Continental Congress, National Archives.

1. The endorsement states that the motion was referred to the Secretary at War. According to the *Journals*, the report of the Secretary was delivered July 26 and debated August 12. H's motion was negatived (*JCC*, XXIV, 441).

To Elizabeth Hamilton

Philadelphia
July 22d. 1783

I wrote you my beloved Betsey by the last post, which I hope will not meet with the fate that many others of my letters must have met with. I count upon setting out to see you in four days; but I have been so frequently disappointed by unforeseen events, that I shall not be without apprehensions of being detained, 'till I have begun my journey. The members of Congress are very pressing with me not to go away at this time as the house is thin, and as the definitive treaty is momently expected.

Tell your father that Mr. Rivington[1] in a letter to the South Carolina delegates has given information coming to him from Admiral Arbuthnot,[2] that the Mercury-frigate is arrived at New York with the definitive treaty, and that the city was to be evacuated yesterday by the treaty.

I am strongly urged to stay a few days for the ratification of the treaty; at all events however I will not be long from My Betsey.

I give you joy my angel of the happy conclusion of the important work in which your country has been engaged. Now in a very short time I hope we shall be happily settled in New York.

My love to your father. Kiss my boy a thousand times. A thousand loves to yourself. A Hamilton

ALS, Hamilton Papers, Library of Congress.
1. James Rivington, after his printing press in New York had been destroyed late in 1775 by the Sons of Liberty (see H to John Jay, November 26, 1775), had gone to England. Appointed the King's printer in New York, he returned to America in October, 1777, and began publication of *Rivington's New-York Gazette: or The Connecticut, Hudson's River, New-Jersey, and Quebec Weekly Advertiser* (later *The Royal Gazette*).
2. It was Admiral Robert Digby, the naval commander in the American station, not Admiral Marriot Arbuthnot.

To Robert R. Livingston [1]

Princeton [New Jersey]
July 23d. 1783

It happens My Dear Sir that both Mr. Maddison and myself are here. We have talked over the subject of your letter to him,[2] and need not assure you how happy we should both be to promote your wish; but the representation continues so thin, that we should have little hope that any thing which is out of the ordinary course and has somewhat of novelty in it could go through. We therefore have concluded it would be to no purpose to make the experiment in the present state of things; but shall *sound* towards a more full representation; though we fear the strictness of the ideas of many Gentlemen will be a bar to the success of the measure. You shall hear from me further on the subject. Mr. Maddison does not write himself as this letter contains both our ideas but he presents his compliments and the assurances of his esteem.

The future destination of Congress cannot now be ascertained. There is an address signing from the citizens of Philadelphia amounting to an invitation to return. Many are of opinion on conciliatory principles, that it will be prudent to do it, till the question respecting permanent residence is decided. Others are much disinclined to a return from different motives.

We have nothing new except an annunciation from Mr. Rivington in a letter to Mr. Izard of the arrival of the definitive treaty.[3] He adds that New York was by the treaty to have been evacuated the

21st of this month. When we are more enlightened I will write you details or rather I will bring them.

We have been for some time in point of representation at sixe's and sevens; when we get to nine I will not forget the money commission you gave me.

Present me respectfully to Mrs. Livingston & the rest of the ladies

Adieu My Dr Sir   Yr. Obed servt   A Hamilton

ALS, New-York Historical Society, New York City.

1. After his retirement as Secretary for Foreign Affairs in May, 1783, Livingston returned to New York. This letter is addressed to him at "Clermont," his country estate.

2. On July 15, 1783, Livingston wrote to James Madison:

"I have this moment been informed that the definitive treaty is concluded & in consequence of it give you this trouble. I believe I mentioned to you that if Congress had made no appointment of a secretary for foreign affairs before the arrival of the treaty it would give me great pleasure to be permitted to sign it in that character & thus conclude my political carrier. . . .

"I should write Coll Hamilton also on this subject having before mentioned it to him but I presume he must by this time be upon his return if however he should still be with you as I have the fullest confidence in his friendship I pray you to show him this. . . ." (New-York Historical Society.)

3. James Rivington, publisher of *The Royal Gazette*, had written to Ralph Izard, a delegate to the Continental Congress from South Carolina, that the frigate *Mercury* had arrived in New York with the definitive peace treaty.

Continental Congress
Report on a Memorial of Lieutenant Colonel Jean Baptiste de Ternant

[Princeton, New Jersey] July 23, 1783

The Committee on the letter from the Secretary at War respecting Lt Col Ternant submit the following [r]esolution:

That Lt Col Ternant be informed that Congress in continuing General Armand in the command of his corps at the time of his promotion to his present rank had reasons of a peculiar nature without any intention derogatory to the merit of Lt. Col Ternant of whose useful and distinguished services in the several confidential and important stations in which he has been employed they entertain a just sense.

That Lt. Col Ternant receive the emoluments of Lt Col Commandant.[1]

AD, Papers of the Continental Congress, National Archives.

1. On March 26, 1783, Congress promoted Colonel Charles Armand to the rank of brigadier general. On May 14, the Secretary at War wrote to Congress that Lieutenant Colonel Jean Baptiste de Ternant believed "the continuance of General Armand in the command of the Corps conveys a tacit reflection on him." The Secretary recommended the promotion of Ternant to the rank of colonel (JCC, XXIV, 344–45). The committee to which the Secretary's letter was referred changed membership several times (JCC, XXIV, 435, note 1). When the report was made, the committee consisted of H, James McHenry, and Richard Peters.

The endorsement states that the report was delivered July 23, but there is no record in the Journals that it was read on that day. It is printed in the Journals under date of September 27, 1783, and the endorsement states that it was passed, except for the last paragraph, on that date.

To John Jay [1]

[Philadelphia, July 25, 1783]

Dear Sir

Though I have not performed my promise of writing to you, which I made you when you left this country, yet I have not the less interested myself in your welfare and success. I have been witness with pleasure to every event which has had a tendency to advance you in the esteem of your country; and I may assure you with sincerity, that it is as high as you could possibly wish. All have united in the warmest approbation of your conduct. I cannot forbear telling you this, because my situation has given me access to the truth, and I gratify my friendship for you in communicating what cannot fail to gratify your sensibility.

The peace which exceeds in the goodness of its terms, the expectations of the most sanguine does the highest honor to those who made it. It is the more agreeable, as the time was come, when thinking men began to be seriously alarmed at the internal embarrassments and exhausted state of this country. The New England people talk of making you an annual *fish-offering* as an acknowlegement of your exertions for the participation of the fisheries.

We have now happily concluded the great work of independence, but much remains to be done to reach the fruits of it. Our prospects are not flattering. Every day proves the inefficacy of the present confederation, yet the common danger being removed, we are receding instead of advancing in a disposition to amend its defects. The road to popularity in each state is to inspire jealousies of the power of Congress, though nothing can be more apparent than that they have no power; and that for the want of it, the resources of the country during the war could not be drawn out, and we at this moment experience all the mischiefs of a bankrupt and ruined credit. It is to be hoped that when prejudice and folly have run themselves out of breath we may return to reason and correct our errors.

After having served in the field during the war, I have been making a short apprenticeship in Congress; but the evacuation of New York approaching, I am preparing to take leave of public life to enter into the practice of the law. Your country will continue to demand your services abroad.[2]

The bearer of this is Mr. Carter, who with Mrs. Carter are making a jaunt to Europe.[3] I presume you have heard of my connection in the family. Your acquaintance with Mr Carter makes it unnecessary I should request your civilities to him, which my friendship for him would otherwise do in the warmest manner. I anticipate the pleasure which Mrs. Jay and Mrs. Carter will enjoy in the society of each other, possessed as they both are of every quality to please and endear. I beg you to present me most respectfully to Mrs. Jay and to be assured of the affection and esteem of Dr. Sir   Your Obedient servant   Alexr. Hamilton

Philadelphia
July 25. 1783.
His Excelly John Jay Esqr

ALS, Windsor Castle, England.
  1. In the spring of 1782 Jay had gone to Paris to begin his work as joint commissioner for negotiating a peace with Great Britain. When this letter was written, Jay was in Paris.
  2. The paragraph which follows is not printed in *HCLW*, IX, 381–82 or in William Jay, *Life of John Jay* (New York, 1833), II, 122. On the receiver's copy it is crossed out, but this was probably done at a later date.
  3. John Carter (John B. Church) went to Europe to arrange payment of money owed to him for supplying the French forces during the Revolution. He was accompanied by his wife, Angelica Schuyler Church, and his business partner, Jeremiah Wadsworth.

To George Clinton

[Princeton, New Jersey, July 27, 1783]

Sir

A few days since I was honored with Your Excellency's letter of the   ;[1] and was glad to find your ideas on the subject corresponded with mine.[2]

As I shall in a day or two take leave of Congress, I think it my duty to give my opinion to the legislature on a matter of importance to the state, which has been long depending and is still without a prospect of termination in the train in which it has been placed. I mean the affair of the grants.[3] It is hazardous to pass a positive judgment on what will happen in a body so mutable as that of Congress; but from all I have seen, I have come to a settled opinion, that no determination will be taken and executed by them in any other manner, than in that prescribed by the confederation. There is always such a diversity of views and interests, so many compromises to be made between different states, that in a question of this nature, the embarrassments of which have been increased by the steps that have preceded, and in which the passions of the opposite sides have taken a warm part, decision must be the result of necessity. While Congress have a discretion they will procrastinate; when they are bound by the constitution they must proceed.

It is therefore my opinion that it will be adviseable for the Legislature when they meet to review the question; and either to relinquish their pretensions to the country in dispute, or to instruct their delegates, if a decision is not had within a limited time to declare the submission to Congress revoked and to institute a claim according to the principles of the confederation.

It would be out of my province to discuss which side of the alternative ought in policy to prevail but I will take the liberty to observe that if the last should be preferred it would be expedient to remove every motive of opposition from private claims, not only by confirming in their full latitude previous to the trial the possessions of the original settlers, but even the grants of the usurped government. It may happen that it will be eventually necessary to employ force; and in this case, it would be of great importance that neither the inhabitants of the grants, nor powerful individuals in other states, should find their private interest in contradiction to that of the state. This has already had great influence in counteracting our wishes, would continue to throw impediments in the way of ulterior measures, and might at last kindle a serious flame between the states.

I communicated to Your Excellency in a former letter that I had declined pressing the application of the legislature to Congress respecting the state troops for garrisoning the frontier posts, because temporary provision had been made in another way,[4] which would save the state the immediate expence and because there was a prospect of some general provision for the defence of the frontiers on a Continental establishment, which was to be preferred on every account.[5] A report for this purpose is now before Congress; but the thinness of representation has for some time retarded and still retards its consideration.

The definitive treaty is not yet arrived, but from accounts, which though not official appear to deserve credit, it may be dayly expected. A Gentleman known and confided in has arrived at Philadelphia, who informs that he saw a letter from Doctor Franklin to Mr. Barkeley[6] telling him that the definitive treaties were signed the 27th of May between all the parties—that New York was to be evacuated in six months from the ratification of the preliminaries in Europe, which will be the 12th or fifteenth of next month.

As it is not my intention to return to Congress I take this opportunity to make my respectful acknowledgement to the legislature for the honorable mark of their confidence conferred upon me, by having chosen me to represent the state in that body. I shall be happy if my conduct has been agreeable to them.

With perfect respect I have the honor to be Yr. Excellency's Most Obedient servant   Alex Hamilton

Princeton
July 27. 1783

ADfS, Hamilton Papers, Library of Congress.
1. Space left blank in MS.
2. Clinton's letter has not been found. In H's letter dated June 29, he had expressed to Clinton his disapproval both of the role played by the Supreme Executive Council of Pennsylvania during the mutiny of troops in Philadelphia and the hasty removal of Congress to Princeton. Clinton apparently agreed with H's opinions.

3. For information on the New Hampshire Grants, see "Motion on Vermont," December 5, 1782. The Vermont problem was again considered by Congress on May 26, 1783 (*JCC*, XXIV, 367).

4. See the Continental Congress report of May 12 in which Washington was directed to garrison the frontier with Continental troops. For the determination of the New York legislature that the frontier should be garrisoned by state troops, see the enclosure to Clinton to William Floyd and H of April 1, 1783. H also discussed the problem of garrisoning the posts in his letter to Clinton on June 1, 1783.

5. The reference is to the "Report on a Military Peace Establishment" delivered on June 18.

6. Thomas Barclay, a friend of Benjamin Franklin, who in November, 1782, was appointed by the Continental Congress commissioner for adjusting its accounts in Europe.

Continental Congress
Unsubmitted Resolution Calling for a Convention to Amend the Articles of Confederation [1]

[Princeton, New Jersey, July, 1783]

Whereas in the opinion of this Congress the confederation of the United States is defective in the following essential points, to wit:

First and generally in confining the power of the fœderal government within too narrow limits, withholding from it that efficacious authority and influence in all matters of general concern which are indispensable to the harmony and welfare of the whole—embarrassing general provisions by unnecessary details and inconvenient exceptions incompatible with their nature tending only to create jealousies and disputes respecting the proper bounds of the authority of the United States and of that of the particular states, and a mutual interference of the one with the other.

Secondly. In confounding legislative and executive powers in a single body, as that of determining on the number and quantity of force, land and naval, to be employed for the common defence, and

AD, Hamilton Papers, Library of Congress.

1. The endorsement, in the writing of H, reads: "Resolution intended to be submitted to Congress at Princeton in 1783; but abandoned for want of support."

As the first session of Congress in Princeton was held on June 30 and as H left Congress at the end of July, this resolution must have been written during July. It is impossible to determine its precise date or the delegates with whom H probably consulted before he abandoned it for want of support. In *JCHW*, II, 269-75, and *HCLW*, I, 305-14, this resolution is dated June 30, 1783.

of directing their operations when raised and equipped with that of ascertaining and making requisitions for the necessary sums or quantities of money to be paid by the respective states into the common treasury; contrary to the most approved and well founded maxims of free government which require that the legislative executive and judicial authorities should be deposited in distinct and separate hands.

Thirdly. In the want of a Fœderal Judicature having cognizance of all matters of general concern in the last resort, especially those in which foreign nations, and their subjects are interested; from which defect, by the interference of the local regulations of particular states militating directly or indirectly against the powers vested in the Union, the national treaties will be liable to be infringed, the national faith to be violated and the public tranquillity to be disturbed.

Fourthly. In vesting the United States in Congress assembled with the *power of general taxation,* comprehended in that of "ascertaining the necessary sums of money to be raised for the common defence and of appropriating and applying the same for defraying the public expences"—and yet rendering that power, so essential to the existence of the union, nugatory, by witholding from them all controul over either the imposition or the collection of the taxes for raising the sums required; whence it happens that the inclinations not the abilities of the respective states are in fact the criterion of their contributions to the common expence; and the public burthen has fallen and will continue to fall with very unequal weight.

5thly. In fixing a rule for determining the proportion of each state towards the common expence which if practicable at all, must in the execution be attended with great expence inequality uncertainty and difficulty.

6thly. In authorising Congress "to borrow money or emit bills on the credit of the United States" without the power of establishing funds to secure the repayment of the money borrowed or the redemption of the bills emitted; from which must result one of these evils, either a want of sufficient credit in the first instance to borrow, or to circulate the bills emitted, whereby in great national exigencies the public safety may be endangered, or in the second instance, frequent infractions of the public engagements, disappointments to lenders, repetitions of the calamities of depreciating paper, a continuance of the injustice and mischiefs of an unfunded debt, and first or last the annihilation of public credit. Indeed, in authorising Congress at all to emit an *unfunded* paper as the sign of value, a resource which though useful in the infancy, of this country, indispensable in the commencement of the revolution, ought not to continue a formal part of the constit[u]tion, nor ever hereafter to be employed, being in² its nature pregnant with abuses and liable to be made the engine of imposition and fraud, holding out temptations equally pernicious to the integrity of government and to the morals of the people.

7thly. In not making proper or competent provision for interior or exterior defence: for interior defence, by leaving it to the individual states to appoint all regimental officers of the land forces, to raise the men in their own way, to cloath arm and equip them at the expence of the United States; from which circumstances have resulted and will hereafter result, great confusion in the military department, continual disputes of rank, languid and disproportionate levies of men, an enormous increase of expence for want of system and uniformity in the manner of conducting them, and from the competitions of state bounties; by an ambiguity in the 4th clause of the 6th article, susceptible of a construction which would devolve upon the particular states in time of peace the care of their own defence both by sea and land and would preclude the United states from raising a single regiment or building a single ship, before a declaration of war, or an actual commencement of hostilities; a principle dangerous to the confederacy in different respects, by leaving the United states at all times unprepared for the defence of their common rights, obliging them to begin to raise an army and to build and equip a navy at the moment they would have occasion to employ them, and by putting into the hands of a few states, who from their local situations are more immediately exposed, all the standing forces of the country; thereby not only leaving the care of the safety of the whole to a part which will naturally be both unwilling and unable to make effectual provision at its particular expence, but also furnishing grounds of jealousy and distrust between the states; unjust in its operation to those states,

2. In MS, "it."

in whose hands they are by throwing the exclusive burthen of maintaining those forces upon them, while their neighbours immediately and all the states ultimately would share the benefits of their services: For exterior defence, in authorising Congress "to build and equip a navy" without providing any means of manning it, either by requisitions of the states, by the power of registering and drafting the seamen in rotation, or by embargoes in cases of emergency to induce them to accept employment on board the ships of war; the omission of all which leaves no other resource than voluntary inlistment, a resource which has been found ineffectual in every country, and for reasons of peculiar force in this.

8thly. In not vesting in the United States a general superintendence of trade, equally necessary in the view of revenue and regulation; of revenue because duties on commerce, when moderate, are one of the most agreeable and productive species of it, which cannot without great disadvantages be imposed by particular states, while others refrain from doing it, but must be imposed in concert, and by laws operating upon the same principles, at the same moment, in all the states, otherwise those states which should not impose them would engross the commerce of such of their neighbours as did; of regulation because by general prohibitions of particular articles, by a judicious arrangement of duties, sometimes by bounties on the manufacture or exportation of certain commodities, injurious branches of commerce might be discouraged, favourable branches encouraged, useful products and manufactures promoted; none of which advantages can be as effectually attained by separate regulations, without a general superintending power; because also, it is essential to the due observance of the commercial stipulations of the United States with foreigner powers, an in[ter]ference with which will be unavoidable if the different states have the exclusive regulation of their own trade and of course the construction of the treaties entered into.

9thly. In defeating essential powers by provisos and limitations inconsistent with their nature; as the power of making treaties with foreign nations, "provided that no treaty of commerce shall be made whereby the legislative power of the respective states shall be restrained from imposing such imposts and duties on foreigners as their own people are subjected to, or from prohibitting the importation or exportation of any species of goods or commodities whatso-ever," a proviso susceptible of an interpretation which includes a constitutional possibility of defeating the treaties of commerce entered into by the United States: As also the power "of regulating the trade and managing all affairs with the Indians not members of any of the states *provided* that the legislative right of any state within its own limits be not infringed or violated"—and others of a similar nature.

10thly. In granting the United States the sole power "of regu-lating the alloy and value of coin struck by their own authority, or by that of the respective states" without the power of regulating the foreign coin in circulation; though the one is essential to the due exercise of the other, as there ought to be such proportions main-tained between the national and foreign coin as will give the former a preference in all internal negotiations; and without the latter power, the operations of government in a matter of primary impor-tance to the commerce and finances of the United States will be ex-posed to numberless obstructions.

11thly. In requiring the assent of *nine* states to matters of prin-cipal importance and of seven to all others, except adjournments from day to day; a rule destructive of vigour, consistency or expedi-tion in the administration of affairs, tending to subject the *sense* of the majority to *that* of the minority, by putting it in the power of a small combination to retard and even to frustrate the most neces-sary measures and to oblige the greater number, in cases which re-quire speedy determinations, as happens in the most interesting con-cerns of the community, to come into the views of the smaller, the evils of which have been felt in critical conjunctures and must always make the spirit of government, a spirit of compromise and expedient, rather than of system and energy.

12thly. In vesting in the Fœderal government the sole direction of the interests of the United States in their intercourse with foreign nations, without empowering it to pass all general laws in aid and support of the laws of nations; for the want of which authority, the faith of the United States may be broken, their reputation sullied, and their peace interrupted by the negligence or misconception of any particular state.[3]

3. At this point H left a blank space. He apparently intended to add other instances of the defectiveness of the Articles of Confederation.

And Whereas experience hath clearly manifested that the powers reserved to the Union in the Confederation are unequal to the purpose of effectually d[r]awing forth the resources of the respective members for the common welfare and defence; whereby the United States have upon several occasions been exposed to the most critical and alarming situations; have wanted an army adequate to their defence and proportioned to the abilities of the country—have on account of that deficiency seen essential posts reduced, others eminently endangered, whole states and large parts of others overrun and ravaged by small bodies of the enemy's forces—have been destitute of sufficient means of feeding, cloathing, paying and appointing that army, by which the troops, rendered less efficient for military operations, have been exposed to sufferings, which nothing but unparallelled patience perseverance and patriotism could have endured—whereby also the United States have been too often compelled to make the administration of their affairs a succession of temporary expedients, inconsistent with order œconomy energy or a scrupulous adherence to the public engagements; and now find themselves at the close of a glorious struggle for independence, without any certain means of doing justice to those who have been its principal supporters—to an army which has bravely fought and patiently suffered—to citizens who have chearfully lent their money, and to others who have in different ways contributed their property and their personal service to the common cause; obliged to rely for the only effectual mode of doing that justice, by funding the debt on solid securities, on the precarious concurrence of thirteen destinct deliberations, the dissent of either of which may defeat the plan and leave these states at this early period of their existence involved in all the disgrace and mischiefs of violated faith and national bankruptcy.

And Whereas notwithstanding we have by the blessing of providence so far happily escaped the complicated dangers of such a situation, and now see the object of our wishes secured by an honorable peace, it would be unwise to hazard a repetition of the same dangers and embarrassments in any future war in which these states may be engaged, or to continue this extensive empire under a government unequal to its protection and prosperity.

And Whereas it is essential to the happiness and security of these states, that their union, should be established on the most solid foundations, and it is manifest that this desireable object cannot be effected but by a government capable both in peace and war of making every member of the Union contribute in just proportion to the common necessities, and of combining and directing the forces and wills of the several parts to a general end; to which purposes in the opinion of Congress the present confederation is altogether inadequate.

And Whereas on the spirit which may direct the councils and measures of these states at the present juncture may depend their future safety and welfare; Congress conceive it to be their duty freely to state to their constituents the defects which by experience have been discovered in the present plan of the Fœderal Union and solemnly to call their attention to a revisal and amendment of the same:

Therefore Resolved that it be earnestly recommended to the several states to appoint a convention to meet at ⁴ on the day of with full powers to revise the confederation and to adopt and propose such alterations as to them shall appear necessary to be finally approved or rejected by the states respectively—and that a Committee of be appointed to prepare an address upon the subject.

4. The spaces in this paragraph were left blank in the MS.

Defense of Congress [1]

[July, 1783] [2]

However men actuated by private pique or party views may take pleasure in stigmatizing the conduct of Congress with or without

AD, Hamilton Papers, Library of Congress. In *JCHW*, II, 283–87, this document is printed without date under the title "Vindication of Congress." Lodge (*HCLW*, I, 431) incorrectly assumed that this MS was part of H's "Full Vindication" written in 1774.

1. The last paragraph suggests that this MS was an introduction to a longer essay justifying the removal of Congress from Philadelphia to Princeton after the failure of the Pennsylvania authorities to satisfy Congress that adequate measures had been taken to suppress the mutiny of Pennsylvania soldiers. Possibly the article was written for one of the Philadelphia newspapers, for H refers to "the removal of Congress from *this* city."

2. This document must have been written after the removal of Congress from Philadelphia, June 30, 1783, and before H left Congress at the end of July.

reason, considerate and good men who are solicitous for the honor of their country will act upon very different principles. They will view with regret those instances in which the measures of that body may be really intitled to blame, will be cautious how they bestow it where it is not merited, and will always examine with candour before they condemn. Though it is certainly true that the infallibility of that or any other body is a doctrine to be reprobated in a free country, and a servile complaisance to its errors would be as dangerous as despicable; yet it must be allowed that an opposite extreme may be little less pernicious. A captious disposition to arraign without examination, to accumulate undistinguishing censure, to excite jealousies against the phantom without the substance of power, to blame for defects in the constitution itself not in the administration of it, is a vice of nearly as mischievous a tendency in the public mind as a blind and superstitious reverence. In the present circumstances of this country most evil is to be apprehended from the prevalency of the former spirit; for new governments emerging out of a revolution, are naturaly deficient in authority and require that every effort should be made to strengthen not to undermine the public confidence. This observation applies with peculiar force to the government of the union; the constitutional imbecillity of which must be apparent to every man of reflexion.

It is therefore painful to hear, as is too fashionable a practice, indiscriminate censures heaped upon Congress for every public failure and misfortune; without considering the intire disproportion between the means which that body have it in their power to employ and their responsibility. It is equally exceptionable to see all the errors of their predecessors concentered in a mass of accusation against the subsisting body. If there have been meritorious acts performed by Congress at any period of the revolution, all the praise of it is confined to the immediate actors; if there have been faults committed they descend with increasing odium upon all who come after. The good deeds of Congress die or go off the stage with the individuals who are the authors of them; but their mistakes are the inheritance of all those who succeed.

It is true Congress in a political capacity are perpetual; but the individuals who compose it in fact undergo frequent changes. It is not more reasonable to charge any present set of members for the mismanagement of a former set allowing it to be real; than it would be to impute to George 3 the crimes adulteries or murders of Henry the 8th. It is a principle of the English law that the King never dies; and yet no man in his senses on account of this fiction of the law will transfer to the reigning monarch the infamy of his predecessor's misconduct. It is not less unjust or absurd to blame a subsisting Congress the greater part of whose members have had no agency in the measures which are the objects of crimination, for the ill consequences of those measures.

It is not much to be wondered at that this error should exist among the uninformed parts of the community, who can only be expected to have general notions of Congress without any precise ideas of their constitution—and who therefore will be disposed to view them always under the same form without attending to the changes which the body is continually undergoing. But when men more enlightened fall into the same fallacy it is an argument of disingenuous intentions, and proves them to be under the influence of passion of prejudice or of something worse.

The chief topics of clamour against Congress are either positive breaches of faith by avowed departures from express stipulations as the reduction of the Continental money from forty to one, or negative, as the general nonperformance of the public engagements.

As to those of the first kind without entering into a discussion of particular instances, without examining whether those which may have happened may have been produced by inexperience, necessity, levity or design, it will be sufficient in justification of the present Congress to say that a large majority of them had no share whatever in those acts which are the subject of complaint. And as to those of the last kind, there always has been and is a conclusive and satisfactory answer to be given for Congress. The power of raising money is not vested in them. All they can do is to assign their quotas to the several states and to make requisitions from them. This they have not failed to do in the most ample manner; and if the states do not comply to enable them to execute their engagements, the delinquency is not to be charged upon Congress.

Should it be said that Congress ought not to have made engagements without the power of fulfilling them, this is to say that they ought to have given up the contest and to have betrayed the liberty

of America. It was necessary to incur debts to support the revolu-
ion; and no man who is a sincere friend to it, can be serious in advancing the position that this essential resource ought not to have
been employed from a scruple of that nature. If Congress indeed
after a definitive conclusion of the peace consent to be the instruments of future engagements, without more effectual provision at
their disposal, they will then merit the indignation of every honest
man.

But the present Congress have more than this general argument to
offer in their vindication. They can say with truth that so far from
having committeed any positive violations of faith, they have
manifested an uniform and anxious solicitude for the restoration of
public credit, and for doing complete justice to every class of public
creditor. Having found by repeated and dayly experience that the
provisions of the confederation were unequal to the purpose; they
have had recourse to extraordinary expedients. Their plan of the
    [3] for funding the public debt is now depending before the
several legislatures, nor is it possible for them to give a more decisive
proof of their disposition to justice than is contained in that plan.

Congress stand in a very delicate and embarrassing situation: on
one hand they are blamed for not doing what they have no means
of doing on another their attempts are branded with the imputations of a spirit of encroachment and a lust of power.

In these circumstances it is the duty of all those who have the
welfare of the community at heart to unite their efforts to direct
the attention of the people to the true source of the public disorders
the want of an efficient general government and to impress upon
them this conviction that these states to be happy must have a
stronger bond of Union and a Confederation capable of drawing
forth the resources of the Country. This will be a more laudable occupation than that of cavilling against measures, the imperfection of
which is the necessary result of the constitution.

It may appear extraordinary that these observations should be
introductory to remarks on the transaction which at this time principally engages the public attention—to wit the removal of Congress
from this city; but there is a chain of ideas which naturally connects

3. April 18, 1783. This space was left blank by H. For information about this
plan, see H to George Clinton, May 14, 1783.

the general opinion of Congress with the judgment to be passed upon their conduct in this particular instance. This chain will easily be traced by men of discernment.[4]

4. The MS is incomplete.

To John Chaloner

[*New York, August 2, 1783.* On August 14, 1783, Chaloner wrote to Hamilton: "Your favr of the 2nd. reached me the 12th Instant." *Letter not found.*]

From Richard Soderstrom [1]

Boston, August 4, 1783. Asks Hamilton to serve as attorney in Soderstrom's suit against James Jarvis.

ALS, Hamilton Papers, Library of Congress.
1. Soderstrom, a prominent Boston merchant, was a member of an insurance company established by John Hurd of that city.

To James Duane [1]

[New York, August 5, 1783]

Dr. Sir

Mrs. Schuyler having some business in this city obliged me to pass into it. I do not find that the definitive treaty is here, though I am inclined to believe that definitive orders have been received respecting the evacuation, and advice of the sailing of a fleet of transports for that purpose. A new embarkation of German troops is going on. But upon the whole I do not imagine the evacuation will be completed 'till after the September equinoxes. Some late indictments in our state have given great alarm here.[2] Many who have all along talked of staying now talk of going. We have already lost too large a number of valuable citizens.

I am with great regard D Sir   Yr Obed ser   A Hamilton
New York Aug 5th

Through forgetfulness I left a small tavern Bill at Princeton unpaid
—for a few dinners. Do me the favour of paying it for me. I mean
the Tavern where we dined together.

ALS, New-York Historical Society, New York City.
1. Duane, along with H and others, was appointed a New York delegate
to the Continental Congress in 1782. (See "Commission as Delegate," October
25, 1782.) Although his term of office began in November, 1782, Duane did not
attend the Congress until July 16, 1783.
2. The reference, of course, is to the prosecution of Loyalists.

To Robert R. Livingston

[Albany, August 13, 1783]

Dr. Sir

I arrived here two days ago. Being in company with Mrs. Schuyler
I was induced, in complaisance to her, to pass through New York.
But I was sorry not to find any satisfactory ground to believe that
the suspicions entertained of the arrival of the definitive treaty were
well founded; though Rivington[1] when it is mentioned to him
shrugs up his shoulders and looks significantly; and Sir Guy[2] has
never explicitly denied its having been received by the Mercury.
Measures however seem to be taking in earnest towards an evacuation. A second and a considerable detachment of Germand troops
is embarking. Intelligence is current of the sailing of a large fleet of
transports from England. Yet I do not think the British will take
leave before the *ides* of October.

The spirit of emigration has greatly increased of late. Some violent
papers sent into the city have determined many to depart, who
hitherto have intended to remain. Many merchants of second class,
characters of no political consequence, each of whom may carry
away eight or ten thousand guineas have I am told lately applied
for shipping to convey them away. Our state will feel for twenty
years at least, the effects of the popular phrenzy.

The subject you wrote to Maddison and myself about we have
since attended to; but we found that nothing could be done in it.
Such a thing would always be difficult there; and unluckily it is to
be feared that a certain influence has of late increased not friendly
to that line of thinking and acting which we call proper.[3]

I left in charge with several of my friends who have promised their attention to it, the business of an extra-allowance.[4] There was when I came away a prospect of a full representation. I flatter myself it will not be neglected. I am very truly & cordially Dr Sir   Yr. Obedient ser   **A Hamilton**

I beg your care of the inclosed.

My respects to the ladies, with those of Mrs. H— Augt. 13. 1783

The Hon. Mr. Livingston

ALS, New-York Historical Society, New York City; copy, Bancroft Transcripts, MS Division, New York Public Library.
   1. Late in July, James Rivington had written the South Carolina delegates in Congress that the frigate *Mercury* had arrived in New York with the definitive peace treaty. (See H to Elizabeth Hamilton, July 22, 1783, and H to Livingston, July 23, 1783.)
   2. Sir Guy Carleton who had succeeded Sir Henry Clinton as commander of the British forces in North America in May, 1782.
   3. See H to Livingston, July 23, 1783, note 2.
   4. See Livingston to H, June 5, 1783.

From John Chaloner [1]

Philada August 14. 1783

Dear Sir

Your favr of the 2nd.[2] reached me the 12th Instant. Mrs. Dunkin is doubtfull whether She can procure the Chintz or not if she does it shall be forwarded as you directed immediately. Herewith the General [3] will receive a Cape Letter from Mr Carter. The Pilot was a long while returning with it. Your draft on me I shall duly honour on Acct of Mr. Carter [4] tho he omitted in his hurry to speak to me on the Subject.[5] Mrs. Chaloner joins me in our best Compliments to you and your good Lady also to the Generals family and Mrs. Van Ransellar [6] all of whom we hope are well. I shall embrace in the first Oppo. of communicating every information I obtain of our friends Wayfare and I remain with The greatest respect   Sir   Your most Obdt Servant

The Honble A Hamilton Esqr
Albany

LC, Historical Society of Pennsylvania.
   1. Chaloner, a Philadelphia merchant, was assistant commissary of purchases for the Continental Army during the Revolution. After the war, in associ-

ation with Charles White, his business was conducted under the firm name of Chaloner and White.

Chaloner, while contracting for the Philadelphia office of the commissary department, had come to the attention of Jeremiah Wadsworth, commissary general of purchases and business partner of John Carter (John B. Church). All the business affairs of Wadsworth and Carter in Philadelphia were conducted through John Chaloner, and when in 1784 the partners were in Europe, Chaloner received the largest share of the thousands of pounds of merchandise they shipped from Europe to America. The partnership of Wadsworth and Carter was dissolved at the end of July, 1785; but, principally because Chaloner had mishandled their affairs, several years were required for Chaloner to settle his accounts with the partners.

2. Letter not found.

3. Philip Schuyler, at whose home in Albany H was living at this time.

4. Carter (or Church) had left the United States for Europe in late July, 1785. (See H to John Jay, July 25, 1783, note 3.)

5. See note 1.

6. Presumably Margarita (Margaret) Schuyler Van Rensselaer, Philip Schuyler's daughter.

To James Duane

Albany, August 20, 1783. Requests information concerning 40,000 acres of land in Tryon County on which Abel James holds a mortgage.

ALS, New-York Historical Society, New York City.

To George Clinton

[*Albany, August 20, 1783.* On August 20, 1783, Hamilton wrote to Philip Van Rensselaer: "I send you a line to the Governor." *Letter not found.*]

To Philip Van Rensselaer [1]

[Albany, August 20, 1783]

Dr Sir

I find on examination that the Cash I could spare is so trifling that it would be of little use to you. I send you a line to the Governor [2] which is at your service. I imagine there may be about £50 due me. The letter accompanying this gives the Govr. an account of the time I was at Congress. He will calculate according to the allowance made by the state. If I can dispose of a bill on Philadelphia, I shall have it in my power to offer you a further sum.

I am Dr S　Yr. friend & ser　　　　　　　　　　　A Hamilton
Aug. 20.

ALS, MS Division, New York Public Library.
　1. Van Rensselaer was the commissary of public stores for the Northern Department.
　2. Letter not found.

To John Canfield [1]

Albany, August 30, 1783. Asks Canfield to sell a farm which belongs to John Carter [2] and is located in Salisbury, Connecticut.

ALS, Courtesy of the Sons of the Revolution, Headquarters, Fraunces Tavern, New York City.
　1. Canfield, a lawyer in Sharon, Connecticut, was a member of the state legislature.
　2. John B. Church.

From Robert R. Livingston

ClerMont [New York] 30th. Augt. 1783

Dr Sir

I felt a resentment at hearing that you had passed without stoping at Clermont that your friendly letter of the 13th. has hardly yet calmed. Abstracted from the pleasure of seeing you I had a thousand political inquiries to make for I have not yet been able to philosophize myself into that tranquil indifference which is perhaps necessary to ones happiness. I am much obliged to you for the attention you have given to the matter I mentioned without being greatly disappointed at its want of success.[1] I consider it as a feather that would have graced my cap But do not feel much pain at going as plain as my neighbours. The affair of the allowance & commission is of more serious import in the present state of my finances but I am less sanguine on that point than you appear to be and scarce know a man in your absence on whom I can rely for carrying it thro'.[2]

I seriou[s]ly lament with you the violent spirit of persecution which prevails here and dread its consequences upon the wealth commerce & future tranquilily of the state. I am the more hurt at it because it appears to me almost unmixed with pure or patriotic motives. In some few it is a blind spirit of revenge & resentment but in more it is the most sordid interest. One wishes to possess the house of some wretched Tory another fears him as a rivale in his trade or commerce & a fourth wishes to get rid of his debts by shaking of his creditor or to reduce the price of Living by depopulating the town. It is a sad misfortune that the more we know of our fellow creatures the less reason we have to esteem them. Tho perhaps philosophically considered this may be designed to weaken attatchments which habit alone would otherwise render too strong for our duties to heaven & ourselves—as violent exercise tires & puts us out of breath as we approach the end of the course to prevent the active soul from wearing out its weaker companion by lengthening the race.

Mrs. Livingston & my sisters return their comps. to Mrs. Hamilton to whom you will be pleased also to present mine.

I am Dr Sir with the truest esteem & regard   Your Most Obt hum Servt

ADf, New-York Historical Society, New York City.
   1. See H to Livingston, July 23 and August 13, 1783.
   2. See Livingston to H, June 5, 1783.

To Richard Soderstrom

[*New York, August 30, 1783.* On the envelope of a letter which Soderstrom wrote to Hamilton on August 4, 1793, Hamilton wrote: "Answered 30th by the post." *Letter not found.*]

James Duane and Ezra L'Hommedieu to Alexander Hamilton and William Floyd

Prince Town [New Jersey] Sept. 1. 1783

Honorable Gentlemen,

We enclose you an Extract of Dispatches from his Excellency our Governor received this Day, respecting the Instructions of the Legislature at their last Sessions for the Security of the Western Posts.[1]

You will be pleased to observe that an official Report on a subject so interesting to the State is deemed to be necessary; as well as a particular Detail of the Motives which influenced Congress, against the declared sense of the State, to give Directions to the Commander in Chief for garrisoning those Posts with Continental Troops.[2] This is a Duty to which, not having been present at the Debates, we find ourselves incompetent. We can therefore only refer his Excellency and the Legislature to you, our worthy Colleagues, who being fully possessed of the Facts, can alone give the necessary official Information.[3]

With Sentiments of the most perfect Esteem and Regard we have the Honour to be Gent. Your most Obedient   Humble Servants

Jas. Duane

Ezra LHommedieu [4]

The Honorable Colos. William Floyd & Alexander Hamilton

LS, in writing of Ezra L'Hommedieu, Hamilton Papers, Library of Congress; Df, in writing of L'Hommedieu, New-York Historical Society. In *JCHW*, I, 399–400, this letter is dated 1783.

1. See George Clinton to H and William Floyd, April 1, 1783; "Report on the Garrisoning of Frontier Posts by Continental Troops," May 12, 1783; H to Clinton, June 1, 1783; and H to Clinton, July 27, 1783.

The extract from Clinton's letter, dated August 23, 1783, reads as follows: "I would take this Oppertunity also of calling your attention to concurrent Resolutions of the Legislature respecting the garrisoning of the Western Posts in this State which by the provisional Treaty are to be evacuated by the British. These Resolutions were in the Tenor of Instructions to our Delegates and were immediately transmitted to them, but as I have not been favoured with any official Information of the Result I submit it to you whether some Report on a Subject so interesting to the state may not be necessary for the Satisfaction of the Legislature. From informal Communications made to me by the Commander in Chief, I have Reason to believe that he has Directions from Congress for garrisoning those Posts with continental Troops and that he is making Arrangements for that purpose. But as you will observe that as it was the Sence of the Legislature that those Posts should have been garrisoned by the State an Explination on the Subject becomes the more necessary; and it is now for this Reason alone I would request that you would be pleased to favor me with a particular Detail of the Motives which influenced the Determination of Congress on this Occasion; for it will readily be perceived that should Congress at this late Day accede to the Propositions made by the State it might be impractable to carry them into execution, especially as I have not ventured, in the State of uncertainty in which I was left, to incur the Expence which the necessary Preparations for the Purpose would have required." (Hamilton Papers, Library of Congress.)

The concurrent resolution of the legislature was enclosed in Clinton to H and Floyd, April 1, 1783.

2. In a letter dated July 27, 1783, H had explained to Clinton his reasons for not introducing in Congress the legislature's request that the frontier posts be garrisoned by state troops.

3. On September 3, L'Hommedieu sent Governor Clinton the following account of H's action on the concurrent resolution:

"We have also wrote to Colos. Floyd & Hamilton to make the Report as we were not here, when that Business was under Consideration. A few Evenings before the Receipt of your Excellencys Letter, I was informed by My Colleague that such an Instructions had been left with him by Colo. Hamilton who received the same early from the Legislature and had suppressed it, so that it had not been known to any Person in Congress, he having determined that it was best for the state that the Posts should be garrisoned with Continental Troops. Whether Colo. Floyd was acquainted with the Instructions I am not able to learn. It was new to me." (*Public Papers of George Clinton*, VIII, 249.)

4. L'Hommedieu had arrived in Princeton to attend the Continental Congress on August 7.

From James Duane

[*Princeton, New Jersey, September 8, 1783*. On September 26, 1783, Hamilton wrote to Duane: "I received last night your letter of the 8th. instant." *Letter not found.*]

To James Duane

[Albany, September 14, 1783]

Dr. Sir

The enclosed was delivered me by Doctr. Schuyler [1] with a request to transmit it to one of the delegates of the state for patronage. He assures me that what he asks has been done in similar cases; particularly for some Hospital surgeons belonging to the State of Pensylvania. If so there will prob⟨ably⟩ be no difficulty in the case. I beg l⟨eave⟩ to recommend it to your attention.

Doctor Schuyler has served with reputation and deserves well of the public; as I am informed from authority which I credit.

I have the honor to be D Sir   Yr. Obed serv.   A Hamilton

Albany
Sep. 14. 1783
The Honble Mr. Duane

ALS, Papers of the Continental Congress, National Archives.
1. Nicholas Schuyler was appointed a surgeon's mate in the general hospital of the Northern Department in January, 1777. In June, 1778, he was appointed surgeon to the regiment commanded by Colonel Moses Hazen. Schuyler petitioned Congress for the depreciation of his pay while he was regimental surgeon. His memorial is in the Papers of the Continental Congress, National Archives.

To John Dickinson [1]

[Albany, September 25–30, 1783] [2]

Sir,

Having always entertained an esteem for you personally I could not without reluctance yield to impressions that might weaken that sentiment, and it is with pain I find myself drawn by circumstances to animadvert upon the late message from the Executive Council to the Assembly of Pensylvania relative to the mutiny in a manner which may seem to impeach the candor of those who were the authors of it.[3] But it will be impossible for persons who have read the report of the Committee and the message of the Council, however inclined to make allowances for the force of involuntary biass, not to conclude that on one side or the other the facts have been wilfully discoloured. I decline any attempt to set the public opinion right upon this subject, because after all that can be said the judgments of men will eventually be determined by personal and party prepossessions. So far as I am concerned, I persuade myself those who are acquainted with me will place intire confidence in my fairness and veracity. I doubt not Your Excellency's friends will be equally partial to you and those of the council to them. But though I should dispair of rectifying or fixing the public opinion by an appeal to the public, and though I have seen too much of the ridicule thrown upon such appeals from men in official stations, and of the ill ef-

ADf, Hamilton Papers, Library of Congress.

1. In *JCHW*, I, 374–93, the addressee of this letter is incorrectly given as Joseph Reed. It is impossible to determine whether this letter was actually sent to John Dickinson. Neither the receiver's copy nor a reply by Dickinson has been found.

2. The MS is undated. As it was written in reply to a message of Dickinson to the Pennsylvania Assembly dated August 18, 1783, which did not appear in *The Pennsylvania Gazette* until September 24, 1783, H's answer has been dated September 25–30, 1783.

3. H, as a member of Congress, had met with the Supreme Executive Council of Pennsylvania on June 21, 22, and 23, 1783, in reference to the mutiny of soldiers of the Pennsylvania line. On June 24 a report on the conference in the writing of H was submitted to Congress. On August 18 Dickinson, president of the Supreme Executive Council of Pennsylvania, sent an account of the mutiny to the state's General Assembly. Dickinson's message is printed in "Minutes of the Supreme Executive Council of Pennsylvania." *Pennsylvania Colonial Records* (Harrisburg, 1853), XIII, 654–66.

fect they have had upon the national character, not to be willing to sacrifice the desire of justifying myself to considerations of prudence and propriety; yet I cannot forbear indulging my feelings so far as to enter into a few explanations with Your Excellency, submitting the justness of them to the testimony of your own mind.

As this is a mere private discussion I address myself to your Excellency in particular; and the rather as from the stile and manner of the message, I take it for granted you had the principal agency in it; and I shall consider on the same grounds the notes in
paper of the   [4] as a commentary on the report of the Committee by yourself, in aid of the message.

4. Spaces left blank in MS. The message appeared in *The Pennsylvania Gazette* on September 24, 1783. The notes to which H refers and which appear with the message in both the *Gazette* and in the *Pennsylvania Colonial Records* read as follows:

"The committee of Congress, in their report, have fallen into several mistakes by confounding facts and sentiments, and representing them as happening or expressed at times when they had not happened, or were not expressed. These mistakes were owing no doubt to the quick succession of circumstances, and the ideas that, without noticing dates, in consequence took possession of the mind.

"The obvious construction of the first report is, that the committee informed Council of the letter to Congress from the board of serjeants, though not a single member of Council, nor the secretary, has any remembrance of its being mentioned by them, nor does any member of Council now know what that message was. The argument annexed to it in the report is no more recollected.

"The committee say, that Council informed them 'the exertions of the militia were not to be expected from a repetition of the insult which had happened.' Though the Council only said, they could not be sure that such another insult would produce those exertions.

"In short, to shew the extreme inaccuracy with which these reports, to be entered upon the minutes of Congress, and preserved among the archives of the empire, have been composed, it is necessary only to attend to that part where the committee say, they represent to Council 'that Congress would probably continue to pursue *the object of having the soldiers in their power*, unless it should be superceded by unequivocal demonstrations of submission on the part of the mutineers—that they had hitherto given no satisfactory evidence of this disposition, having lately presented the officers they had chosen to represent their grievances with a formal commission in writing, enjoining them if necessary to use compulsory means for redress, and menacing them with death in case of their failing to execute their views.'

"The conference, in which the committee say they made this representation, was held according to their own report on the *twenty-third* of *June*. It began at 10 'clock in the morning. The commission from the mutineers to the officers bears date, and was presented to the officers on that day, about 8 o'clock in the morning. It is highly improbable that the committee should have discovered its contents, in the two hours that intervened between its being *presented*, and *their meeting* the Council; and the improbability is increased

I take up the matter individually, because I mean to treat it on a private footing; and because though I do not acknowlege any peculiar responsibility, it happened to be my lot as Chairman principally to conduct the conferences on the part of the Committee.

I regard the whole of this business as a most unfortunate one; in which probably none of the actors will acquire great credit. I deplore it as tending to interrupt the harmony between Congress and a respectable a meritorious member of the Union. Who were right or who were wrong is a question of less importance than how mutual irritations may be best treated? Whatever revives or continues the former is to be regretted. I lament to be under any inducement to discuss circumstances that relate to it in the remotest degree. Nothing but an attack upon the ingenuousness of my conduct could have called me to it. Its prudence either collectively or individually would patiently have been consigned to the lash of censure and cri[ti]cism merited, or unmerited.

Happily in the present case the members of the Committee have a strong ground from which they cannot easily be forced. Apprehensive of misconception, I will not say of misrepresentation, they tried to render it impossible by written documents. The presumption with impartial minds cannot fail to be in favour of that side which gave so decisive a proof of its disposition to fairness as to endeavour to put it out of its own power to misrepresent.

The professed scruples of the Council cannot be admitted to have any weight. Usage and the plainest rules of propriety will dictate that it never could have wounded the dignity or delicacy of the executive of any state, to have given to a Committee of Congress appointed to confer on a subject of moment, a written answer to a request in writing after previous explanations.[5] The fact stated speaks

----

by this circumstance, that not a member who was in Council knew any thing of the commission, nor remembers to have heard a single syllable respecting it mentioned by the committee during the whole conference. The first knowledge Council had of the commission was on the *twenty-fourth*, when they received the letter from Captain *Chrystie*, and that same day they sent a copy of it to Congress by their Secretary."

5. On June 22, 1783, H and Oliver Ellsworth, at the request of Congress, asked the Supreme Executive Council of Pennsylvania for its opinion concerning the use of the state militia to suppress the mutiny. On June 23, H and Ellsworth wrote to Dickinson "to request the determination of the council in writing." The Council refused to give a written reply stating that it would do so only if Congress, and not a committee of Congress, requested it. See H's report dated June 24, 1783.

for itself. The consequences show that the precaution of the Committee was well judged and that it would have been well for the Council to have concurred. In the present case it might be observed, that there was in the first instance a written application from Congress to the Council in the customary form of resolutions;[6] and though a Committee was authorised to confer and explain, a formal and authentic answer might reasonably have been expected by Congress and when desired by the Committee should have been understood as desired on their behalf.

There is an awkwardness in reasoning upon self evident positions, but as the Council have by their conduct in the first instance and by their message since put forward a doubt upon the subject and made it a point of importance, I shall be excused for examining it a little further. On what could the objection of the Council be founded? They say it had been unusual. Admitting the fact, was the mere novelty of the thing a sufficient reason against it? If there was no apparent inconvenience in making a new precedent, if on the contrary there was a manifest convenience in it, ought not such a punctilio to have given way to considerations of utility?

Was it derogatory to the dignity of the Council? Surely if they communicate in writing with the executive servants of Congress, even those in subordinate stations, as is the practice of every day and as is indispensable to the prosecution of public business, they might at less expence of dignity pursue the same mode with a part of that body itself.

The distinction taken by the Council in their message to the assembly, respecting the responsibility of such executive officers, as not applicable to a Committee,[7] if it amounts to any thing, proves only this—that such officers ought in prudence to take greater

6. See "Resolutions on Measures to be Taken in Consequence of the Pennsylvania Mutiny," June 21, 1783.

7. The message of the president and Council to the Assembly had stated that ". . . it might be very proper for responsible officers [of Congress] to ask for answers in writing, to justify themselves to their superiors, and a generous condescension in the persons from whom they were solicited, would induce them to comply; but, the committee were a part of the body representing the sovereignty of the United States, and we had the honor of representing the sovereignty of this State, that *conferences*, especially between persons vested with such authorities, were intended to obtain a free and full communication of sentiments, without the intervention of writing, and that no inconvenience could be apprehended from proceeding in this usual method, as each party could rely upon the integrity of the other." (*The Pennsylvania Gazette*, September 24, 1783.)

precautions for their own justification than a Committee of Congress need to do. It is not to be inferred, if a Committee of Congress acting ministerially think it expedient to use circumspection, that those with whom they are transacting business can with propriety refuse to join with them in that mode which is best adapted to precision and certainty.

But indeed the ground of the d⟨istinction⟩ [8] is erroneous. A committee of Congress act in ⟨a⟩ ministerial capacity and are therefore responsi⟨ble to⟩ the body to which they belong as well as the servants of that body though in a different manner. If it be said they do not act ministerially but stand in the place of Congress, then the Council upon their own principles ought to have complied with their request.

To diminish the exceptionableness of their refusal, it is true, as stated by the Council that though they said they could not *condescend* to do what the Committee had asked yet they declared themselves to *grant* an answer in writing, if Congress should request it; and that they proposed that the Committee should put their verbal answer in writing to be afterwards perused and examined by them.

The answer of the Committee as I doubt not Your Excellency will recollect was—as to the first point that Congress in all probability would not make the request, having determined (as the Council had been already informed) not to resume their deliberations in the city till effectual measures had been taken to suppress the mutiny—and should they assemble would naturally feel a delicacy in requesting what had been denied to their Committee. And as to the second point, that the Council having judged it inexpedient to give a written answer, the Committee would content themselves with making the most accurate report in their power, relying upon the confidence of the body to which they belonged and upon the candour of the council.

Your Excellency is too good a judge of human nature as well as of the force of language not to have perceived at the time of effect which the refusal of the Council had upon my mind. I own it struck me either as an uncandid reserve or an unbecoming stateliness; and in either supposition a disrespect to the body of which the Committee were members.

Though nothing enters less into my temper than an inclination

8. The material in broken brackets is taken from *JCHW*, I, 377.

to fetter business by punctilio, after the Council had discovered, such overweening nicety, I should have thought it a degradation to my official character to have consented to their proposal.

The desire of self justification is so natural that I should not have been surprised to have seen the transactions which are the subject of the council's message receive a colouring favourable to their purpose. But I did not expect to find material facts either suppressed or denied.

The report made by the Committee on the first interview with the Council was I acknowlege from memory and therefore I admit the possibility of error; but so far as my memory can be relied on the representation was just. And I am certain that there is a mistake in the insinuation, that the circumstance of the message sent to Congress by the Board of serjeants, was not mentioned at all to the Council, for I have a note of it taken immediately after the first conference subsequent to the mutiny.[9] The affair, by the event of

[10] having assumed a more serious aspect I kept a regular minute of the proceedings a summary of which made up our report to Congress and which I shall annex at large to this letter for your Excellency's perusal.[11]

The message intirely omits the declaration of the Council that

and the note says, that the Council only declared, "that they could not be sure, that such another insult would produce those exertions." [12] The difference in this article is of great importance. The

9. In his "Report on Conference with the Supreme Executive Council of Pennsylvania on the Mutiny," dated June 20, 1783, H wrote that he had informed the Council of the danger of allowing the Lancaster troops to join the soldiers in the barracks in Philadelphia. The soldiers in Philadelphia, H reported, "had manifested a dangerous spirit by an insolent and threatening message sent to Congress in the name of a Board of serjeants and who it was apprehended would be ready to make common cause with those on their march for mutinous purposes." In a message to the Pennsylvania Assembly, the Council denied that the committee had informed it of the message from "the Board of serjeants."

10. At this point H left a blank space in the MS. He presumably intended to fill in the date on which the Pennsylvania troops surrounded the "place where Congress were assembled." This took place on Saturday, June 21, 1783.

11. For the report, see "Report of a Committee Appointed to Confer with the Supreme Executive Council of Pennsylvania on the Mutiny," June 24, 1783. The "minutes" have not been found.

12. In their report dated June 24, H and Oliver Ellsworth informed Congress that the Pennsylvania Council had told them:

declaration made so deep an impression at the time, that almost the precise words remained in my memory. They were twice repeated as well when we saw Your Excellency alone in your own house in the morning, as when you delivered to us in the Council chamber the determination of the Council. Mr. Elseworth [13] in half an hour afterwards repeated them to several members of Congress assembled at the Presidents house, and in a few hours from that time I committed them to writing. I cannot suppose Your Excellency's recollection fails you in this particular and I must pointedly appeal to your candour.

To show the inaccuracy with which the report of the Committee was composed it is observed in the notes with respect to that part which relates to the commission given by the mutineers to the officers, whom they had chosen to represent them, that only two hours intervened between that event and the conference with the Council—and that it was very improbable the knowlege of it could have so early reached the Committee. It is added that none of the Council remembers to have heard a single syllable respecting it during the whole conference.[14]

As to the argument drawn from the short interval between the delivery of the commission and the conferrence, it will be sufficient to say that the Committee held a constant communication with General St Clair [15] and that he kept a vigilant eye upon all the motions of

----

"That the Militia of the city in general were not only ill provided for service, but disinclined to act upon the present occasion. That the Council did not believe any exertions were to be looked for from them, except in case of further outrage and actual violence to person or property. That in such a case a respectable body of citizens would arm for the security of their property and of the public peace; but it was to be doubted what measure of outrage would produce this effect; and in particular it was not to be expected merely from a repetition of the insult which had happened."

H probably intended to insert this extract from the committee report in the blank space which he left in the MS.

In the notes attached to the message it was denied that the last statement quoted had been made, and it was asserted that the Council had said only that "they could not be sure that such another insult would produce those exertions" (*The Pennsylvania Gazette*, September 24, 1783).

13. Oliver Ellsworth.

14. In a note to the address of the Supreme Executive Council to the Assembly, an example was given of what was termed "the extreme inaccuracy" of the report which H and Ellsworth presented to the Continental Congress. See footnote 4, fourth and fifth paragraphs.

15. Major General Arthur St. Clair. See "Report of a Committee Appointed to Confer with the Supreme Executive Council of Pennsylvania on the Mutiny," June 24, 1783, note 4.

the mutineers—that his access to them was easy—that the fact in question was a matter of immediate notoriety—that two hours were abundant time for a thing of that nature to be conveyed from the barracks to General St Clairs quarters and that one of the Committee had *actually seen* and obtained the intelligence from him, a little time before the interview with the Council commenced. It is much more extraordinary that the Council should have been apprized of it so late than that the Committee should have known it so early. As to the memory of the Council it is unfortunate it should have been so fallible as it is said to have been; but I would rather suppose in the quick succession of circumstances, the matter had escaped their recollection than that my minutes as well as my memory should have deceived me. I will recollect also that Your Excellency when it was mentioned acknowleged that it rather contradicted the pacific appearance which the conduct of the troops in other respects wore.

These are the essential differences in point of fact between the report of the Committee and the message of council. The whole complexion indeed of the one materially varies from the other, but the most common observer must have noticed how different an aspect the same facts will bear differently dressed and arranged. It was to avoid this we proposed to reduce them to writing; but as this has not been done, spectators must judge from the situation of the parties and the course of the transactions which side has given the justest relation.

I cannot however forbear remarking that I see expressions of civility on the part of the Committee making a figure in the message very different from their genuine intention; being introduced in a manner that gives them the air of concessions in favour of the conduct of the Council. Your Excellency will certainly recollect that the Committee were very remote from a concurrence in sentiment with the Council; and though they did not presume to judge of the disposition of the citizens strongly urged the expedience and necessity of calling out the Militia and facility of employing them with success against an unofficered and disorderly body of mutinous soldiers. It is true also that they acknowleged the candour with which the Council exposed to them what they deemed the temper of their citi⟨zens⟩ and their own difficulties and embarrassments which were no doubt delineated with great energy of language and display of circumstances. But they certainly never admitted the candour of refusing an answer in writing which was a part of the *business* transacted with the Council; nor did they *withdraw* without giving an intelligible intimation of their sense of this proceeding.

I was also surprised to see any part of the private and confidential conversation I had with your Excellency ushered into the message from the council and moulded into such a shape as to imply by an obvious construction an approbation of their reasons. Your Excellency will admit the following state of this transaction to be a just one.[16]

I waited upon the Council to correct a piece of information I had given them respecting ammunition; but even this is mistated, as will be seen by my minutes.[17] Having done this my official business ended when I was taken aside by Your Excellency and a conversation passed in declared confidence. You informed me that a meeting of the Militia officers was then holding and in consultation with the Council about eventual measures (in consequence as I conjectured of a communication to you the preceding evening from the delegates of the state of the intention of Congress to remove from the city in case they did not receive satisfactory assurances of support) you added that you hoped nothing would be precipitated; but that proper allowances would be made for the situation of the Council.

I understood your observation, with reference to the departure of Congress, and replied to this effect—that I viewed the departure of

16. The address of the Supreme Executive Council of Pennsylvania stated that in a conference on June 22 between the Council and a committee of Congress the committee maintained that any quantity of ammunition could be supplied the state in fifteen minutes.

On June 24, according to the Council report, one of the committee of Congress members came to the Council chamber and

". . . informed the President, that he thought himself bound to give him notice of a great mistake that had been committed by the person, from whom he had received his intelligence concerning the ammunition, that person having, in a late conversation, told him there were not more than 200 musquet cartridges to be found. The President took this opportunity of again desiring, that Council might not be precipitated into measures not adapted to the present circumstances; that the soldiers had now been quiet for *three* days, and we expected *every hour* to hear from their committee. The gentleman said, that no report in writing had yet been made to Congress, and that for his part he should be for taking some time to make it, for the reasons that had been mentioned." (*The Pennsylvania Gazette*, September 24, 1783.)

17. H's minutes have not been found, and this event is not mentioned in the report. See note 11.

Congress as a delicate measure, including consequences important to the national character abroad and critical with respect to the state of Pensylvania and in particular the city of Philadelphia. That the triumph of a handful of mutinous soldiers permitted in a place which is considered as the capital of America to surround and in fact imprison Congress without the least effort on the part of the citizens to uphold their dignity and authority, so as to oblige them to move from the place which had been their residence during the revolution, would it was to be feared be viewed at a distance as a general disaffection of the citizens to the fœderal government, might discredit its negotiations and affect the national interests. That at home it might give a deep wound to the reputation of Pensylvania might draw upon it the resentments of the other states and sow discord between Congress and the state. That the removal of Congress would probably bring the affair to a crisis and by convincing the mutineers that extremities were intended, would either intimidate them into a submission or determine them to immediate excesses. That impressed with these considerations, and still hoping, notwithstanding some appearances to the contrary, that the mutineers might be sincere in their professions of submission, or that the Council on further examination would find it in their power to act with vigour, I had declined giving my assent to a report in writing which would necessarily be followed by the departure of Congress. That though the Committee had no discretion by the powers under which they acted, but were bound by the tenor of their instructions, the moment they did not receive, "satisfactory assurances of prompt and adequate exertions on the part of the state for supporting the public authority" to advise the adjournment of Congress to Trenton or Princeton—and I therefore considered the delay of this advice as at their extreme peril, yet as to myself, I should persist in it 'till the result of the present consultation with the Militia officers or 'till some new circumstance should turn up to explain the designs of the mutineers. That in persuing this line of conduct, I should counteract the sense of some Gentlemen whose feelings upon the occasion were keen and the opinions of others who thought the situation of Congress under the existing circumstances extremely awkward precarious and unjustifiable to their constituents.

Your Excellency approved my intention, wished for time and

promised if any new resolution should be taken to give me immediate notice of it.

The Meeting of the Militia officers dissolved.[18] I heard nothing from Your Excellency. General St Clair about two in the afternoon informed the Committee that the officers appointed by the Soldiers to manage their business had in the first instance refused to give him an account of their transactions—that which was only extracted from them by a peremptory demand. He mentioned to us the instructions they had received from the soldiers which contained faint and affected concessions mixed with new and inadmissible claims. The whole affair wore the complexion of collusion between the officers of the Committee and the soldiery and of a mere amusement on their part 'till they could [19] gain fresh strength and execute their project whatever it might be with greater advantage.

This behaviour of the officers gave the affair a new and more serious aspect and overcame my opposition to the report. Mr. Peters [20] on hearing the relation of General St Clair declared at once that he thought the Committee had then no alternative; at least what he said was understood in this sense by General St Clair, Mr Elseworth and myself. If I am not much mistaken General St Clair also expressed his opinion that Congress were unsafe in the city.

The ideas I suggested to Your Excellency in the conversation I have mentioned, were substantially expressed to several members of Congress as the motives of my delay—and particularly I recollect to Mr. Maddison, with these observations in addition. That though I was fully convinced Congress under an immediate view of circumstances, would in reality be justified in withdrawing from a place where such an outrage to government had been with impunity perpetrated by a body of armed mutineers, still for several days in complete command of the city and where either the feebleness of public councils or the indisposition of the citizens afforded no assurance of protection and support; yet as the opinions of men would be governed by events, and as the most probable event was that the

18. The Pennsylvania Supreme Executive Council met with the militia officers in the Philadelphia area on the morning of June 24.

19. In MS "good."

20. Richard Peters, along with H and Oliver Ellsworth, was a member of the committee appointed on June 19 to take effective measures to deal with the mutiny.

removal of Congress, announcing decisive measures of coertion to the soldiery would awe them into submission, there was great danger that the reputation of Congress would suffer by the easy termination of the business, and that they would be accused of levity timidity or rashness.

Though not within the scope of my original intention I will indulge a few additional reflections on this subject.

I am sensible, that the Council in some respects stand upon advantageous ground in this discussion. Congress left the city because they had no forces at hand, no jurisdiction over the Militia and no assurances of effectual support from those who had. The Council, as the Executive of the state, were necessitated to remain on the spot. Soon after Congress removed, the Mutineers were deserted by their leaders and surrendered at discretion.

The Multitude will be very apt to conclude that the affair was of triffling consequence that it vanished under its own insignificance— that Congress took up the matter in too high a tone of authority— that they discovered a prudish nicety and irritability about their own dignity—that the Council were more temperate more humane and possessed of greater foresight.

The byass in favour of an injured army—the propensity of the human mind to lean to the speciousness of professed humanity rather than to the necessary harshness of authority—the vague and imperfect notions of what is due to public authority in an infant popular government—and the insinuating plausibility of a well constructed *message* will all contribute to that conclusion.

But let us suppose an impartial man of sense well acquainted with facts to form an argument upon the subject. It appears to me he might naturally fall into this train of combination.

It is a well known fact that from the necessities of the war or the delinquencies of the several states Congress were not enabled to comply with their engagements to the army, which after a glorious and successful struggle for their country, much suffering, exemplary patience and signal desert, they were compelled by the irresistible dictates of an empty treasury and a ruined credit to disband, after having given strong indications of their discontent and resentment of the public neglect. A large part of the army suffer themselves to be patiently dismissed; a particular corps of four or five hundred men stationed in the place where Congress reside, refuse to accept their discharges but on certain specified conditions. They even go further and stimulated by their injuries, or encouraged and misled by designing persons are emboldened to send a threatening message to Congress declaring to them that unless they would do them justice immediately, they would find means of redress for themselves. Measures are indirectly taken to appease this disorder and give the discontented soldiers as much satisfaction as the situation of things will permit. Shortly after accounts are received that another corps at   [21] miles distance have also mutinied, and that a part of them to the number of about Eighty men are on their march to join those who had already discovered so refractory a disposition. A Committee of Congress is immediately appointed to confer with the Executive of the State on the measures proper to be persued in this exigency. That Committee in the first instance suggests to the Council the expedience of calling out a body of Militia to intercept the detachment of mutineers on its march and represent the danger of the progress of the spirit of mutiny and of future outrages should those on their march be suffered without molestation to join a more numerous corps in the same temper with themselves. The Council urge a variety of difficulties: the shortness of the time to collect the Militia, before the mutineers would arrive, the reluctance with which the citizens would obey a call against men whom they consider as meritorious and injured and the like. The Committee perceiving the unwillingness of the Council to employ the Militia desist from pressing and recur to expedients. The day after the mutineers march in triumph into the city and unite themselves with those who are already there; and the following day the whole body assemble in arms throw off all obedience to their officers and in open defiance of government march to the place which is the usual seat of Congress and the Council of the state, while both are actually sitting, surround it with guards and send a message to the council, demanding authority to appoint themselves, officers to command them, with absolute discretion to take such measures as those officers should think proper to redress their grievances; accompanied with a threat that if there was not a compliance in twenty minutes, they would let

21. Space left blank in MS. H is referring to the soldiers from Lancaster, Pennsylvania.

in an injured soldiery upon them and abide the consequence. The members of Congress who were at the time assembled request General St Clair, who happened to be present, to take such measures as he should judge expedient without committing the honor of government to divert the storm and induce the troops to return to their quarters without perpetrating any acts of violence. General St Clair in concert with the Council grants the mutineers permission to elect out of officers then or formerly in commission such as they should confide in to represent their grievances to the Council, with a promise that the Council would confer with the persons elected for that purpose. Having obtained this promise the mutineers return to their quarters, in military parade, and continue in open defiance of government.

The concession made was a happy compromise between an attention to dignity and a prudent regard to safety. Men who had dared to carry their insolence to such an extreme and who saw no opposition to their outrages were not to be expected to retreat without an appearance at least of gratifying their demands. The slightest accident was sufficient to prompt men in such a temper and situation to tragical excesses.

But however it might become the delicacy of government not to depart from the promise it had given, it was its duty to provide effectually against a repetition of such outrages and to put itself in a situation to give instead of receiving the law; and to manifest that its compliance was not the effect of necessity but of choice.

This was not to be considered as the disorderly riot of an unarmed mob but as the deliberate mutiny of an incensed soldiery carried to the utmost point of outrage short of assassination. The licentiousness of an army is to be dreaded in every government; but in a republic it is more particularly to be restrained, and when directed against the civil authority to be checked with energy and punished with severity. The merits and sufferings of the troops might be a proper motive for mitigating punishment when it was in the power of the government to inflict it—but it was no reason for relaxing in the measures necessary to arrive at that situation. Its authority was first to be vindicated and then its clemency to be displayed.

The rights of government are as essential to be defended as the rights of individuals. The security of the one is inseparable from that of the other. And indeed in every new government, especially of the popular kind the great danger is that public authority will not be sufficiently respected.

But upon this occasion there were more particular reasons for decision.

Congress knew there were within two or three days march of the city a more considerable body of the same corps part of which had mutinied and come to town and had been the chief actors in the late disorder—that those men had with difficulty been kept by the exertions of their officers from joining the insurgents in the first instance—that there was another corps in their neighbourhood which a little time before had also discovered symptoms of mutiny—that a considerable part of the same line which were in mutiny in town was every moment expected to arrive from the Southward, and there was the greatest reason to conclude would be infected with the same spirit on their arrival, as had presently happened in the case of a small detachment which had joined a few days before—that there were besides large numbers of disbanded soldiers scattered through the country in want and who had not yet had time to settle down to any occupation and exchange their military for private habits—that some of these were really coming in and adding themselves to the revolters—that an extensive accession of strength might be gained from these different quarters—and that there were all the sympathies of like common distresses and resentments to bring them together and to unite them in one cause. The partial success of those who had already made an experiment would have been a strong encouragement to others—the rather as the whole line had formerly mutinied not only with impunity but with advantage to themselves.

In this state of things decision was most compatible with the safety of the community as well as the dignity of government. Though no general convulsion might be to be apprehended serious mischiefs might attend the progress of the disorder. Indeed it would have been meanness to have negotiated and temporised with an armed banditti of four or five hundred men, who in any other situation than surrounding a defenceless senate could only become formidable by being feared. This was not an insurrection of a whole people—it was not an army with their officers at their head demanding the justice of their country—either of which might have made caution and concession respectable. It was a handful of mutinous soldiers, who had equally violated the laws of discipline as the rights of public authority.

Congress therefore wisely resolve that "it is necessary that effectual measures be immediately taken for supporting the public authority" and call upon the state in which they reside for the assistance of its militia at the same time that they send orders for the march of a body of regular forces as an eventual resource.

There was a propriety in calling for the aid of the Militia in the first place, for different reasons. Civil government may always with more peculiar propriety resort to the aid of the citizens to repel military insults, or encroachments. Tis there it ought to be supposed where it may seek its surest dependence especially in a democracy, which is the creature of the people. The citizens of each state are in an aggregate light the citizens of the United states and bound as much to support the representatives of the whole as their own immediate representatives. The insult was not to Congress personally it was to the government to public authority in general; and was very properly put upon that footing. The regular forces which Congress could command were at a great distance, and could not but in a length of time be brought to effecuate their purpose. The disorder continued to exist on the spot where they were, was likely to increase by delay and might be productive of sudden and mischievous effects by being neglected. The city and the bank were in immediate danger of being rifled and perhaps of suffering other calamities. The citizens therefore were the proper persons to make the first exertion.

The objection that these were not the objects of the care of Congress can only serve to mislead the vulgar. The peace and safety of the place which was the immediate residence of Congress *endangered too by the troops of the United States* demanded their interposition. The President of the State of Pensylvania was himself of this opinion having declared to a member of that body that as their troops were the offenders it was proper for them to declare the necessity of calling out the Militia as a previous step to its being done.

Nor is there more weight in the supposition that the danger was inconsiderable and that from the pacific appearances of the troops it was to be expected the disorder would subside of itself. The facts were that the troops still continued in a state of mutiny—had made no submissions—nor offered any—and that they affected to negotiate with their arms in their hands. A band of mutinous soldiers in such a situation uncontrouled and elated [by] their own power was not to be trusted. The most sudden vicissitudes and contradictory changes were to be expected; and a fit of intoxication was sufficient at any moment with men who had already gone such lengths to make the city a scene of plunder and massacre. It was the height of rashness to leave the city exposed to the bare possibility of such mischiefs.

The only question in this view is whether there was greater danger to the city in attempting their reduction by force than in endeavouring by palliatives to bring them to a sense of duty. It has been urged and appeared to have operated strongly upon the minds of the Council, (Your Excellency will recollect that in our private conversation, you urged this consideration and appealed to my military experience & that I made substantially the observations which follow) that the soldiers being already embodied accustomed to arms and ready to act at a moments warning it would be extremely hazardous to attempt to collect the citizens to subdue them as the mutineers might have taken advantage of the first confusions incident to the measure to do a great deal of mischief before the Militia could have assembled in equal or superior force.

It is not to be denied but that a small body of disciplined troops headed and led by their officers with a plan of conduct could have effected a great deal in similar circumstances; but it is equally certain that nothing can be more contemptible than a body of men used to be commanded and to obey when deprived of the example and direction of their officers. They are infinitely less to be dreaded than an equal number of men who have never been broken to command, nor exchanged their natural courage for that artificial kind which is the effect of discipline and habit. Soldiers transfer their confidence from themselves to their officers, face danger by the force of example the dread of punishment and the sense of necessity. Take away these inducements and leave them to themselves they are no longer resolute than 'till they are opposed.

In the present case it was to be relied upon that the appearance of opposition would instantly bring the mutineers to a sense of their insignificance and to submission. Conscious of their weakness from the smallness of their numbers—in a populous city and in the midst of a populous country—awed by the consequences of resisting government by arms, and confounded by the want of proper leaders and proper direction, the common soldiers would have thought of nothing but making their peace by the sacrifice of those who had been the authors of their misconduct.

The idea therefore of coertion was the safest and most prudent, for more was to be apprehended from leaving them to their own passions than from attempting to controul them by force. It will be seen by and by how far the events justly appreciated corresponded with this reasoning.

Congress were not only right in adopting measures of coertion; but they were also right in resolving to change their situation if proper exertions were not made by the particular government and citizens of the place where they resided. The want of such exertions would evince some defect, no matter where, that would prove they ought to have no confidence in their situation. They were to all intents and purposes in the power of a lawless armed banditti enraged whether justly or not against them. However they might have had a right to expose their own persons to insult and outrage, they had no right to expose the character of representative, or the dignity of the states they represented or of the Union. It was plain they could not with propriety in such a state of things proceed in their deliberations where they were and it was right they should repair to a place where they could do it. It was far from impossible that the mutineers might have been induced to seize their persons as hostages for their own security as well as with a hope of extorting concessions. Had such an event taken place the whole country would have exclaimed, why did not Congress withdraw from a place where they found they could not be assured of support— where the government was so feeble or the citizens so indisposed as to suffer three or four hundred mutinous soldiers to violate with impunity the authority of the United States and of their own state?

When they resolved to depart on the want of adequate exertions, they had reason to doubt their being made from the disinclination shown by the Council to call out the militia in the first instance; and when they did actually depart they were informed by the Council that the efforts of the citizens were not to be looked for even from a repetition of the outrage which had already happened and it was to be doubted what measure of outrage would produce them. They had also convincing proof that the mutiny was more serious than it had even at first appeared by the participation of some of the officers.

To throw the blame of harshness and precipitancy upon Congress it is said that their dignity was only *accidentally* and *undesignedly* offended.[22] Much stress has been laid upon the message from the soldiery being directed to the Council and not to them. All this however is very immaterial to the real merits of the question. Whatever might have been the first intention of the mutineers in this particular act whether it proceeded from artifice or confusion of ideas, the indignity to Congress was the same. They knew that Congress customarily held their deliberations at the state house; and if it even be admitted that they knew saturday to be a day of usual recess, which perhaps is not altogether probable, when they came to the place they saw and knew Congress to be assembled there. They did not desist in consequence of this; but proceeded to station their guards and execute their purposes. Members of Congress went out to them—remonstrated with them—represented the danger of their proceedings to themselves and desired them to withdraw, but they persisted until they obtained what they supposed a part of their object. A majority of the same persons had some days before sent a message almost equally exceptionable to Congress; and at the time they scarcely spoke of any other body than Congress; who indeed may naturally be supposed to have been the main object of their resentments: for Congress having always appeared to the soldiery to be [the] body who contracted with them and who had broken faith with them. It is not to be supposed they were capable of investigating the remote causes of the failures so as to transfer the odium from Congress to the state.

But the substantial thing to be considered in this question is the violation of public authority. It cannot be disputed that the mutiny of troops is a violation of that authority to which they owe obedi-

22. Dickinson wrote that the Supreme Executive Council "could not bear to avenge the dignity of Congress, *accidentally* and *undesignedly* offended, by shedding the blood of men whom they considered as having fought and suffered for the *American* cause" (*The Pennsylvania Gazette*, September 24, 1783).

SEPTEMBER 1783   457

ence. This was in the present case aggravated to a high degree of atrociousness by the gross insult to the government of Pensylvania, in the face of Congress and in defiance of their displeasure. It was further aggravated by continuing in that condition for a series of time.

The reasons have been assigned that made it incumbent upon Congress to interpose; and when they called upon the state of Pensylvania not only to vindicate its own rights but to support their authority—the declining a compliance was a breach of the confederation and of the duty which the state of Pensylvania owed to the United States. The best apology for the government of Pensylvania in this case is that they could not command the services of their citizens. But so improper a disposition in the citizens if admitted must operate as an additional justification to Congress in their removal.

The subsequent events justly appreciated illustrate the propriety of their conduct. The mutineers did not make voluntary submissions in consequence of negotiation persuasion or conviction. They did not submit 'till after Congress had left the city publishing their intentions of coertion, 'till after there had been an *actual call* upon the Militia—till their leaders and instigators alarmed by the approach of force and the fear of being betrayed by the men fled. They were reduced by coertion not overcome by mildness. It appears too that while they were professing repentance and a return to their duty, they were tampering with the troops at York Town and Lancaster to increase their strength—and that two officers at least were concerned in the mutiny, who by their letters since, have con⟨fessed⟩ that some project of importance was in contemplation.

The call for the militia was made the day after it had been pronounced ineligible by the Council.[23] There could have been little change in that time either in the temper or preparation of the citizens. The truth is that the departure of Congress brought the matter to a crisis and that the Council were compelled by necessity to do what they ought to have done before through choice.

It is to be lamented that they did not by an earlier decision, prevent

23. When the Supreme Executive Council learned, on June 24, that the soldiers were planning an attack on the Bank of North America, it ordered that a guard be placed there. On June 25, fearing that the mutinous troops would engage in violence, the Council finally ordered the state militia into service.

the necessity of Congress taking a step which may have many disagreeable consequences. They then would [24]

24. The remainder of the MS is missing. On the last page of the MS there
are several notes in the writing of Colonel Timothy Pickering and signed "T.P."

To James Duane

Albany 26 Sepr. 1783

Dr. Sir,

I received last night your letter of the 8th. instant,[1] accompanied
by one from Mr. L'hommedieu and yourself to Mr. Floyd and myself.[2] I shall in consequence write to the Governor on the subject;
though if I recollect right, I did in an official letter to him mention
all that I can now say though perhaps at greater length—to wit that
the resolutions of the senate & Assembly were committed for consideration and that it appeared to be the prevailing opinion of
Congress to postpone a determination on them 'till they had settled
a permanent plan for a peace establishment, comprehending of course
a provision for the garrison in this state; making in the mean time
temporary provision out of the troops already in Continental pay
and service. Be pleased to communicate this to Mr. L'Hommedieu
with my compliments.

Perceiving your uneasiness lest any accident should happen to Mr
Carter's[3] papers if left, I did as you proposed, force open the box
and took them out, afterwards closing it again; and communicated
my having done it to you in Congress; but you were so much engaged at the time that it appears it did not remain in your memory.

General Schuyler & the ladies present their compliments.

I am Dr Sir   Yr. affectionate & Humble servt   A Hamilton

I take the liberty to inclose a letter to Mrs. J Morris [4] for more safe
conveyance; which I beg the favour of you to forward.

The Honble Mr. Duane

ALS, New-York Historical Society, New York City.
 1. Letter not found.
 2. The letter from Duane and Ezra L'Hommedieu to H and William Floyd
is dated September 1, 1783. The controversy over whether the frontier posts
should be garrisoned by state or Continental troops can be followed in the documents listed in note 1 of that letter.

3. John Carter (John B. Church).
4. Presumably Mrs. Jacob Morris of Philadelphia whose husband was deputy quartermaster of the Continental Army during the American Revolution.

From John Jay

Passy [France] 28 Septr. 1783

Dear Sir:

Mr. Carter [1] lately delivered to me your friendly letter of the 25 July last. You was always of the Number of those whom I esteemed, and your Correspondence would have been both interesting & agreable.

I had heard of your marriage, and it gave me Pleasure, as well because it added to your Happiness, as because it tended to fix your Residence in a State of which I long wished you to be and remain a citizen.

The Character and Talents of Delegates to Congress daily becomes more and more important, and I regret your declining that appointment at this interesting Period. Respect however is due to the Considerations which influence You; but as they do not oppose your accepting a Place in the Legislature, I hope the Public will still continue to derive advantage from your Services. Much remains to be done, and Labourers do not abound.

I am happy to hear that the Terms of Peace, and the Conduct of your Negociat⟨ions⟩ give general Satisfaction—But there are some of our Countrymen it seems who are not content, and that too with an article which I thought to be very unexceptionable, vizt. the one ascertaining our Boundaries. Perhaps those Gentlemen are Latitudinarians.

The american news papers for some months past contain advices which do us Harm. Violencies and associations against the Tories pay an ill compliment to Government and impeach our good Faith in the opinions of some, and our magnanimity in the opinion of many. Our Reputation also suffers from the apparent Reluctance to [taxes] [2] and the Ease with which we incur Debts without providing for their Payment. The Complaints of the army—The Jealousies respecting Congress—the Circumstances which induced their leaving Philadelphia— [3] and the too little appearance of a national Spirit pervading uniting and invigorating the Confederacy, are considered as omens which portend the Diminution of our Respectability, Power and Felicity. I hope that as the wheel turns round other & better Indications will soon appear. I am persuaded that america possesses too much wisdom and virtue, to permit her brilliant Prospects to fade away for want of either.

The Tories are almost as much pitied in these Countries, as they are execrated in our's. An undue Degree of Severity towards them would therefore be impolitic as well as unjustifiable: They who incline to involve that whole Class of Men in indiscriminate Punishment and Ruin, certainly carry the Matter too far—it would be an Instance of unnecessary Rigour and unmanly Revenge without a parallel except in the annals of religious Rage in Times of Bigotry and Blindness. What does it signify where nine tenths of these People are buried? I would rather see the Sweat of their Brows fertilize our Fields, than those of our Neighbours which it would certainly water those Seeds of Hatred, in [4]

Victory and Peace should in my opinion be followed by Clemency, Moderation and Benevolence; & we should be careful not to sully the Glory of the Revolution by licenciousness and Cruelty. These are my Sentiments, & however unpopular they may be, I have not the least Desire to conceal or disguise them.

Mr. & Mrs. Carter are well, and our Endeavours shall not be wanting to render Paris agreable to them.

Be pleased to present our best Compliments to Mrs Hamilton, and believe me to be with great Regard & Esteem   Dear Sir   Your most obt. & hble servt.   John Jay

Col. A. Hamilton

ALS, Hamilton Papers, Library of Congress.
   1. John Carter (John B. Church).
   2. This word was taken from *JCHW*, I, 401.
   3. Jay was referring to the removal of Congress from Philadelphia to Princeton in June, 1783, because of the mutiny of the Pennsylvania troops. See "Report of a Committee Appointed to Confer with the Supreme Executive Council of Pennsylvania on the Mutiny," June 24, 1783.
   4. Approximately four lines of MS are obliterated at this point.

To George Washington

[Albany, September 30, 1783]

Sir

I think I may address the subject of this letter to Your Excellency with more propriety than to any other person, as it is purely of a military nature, as you are best acquainted with my services as an officer, and as you are now engaged in assisting to form the arrangements for the future peace establishment.

Your Excellency knows that in March 82, I relinquished all claim to any future compensation for my services, either during the residue of the war, or after its conclusion—simply retaining my rank.[1] On this foundation I build a hope that I may be permitted to preserve my rank, in the peace establishment, without emoluments and un-attached to any corps—as an honorary reward for the time I have devoted to the public. As I may hereafter travel I may find it an agreeable circumstance to appear in the character I have supported in the revolution.

I rest my claim solely on the sacrifice I have made; because I have no reason to believe that my services have appeared of any value to Congress—as they declined giving them any marks of their notice, on an occasion, which appeared to my friends to intitle me to it, as well by the common practice of sovereigns as by the particular practice of this country in repeated instances.

Your Excellency will recollect, that it was my lot at York Town to command as senior officer a successful attack upon one of the enemy's redoubts, that the officer who acted in a similar capacity in another attack made at the same time, by the French troops has been handsomely distinguished in consequence of it by the government to which he belongs,[2] and that there are several examples among us where Congress have bestowed honors upon actions, perhaps not more useful nor apparently more hazardous.

These observations are inapplicable to the present Congress, further than as they may possibly furnish an additional motive to a compliance with my wish.

The only thing I ask of Your Excellency is that my application may come into view in the course of the consultations on the peace establishment.[3]

I have the honor to be With sincere esteem   Your Excellency's Most Obed servant   Alex Hamilton

Albany Sepr. 30th. 1783
His Excelly General Washington

ALS, Hamilton Papers, Library of Congress; copy, Hamilton Papers, Library of Congress.

1. See the two letters which H wrote to Washington on March 1, 1782.

2. The officer who commanded the attack on the other enemy redoubt was Antoine Charles du Houx, Baron de Vioménil. Upon his return to France, Vioménil had been made commander of the Order of Saint-Louis and a lieutenant general.

3. For an explanation of congressional consideration of a peace establishment, see "Report on a Military Peace Establishment," June 18, 1783, note 1. The plan for a peace establishment, drafted by H, was introduced in Congress on June 18, 1783, considered by a committee for four months, and reintroduced on October 23. It was not accepted by Congress.

To George Washington [1]

[Albany, September 30, 1783]

Dr. Sir

As I flatter myself I may indulge a consciousness that my services have been of some value to the public, at least enough to merit the small compensation I wish, I will make no apology to your Excellency for conveying through you that wish to Congress. You are able to inform them if they wish information, in what degree I may have been useful, and I have intire confidence that you will do me justice.

In a letter which I wrote to you several months ago I intimated that it might be in your power to contribute to the establishment of our Fœderal union upon a more solid basis. I have never since explained myself.[2] At the time I was in hopes Congress might have been induced to take a decisive ground—to inform their constituents of the imperfections of the present system and of the impossibility of conducting the public affairs with honor to themselves and advantage to the community with powers so disproportioned to their responsibility; and having done this in a full and forcible manner, to adjourn the moment the definitive treaty was ratified. In retiring at the same juncture I wished you in a solemn manner to declare to the people your intended retreat from public concerns, your opinion of the present government and of the absolute necessity of a change.

Before I left Congress I dispaired of the first and your circular letter to the states had anticipated the last.[3] I trust it will not be without effect though I am persuaded it would have had more combined with what I have mentioned. At all events, without compliment Sir, It will do you honor with the sensible and well meaning; and ultimately it is to be hoped with the people at large—when the present epidemic phrenzy has subsided.

I am Dr. Sir with sincere esteem   Your obedient serv

Alex Hamilton

Mrs. Hamilton presents her compliments to Mrs. Washington
Sepr. 30
I beg the favour of Your Excellency to forward the inclosed to General Greene [4]

General Washington

ALS, George Washington Papers, Library of Congress; copy, Hamilton Papers, Library of Congress.

1. The preceding letter to Washington, also dated September 30, probably was enclosed in this letter. H presumably intended his first letter as a public communication, his second as a private communication. He apparently wished Washington to refer the public letter to Congress.

2. H is probably referring to his letter of March 24, 1783, in which he congratulated Washington on the conclusion of the war, expressed his conviction that "it now only remains to make solid establishments within to perpetuate our union," and concluded that Washington's help would be needed to preserve the union of the states.

3. Washington's circular to the states, dated June 8, 1783, is in *GW*, XXVI, 483–96.

4. See H to Major General Nathanael Greene, October 1, 1783.

To Major General Nathanael Greene

[Albany, October 1, 1783]

By this time I presume My Dear General you have returned to your ancient residence. I had the pleasure of seeing Mrs. Greene at New York; and was induced by her to hope you would be prevailed upon to become a fellow citizen of ours. I know you have long had a partiality for our state; but I have been afraid, and have not yet banished my apprehensions, that your new Mistress would detach you from your old. I could not indeed very much blame your inconstancy when I consider how much South Carolina has done to attach you to her. Yet now you have revisited the ruddy and health-teeming countenance of our Northern lass, I am not without expectation that you may prefer it to the palefaced charms of the one you have left behind. I know besides that she will have a powerful advocate in one that will have a powerful influence with you.[1]

Mr. Carter[2] sometime before he left this informed me that he had sent a Bond of Mr. Kinlocks to you to be renewed by him—and which was to be transmitted to me by you. I have some confused idea that he afterwards mentioned something to me on the subject, which however I have forgotten. But I shall be glad to receive a line from you to inform me whether the Bond has been renewed or not and what has been done with it.[3]

Let me assure you that no one interests himself more warmly in your health and happiness than myself, and request that you will present my affectionate compliments to Mrs. Greene. Mrs. Hamilton joins hers to you both   Dr Sir   Yr. affect & Obed ser   A Hamilton

Albany October 1st 1783
General Greene

ALS, Hamilton Papers, Library of Congress.
   1. In 1783 Greene, after a visit to his former home in Coventry, Rhode Island, had returned to South Carolina where he owned property.
   2. John B. Church.
   3. For information on this bond see H to Greene, June 10, 1783.

To George Clinton

Albany Octr. 3d. 1783

Sir

I have lately received from Messrs. Duane and Lhommedieu an extract of a letter from Your Excellency to the Delegates of the 23d. of August last requesting "a particular detail of the motives which influenced the determination of Congress" respecting the application of the legislature to have their state troops released from Continental pay, for the purpose of garrisoning the frontier posts.[1]

In my letters to Your Excellency of the 1st of June and 27th of July, which were intended to be official, I summarily informed you that Congress had made temporary provision for garrisoning the frontier posts and that a plan was under deliberation relative to a peace establishment, which would of course embrace that object permanently—that such temporary provision being made at the common expence, and a general plan being under consideration for the future, I had declined pressing a compliance with the application of the Legislature, conceiving it to be more for the interest of the state that the expence should be jointly borne than that it should fall exclusively upon itself.

I did not enter into a more full detail upon the subject because the business continued to the time I left Congress in an undecided state and it was impossible to judge what views would finally prevail. The concurrent resolutions of the two houses had been immediately on their receipt referred to a Committee appointed to report on a peace establishment who had suspended their report on these resolutions 'till it should appear, what would be the fate of a general plan, which had been submitted.[2]

As to the motives that influenced Congress in making the provision they did make, rather than immediately assenting to the application of the state—as far as I was able to collect them they were these. The opinions of many were unsettled as to the most eligible mode of providing for the security of the frontiers, consistent with the constitution, as well with respect to the general policy of the union, as to considerations of justice to those states, whose frontiers were more immediately exposed. A considerable part of the house ap-

ADfS, Hamilton Papers, Library of Congress.

1. Clinton wanted information on the congressional resolution of May 12, 1783 (see "Report on the Garrisoning of Frontier Posts by Continental Troops," of that date), which provided that posts evacuated by the British be garrisoned by Continental troops who had enlisted for three years. In addition to the letters from H to Clinton which are referred to in the second paragraph of this letter, see Clinton to H and William Floyd, April 1, 1783; James Duane and Ezra L'Hommedieu to H and Floyd, September 1, 1783; and H to Duane, September 26, 1783.

2. The concurrent resolutions were an enclosure in Clinton's letter of April 1, 1783, to H and Floyd. For information on the committee on the peace establishment, see "Report on a Military Peace Establishment," June 18, 1783.

peared to think, from reasons of a very cogent nature, that the well being of the Union required a fœderal provision for the security of the different parts and that it would be a great hardship to individual states peculiarly circumstanced to throw the whole burthen of expence upon them by recurring to separate provisions in a matter the benefit of which would be immediately shared by their neighbours & ultimately by the Union at large—that indeed it was not probable particular states would be either able or *upon experiment,* willing to make competent provision at their separate expence and that the principle might eventually excite jealousies between the states unfriendly to the common tranquillity.

I freely confess I was one who held this opinion.

Questions naturally arose as to the true construction of the articles of confederation upon this head—questions as delicate as interesting and as difficult of solution.[3] On one hand it was doubted whether Congress were authorised by the confederation to proceed upon the idea of a fœderal provision—on the other it was perceived that such a contrary construction would be dangerous to the union, including among other inconveniences, this consequence, that the United States in Congress, cannot raise a single regiment, or equip a single ship for the general defence 'till after a declaration of war or an actual commencement of hostilities.

In this dilemma, on an important constitutional question, other urgent matters depending before Congress and the advanced season requiring a determination upon the mode of securing the Western posts in case of a surrender this fall, all sides of the house concurred in making a temporary provision in the manner which has been communicated.

My apprehension of the views of the legislature was simply this, that looking forward to a surrender of the posts and conceiving from some expressions in the articles of confederation, that separate provision was to be made for the frontier garrisons, they had thought it expedient to apply the troops already on foot to that purpose and to propose to Congress to give their sanction to it.

3. Article 6 of the Articles of Confederation provided: "Nor shall any body of forces be kept up by any State, in time of peace, except such number only as, in the judgment of the United States, in Congress assembled, shall be deemed requisite to garrison the forts necessary for the defence of such State." As H suggested, the Articles of Confederation contained no explicit prohibition of a Continental peace establishment.

Under this apprehension, reflecting besides that those troops were engaged only for a short period, upon a very improper establishment to continue, on account of the enormous pay to the private men, and that the expence which is now shared by all and which would have fallen solely upon the state, had the application been complied with—would probably be at the rate of nearly Eighty thousand dollars per annum, a considerable sum for the state in its present situation. I acknowlege to your Excellency that I saw with pleasure rather than regret, the turn which the affair took. I shall be sorry however if it has contravened the intentions of the legislature.

I will take the liberty to add upon this occasion, that it has always appeard to me of a real importance to this state in particular, as well as to the Union in general that Fœderal rather than state provision should be made for the defence of every part of the confederacy in peace as well as in war. Without entering into arguments of general policy, it will be sufficient to observe that this state is in all respects *critically situated*. Its relative position shape and intersections viewed on the map strongly speak this language—strengthen the confederation—Give it exclusively the power of the sword. Let each state have no forces but its Militia.

As a question of mere œconomy the following considerations deserve great weight: The North River facilitates attacks by sea and by land, and besides the frontier forts all military men are of opinion that a strong post should be maintained at West Point or some other position on the lower part of the River. If Canada is well governed it may become well peopled and by inhabitants attached to its government. The British Nation while it preserves the idea of retaining possession of that Country may be expected to keep on foot there a large force. The position of that force either for defence or offence will necessarily be such as will afford a prompt and easy access to us. Our precautions for defence must be proportioned to their means of annoying us; and we may hereafter find it indispensable to increase our frontier garrisons. The present charge of a competent force in that quarter thrown additionally into the scale of those contributions which we must make to the payment of the public debt and to other objects of general expence, if the Union lasts, would I fear enlarge our burthen beyond our ability: that charge hereafter increased as it may be would be oppressively felt by people. It includes not only the expence of paying and subsisting the necessary number of troops, but of keeping the fortifications in repair probably of creating others and of furnishing the requisite supplies of military stores.

I say nothing of the Indian nations because though it will be always prudent to be upon our guard against them; yet I am of opinion we may diminish the necessity of it by making them our friends; and I take it for granted there cannot be a serious doubt any where as to the obvious policy of endeavouring to do it. Their friendship alone can keep our frontiers in peace. It is essential to the improvement of the furr trade an object of immense importance to the state. The attempt at the total expulsion of so desultory a people is as chimerical as it would be pernicious. War with them is as expensive as it is destructive. It has not a single object, for the acquisitions of their lands is not to be wished 'till those now vacant are settled—and the surest as well as the most just and humane way of removing them is by extending our settlements to their neighbourhood. Indeed it is not impossible they may be already will[ing] to exchange their former possessions for others more remote.

The foregoing considerations would lose all force if we had full security that the rest of the world would make our safety and prosperity the first object of their reverence and care; but an expectation of this kind would be too much against the ordinary course of human affairs—too visionary to be a rule for national conduct.

It is true our situation secures us from conquest, if internal dissentions do not open the way; but when Nations now make war upon each other the object seldom is total conquest—partial acquisitions, the jealousy of power, the rivalship of dominion or of commerce, sometimes national emulation and antipathy are the motives. Nothing shelters us from the operation of either of these causes. The fisheries, the furr trade, the navigation of the lakes and of the Mississippi—the Western territory—the Island[s] in the West Indies with referrence to traffic, in short the passions of human nature are abundant sources of contention and hostility.

I will not trespass further on Your Excellency's patience; I expected indeed that my last letter would have finished my official communications; but Messrs. Duane and Lhommedieu having transmitted the extract of your letter to Mr. Floyed and myself in order that we might comply with what your Excellency thought would be expected by the Legislature, it became my duty to give this explanation. Mr. Floyed having been at Congress but a little time after the concurrent resolutions arrived and being now at a great distance from me occasions a separate communication.

I have the honor to be With perfect respect   Your Excellys Most Obed serv   A Hamilton

NB

I did not at the time inclose the resolution directing the general to provide for garrisoning the frontier posts because, I understood it would in course be transmitted to you by the President or the Secretary at War.[4]

4. The resolution, in the writing of H, was dated May 12, 1783.

From James Madison

Princeton [New Jersey] Octr. 16. 1783

Dear Sir

Your favor of the 6th. of July by some singular ill luck never found its way to my hands till yesterday evening.[1] The only part that now needs attention is a request that I will answer the following Question "What appeared to be my idea and disposition respecting the removal of Congress—did I appear to wish to hasten it, or did I not rather show a strong disposition to procrastinate it?"[2] If this request had been recd. at the time it ought it might have been answered as fully as you then wished. Even after the delay which has taken place, my recollection enables me with certainty to witness that the uniform strain of your sentiments as they appeared both from particular conversations with myself, and incidental ones with others in ⟨my⟩[3] presence, was opposed to the removal of Congress except in the last necessity; that when you finally yielded ⟨to⟩ the measure it appeared to be more in compliance with the peremptory expostulations of others than with any disposition of your own mind, and that after the arrival of Congress at Princeton your conversation shewed that you recieved the removal ⟨rather⟩ with regret than with pleasure.

Perhaps this obedience to your wishes may be too ⟨late⟩ to answer the original object of them; But I could not ⟨lose⟩ such an opportunity of testifying the esteem & regard with ⟨which I am Dr. Sir Yr. very Humle. servt.   J. Madison Jr.⟩

AL[S], Hamilton Papers, Library of Congress; copy, Hamilton Papers, Library of Congress.

1. H wrote to Madison on June 29, 1783, to ask for the same information that he requested in his letter of July 6. The letter of June 29 apparently was never sent.

2. H's inquiries were made soon after Congress, intimidated by mutinous soldiers in Philadelphia, had resolved to move to Princeton.

3. The material in broken brackets is taken from a copy of the original in the Hamilton Papers, Library of Congress.

From George Washington [1]

Rocky Hill [New Jersey] 18th Octr. 1783

Dear Sir,

I am favoured with your two letters of the 30th September.

The debate on Indian Affairs which I believe is got through,[2] and that on the residence of Congress wch. is yet in agitation[3] has entirely thrown aside for sometime the consideration of the peace establishment.[4] When it is resumed I will take care that your application comes into view and shall be happy if any thing in my power may contribute to its success being with great truth   Dr. Sir   Yr. most obedt. servt.   Go: Washington

Colonel Hamilton.

Copy, Hamilton Papers, Library of Congress.

1. This copy was apparently made by Octavius Pickering, for at the bottom of the MS there appears the following sentence: "Examined with the original— Octavius Pickering."

2. In September, 1783, Congress considered both the purchase of Indian lands within the state of Pennsylvania by that state and a proclamation prohibiting all persons from settling on Indian lands not within the limits of their respective states. In October, Congress received a lengthy committee report on Indian affairs.

3. After its removal to Princeton in late June, 1783, Congress received offers of a permanent residence from several states. The subject of the future residence of Congress was debated during September and early October.

4. For information on the peace establishment see "Report on a Military Peace Establishment," June 18, 1783.

Oath of Allegiance [1]

Albany, October 20, 1783. On this date Hamilton signed an oath of allegiance to the State of New York. The oath, signed by six other lawyers, reads as follows: "I ——————— do solemnly without any mental reservation or Equivocation whatsoever swear and declare and call God to witness That I renounce and adjure all allegiance to the King of Great Britain; and that I will bear true faith & allegiance to the State of New York, as a free and Independent State, and that I will in all things to the best of my knowledge & ability Do my duty as a good and faithful Subject of the said State ought to do. So help me God."

DS, Mr. Hall Park McCullough, North Bennington, Vermont.

1. The oath taken by H was prescribed by the New York legislature. On March 26, 1781, the legislature adopted "An Act for the better securing the independence of this State," which provided that every person elected or appointed to public office should take an oath of allegiance to the state. At the next session of the legislature, meeting in the fall of 1781, it was enacted that "every attorney, solicitor or counsellor at law" also should take the oath (*Laws of the State of New York*, I, 355, 420).

Oath for the Faithful Execution of Office [1]

Albany, October 20, 1783. On this date Hamilton signed an oath for the faithful execution of his office. The oath, signed by five other lawyers, reads as follows: "I AB. chosen or appointed [as the Case may be] [2] to the office of [here insert the officer's Title of Office] Do solemnly in the presence of almighty God before whom I expect to answer for my conduct promise and swear, that I will in all things to the best of my knowledge and ability faithfully perform the Trust reposed in me. So help me God." After his signature Hamilton wrote: "20th. of October 1783 qualified as an Attorney & Counsellor in the Supreme Court and also as solicitor and Counsellor in the Court of Chancery."

DS, Mr. Hall Park McCullough, North Bennington, Vermont.

1. This oath was prescribed by the New York legislature in "An Act requiring all persons holding offices or places under the government of this State to take the oaths therein prescribed and directed" (*Laws of the State of New York*,

I, 13–14). The oath taken by H was required of "all other ministerial officers in this State."

2. All brackets in this document appear in the original.

From James McHenry [1]

Princeton [New Jersey] 22 [–23] Octbr. 1783.

Dear Hamilton.

I obey you. The homilies you delivered in Congress are still recollected with pleasure. The impressions they made are in favor of your integrity and no one but believes you a man of honor and republican principles. Were you ten years older and twenty thousand pounds richer, there is no doubt but that you might obtain the suffrages of Congress for the highest office in their gift. You are supposed to possess various knowlege, useful—substantial—and ornamental. Your very grave and your cautious—your men who measure others by the standard of their own creeping politics think you sometimes intemperate, but seldom visionary, and that were you to pursue your object with as much cold perseverance as you do with ardor and argument you would become irresistable. In a word, if you could submit to spend a whole life in depicting a fly you would be in their opinion one of the greatest men in the world. Bold designs—measures calculated for their rapid execution—a wisdom that would convince from its own weight—a project that would surprise the people in greater happiness, without giving them an opportunity to view it and reject it, are not adapted to a council composed of discordant elements, or a people who have thirteen heads each of which pay superstitious adoration to inferior divinities.

I have been deterred from day to day from sending you the extract you desire by a proclamation on the subject which I expected would have passed. It is still in dubio. I have reported on Fleury's [2] case on the principle you recommend. I fear his half pay will not be granted.[3]

Congress some time ago determined to fix their fœderal Town on the Delaware near Trenton. Yesterday they determined to erect a second fœderal Town on the Potomac near George Town: and to reside equal periods (not exceeding one year) at Annapolis & Trenton till the buildings are completed. We adjourn the 12 of next month to meet at Annapolis the 26.

Adieu my dear friend and in the ⟨da⟩ys of your happiness drop a line to yours   James McHenry

Octbr. 23d

our examplification of the treaty has passed and will be transmitted to the State officially.[4]

ALS, Hamilton Papers, Library of Congress.
    1. McHenry, who was elected to the Continental Congress on May 12, 1783, attended Congress intermittently from June, 1783, to June, 1784.
    2. François Louis Teisseydre, Marquis de Fleury.
    3. McHenry was chairman of a committee to which the Secretary at War submitted a report concerning Lieutenant Colonel Fleury. The committee reported that Fleury was entitled to half pay "or commutation and other emoluments allowed to officers continuing in the service to the end of the war" (JCC, XXV, 644).
    4. McHenry is referring to the congressional resolution of October 22, 1783, which stated that copies of the provisional articles of peace between the United States and Great Britain and the ratification of those articles be sent to each state (JCC, XXV, 661).

From John Chaloner [1]

Philada Octr 24, 1783

Sir,

Mr. Maley [2] presented me your draft amounting to One hundred twenty five dollars which I have paid him. I have not yet reced any intelligence of our friend [3] but in daily expectation of it—the moment I receive the advice if no private opportunity offers I will dispatch an Express to you with the Intelligence. Mrs. Chaloner joins me in Compliments to you & your Laday & I remain   Dear Sir Your most Obdt Servt

Mr A Hamilton

LC, Historical Society of Pennsylvania, Philadelphia.
    1. Chaloner, under the firm name of Chaloner and White, transacted business for John Barker Church whose legal affairs had been entrusted to H.
    2. Presumably William Maley, a Philadelphia ship captain.
    3. Probably John Barker Church who had gone to France in July, 1783.

From Hugh Knox [1]

St Croix Octr. 27th 1783

Dear Colonel Hamilton!

My old & good friend. Faith between you and me, it hath puzzled me very much to account for your long Silence. Three years have now Elapsed since my last from you, tho' I have wrote you frequently in that time. Can any thing have happened on my part, which Should have So long deprived me of the pleasure of hearing from you? When you were Covered with the dust of the Camp, & had cannon balls whistling thick about your ears, you used to Steal an hour's Converse with an old friend every 5 or 6 months; & now, in a time of profound peace & tranquillity, you cannot, it Seems, find *two minutes* for this kind office. I think I know you too Well, to Suppose you could take offence at any free Strictures on the times which might have dropped from my pen in the Confidence of friendship, when you know how firmly & enthusiastically I was attached to the Cause in which you were Embark'd. Or, Since your Marr⟨iage to t⟩he amiable Miss Schyler, are you So loss'd in ⟨– – –⟩ as to render you forgetful of your other friends? ⟨Or⟩ are you grown too rich & proud, to have a good Memory? Or are you so Engaged in Writing the History of the American War (Cujus Maxima pars facisti, & which you know I have appointed you to) that you have no time to write letters? Or— or— or— pray what is it? Pray make Haste to Explain this Strange Mystery!

This Hasty line goes to you in the Care of Lawyer Peter Markoe Esqr. Son of Abraham Markoe Esqr. of this Island, now Settled in Philadelphia. To this Young man's learning, Genius & merit you cannot be a stranger. He thinks of practising law (I believe) in Philadelphia, for which he is well qualified, having Studied that Science in the Temple, & having those talents which must needs render him eminent in that line. Uncertain where your present residence is, whether in the State of York, Jersey or Pennsylvania, I can only Say, that if your influence or recommendation can promote his prosperity, they will not be wanting I believe on your part.

Mr. & Mrs. Mitchell have, I hear, left these Islands and gone to

America. I have not hear'd from them or of them Since their Departure.[2] I am Sorry to Inform you that no Justice Seems to be done
in the dealing of Mr Litton; & that as things are Situated & perplexed,
I fear little will come out of it for Any of the Heirs.[3]

With a humble tender of Mrs Knox's & my best respects & Kind-
est Wishes to ⟨your lady⟩, Self & family, I remain   My [--] respected friend   Yours Unalterably   Hugh Knox

ALS, Hamilton Papers, Library of Congress.
    1. Knox, a Presbyterian minister who settled on St. Croix in 1772, had
helped H make arrangements to come to the mainland.
    2. George Mitchell and his wife, Ann Venton Mitchell. Mrs. Mitchell, the
daughter of James Lytton and Ann Fawcett Lytton, married John Venton
with whom, in 1762, she had gone to New York. In 1770, she returned to St.
Croix to claim her share of her father's estate. In 1780, three years after the
death of John Venton, she married George Mitchell, a native of Scotland who
had gone to St. Croix from Virginia. Probably in 1783, they returned to America and settled in Burlington, New Jersey. Mrs. Mitchell was H's cousin. Her
mother was the sister of H's mother, Rachel Lavien.
    3. Knox probably is referring to the settlement of the estate of James Lytton,
H's uncle-in-law, who had died in 1769. Litigation over the estate continued
for two decades.

Army Promotion [1]

[Princeton, New Jersey, October 28, 1783]

In pursuance of an Act of Congress of the 30th. day of September
1783.[2]

Lieutenant Colonel Alexander Hamilton is to take rank as Colonel
by brevet in the Armies of the United States of America.

Given under my hand at Princeton the 28th. Day of October 1783.

                                      Elias Boudinot   Presidt.
B: Lincoln.

DS, RG 233, Records of the Committee on Pensions, 14th Congress, National
Archives.
    1. For an account of H's services and retention in the Army, see "Petition
to the New York Legislature," February 4, 1784, and the two letters he wrote
to George Washington on March 1, 1782.
    2. The congressional resolution reads as follows: "Resolved, that the Secre-
tary at War issue to all Officers in the Army under the rank of Major General
who hold the same rank now that they held in the year 1777, a brevet Commission, one grade higher than their present rank having respect to their seniority"
(JCC, XXV, 632).

From George Washington

Rocky Hill [New Jersey] Novr. 6th. 1783

Dear Sir,

The enclosed is a letter which I had written, and was about to dispatch at the date of it;[1] but upon second thoughts, determined to Postpone it, and try, if from the importance of the matter, I could not bring forward the Peace Establishment, previously.

I have tryed it, in vain. Congress, after resolving on the   [2] of last Month to adjourn upon the 12th. of this, did, equally unexpectedly & surprizingly to me, finish their Session at this place the day before yesterday; without bringing the Peace Establishment, or any of the many other pressing matters, to a decision.[3]

Finding this was likely to be the case, I shewed your letter to some of your particular friends,[4] and consulted them on the propriety of making known your wishes; with my testimonial of your Services to Congress; but they adviced me to decline it, under a full persuasion that no discrimination would, or indeed could be made at this late hour as every other Officer from the highest to the lowest grades (not in actual command) were retiring without the retention of Rank—and that the remainder upon a Peace establishment (if a Continental one should ever take place) would come in upon the New System, under fresh appointments; so that unless you wished to come into actual command again, (which none supposed) they saw no way by which you could preserve your Rank.

I have the pleasure to enclose you a Brevet; giving you the Rank of full Colonel;[5] and with best respects to Mrs. Hamilton & General Schuyler & family I am   Dr Sir   Yr. Most Obed Servt.

Go: Washington

Colo. Hamilton

ALS, Hamilton Papers, Library of Congress; ADfS, George Washington Papers, Library of Congress.

1. This is presumably a reference to Washington to H, October 18, 1783.

2. Space left blank in MS. On October 21, 1783, Congress resolved to adjourn on November 12 and to meet in Annapolis on November 26. Adjournment, however, took place on November 4.

3. The report on a military peace establishment was introduced in Congress on October 23, 1783. No action was taken on it before the Congressional recess on November 4.

4. See the two letters H wrote to Washington on September 30, 1783.
5. See "Army Promotion," October 28, 1783.

From John Chaloner

Philada Novr 26 1783

Dear Sir

Doubtless you have seen the advertisement by order of the directors of the Bank calling on the Stockholders to attend the election at the Bank on the Second Monday in January for the appointment of directors for the Insuing year informing them that at the same time several important Matters respecting the institution, will be submitted to their consideration, particularly the propriety of enlarging the Capital Stock, by opening a new Subscription for One thousand additional Shares.[1]

The plann proposed is to sell the additional Shares at five hundred Dollars each & the new & old Shares jointly to draw dividends on four hundred & fifty Dollars the new Share of coarse sink fifty Dollars to the Original Stock.

I have as yet reced no Letters from our Friends Wadsworth & Carter.[2] Mr. Austin[3] this day informed me that his Brother in Law Charles Hopkins[4] who was sent out by them & now returnd reced a Letter in London from Mr Gibbs of LOrient[5] advising of their arival.

I hope soon to have the pleasure of covering you Letters from them. Mrs Chaloner joins me in Compliments to you & your good Lady Mr & Mrs Schuyler & Mr & Mrs Renseller[6]

I am Dear Sir   Your most Obdt hble Servt

LC, Historical Society of Pennsylvania, Philadelphia.

1. The Bank of North America, approved by Congress in 1781, opened its doors in January, 1782. A private bank under governmental auspices, the Bank of North America had a capitalization of $400,000 subscribed in shares of $400 in gold or silver. It was managed by twelve directors who annually selected from among their number a president. In the election one share equalled one vote. The largest stockholder was Jeremiah Wadsworth. The next largest was John B. Church, whose legal affairs were handled by H.

Late in 1783, the stockholders voted to enlarge the stock by a second issue of 1,000 shares.

2. Wadsworth and Church (John Carter) had sailed for France in July, 1783. During their absence some of their American business affairs were handled by Chaloner.

3. Probably J. L. Austin, a Boston merchant engaged in the French trade.

4. Charles Hopkins was the brother of Theodore Hopkins of Hartford, with whom Jeremiah Wadsworth was associated in business. During the American Revolution Theodore Hopkins had gone abroad as Wadsworth's business representative. Presumably Charles Hopkins in association with his brother also transacted business for Wadsworth or for Wadsworth and Church.

5. William Gibbs was a Boston merchant who after the Franco-American treaty of 1778 engaged in the French-American trade at L'Orient in France.

6. Mr. and Mrs. Stephen Van Rensselaer. Mrs. Van Rensselaer was H's sister-in-law.

To George Clinton [1]

New York, December 1, 1783. Writes as the legal representative of "Mrs. Chamier, widow and Administratrix of Daniel Chamier deceased." Asks that George Birks, who owed money to Daniel Chamier, be "apprehended" and compelled to appear in court.

ADS, Chicago Historical Society.
    1. This memorial was sent to the governor because of the absence of proper officers of government in New York City which recently had been evacuated by the British.

Alexander Hamilton, John Laurance, Morgan Lewis, and Richard Varick to Thomas Mifflin [1]

[New York, December 10, 1783]

Sir,

Being concerned as Council for a number of persons, who, since the annunciation of the provisional treaty have been indicted under the confiscation laws of this state for the part they are supposed to have taken in the late war,[2] we are induced at the desire of our clients and in their behalf, to apply to Congress through your Excellency for an exemplification of the definitive treaty.[3] We take it for granted that ere this it will have been proclaimed for the information and direction of the respective states; but as there is a great strictness in the Courts of this State, it will we apprehend, be necessary to be able to produce an ex⟨emplif⟩ication of the treaty under the seal of the United States. In a matter so interesting to a great number of individuals (for it does not belong to us to urge considerations of national honor) we hope we shall be excused when we observe that there appears to us no probability that the legislature of this state will interpose its authority to put a stop to prosecutions 'till the definitive treaty is announced in form. In the mean time a period is limited for the appearance of the indicted persons to plead to their indictments, and if they neglect to appear within the time judgment by default will be entered against them. It is therefore of great consequence to them, that we should have in our possession as speedily as possible an authentic document of the treaty and of its ratification by Congress; and we on this account pray an exemplification of both.

We persuade ourselves that the justice and liberality of Congress will induce a ready compliance with our prayer; which will conduce to the security of a great number of individuals who derive their hopes of safety from the national faith.

We have the honor to be with perfect respect   Your Excellency's
Most Obedient and humble servants   John Laurance
                                                                         Alex Hamilton
                                                                         Morgan Lewis
                                                                         Richd. Varrick

City of New York
December 10th. 1783
His Excellency The President of Congress

LS, in the writing of H, Papers of the Continental Congress, National Archives; DfS, in the writing of H, Hamilton Papers, Library of Congress. The draft, dated December 8, differs in minor respects from the receiver's copy.

1. Laurance, Lewis, and Varick, like H, were New York lawyers. Mifflin was at this time President of Congress.

2. As early as 1775, the Provincial Congress of New York had provided for the sequestration of Tory property and had appointed commissioners of sequestration in seven counties. Subsequent laws disfranchised the Loyalists, provided for the removal or imprisonment of dangerous adherents to the King, and disbarred Loyalist lawyers. Confiscation was provided for by an act passed October 22, 1779, which attainted many Loyalists and made their estates forfeit. The extensiveness of anti-Tory legislation in New York is revealed by a 186-page volume. Entitled *Laws of the Legislature of the State of New York in Force Against the Loyalists and Affecting the Trade of Great Britain* (London, 1786), it reprints twenty-four Tory laws and eight trade laws of 1778 to 1785.

3. The definitive treaty had arrived on November 22, 1783, but because of the lack of a quorum ratification was delayed until January 14, 1784.

To John Chaloner

[*New York, December 11, 1783*. On December 18, 1783, Chaloner wrote to Hamilton: "I have consulted the president of the Bank respectg the information you required in your Letter of the 11th. Instant." *Letter not found.*]

To John B. Church

[*New York, December 12, 1783*. On February 7, 1784, Church wrote to Hamilton: "I received a few Days since my Dear Sir your Favor of the 12th Decemr." *Letter not found.*]

Thomas Mifflin to Alexander Hamilton, John Laurance, and Richard Varick

Annapolis December 17th: 1783

Gentlemen

Yesterday I received the letter you did me the honor to write to me on the 10th: instant,[1] and laid it before Congress; but as seven States only have met, the Subject of it cannot be taken up so soon as its Importance requires.

I will transmit to you an authenticated copy of the Ratification of the definitive Treaty the moment that Congress shall put it into my power.

I am with much Respect & Esteem   Gentlemen   Your obedt: & hble Servt: Thomas Mifflin

LC, Papers of the Continental Congress, National Archives.

1. Although Morgan Lewis's name appears at the end of the letter sent to Mifflin, Mifflin does not include him as an addressee.

From John Chaloner

Philada Decr [18] [1] 1783

Dear Sir

I have consulted the president of the Bank [2] respectg the information you required in your Letter of the 11th. Instant.[3] He informs me that you must send a regular Power of attorney reciteing the power left by John Carter, that it must be attested by one of the chief Magistrates of your City authourizing whom you please to receive the dividend & vote for Mr Carter's Shares.[4] I wrote you some time past on this subject & forwarded your Letters from Mr Carter but as they were sent on to Albany It is propable you have not reced it—for which reason I now trouble you with duplicate.[5]

I am with great Respect   Sir   Your most Obdt Servt
Alexr Hammilton Esqr.

LC, Historical Society of Pennsylvania, Philadelphia.
  1. This letter is incorrectly dated "Decr 8," for Chaloner in the first sentence refers to H's letter of "the 11th Instant." As the letter following in the letter book is dated December 18, this letter was also probably written on that date.
  2. The president of the Bank of North America, Thomas Willing.
  3. Letter not found.
  4. H was the legal representative of John Carter (John B. Church). The shares to which Chaloner refers were share of stock of the Bank of North America owned by Church.
  5. Letters not found.

To Samuel Loudon [1]

[New York, December 27, 1783]

Mr. Loudon,

I Observe in Mr. Holt's paper [2] of this day, a nomination for the ensuing election, in which my name is included.[3] I thank the authors of it for the honour they intended me; but being determined to decline public office, I think it proper to declare my determination, to avoid in any degree distracting the votes of my fellow citizens.

Alex. Hamilton

Saturday, Dec. 27, 1783

The New-York Packet. And the American Advertiser, December 29, 1783.
    1. Loudon was the publisher of *The New-York Packet*.
    2. From 1766 through January, 1782, John Holt had published *The New-York Journal, and General Advertiser*. On November 22, 1783, he began publishing *The Independent New-York Gazette*.
    3. On December 27, 1783, an election was held in New York City for state senators for the southern district and state representatives from the city and county of New York. H was one of those named as a candidate for the Assembly.

To Elizabeth Hamilton

[Albany, 1783–1789] [1]

I arrived My Dear Betsey at this place yesterday Evening not so much fatigued as I expected to have been but with my Cold somewhat increased. I am however better to day and hope to finish my business so as to return on Thursday. If a Vessel offers at the time and a fair wind I may take that mode of conveyance.

I hope you have been attentive to your medicine. Remember *Mrs. Powel* on the *advantages* of health and *disadvantages* of the want of it. Consider how much pain you suffer and how much *pleasure* you lose, by your present situation; and for both our sakes omit nothing that can make you better. Adieu My Betsey. I look forward with eagerness to a return to your bosom   Yrs.   A H
Albany
Saturday

ALS, Hamilton Papers, Library of Congress.
    1. The Hamiltons moved to 57 Wall Street in November, 1783. Since this letter is addressed to Elizabeth at that address, it has been dated 1783–1789.

From Jacobus Swartwout [1]

[*New York, 1783.*] Requests that Hamilton serve as attorney in a suit brought against Swartwout by John Thurman for nonpayment of debt.

ALS, Hamilton Papers, Library of Congress.
    1. Swartwout was a member of the New York Assembly from Dutchess County in 1777 and 1778 and from 1780 to 1783.

1 7 8 4

A Letter from Phocion to the Considerate Citizens of New York [1]

[New York, January 1–27, 1784]

While not only every personal artifice is employed by a few heated and inconsiderate spirits, to practise upon the passions of the people, but the public papers are made the channel of the most

A Letter from Phocion to the Considerate Citizens of New-York On the Politics of the Day (New York, Printed by Samuel Loudon, 1784).

1. During 1783 H had criticized in private letters the way in which Loyalists were treated in New York State. His first *Letter from Phocion* was a public indictment of the majority in the state legislature and the inhabitants of New York City who in violation of the fifth and sixth articles of the treaty of peace not only refused to restore confiscated Loyalist property, but ignored the prohibition against further confiscation or prosecution.

H's first *Letter from Phocion* was prompted by the events following the evacuation of New York City by the British in November, 1783, and the re-establishment of government by the Patriots. As early as October 23, 1779, the New York legislature had provided for the temporary government of the section of the state under British control. A Council for the Southern District—comprising the counties of New York, Suffolk, Kings, Queens, and Richmond—was established to assume control of the administration of the section whenever the British left it. The power of the council was to end as soon as the legislature convened and established a permanent government. See "An Act to provide for the temporary government of the southern parts of this State, whenever the enemy shall abandon or be dispossessed of the same, and until the legislature can be convened" (*Laws of the State of New York,* I, 192–93).

On December 10, 1783, soon after the evacuation of New York City by the British, the Council for the Southern District announced that an election of aldermen and assistant aldermen would be held on December 15. On December 29, the Council gave the city's electors the right to choose representatives to the state legislature.

The treatment of the Loyalists—and the term included those who had remained in New York City during the British occupation—immediately became an issue. Articles in the Patriot press insisted that all Loyalists should make a "voluntary departure" or face the possibility of exile. During the election of representatives to the state legislature (December 29, 1783, to January 5, 1784) denunciation of the Tories was particularly virulent. Some weeks later New York Patriots organized a Whig Society, one purpose of which was to put pressure on the aldermen to take action against the Tories.

The session of the New York legislature which met in 1783 had passed several anti-Tory laws, among them an act entitled "An Act declaratory of inflammatory and pernicious doctrines, tending to the subversion of all private security and genuine liberty; it would be culpable in those who understand and value the true interests of the community to be silent spectators. It is, however, a common observation, that men, bent upon mischief, are more active in the pursuit of their object, than those who aim at doing good. Hence it is in the present moment, we see the most industrious efforts to violate, the constitution of this state, to trample upon the rights of the subject, and to chicane or infringe the most solemn obligations of treaty; while dispassionate and upright men almost totally neglect the means of counteracting these dangerous attempts. A sense of duty alone calls forth the observations which will be submitted to the good sense of the people in this paper, from one who has more inclination than leisure to serve them; and who has had too deep a share in the common exertions in this revolution, to be willing to see its fruits blasted by the violence of rash or unprincipled men, without at least protesting against their designs.

The persons alluded to, pretend to appeal to the spirit of Whiggism, while they endeavour to put in motion all the furious and dark passions of the human mind. The spirit of Whiggism, is generous, humane, beneficent and just. These men inculcate revenge, cruelty, persecution, and perfidy. The spirit of Whiggism cherishes legal liberty, holds the rights of every individual sacred, condemns or punishes no man without regular trial and conviction of some crime declared by antecedent laws, reprobates equally the punishment of the citizen by arbitrary acts of legislature, as by the lawless combinations of unauthorised individuals: While these men are advocates for expelling a large number of their fellow-citizens unheard, untried; or if they cannot effect this, are for disfranchising them, in the face of the constitution, without the judgment of their peers, and contrary to the law of the land.

---

the Alienism of Persons therein described." This alien bill, however, did not become law, for it was vetoed by the Council of Revision whose objections were presented to the legislative session which convened in January, 1784. It was the arguments employed by the partisans of this act to which H referred in both the first *Letter from Phocion* and the *Second Letter from Phocion.* The legislature reconsidered the law on February 11, 1784, and, accepting the objections of the Council, did not repass it. H's first *Letter from Phocion* probably was written between January 1, a time at which anti-Tory sentiment in New York was especially great, and January 27, when Gouverneur Morris mentioned the pamphlet in a letter to H of that date.

The 13th article of the constitution declares, "that no member of this state shall be *disfranchised* or *defrauded of any of the rights or privileges* sacred to the subjects of this state by the constitution, unless *by the law of the land or the judgment of his peers.*" If we enquire what is meant by the law of the land, the best commentators will tell us, that it means *due process of law, that is, by indictment or presentment of good and lawful men,** and trial and conviction in consequence.

It is true, that *in England,* on extraordinary occasions, attainders for high treason, by act of parliament have been practiced, but many of the ablest advocates for civil liberty have condemned this practice, and it has commonly been exercised with great caution upon individuals only by name, never against *general descriptions* of men. The sense of our constitution on this practice, we may gather from the 41st article, where all attainders, other than for crimes committed during the late war, are forbidden.

If there had been no treaty in the way, the legislature might, by *name,* have attainted particular persons of high treason for crimes committed during the war, but independent of the treaty it could not, and cannot, without tyranny, disfranchise or punish whole classes of citizens by general discriptions, without trial and conviction of offences known by laws previously established declaring the offence and prescribing the penalty.

This is a dictate of natural justice, and a fundamental principle of law and liberty.

Nothing is more common than for a free people, in times of heat and violence, to gratify momentary passions, by letting into the government, principles and precedents which afterwards prove fatal to themselves. Of this kind is the doctrine of disqualification, disfranchisement and banishment by acts of legislature. The dangerous consequences of this power are manifest. If the legislature can disfranchise any number of citizens at pleasure by general descriptions, it may soon confine all the votes to a small number of partizans, and establish an aristocracy or an oligarchy; if it may banish at discretion all those whom particular circumstances render obnoxious, without hearing or trial, no man can be safe, nor know when he may be the

* Coke upon Magna Charta, Chap. 29, Page 50.²
2. Coke's comment on the Magna Carta is in his *The Second Part of the Institutes of the Laws of England,* Vol. I, Ch. 29, p. 50.

innocent victim of a prevailing faction. The name of liberty applied to such a government would be a mockery of common sense.

The English Whigs, after the revolution, from an overweening dread of popery and the Pretender, from triennial, voted the parliament septennial. They have been trying ever since to undo this false step in vain, and are repenting the effects of their folly in the overgrown power of the new family. Some imprudent Whigs among us, from resentment to those who have taken the opposite side, (and many of them from worse motives) would corrupt the principles of our government, and furnish precedents for future usurpations on the rights of the community.

Let the people beware of such Counsellors. However, a few designing men may rise in consequence, and advance their private interests by such expedients, the people, at large, are sure to be the losers in the event whenever they suffer a departure from the rules of general and equal justice, or from the true principles of universal liberty.

These men, not only overleap the barriers of the constitution without remorse, but they advise us to become the scorn of nations, by violating the solemn engagements of the United States. They endeavour to mould the Treaty with Great-Britain, into such form as pleases them, and to make it mean any thing or nothing as suits their views. They tell us, that all the stipulations, with respect to the Tories, are merely that Congress will recommend, and the States may comply or not as they please.

But let any man of sense and candour read the Treaty, and it will speak for itself. The fifth article is indeed recommendatory; but the sixth is as positive as words can make it. *"There shall be* no future confiscations made, nor prosecutions commenced against any person or persons, for, or by reason of the part which he or they may have taken in the present war, and no person shall, on that account, suffer any future loss or damage, either in his person, liberty, or property."

As to the restoration of confiscated property which is the subject of the fifth article, the states may restore or not as they think proper, because Congress engage only to recommend; but there is not a word about recommendation in the 6th article.

Quotations are made from the debates in Parliament to prove that the whole is understood as recommendatory; but the expressions in those quotations, turn altogether upon those persons who have been actually proscribed and their property confiscated; they have no relation to those who come under the sixth article, or who might be the objects of future prosecution or punishment. And to this it may be added, that it is absurd and inadmissible in fair reasoning, to combat the plain and authentic language of solemn treaty by loose recitals of debates in newspapers.

The sound and ingenuous construction of the two articles taken collectively, is this—that where the property of any persons, other than those who have been in arms against the United States, had been actually confiscated and themselves proscribed, there Congress are to recommend a restoration of estates, rights and properties; and with respect to those who had been in arms, they are to recommend permission for them to remain a twelvemonth in the country to solicit a like restoration: But with respect to all those who were not in this situation, and who had not already been the objects of confiscation and banishment, they were to be absolutely secured from all future injury to person, liberty or property.

To say that this exemption from positive injury, does not imply a right to live among us as citizens, is a pitiful sophistry; it is to say that the banishment of a person from his country, connexions and resources (one of the greatest punishments that can befal a man) is no punishment at all.

The meaning of the word *liberty* has been contested. Its true sense must be the enjoyment of the common privileges of subjects under the same government. There is no middle line of just construction between this sense and a mere exemption from personal imprisonment! If the last were adopted, the stipulation would become nugatory; and by depriving those who are the subjects of it, of the protection of government, it would amount to a virtual confiscation and banishment; for they could not have the benefit of the laws against those who should be aggressors.

Should it be said that they may receive protection without being admitted to a full enjoyment of the privileges of citizens, this must be either matter of right under the treaty, or matter of grace in the government. If the latter, the government may refuse it, and then the objection presents itself, that the treaty would by this construction be virtually defeated; if matter of right, then it follows that more is intended by the word liberty, than a mere exemption from imprisonment, and where shall the line be drawn—not a capricious and arbitrary line, but one warranted by rational and legal construction?

To say that by espousing the cause of Great-Britain they became aliens, and that it will satisfy the treaty to allow them the same protection to which aliens are entitled is to admit that subjects may at pleasure renounce their allegiance to the state of which they are members, and devote themselves to a foreign jurisdiction; a principle contrary to law and subversive of government. But even this will not satisfy the treaty; for aliens cannot hold real property under our government; and if they are aliens, all their real estates belong to the public. This will be to all intents and purposes, a confiscation of property. But this is not all, how does it appear that the persons who are thus to be stripped of their citizenship, have been guilty of such an adherence to the enemy, as in legal contemplation amounts to a crime. Their merely remaining in their possessions under the power of the conqueror does not imply this; but is executed by the laws and customs of all civilized nations. To adjudge them culpable, they must be first tried and convicted; and this the treaty forbids. These are the difficulties involved, by recurring to subtle and evasive instead of simple and candid construction, which will teach us that the stipulations in the treaty, amount to an amnesty and act of oblivion.

There is a very simple and conclusive point of view in which this subject may be placed. No citizen can be deprived of any right which the citizens in general are entitled to, unless forfeited by some offence. It has been seen that the regular and constitutional mode of ascertaining whether this forfeiture has been incurred, is by legal process, trial and conviction. This *ex vi termini*, supposes prosecution. Now consistent with the treaty there can be no future prosecution for any thing done on account of the war. Can we then do by act of legislature, what the treaty disables us from doing by due course of law? This would be to imitate the Roman General, who having promised Antiochus to restore half his vessels, caused them to be sawed in two before their delivery; or the Plataeæ, who having promised the Thebans to restore their prisoners, had them first put to death and returned them dead.

Such fraudulent subterfuges are justly considered more odious than an open and avowed violation of treaty.

When these posture-masters in logic are driven from this first ground of the meaning of the treaty; they are forced to that of attacking the right of Congress to make such a stipulation, and arraigning the impudence of Great-Britain in attempting to make terms for our own subjects. But here as every where else, they are only successful in betraying their narrowness and ignorance.

Does not the act of confederation place the exclusive right of war and peace in the United States in Congress? Have they not the sole power of making treaties with foreign nations? Are not these among the first rights of sovereignty, and does not the delegation of them to the general confederacy, so far abridge the sovereignty of each particular state? Would not a different doctrine involve the contradiction of *imperium in imperio?* What reasonable limits can be assigned to these prerogatives of the union, other than the general safety and the *fundamentals* of the constitution? Can it be said that a treaty for arresting the future operation of positive acts of legislature, and which has indeed no other effect than that of a pardon for past offences committed against these acts, is an attack upon the fundamentals of the state constitutions? Can it be denied that the peace which was made, taken collectively, was manifestly for the general good; that it was even favourable to the solid interests of this country, beyond the expectation of the most sanguine? If this cannot be denied; and none can deny it who know either the value of the objects gained by the treaty, or the necessity these states were under at the time of making peace?—It follows that Congress and their Ministers acted wisely in making the treaty which has been made; and it follows from this, that these states are bound by it, and ought religiously to observe it.

The *uti possiedetis, each party to hold what it possesses,* is the point from which nations set out in framing a treaty of peace; if one side gives up a part of its acquisitions, the other side renders an equivalent in some other way. What is the equivalent given to Great-Britain for all the important concessions she has made. She has rendered the capital of this state and its large dependencies. She is to surrender our immensely valuable posts on the frontier, and to yield to us a vast tract of western territory, with one half of the Lakes, by which we shall command almost the whole furr trade; she renounces to us her claim to the navigation of the Mississippi, and admits us a share in the fisheries, even on better terms than we formerly enjoyed it. As she was in possession by right of war of all these objects, whatever may have been our original pretensions to them, they are by the laws of nations to be considered as so much given up on her part; and what do we give in return? We stipulate that there shall be no future injury to her adherents among us. How insignificant the equivalent in comparison with the acquisition! A man of sense would be ashamed to compare them: A man of honesty, not intoxicated with passion, would blush to lisp a question of the obligation to observe the stipulation on our part.

If it be said that Great-Britain has only restored to us what she had unjustly taken from us, and that therefore we are not bound to make compensation—This admits of several answers. First, That the fact is not true, for she had ceded to us a large tract of country to which we had even no plausible claim: Secondly, That however the principle of the objection might have been proper to prevent our promising an equivalent, it comes too late after the promise has been made: Thirdly, That as to the external effects of war, the voluntary law of nations knows no distinction between the justice or injustice of the quarrel; but in the treaty of peace puts the contracting parties upon an equal footing; which is a necessary consequence of the independence of nations; for as they acknowledge no common judge, if in concluding peace both parties were not to stand upon the same ground of right, there never could be an adjustment of differences or an end of war. This is a settled principle.

Let us examine the pretext upon which it is disputed. Congress, say our political jugglers, have no right to meddle with our internal police. They would be puzzled to tell what they mean by the expression. The truth is, it has no definite meaning; for it is impossible for Congress to do a single act which will not directly or indirectly affect the internal police of every state. When in order to procure privileges of commerce to the citizens of these states in foreign countries, they stipulate a reciprocity of privileges here, does not such an admission of the subjects of foreign countries to certain rights within these states operate, immediately upon their internal police? And were this not done, would not the power of making commercial treaties vested in Congress, become a mere nullity? In short if nothing was to be done by Congress that would affect our internal police, in the large sense in which it has been taken, would not all the powers of the confederation be annihilated and the union dissolved?

But say they again, such a thing was never heard of as an indemnity for traiterous subjects stipulated in a treaty of peace. History will inform them that it is a stipulation often made. Two examples shall be cited: The treaty of Munster which put an end to the differences between Spain and the United Provinces, after the revolution of those provinces: The treaty concluded in 1738, between the Empire, France, Spain, Poland, and several other powers, called the Christian peace. The war which preceded this treaty was one of the most complicated in which Europe had been engaged; the succession to the Spanish Monarchy, and the right to the throne of Poland had been included in it, Stanislaus having been obliged to abdicate the crown. Different parts of the nations concerned had taken opposite sides. Many of the German Princes had been in arms against the Empire to which they owed obedience: This treaty not only mutually stipulates indemnity to the subjects of the respective powers, but even restitution of *property* and *offices*. The Emperor, who contracted in behalf of the Empire, has much less extensive powers as head of the Empire, than Congress as representative of the United States.

But let it be admitted that Congress had no right to enter into this article. Do not equity and prudence strongly urge the several states to comply with it? We have in part enjoyed the benefit of the treaty; in consequence of which, we of this state are now in possession of our capital; and this implies an obligation in conscience, to perform what is to be performed on our part. But there is a consideration which will perhaps have more force with men, who seem to be superior to conscientious obligations; it is that the British are still in possession of our frontier posts, which they may keep in spite of us; and that they may essentially exclude us from the fisheries if they are so disposed. Breach of treaty on our part will be a just ground for breaking it on theirs. The treaty must stand or fall together. The wilful breach of a single article annuls the whole.* Congress are appointed by the constitution to manage our foreign concerns. The nations with whom they contract are to suppose they understand their own powers and will not exceed them. If they do it in any instance, and we think it proper to disavow the act, it will be no apology to those with whom they contract that they had exceeded their authority. One side cannot be bound unless the obligation is reciprocal.

Suppose then Great-Britain should be induced to refuse a further compliance with the treaty, in consequence of a breach of it on our part, what situation should we be in? Can we renew the war to compel a compliance. We know, and all the world knows, it is out of our power? Will those who have heretofore assisted us take our part? Their affairs require peace as well as ours, and they will not think themselves bound to undertake an unjust war to regain to us rights which we have forfeited by a childish levity and a wanton contempt of public faith.

We should then have sacrificed important interests to the little vindictive selfish mean passions of a few. To say nothing of the loss of territory, of the disadvantage to the whole commerce of the union, by obstructions in the fisheries; this state would loose an annual profit of more than £.50,000 *Sterling*, from the furr trade.

But not to insist on possible inconveniences, there is a certain evil which attends our intemperance, a loss of character in Europe. Our Ministers write that our conduct, hitherto, in this respect, has done us infinite injury, and has exhibited us in the light of a people, destitute of government, on whose engagements of course no dependence can be placed.

* Vatel, Book 4, Ch. 4, § 47.[3] Grotius, Book 3, Ch. 19, § 14.[4]

3. *The Law of Nations; or Principles of the Law of Nature: Applied to the Conduct and Affairs of Nations and Sovereigns. By M.d. Vattel. . . . Translated from the French,* 2 Vols. (London: Printed for J. Newberry, J. Richardson, S. Crowder, T. Caston, T. Longman, B. Law, J. Fuller, J. Coote, and G. Kearsley, 1760).

4. *The Rights of War and Peace, in Three Books. Wherein are explained, The Law of Nature and Nations, and The Principal Points relating to Government. Written in Latin by the Learned Hugo Grotius, And Translated into English. To which are added, All the large Notes of Mr. J. Barbeyrac, Professor of Law at Groningen, And Member of the Royal Academy of Sciences at Berlin* (London: Printed for W. Imys and R. Manby, J. and P. Knapton, D. Brown, T. Osborn, and E. Wicksteed, 1738).

The men who are at the head of the party which contends for, disqualification and expulsion, endeavoured to inlist a number of people on their side by holding out motives of private advantage to them. To the trader they say, you will be overborne by the large capitals of the Tory merchants; to the Mechanic, your business will be less profitable, your wages less considerable by the interference of Tory workmen. A man, the least acquainted with trade, will indeed laugh at such suggestion. He will know, that every merchant or trader has an interest in the aggregate mass of capital or stock in trade; that what he himself wants in capital, he must make up in credit; that unless there are others who possess large capitals, this credit cannot be had, and that in the diminution of the general capital of the State, commerce will decline, and his own prospects of profit will diminish.

These arguments, if they were understood, would be conclusive with the Mechanic: "There is already employment enough for all the workmen in the city, and wages are sufficiently high. If you could raise them by expelling those who have remained in the city, and whom you consider as rivals, the extravagant price of wages would have two effects; it would draw persons to settle here, not only from other parts of this State, but from the neighbouring States: Those classes of the community who are to employ you, will make a great many shifts rather than pay the exorbitant prices you demand; a man will wear his old cloaths so much longer before he gets a new suit; he will buy imported shoes cheap rather than those made here at so dear a rate: The owner of a house will defer the repairs as long as possible; he will only have those which are absolutely necessary made; he will not attend to elegant improvement, and the like will happen in other branches. These circumstances will give you less employment, and in a very little time bring back your wages to what they now are, and even sink them lower. But this is not all: You are not required merely to expel your rival mechanics, but you must drive away the rich merchants and others who are called Tories, to please your leaders, who will persuade you they are dangerous to your liberty (though in fact they only mean their own consequence.) By this conduct you will drive away the principal part of those who have the means of becoming large undertakers. The Carpenters and Masons in particular, must be content with patching up the houses already built and building little huts upon the vacant lots, instead of having profitable and durable employment in erecting large and elegant edifices."

There is a certain proportion or level in all the departments of industry. It is folly to think to raise any of them, and keep them long above their natural height. By attempting to do it the œconomy of the political machine is disturbed, and till things return to their proper state, the society at large suffers. The only object of concern with an industrious artisan, as such, ought to be, that there may be plenty of money in the community, and a brisk commerce to give it circulation and activity. All attempts at profit, through the medium of monopoly or violence, will be as fallacious as they are culpable.

But say some, to suffer these wealthy disaffected men to remain among us, will be dangerous to our liberties; enemies to our government, they will be always endeavouring to undermine it and bring us back to the subjection of Great-Britain. The safest reliance of every government is on mens interests. This is a principle of human nature, on which all political speculation to be just, must be founded. Make it the interest of those citizens, who, during the revolution, were opposed to us to be friends to the new government, by affording them not only protection, but a participation in its privileges, and they will undoubtedly become its friends. The apprehension of returning under the dominion of Great Britain is chimerical; if there is any way to bring it about, the measures of those men, against whose conduct these remarks are aimed, lead directly to it. A disorderly or a violent government may disgust the best citizens, and make the body of the people tired of their Independence.

The embarrassed and exhausted state of Great-Britain, and the political system of Europe, render it impossible for her ever to re-acquire the dominion of this country. Her former partizans must be convinced of this, and abandon her cause as desperate. They will never be mad enough to risk their fortunes a second time in the hopeless attempt of restoring her authority; nor will they have any inclination to do it, if they are allowed to be happy under the government of the society in which they live. To make it practicable, if they should be so disposed, they must not only get the government of this state, but of the United States into their hands. To suppose this possible, is to suppose that a majority of the numbers, property and abilities of the United States has been and is in opposition to the revolution. Its success is a clear proof that this has not been the case; and every man of information among us, knows the contrary. The supposition itself would show the absurdity, of expelling a small number from the city, which would constitute so insignificant a proportion of the whole, as without diminishing their influence, would only increase their disposition to do mischief. The policy in this case would be evident, of appealing to their interests rather than to their fears.

Nothing can be more ridiculous than the idea of expelling a few from this city and neighbourhood, while there are numbers in different parts of this and other states, who must necessarily partake in our governments, and who can never expect to be the objects of animadversion or exclusion. It is confirming *many* in their enmity and prejudices against the state, to indulge our enmity and prejudices against a few.

The idea of suffering the Tories to live among us under disqualifications, is equally mischievous and absurd. It is necessitating a large body of citizens in the state to continue enemies to the government, ready, at all times, in a moment of commotion, to throw their weight into that scale which meditates a change whether favourable or unfavourable to public liberty.

Viewing the subject in every possible light, there is not a single interest of the community but dictates moderation rather than violence. That honesty is still the best policy; that justice and moderation are the surest supports of every government, are maxims, which however they may be called trite, at all times true, though too seldom regarded, but rarely neglected with impunity. Were the people of America, with one voice, to ask, What shall we do to perpetuate our liberties and secure our happiness? The answer would be, "govern well" and you have nothing to fear either from internal disaffection or external hostility. Abuse not the power you possess, and you need never apprehend its diminution or loss. But if you make a wanton use of it, if you furnish another example, that despotism may debase the government of the many as well as the few, you like all others that have acted the same part, will experience that licentiousness is the fore-runner to slavery.

How wise was that policy of Augustus, who after conquering his enemies, when the papers of Brutus were brought to him, which would have disclosed all his secret associates, immediately ordered them to be burnt. He would not even know his enemies, that they might cease to hate when they had nothing to fear.

How laudable was the example of Elizabeth, who when she was transfered from the prison to the throne, fell upon her knees and thanking Heaven, for the deliverance it had granted her, from her bloody persecutors; dismissed her resentment. "This act of pious gratitude says the historian, seems to have been the last circumstance in which she remembered any past injuries and hardships. With a prudence and magnanimity truly laudable, she buried all offences in oblivion, and received with affability even those, who had acted with the greatest virulence against her." She did more—she retained many of the opposite party in her councils.

The reigns of these two sovereigns, are among the most illustrious in history. Their moderation gave a stability to their government, which nothing else could have affected. This was the secret of uniting all parties.

These sentiments are delivered to you in the frankness of conscious integrity, by one who *feels* that solicitude for the good of the community which the zealots, whose opinions he encounters profess, by one who pursues not as they do, the honour or emoluments of his country, by one who, though he has had, in the course of the Revolution, a very *confidential* share in the public councils, civil and military, and has as often, at least, met danger in the common cause as any of those who now assume to be the guardians of the public liberty, asks no other reward of his countrymen, than to be heard without prejudice for their own interest. PHOCION.

P. S. While the writer hopes the sentiments of this letter will meet the approbation of discreet and honest men, he thinks it necessary to apologize for the hasty and incorrect manner. Perhaps too, expressions of too much asperity have been employed against those who take the lead in the principles which are here opposed; and feelings of indignation against the pernicious tendency of their measures, have not admitted sufficient allowances for what is, in some instances, an honest, though mistaken, zeal. Though the writer entertains the worst opinion of the motives of many of them, he believes there are some who act from principle.

To John Chaloner

[*New York, January 8, 1784. On January 21, 1784, Chaloner wrote to Hamilton: "I have before me yours of the 8th. & 15th Instt." Letter of January 8 not found.*]

To John Chaloner

[*New York, January 15, 1784. On January 21, 1784, Chaloner wrote to Hamilton: "I have before me yours of the 8th. & 15th Instt." Letter of January 15 not found.*]

From John Chaloner

Philada. Jany. 21st: 1784

Dear Sir

I have before me yours of the 8th. & 15th Instt.[1] Yesterday I waited on the President of the Bank[2] with your power of Attorney.[3] He thought it sufficient had Mr Carters to you accompanied it, but for want thereof they could not pay me his dividend. You must therefore send me Mr Carters original Power of Attorney to you. Your draft favour of Mr Hoffman[4] I will take up. A Mr P Thompson[5] applied to me for some money on your Account saying you promised to write me on the subject. Must I pay him & how much?

The Bank have agreed to enlarge their shares the new subscriber to pay 500 Dollars—50 of which he gives to the Old Stock as a premium for coming into the partnership.[6] This measure has occasioned some of the wealthiest Merchants to Combine & establish a new Bank. Subscriptions[7] I beleive will be soon open at four hundred dollars a share. I have not a doubt from the Characters that I hear are engaged in this matter but that it will be a permanent source and profitable as the present one, & will I doubt not have the preference whilst the Old Stock is encumbered with the Clog of fifty Dollars advance. If any oppo to London pray advise our friends of this measure.

I am in haste Dear Sir   Your most Obdt Servt   John Chaloner

ALS, Hamilton Papers, Library of Congress; LC, Historical Society of Pennsylvania, Philadelphia.
    1. Letters not found.
    2. The president of the Bank of North America was Thomas Willing.
    3. On December 18, 1783, Chaloner had written to H that in order to receive the dividend on the shares of stock owned by John Carter (John B. Church) in the Bank of North America. H had to submit a power of attorney.
    4. Chaloner is perhaps referring to Nicholas Hoffman, a New York merchant who was a Loyalist during the American Revolution. In 1784, H represented Hoffman in proceedings arising out of the confiscation of Hoffman's estate.
    5. P. Thompson may have been Philip Thompson for whom H had signed a memorial to the Supreme Executive Council of Pennsylvania on February 22, 1783.
    6. The initial shares of stock had cost $400. According to Chaloner (Chaloner to H, November 26, 1783), the new stock, while costing $500, would be valued at $450 in the distribution of dividends; the remaining $50 would be added to the value of the initial shares.
    7. Dissatisfied with the policies of the Bank of North America, a group of promoters announced in January, 1784, a plan to petition the legislature for a charter for a second bank to be known as the Bank of Pennsylvania. Among the subscribers to the new bank, as Chaloner indicated, were some of the socially prominent and wealthy merchants of Philadelphia. They were apparently motivated, not by antagonism to the Bank of North America, but by a desire to share in the profits which that bank had made.

From Gouverneur Morris [1]

Philadelphia 27 Jany 1784

My dear friend

I arrived here on Thursday Evening, after a mighty disagreable Ride, and a mighty whimsical Accident in crossing the Delaware, the Particulars of which I shall reserve till we meet. As I promised to write you the Politics and News of Philadelphia, I will do it this Day; for the Snow Storm rages so incessantly that I can't go abroad. This you will say bodes a long Letter, and I fear you will not be mistaken.

AL, Columbia University Libraries.
    1. In the autumn of 1783, Morris returned to New York where he visited his mother at "Morrisania," the family estate. He intended to practice law in New York City, but because of business ties in Philadelphia he returned to that city (Jared Sparks, The Life of Gouverneur Morris [Boston, 1832], I, 264-65).

I would entertain you with a *splendid* Account of those Illuminations and fire Works, which, if we may believe the Philadelphia News Papers, were *to have been* the most splendid imaginable;[2] but I arrived too late, & only know by Hearsay the Accident which happened to them, and which you may know too by consulting the News Papers. The Exhibition would have been perfectly ridiculous, but for the Death of one Spectator, & the Wounds of others. These are Subjects on which Pleasantry is misplaced. I have been however to see the Place, which was to have been the most splendid of all possible Places, and truly if the Projectors had intended to fire their City, it was an ingenious Invention. Only think of a large wooden Stage, raised in the Middle of a Street, to hang Canvass on, with a Number of Lamps o[n] the Inside, & no precautions against the Flames. You will perhaps be curious, as I was, to know what put it into their Heads. The Account I received is to this Effect. The Quakers, who have more than one Reason for not illuminating their Houses, and some others who have (on this Occasion) at least one Reason for the same Thing, wished to serve both their Class and their Principles. But how was this to be brought about, without offending certain Persons, whose Whiggism consists in abusing the Tories? The President[3] (who is said to be clever at Expedients) undertook the Task. The Mountain labored long and hard, & then outpopp'd Captain Peale.[4] This is a Politician by Birth, & a Painter by Trade, whose History, like that of the ancient Nobles, can be traced back till it is lost in the Clouds of Obscurity. He it seems is one of those who have supported the Revolution by the Powers of

2. Late in November, 1783, the Pennsylvania Assembly appointed a committee to report on arrangements for a "public demonstration of joy" upon the signing of the definitive treaty of peace between the United States and Great Britain. On December 2, 1783, the Assembly resolved

". . . that a triumphal Arch be erected at the upper end of High or Market street, between Sixth and Seventh streets, to be embellished with illuminated paintings and suitable inscriptions; and that some fire works be prepared for the occasion.

"That such an exhibition in point of elegance as well as in regard to the convenience and safety of the spectators will prove most generally acceptable; it being intended there should be no other illuminations in the city." (*Pennsylvania Archives*, X, 149.)

The definitive treaty was ratified on January 14, 1784.

3. John Dickinson was president of Pennsylvania.

4. Charles Wilson Peale, the famous portrait painter, moved to Philadelphia in 1776. He was engaged in active service during the Revolution, and he also held several public offices.

Eloquence, notably displayed at the Corners of Streets, to such Audiences as can usually be collected in such Places. In order to secure the aforesaid Whigs, Captain Peale was employed to prepare Decorations & Devices for the triumphal Arch, & to superintend the Expenditure of the Sum of six hundred Pounds, appropriated by Government to the splendid Exhibition. At the same Time all Illuminations were forbidden, & by a wise Foresight, Squibbs were also prohibited. This you see is the age of Coalitions; and so, blessed be the Peacemakers.

A Man who arrives in this City from New York, beholds a Scene as perfectly new as if he went to the Moguls Dominions. The Philadelphians, long famous for their Progress in the Arts, have already compleated what we have but just begun. For the violent Whigs and the violent Tories, who turned their Backs upon every Body else about two years ago, have each performed a Semi Circle and met at the opposite Point. You know the present Influence is the Banko-mania and this Day's News Paper gives us the Plan of the intended Pensilvania, or, as some call it, Coalition Bank.[5] That you may judge of the propriety of the latter Name, I will give you the Characters of the Parties named in the Advertisement, as I had them at Breakfast from our friend.

The first is Samuel Howel.[6] A quaker who would have been a Whig, if he had not been afraid; but as Providence had otherwise ordained, he remitted his Property to the House of Hopes[7] in Amsterdam at the begining of the Contest. With them it remained during the War & in Return for this Confidence, several Dutch men have brought him Letters of Recommendation from that House. This Circumstance has raised the Idea that he possesses great Credit abroad, which Credit will, it is supposed give Stability to the Bank. Be this as it may, he is said to be an honest Man, which is no bad thing in any Case.

5. For information on the Bank of Pennsylvania, see John Chaloner to H, January 21, 1784, note 7.

6. Howell, an eminent Philadelphia merchant, was described by John Chaloner as one who professed republican principles and who "altho a Quaker was long confined in Gaol by the British" (Chaloner to Jeremiah Wadsworth and John B. Church, February 14, 1784, Connecticut Historical Society, Hartford). After the evacuation of Philadelphia by the British, Howell served as a member of the Pennsylvania General Assembly.

7. House of Hope, a Dutch banking house founded by Henry Hope.

The next is Archibald McCall.[8] A good name would be to him a good Purchase. And yet all his Conduct is swayed by the gentler Affections. He loved the british Cause so well, that he would have resigned his Neck to serve it, but for the greater Lover he bore himself. And in Order that he might reconcile those contrarient Emotions he took a full Share in the Labor of depreciating our Money & transmitting Intelligence. To these patriotic Deeds his Benignity added the charitable one of supplying small Sums, to Men in Distress, at a moderate Interest; such as five, or ten, per Cent per Month, according to their Necessities.

Next comes John Bayard.[9] You may remember that when we met last Summer, at Poughkeepsie, you lent me a Pamphlet written by General Cadwallader.[10] This is the Colo. Bayard whose Sensibilities are recorded in that Pamphlet. The Colo. is as good a Whig, tho not quite so great a Man as Captain Peale.

The next (Edward Shippen) [11] has the Misfortune to be general Arnold's Father in Law, but he bears no Resemblance to his Son except that their political Principles were the same from Arnold's Defection 'till the Treaty of Peace.

Close on his Heels comes George Emlen.[12] In many Traits of Character there is a strong Resemblance between him & McCall. But if McCall has more of the milk of human kindness, Friend Emlem as far exceeds him in the Meekness of Christian Love. He has therefore a more pious Charity, & seeks more distressed Objects on which

8. McCall, a member of a merchant family with extensive commercial connections, before the Revolution engaged in trade in both the East and West Indies. He was described by John Chaloner as a wealthy merchant who was "perfectly neuter during the War" (Chaloner to Wadsworth and Church, February 14, 1784, Connecticut Historical Society.)

9. Bayard, a Philadelphia merchant, served during the Revolution both as a soldier and as a member of the Pennsylvania legislature. In the seventeen-eighties as before the war, Bayard was active in the mercantile life of Philadelphia.

10. For information on this pamphlet, see Brigadier General John Cadwalader to H, March 2, 1783.

11. Shippen, a distinguished member of the Philadelphia bar, was a Loyalist during the American Revolution. His Loyalism was not a serious handicap to his career, for in 1784 he was appointed president of the Court of Common Pleas of Philadelphia County, and he subsequently became justice of the peace, president of the Court of Quarter Sessions and General Jail Delivery, judge of the High Court of Errors and Appeals, and a member of the Pennsylvania Supreme Court.

12. Emlen, like most of the other supporters of the Bank of Pennsylvania, was a Philadelphia merchant.

to exercise it. This superior Endowment has been justly rewarded, in some Instances, with twelve per Cent per Month. See how good a Thing it is to be Merciful to the Poor.

Jared Ingersol [13] comes next. He is a good Whig a worthy young Man and his Friends are sorry to see him in such Company.

Thomas Fisher [14] is a quaker and a Tory, but John Steinmetz [15] is one of those Whigs who staid in Philadelphia when the Enemy took Possession. It was during that Period perhaps, that he learnt of McCall & Emlen the Practice of monthly Loans, which he has since pursued with no small Degree of Edification. It is supposed that these good Christians, in establishing the Coalition Bank, are actuated by the laudable Desire of extending their monthly Charities. For if by their Influence over the Corporation, they can obtain its Funds; as they will thereby procure Money at one half per Cent per Month, they may afford particular Accomodations for two and an half, or three per Cent, according to Circumstances; which will you know be a great Relief to the Poor. This single Consideration will shew the Use of the Institution.

Tench Coxe [16] comes next in the List. I believe you know him, for I think you mentioned to me the Anecdote of his being excluded from the dancing Assembly, on Account of Toryism.

David Rittenhouse [17] is known to the World. If the Representation given of the other Characters be true, your Sensibility will be wounded (as Mine was) to see his Name in this Place.

13. Jared Ingersoll, Jr., a native of Connecticut, did not share the Loyalist sympathies of his well-known father. After law studies in England, Ingersoll returned to Philadelphia where he became one of the foremost lawyers of that city.

14. Fisher, son of the prominent Quaker merchant, Joshua Fisher, was a partner in the firm of Joshua Fisher and Sons which before the Revolution had established a line of packet ships between Philadelphia and London. During the war Fisher refused to sign a loyalty oath and was exiled to Winchester, Virginia.

15. Steinmetz was described by John Chaloner as a wealthy merchant "professing republican principles" (Chaloner to Wadsworth and Church, February 14, 1784, Connecticut Historical Society). In 1780, Steinmetz was elected a member of the Pennsylvania Assembly.

16. Before the Revolution Tench Coxe was a member of the Philadelphia firm of Coxe, Furman and Coxe. Coxe, whether because of royalist sympathies or a desire to protect his family's business, left Philadelphia soon after the outbreak of the Revolution and joined the British. Returning to Philadelphia with the army of General William Howe, Coxe, who was soon again active in the commercial life of the city, became an ardent Whig.

17. Rittenhouse was the well-known astronomer and mathematician.

Samuel Pleasants [18] & Joseph Swift [19] are tories, & not remarkable for any Thing else; which cannot be said of Jeremiah Warder.[20] Of the same Religion with the pious Emlene, and of equal political merit, he exceeds him in some of the moral Qualities; and chiefly in Fortitude, justly considered as the Base of every other Virtue. A remarkable Instance of it was exhibited in the Affair of one Mease,[21] late Cloathier General. This Man was prosecuted for Fraud, yet some how or other, he was acquitted, altho Jeremiah in his Zeal for the Conviction of so capital an Offender, affirmed both the Thing which was, & the Thing which was not. This Conduct, by which he risqued his Ears for the Good of his Country, has very justly endeared him to all Ranks and orders of Men.

Peter Knight [22] and Robert Knox [23] are good Sort of Men, & as they bear Whig Characters, they Mark with true Distinctions of Light and Shade the Merits of the Coalition. Your Friend Phocion [24] has written a Book in Favor of Moderation, He certainly means well, but if he were here he would see what goodly Fruit is produced, in the Fulness of time, from those Seeds of Contention which he has labored to destroy; and he would find out the Truth of that old Proverb, "the farthest Way about, is the nearest Way Home."

18. Pleasants, an affluent Quaker merchant, was exiled for a short time during the Revolutionary War, but was permitted to return to Philadelphia in 1778. John Chaloner described him as a Tory merchant whose "relations and family has been much connected with the proprietary family" (Chaloner to Wadsworth and Church, February 14, 1784, Connecticut Historical Society).

19. Swift, a captain in the Pennsylvania Loyalists, returned to his mercantile business at the end of the war. He was later elected an alderman of the city of Philadelphia.

20. Jeremiah Warder, Jr., was a well-known Philadelphia merchant who was described by John Chaloner as "perfectly neuter during the War" (Chaloner to Wadsworth and Carter, February 14, 1784, Connecticut Historical Society).

21. James Mease was clothier general in 1777 and 1778.

22. Knight was a Philadelphia lumber merchant.

23. Knox was a Philadelphia merchant and a member of the Pennsylvania Assembly.

24. See "A Letter from Phocion to the Considerate Citizens of New York," January 1–February 11, 1784.

To Francisco de Miranda [1]

[New York, January–July, 1784]

Col Hamiltons Compliments to Col Miranda; is much obliged to him for the paper.

Wednesday

AD, Academia Nacional de la Historia, Caracas, Venezuela.

1. Miranda, Spanish-American adventurer and soldier, served with the French during the American Revolution. After the war, when his attempts to achieve the independence of Spanish America were discovered, he fled first to the United States and then to England.

Miranda was in New York from January to July, 1784 (Robertson, *The Life of Miranda*, I, 40–46). This letter must have been written during that time.

From John Chaloner

Philada Febry 2. 1784

Dear Sir

I wrote you the 21st Ulto Copy of which you have annexd. At that period few or no Subscriptions to the Bank of Pensylvania had taken place but its progress has been so rapid as to obtain Seven hundred & fifteen shares on friday last. Thursday next they choose directors & begin to prepare for business. Its Constitution or at least the proposed Constitution is exactly the same as the Bank of No America except the controul & restriction which the Finnancier has over it & they do not make their notes equal with Specie to tax getherers—by this I mean there is no compulsion on the tax collectors to receive them as such: with them it will be matter of choice it is not so with the Bank of No America. The president of the State the Speaker of Assembly & the Chief Justice are all times to have a right of inspecting into its state & situation.[1]

The Subscriptions to the old Bank open this day on the terms I mentioned in my last.[2] I believe no Stock of the former proprietors are to be bought [3] without considerable advance 20 to 25 ℔ Cent.[4]

Your draft was sent me for acceptance on Saturday by your friend Mr Gouvernieur Morris. I informed him I would pay it as soon as you forwarded me Mr Carters power of attorney to you[5] & desired his young man to acquaint him if it was not convenient for him to wait until then I would immediately accept it. I have heard no more of it & suppose him satisfied therewith—if not I will immediately pay it. Mrs. Chaloner joins me in Compts to Mrs. Hammilton & yourself & I remain   Dear Sir   Your much obliged hble Servt   John Chaloner

Alexr Hammilton Esqr

ALS, Hamilton Papers, Library of Congress; LC, Historical Society of Pennsylvania, Philadelphia.

1. For information on the Bank of Pennsylvania, see Chaloner to H, January 21, 1784, note 7.
2. Chaloner to H, January 21, 1784.
3. In MS, "bot."
4. The stock of the bank, issued at its inception, had increased in value during the bank's first two years of operation. By January, 1784, its value was estimated at from 15 to 25 percent above its initial value.
5. See Chaloner to H, January 21, 1784.

Petition to the New York Legislature [1]

[New York, February 4, 1784]

To The Honorable The Representatives of the State of New York
   In Senate and Assembly
   The Memorial and Petition of Alexander Hamilton humbly sheweth

   That Your Memorialist early in the year 1776 entered into the service of this State having been previously a resident therein, in the command of a company of Artillery raised for its particular defence, and continued in the command of that company till 1777 when he was called by His Excellency General Washington to occupy a place in his family; in which station he acted 'till the year 1781.

   That he made the campaign of 1781 at the head of a corps of light infantry, composed principally of the troops of this state; after which he obtained leave of absence from the Commander in Chief; the situation of public affairs then affording no probability of future activity in the military line.

   That though he retained his rank in the army to be ready to return into military service, if any unforeseen change of circumstances should still require exertions in that line; yet from scruples of delicacy, he voluntarily relinquished his pay from the end of the year 1781 and with it his right to half pay and other allowances made to officers after the war.[2]

That by a settlement of his account of pay and subsistence to that period, there was found a ballance due him of three thousand five hundred and twenty five dollars; of which there still remains due Two thousand Eight hundred and twenty dollars; for which he has a certificate from the treasury of the United States.

Your Memorialist observing the delays and obstacles that occur in any Continental provision for the payment of public debts is induced to pray that the Honorable the Legislature would be pleased to grant him in lieu of his present certificate securities similar to those which have been given to the officers in general, who were previous to the war citizens of this state; which prayer he flatters himself will be the more readily granted, not only as there remain very few who have not already been comprehended in the provisions made by the state but as the sacrifice already mentioned of so large a part of his claims upon the public encourages him to expect, that he will not be left as to the residue, upon a worse footing than the generality of his fellow citizens in the same circumstances.

With full confidence in the equity and generosity of the Legislature Your Memorialist respectfully submits his prayer.

Alexander Hamilton

New York 4th. of February 1784

ADS, Lilly Library, Indiana University, Bloomington.
1. H petitioned the New York legislature to assume the debt owed him by Congress because the legislature not only had provided compensation for the depreciation of the pay of soldiers from the state serving in the Continental Army, but it had also by a number of acts provided for the settlement of the accounts of specified officers. See *Laws of the State of New York*, I, 298–303, 335–36, 361, 385–86, 430, 456–58, 541–42.

H's petition was received by the New York Assembly on February 4 and referred to a committee. It was read in the Senate on February 9 and referred to a committee of the whole. The journals of neither the Assembly nor Senate reveal the disposition of his petition.

2. See the two letters H wrote to George Washington on March 1, 1782.

To John Chaloner

[*New York, February 5, 1784.* On February 12, 1784, Chaloner wrote to Hamilton: "Your two favours of the fifth & Eighth Instant are both reced." *Letter of February 5 not found.*]

From John B. Church [1]

Paris Feby. 7th 1784

I received a few Days since my Dear Sir your Favor of the 12th Decemr.[2] I observed your Account of the Project of the Bank, I fear by Letters I have Received from Chaloner that the Plan will be carried into Execution before this Reaches you,[3] if it is and the Shares are not all taken up pray buy for me Two hundred and fifty Shares. I shall direct Chaloner to draw on me to supply you with the money; if the Plan is not decided on before you receive this, I am clear for the Augmentation[4] propos'd and beg you immediately on its being determined to buy for me the 250 shares abovementioned. It will be necessary to keep your Intentions a secret, as I have no doubt but there are some People who hope by this Increase to buy largely and prevent us from a preponderance in the Bank which is to us a very capital Object;[5] and if we want Funds for a Bank that we may establish in New York the Bank Shares will be always saleable. I should be sorry if Mr. Sayre should effect his Establishment before we are able to Return and carry our Plan into Execution, but I shall be astonish'd if Men of Property are weak and credulous enough to give him their Confidence.[6] We are taken measures to vest our Property in America by exporting from here and England a large Quantity of ready money Articles and I hope that we shall be at New York in June or July.[7]

I have heard nothing from Genl Schuyler nor do you say a Word about him or the Family & I wish to know whether he has made the Purchases I requested him to make for me.

The Power respecting the Bank Stock gives you a Right to sell and transfer, so that if there is any Difficulty about voting you can transfer the Shares into your own Name which will obviate every Difficulty.

I hope by this Time order and good Government prevail in the State and that Lenity and moderation have taken Place of Violence and Resentment. I shall be glad if Moses can carry his Vindue Scheme into Execution as I think it will prove a very beneficial one.[8]

Angelica joins me in Love to Mrs. Hamilton and yourself she is very well the little maid [9] is fat and handsome. Phil [10] is in Pension he jabbers now more French than English. The inclement Weather prevents our leaving Paris but I think we shall set out in 10 or 12 Days, they have experienc'd here the severest Winter that has been felt for many Years. Adieu My Dear Sir. I am very sincerely and affectionately   Your Friend & Servant   J B Church

ALS, Hamilton Papers, Library of Congress.
  1. John B. Church (John Carter) and Jeremiah Wadsworth had gone to France in July, 1783, to settle accounts owed them by the French government. During the American Revolution they had furnished supplies for the French forces in America.
  2. Letter not found.
  3. Church is referring to the proposed plan for increasing the stock of the Bank of North America by the sale of additional shares of stock. See John Chaloner to H, January 21, 1784.
  4. Church presumably authorized H to cast the votes to which his ownership of stock entitled him.
  5. Church and Wadsworth had a "preponderance in the Bank," for Wadsworth was the largest stockholder and Church the second largest.
  6. The "Mr. Sayre" to whom Church is referring was probably Stephen Sayre, a London banker. Sayre was connected with a group of New Yorkers who late in 1783 made plans for establishing a bank in New York. On February 12, 1784, proposals were published for a bank to be known as the "Bank of the State of New York." The amount of capital was to be $750,000 consisting of 750 shares at $1,000 a share. One-third of the subscription was to be paid in cash, and the remaining two-thirds was to consist of landed security, given by mortgage or conveyed in trust. Subscription books were opened at 6 Wall Street by Stephen Sayre and John Stephens. It was for this bank that Robert R. Livingston applied on February 17, 1784, to the New York Assembly for an act of incorporation. See H to Church, March 10, 1784.
  7. For an account of the business activities of Church and Wadsworth while in Europe, see John D. R. Platt, "Jeremiah Wadsworth: Federalist Entrepreneur" (unpublished doctoral dissertation, Columbia University, 1955), 47–68.
  8. Because of the illegibility of the MS, the meaning of this sentence cannot be determined. The man to whom Church is referring could be either "Moses" (possibly Isaac Moses, a New York merchant) or "Moris" (perhaps Robert Morris, the Superintendent of Finance).
  9. Catherine Church.
  10. Philip Church.

To John B. Church

[*New York, February 7, 1784.* On May 2, 1784, Church wrote to Hamilton: "I have within a few Days Received your Favors of the 7th and 18th Feby. and 6th March." *Letter of February 7 not found.*]

To John Chaloner

[*New York, February 8, 1784.* On February 12, 1784, Chaloner wrote to Hamilton: "Your two favours of the fifth & Eighth Instant are both reced." *Letter of February 8 not found.*]

From John Chaloner

Philada. Febry 12th 1784

Dear Sir

Your two favours of the fifth & Eighth Instant are both reced, the latter covering Mr Carters power of Attorney to you.[1] The utillity of another bank to the Mercantile Interest is very evident[2] the rapid progress of the New one has already in some Instances dictated to the Old. I will mention a Case. On application with your power of Attorney to me, I was told it was irregular & could not receive the Dividends on Mr Carters Shares untill his power was lodg'd. I informd them I was sorry they did not inform me of this, when I enquired of them what authority was necessary, to enable me to receive the devidents on those Shares—that you had done all that they informd me was requisite, & was now drawing on me for the money—a bill for a part had come to hand. Mr Willing[3] said it could not be help'd, but I must get the power, & in the mean time if I required it he would pay the draft. I told him on that Account it was not material, here ended the matter. Some few days afterwards, when the subscribers to the New bank were in No Sufficient to choose directors, I waited on them with a letter from Mr Peter Colt,[4] in favour of whom J. Wadsworth had executed & lodg'd at the bank a power of Attorney. Colts letter was to the Cashier,

informing that J Wadsworth had wrote him that he executed &
lodged a power of Attorney at the bank for him to receive his dividend on his Shares of Stock & in consequence thereof had drawn on
him the Cashier in favour of me for the amt of J Wadsworths
dividend, on his several shares, it was immediately accepted, & the
dividends placed to my Credit, & altho then I had not received nor
heard nothing from you respecting Mr Carters power, they offerd
to place his shares also to my Credit. Both your drafts are come to
hand & duly honourd. The Subscriptions in both banks are nearly
compleated.[5] Both are under the auspices of Wealthy Merchants.
The Stockholders to the New One are most Numerous, and composed generally of People who have but little Interest in the Old
One, a very great proportion are Men distinguished from neutrality
in the late Contest: Many of them have been punishd for Tories.[6]
I think they will equal the Old bank in business & their directors are
Men of the first Rank of Merchants before the war.[7] After their Subscriptions were so Numerous as to render their Success beyond a
doubt, I subscribed 8 Shares for Mr Church & 2 for myself. I think
both Wadsworth & him would wish to be Interested especially as
the Old Bank will at their pleasure augment & increase their Subscriptions it is next to impossiable for them to continue their influence if necessary. If they pursue their Scheme of bankg in New
York[8] & should want their bills taken up here, they Stand a Chance
of makg better terms if two are established & they Interestd in both
than with one only & both will I doubt not share equal dividends
to what the Old has already done. I congratulate you on Mr Church's
reception with his Family in London, Mrs Chaloner joins me in
Compliments to Mrs Hamilton & I remain Dr Sir   Your most Obdt
Servt
Alexr Hamilton Esqr

LC, Historical Society of Pennsylvania, Philadelphia.
    1. Neither the letters nor the power of attorney has been found.
    2. The new bank was the Bank of Pennsylvania. See Chaloner to H, January
21, 1784.
    3. Thomas Willing, president of the Bank of North America.
    4. The pre-Revolutionary business activities of Peter Colt of New Haven,
Connecticut, consisted chiefly of trade with the West Indies. From 1777 until
1780 he was deputy commissary for the Eastern Department. After he resigned
that position he became a business aide of Jeremiah Wadsworth. He not only
sold goods to Wadsworth, the contractor for supplying the French troops in

America, but as Wadsworth's representative he traveled with the French army to handle the distribution of goods. In 1783, Colt opened a store in Hartford. He continued, however, to manage some of Wadsworth's business affairs.

5. The newly formed Bank of Pennsylvania and the Bank of North America.

6. In MS, "Toris."

7. For a description of the leading promoters of the bank, see Gouverneur Morris to H, January 27, 1784.

8. See John B. Church to H, February 7, 1784, for information on Wadsworth's and Church's interest in a New York bank.

To John Chaloner

[*New York, February 12, 1784.* On February 17, 1784, Chaloner wrote to Hamilton: "Yours of the 12th. Instant I have just reced." *Letter not found.*]

From John Chaloner

Philada Febry 17th. 1784

Dear Sir

Yours of the 12th. Instant I have just reced [1] & am glad to find your Sentiments coinside with mine respecting the deposit of Bank Stock. I will immediately subscribe two thousand dollars for Mr Church. By the very next oppo. I will send a Sketch of the Acct between us.

I am with respect   Sir   Your most Obdt Servt

A Hamilton Esqr.

LC, Historical Society of Pennsylvania, Philadelphia.
   1. Letter not found.

To Egbert Benson

[*New York*] *February 18, 1784.* "I am engaged in several causes depending on the Trespass law on the side of the defendants. Three of my Clients who are British Merchants are anxious to have your assistance. . . . The actions are brought in the Mayor's Court; so that I suppose the argument will come on in about five weeks. Will it be convenient for you to be here?"

ALS, Lloyd W. Smith Collection, Morristown National Historical Park, Morristown, New Jersey.

To John B. Church

[*New York, February 18, 1784.* On May 2, 1784, Church wrote to Hamilton: "I have within a few Days Received your Favors of the 7th and 18th Feby. and 6th March." *Letter of February 18 not found.*]

To Gouverneur Morris [1]

New York Feby. 21. 1784

I duly received my dear Sir your letter of the 27th: of January and I would have sooner told you how much pleasure it gave me, if I had had time; but legislative folly has afforded so plentiful a harvest to us lawyers that we have scarcely a moment to spare from the substantial business of reaping. Today being sunday I have resolved to give an hour to friendship and to you. Good people would say that I had much better be paying my devotions to the *great* [2]

⟨devotions I mean; for with so lively an imagination as yours it is necessary to be explicit, lest you should be for making a different association that would not suit me quite as well.

To say that I was amused with your letter was to say what must have happened of course; a good theme in good hands could not fail to be amusing. The coalition you mention is not to be wondered at, though in a political light it is whimsical enough; but the meeting of extremes at the same point is a common case. I expect in another year to see our political antipodes in this city shaking hands, but whenever it happens it will not affect me as it seems to have done you in the instance you mention, because probably I shall not have the same reasons. To be serious:

The erection of a new bank in Philadelphia does not appear to me an evil to the community.[3] The competition may indeed render the large profits of⟩ the old bank less permanent; but they will always remain considerable enough; and the competition will cause business to be done on easier and better terms in each to the advancement of trade in general. If I reason wrong correct me. That a stock holder of the old bank should feel his interest wounded—that those who have made their property in it subservient in some measure to the support of the revolution should feel a degree of indignation at the kind of rivalship which has started up—are both natural sensations —but that large profits should produce rivalship—that men in a matter of this kind should empl⟨oy their money⟩ where they expect the greatest advantage ⟨and the cheapest⟩ market in purchasing [4]

⟨second bank *has been* established, I think you will, on reflection, agree with me that they ought to wish to be interested in both the institutions, and that therefore it is the duty of those who have the laying out of their money to purchase in the new bank, on the principle I have hinted at as well as the circumstances of a lower price. The whole of this business, my dear friend, is a mere mercantile speculation, and I am sure when there has been time to cool down the considerate proprietors of the old bank will blame nobody for adventuring upon mere mercantile principles. To you I need not say that it is chimerical to expect any other will prevail.

Were I to advise upon this occasion, it would be as soon as possible to bring about a marriage or, perhaps what you will prefer, an intrigue between the old bank and the new. Let the latter be the wife or, still to pursue your propensity, the mistress of the⟩ former. As a mistress (or you'll say a wife) it is to be expected she will every now and then be capricious and inconstant; but in the main it will [be to] the interest of both husband and wife that they should live well together and manage their affairs with good humour and concert. If they quarrel they will not only expose themselves to the gibes of their neighbours, but the more knowing part of these will endeavour to keep them by the ears in order to make the favours of each more cheap, and more easily attainable.

I ought in return to give you an account of what we are doing here; but I will in the lump tell you that we are doing those things which we ought not to do, and leaving undone those things which we ought to do. Instead of wholesome regulations for the improvement of our polity and commerce; we are labouring to contrive methods to mortify and punish tories and to explain away treaties.

Let us both erect a temple to time; only regretting that we shall not command a longer portion of it to see what will be the event of the American drama.

Adieu very sincerely   Yr. Affectionate   A Hamilton
New York Feby. 21. 1784
G Morris Esqr

ALS, Hamilton Papers, Library of Congress. In *HCLW*, IX, 399, this letter is incorrectly dated March 21, 1784.

1. Morris had resigned as assistant to the Superintendent of Finance late in 1783. In January, 1784, he returned to Philadelphia from a visit to his ancestral home "Morrisania."

2. At this point a part of the MS is missing. The bracketed portions of this letter are taken from *HCLW*, IX, 400–02. Although the MS was partially destroyed when it was copied by Lodge, he printed much more of the letter than is now preserved.

3. H is referring to the attempt to create a rival—the Bank of Pennsylvania—to the Bank of North America.

4. At this point a part of the MS is missing.

Constitution of the Bank of New York [1]

[New York, February 23, 1784–March 15, 1784] [2]

CONSTITUTION
Article 1st.

That the Bank shall be called by the Name and Title of the Bank of New York.

D, Hamilton Papers, Library of Congress.

1. Scholars have unanimously attributed the "Constitution of the Bank of New York" to H (Hamilton, *History*, III, 46; Schachner, *Hamilton*, 182; Mitchell, *Hamilton*, 348; Allan Nevins, *History of the Bank of New York*, 8). Attached to the "Constitution" in the Hamilton Papers, Library of Congress, there is a scrap of paper on which there appears in H's writing the words "Constitution of the Bank of New York." Whether this was the endorsement of an unlocated or lost draft of the "Constitution" or whether H appended it to a copy of the "Constitution" made by someone else cannot be determined. The only available evidence consists of the document, not in H's writing, in the Hamilton Papers, and two letters (H to John B. Church, March 10, 1784; H to Nicholas Low, December 21, 1791).

On February 23, 1784, the following announcement appeared in *The New-York Packet. And the American Advertiser:* "BANK. It appearing to be the disposition of the Gentlemen in this City, to establish a BANK on liberal principles, the stock to consist of specie only; they are therefore hereby invited to meet To-Morrow Evening at Six o'clock at the Merchant's Coffee House; where a plan will be submitted to their consideration." The establishment of a specie bank was prompted in part by a project headed by

–2–

That the Capital Stock consist of Five Hundred Thousand Dollars
in Gold or Silver, divided into One Thousand Shares of Five Hundred Dollars each Share and that a Majority of all the Directors may
at their discretion open new Subscriptions for encreasing the Capital
Stock, when they shall judge it for the Interest of the Bank so to
do, provided the said New Subscriptions do not exceed the Sum of
Five Hundred Thousand Dollars.

–3–

That Thirteen Directors be annually chosen by a Majority of Votes,
who are to have the sole Conduct and Management of the Bank.
At the first General Election, the President and Cashier are to be
elected by the Subscribers to the Bank, but for ever afterwards the
Thirteen Directors are to chuse a President from among themselves;
and the Cashier as well as every other Person employed in the Bank
is to be appointed and paid by them and be under their immediate
controul.

–4th–

That the first Election be on the 15th. day of March 1784; that the
next General Election for thirteen Directors shall be on the Second
Monday in May 1785; and so continue Yearly and every Year, but
in case of any Vacancy in the Direction by Death, Resignation or
otherwise, public notice shall be given within one Week after such

---

Robert R. Livingston to form a land bank. See Church to H, February 7,
1784, and H to Church, March 10, 1784.

At the meeting of February 24, 1784, at the Merchant's Coffee House, Alexander McDougall was made chairman, and plans for a bank were approved.
Late in 1783 H had been directed by Church to establish a New York bank
which would be dominated by Church and Jeremiah Wadsworth. This project,
however, was anticipated by some New York merchants who met on February
24 and established a specie bank which presumably was similar to that which
H was attempting to organize for Church and Wadsworth. Deciding "to fall
in with them," H endeavored to see that Church had "a proper weight" in the
affairs of the bank (H to Church, March 10, 1784). On March 15, the bank
was formally organized, five hundred shares having been subscribed. Alexander
McDougall was elected president and William Seton cashier. The directors
were Samuel Franklin, Robert Bowne, Comfort Sands, H, Joshua Waddington,
Thomas Randall, William Maxwell, Nicholas Low, Daniel McCormick, Isaac
Roosevelt, John Vanderbilt, and Thomas B. Stoughton.

2. The "Constitution" must have been written between February 23, 1784,
the date of the announcement of a meeting to form the Bank of New York,
and March 15, the date on which, according to the "Constitution," the first
election of directors was to be held.

an Event, that the Vacancy may be filled; the Election to be within fourteen days after such notice.

5th.

That every Holder of one or more Shares to the Number of Four, shall have One Vote for each Share—A Subscriber of Six Shares shall have Five Votes, Eight Shares, Six Votes, and Ten Shares, Seven Votes, and One Vote for every Five Shares above Ten.

–6th–

That no Stockholder after the first Election shall be entitled to Vote, unless such person has possessd the Stock three months previous to the day fixed for an election of Directors or any other General purpose; And if any Stockholder (who shall have been a Resident in this State at least Twelve months immediately preceeding such Election) should be absent, he shall be entitled to Vote by Proxy properly appointed; but in no other case shall any Vote be admitted by Proxy.

–7th–

That no Person shall be eligible to Serve in the Office of Director unless he be a Stockholder.

–8th–

That the Board of Directors determine the manner of doing business and the Rules and Forms to be pursued, appoint and employ the various Clerks and Servants, which they may find necessary, and dispose of the Money and credit of the Bank for the interest and benefit of the Proprietors; but they are not to employ the money or Credit of the Bank in the drawing or negotiating of any Foreign Bill or Bills of Exchange, or advance a Loan to any Foreign Power whatever.

–9th–

That if at any time it shall be the opinion of a Majority of the Directors that any of their Body are guilty of neglect of Duty or any Mal Practice whereby the Interest of the Bank is or may be affected, such majority of the Directors with or without the consent of the President, may advertise for a general Meeting of the Stockholders to lay before them a Complaint of such neglect of Duty or breach of Trust, and if it appears to the Stockholders to be well founded such Director or Directors may be removed by a majority of Votes.

–10th–

That if any of the Directors shall convert any of the Money or Property of the Bank to his own particular use, or be guilty of fraud or Embezzlement, he shall forfeit his whole share of Stock to the Company and be expelld the Direction by a Majority of all the Directors and thereby rendered incapable of ever serving again in that Office

–11th–

That no President or Director shall receive any other Emolument for his attendance on the Duties of his Office than such as shall be fixed and agreed to by a majority of Votes at a General Election.

–12th–

That there shall be a Meeting of the Directors Quarterly for the purpose of regulating the affairs of the Bank and not less than Seven shall constitute a Board, who may adjourn from time to time; and the President if necessary may call a Meeting of the Directors at any intermediate time; At every Meeting of the Directors all Questions are to be decided by a majority of Votes.

–13th–

That the President or a Majority of the Directors shall have Power to call a General Meeting of the Stockholders by an Advertisement in the public Papers whenever it appears to them there is urgent occasion.

14th.

That the Cashier and every principal Clerk do give a Security for their Trust to such an Amount as a Majority of all the Directors shall require.

–15th–

That all Notes issued by the Bank, shall be Signed by the President for the Time being, or any Director who may be fixed upon by the Board for that Purpose, and Counter Signed by the Cashier, or in his absence by a Clerk to be appointed by the Directors.

–16th–

That no Stockholder shall be accountable to any Individual or the Public for Money lodged in the Bank for a greater Sum than the amount of his Stock.

–17th.–

That such a Dividend on the Profits of the Bank as a Majority of all the Directors shall determine to make, shall be declared at least fourteen days previous to the General Election in May 1785; and that all Subsequent Dividends shall be made half yearly.

–18th.–

That all Shares shall be transferable, such Transfer to be made by the Proprietor or Proprietors or his her or their lawful Attorney in Books kept at the Bank for that purpose, which Books shall be always kept open at the usual Office Hours except on particular days previous to the declaring a Dividend of which due Notice shall be given.

–19th–

That the President and Directors shall Petition the Legislature to incorporate the Subscribers or Stockholders under the Name and Title of the President Directors and Company of the Bank of New York, and to pass Laws for inflicting the most exemplary punishment on those who may commit Fraud or Embezzlement; and also to punish the Counterfeiters of Bank Notes and Checks in the like exemplary manner, with such other Clauses in the Act as they shall judge necessary and proper for the Security of the Stockholders and the Public.

–20th–

That the Constitution shall be fairly transcribed upon Parchment and remain at the Bank; the President and Directors when chosen, and prior to the opening of the Bank, shall severally Sign and Seal the same, and take an Oath or Affirmation before a Magistrate, that he will to the best of his Knowledge and abilities conduct the business of the Bank for the Interest and benefit of the Proprietors and agreable to the true intent and meaning of the Constitution which Oath or Affirmation shall also be taken by every future Director when chosen, and before he enters upon the execution of his Trust.

Outline of a Charter for the Bank of New York[1]

[New York, February 23–March 15, 1784][2]

PLAN FOR THE INCORPORATION OF A BANK

1st: The Stile of the Bank to be "The Bank of New-York."

2. The Capital Stock not to Exceed 1,000,000 Dollars; each Share consisting of 500 Dollars.

3. The Subscribers to Elect on the 2d. Monday of May, in each year thirteen Directors to Conduct the Affairs of the Bank, who shall be authorised to Chuse a President; the Mode of Election to be determined by a Majority of the Stockholders.

4. Two permanent Officers of the State, together with the Treasurer to be appointed by the Government as Inspectors of the Bank; who shall at all Times have free Access to its Books, Papers and Deliberations.

5th: In Case the United States should think proper to deposit any Part of their Funds in the Bank, The Commissioners of the Treasury to have the like Inspection, as specified in the preceding Article.

6th. One Fifth of the Actual Stock of the Bank to be always let out on landed Security to the Several Counties of the State, according to such Quotas, and in such manner as the Legislature shall appoint; the Sums lent to be paid by Installments in four years with lawful Interest. The Interest for the first Year to be deducted at the Time of Advancing the money: The Bank to be Judge of the Sufficiency of the Security.

7th. The Bank to make all Payments in Gold or Silver Coin or Bank Notes, at the Election of the Receiver, and not to be obliged to Receive any other Species of money.

8th. If at any Time the Dividend of the Bank should Exceed Eight per Cent; the Surplus to be added to the Capital in Proportion to the Shares held by each Subscriber; and this Surplus to be also lent on landed Security, in addition to the one Fifth Part of the Stock, as Specified in the 6th. Article, and on the Same Conditions.

9th. The Bank never to Engage in Trade.

10th. The Charter to be in Force for Fifteen Years.

D, Hamilton Papers, Library of Congress.

1. The officers of the Bank of New York (see "Constitution of the Bank of New York," February 23–March 15, 1784) were enjoined by its constitution to apply to the legislature for incorporation. The application was accordingly made (H to John B. Church, March 10, 1784), and was read in the Senate on March 18 (New York Senate *Journal*, 1784, 63).

Although this document, like the "Constitution of the Bank of New York," has been attributed to H, there is no evidence, apart from the copy in an unidentified handwriting which is in his papers in the Library of Congress, that he was the author. The New York Assembly *Journal*, 1784, 27, records the receipt of a petition from H, but this was doubtless a petition requesting that he be granted state securities in exchange for continental certificates. See "Petition to the New York Legislature," February 4, 1784.

2. See "Constitution of the Bank of New York," February 23–March 15, 1784, note 2.

To Robert Bayard [1]

New York, March 6, 1784. "Mrs. Naomi Dunbar widow of Daniel Dunbar has retained me as Council in a suit which she expects will shortly be brought in behalf of the state for a house and lot in this city sold by you to her husband. . . . Mrs. Dunbar therefore wishes . . . that you would procure and send over to her a proper conveyance for the house and lot."

ALS, Mr. Justin G. Turner, Los Angeles, California.

1. Bayard was a wealthy merchant and a former Loyalist. His estate had been confiscated by an act of attainder of October 22, 1779. He was William Bayard's brother.

To John B. Church

[*New York, March 6, 1784.* On May 2, 1784, Church wrote to Hamilton: "I have within a few Days Received your Favors of the 7th and 18th Feby. and 6th March." *Letter of March 6 not found.*]

To John B. Church

New York, March 10th. 1784

My Dear Sir

In my last to you [1] I informed you that a project for a land bank had been set on foot by Mr. Sayre [2] as the ostensible Parent; but that I had reason to suspect the Chancellor was the true father.[3] The fact has turned out as I supposed; and the Chancellor with a number of others have since petitioned the Legislature for an exclusive charter for the proposed bank. I thought it necessary not only with a view to your project, but for the sake of the commercial interests of the state to start an opposition to this scheme; and took occasion to point out its absurdity and inconvenience to some of the most intelligent Merchants; who presently saw the matter in a proper light and began to take measures to defeat the plan.

The Chancellor had taken so much pains with the country members, that they all began to be persuaded that the land bank was the true Philosophers stone that was to turn all their rocks and trees into gold—and there was great reason to apprehend a majority of the Legislature would have adopted his views. It became necessary to convince the projectors themselves of the impracticability of their scheme and to counteract the impressions they had made by a direct application to the Legislature. Some of the Merchants to effect these purposes set on foot a subscription for a money-bank and called upon me to subscribe.[4] I was a little embarrassed how to act but upon the whole I concluded it best to fall in with them, and endeavour to induce them to put the business upon such a footing as might enable you with advantage to combine your interests with theirs; for since the thing had been taken up upon the broad footing of the whole body of the Merchants, it appeared to me that it never would be your interest to persue a distinct project in opposition to theirs; but that you would prefer, so far as you might choose to employ money in this way, to become purchaser in the general bank. The object, on this supposition, was to have the bank founded on such principles as would give you a proper weight in the direction. Unluckily for this purpose I entered rather late into the measure: proposals had been agreed upon, in which among other things it was settled that no stockholder to whatever amount should have more than seven votes, which was the number to which a holder of ten shares was to be intitled. At an after meeting of some of the most influential characters I engaged them so far to depart from this ground as to allow a vote for every five shares above ten.

The stockholders have since thought proper to appoint me one of the directors. I shall hold it till Wadsworth and you come out and if you choose to become parties to this bank, I shall make a vacancy for one of you. I enclose you the constitution and the names of the President directors and Cashier.[5]

An application for a Charter has been made to the Legislature with a petition against granting an exclusive one to the land bank. The measures which have been taken appear to have had their effect upon the minds of the partizans of the land bank.[6]

The affairs of the bank in Pensylvania [7] appear to be in some confusion. They have stopped discounts; but I have no apprehension that there is any thing more in the matter than temporary embarrassment, from having a little overshot their mark in their issues of paper, and from the opposition which the attempt to establish a new bank had produced.[8]

I have had no tolerable offer for your land in Connecticut. Forty shillings that currency per acre has been the highest but I have written to Mr Campfield [9] requesting him to inform himself well of the value of the land; and if he thinks it is not worth more to accept the offer. I am told he is a judicious and honest man and I presume the land where it is will never be worth anything to you if it remains unsold. Betsey joins me in best affections to Mrs. C & yourself. Our Compliments to W.[10]

I am most sincerely Dr sir   Yr. affectionate friend & servant
A Hamilton

ADfS, Hamilton Papers, Library of Congress.

1. Letter not found.

2. Stephen Sayre, a London banker. See Church to H, February 7, 1784, note 6.

3. Robert R. Livingston. For an explanation of the attempt of Sayre and Livingston to organize a bank, see Church to H, February 7, 1784, note 6.

4. See "Constitution of the Bank of New York," February 23–March 15, 1784.

5. The names of the president, cashier, and directors are given in "Constitution of the Bank of New York," February 23–March 15, 1784, note 1.

6. On February 17, 1784, Robert R. Livingston and others had petitioned the Assembly for "Letters of Incorporation" for a land bank. It was not until March 18, 1784, that the petition of the "President, Directors, and Company of the Bank of New York" for an "Act of Incorporation" was read in the Senate.

7. The Bank of North America.

8. For information on the attempt to establish the Bank of Pennsylvania, see John Chaloner to H, January 21, 1784.

9. On August 30, 1783, H had written to John Canfield of Sharon, Con-

necticut, requesting him to sell a farm owned by John B. Church in the township of Salisbury.

10. Jeremiah Wadsworth, who was in Europe with Church.

From John Chaloner

Philada. March 16, 1784

Sir

Herewith you have a letter from Mr Church which came to hand by the last Post.[1] Yesterday at a meeting of the Stockholders of the New Bank they agreed to withdraw their Petition for a Charter & that Institution does not go on.[2] You will please therefore to give order respectg the monies I subscribed on acct of Mr Church for that Purpose.

I am with great respect Sir   Your

A Hamilton Esqr

⅌ Post

LC, Historical Society of Pennsylvania, Philadelphia.

1. Letter not found.

2. To prevent the creation of a rival bank (see Chaloner to H, January 21, 1784), the Bank of North America altered its original plan to issue 1,000 shares of stock by enlarging the issue to 4,000 shares. As the enlarged stock issue made it possible for them to share in the profits of an established institution, the promoters of the Bank of Pennsylvania gave up their plan to form a rival bank.

To Gouverneur Morris [1]

[New York, March 21, 1784]

Dr. Sir

Permit me to introduce to Your acquaintance and attention Mr Seaton Cashier of the Bank of New York.[2] He is just setting out for Philadelphia to procure materials, and information in the forms of business. I recommend him to you, because I am persuaded you will with pleasure facilitate his object. Personally I dare say you will be pleased with him.

He will tell you of our embarrassments and prospects. I hope an incorporation of the two banks which is evidently the interest of both has put an end to differencies in Philadelphia.[3] Here a wild and impracticable scheme of a land bank stands in our way; the projectors of it persevering in spite of the experience they have that all the mercantile and monied influence is against it.[4]

March 21

G M Esqr.

AL[S], Hamilton Papers, Library of Congress.
    1. *JCHW*, I, 416, and *HCLW*, IX, 399, give Thomas FitzSimons, a director of the Bank of North America, as the recipient of this letter. It was addressed to Gouverneur Morris, for on the lower left-hand margin of the MS are the initials "G.M." in H's writing. The same or a similar letter may have been sent to FitzSimons, for William Seton on March 27, 1784, wrote to H: "Allow me now particularly to thank you for your kind letter to Mr. Fitzsimmons."
    2. William Seton, a New York merchant, had been a passive Loyalist during the American Revolution. At the organization meeting of the Bank of New York on March 15, 1784, he was elected cashier of that institution.
    3. See John Chaloner to H, March 16, 1784.
    4. See John B. Church to H, February 7, 1784.

To John Chaloner

[*New York, March 22, 1784.* On March 25, 1784, Chaloner wrote to Hamilton: "Yours of the 22d Instant I have just now reced." *Letter not found.*]

From John Chaloner

Philada March 25 1784

Dear sir

Yours of the 22nd Instant [1] I have just now reced and shall attend to your directions. I never charge Mr Church Commissions on receiving Cash because the charge of Commissions on his property in my hands is considerable large but if this transaction is not for him, I ought to have a small Comm[issio]n. I have reced the Package for Mrs Hamilton, & will forward it by the first Vessell to New York. I do not apprehend any danger of being shut out from the Bank, unless they sho'd in April next when the Stockholders meets lessen the number of shares proposed for sale. The Bank do very little discounts at present, & I think they have no prospect of making such large dividends in future as they have done. The Specie has and is going very fast out of the Country: I think our friends will be too late to execute their object & I fear the great exports of Specie will dissolve all the *Banks* in a very little time. Our Assembly has applied to the Bank for two hundred thousand pounds on Loan, to be taken up by such of the Inhabitants as could mortgage Value for the security thereof, paymt of which to be made in Gales as may be agreed on.[2] The application I believe was made in consequence of Mr Wilsons[3] promise on behalf of the Bank, that they would lend on this plan 200,000 Dollars—and 300,000 for the purpose of paying their Quota of 82 & 83-taxes. The Bank informd the Committee applying, that their situation at present would not admit of their complying with their request but that they were chearfully disposed to do it as soon as circumstances would admit, which they hoped would not be long. The Committee then asked for a Credit on £200,000 paper to be issued by them, & the Bank to receive it as Specie. This they positively & pointedly refused. The Committee suggested that it was in their power, & they should make paper money to alleviate the distresses of the Country if they could not borrow, here ended the Conferrence. From all which consided with the disposition of the house to make paper money, It is not unlikely but that events may take place hear in a Year or less. At present the Season is to far advanced to go into the measure, otherwise it would be effected this session, another House may think differently, but as it is the universal cry of the People of the back Countries, it is full likely they will be of similar sentiments and oppinions with the Present.

Mrs Chaloner joins me in Compliments to Mrs Hamilton & I remain with the greatest respect   Dr Sir   Your most Obdt Servt

Alexr Hamilton Esqr

LC, Historical Society of Pennsylvania, Philadelphia.

1. Letter not found.

2. In a letter to John B. Church and Jeremiah Wadsworth, dated March 25, 1784, Chaloner described the loan in greater detail. The Assembly wished to borrow the money, he wrote, "on a plan similar to one adopted here a short time before the War which accomodated Many People with money on very easy terms. The Plan was: Money was struck and loaned to Individuals at Common Interest—they Mortgaging Property three times the value of the money—but the borrower had the Privilege of paying off his debt in Stipulated Cash" (Jeremiah Wadsworth Papers, Connecticut Historical Society, Hartford).

3. James Wilson, a Philadelphia lawyer, was at this time a member of the Continental Congress and a director of the Bank of North America.

From William Seton [1]

Philadelphia 27 March 1784

Dear Sir

You will have seen by my Letters to the Direction how I have proceeded since my coming here. Allow me now particularly to thank you for your kind Letter to Mr: Fitzsimmons, as from him I have already received every assistance and shall derive every necessary Information: [2] I find he is the Leading Man in the Direction of the Bank of North America abstracted from its connection with the State, which part of its business I have no need to pry into.

You will observe by my Letter of this day to our President [3] that I have been requested to postpone my Visits to the Bank until they shall be well informed that the Bank of New York has or actually will obtain a Charter. Altho' I am confident this is only an ostensible reason for not wishing to see me at the Bank, it will be highly necessary I should be regularly informed of what is doing in this respect, that I may be able to speak fully and with firmness to the Subject; therefore exclusive of any Letter the Direction may write to me, I trust you will be kind enough to communic⟨ate⟩ whatever may appear to you, essential for me to know.

The fact is, (and which cannot be communicated to ⟨you⟩ and therefore not mentioned in my Official Letter) their moti⟨ve in not⟩ wishing to see me at the Bank just now, arises from their being at present in very great confusion—the Opposition of the New Bank began it,[4] and being pressed so hard by this Opposition, they were obliged to lay themselves so open, that it evidently appeared if carried further it would strike too fatal a Blow, therefore for the safety of the Community at large it became absolutely necessary ⟨to⟩ drop the Idea of a New Bank and to join Hand in Hand to relieve the Old Bank from the Shock it had received; Gold and Silver had been extracted in such amounts that Discounting was stopd, and for this fortnight past not any business has been done at ⟨the⟩ Bank in this Way; the distress it has occasioned to those dependent on Circulation and engaged in large Speculations, is severe, and as if their

Cup of Misery must overflow, by the last arrival from Europe, Intelligence is received that no less a Sum than £60,000, Sterling of Mr. Morris Bills drawn for the Dutch Loan are under Protest. It is well known that by some means or other the Bank must provide for this Sum. The Child must not desert its Parent in distress—and such is their Connection that whatever is fatal to the one, must be so to the other; however the Man who has more than once by his consumate abilities saved the American Empire from Ruin, will no doubt be found equal to overcome these temporary Inconveniencies and to restore universal Confidence and good order.

I trust you will be guarded in your conversation with others on this Subject, least it might recoil on me, and not only place me in a disagreable Situation but defeat the purposes of my coming here.

I have had several Interviews with our friend Govr: Morris; he is for making the Bank of New York a Branch of the Bank of North America, but we differ widely in our Ideas of the benefits that would result from such a Connection.

If it will not be intruding too much upon your time and goodness may I request that you will now and then inform me what is doing by our Legislature—and permit me to assure you that it will ever give me singular pleasure to have it in my power to evince the respect and esteem with which I am   Dear sir   Your Obedient and very Humble Servant   Wm Seton

ALS, Hamilton Papers, Library of Congress.
    1. Seton was cashier of the Bank of New York.
    2. Thomas FitzSimons, a director of the Bank of North America. For information on H's letter to FitzSimons, see H to Gouverneur Morris, March 21, 1784, note 1.
    3. Alexander McDougall.
    4. For information on "the New Bank"—the Bank of Pennsylvania—see John Chaloner to H, January 21, 1784.

From Hugh Seton [1]

[*England, March 30, 1784.* On June 18, 1784, Hamilton wrote to Seton: "I have been duely honored with your letter of the 30th. of March." *Letter not found.*]

    1. Hugh Seton of Leicester Fields, County of Middlesex, England, was the partner of John Ballantyne of Bologne, France, in the firm of Charles and

Hugh Smith and Company. Seton asked H to collect a debt for him. **See** H to Seton, June 18, 1784.

To ————————

New York, March 31, 1784. "I have considered the Patent to Mr. Woolley and am in doubt whether it is valid or not so far as it gives an exclusive right of ferriage; as this may be construed into a monopoly."

ALS, Bank of New York, New York City.

From Jacob Le Roy [1]

Greenwich [Connecticut] March, 1784. Instructs Hamilton to collect interest on money owed to Le Roy by John Reade.

ALS, Hamilton Papers, Library of Congress.
    1. Le Roy was a member of the New York merchant firm of Jacob Le Roy and Sons.

Promissory Note from John Campbell to Stephen Rapalje

[New York, April 1, 1784.] Hamilton engages to pay promissory note from John Campbell [1] to Stephen Rapalje [2] if Campbell defaults.

D, in writing of H, signed by John Campbell and H, Hamilton Papers, Library of Congress.
    1. Campbell was a merchant who lived at 31 Hanover Square, New York City.
    2. Rapalje was a New York merchant.

To Gouverneur Morris [1]

[New York, April 7, 1784]

Pardon me My Dr. Sir for not sooner having obeyed your orders with respect to the inclosed. I part with it reluctantly; for that is so rare an article, that when we get so much of it in so small a compass we can not easily consent to be dispossessed of it.

I am very happy to hear of the union of your two banks; for you will believe me when I tell you, that on more deliberate consideration, I was led to view the competition in a different light from that in which it at first struck me.[2] I had no doubt that it was against the interests of the proprietors; but on a super[fi]cial view I perceived benefits to the community which on a more close inspection I found were not real.

You well call our proceedings here *strange doings;* if some folks were paid to counteract the prosperity of the state, they could not take more effectual measures than they do. But it is in vain to attempt to kick against the Pricks.

Discrimination bills—Partial taxes—schemes to engross public property in the hands of those who have present power—to banish the real wealth of the state and substitute paper bubbles are the only dishes that suit the public palate at this time.

Permit me to ask your opinion on a point of importance to the NY bank—the best mode of receiving and paying out Gold. I am aware of the evils of that which has been practiced upon in Philadelphia—*weighing it in quantities*—but I cannot satisfy myself about a substitute; unless there could be a coinage.

Favour me with your sentiments on this subject as soon as you can.

Believe me with equal warmth and sincerity. Yrs.   AH

N York
April 7. 1784
G Morris Esqr

ALS, Hamilton Papers, Library of Congress.
1. Morris was at this time practicing law in Philadelphia.
2. The Bank of North America had prevented the creation of a rival institution, the Bank of Pennsylvania, by enlarging its capital stock to allow the participation of many of the promoters of the rival bank in the Bank of North America.

Second Letter from Phocion [1]

[New York, April, 1784]

The little hasty production, under the signature of Phocion, has met with a more favourable reception from the public, than was expected. The force of plain truth has carried it along against the

A Second Letter from Phocion to the Considerate Citizens of New-York. Containing Remarks on Mentor's Reply (New-York, Printed by Samuel Loudon, 1784).

1. The Philadelphia edition of H's *Second Letter from Phocion* was entitled *Colonel Hamilton's Second Letter, from Phocion to the Considerate Citizens of New-York on the Politics of the Times, in Consequence of the Peace: Containing Remarks on Mentor's Reply* (Philadelphia, Printed and Sold by Robert Bell in Third Street, 1784). H's first Letter from Phocion is dated January 1–February 11, 1784.

H's *Second Letter from Phocion* was written in reply to *Mentor's Reply to Phocion's Letter; With Some Observations on Trade. Addressed to the Citizens of New-York* (New York, Printed by Shepard Kollock, No. 22, Hanover-Square, 1784).

The authorship of *Mentor's Reply* generally has been ascribed to Isaac Ledyard (E. Wilder Spaulding, *New York in the Critical Period* [New York, 1932], 129; John B. McMaster, *A History of the People of the United States* [New York, 1918], I, 127–28; Stokes, *Iconography of Manhattan*, V, 1183; Hamilton, *History*, III, 38). There is, however, no evidence that he was the author.

During the Revolution Isaac Ledyard served as a surgeon's mate in the First New York Regiment from March to November, 1776, and as assistant purveyor of the hospital department from October, 1780, to July, 1782. Nothing is known of his career after the Revolution. An Isaac Ledyard of Newtown, Queens County, is listed in the first United States census (*Heads of Families . . . 1790*, 152). In 1792, Ledyard wrote to H a series of letters dealing with the political situation in New York, and on March 27, 1792, he wrote to H concerning two petitions which he had sent to the United States Congress.

Given Ledyard's obscurity and the fact that he and H were political allies in 1792 and presumably earlier, there is little reason to assume that he wrote *Mentor's Reply*.

Mentor's Reply contains only the date 1784. It probably was written during February or March, 1784, for it must have been published soon after the first *Letter from Phocion* appeared. In the preface to his pamphlet "Mentor" wrote: "The Author feels himself constrained to beg his readers indulgence, for the hasty manner, which the scantiness of his time (not being able to devote but three evenings to it) has obliged him to observe in preparing this address." The address was reprinted in Philadelphia late in March, 1784.

H's *Second Letter from Phocion* was probably written during April, 1784. Toward the end of his letter H refers to a bill "depending before the House of Assembly, for putting various descriptions of persons out of the protection of government" and adds that he does not believe that such a measure "can obtain the sanction of the majority." The bill to which he referred was "An Act to Preserve the Freedom and Independence of this State, and for other stream of prejudice; and the principles, it holds out, have gained ground, in spite of the opposition of those, who were either too angry, or too much interested to be convinced. Men of this description, have, till lately, contented themselves with virulent invectives against the Writer, without attempting to answer his arguments; but alarmed at the progress of the sentiments advocated by him, one of them has at last come forward with an answer; with what degree of success, let those, who are most partial to his opinion, determine.

To say, that the answer of Mentor is a feeble attempt, would be no derogation from his abilities; for, in fact, the cause he espouses, admits of nothing solid; and, as one of its partizans, he is only to be blamed for not knowing its weak sides better, than to have been tempted to expose it to the experiment of a defence.

But, before I enter farther into the subject, I shall take occasion to acknowledge, with regret, the injudicious appearance of warmth in my former letter; [2] calculated, with many minds, to raise prejudices against the truths it contains, and liable to be misrepresented into a general censure on that part of the community, whose zeal, sacrifices and sufferings must ever render them respectable to the true friends of the revolution. I shall only observe in apology (as is truly the case) that whatever severity of animadversion may have been indulged, was wholly directed against a *very small* number of men, who are manifestly aiming at nothing, but the acquisition of power and profit to themselves; and who, to gratify their avidity for these objects, would trample upon every thing sacred in society, and overturn the foundations of public and private security. It is difficult for a man, conscious of a pure attachment to the public weal, who sees it invaded and endangered by such men, under specious but false pretences, either to think, or to speak of their conduct, without indignation. It is equally difficult for one, who in questions

---

Purposes therein mentioned," passed by the legislature on May 12, 1784. The title of this act was changed several times between its introduction, early in March, 1784, and its final passage. The *Second Letter from Phocion* must have been written before May 3, the date on which the act was passed by the legislature and sent to the Council of Revision.

That H's *Second Letter from Phocion* was written in April, 1784, is also suggested by the fact that it was advertised as separately published in *The Pennsylvania Gazette*, April 14, 1784.

2. "Mentor" accused the author of *A Letter from Phocion* of displaying "in an eminent degree, that great disqualification for a statesman, an uncontroulable warmth of temper."

that affect the community, regards *principles* only, and not *men*, to look with indifference on attempts to make the great principles of social right, justice and honour, the victims of personal animosity or party intrigue.

More tenderness is indeed due to the mistakes of those, who have suffered too much to reason with impartiality, whose honest prejudices, grown into habits by the impressions of an eight years war, cannot at once accommodate themselves to that system which the public good requires, and whose situations are less favourable to distinguishing between doctrines invented to serve the turn of a revolution, and those which must give permanent prosperity to the state.

These observations I have thought proper to premise, in justice to my own intentions, and I shall now proceed, as concisely as possible, to examine the suggestions of Mentor, interspersing as I go along, some remarks on objections which though omitted by him, have been urged in other shapes against the principles of Phocion.

Mentor proposes to treat the sentiments of Phocion as a political novelty, but if he is serious, it is a proof that he is not even "tolerably well informed." They are as old as any regular notions of free government among mankind, and are to be met with, not only in every speculative Writer, on these subjects, but are interwoven in the theory and practice of that code, which constitutes the law of the land. They speak the common language of this country at the beginning of the revolution, and are essential to its future happiness and respectability.

The principles of all the arguments I have used or shall use, lie within the compass of a few simple propositions, which, to be assented to, need only to be stated.

First, That no man can forfeit or be justly deprived, without his consent, of any right, to which as a member of the community he is entitled, but for some crime incurring the forfeiture.

Secondly, That no man ought to be condemned unheard, or punished for supposed offences, without having an opportunity of making his defence.*

* *Vide* Address of Congress to the people of Great Britain, September 5, 1774.[3]

3. The date given by H is incorrect. *The Address of Congress to the People of Great Britain* was read in, and approved by, Congress on October 21, 1774 (see *JCC*, I, 81–90).

Thirdly, That a crime is *an act* committed or omitted, in violation of a public law, either forbidding or commanding it.†

Fourthly, That a prosecution is in its most precise signification, an *inquiry* or *mode of ascertaining*, whether a particular person has committed, or omitted such *act*.

Fifthly, That *duties* and *rights* as applied to subjects are reciprocal; or in other words, that a man cannot be a *citizen* for the purpose of punishment, and not a *citizen* for the purpose of privilege.

These propositions will hardly be controverted by any man professing to be a friend to civil liberty. The application of them will more fully appear hereafter.

By the declaration of Independence on the 4th of July, in the year 1776, acceded to by our Convention on the ninth, the late colony of New-York became an independent state. All the inhabitants, who were subjects under the former government, and who did not withdraw themselves upon the change which took place, were to be considered as citizens, owing allegiance to the new government, This, at least, is the legal presumption; and this was the principle, in fact, upon which all the measures of our public councils have been grounded. Duties have been exacted, and punishments inflicted according to this rule. If any exceptions to it were to be admitted, they could only flow from the *indulgence* of the state to such individuals, as from peculiar circumstances might desire to be permitted to stand upon a different footing.

The inhabitants of the southern district, before they fell under the power of the British army, were as much citizens of the state as the inhabitants of other parts of it. They must, therefore, continue to be such, unless they have been divested of that character by some posterior circumstance. This circumstance must, either be—

Their having, by the fortune of war, fallen under the power of the British army.

Their having forfeited their claim by their own misconduct.

Their having been left out of the compact by some subsequent association of the body of the state, or

Their having been dismembered by treaty.

† Blackstone, Vol. IV, page 5.⁴

4. H's reference is, of course, to Sir William Blackstone's *Commentaries on the Laws of England*, presumably to the American edition printed in 1771. The sentence to which Blackstone is given as a reference is, except for H's omission of two words, an exact quotation.

The first of these circumstances according to the fundamental principles of government, and the constant practice of nations could have no effect in working a forfeiture of their citizenship. To allow it such an effect, would be to convert misfortune into guilt; it would be in many instances, to make the negligence of the society, in not providing adequate means of defence for the several parts, the crime of those parts which were the immediate sufferers by that negligence. It would tend to the dissolution of society, by loosening the ties which bind the different parts together, and justifying those who should for a moment fall under the power of a conqueror, not merely in yielding such a submission as was exacted from them, but in taking a willing, interested and decisive part with him.

It was the policy of the revolution, to inculcate upon every citizen the obligation of renouncing his habitation, property, and every private concern for the service of his country, and many of us have scarcely yet learned to consider it as less than treason to have acted in a different manner. But it is time we should correct the exuberances of opinions propagated through policy, and embraced from enthusiasm; and while we admit, that those who did act so disinterested and noble a part, deserve the applause and, wherever they can be bestowed with propriety the rewards of their country, we should cease to impute indiscriminate guilt to those, who, submitting to the accidents of war, remained with their habitions and property. We should learn, that this conduct is tolerated by the general sense of mankind; and that according to that sense, whenever the state recovers the possession of such parts as were for a time subdued, the citizens return at once to all the rights, to which they were formerly entitled.

As to the second head of forfeiture by misconduct, there is no doubt, that all such as remaining within the British lines, did not merely yield an obedience, which they could not refuse, without ruin; but took a voluntary and interested part with the enemy, in carrying on the war, became subject to the penalties of treason. They could not however, by that conduct, make themselves aliens, because though they were bound to pay a temporary and qualified obedience to the conqueror, they could not transfer their eventual allegiance from the state to a foreign power. By becoming aliens too, they would have ceased to be traitors; and all the laws of the state passed during the revolution, by which they are considered and punished as subjects, would have been, by that construction, unintelligible and unjust. The idea indeed of citizens transforming themselves into aliens, by taking part against the state, to which they belong, is altogether of new-invention, unknown and inadmissible in law, and contrary to the nature of the social compact.

But were this not the case, an insurmountable difficulty would still remain, for how shall we ascertain who are aliens or traitors, let us call them which we will. It has been seen that the boundaries of the British lines cannot determine the question; for this would be to say, that the merely falling under the power of the British army, constituted every man a *traitor* or an *alien*. It would be to confound one third of the citizens of the state in promiscuous guilt and degradation, without evidence, or enquiry. It would be to make crimes, which are in their nature personal and individual, aggregate and territorial. Shall we go into an enquiry to ascertain the crime of each person? *This would be a prosecution;* * and the treaty forbids all future prosecutions. Shall the Legislature take the map and make a geographical delineation of the rights and disqualifications of its citizens? This would be to measure innocence and guilt, by latitude and longitude. It would be to *condemn* and *punish*, not one man, but thousands for *supposed offences*, without giving them an opportunity of making their defence. God forbid that such an act of barefaced tyranny should ever disgrace our history! God forbid that the body of the people should be corrupt enough to wish it, or even to submit to it!

But here we are informed by Mentor, that the treaty, instead of offering any obstacles to the views of those, who wish to metamorphose their fellow citizens into aliens, is precisely the thing which removes the difficulty.[5] Mentor is thus far right; that if they are aliens at all, it must be by some stipulations in the treaty, but it requires not a little dexterity to shew, that such a stipulation exists.

---

* *Vide* proposition 4*th.*

5. In the passage to which H is referring, "Mentor" had written:
"But it is by treaty, that they become aliens or subjects of England. By the treaty England adopted them as subjects, and by ratifying that treaty, the states and this state, from the share she had in it, consented to that adoption. And this is the great benefit of the treaty to them, which Phocion says, we would violate; whereas it appears that we, who he dubs heated and designing men, are the real supporters of it."

If it exists at all, it must be collected from the 5th and 6th articles. Let us, by analyzing these articles, try if we can find it out.

The fifth article speaks in the first clause of *real British subjects* whose estates *had been confiscated*, and stipulates that Congress shall recommend a restitution.

In the second clause it speaks of *persons resident* in districts in the possession of the British forces, who had not borne arms against the United States of whose estates, *also confiscated*, Congress are in like manner to recommend a restitution.

In the third clause, persons of every other description are comprehended, who are to be permitted to remain twelve months unmolested, in any of the states, to solicit a restoration of their property, which *had been confiscated;* Congress recommending, even with respect to them, a restitution, on condition of their refunding to the present possessors, where there had been a sale, the bona fide price given by them for the estates in their possession.

It is apparent from the dissection of the article, that the inhabitants in the Southern district, possessed by the British army, are not confounded in one general mass of alienism, as has been asserted. We find the express words of description are *real British subjects*, and as contradistinguished from them, *persons resident* in districts within the possession of the British arms. These last, by the *letter* as well as the spirit of the article are deemed *not British subjects*.

There is no intelligible medium, between a real British subject, and one that is not a British subject at all. A man either *is* or *is not* the subject of a country. The word *real*, as applied to the affirmative, is a redundancy. Its natural contrasts are *fictitious* or *pretended*. If we should call the persons of other descriptions in the article *fictitious* or *pretended* British subjects, instead of justifying, it would exclude the construction given by Mentor. For if they were only *fictitious* or *pretended* British subjects, they must be real American subjects; or in other words, if they were not *real* British subjects, which by necessary implication they are declared not to be, they must of necessity be American subjects.

The phrase *real British subjects*, strictly considered, is innaccurate; but its practical import, with the help of a little candor, is easily fixed. It is well known that in this and other states, the property of persons, who had never been subjects of this country, before or after the revolution, but who had truly been subjects of Great-Britain, had in many instances been confiscated. Sir Henry Clinton, the late Governor Tryon, Lord Dunmore, are examples among us of the real British subjects in the contemplation of the treaty. All the rest are of course American subjects.

To understand the fifth and sixth articles relatively, it is necessary to remark that all the different classes described in the fifth article agree in one *common quality;* they are all persons whose *property had been already confiscated.* I have placed this fact in a pointed view; because it shews incontestibly, that the persons who are the objects of the fifth article, and those who are the objects of the sixth, are totally different. The one relates to persons whose property had been confiscated, and *aims* at restitution; the other relates to those whose property had not yet been confiscated, who were not actually suffering the sentence of the law, and has for object to prevent future prosecutions, confiscations, or injuries to individuals on account of their conduct in the war.

This distinction solves the seeming contradiction between the fifth and sixth articles; the former providing for the future residence of persons of a particular description within the state for a twelve month; the other prohibiting all future injury or damage to persons, liberty or property. At first sight, the great extent of the latter provision appears to supercede, and render absurd, the former; but the two articles are reconciled, by considering those, who had already suffered the sentence of the law, as not within the purview of the sixth article, to arrest or remit that sentence; while all others against whom sentence had not passed, are within the protection of the sixth article. It does not operate with a retrospective and restorative influence, but looks forward and stops the future current of prosecution and punishment.

To illustrate, in a more striking manner, the fallacy of Mentor's comment upon the treaty, I shall give a recital of it, with some explanatory additions, the fairness of which I think will not be disputed.

"In the sixth article (says he) it is provided that *no one shall suffer* in his person, liberty, or property, on account of the part he may have taken in the war;" and yet though no one, consistently with the treaty, can hereafter suffer in either of those respects, yet many, consistently with the treaty, may be declared aliens, may be stripped of the most valuable rights of citizenship, and may be banished from the state, without injury to person, liberty, or property, "The fifth article," though it speaks of none but those who have already had their estates confiscated, "describes the persons provided for by the sixth," which indeed says, that there *shall be* no future prosecutions, nor confiscations, nor injury to person, liberty, or property; but this only means, that there shall be no future prosecutions commenced against those, who have been already *attainted and banished*, nor confiscations made of the estates of those whose estates *have been already confiscated*, nor injuries done to the persons, liberty, and property, of those, who are already to be esteemed *dead in law* by attainder and exile; but with respect to all those who have not been already *attainted, banished*, and *subjected to confiscation*, (the only persons comprehended in the fifth article and provided for in the sixth) we may prosecute, banish, confiscate, disfranchise, and do whatever else we think proper. The fifth article stipulates the good offices of Congress for those, who have been already ruined, and the sixth benignly takes care that they shall not be ruined a second time; but leaves all others to their destiny and our mercy. "The fifth article, distinguishes, the persons who are the objects of it, into three classes—First, those who are real British subjects—The second, those" (meaning British subjects who were not real British subjects, described by the appellation of persons resident in districts in the possession of the British forces) "who had not taken arms against the country—The third class are described by the provision that is made for them, viz. They shall have liberty to go into any part of the United States for twelve months to solicit a restoration of their estates, that may have been confiscated. This class must be those who belonging to America, have taken arms against their country. The first and second class it is agreed, that Congress shall recommend to the states a restoration of their property. The third it seems were too infamous for the English minister to ask any consideration for, except the wretched privilege of asking it for themselves," though in fact, with respect even to them, it is expressly stipulated, that Congress shall recommend a restoration of their estates, rights and properties, on paying to the present possessors the bona fide price given for them, where there has been an actual sale. "But (continues he) I can find no where even a request, and that only implied, that any of the three classes may dwell among us, and enjoy the immunities and privileges of citizens; for the first class are considered as former subjects; the second and third as acquired subjects of England," *acquired* but not *real*.

Thus we see, by taking the out-lines of Mentor's construction, and filling up the canvass in a manner suited to the design, the whole is a groupe of absurdities; or in other words by connecting the consequences with the principles of his comment, on the treaty, the result is too ridiculous not to strike the meanest understanding.

It must appear by this time manifest, that there is nothing in the terms of the treaty, which countenances the supposition, that those who have been within the British lines are considered and stipulated for as aliens. One ground, upon which this idea has been originally adopted, was that it would have been improper to have stipulated for them at all, if they were not aliens; but I have shown in my former letter, that a stipulation for subjects, in similar circumstances, has been far from unprecedented.

A good criterion by which to determine the meaning of the treaty, in this respect, is to recur to the impressions that it made, on its first appearance; before there had been time to contrive and substitute an artificial to the natural and obvious sense of the words. Every man, by appealing to his own bosom, will recollect, that he was at first struck with an opinion that the disaffected were secured from every future deprivation and injury whatever; and however many may have been chagrined at the idea, that they should be admitted to a party of privileges with those who had supported the revolution, none doubted that this was the sense of the treaty. Indeed the principal doubt seemed to be, in the first instance, whether the sixth article was not so broad, as to protect even those, who had been attainted, from personal injury, in case of their return within the state.

I shall not, in this place, revive the question of the power of Congress to make this stipulation; not only because Mentor appears to have conceded this point, and to acknowledge our obligation to a faithful observance of the treaty; but because what has been offered in my former letter on this head, must continue to appear to me to be absolutely conclusive; until some satisfactory limits can be assigned to the powers of war, peace and treaty, vested in Congress, other than those I have mentioned,—the public safety and the fundamental constitutions of the society.

When any different and intelligible line shall be drawn—I will give up the question, if I cannot shew it is inadmissible in practice.

The common interests of humanity, and the general tranquility of the world, require that the power of making peace, wherever lodged, should be construed and exercised liberally; and even in cases where its extent may be doubtful, it is the policy of all wise nations to give it latitude rather than confine it. The exigencies of a community, in time of war, are so various and often so critical, that it would be extremely dangerous to prescribe narrow bounds to that power, by which it is to be restored. The consequence might frequently be a diffidence of our engagements, and a prolongation of the calamities of war.

It may not be improper, in this place, to answer an objection which has been made to a position contained in my former letter. It is there laid down as a rule, that the breach of a single article of a treaty annuls the whole. The reason of this rule is, that every article is to be regarded as the consideration of some other article.

This has given occasion to observe, that a breach of the treaty on the part of the British, in sending away a great number of negroes, has upon my principles long since annihilated the treaty, and left us at perfect liberty to desert the stipulations, on our part.[6]

This admits of an easy and solid answer. The breach of one article annuls the whole; if the side injured by it chooses to take advantage of it to dissolve the treaty; * but if its interest dictates a different conduct it may wave the breach and let the obligation of the treaty continue. The power of determining whether the treaty has been broken properly belongs to that body who made it. Congress have

---

* Vatel. P. 130, § 48.[7]

6. The observation described in this paragraph was not made by "Mentor." It was, as H states, commonly argued that since the British had refused to abide by the provision of the peace treaty which stipulated that the British should not carry away "negroes or other property of the American inhabitants" the treaty was not binding on the United States.

7. H's reference is, of course, to one of the many editions of Vattel's *The Law of Nations*. His material is taken from Book IV, Ch. IV, p. 130, Sections 46–49.

wisely taken a different course, and instead of reviving the state of hostility by declaring the treaty void, have proceeded upon the presumption of its continuing in force; and by subsequent acts have given it additional validity and strength. The definitive treaty has been since concluded, and proclaimed with a remarkable solemnity and energy for the observance of the citizens of the United States.

The third mode mentioned, by which the inhabitants of the southern district may have lost their rights of citizenship, is their having been left out of the compact by some subsequent association of the body of the state. The fact however is directly the reverse; for not only the constitution makes provision for the representation of the people of the southern district in the Legislature, but during the whole war, by an ordinance of the Convention, who framed the constitution, an actual representation has been kept up in a manner, the regularity of which (whatever might have been the expedience of it) was more than questionable; as all elections were suspended in that part of the state. This circumstance of a constant representation of the inhabitants of the Southern district in the Legislature, during the war, is in a rational as well as a legal light a conclusive refutation of the pretended alienism of those inhabitants by any event of the war, or by any other matter that applies to them in a collective view antecedent to the treaty of peace. To this it may be added, that a variety of the laws of the state, in the course of the war, suppose and treat the inhabitants of the Southern district as subjects; owing allegiance to the state, and consequently having the rights which subjects in general enjoy under the government.*

The argument is still stronger when we attend to what has been done by the government since the restoration of its jurisdiction in the Southern district. We did not wait till a bill of naturalization was passed, to remove the disabilities of the inhabitants, before we proceeded to elections.[8] We did not confine those elections to such persons only, as had resided without the British lines, but left them open to all descriptions of persons, who would choose to take the oath prescribed for that purpose, by the Council. Few indeed in

* *Vide*, Position 5th.

8. The elections were those of December, 1783, authorized by the Council for the Southern District for the selection of city aldermen and representatives to the state legislature. See *A Letter from Phocion*, January 1–February 11, 1784, note 1.

this city, besides those who had been absent, did in fact vote at the elections; but a considerable number did in the counties. And if we should admit the doctrine of the general alienism of the inhabitants of the Southern district, either before, or in consequence of the treaty of peace, a curious question not easy to be solved, would arise as to the validity of the election of many individuals now holding seats in Senate and Assembly. So far as an act of government can decide the point in controversy, it is already decided. The Council for the temporary government of the Southern district in appointing the mode of election—the conduct of the legislature since in admitting the members elected in that mode, are unconstitutional; or the inhabitants at large of the Southern district, either by the treaty, or any antecedent circumstance, are not aliens.

I have dwelt the more largely on this head, not only because the idea of a general alienism of the inhabitants of the Southern district is the ground Mentor has taken; but because some persons who have it in their power to make a mischievous use of it, are endeavouring to give it circulation, where, if it could prevail, it might lead to pernicious consequences. Pressed by the difficulty of discriminating those, who may have forfeited the rights of citizenship from those who have not, without a manifest violation as well of the constitution, as of the treaty of peace, they are willing if possible to devise some general expedient to evade both; and the one they have hit upon is, to declare all those aliens, who lived within the British lines during the war, on the miserable pretence that they are made such by the treaty.[9]

Thus we have another example how easy it is for men to change their principles with their situations—to be zealous advocates for the rights of the citizens when they are invaded by others, and as soon as they have it in their power, to become the invaders themselves—to resist the encroachments of power, when it is the hands of others, and the moment they get it into their own to make bolder

9. The 1783 session of the New York legislature had passed an act entitled "An Act declaratory of the Alienism of Persons therein described." See *A Letter from Phocion*, January 1–February 11, 1784, note 1. The act, which the legislature did not re-enact over the veto of the Council of Revision, declared that all subjects of New York who adhered to the enemy had renounced their allegiance to the state and were thus aliens. As H must have known of the Council's veto of the act, he was at this point referring to the continued acceptance by many New Yorkers of the ideas embodied in the act.

strides than those they have resisted. Are such men to be sanctified with the hallowed name of patriots? Are they not rather to be branded as men who make their passions, prejudices and interests the sole measure of their own and others rights?

This history of mankind is too full of these melancholy instances of human contradiction.

Having mentioned the oath directed to be prescribed to electors in the Southern district, by the Council for the temporary government; I shall take occasion, in this place, with freedom, but with respect, to examine the propriety of that measure.[10]

This measure was founded upon an act of the legislature of this state passed in the year   [11] declaring, that persons who had been guilty of certain matters particularized in that act, should be forever after disqualified from voting at all public elections. I confine myself for the sake of brevity to the general idea of the act. The embarrassment with the Council, no doubt, was, how to ascertain the persons who had incurred the disability. As the matters, to which that disability related, were of a specific nature, it was necessary, they should be specifically ascertained before the law could have its effect.

The Council, therefore, could not satisfy that law, by declaring all those disqualified, who had resided within the British lines during the war. They would not leave the operation of it to a course of judicial investigation and decision, because this would be to fly in the face of the treaty, and appearances were to be preserved. This consideration was strengthened by another. The course of the law must have been dilatory. The elections were to be entered upon. It was deemed inexpedient, that the voice of the citizens at large (which must have been the case if the act of the legislature, in question, had been left to its natural course) should govern these elections. If the returning citizens were not at this juncture gratified, tumults were by some apprehended.

This was a plausible step, and on that account the more dangerous. If we examine it with an unprejudiced eye, we must acknowledge

10. In its call for an election in December, 1783, the Council for the Southern District had stipulated that Loyalists who had taken an oath of allegiance to the state were to be allowed to vote.

11. Space left blank in original. The act to which H is referring was dated March 27, 1778 (*Laws of the State of New York*, I, 28–36).

not only that it was an evasion of the treaty, but a subversion of one great principle of social security, to wit, that every man shall be presumed innocent until he is proved guilty: This was to invert the order of things; and instead of obliging the state to prove the guilt, in order to inflict the penalty, it was to oblige the citizen to establish his own innocence, to avoid the penalty. It was to excite scruples in the honest and conscientious, and to hold out a bribe to perjury.

That this was an evasion of the treaty, the fourth proposition already laid down will illustrate. It was a mode of inquiry who had committed any of those crimes to which the penalty of disqualification was annexed, with this aggravation, that it deprived the citizen of the benefit of that advantage which he would have enjoyed by leaving, as in all other cases, the burthen of the proof upon the prosecutor.

To place this matter in a still clearer light, let it be supposed, that instead of the mode of indictment and trial by jury, the legislature was to declare that every citizen who did not swear he had never adhered to the King of Great-Britain, should incur all the penalties which our treason laws prescribe. Would this not be a palpable evasion of the treaty, and a direct infringement of the constitution? The principle is the same in both cases, with only this difference in the consequences; that in the instance already acted upon, the citizen forfeits a part of his rights,—in the one supposed he would forfeit the whole. The degree of punishment is all that distinguishes the cases. In either justly considered, it is substituting a new and arbitrary mode of prosecution to that antient and highly esteemed one, recognized by the laws and the constitution of the state; I mean the trial by jury.

Let us not forget that the constitution declares that trial by jury in all cases in which it has been formerly used, should remain inviolate forever, and that the legislature should at no time, erect any new jurisdiction which should not proceed, according to the course of the common law. Nothing can be more repugnant to the true genius of the common law, than such an inquisition as has been mentioned into the consciences of men.

A share in the sovereignty of the state, which is exercised by the citizens at large, in voting at elections is one of the most important rights of the subject, and in a republic ought to stand foremost in the estimation of the law. It is that right, by which we exist a free people; and it certainly therefore will never be admitted, that less ceremony ought to be used in divesting any citizen of that right, than in depriving him of his property. Such a doctrine would ill suit the principles of the revolution, which taught the inhabitants of this country to risk their lives and fortunes in asserting their *liberty;* or in other words, their *right* to a *share* in the government. That portion of the soverignty, to which each individual is entitled, can never be too highly prized. It is that for which we have fought and bled; and we should cautiously guard against any precedents, however they may be immediately directed against those we hate, which may in their consequences render our title to this great privilege, precarious. Here we may find the criterion to distinguish the genuine from the pretended whig. The man that would attack that right, in whatever shape, is an enemy to whiggism.

If any oath, with retrospect to past conduct, were to be made the condition, on which individuals, who have resided within the British lines, should hold their estates; we should immediately see, that this proceeding would be tyrannical, and a violation of the treaty, and yet when the same mode is employed to divest that right, which ought to be deemed still more sacred, many of us are so infatuated as to overlook the mischief.

To say that the persons, who will be affected by it, have previously forfeited that right, and that therefore nothing is taken away from them, is a begging of the question. How do we know who are the persons in this situation? If it be answered, this is the mode taken to ascertain it, the objection returns, 'tis an improper mode, because it puts the most essential interests of the citizen upon a worse footing, than we should be willing to tolerate where inferior interests were concerned; and because to elude the treaty it substitutes to the established and legal mode of investigating crimes, and inflicting forfeitures, on that is unknown to the constitution, and repugnant to the genius of our law.

Much stress has been laid upon a couple of unmeaning words in the act, to enforce the penalties of which, the oath was invented. It is declared, that the persons, who have done the several things enumerated in the act, shall be *ipso facto* disqualified. These words of potent sound, but of little substance, have been supposed to include wonderful effects. Let us see if we can give them any definite meaning. If a man commits murder, by the very act *ipso facto*, he incurs the penalty of death; but before he can be hanged, we must enquire whether he has certainly committed the fact. If a man has done any of those things which are declared sufficient to disqualify him from voting, though by the very act, *ipso facto* he incurs the penalty of the law, yet before he can be actually disqualified, we must enquire whether he has really done the act. From this we perceive the words *ipso facto* are mere expletives, which add nothing to the force or efficacy of the law.

It has been said too, that an oath to determine the qualifications of electors, is an usual precaution in free governments; but we may challenge those who make the assertion, to show that retrospective oaths have ever been administered, requiring electors to swear that they have not been guilty of past offences. In all the violence of party which has at different periods agitated Great Britain, nothing of this kind has ever been adopted; but even where religious fanaticism has given an edge to political opposition, and in an undecided contest for the crown, they have never gone further than to prescribe oaths for testing present dispositions towards the government on general principles, without retrospection to particular instances of past mal-conduct. The practical notions of legal liberty established in that country by a series of time would make such an experiment too odious to be attempted by the government. Wise men have thought that even there, they have carried the business of oaths to an exceptionable length; but we who pretend a purer zeal for liberty, in a decided contest, after a formal renunciation of claims by the adverse party, are for carrying the matter to a still more blameable extreme.

Men, whose judgements and intentions I respect, were promoters of the measure, which has occasioned this digression; some from the contagion of popular opinion; others from the too strong impressions of momentary expedience, and a third class from the insensible bias of some *favourite pursuit*.

As to the fourth method in which the inhabitants of the Southern district may have lost their rights of citizenship, a dismemberment by treaty, I have naturally been drawn, under the third head, into a discussion of this, and I trust have shown to the full satisfaction of all candid men, that there is not a shadow of foundation to suppose that such a dismemberment, is in the contemplation of the treaty. A few short remarks shall conclude what I intend to say on this article.

It is a case, without precedent, that a nation in surrendering its acquisitions in war, to the state from which those acquisitions were made, should stipulate for the inhabitants of the country given up as for *its own* subjects. To do it would be both useless and absurd; unless, because the country being surrendered, no reasonable advantage could be derived from retaining the allegiance of its inhabitants; absurd, because the district of territory surrendered being given up as a part of the state, to which the surrender is made, it would be contradictory, by the same act, to acknowledge the right of that state to the *part* given up, and yet to hold up a claim to the allegiance of its inhabitants.

The surrender (for the question does not relate to *original cessions*) carries in itself a decisive implication, that the inhabitants of the country surrendered, are the subjects of the power to which the surrender is made; and the presumption in this case is so strong that nothing but the most positive and unequivocal exceptions in the treaty would be sufficient to defeat it. Laboured constructions to give the treaty that complexion are inadmissable; for if there were room to doubt, the doubt, in just reasoning, should be interpreted against the position, that the inhabitants of the country surrendered were the subjects of the power by which the surrender was made.

The only additional remark I shall make on this head is this: Though we are under great obligations to our ministers for the substance of the treaty, which comprehends all the essential interests of this country; we must acknowledge that the language of it is, in many respects, defective and obscure. The true rule in this case is, not to have recourse to artifical and far-fetched interpretation; but to admit such meanings as the simple and proper import of the words conveys. When therefore it is said in the sixth article. "that there shall be no future prosecutions commenced, nor confiscations made, nor damage done to person, liberty, or property, of any person or persons, on account of the part taken by them in the war," as the natural and obvious scope of the words presents a full amnesty and indemnity for the future; we should not torture our imaginations to pervert them to a different sense.

It has been urged, in support of the doctrines under consideration, that every government has a right to take precautions for its own security, and to prescribe the terms on which its rights shall be enjoyed.[12]

All this is true when understood with proper limitations; but when rightly understood will not be found to justify the conclusions, which have been drawn from the premises.

In the first formation of a government the society may multiply its precautions as much, and annex as many conditions to the enjoyment of its rights, as it shall judge expedient; but when it has once adopted a constitution, that constitution must be the measure of its discretion, in providing for its own safety, and in prescribing the conditions upon which its privileges are to be enjoyed. If the constitution declares that persons possessing certain qualifications shall be entitled to certain rights, while that constitution remains in force, the government which is the mere creature of the constitution, can divest no citizen, who has the requisite qualifications, of his corresponding rights. It may indeed enact laws and annex to the breach of them the penalty of forfeiture; but before that penalty can operate, the existence of the fact, upon which it is to take place, must be ascertained in that mode which the constitution and the fundamental laws have provided. If trial by jury is the mode known and established by that constitution and those laws, the persons who administer the government in deviating from that course will be guilty of usurpation. If the constitution declares that the legislative power of the state shall be vested in one set of men and the judiciary power in another; and those who are appointed to act in a legislative capacity undertake the office of judges, if, instead of confining themselves to passing laws, with proper sanctions to enforce their observance, they go out of their province to decide who are the violators of those laws, they subvert the constitution and erect a tyranny. If the constitution were even silent on particular points those who are intrusted with its power, would be bound in exercising their discretion to consult and pursue its spirit, and to conform to the dictates of reason and equity; if, instead of this, they should undertake to declare whole classes of citizens disfranchised and excluded from the common rights of the society, without hearing, trial,

12. This was an argument used in *Mentor's Reply*.

examination or proof; if, instead of waiting to take away the rights of citizenship from individuals, till the state has convicted them of crimes, by which they are to lose them, before the ordinary and regular tribunal, they institute an inquisition into mens consciences, and oblige them to give up their privileges, or undertake to interpret the law at the hazard of perjury; they expose themselves to the imputation of injustice and oppression.

The right of a government to prescribe the conditions on which its privileges shall be enjoyed, is bounded with respect to those who are already included in the compact, by its original conditions; in admitting strangers it may add new ones; but it cannot without a breach of the social compact deprive those, who have been once admitted of their rights, unless for some declared cause of forfeiture authenticated with the solemnities required by the subsisting compact.

The rights too of a republican government are to be modified and regulated by the principles of such a government. These principles dictate, that no man shall lose his rights without a hearing and conviction, before the proper tribunal; that previous to his disfranchisement, he shall have the full benefit of the laws to make his defence; and that his innocence shall be presumed till his guilt has been proved. These with many other maxims, never to be forgotten in any but tyrannical governments, oppose the aims of those who quarrel with the principles of Phocion.

Cases indeed of extreme necessity are exceptions to all general rules; but these only exist, when it is manifest the safety of the community is in imminent danger. Speculations of possible danger never can be justifying causes of departures from principles on which in the ordinary course of things all private security depends—from principles which constitute the essential distinction between free and arbitrary governments.

When the advocates for legislature discriminations are driven from one subterfuge to another, their last resting place is—that this is a new case, the case of a revolution. Your principles are all right say they, in the ordinary course of society, but they do not apply to a situation like ours. This is opening a wilderness, through all the labyrinths of which, it is impossible to pursue them: The answer to this must be, that there are principles eternally true and which apply to all situations; such as those that have been already enumerated—that we are not now in the midst of a revolution but have happily brought it to a successful issue—that we have a constitution formed as a rule of conduct—that the frame of our government is determined and the general principle of it is settled—that we have taken our station among nations have claimed the benefit of the laws which regulate them, and must in our turn be bound by the same laws—that those eternal principles of social justice forbid the inflicting punishment upon citizens, by an abridgement of rights, or in any other manner, without conviction of some specific offence by regular trial and condemnation—that the constitution we have formed makes the trial by jury the only proper mode of ascertaining the delinquences of individuals—that legislative discriminations, to supersede the necessity of inquiry and proof, would be an usurpation on the judiciary powers of the government, and a renunciation of all the maxims of civil liberty—that by the laws of nations and the rules of justice, we are bound to observe the engagements entered into on our behalf, by that power which is invested with the constitutional prerogative of treaty—and that the treaty we have made in its genuine sense, ties up the hands of government from any species of future prosecution or punishment, on account of the part taken by individuals in the war.

Among the extravagancies with which these prolific times abound, we hear it often said that the constitution being the creature of the people, their sense with respect to any measure, if it even stand in opposition to the constitution, will sanctify and make it right.

Happily, for us, in this country, the position is not to be controverted; that the constitution is the creature of the people; but it does not follow that they are not bound by it, while they suffer it to continue in force; nor does it follow, that the legislature, which is, on the other hand, a creature of the constitution, can depart from it, on any presumption of the contrary sense of the people.

The constitution is the compact made between the society at large and each individual. The society therefore, cannot without breach of faith and injustice, refuse to any individual, a single advantage which he derives under that compact, no more than one man can refuse to perform his agreement with another. If the community have good reasons for abrogating the old compact, and establishing a new one, it undoubtedly has a right to do it; but until the compact is dissolved with the same solemnity and certainty with which it was made, the society, as well as individuals, are bound by it.

All the authority of the legislature is delegated to them under the constitution; their rights and powers are there defined; if they exceed them, 'tis a treasonable usurpation upon the power and majesty of the people; and by the same rule that they may take away from a single individual the rights he claims under the constitution, they may erect themselves into perpetual dictators. The sense of the people, if urged in justification of the measure, must be considered as a mere pretext; for that sense cannot appear to them in a form so explicit and authoritative, as the constitution under which they act; and if it could appear with equal authenticity, it could only bind, when it had been preceded by a declared change in the form of government.

The contrary doctrine serves to undermine all those rules, by which individuals can know their duties and their rights, and to convert the government into a government of *will* not of *laws*.

There is only one light on Mentor's plan in which this subject remains to be considered—the danger to the government, from suffering persons to reside among us, who have an aversion to our constitution; either by their becoming auxiliaries to future attempts of the British nation to recover their lost authority; or by their contributing to corrupt the principles and change the form of our government.

My observations on this subject, in my former letter, I believe remain unshaken, by what Mentor has opposed to them. I shall however add a few others.

The restoration of British authority in this country, is too chimerical to be believed even by Mentor himself; though he makes some faint essays to induce the supposition.[13]

Why did Great Britain make peace with America? Because the necessity of her affairs compelled her to it. In what did this necessity

13. "Mentor" argued that the present ministry and King of England did not wish a reunion of England and America. But, he added, "suppose the inclination of the present King should not lead him to reclaim the country; yet, his son, when he comes to the throne, may be ambitious for the glory of recovering the lost dominion of his father. And as to the difficulty of obtaining money from parliament to carry on an unreasonable war, the rapid corruption of that people will probably soon remove it."

consist? In every species of embarrassment and disorder, that a nation could experience. Her public debt had almost arrived at that point, when the expences of a peace establishment were nearly equal to all the revenues they were able to extract from exhausting the sources of taxation. Had they carried on the war, 'till they had exceeded this point, a bankruptcy would have been the inevitable consequence. We perceive, as it is, the great difficulties that are acknowledged by every succession of ministers, in devising means to retrieve the affairs of the nation.

The distractions of the government, arising from those embarrassments, are scarcely paralleled in any period of British history. Almost every sitting of parliament is a signal of a change of ministry. The King at variance with his ministers—the ministers unsupported by parliament—the lords disagreeing with the commons; the nation execrating the King, ministers, lords and commons; all these are symptoms of a vital malady in the present state of the nation.

Externally the scene is not brighter: The affairs of the East India settlements are in the most perplexing confusion, and Ireland seems to be ready to dismember itself from the British empire.

It may be said that these are temporary mischiefs, which may be succeeded by greater tranquility, prosperity and power. The future situation of Great Britain is a problem which the wisest man cannot solve. In all appearance, it will be a considerable time, before she can recover from the pressure of the evils under which she now labours, to be in a condition to form enterprizes against others: When that period may arrive our strength and resources will have greatly increased—the habits of men attached to her will have worn out—and it is visionary to suppose that she will then entertain a disposition to renew her attempts upon a country, increased in strength and resources, exerting its forces under an established constitution, fortified by foreign alliances, which her acknowledged independence will at all times command; when she reflects that that country, in the tumult of a revolution, and in a state of comparative impotence, baffled all her efforts, in the zenith of her power.

To an enlightened mind it will be sufficient to say, upon this subject, that independent of our own means of repelling enterprises against us, Europe has been taught by this revolution to estimate the danger to itself of an union of the two countries, under the same government, in too striking a manner, ever to permit the re-union, or tolerate the attempts of Great Britain towards it.

The danger, from a corruption of the principles of our government, is more plausible, but not more solid. It is an axiom that governments form manners, as well as manners form governments. The body of the people of this state are too firmly attached to the democracy, to permit the principles of a small number to give a different tone to that spirit. The present law of inheritance making an equal division among the children, of the parents property, will soon melt down those great estates, which if they continued, might favour the power of the *few*. The number of the disaffected, who are so, from speculative notions of government, is small: The great majority of those, who took part against us, did it from accident, from the dread of the British power, and from the influence of others to whom they had been accustomed to look up. Most of the men, who had that kind of influence are already gone: The residue and their adherents must be carried along by the torrent; and with very few exception, if the government is mild and just, will soon come to view it with approbation and attachment.

Either the number of mal-contents in the state is small or it is considerable. If small, there can be no room for apprehensions; if great, then opposition to the government is only to be overcome by making it their interest to be its friends, or by extirpating them from the community. A middle line which will betray a spirit of persecution in the government, but will only extend its operation to a small number, will answer no other purpose than to disable a few, and inflame and rivet the prejudices of the rest; by exhibiting the temper of government in a harsh and unconciliating light. We shall then in truth have a considerable faction in the state ready for all innovations.

The impracticability of such a general extirpation suggests the opposite conduct as the only proper one.

There is a bigotry in politics, as well as in religions, equally pernicious in both. The zealots, of either description, are ignorant of the advantage of a spirit of toleration: It was a long time before the kingdoms of Europe were convinced of the folly of persecution, with respect to those, who were schismatics from the established church. The cry was, these men will be equally the disturbers of the hierarchy and of the state. While some kingdoms were impoverishing and depopulating themselves, by their severities to the non-conformists, their wiser neighbours were reaping the fruits of their folly, and augmenting their own numbers, industry and wealth, by receiving with open arms the persecuted fugitives. Time and experience have taught a different lesson; and there is not an enlightened nation, which does not now acknowledge the force of this truth, that whatever speculative notions of religion may be entertained, men will not on that account, be enemies to a government, that affords them protection and security. The same spirit of toleration in politics, and for the same reasons, has made great progress among mankind, of which the history of most modern revolutions is a proof. Unhappily for this state, there are some among us, who possess too much influence, that have motives of personal ambition and interest to shut their minds against the entrance of that moderation, which the real welfare of the community teaches.

Our neighbours seems to be in a disposition to benefit by our mistakes; and the time will not be very remote, if the schemes of some men can prevail, when we shall be ashamed of our own blindness, and heap infamy upon its promoters.

It is remarkable, though not extraordinary, that those characters, throughout the states, who have been principally instrumental in the revolution, are the most opposed to persecuting measures. Were it proper, I might trace the truth of this remark from that character, which has been the first in conspicuousness, through the several gradations of those, with very few exceptions, who either in the civil or military line have borne a distinguished part. On the other hand I might point out men who were reluctantly dragged into taking a part in the revolution; others who were furious zealots in the commencement of the dispute, that were not heard of to any public purpose, during the progress of it, and others who were fluctuating, according to the tide of good or ill-fortune, all of whom now join in the cry with a third class, more imprudent but much more respectable, and endeavour by the loudness of their clamours to atone for their past delinquencies.

As to Mentor's commercial reveries, I shall decline bestowing many remarks upon them, not only because they are not immediately connected with the general subject, but because there is little danger of their making any proselytes; [14] while men are convinced that the prosperity of the national commerce depends as much upon the extent of its capital as that of an individual—that to confine trade to any particular description of men, in exclusion of others who have better means of carrying it on, would be, if practicable, to make the people at large tributary to the avarice of a small number, who were to have the benefit of the monopoly—that in the present situation of things, a very small proportion of those, intended to be benefited, who have the means to avail themselves of the advantage, would reap all its fruits even at the expence and to the prejudice of the greater part of those who were meant to be favoured—that the fewer hands trade is confined to the less will be its activity, and the less the degree of employment afforded to other classes of the community; and, in short, that all monopolies, exclusions and discriminations, in matters of traffick, are pernicious and absurd.

SINCE writing the foregoing, I have learned, that a bill is depending before the House of Assembly, for putting various descriptions of persons out of the protection of government.[15] I have too much respect for the wisdom and virtue of that body to suppose a measure of this nature can obtain the sanction of the majority. What is the plain language of the proposal? There are certain persons, who are obnoxious to public resentment. The treaty forbids us to proceed against them in a legal way. Let us therefore by an unconstitutional exertion of power evade the treaty, however dangerous the precedent to the liberty of the subject, and however derogatory to the honour of the nation. By the treaty we stipulate, that *no person* or *persons* shall *suffer* on account of the part they may have taken in the war, any damage to person, liberty, or property; and yet by taking away the protection of government, which they would enjoy under the subsisting laws, we leave them to *suffer* whatever injury to either, the

14. "Mentor" argued that the city of New York would not suffer if departing Tories took with them large quantities of money. The economic health of New York, he wrote, was not dependent on the quantity of money but on trade, a trade which would not diminish if the Loyalists left. He also recommended that all foreign merchants be excluded from New York.
15. This bill was passed in May under the title of "An Act to Preserve the Freedom and Independence of this State, and for other Purposes therein mentioned" (*Laws of the State of New York*, I, 772–74). The same bill, under varying titles, was debated by the legislature from March until its passage.

rashness of individuals who are the *subjects* of the state, may think proper to inflict. What would this be but to imitate the conduct of a certain General, who having promised that he would not spill the blood of some prisoners, who were about to surrender by capitulation, after he had them in his power, had them all strangled to death? Words in every contract are to be construed so as to give them a reasonable effect. When it is stipulated, that a man shall not suffer in person, liberty, or property, it does not merely mean, that the state will not inflict any positive punishment upon him; but also that it will afford him protection and security from injury. The very *letter* as well as the *spirit* of the stipulation imports this. He *shall not suffer* any damage, are the words of the treaty.

The scheme of putting men out of the protection of the law, is calculated to transfer the scepter from the hands of government to those of individuals—it is to arm one part of the community against another; it is to *enact* a civil war. If unhappily for the state, this plan could succeed, no man can foresee the end of it. But the guardians of the rights of the community will certainly, on mature deliberation reject it.

Feeling for the honour of the state, if expulsions must take place, if the constitution and the faith of the United States, must be sacrificed to a supposed political expedience. I had much rather see an open avowal of the principles upon which we acted, than that we should cloth the design with a viel of artifice and disguise, too thin not to be penetrated by the most ordinary eye.

I shall now with a few general reflections conclude.

Those, who are at present entrusted with power, in all these infant republics, hold the most sacred deposit that ever was confided to human hands. 'Tis with governments as with individuals, first impressions and early habits give a lasting bias to the temper and character. Our governments hitherto have no habits. How important to the happiness not of America alone, but of mankind, that they should acquire good ones.

If we set out with justice, moderation, liberality, and a scrupulous regard to the constitution, the government will acquire a spirit and tone, productive of permanent blessings to the community. If on the contrary, the public councils are guided by humour, passion and prejudice; if from resentment to individuals, or a dread of partial inconveniences, the constitution is slighted or explained away, upon every frivolous pretext, the future spirit of government will be feeble, distracted and arbitrary. The rights of the subject will be the sport of every party vicissitude. There will be no settled rule of conduct, but every thing will fluctuate with the alternate prevalency of contending factions.

The world has its eye upon America. The noble struggle we have made in the cause of liberty, has occasioned a kind of revolution in human sentiment. The influence of our example has penetrated the gloomy regions of despotism, and has pointed the way to inquiries, which may shake it to its deepest foundations. Men begin to ask every where, who is this tyrant, that dares to build his greatness on our misery and degradation? What commission has he to sacrifice millions to the wanton appetites of himself and the few minions that surround his throne?

To ripen inquiry into action, it remains for us to justify the revolution by its fruits.

If the consequences prove, that we really have asserted the cause of human happiness, what may not be expected from so illustrious an example? In a greater or less degree, the world will bless and imitate!

But if experience, in this instance, verifies the lesson long taught by the enemies of liberty; that the bulk of mankind are not fit to govern themselves, that they must have a master, and were only made for the rein and the spur: We shall then see the final triumph of despotism over liberty. The advocates of the latter must acknowledge it to be an *ignis fatuus,* and abandon the pursuit. With the greatest advantages for promoting it, that ever a people had, we shall have betrayed the cause of human nature.

Let those in whose hands it is placed, pause for a moment, and contemplate with an eye of reverence, the vast trust committed to them. Let them retire into their own bosoms and examine the motives which there prevail. Let them ask themselves this solemn question —Is the sacrifice of a few mistaken, or criminal individuals, an object worthy of the shifts to which we are reduced to evade the constitution and the national engagements? Then let them review the arguments that have been offered with dispassionate candour; and if they even doubt the propriety of the measures, they may be about to adopt, let them remember, that in a doubtful case, the constitution ought never to be hazarded, without extreme necessity.

PHOCION

From John Chaloner

Philada May 1. 1784

Sir,

Inclosed you have Captn Wades recet for the Box I reced of the Consul of france which I hope will come safe to hand.[1] I shall write you on the Subject of the Bank as soon as I am well informd of the business transacted Yesterday at a meeting of the Stockholders. I have not a doubt but that the money can be better employed & with equal security.

I am Sir   Your most Obdt Servt

Mr Alexr Hamilton

LC, Historical Society of Pennsylvania, Philadelphia.
   1. Presumably a French consul had turned over to Chaloner correspondence or goods from John B. Church who was then in France. Captain Wade, in turn, was entrusted by Chaloner to transport the box to H in New York City.

From John B. Church

London May 2d: 1784

My Dear Sir

I have within a few Days Received your Favors of the 7th & 18th Feby. and 6th March.[1] I am sorry to see the Proprietors of the old Bank at Philada. have acted so weak a Part as to cause an unnecessary Opposition; I fear they will by the Conduct they have pursued decrease their future Dividends, and I really believe the new Bank will be more beneficial than the old.[2]

The Establishment of the New York Bank has determined Wadsworth and myself to give up all Thoughts of carrying our banking Plan into Execution,[3] but I should be glad to be interested in the Shares of that Bank if they are not disposed of, and I shall write Chaloner to employ my monies in his Hands that Way.

Almost all the Elections for a new Parliament are at an End. Mr. Pitt and the Administration will have a great majority altho' they will not be able to prevent Mr. Fox being elected for Westminster, but it is said he will make no Opposition this session, but that the minister will get thro his Business as quick as possible and that the East India Business is to be deferr'd untill the next Session of Parliament.[4] I think Britain is in a fair way of loosing shortly her Possessions in that Part of the World.

I find the People of New haven have opened their Doors to the Loyalists they have done wisely, and I hope New York will open their Eyes and follow the Example.

What is become of the Fœderal Government? will the States invest Congress with the necessary Powers to fund the Debt, and do other Acts which are essentially necessary for the well being of the States?

Mrs. Church is well she joins me in Love to Mrs. Hamilton and yourself I am   Dear Sir   Your faithful & sincere Friend   J B Church

P.S.   By the first Ship I will send you out such new Law Publications as I shall be inform'd are likely to prove agreable to you.

ALS, Hamilton Papers, Library of Congress.
    1. Letters not found.
    2. Church is referring to the attempt by a group of Philadelphia merchants to create the Bank of Pennsylvania as a rival to the Bank of North America. See John Chaloner to H, January 21, 1784.
    3. See "Constitution of the Bank of New York," February 23, 1784–March 15, 1784, note 1.
    4. Church is referring to the alleged mismanagement of Indian affairs by the East India Company.

From John Campbell

Montreal 10th. May 1784

Dr. Sir,

I am happy to have the Satisfaction to Inform you that If I could by any means find a Safe Opportunity at Present I have in my power to remit you the Cash to pay those people that you was my Security too. As I only arrived here the 29th. of last Month, I beg you may not think it Strange you not Recd. the mony by this.[1] I hope you'll rest assured that when ever I can with any Safety Send it to you that I will take the Satissfaction to Comply.

I have the honour to be sir   Your most obt.   John Campbell

Col. Arch Hamilton

ALS, Hamilton Papers, Library of Congress.
   1. See "Promissory Note from John Campbell to Stephen Rapalje," April 1, 1784.

To John B. Church

[*New York, May 16, 1784.* On the envelope of a letter that Church wrote to Hamilton on February 7, 1784, Hamilton wrote: "From & to Mr. Carter May 16, 1784." *Letter not found.*]

To Hugh Knox

[*New York, May 17, 1784.* On July 28, 1784, Knox wrote to Hamilton: "After a long long Chasm in Our Epistolary Intercourse, I received your favour of the 17th. of May last." *Letter not found.*]

To John Chaloner

[New York] May [17–]18th. 1784

Dr Sir.

By this post will come to you a letter from General Schuyler, in which you will perceive he has desired me to draw upon you for a sum of money. The object is to pay for a lot purchased for Mr Carter.[1] The amount of the sum wanted is £2800 this Currency. A bill upon Philadelphia cannot be sold here ⟨without⟩ considerable discount. I am therefore to request you will forward it by *trusty persons* coming on to this city. Seven hundred pounds are immediately wanted for a first payment. The residue you can send on, a little more at your leisure, but the whole as speedily as convenient. Pray Mr Dear sir, Let this matter engage your particular attention;

for we may otherwise lose the lot—which is deemed a very beneficial purchase and will peculiarly suit Mr. Church.

If you have not yet done it you will please to vest the two thousand dollars in your hands in the dividend account in bank shares for Mr Church.[2]

I wish much to hear from you on the present situation of the bank. What has occasioned the late embarrassments. How far they are surmounted &c. What is the present plan of voting. How the new shares sell &c.[3]

Do me the favour to inquire of Mr. Oster[4] who committed to his care the box for Mrs. H—as she has received no letter respecting it.

Mrs. H joins in Compliments to Mrs. C. Believe me to be very truly Yr Obed ser   A Hamilton

May 17th. 1784
Mr. Chaloner

ALS, Historical Society of Pennsylvania, Philadelphia.
1. See John B. Church to H, February 7, 1784.
2. Presumably in shares of the Bank of North America.
3. For an account of the financial difficulties of the Bank of North America at this time, see William Seton to H, March 27, 1784.
4. Oster was a French consul who was probably stationed at Philadelphia. See Chaloner to H, May 1, 1784.

From John Chaloner

Philada May 26. 1784

Dear Sir

Yours of the 18 Inst came duly to hand I have expectation of a bill on your City for the amt of your first payment or thereabouts. I shall certainly receive it in a day or two & will forward it immediately.

The Present situation of the Bank is unknown to any but the directors thereof. What has occasioned the late embarrassments is also unknown. They are so far surmounted as to enable them to discount again. The Plan of Voting on all occasions is confind to twenty in any one Person let him own what No of Shares he pleases.

Not many of the new shares are sold. The worst of consequences attending the Bank is to be apprehended from the present desire of emitting paper money.[1] It will certainly take place in August next —but whether legal tender or not is uncertain—but I think it very propable.

I am D sir   Your most Obdt Servt   John Chaloner
Col Alexr Hamilton

ALS, Hamilton Papers, Library of Congress; LC, Historical Society of Pennsylvania, Philadelphia.
    1. See Chaloner to H, March 25, 1784.

From Matthew Visscher [1]

May 27, 1784. Lists persons against whom judgments have been entered under the Confiscation Law.

ALS, Hamilton Papers, Library of Congress.
    1. Visscher was an Albany lawyer who was clerk of the city and county of Albany.

From Egbert Benson

May 28, 1784. "There is an Ejectment depending in the Supreme Court for Lands in this County [1] for the Family of the Rooseboom's agt: Pearsall Brown, in which the Lessors of the Plf: request You will consider Yourself retained as Council on their Behalf. . . . I have a similar Request to you from the Devisees of Catharine Brett, who claim a considerable Tract in the Rumbout Precinct in this County distinguished by the Name of the *Gore*."

ALS, Mr. William N. Dearborn, Nashville, Tennessee.
    1. Dutchess County.

From John Chaloner

Philada May 31. 1784

Dear Sir,

Inclosed you have a list of sundry bills Exchd herewith. Should any of the Persons on whom Mr Macarty [1] has drawn decline acceptance because of the time: You have his consent to grant them

any indulgence on this head. I have forwarded them to you because
he has confidence that they will be paid & if so will prevent my sending on Money and also because he is a particular acquaintance of
our friends W & C,[2] and by them particularly recommended to me.
They have largely assisted him in money matters & he means to apply
this towards reimberseing them. I shall continue to forward bills to
amt of the paymt as fast as I can possibly procure them in the mean
time I remain

Dear Sir   Your most Obdt Servt

Col Alexr. Hamilton

LC, Historical Society of Pennsylvania, Philadelphia.
1. William Macarty was a Pennsylvania merchant who, having gone bankrupt and having received a general discharge from his creditors, went to
L'Orient, France in 1784 to re-establish himself in business. Some of the
capital for his new business venture was supplied by Jeremiah Wadsworth.
Macarty asked Chaloner to collect the debts owed him in America.
2. Jeremiah Wadsworth and John B. Church.

To Egbert Benson

[*New York, June 8, 1784.* The catalogue description of a letter
to Benson from Hamilton reads: "Mainly on legal business, concluding: 'No thing new here except that the Whigs by way of emi-
nence (as they distinguish themselves) are degenerating fast into a
very peaceable set of people.'" *Letter not found.*]

ALS, sold at Anderson Galleries, May 9, 1912, Lot 65.

To Marquis de Chastellux [1]

[New York, June 14, 1784]

Monsieur Le Chevalier

Colonel Clarkeson,[2] who will have the honor of delivering you
this, being already known to you, I give him this letter more for
the sake of renewing to you the assurances of my attachment and
esteem, than from a supposition that he will stand in need of any
new title to your attention. I will therefore only say of him that his
excellent qualities cannot be known without interesting those to

whom they are known and that from a personal and warm regard for him I should be happy, if any thing I could say could be an additional motive for your countenance and civilities to him.

I speak of him in the capacity[3] of a friend: As the messenger of Science he cannot fail to acquire the patronage of one of her favourite ministers. He combines with the views of private satisfaction which a voyage to Europe cannot but afford, an undertaking for the benefit of a Seminary of learning lately instituted in this state.[4]

Learning is the common concern of Mankind; and why may not poor republicans who can do little more than wish her well, send abroad to solicit the favours of her patrons and friends? Her ambassador will tell you his errand. I leave it to your *Mistress* to *command* and to the Trustees of the institution to *ask* your interest in promoting his mission.

Permit me only to add that if there is any thing in this country by which I can contribute to your satisfaction nothing will make me happier at all times than that your commands may inable me to give you proofs of the respectful and affectionate attachment with which I have the honor to be   Monsieur Le Chevalier   Your most Obedient and humble servant   A H

New York
June 14. 1784
The Chevalier De Chastelus

ADfS, Hamilton Papers, Library of Congress.

1. François Jean, Chevalier de Chastellux (known after 1783 by the title of marquis), came to America in 1780 as a major general in the army commanded by Rochambeau. The purpose of his trip was not only to engage in military exploits but to study the territory and customs of America. His observations were published in 1786 under the title *Voyages dans l'Amérique Septentrionale en 1780–81–82.*

2. Colonel Matthew Clarkson, a member of a family prominent in the political and mercantile affairs of New York, served during the American Revolution as aide-de-camp to Major General Benedict Arnold and later on the staff of Major General Benjamin Lincoln. Among many other offices which he held after the war, he was a regent of the University of the State of New York.

In 1784, he was authorized to go to France and the United Netherlands to solicit benefactions for the newly instituted university and to purchase "such philosophical apparatus for the College [Columbia] as Dr. Franklin, Mr. Adams and Mr. Jefferson, Ministers of the United States should advise" (Stokes, *Iconography of Manhattan,* V, 1192).

3. The word "capacity" is crossed out on the MS by either H or someone else at a later date.

4. The University of the State of New York was organized by the legislature in 1784.

From John B. Church

Paris June 15th 1784

My Dear Sir

I arrived here three Days since, and cannot let slip the Opportunity which the Departure of the Marquis de la Fayette offers me to drop you a Line.[1] I cannot say how long I shall remain here, but I shall not exceed next week, unless a Treaty that Wadsworth and myself are about entering on with the Farmers General to supply them with Tobacco should take Place in which Case I may be detained here some Time.[2] I propose spending the next Winter here with Mrs. Church, and in May following shall take my Passage for America where I hope to embrace Mrs. Hamilton and yourself. Of public Affairs it is needless to write you as the Marquis will furnish you more ample Information than I possibly can. Wadsworth will go to America immediately on our Return to England and by him I shall write you and more fully. Present my best and most affectionate Wishes to Mrs. Hamilton and believe me most cordially
Yours & &   J B Church

Alexr Hamilton Esqr.

ALS, Hamilton Papers, Library of Congress.
1. Lafayette sailed for America on July 1, 1784.
2. The Farmers General, a group of financiers to whom collection of many indirect taxes was farmed out, had a monopoly on the importation of tobacco Church was interested in the restrictions imposed by the Farmers General on the tobacco trade because John Chaloner, his American correspondent, shipped Virginia tobacco to France "on account and Risque of Messrs. Wadsworth and Carter" (Platt, "Jeremiah Wadsworth," 93). Wadsworth and Church did not succeed in securing a treaty. Instead, the Farmers General made a contract with Robert Morris early in 1785.

To James Bowne [1]

[New York, June 17, 1784. Requests that Bowne "Let me know if you please Whether Philip Palmer and Joseph Palmer are both alive

or not, and whether Mr. Leonard Lawrence is Executor or Admin-
istrator to his father." [2] *Letter not found.*]

ALS, sold at American Art Association Galleries, November 24, 1924, Lot
329.
   1. Bowne was a member of the firm of Bowne and Company of New York
City, stationers and printers, founded by Daniel Bowne in 1775.
   2. Extract taken from American Art Association Galleries catalogue.

To John B. Church

[*New York, June 18, 1784.* On July 24, 1784, Church wrote to
Hamilton: "Two Days since Coll Clarkson arrived and brought me
your Favor of the 18th June." *Letter not found.*]

To Hugh Seton [1]

New York June 18th 1784

Sir

   I have been duely honored with your letter of the 30th of March; [2]
and am much flattered by the confidence you have reposed in me. I
should with pleasure have undertaken to execute your wishes had
I been in a situation that left me at liberty to do it; but it has happened that Mr. Wilkes [3] sometime since applied to me on the same
subject; and though I was not absolutely retained by him, yet as
I had been consulted on the business, I should conceive it improper
to act against him. In this dilemma as you were at a great distance,
and he might elude your persuit before you could make a new
choice of a person to manage the affair for you, I thought it my duty
to transfer the trust to some person on the spot to whose judgment
and integrity your interests might be safely committed. I have fixed
upon Mr. Samuel Jones [4] for this purpose; a Gentleman as distinguished for his probity as for his profession[al] knowlege; and have
accordingly substituted him in my place.
   He has had Mr. Wilkes arrested upon your demand, who not being
able to obtain bail is of course in prison. This has been done in persuance of your intimation that Mr. Wilkes friends are able to do
something for him; and it is to be hoped that rather than suffer him
to lie in jail they will either satisfy or become bound for at least

a part of your demand. This seems to be your only resource; for he has no property in this Country and has been of late in no way of acquiring any.

He did not (as you had been informed) accompany Mrs. Hayley [5] to this Country; but it is reported that she has lately arrived at Boston.

I am requested by Mr. Jones to mention to you that it will be necessary you should furnish him with the account of sales rendered by Mr. Wilkes, and at the same time with the bills of exchange which he accepted. He wishes to be possessed of these as evidence in case of a controverted suit. You mention that the bills of Exchange were sent to New York but you do not say to whom. On tracing the matter we have reason to conclude they were sent to Mr. McAdam; [6] but as he is now in England, we cannot have recourse to him to obtain them.

Circumstanced as I am, I must now take leave of this business; without acting hereafter on either side.

But as a just representation of facts is always most conducive to the settlement of disputes, and may enable you the better to judge what course it will [be] proper for you to persue, I think it incumbent upon me, from the confidence you have been pleased to repose in me, to inform you that I have taken pains to ascertain the quality and condition of the wines of both cargoes on their arrival in this Country; and the result of my inquires of Gentlemen who could not be mistaken in the matter and on whose veracity I can depend has been, that the wine of the second as well as of the first cargo was in general either damaged or of indifferent quality; and necessarily sold at very low rates.

I am inclined to suspect that Mr. Wilkes intention will be to endeavour to procure an act of insolvency in his favour at the next meeting of the Legislature (continuing in the mean time in confinement) and that he will in this expectation rather discoura⟨ge⟩ his friends from becoming sureties for him.

I think with proper management on the part of those concerned for you, it will be very difficult for him to succeed in this scheme; but moderation in your behalf will be best calculated to frustrate this experiment and lay him under a necessity of calling in the aid of his friends.

I persuade myself you will do justice to the motives of these intimations; and though I have it not in my power to serve you upon the present occasion, will permit me to make you an offer of my best services upon every other; and to assure you that I am with much consideration and esteem— Sir Your Obedient and humble servant

ADf, Hamilton Papers, Library of Congress.

1. Seton was a partner with John Ballantyne of Bologne, France, in the firm of Charles and Hugh Smith and Company. For other correspondence relating to this case, see H to Seton, January 1, 1785; Seton to H, February 2, 1785; John Wilkes to H, November 8, 1785; H to Wilkes, November 8, 1785; and Wilkes to H, November 9, 1785.

2. Letter not found.

3. John De Ponthieu Wilkes, the son of Israel Wilkes, father of Commodore Charles Wilkes, and nephew of John Wilkes, the famous English agitator. The conclusions reached in both *HCLW*, IX, 406–09, and Schachner, *Hamilton*, 449–50, on the identity of John Wilkes are incorrect. There is no doubt as to the identity of the man concerned in this case. Seton sent H a power of attorney dated March 27, 1784, in which it is stated that H was "in our Names to ask Demand Sue for Recover and receive of and from John Wilkes otherwise John De ponthieu Wilkes" (MS Division, New York Public Library). Wilkes had sold goods for Charles and Hugh Smith and Company for which he owed £7400.

4. Samuel Jones, lawyer, later chief justice of New York. The power of attorney from H to Jones was dated June 16, 1784 (MS Division, New York Public Library).

5. Mary Wilkes Stark Hayley. Mary Wilkes was the youngest sister of John Wilkes, the English agitator. She came to America after the death of her second husband, George Hayley. After living in the United States for some time, she married a Mr. Jefferys and returned to England.

6. John Loudoun McAdam came to America in 1770 to live with his uncle, a New York City merchant. He formed the firm of McAdam, Watson and Company. After the Revolution he returned to England.

From Clement Richard [1]

New York, June 24, 1784. Discusses a legal controversy between Richard and Gommes.[2] Agrees to give half of any damages received from Gommes to the New York City poorhouse.

ALS, Hamilton Papers, Library of Congress. This letter is in French.

1. Richard was a merchant of Santo Domingo.

2. This could be either Isaac Gomez or Moses Gomez, both of whom were New York City merchants.

From Matthew Visscher

June 29, 1784. Sends information on judgments entered against Joshua de St. Croix and James Leonard.

ALS, Hamilton Papers, Library of Congress.

From Gouverneur Morris

Philadelphia 30 June 1784

Dear Hamilton

This is rather a late Period to acknowlege yours of the seventh of April. I have lived in the constant Intention to answer it & I now execute my Purpose. But why not sooner? Procrastination is the Thief of Time says Doctor Young. I meant to have written fully on the Subject of the Gold. But I waited some Informations from Annapolis [1] on the Probability of a Mint. [2] I afterwards intended a long Letter upon a Subject I mentioned to Mr. Seton [3] viz a Coalition between your Bank and the national Bank. I do not find either Party inclined to it. And yet both would be the better for it. You I believe will soon be out of B[ank] Cash unless it should take Place. I would say a great Deal on this Subject but it would be very useless. When you find your Cash diminish very fast remind Seton of my Predictions and let him tell you what they were. If the Legislature should attempt to force Paper Money down your Throats it would be a good Thing to be somewhat independent of them. But I must check myself or I shall go too far into a Business which would plague us both to no Purpose. It shall be left therefore untill we meet.

This Letter was intended for nothing else than to assure you of the Continuance of my Esteem. Present me (if you do not dislike the Term) affectionately to Mrs. Hamilton. At any Rate believe me   very affectionately yours   Gouv Morris

ALS, Hamilton Papers, Library of Congress.
  1. The Continental Congress was meeting at Annapolis.
  2. As early as 1782, Gouverneur Morris, then the assistant financier, had drawn up a plan for an American coinage. Although the subject was discussed in Congress, nothing was done until 1784 when Thomas Jefferson was ap-

pointed one of a committee to consider the coinage. Jefferson, relying on Morris's plan but making important changes in it, recommended a plan to Congress. It was not until 1786, however, that Congress decided on the coins to be used and thus made necessary the establishment of a mint. Consonant with a recommendation made by the Board of Treasury, the Continental Congress adopted on October 16, 1786, "An Ordinance for the establishment of the Mint of the United States of America, and for regulating the value and alloy of Coin" (JCC, XXXI, 876).

3. William Seton, cashier of the Bank of New York, had been sent to Philadelphia to consult with officials of the Bank of North America.

From Ezekiel Forman [1]

Philadelphia, July 4, 1784. Asks for information concerning an act of the New York legislature "relative to debts due to persons who were Residents of Your State, and whose Estates have been forfeited."

ALS, Hamilton Papers, Library of Congress.
1. Forman had been a New Jersey Loyalist who joined the British army. He was taken prisoner and later released in Pennsylvania. When this letter was written, he was practicing law in Philadelphia.

From John Chaloner

Philada July 14, 1784

Dear Sir

Inclosed you have Mr Peter Whiteside's [1] draft on Messrs. James Buckannan & Co.[2] for One thousand Dollars at six days Sight, Mr Thomas Irwin [3] on Captn Geo Geddes [4] at 5 days sight for twenty three pounds 9/2, & James Bowne on William Bowne [5] at twenty days for seventy five dollars, making on the whole four hundred twenty six pounds 11/8 which I doubt not will meet due honour. This I have charg'd to Mr Church. I have hitherto neglected vesting Mr Church's money in Bank Stock in hopes of buying it under par. None as yet offerd & I must therefore buy at par unless you think otherwise. I purchased a little while before I reced your Orders under par which encouraged me to expect it now.

I am applied to for an obligation of Mr Traceys [6] to Mr Church for Bank Stock their agents being desireous to discharge it. If you are in possession of the obligation please to forward it that payment may be reced.

Mr Macarty [7] will give you directions respecting Mr Woodwards [8] bill and any others that I have remitted you payable to him.

Mrs Chaloner joins me in Compliments and I remain   Sir   Your most Obdt hble Servt

Alexr Hamilton Esqr

LC, Historical Society of Pennsylvania, Philadelphia.
    1. Whitesides was a leading Philadelphia merchant.
    2. James Buchanan, a New York merchant, was a stockholder in the recently formed Bank of New York.
    3. Irwin was a Philadelphia merchant and shipowner.
    4. Captain George Geddis of Philadelphia.
    5. Members of the firm of Bowne and Company of New York, stationers and printers, founded by Daniel Bowne in 1775.
    6. Probably Nathaniel Tracy of Newburyport, Massachusetts, a stockholder in the Bank of North America.
    7. For information on William Macarty, see Chaloner to H, May 31, 1784.
    8. Probably John Woodward, a New York City merchant.

To Richard Varick [1]

[New York] July 23, 1784. "Mr. Laurance [2] & myself who have been retained by Mr. R. Smith being about to leave Town, I have recommended Mr. Smith to you in our absence."

ALS, Humanities Research Center, The University of Texas.
    1. Varick was recorder for New York City.
    2. John Laurance, a New York lawyer.

From John B. Church

London July 24th 1784

Dear Sir

I wrote you last from France by M de la Fayette [1] two Days since Coll Clarkson [2] arrived and brought me your Favor of the 18th June.[3] I am glad to find by him that your violent Party in New York begins to moderate. I hope shortly that Humanity and good Policy will replace Violence and Folly. If the Bank is not solidly established I do not wish to be concerned in it.[4] Wadsworth is gone to Ireland from whence he will return to Liverpool and embark at that Place in a few Days for America. I cannot Return before next Spring, when I hope to have the Happiness to embrace you, tomorrow we set out for Yarmouth to spend a Month by the SeaSide. I have directed a Merchant here to ship a Machine for the Purpose of copying Letters and Writings, his Correspondent will deliver it you. I think you will find it very usefull as it saves a great Deal of Time and without the Trouble of copying you can preserve Copy of private Writings you do not chuse to trust to others to copy. Angelica is well she joins me in best Affections to Mrs. Hamilton and yourself. I am   My Dear Sir with sincere Esteem   Yours &c. &c.

J B Church

Alex Hamilton Esqr.

ALS, Hamilton Papers, Library of Congress.
1. See Church to H, June 15, 1784.
2. Matthew Clarkson. See H to Marquis de Chastellux, June 14, 1784.
3. Letter not found.
4. The Bank of New York, which was organized in March, 1784, opened for business in June.

To Elizabeth Hamilton

[Albany, July 28–31, 1784] [1]

I arrived here My beloved Betsey the fifth day after we set out, the three first days with every favourable circumstance but the two last through very bad weather. I am however as well as I can be absent from you and my darling boy [2]—nor was I ever more impatient to be at home. I can have little pleasure elsewhere. I hope and persuade myself My Betsey is not less desirous for my return. Saturday is the day appointed for commencing our journey back.

Your papa [3] has not enjoyed good health of late but is better & all the family well. He will not leave this for the city in less than Eight days.

Johnny's [4] affair will shortly terminate without any other inconvenience than a few days confinement   Adieu My Angel love me as I do you   Yrs. for ever

⟨Peggy⟩ [5] gives her love to you

ALS, Mr. George T. Bowdoin, New York City.
1. This letter is undated. H speaks of only one child. As Philip was born in 1782 and Angelica was not born until September, 1784, the letter was probably written during the interval between those two years. He writes, furthermore, from Albany to Elizabeth in New York City. From 1782 to

1784, there is evidence of only one short period when H was in Albany and Elizabeth in New York City. On July 23, 1784, H wrote to Richard Varick that he was going out of town. Since he wrote to Elizabeth that the trip took five days, this letter has been dated July 28–31, 1784.

2. Philip Hamilton.

3. Philip Schuyler.

4. Presumably either John B. Schuyler, Philip Schuyler's son, or John C. Schuyler, Philip Schuyler's nephew, who was studying law with H.

5. Margarita (or Margaret) Schuyler Van Rensselaer, Elizabeth's sister.

From Hugh Knox

St Croix July 28th. 1784.

My dear Sir

After a long long Chasm in Our Epistolary Intercourse, I received your favour of the 17th. of May [1] last by the hands of Mr. Beekman.[2] That Gentleman's General Account of you has given me, & your other friends here, a vast deal of pleasure. For, believe me, I have always had a just & secret pride in having Advised you to go to America, & in having recommended you to Some of my old friends there; Since you have not only *Answered*, but even far *Exceeded*, our most Sanguine hopes & Expectations. I am glad to find that your popularity increases, & that your fine talents are coming into play, in a way that Contributes so much to your own honour & Emolument, & to the Good of the public. Perhaps Camps & marches & the hardy deeds of War, may have a little fortified & Steel'd your Constitution (which used to be rather delicate & frail). But be Ware you do not enfeeble & impair it again, by plunging into intense Studies, & the anxieties of the Bar: For I know your laudible Ambition to Excell, & that you will Strain Every Nerve to be among the first of your profession. And, great as your talent are, I should imagine that the accurate Study of So Complex & Voluminous a Science as the law, & Acquireing all the habits of a pleader, would cost you a deal of Labour.

Your Matrimonial Connection, I should think, might Enable you to live at your ease (I do not mean the *Otium ingloriosum*, but the otium honestum) As a Gentleman of Independent fortune, & to pursue Studies more pleasing to yourself & perhaps more profitable to the Common-wealth, & to posterity. You guess at the meaning of this hint. But you are certainly a better Judge of the propriety & Expediency of your present pursuits, than I can possibly be.

I sincerely wish you joy of your fine boy, & hope he may inherit all the powers & Virtues of his father, & of his amiable mother, who was not, I presume, born when I left the Continent. May every Species of happiness attend & beatify your Self & dear family! This is indeed a Cheap Offering, but it is a very cordial & Sincere one; & Who knows but it may be heard in heaven?

What Could have become of all the letters I have wrote you? Indeed, many of them were intended as recommendations of individuals to your friendly attentions: and therefore might have rested with these individuals. One of these went with Doctor Finlay,[3] & another By Peter Marcoe[4] Esqr., now with his father at Philadelphia, designing the practice of the Law.

I hinted to Doctor Stevens[5] your complaint of his remisness. He declares he has wrote you more than once, altho' he hath not before hear'd from [you]. He will undoubtedly write you by Mr Beekman. The doctor has an Extensive & lucrative practice, & is much & deservedly esteemed in his profession. But whither his torturing so many dogs & other quadrupedes in Edinburgh, in his Experiments on the *Succus gastricus* of the Stomach, may not have a little injured his sensibility, & made him a cooler friend & less cordial companion, I cannot take upon me to Say. He sometimes talks much of going to America, & I believe would do exceedingly well there in One of the Capitals, as he has a fine address, & Great merit & Cleverness.

But I believe I have wearied you, & Shall not add to the prolixity, but by Saying, That I am [with] Great Esteem & invariable Attachment, My Dear Sir   Your very affectionate Servt: Hugh Knox

ALS, Hamilton Papers, Library of Congress.
    1. Letter not found.
    2. David Beekman, member of a prominent New York merchant family, had been a partner in the St. Croix firm of Beekman and Cruger for which H had worked as a clerk. Beekman had become a planter in St. Croix.
    3. The Reverend James Finley of Chester County, Pennsylvania.
    4. Peter Markoe, son of Abraham Markoe of St. Croix.
    5. Edward Stevens, boyhood friend of H and his classmate at King's College, studied medicine at the University of Edinburgh. Stevens began practice in St. Croix in February, 1783.

From Hugh Seton

[*England, August 1, 1784.* On February 2, 1785, Seton wrote to Hamilton: "I only trouble you with these few Lines to mention the Earnest Wish I have to hear of your Receipt of Mine of 1st. August." *Letter not found.*]

From Marquis de Fleury [1]

[Tenerife, Canary Islands, August 4, 1784]

Colonel fleury's Complimens, to his former friend Colonel hamilton; he has written several Letters to him from the west indias, & france, but Received no answer. & he tis now going to take the Command of a Regiment at the island of france, & does not expect to hear from him, but he shall for ever remember with pleasure, that Col. hamilton was a friend of his in america, & wish him all kinds of happiness and fortune:—

he begs, he would present his Rispects to Mrs. hamilton.
Canary islands: teneriffe: august 4th. 1784:

ALS, Hamilton Papers, Library of Congress.
1. In 1781, after the Battle of Yorktown, François Louis Teisseydre, Marquis de Fleury, went to France. Returning to America in 1782 and finding the war almost over, he went to South America. He returned to France in 1784.

To Ezekiel Forman

[*New York, August 4, 1784.* On October 18, 1784, Forman wrote to Hamilton: "I am favored with your Letter of the 20th past and . . . one written the 4th. August." *Letter of August 4 not found.*]

To Samuel Blachley Webb [1]

[New York, August 7, 1784] [2]

Mr. Hamilton requests the pleasure of General Webbes Company at dinner on Monday at four oClock.
Saturday

AL, Yale University Library.
1. Webb was a native of Connecticut who before his retirement from the Army in 1783 had been made a brigadier general. Webb settled in New York City after the war.
2. This letter is undated but the endorsement reads: "7th. August 1784."

To John Chaloner

[New York, August 14, 1784]

Dr. Sir

I received in due time your letter of 14 of July.

The bills sent by you which have been paid and will be paid are

on James & Alex Stewart [1] . . . . . £	600
ditto	300
on Delafield [2]	149. 4
James Buchanan & Co	400
on Cap G. Geddes	23. 9.2
William Bowne [3]	30
	1502.13.2

The Drafts on Lowe and Woodward [4] I return by Mr. Mc.Cartys [5] desire who will have explained to you.

The ballance due on the lot will be £1297.7.10 which bears interest at seven ₱ Cent. If you are in Cash on Mr. Church's account, I shall be obliged to you as soon as possible to forward that ballance; the rather as from particular circumstances there is some little hazard in the title 'till the transaction is completed.

I inclose you Messrs. Nathaniel and John Traceys [6] obligation to Mr. Church for Twenty five shares of bank Stock, agreeable to your request.

Mrs. Hamilton tells me that Mrs. Church informs her she has sent to your care a box of sheeting for her—and there is some other thing which she does not recollect for Mrs. Schuyler. She requests you will be so good as to forward these articles.

Mrs. H joins in compliments to Mrs. C.

Believe me to be   With great regard Dr Sir   Your Obed Servt
A Hamilton

New York
Augt. 14th. 1784
Mr. J Chaloner

ALS, Hamilton Papers, Library of Congress.

1. James and Alexander Stewart were New York merchants, and stockholders in the Bank of New York.

2. John Delafield was listed in *The New York Directory for 1786* as a broker.

3. For an identification of Buchanan, Geddes, and Bowne, see Chaloner to H, July 14, 1784.

4. Lowe was doubtless Nicholas Low, a prominent New York merchant. Woodward was the John Woodward to whom Chaloner referred in his letter to H of July 14, 1784.

5. For information on William Macarty, see Chaloner to H, May 31, 1784.

6. Nathaniel and John Tracy were merchants of Newburyport, Massachusetts. Nathaniel was listed among the first stockholders of the Bank of North America.

From John Chaloner

Philada Augt 27, 1784.

Dear Sir

Your letter of the 14th Inst was deliverd to me late last evening, incloseing Messrs Traceys obligation.[1] I shall inform their agent and get the Shares transferd immediately. I will forward the money you request in the course of next week.

Mr Church wrote me sometime in Feby last that I should receive by the Dauphin three boxes, two marked JBC—and one marked PS —which is a box of garden seeds for General Schuyler.[2] This vessell arived about the middle of June & I reced by her no boxes answering Mr Churchs's description. I have a large number of Boxes & other Packages all marked WC & No. There are three boxes distinguished by their numbers as Mr Church's private property & propably one of them is intended for Genl Schuyler. If by their contents you or Genl Schuyler can designate which belongs to him I will forward it immediately.

Mrs Chaloner joins me in Compliments to Mrs Hamilton & I remain with great regard   Dr Sir   Your most obdt hble Servant

John Chaloner

ALS, Hamilton Papers, Library of Congress.

1. The obligations of Nathaniel and John Tracy to John B. Church for twenty-five shares of bank stock.

2. Philip Schuyler.

To Samuel Blachley Webb

[New York, August 30, 1784]

Col Hamilton will do himself the pleasure to dine with General Web tomorrow

Augt. 30th.

AL, Yale University Library.

From John Trumbull [1]

Hartford, September 4, 1784. "On receiving your letter [2] I was sorry to find, that you had not mentioned the names of those Merchants, who compose the firm of Turnbull, Marmie & Co.—without which, you are sensible, that any Writ I could draw must abate. I have not been able to discover them by my enquiries in this place; but fearing least the Property mentioned in Mr. Duer's [3] letter might be removed, I have dispatched an Officer to attach it. I desire you to send me the names, places of Residence &c of that Company, as soon as possible, that I may be able to secure it effectually before any advantage can be taken of mistakes in the description I have given in the writs."

ALS, New-York Historical Society, New York City.
    1. John Trumbull, lawyer and poet, was a first cousin of Jonathan Trumbull, governor of Connecticut during the American Revolution.
    2. Letter not found.
    3. William Duer.

To Ezekiel Forman

[*New York, September 20, 1784.* On October 18, 1784, Forman wrote to Hamilton: "I am favored with your Letter of the 20th past." *Letter not found.*]

From John B. Church

London Septr. 25th 1784

My Dear Sir

It is an age since I had the Pleasure of Receiving a line from you altho' several Vessells have lately arrived from New York. By the Mentor Captn. Lawton I sent you address'd to the Care of Mr. Nathl. Shalor [1] a Machine for the Purpose of copying writings with Paper Ink and every Thing belonging to it, I wish you may find it of Use to you. Mrs. Church has spent six weeks at Yarmouth and bathed in the Sea, she has Received very great Benefit from it and her Health is much mended, I think we shall go to Paris about the End of next month and stay there 2 or 3 months when we shall return here and the Beginning of April take our Passage to America. There is every Appearance of a war between the Emperor and the Dutch [2] and it is most probable France will take Part with the latter, in this Case I fear their Attention will be so wholly engross'd by the War that they will pay no Attention whatever to America, with respect to this Country, there is not even a Shadow of a Disposition to enter into any commercial Treaty with America, and the merchants and Tradesmen are much sour'd by the frequent American failures which take Place with great Rapidity; the Loyalists here are a great Burden to the Government, and they know not how to ascertain the Real Losses they have sufferd for the Estimates presented to the Commissioners are swell'd to a most enormous Sum, it is in Agitation to appoint Commissioners in every State of America to estimate the Real losses of the Loyalists. Phil and the little Maid are in Perfect Health. [3] Angelica joins me in Love to Mrs Hamilton and yourself. I am very sincerely

Your's

J B Church

Mr Hamilton

ALS, Hamilton Papers, Library of Congress.

1. Nathaniel Shaler, a merchant of New York City, was a frequent correspondent of Jeremiah Wadsworth, Church's business partner. Shaler and Wadsworth (and presumably Church) were occasionally involved in business partnerships.

2. Joseph II, Emperor of the Holy Roman Empire, had demanded free

navigation of the Scheldt. When the States General refused his demands, Austrian ships were ordered to navigate the river. In October, 1784, the Dutch sought to prevent it, and the Emperor broke off diplomatic relations.

3. The son and daughter of John B. and Angelica Church.

From Timothy Pickering [1]

Philadelphia, September 30, 1784. Encloses legal papers to be used by Hamilton in "execution of the will of . . . John Holt, late of New-York printer deceased."

ALS, Hamilton Papers, Library of Congress.

1. After the war Pickering, a native of Massachusetts, settled in Philadelphia where he became a merchant.

To Samuel Blachley Webb

[New York, September, 1784]

Colo Hamilton presents his compliments to Genl Webb requests the favor of his company to dinner on saturday next at four OClock.

Friday Morn

Letter in unidentified handwriting, Yale University Library.

From Marquis de Lafayette

Albany October the 8th 1784

Dear Hamilton

With all the warmth of my long and tender friendship I Congratulate You Upon the Birth of Your daughter,[1] and Beg leave to present Mrs Hamilton With my most Affectionate Respects.

Several delays Have Retarded the Oppening of the treaty and When I was Upon the Ground, it Has Been found that my influence with the Indians Both friendly and Hostile tribes, was much Greater than the Commissioners and Even myself Had Conceived—so that I Was Requested, Even By Every one of the *those* [tribes] to Speak to *those* Nations.[2] There were Some, more or less, from Each Tribe. I stayed as long as the Commissioners thought I Could do them some Good, and that Has Rather Cramped my private plans of Visits.

Now my dear friend, I am Going to Hartford, Boston, Newport, from thence By Water to Virginia, in order to save time, and about the twentieth of Next Month I Hope to Be Again With You in New york. But Before that time will write You from Newport.

Adieu, My dear Hamilton, Most affectionately I am   Yours
                                                    Lafayette

I am told Mr Jay is not determined Upon Accepting.[3] I much wish He may Consent to it, the more so as His probable successor A.L.[4] does not Hit my fancy; indeed I very much wish Mr Jay may accept the Office.

ALS, Hamilton Papers, Library of Congress.
    1. Angelica Hamilton, H's oldest daughter, who was born in 1784.
    2. Lafayette arrived in the United States in August, 1784. After visiting Washington at Mount Vernon, he traveled to Baltimore and New York City. On September 23 he reached Albany where he met commissioners of Congress who were going to Fort Schuyler to negotiate a treaty with the Indians. With Victor Louis Charles de Riquet, Chevalier de Caraman, and the Marquis de Barbé-Marbois, Lafayette went up the Hudson to Fort Schuyler where he participated in the negotiations.
    3. On July 24, 1784, Congress offered John Jay the position of Secretary for Foreign Affairs.
    4. Probably Arthur Lee of Virginia.

Petition of the President, Directors, and Stockholders of the Bank of New York [1]

New York, October 8, 1784. On this date the President, Directors, and Stockholders of the Bank of New York petitioned "the Honorable The Representatives of the State of New York in Senate and Assembly convened" for the passage of "an Act to incorporate the Subscribers to the said Bank by the Name and Stile of the President Directors and Company of the Bank of New York." The petition set forth arguments on the usefulness of banks in general and the advantages of the Bank of New York to the state.

DS, Bank of New York, New York City.
    1. This document was signed by H and eleven other of the bank's stockholders.
    According to Broadus Mitchell (Hamilton, 351), the petition of October 8, 1784, "is obviously, from logic and style, the work of Hamilton." No conclusive evidence, however, substantiates the claim for H's authorship.

For information on the Bank of New York, see "Constitution of the Bank of New York," February 23–March 15, 1784.

Soon after its inauguration the Bank of New York applied to the New York legislature for incorporation. See "Outline of a Charter for the Bank of New York," February 23–March 15, 1784. Despite its failure to secure a charter, the bank opened on June 9, 1784. The bank did not obtain a charter until 1791.

Baron von Steuben to James Duane [1]

[New York, October 11, 1784]

The flattering token of their regard with which the Mayor Recorder & Alderman of the metropolis of a state distinguished for its exertions in the late revolution have honored me, derives additional value from the characters of the respectable individuals who compose that body and from the very obliging manner in which it is conferred.

The degree of my zeal for the common cause of America will best be appreciated by recurring to the manner, in which at a late period of life I embarked my reputation honor and future hopes in the glorious struggle for liberty and independence. And 'tis only by appealing to that zeal, I am able to convey an idea of the price I set on the approbation of those upon the basis of whose virtue so noble a fabric has been erected.

I can never cease to be happy in the reflection that my services may have had some share in the great work; nor can I doubt that those services such as they are may safely be referred to the justice and generosity of the country to which they were rendered.

The knowlege I acquire of the character of the inhabitants of this state, makes my residence among them, every day more agreeable, and there is nothing I desire more than opportunities of cultivating their friendship and giving them proofs of my esteem.

Df, in writing of H, New-York Historical Society, New York City.

1. Duane was mayor of New York City.

On October 8, 1784, Duane submitted to the Common Council of New York City the draft of an address to Baron von Steuben recounting the Baron's distinguished service during the American Revolution, and a certificate granting him the freedom of the city. The address and certificate were presented to von Steuben on October 11, the day on which he probably presented this reply written by H.

From Ezekiel Forman

Philadelphia, October 18, 1784. "I am favored with your letter of the 20th past and . . . one written the 4th. August.[1] I want you to Write Wade and [John] Philips of Philadelphia, demanding payment of their Bond."

ALS, Hamilton Papers, Library of Congress.
   1. Neither letter has been found.

From Marquis de Lafayette

Boston october the 22d 1784

My dear Hamilton

Every step I move there Comes upon me a Happy Necessity to Change my plans. The Reception I met with in Boston [1] no Words Can describe—at least it is impossible to Express what I Have felt. Gratitude as well as propriety Conspired With all other inducements to keep me Here Some time longer. Rhode island and New Hampshire I must visit—and intend embarking By the first or second day of next month for Virginia in the Nimph frigat which Has Been Sent on my Account. In less than four weeks time from this day I Hope to Be with Congress, and When my Business there is Concluded, will Come to New york where I Hope we will spend some days together. My stay in Your City Has Been too short—far inadequate to the feelings of my gratitude, and to the Marks of goodness Bestowed upon me. But this time I will Be some days longer with my New york friends.

Upon Reflecting to my Situation, my Circumstances, my love for America, and Yet the motives that might render it improper for Her, to employ me in a public Capacity, I have Confined myself to a plan which, at the same time it gratifies my Attachment, And Serves the United States, Cannot Have Any shadow of inconvenience—after Having told me they know my zeal, I wish Congress to add they want me to Continue those friendly and I might say patriotic exertions—that in Consequence of it, their Ministers at

Home, and their Minister Abroad will Have a standing order to look to me as one whose information, and exertions will ever Be employed to the Service of the United States, and When they think it is Wanted to Communicate With me Upon the affairs of America—that Congress will, whenever I think it proper, Be glad of my Correspondance.

Upon that General scale, every Minister may Conceal from me what He pleases, may write to me, Only when He pleases, and should He ever think my assistance is wanting, He Has a title to ask, I Have one to give it—and my Commission with America is for ever Kept, without Giving jealousy, Upon Such a footing as will Remain at the disposition of Each public servant of Congress.

It seems to me, my dear friend, this idea already met with your approbation. In Case it does, do promote it with your delegates and others. If it does not, write it to me By the Bearer whom I send By land to Apologize to the General for my delays.

My affectionate Respects wait upon Mrs Hamilton. I give my Blessing to the little family—adieu   Yours forever   Lafayette

Our friend Knox Has Been Most affectionate and Kind to me.

I Have written to Wadsworth,[2] and spoken to Bostonians Respecting the Baron's ⟨affairs⟩.[3] I wish to do the same in Virginia, Maryland and elsewhere.

ALS, Hamilton Papers, Library of Congress.
    1. Boston, where he arrived on October 15, was one of the many cities visited by Lafayette on his American tour of 1784.
    2. Presumably Jeremiah Wadsworth.
    3. Lafayette is referring to Baron von Steuben's claim for compensation for his services in the American Revolution. See "Report on the Claim of Baron von Steuben," December 30, 1782. The word in broken brackets is taken from *JCHW*, I, 423.

To John Chaloner

[New York, November 11, 1784]

Dr Sir

Mrs. Renselaaer[1] has requested me to write to you concerning a negro, Ben, formerly belonging to Mrs. Carter[2] who was sold for a term of years to Major Jackson.[3] Mrs. Church has written to her sister that she is very desirous of having him back again; and you are requested if Major Jackson will part with him to purchase his remaining time for Mrs. Church and to send him on to me.

There are also some boxes intended for the family sent to your care. The[re] is one of *sheeting* for Mrs. Hamilton. There is another of Garden seed and another with what Mrs. Church calls a Beauatrice for Mrs. Schuyler. If you can distinguish these boxes you will oblige the ladies by forwarding them to me.

I will be much obliged to you to send me a sketch of my account with you containing all the sums furnished on Mr Churches account

I am with great regard   Dr Sir Your obed servant

Alexr. Hamilton

New York
Novr. 11. 1784
Mr J Chaloner

ALS, Historical Society of Pennsylvania, Philadelphia.
  1. Margarita Schuyler Van Rensselaer, H's sister-in-law.
  2. Angelica Schuyler Church, H's sister-in-law.
  3. Major William Jackson was assistant secretary at war.

To Francisco de Miranda

Introductory Note

According to his biographer (Robertson, *The Life of Miranda*, I, 43), Miranda, while in New York City in 1784, devised a plan for the liberation of Venezuela which he revealed to Henry Knox and Hamilton. In the Miranda papers there are four lists of names, three of which are in the writing of Hamilton, and one of which is in an unidentified handwriting but which is designated, presumably in Miranda's writing, "Note of Mr. hamilton." To facilitate references to them, the lists have been designated in the order in which they appear in the Miranda papers by the numerals I, II, III, IV.

It is not possible to state definitely the purpose of these lists. According to a memoir which he wrote in 1792, Miranda recalled that "In the year 1784, in the city of New York, I formed a project for the liberty and independence of the entire Spanish-American Continent with the cooperation of England. That nation was naturally much interested in the design, for Spain had furnished a precedent by forcing her to acknowledge the independence of her colonies in America" (Robertson, *The Life of Miranda*, I, 43–44). Miranda later wrote, in a letter to Hamilton dated November 4, 1792, of "those grand & beneficial projects we had in Contemplation . . . in our Conversation at New Yorek." Hamilton did not explain his relationship to Miranda until fourteen years later when he wrote on a letter which Miranda had written to him on February 7, 1798, the following comment. "Several years ago this man was in America much heated with the project of liberating S Am from the Spanish Domination. I had frequent conversation with him on the subject and I presume expressed ideas favorable to the object and perhaps gave an opinion that it was one to which the UStates would look with interest."

As printed in the *Archivo del General Miranda. Negociaciones, 1770–1810,* XV, 72–77, the "Lista de Oficiales" is followed by a document entitled "Of the supposed expences of raising clothing and arming, *five thousand men,* fully officered, and divided into proportions, of Infantry Cavalry, and Artillery." At the end of the document is written "Boston 23d. November 1784." The juxtaposition of the two documents and the fact that the "Lista de Oficiales" is prefaced by the statement that it was a "*Nota de* Mr. Hamilton" suggests that Hamilton was the author of both. "The supposed expences of raising clothing and arming, *five thousand men*" is not, however, in the writing of Hamilton. That it was written at Boston, and the handwriting, suggest that Henry Knox was the author.

The date given these lists is based on the date of the document "Of the supposed expences" described in the preceding paragraph.

[New York, November 23, 1784]

I[1]
Note of Mr. hamilton

General Washington.	General Du Portail . . !
Major general Green.—!	General Wayne.
General Knox.—!	General Williams.
General St. Clair.	Colonel Dearborn.!
General M Dougall.	Colonel Brook!
Marquis Lafayette.	Colonel Putnam.!
Major général Baron de Steuben.!	Colonel hull.

II[2]

General Washington
Major General Greene!
General Knox!
General St Clair
General M Dougall
Marquis La Fayette
Major General Baron De Steuben!
General Du Portail!
General Wayne
General Williams

III[3]

Col Lee!
Col Washington
Col Pinckney

Lt Col Laurens!

Lt Colonel Burr

Lt Colonel Harrison Secretary to the
  Commander in Chief!

Lt Col Gouvion!

Lt Col Fleury!

IV [4]

Colonel Dearborn

Colonel Brook

Colonel Putnam

Lt Colonel Hull—

Colonel Olney!

Major Dexter

Col Huntington

Lt Col Fish!

Colonel Ogden

Colonel Barber!

Col Walter Stewart

Col Richard Butler

Lt Col Harmar!

Major Edwards

1. D, Academia Nacional de la Historia, Caracas, Venezuela.
2. AD, Academia Nacional de la Historia.
3. AD, Academia Nacional de la Historia.
4. AD, Academia Nacional de la Historia.

From John Chaloner

Philada Novemr 25. 1784.

Dear Sir

Inclosed you have bill of Lading for two boxes remaining in my
care for Mr Church. I suppose these must contain the several articles
wanted by the Ladies as they are the only packages in my possession
that does not contain Merchandize directed for Sale. Mr Church
informed me that a package would be sent by the same Vessell that
brought those, containing things for his use and which he desired
me to retain for him untill he came over. No package of such mark

or description is come to hand—those are said to be for his use and one of them may propably be the one he intended to describe—if by examining the contents of them they or either of them should turn out to contain things different than what was intended for the Ladies will you please to have them taken care of for Mr Church.

Major Jackson declines parting with Ben[1] But says when Mrs Church returns he will let her have him should she request it but will not part with him to any body else.

I will send you the account you desired in a few days. Mrs Chaloner joins me in Compliments to the Ladies and I remain with respect Dr Sir   Your most Obdt Serv   John Chaloner

ALS, Hamilton Papers, Library of Congress.
1. See H to Chaloner, November 11, 1784.

To John Jay [1]

[New York, December 7, 1784]

Dear Sir

The Baron De Steuben has informed me that he is about to set out for Trenton, where he expects to make application to Congress for a final settlement of his pretensions.[2] I feel myself so much interested in the success of his intended application, that I cannot forbear taking the liberty to recommend his case to your particular patronage. I have been an eye-witness to the services he has rendered this Country. I will venture to say they have been of essential weight in the revolution. 'Tis unquestionably to his efforts we are indebted for the introduction of discipline in the army; and that against a torrent of prejudice and opposition. Tis to that discipline we owe the figure we made with a handful of men in the latter periods of the war. Tis to that discipline we owe savings of different kinds of the utmost importance to our exhausted finances. The Baron De Steuben, whatever pride or personal[i]ty may say, is one of the *few* men who in the military line has rendered *substantial* services to the American cause. Justice demands he should have a liberal compensation. The reputation of our Country will not permit, that he be necessitated to quit us to solicit the bounty of those whom he has not served.

You my Dr Sir, I know will feel properly what justice and national reputation dictate upon this occasion. But your absence from America has perhaps prevented your receiving in some respects just representations of men and things. I flatter myself that which I now make to you will be received as a just one.

The Baron, if he remains in this Country will continue a citizen of New York. It seems to me, circumstanced as we are, it is not a contemptible object to give inducements to stay among us to a man whose military experience would be of singular advantage in forming those establishments to which we may be driven.

I shall not dwell longer on the subject, as I am convinced I need not multiply considerations to induce you to do whatever is possible or proper.

I remain with the most sincere & respectful attachment   Dr Sir
Your Obed ser   Alex Hamilton
NY. Decr. 7, 1784

ALS, The Andre deCoppet Collection, Princeton University Library; copy, The Oneida Historical Society at Utica, New York.
  1. On his return to the United States in July, 1784, Jay was appointed Secretary for Foreign Affairs.
  2. See "Report on the Claim of Baron von Steuben," December 30, 1782.

To Stephen Van Rensselaer

[*New York, December 9, 1784–1788.*[1] "My public engagements have not only left me bare of Cash but have lain me under a necessity to use my credit at the Bank as far as consisstently with delicacy in my station of director I ought to go. . . . The opportunities my profession gives me have taught me to consider partnerships under all circumstances as delicate and hazardous things. . . . I am sure for once they succeed, they ten times involve and embarras the person in that predicament." *Letter not found.*][2]

ALS, sold at Anderson Galleries, May 9, 1912, Lot 64.
  1. In the catalogue this letter is dated December 9, 1783. Since "the Bank" (i.e., the Bank of New York) was not established until March, 1784, the date is inaccurate. H was director of the bank from 1784 to 1788; therefore, the letter has been given the inclusive date of December 9, 1784–88.
  2. Extract taken from the manuscript dealer's catalogue.

To Egbert Benson [1]

New York, December 10, 1784. "When you were in town you mentioned to me some cause which you expected to come on at the circuit and to which you wished me to attend. As the parties have escaped my recollection . . . , I have concluded to write to you on the subject; that you may inform me who are the parties & what the controversy."

ALS, The Huntington Library, San Marino, California.
　1. Part of this letter is missing.

From Baron von Steuben

Trenton ce 14. Dec: [1784]

Mon Ami! J'ai remis Votre lettre a Mr: J.[1] Je le trouve disposé a Seconder mes demandes, Lesquels d'après son opinion je doit presenter au Congres sans perte de tems; quand meme la decision devroit en etre retarde. Ainsi Envoyer moi le Memoire sans delai,[2] je L'attendroi ici a Trenton avant que J'aille a Philadelphie.

Il S'agit de nommer un Secretair ou Ministre de Guerre, Le Gros Candidat du North serat sans doute proposé par ses compatriottes,[3] je n'en connois point d'autre; Si Le Congres avoit deja satisfait a mes pretensions je pourrai bien Entrer en Lice. Dites moi Votre sentimens la dessus.

Le Marquis [4] a pris Congé de moi sans toucher le sujet; pour ne pas Lui Causer de L'Ennui dans un païs ou il ne devroit pas en Avoir —je ne Lui ai pas meme demander si Mr: de Chattelleur [5] Lui avoit remis ma Lettre.

Envoyes moi le Memoire Mon Ami, je Vous Embrasse　Steuben Coll. Hammilton.

ALS, Hamilton Papers, Library of Congress.
　1. See H to John Jay, December 7, 1784. As von Steuben indicates, H's letter to Jay was delivered by von Steuben who attended the Continental Congress which was in session at Trenton.
　2. The memorandum has not been found. It presumably was one of the many letters which H drafted for von Steuben's signature setting forth the Baron's claim for compensation from Congress.

3. On October 30, 1783, Benjamin Lincoln resigned as Secretary at War. A successor was not appointed until a year and a half later. "Le Gros Candidat du North" to whom von Steuben refers was probably Henry Knox who, in March, 1785, succeeded Lincoln.

4. On December 11, 1784, the Continental Congress had made a formal presentation of an address to Lafayette who on December 13 left Trenton where the Congress was in session for New York.

5. Probably the Marquis de Chastellux, a major general in the army of Rochambeau, who came to America in 1780.

From Augustus Van Cortlandt [1]

Yonkers [*New York*] *December 29, 1784.* Sends a citation from Morris Hazard, and a copy of the proceedings against Rufus Herrick.

ALS, Hamilton Papers, Library of Congress.
  1. Van Cortlandt was a New York landowner.

Baron von Steuben to the President of Congress

[*New York, 1784*].[1] In a letter beginning "Nothing could justify my repeated applications to Your Honorable body, but that rigorous lot by which I feel myself oppressed," Hamilton set forth von Steuben's claims to compensation by the Continental Congress.

Df, in writing of H, Mr. Herbert R. Strauss, Chicago.
  1. Because von Steuben sent so many memorials to Congress, any one of which may have been written by H, it is impossible to date this letter precisely. It contains, however, one clue to the date on which it may have been written. In the first paragraph H writes for Steuben: "It is now two years that I have been soliciting the accomplishment of that Indemnification which has been adjudged to me by different Committees of Congress." As von Steuben's first memorial was submitted in December, 1782 (see "Continental Congress. Report on the Claim of Baron von Steuben," December 30, 1782), this memorial presumably was written in 1784.

1 7 8 5

To Hugh Seton [1]

[New York, January 1, 1785]

Sir,

I presume Mr. Jones [2] has ere this informed you of the disagreeable turn of your affair with Mr. Wilkes; [3] but as you first committed it to my management I think it proper to give you some account of its conclusion. As Mr. Jones does not at this time practice, he employed Mr. Burr [4] to issue process against Mr. Wilkes upon which he was put into confinement; pursuant to your expectation that his friends would interpose for his relief. The situation of this Country, by means of the war, affords so many examples of ruined debtors, that the Legislature is disposed to make relief to such persons as easy as possible; and accordingly pass from time to time acts for relief of insolvent debtors without the necessary checks for preventing fraud. While Mr. Wilkes was in confinement an act of this kind [5] passed. Mr. Burr who is a member of the Assembly, of influence and abilities, did every thing in his power to qualify the intended relief with such reasonable checks as would have given you an opportunity of opposing with success Wilkes' discharge; but finding his efforts, in this way, fruitless he took the only step which then remained to disappoint Wilkes of the benefit of the act. He discontinued the suit, and let him out of confinement. The principle of the act was to relieve persons in actual confinement at the time of passing it on surrendering their whole property for the benefit of their Creditors. Wilkes immediately *procured himself* to be arrested by some other person, and has been since discharged under the act. Indeed if it had not then happened there would be now a fresh opportunity; for the Legislature which is sitting are about passing a similar law.

Questions may perhaps be raised with Success hereafter whether Wilkes' discharge was a valid one; as there is no doubt his confinement was voluntary and collusive. But it is best such a discussion should sleep for the present.

I sincerely Sir sympathize with you in the mortification you must experience in being thus baffled, after having suffered so heavy a loss; and I shall be happy if you are satisfied that every thing was done by the persons to whom I committed the business, to secure your interests, which the situation of things permitted.

I remain with much esteem   Sir   Your Obed serv

New York
Jany. 1st 1785

ADf, Hamilton Papers, Library of Congress.
    1. For other correspondence and information concerning this letter, see H to Seton, June 18, 1784; Seton to H, February 2, 1785; John Wilkes to H, November 8, 1785; H to Wilkes, November 8, 1785; and Wilkes to H, November 9, 1785.
    2. Samuel Jones.
    3. John Wilkes.
    4. Aaron Burr.
    5. On October 23, 1784, Wilkes had petitioned the legislature "praying leave to bring in a bill to enable him to deliver up all his effects and property for the benefit of his creditors; and that in consequence thereof he may be discharged from the demands of his creditors, and his person released from confinement" (New York Assembly *Journal*, 1784, 16). On November 24, 1784, "An Act to revive and amend an act entitled 'An act for the relief of insolvent debtors within this State,' passed 17th April 1784" was passed by the New York legislature (*Laws of the State of New York*, II, 27–29).

From Hercules Mulligan [1]

New York, January 7, 1785. At the bottom of an itemized account of money owed Mulligan by Philip Schuyler, Mulligan signed the following receipt: "Recd payment (by the hands of Col. Hammelton) in full."

ADS, Hamilton Papers, Library of Congress.
    1. Despite the reliance by H's biographers on Hercules Mulligan's narrative of the life of H (written sometime between 1810 and 1815), this receipt and an entry in H's "Cash Book" are the only known documents which show any association between H and Mulligan.

To Timothy Pickering [1]

New York, January 7, 1785. "I am mortified in being obliged to acknowlege to you my neglect of the business you committed to my care for your friend Mr. Holt.[2] . . . I have applied to Mrs. Holt. I find she has some time since taken out letters of Administration with the will annexed during the absence of the Executors; a matter in which she never could have found any difficulty. It would indeed be in Mr. Holts power, on coming within the state to take the business out of her hands."

ALS, Massachusetts Historical Society, Boston.
    1. For background to this letter, see Pickering to H, September 30, 1784.
    2. William Holt, brother of John Holt.

From Hugh Seton

[*England, January 8, 1785.* On February 2, 1785, Seton wrote to Hamilton: "I also wrote you a few Lines the 8th of this Month." Since Seton wrote this letter on February 2, he must have been referring to January 8. *Letter not found.*]

From Neil Jamieson [1]

New York, January 10, 1785. Itemizes amounts of money paid for a house in New York City during the British occupation.

ALS, Hamilton Papers, Library of Congress.
    1. Jamieson was the head of the dry goods house of Neil Jamieson and Company located at 933 Water Street, New York City.
    H wrote on the margin of this letter the names of the various British commanders in New York from 1778 to 1783.

To Richard Varick [1]

[New York, January 10, 1785]

Mr. Hamiltons Compliments to the Recorder and to Doctor Bailey [2]—is very sorry that he can't have the pleasure of meeting them this Evening as the weather is bad and he is a good deal indisposed.

Monday Evening

AL, New-York Historical Society, New York City.
1. Varick was the recorder of New York City.
2. Dr. Richard Bailey (Bayley), a native of Connecticut, had studied medicine in New York City and later in London where he was working at the outbreak of the American Revolution. He returned to America as a surgeon in the British army under Howe. In 1777 he resigned his position and settled in New York City where he remained until his death in 1801.

From Philip Schuyler

Albany Jan: 11 1785

My Dear Sir

Your two favors the one advising me of the Beautrice and the other Covering letters from my Children in Europe I have had the pleasure to receive.[1]

Mrs. Schuyler has been much indisposed since my last. We began to be very apprehensive of her situation but our fears are vanished with the untoward Symptoms which occasioned them. She is now so well as to go abroad and we have well grounded hopes of a perfect restoration.

Please to forward the enclosed.

Mrs. Schuyler thinks she has receipts for discharge of the account you inclosed. She will examine her papers in a few days. If she is mistaken I shall advise you of It and beg the favor of you to discharge It.

Congress I hear is at New York.[2] Will you be good enough to communicate now & then what they are about.

I am not yet without hopes of making you a visit with Mrs. Schuyler who Joins me in love & the compliments of the season to you & our Dear Daughter, embrace the little ones for us.

Adieu   I am most affectionately Yours &c. &c.   P Schuyler

Colo. Hamilton

ALS, Hamilton Papers, Library of Congress.
1. Letters not found.
2. The Continental Congress adjourned at Trenton on December 24, 1784, to meet in New York City on January 11, 1785.

From John Chaloner

Philadelphia, January 26, 178[5].[1] Requests the opinion of Hamilton on "a Transaction in which Mr Church[2] is deeply interested," and in which the protested bills of John Holker are involved.

ALS, Hamilton Papers, Library of Congress.
  1. Chaloner mistakenly dated this letter January 26, 1784.
  2. John B. Church.

To John Chaloner

[*New York, February 2, 1785.* On the back of a letter that Chaloner wrote to Hamilton on January 26, 1785, Hamilton wrote: "Answered Feby. 2d." *Letter not found.*]

From Hugh Seton[1]

London 2d. Febry. 1785

Dr. Sir

I only trouble you with these few Lines to mention the Earnest Wish I have to hear of your Receipt of mine of 1st. August[2] inclosing all Mr. Wilkes's[3] Acceptances &c as I am uneasy least they have miscarried & yet Mrs. Laurence of this Place who took the Charge of Sending them out to you tells Me that the Vessell arrived Safe; Present my best respects to Mr Maxwell[4] to whom you recommended Me, I Should have wrote to him but troubled you with this as the Papers were originally Sent you: I also wrote you a few Lines the 8th of this Month.[5] I am ever with very Particular Respect Dr Sir Your most faithfull hum ser   Hugh Seton

ALS, Hamilton Papers, Library of Congress.
  1. For other correspondence concerning this case, see H to Seton, June 18, 1784, and January 1, 1785; John Wilkes to H, November 8, 1785; H to Wilkes, November 8, 1785; and Wilkes to H, November 9, 1785.
  2. Letter not found.
  3. John De Ponthieu Wilkes.
  4. Probably William Maxwell, tobacconist, who was a director of the Bank of New York.
  5. Letter not found.

Attendance at a Meeting of the Society for Promoting the Manumission of Slaves [1]

New York, February 4, 1785. On this date Hamilton attended an organization meeting of the Society for Promoting the Manumission of Slaves held at the Coffee House in New York City. After the proposed constitution of the Society was read and adopted, the Society "Ordered—That Colonel Hamilton, Colonel Troup [2] and Mr. Matlack [3] be a Committee to Report a Line of Conduct to be recommended to the Members of the Society in relation to any Slaves possessed by them; and also to prepare a Recommendation to all such Persons as have manumitted or shall Manumit Slaves to transmit their names and the names and Ages of the Slaves manumitted; in Order that the same may be Registered and the Society be the better Enabled to detect Attempts to deprive such Manumitted Persons of their Liberty."

MS, "Minutes of the Society for Promoting the Manumission of Slaves," New-York Historical Society, New York City.

1. At the first meeting of the society, held on January 25, 1785, a committee was appointed "to draw up a set of Rules for the Government of the said Society," and "the Meeting was then adjourned to the 4th day of February next" (*ibid.*). H was one of thirty-two men who attended the meeting on February 4.
2. Robert Troup.
3. White Matlack.

To Walter Stewart [1]

New York, February 21, 1785. "I have delayed answering the letter you lately wrote me [2] in expectation of Mr. Templetons making some proposals, which it appeared to me he had some thoughts of doing, but as he has not come to any explanation, it is unnecessary to wait any longer for it. All that I can recommend to you to do, is to procure and send out all original letters or orders from Templeton or his partner directing the appropriation of the proceeds of the Cargo to their benefit."

ALS, Columbia University Libraries.

1. Stewart, who had been brevetted a brigadier general at the end of the Revolution, was at this time a Philadelphia merchant.
2. Letter not found.

Committee of Accounts for Columbia College

New York, March 8, 1785. Approves an "Account of the Repairs of the Buildings of Columbia College in this City." [1]

DS, Columbia University Libraries.
1. H was a member of the committee of accounts for Columbia College.

To George Washington

[New York, March 10, 1785]

Dr. Sir,

I am requested by Mr. Oudinarde [1] to transmit you the Inclosed Account. I observed to him that it was a little extraordinary the account had not been presented before; and that it was probable your accounts with the public had been long since closed, and that, by the delay, you may have lost the opportunity of making it a public charge, as it ought to have been. But as the person was very importunate I told him I should have no objection to be the vehicle of conveyance to you. In this view I transmit the account; and remain with much respect   D Sir   Yr Obed & humb   Alex Hamilton

⟨Mrs.⟩ Hamilton joins in compliments to ⟨Mrs.⟩ Washington
New York March 10. 1785

ALS, Hamilton Papers, Library of Congress.
1. Probably one of the two partners of the New York merchant firm of M. and H. Oudenarde at 18 Hanover Square, New York City.

To Thomas Pearsall

[*March 16, 1785.* Pearsall wrote to Hamilton: "I have thy Letter of this date." *Letter not found.*]

From Thomas Pearsall [1]

New York, March 16, 1785. "I have thy Letter of this date.[2] I recollect thy Application to me with a Copy of Oliver Arnolds

Judgment obtained against me in Rhode Island for the Outfit of my Quarter of Sloop Diana. My present Determination is . . . not to pay it, as . . . I never gave Orders either in Writing or Verbally for the outfit."

ALS, Hamilton Papers, Library of Congress.
1. Pearsall was a partner in the firm of merchants in New York City known as Thomas Pearsall and Son.
2. Letter not found.

To Elizabeth Hamilton

[*Westchester, New York, March 17, 1785*. Hamilton wrote to Elizabeth Hamilton: "I have just written to you My beloved by the person who will probably be the bearer of this." *Letter not found.*]

To Elizabeth Hamilton

[Westchester, New York, March 17, 1785]

I have just written to you [1] My beloved by the person who will probably be the bearer of this. Col Burr just tells me, that the house we live in is offered for sale at £2100.[2] I am to request you to agree for the purchase for me, if at that price. If you cannot do better, you may engage that the whole shall be paid in three months; but I could wish to pay half in a short time and the other half in a year. Adieu my Angel   A Hamilton

Chester [3] March 17. 1785

ALS, Hamilton Papers, Library of Congress.
1. Letter not found.
2. The house to which H is referring was probably at 57 Wall Street, his residence during most of the 1780's.
3. "Chester" probably was Westchester, New York.

From Thomas White [1]

New York, March 22, 1785. "[I enclose] a statement respecting the Rents (of the different Lotts on the Vineyard in dispute with the Beekmans) that we have received since the Death of my Father, which I hope will be sufficient both to you and the other Gentlemen Arbitrators of this disagreeable Business to conclude upon."

ALS, Hamilton Papers, Library of Congress.
    1. White was the son of Thomas White, an attainted Loyalist who died during or shortly after the Revolution. His widow was allowed by state law in 1784 to repurchase the lands that had been forfeited by her husband. It was these lands that were in dispute.

To Jeremiah Wadsworth

[*New York, April 1, 1785.* On April 7, 1785, Hamilton wrote to Jeremiah Wadsworth: "In mine to you of the first instant." *Letter not found.*]

From Jeremiah Wadsworth

Hartford April 3d 1785

Dear Sir

I have received very unfavorable accounts respecting Isaac Moses & Co House in Holland.[1] As you have the recet for our Monies I wish you inquire of him if our concerns are so involved in his matters that we shall be liable to any loss in case of his ruine by this misfortune in holland. I am   Dear Sir Your very Hum Servant

Jere Wadsworth

Have you any news from Church[2] by ye last Packet? I have not a line.

Col Hamelton

ALS, Hamilton Papers, Library of Congress.
    1. Isaac Moses, according to *The New York Directory for 1786,* was an auctioneer who was located at 37 Dock Street in New York City. He was also connected in an international partnership with Marcus Elcan of Richmond, Virginia, and with Samuel and Moses Myers of Amsterdam. The dissolution of the firm was announced in a supplement to *The New-York Journal, or the Weekly Register,* of June 23, 1785. The partnership of Wadsworth and Church held some of the firm's notes.
    2. John B. Church who was at this time in England.

To ———

New York, April 7, 1785. Wishes to obtain evidence to assist Alexander Macauley in a dispute between Macauley and John Wardrop.

ALS, Pequot Library, Southport, Connecticut.

To The New-York Packet

[New York, April 7, 1785]

The Subscriber having observed his name included in some of the lists of persons proposed for the ensuing election, and being sincerely desirous of declining public office at the present juncture, thinks it proper to declare his wishes on this head, to prevent the attention of any of his fellow-citizens being diverted from persons, whose convenience and abilities will be better adapted to their services.   Alexander Hamilton.

Loudon's New-York Packet, April 7, 1785.

To Henry Laurens

[*New York, April 6, 1785.* On April 19, 1785, Laurens wrote to Hamilton: "I was yesterday honored by receipt of your very obliging Letter of the 6th." *Letter not found.*]

To Jeremiah Wadsworth

New York April 7th. 1785

Dr. Sir,

In mine to you of the first instant [1] I informed you that the house of Samuel and Moses Myers of Amsterdam had stopped payment in consequence of which an assignment of property had there taken place for the benefit of the *English* and *Dutch* Creditors. How far this assignment will operate cannot now be determined; as we are not sufficiently acquainted with the circumstances. It happened the Mr. Moses, who is one of the partners, called upon me to consult me professionally as to the measures I should think it adviseable for him to pursue.[2] I told him of my having his notes for monies due from him to Mr Church on your partnership;[3] but that as I did not think your interest incompatible with his I should freely give him my council. The first steps I advised him to, was to make an assignment of all partnership effects in Pensylvania, Maryland, Virginia and South Carolina to Trustees for the general benefit of Creditors. My reason for this was that in those states partial attachments would lie for the benefit of the persons making them and I have no doubt but that orders would have arrived from different parts of Europe for that purpose before any sent from here could reach either of those places. The fact has turned out as was supposed.

Mr Moses has lately exhibited a sketch of his affairs; in which he makes out seven thousand pounds more than he owes. But as this is but a sketch—as his affairs are very extensive and complicated—it is probable he cannot ascertain their true state, and it is rather to be apprehended that he draws a flattering picture. There is thus far *every appearance* of *fairness* in his conduct; and his Creditors here seem inclined to be indulgent.

His object is to obtain a letter of license for five years; there will I suspect be great difficulties in this. He urges against an immediate assignment of his whole property that it will probably, by being precipitately disposed of fall greatly short of the real value to the injury of his Creditors as well as him self. On the other hand, however if it remains with him, as he is very enterprising the result must be a mere chapter of accidents. In the state of his affairs, he exhibits £12000 debts of *Isaac Moses* and £21000 property. Your demand is against *Isaac Moses*, so that if his state in this respect be at all accurate and he makes no improper disposition of Isaac Moses' property, you will be safe; as his private property must first be applied to the payment of his private debts and the ballance to the partnership debts; and so *vice versa*. He has assured me he will make no disposition to your prejudice. Upon the whole I am of opinion (as he will have much in his power) that it will be most prudent for your interest not in the first instance to be one of those who shall press; if others begin you can keep pace with them; and by indulgent conduct, if others press, I think Moses will be induced to take care of you. He appears to think him self under peculiar obligations to your concern. His general state of affairs is—

Debts due from himself & Copartnership	£91.000
Good Debts and effects belong to himself and partners........................	98.000
Surplus	£ 7.000

But supposing the worst there seems to be little doubt that he will be able to pay 15/ in the pound.

Should it not be convenient to you to be on the spot yourself, Let me hear from you on this head.

Mr. Burr has delivered me a declaration against Henly.[4] I find it was a partnership business, so the suit not abated as I at first supposed, by Archibald Blairs insolvency.[5] I shall ask some friend of yours on your account to become bail to the action. As an Atty I cannot do this.

By our advices from Albany I have great reason to apprehend General Schuyler is no more. This I consider as a great loss to his family, friends and the public.

With sincere regards. I remain Dr Sir   Your Obedt sert

P.S—Yrs of the third instant is just handed me.
New York
April 7. 1785

Copy, Hamilton Papers, Library of Congress.
  1. Letter not found.
  2. See Wadsworth to H, April 3, 1785, note 1.
  3. The partnership between John B. Church and Jeremiah Wadsworth for supplying the French army in America was continued for some years after the Revolution. It was dissolved in July, 1785.
  4. Probably Archibald Henly whose promissory note to Samuel Donaldson is preserved in H's legal papers, Library of Congress.
  5. Archibald Blair was listed in *The New York Directory for 1786* as a stock-broker.

From Marquis de Lafayette

Paris April the 13th 1785

My dear Hamilton

Altho I have just now writen to McHenry [1] Requesting him to impart My Gazette to you, a very barren one indeed, I feel within myself a Want to tell you I love you tenderly. Your Brother Church

Has sailed for America since which I Had a letter from His lady who is in very good Health.² By an old letter from our friend Greene ³ I Have Been delighted to find He consents to send His son to be educated with mine. The idea makes me very Happy. I wish, dear Hamilton, you would Honour me with the same Mark of your friendship and confidence. As there is no fear of a War I intend ⟨visiting⟩ the ⟨Prussian⟩ and Austrian ⟨troops⟩. In one of your New York Gazettes I find an ⟨Association⟩ Against the slavery of negroes which seems to me ⟨worded⟩ in such a way as to give no offense to the moderate Men in the Southern States.⁴ As I ever Have Been partial to my Brethren of that Colour, I wish if you are one in the Society, you would move, in your own Name, for my Being Admitted on the list. My Best Respects wait on Mrs. Hamilton. I kiss Phil, and the Young lady. Adieu   Your affectionate friend

Lafayette

Mention me most affectionately to the doctor, His lady,⁵ Genl Schuyler and family, your sister Peggy, Fish, Webb,⁶ and all our friends.

ALS, Hamilton Papers, Library of Congress.
 1. James McHenry.
 2. John B. and Angelica Church.
 3. Nathanael Greene.
 4. In 1785 the New York Society for Promoting the Manumission of Slaves and Protecting Such of Them as Have Been or May Be Liberated was founded. H was among the sponsors of the organization. John Jay was elected the first president.
 5. Dr. and Mrs. John Cochran were Elizabeth Hamilton's aunt and uncle.
 6. Nicholas Fish and Samuel B. Webb.

From David Beekman ¹

New York, April 15, 1785. "I yesterday saw Mr. Cor[neliu]s P. Low ² & he is not willing to do anything, & now says the money belongs to the state. He alters his opinion often. Will you be so kind, and take this affair in your hands for me & if you think I can recover it, I beg you will."

ALS, Hamilton Papers, Library of Congress.
 1. Beekman, member of a prominent New York merchant family, had been a partner in the St. Croix firm of Beekman and Cruger for which H had worked as a clerk. Beekman had become a planter on St. Croix.
 2. Low was a merchant in New York City.

From Jeremiah Wadsworth

Hartford April: 17 1785

Dear Sir

I have this moment received a letter from you of the 7th Instant. Our concern with Moses by his sketch of an account exhibited me at New York was in sundry Vessels. I am so well persuaded that in these concerns we shall loose Money, even if Moses pays all his debts that I would willingly give up 5/ in the pound & ⟨– –⟩ & give discharges for 15/ in the pound. I do not ⟨think⟩ I can be at NYork before the end of June & beg you will do every thing you think proper with Moses.[1] I am glad to find by Mr. Colt[2] who left NYork the 14th that Gen Schuyler is not dead.[3] As to Henlys matter[4] I suppose you will be able to decide on examining the papers exhibited by the plantiff the probability of the suits succeeding or not. If there is like to be any considerable ballance due from Henly I would try to & have him set ye final tryal. I pray you to write me when that will be. It has been reported here that Church has wrote you he has resolved to stay in Europe. I find nothing in yr. letter on this Subject & therefore disbelieve it.

I am dear Sir Your very Hume Servant   Jere Wads⟨worth⟩

Col Hamilton

ALS, Hamilton Papers, Library of Congress.
   1. For an account of Isaac Moses's financial affairs, see H to Wadsworth, April 7, 1785.
   2. Peter Colt was a business associate of Wadsworth.
   3. See the last paragraph of H to Wadsworth, April 7, 1785.
   4. Archibald Henly about whose legal affairs H wrote to Wadsworth on April 7, 1785.

From Henry Laurens [1]

Charleston S. Carolina
19. April 1785

Dear Sir

I was yesterday honored by receipt of your very obliging Letter

LC, Long Island Historical Society, Brooklyn, New York.
   1. Henry Laurens returned to the United States in the summer of 1784, and after attending Congress he reached Charleston in January, 1785.

of the 6th. inclosing Mr. Frederic's Narrative.[2] A tissue of Lies. During the Seige of Charleston, when he pretends he carried arms & to have acted in the Trenches, he was at my Mepkin Plantation, whence some time after the Town fell, he joined the temporary Conquerors; he also seduced his Wife, she thro' the persuasion of faithful Scaramouch returned, he was afterward captured by an American Cruizer, carried into George Town & claimed by one of my Attornies, he broke thro' & escaped and had not been heard of till now We learn he is in the Jail of New York.

Scaramouch, Berry & others who know the whole history of my Negroes aver, he never was about the person of our dear departed friend;[3] Our dear friend was too tenacious of propriety to have manumitted a Slave not his own; this is evinced by his conduct to the black Man who was actually with him and who continues with me.

Our dear friend and his father entertained but one opinion respecting Slavery, excepting that his generous Soul would have precipitated a Work, which to make it glorious his father thought he saw could only be accomplished by gradual Steps. Haste would make havoc. Could I but prevail upon my fellow Citizens to prohibit further importations, I should deem it progress equal to carrying all the outworks; my attempts hitherto have been fruitless, I have some ground for beleiving offensive; speaking generally a whole Country is opposed to me, pressing the Business which We had in view would not forward it, nor afford happiness even to the Negroes, witness Frederick's Case. I am acting therefore agreeable to the dictates of my Conscience and the best lights of my understanding. Some of my Negroes to whom I have offered freedom have declined the Bounty, they will live with me, to some of them I already allow Wages, to all of them every proper indulgence, I will venture to say the whole are in more comfortable circumstances than any equal number of Peasantry in Europe, there is not a Beggar among them nor one unprovided with food, raiment & good Lodging, they also enjoy property; the Lash is forbidden; they all understand this declaration as a Substitute—"If you deserve whipping I

2. Letter not found.
3. Henry Laurens's son, John, who was killed in August, 1782.

shall conclude you don't love me & will sell you, otherwise I will never sell one of you, nor will I ever buy another Negro, unless it shall be to gratify a good Man who may want a Wife."

You may remember George in Philadelphia, I had given him absolute freedom before I went last to Europe, he embarked with me, but returned long before I came home, is now about my house and says he does not want to be more free than he is. Yet I beleive no man gets more work from his Negroes than I do, at the same time they are my Watchmen and my friends; never was an absolute Monarch more happy in his Subjects than at the present time I am, how long this will continue is uncertain, but I will endeavor to do right to day.

I think I see the rising gradations to unlimited freedom and view the prospect with pleasure. When We shall be wise enough to stop importation, such happy Families will become more general and time will work manumission or a state equal to it. Policy and Decency will dictate proper reservation; We shall then insure good Servants, good Soldiers, our Strength in time of Need; at present the Number of wretched Slaves, precarious Riches, is our greatest Weakness— but alas! these Southern States are not at this moment in a disposition to be persuaded tho' one should rise from the dead—God forbid our conversion by too long a Delay, shall be the Effect of a direful Struggle.

But to return to Frederic, he was always a very good Lad before the War, contaminated no doubt by bad Examples in that dreadful Scene. He is according to the Law of the Land my property, I paid a valuable consideration for him to those, meaning the British, who debauched and carried him off. If he is to be freed from my claim, let him be a Slave to no other Man, Your Corporation I should think will interpose, If you my dear Sir can prevail upon him to return, I will receive and put him upon a footing with his fellow Servants, without resenting his past Errors, his future Welfare will depend upon his own Behaviour. Whatever Expences may attend I will repay as soon as I am informed, and shall ever thank you for this friendly interference on my Behalf.

Could Frederic read all this he would perceive his Master is not very anxious to remand him to good Quarters, there was a time when he would have been valued at £100. or £150 Sterling—the time is when I only wish to collect my Family. It would grieve me to hear he was enslaved by any one, who has a shorter claim of property in him than I have. I wish to give him a chance of being rescued from Slavery.

My health is somewhat mended since my arrival in Carolina, but a constitution broken down by Long & close confinement of an aged Man, cannot be recovered by increasing Age—for happiness, since receiving the Wound to which We have alluded, ever green, I have learned to be at least half happy by a quiet submission in every Event; comparatively I am very happy, my landed property remains & I am not in debt.

I beg my dear Sir you will do me the honor to present my respectful Compliments to Mrs. Hamilton and to be assured that with great Respect & Esteem I am, your obliged and obedt Servant

To Robert Livingston [1]

[April 25, 1785]

Dr Sir,

Mr. W. Livingston [2] mentioned to me lately in New York, that you would wish to have measures speedily taken concerning the controversy between the Chancellor [3] and yourself. [4] Though I am upon the maturest reflection of opinion that the law is with you; yet you know my sentiments as to the uncertainty of the event. Much will depend on the whim of a jury; and therefore previous to entering upon a prosecution which may be long, complicated and expensive, I should be happy you would honor me with your ideas of the practicability of a compromise, and of the conditions, if any, on which you would think it admissible. Suppose the Chancellor would content himself with one Mill, [5] relinquish all pretensions to erecting more, and bind himself in firm covenants not to do it, would you think it adviseable to close with such a mode of settling the dispute? I should be glad to hear from you on the subject; and in the mean time, I will take measures to sound the Chancellor. Should the matter after all come to extremities, I shall do every thing in my power for your Interests; but if it could be terminated to your satisfaction in an amicable way it would give me pleasure to contribute to it.

It may appear to you, Sir, a little extraordinary that I should take occasion in this professional letter to mention politics; but the situation of the state at this time is so critical that it is become a serious object of attention to those who are concerned for the *security of property* or the prosperity of government, to endeavour to put men in the Legislature whose principles are not of the *levelling kind*. The spirit of the present Legislature is truly alarming, and appears evidently directed to the confusion of all property and principle. The truth is that the state is now governed by a couple of New England adventurers—Ford and Adgate; [6] who make tools of the Yates [7] and their Associates. A number of attempts have been made by this junto to subvert the constitution and destroy the rights of private property; which but for the Council of Revision would have had the most serious effects.[8] All men of respectability, in the city, of whatever party, who have been witnesses of the despotism and iniquity of the Legislature, are convinced, that the principal people in the community must for their own defence, unite to overset the party I have alluded to. I wish you to be persuaded Sir, that I would not take the liberty to trouble you with these remarks with a view to serving any particular turn; but, from a thorough conviction, that the safety of all those who have any thing to lose calls upon them to take care that the power of government is intrusted to proper hands. Much depends on the ensuing election.[9] You Sir have much in your power; and I have no doubt you will have heared from other quarters and from your immediate connections, a like account of public affairs to that which I have now given.

I have the honor to be with the greatest respect & esteem   Sir Your obed & hum ser   Alex Hamilton

April 25, 1785

ALS, MS Division, New York Public Library.
1. Robert Livingston was the third proprietor of Livingston Manor.
2. Walter Livingston was the son of the Robert Livingston to whom this letter was addressed.
3. Robert R. Livingston was chancellor of the State of New York, and a second cousin of the third proprietor of Livingston Manor.
4. After the death of Robert Livingston, the first proprietor of Livingston

Manor, the disposition of his extensive landholdings was for many years the subject of litigation among his descendants.

5. The dispute between Robert Livingston and Chancellor Robert R. Livingston concerned the establishment of grist-mills on a stream known as Roeliff Jansen Kill.

6. Matthew Ford and Jacob Adgate were representatives in the New York Assembly from Albany County.

7. Abraham Yates, Jr., and Robert Yates, both of whom lived in Albany, were prominent supporters of Governor George Clinton. For H's views on these two men, see H to Robert Morris, August 13, 1782.

8. The reference is to the various anti-Tory laws passed in 1784, some of which the Council of Revision had vetoed.

9. The election for the members of the ninth session of the New York legislature was held in the spring of 1785.

From William Cooper and Andrew Craig [1]

Burlington [*New Jersey*] *May 9, 1785.* Ask for information and advice on the progress being made in the sale of 40,000 acres in the Otsego Patent.

LS, Hamilton Papers, Library of Congress.
1. Cooper, who later founded Cooperstown, New York, was the father of James Fenimore Cooper. From 1776 to 1786 Cooper and Craig, both of Burlington, New Jersey, purchased the greater part of the Otsego Patent, which had originally been granted to George Croghan.

To William Duer

[Westchester, New York, May 14, 1785]

My Dear Sir

I wrote you from Albany informing you that the Chancellor had given you till the first of June to bring into Court the money allowed to be due, to wit such part of the principle with interest at five ℀ Cent as became due to 1776 and the residue of the principal which afterwards became due. I am doubtful whether that letter may not be delayed. I do not now recollect precisely the order but it is pretty nearly as I state and I would advise to write to Lansing [1] for greater certainty. The Injunction continues in the mean time, and will continue if the money is brought in 'till the decision of the cause. I believe you will think this determination of the Chancellor a reasonable one; though I wish it could have been put upon a footing more convenient to You.

I congratulate you on your election.[2] I hope you may not find yourself fettered by some of your Colleagues. Abilities like yours ought always to be employed for the public good; and I have no doubt this will be your object. When I left Albany there was every reason to believe, General Schuyler with all his friends (whose views correspond with yours) would be elected in exclusion of Ford, Adgate, Yates [3] &c.

I remain   Affectionately   Yr. friend & servant   Alex Hamilton

Chester [4] 14th May 1785

ALS, Harwood Collection, Library of Congress.
   1. John Lansing, Jr., was an attorney in Albany and presumably involved as counsel in the case about which H was writing.
   2. Duer was elected an assemblyman from New York City to serve in the ninth session of the New York legislature which was to meet in January, 1786.
   3. Matthew Ford, Jacob Adgate, and Abraham Yates, Jr., represented Albany County in the New York legislature. See H to Robert Livingston, April 25, 1785.
   4. "Chester" probably referred to Westchester, New York.

From John Ross [1]

Philadelphia, May 17, 1785. Sends information concerning Ross's share of ownership of the ship *Diligent.*

ALS, Hamilton Papers, Library of Congress.
   1. Ross, a Philadelphia merchant, was an agent for François, Marquis de Barbé-Marbois, the French chargé d'affaires in the United States. H was representing Ross in *Bartholomew Terrasson et al.* v. *Ship Diligent,* a case pending before the New York Court of Admiralty.

From Cornelius Glen [1]

Albany, May 20, 1785. Requests aid in the recovery of money from Daniel Parker and Company.

ALS, Hamilton Papers, Library of Congress.
   1. Glen, an Albany merchant, had been an agent for Daniel Parker during the Revolution.

From John D. Coxe and Tench Coxe [1]

Philadelphia, May 21, 1785. Request Hamilton to represent them and to provide information on lands in dispute between John and Tench Coxe and Robert Lettis Hooper and James Wilson. Request Hamilton to forward certain legal documents to the commissioners of the Land Office of New York.

LS, in writing of John D. Coxe, Hamilton Papers, Library of Congress.
  1. John D. Coxe, a Pennsylvania lawyer, and Tench Coxe, a Philadelphia merchant, were speculating in land in western New York.

From Stephen De Lancey [1]

Scarsdale [New York] May 27, 1785. Asks for information concerning the progress of various legal actions instituted against De Lancey's debtors.

ALS, Hamilton Papers, Library of Congress.
  1. De Lancey was the grandson of Stephen De Lancey, founder of the family in the United States.

From Ezekiel Forman

Philadelphia, May 31, 1785. Asks Hamilton to return John Philips's bond.

ALS, Hamilton Papers, Library of Congress.

From James Hamilton [1]

[*St. Croix, May 31, 1785.* On June 22, 1785, Hamilton wrote to James Hamilton: "I have received your letter of the 31st of May last." *Letter not found.*]

  1. James Hamilton was H's older brother. See H to James Hamilton, June 22, 1785, note 1.

From Jarvis Coles

[*June 7, 1785.* According to the catalogue description of this letter, Coles, on Hamilton's orders, had occupied a house for military purposes. Coles, who after the war was sued by the owner for rent, requested Hamilton to defend him. *Letter not found.*]

ALS, sold at Swann Galleries, March 5, 1943, Lot 37.

To John D. Coxe and Tench Coxe [1]

New York, June 9, 1785. Cannot represent them in their land dispute with Robert Lettis Hooper and James Wilson, as Hooper and Wilson previously have engaged Hamilton's services in the controversy.

ADfS, Hamilton Papers, Library of Congress.
  1. See John D. Coxe and Tench Coxe to H, May 21, 1785.

From James Duane, John Jay, and Robert R. Livingston to Alexander Hamilton and Samuel Jones

[New York] June 9, 1785

At a meeting of the agents appointed by the state of New York to manage their controversy with the Commonwealth of Massachusetts [1]—it is agreed that a general retaining fee be given to Alexander Hamilton and Samuel Jones [2] Esqrs. as Counsellors and Solicitors on the part of this State that the brief already prepared together with the necessary papers be put in their hands—That they compleat the said Brief with as much expedition as possible—That they collect every necessary evidence from the records and order three copies to be made of such Brief for the use of the agents and Counsellors who are to attend the trial [3]

Jas. Duane
John Jay
Robt. R Livingston

Copy, The Huntington Library, San Marino, California; copy, New-York Historical Society, New York City.

1. For information on this controversy, see "Notes on the History of North and South America," December, 1786.

2. Jones, a resident of Oyster Bay, Long Island, had recently been elected to the New York Assembly. He was a partisan of Governor George Clinton.

3. The brief drawn up in this controversy is in H's writing. Jones apparently also served as counsel, for in the James Duane Papers, New-York Historical Society, there is an account from Jones against the agents of the State of New York.

To Samuel Jones

[New York, June 9, 1785] [1]

Dr Sir

The above is a copy of a paper transmitted me this day by Mr. Duane.[2] You will perceive much is expected from us; and unfortunately in the situation of my business little is in my power. I wish to see you in Town as soon [3]

AL, The Huntington Library, San Marino, California.

1. The letter is undated. It was written, as the first line states, on the date on which H received his commission from James Duane (see James Duane, John Jay, and Robert Livingston to H, June 9, 1785).

2. See Duane, Jay, and Livingston to H, June 9, 1785.

3. The remainder of this letter is missing.

From Robert Livingston [1]

Manor Livingston [New York] 13 June 1785

Dr. Sir

Your kind & interesting letter of the 25th. April did not come to my hands before the 23 May, when I was at my Iron works endeavouring to git them repaird & to Sett the Furnace going which gave me much trouble & realy exercised my patience & from whence I return'd last Saterday, much fateagu'd, this troublesome Job, am persuaded will appologise for my not answering your polite letter Sooner.

With regard to the practicabelity of a Compromise with the Gentm. in Question [2] I think it Scarcely possible as his pretentions are so very wild, Romantic & Extensive, in so much that he would if in his power take all & leave me none.

Wherefore I think it most prudent for me, to carry on a sute against him, not only for Building a Griss Mill with two pair of Stones & using my waters but also for the proffitts he has & does, make of it, to my prejudice & damage.

And while I am determind not to possess anything to which he can lay a just clame, so my intention is, not to suffer him to possess any to which I have a just right, this in my judgement is Strictly honest, of corse nothing but the Law can deside us, and the Sooner this is enterd upon the Sooner its hoped it will be determind, am fully resolved not to be frightened by any, or all his threats,[3] from time to time thrown out against me, & mean to have my right, and this perswade my Self a jury will give me.

I will however write Mr Duane [4] on the Subject altho I think a Compromise in this Case inadmissable, and thank you kindly for proposing it.

I do not my good Sir, think it any ways Extraordinary you should make mention of the Politics of the present dangerous times, on the Contrary I feal happy in finding your Sentiments so justly accord with mine, and my Sons, as we observed for some time past the pernitious intentions of those you mention, & in order to prevent, & counter act, as much as in us laid, their politics, and prevent ourselves, & Countrye from ruin, which we clearly Saw rappedly decending on our heads, we did endeavour the last year for an alteration in the representation, but without the desir'd Success, while we stood almost alone, as if no one saw the danger, but ourselves, nor did this falure discourage us, but reather hightend our diligence in this last Election, by Compleating the necessary Junction previous to the day of Election we have so often desired & Endeavourd for; by uniting the interests of the Rensselaer, Schuyler, & our family, with other Gentm. of property in the County in one Interest; by which means we Carryed this last Election to a man as you must have heard from your friends,[5] and I trust we Shall always have the like Success provided we Stick Close to Each other; and our Countryes interest; which is our Sincear desire; and of which we Should be Cautious of letting our Enemyes know anything while that may be dangerous: these Sir, are our Sentiments on the Politcks of the times & our firm resolutions to abide by, and to which Shall now most cordially desire your interest and influence in future, remain with respect & Esteem   Dr. Sir. your Most Humble Servant

Robt. Livingston

Alexander Hamilton Esqr.

ALS, Hamilton Papers, Library of Congress.
   1. Robert Livingston was the third proprietor of Livingston Manor.
   2. For information on Robert Livingston's controversy with Chancellor Robert R. Livingston, see H to Robert Livingston, April 25, 1785.
   3. In MS, "treats."
   4. James Duane.
   5. In the spring election of 1785, John Lansing, Jr., was the only Albany assemblyman to be re-elected. The new representatives were for the most part men who in state politics opposed the policies of Governor George Clinton.

To Jeremiah Wadsworth

New York June 15. 1785

Dr. Sir,

Before I left Town for Albany some time since, I requested Mr. Duer[1] to mention to you, that I believed it would depend upon yourself to be President of the bank here. Since my coming to Town I find you are elected director; and I have no doubt you may be President if you please. I will be much obliged to you to let me know *in confidence* whether the appointment if made will be accepted.[2]

You may imagine Your acceptance is a thing I wish for much. It will be of great advantage to the Institution and not disreputable to yourself. As an Inducement, I think I may safely assure you there is a much better prospect of a Charter with the present Legislature than there has been with any former one. Let me hear from you speedily & believe me to be   Your friend & servt   Alex Hamilton

ALS, Connecticut Historical Society, Hartford.
   1. William Duer.
   2. The two authorized histories of the Bank of New York (Henry W. Domet, *A History of the Bank of New York, 1784–1884* [Cambridge, n.d.] and Nevins, *History of the Bank of New York*) state that Jeremiah Wadsworth was president of the Bank of New York from May, 1785, to May, 1786. John D. Platt in his definitive life of Wadsworth states that Wadsworth resigned his directorship and that he was never influential in the bank's affairs and never elected its president. The sources cited by Platt indicate that he is correct (Platt, "Jeremiah Wadsworth," 148–49).

To Ezekiel Forman

[*New York, June 17, 1785.* On the back of a letter that Forman wrote to Hamilton on May 31, 1785, Hamilton wrote: "Answered June 17th. 1785." *Letter not found.*]

To James Hamilton [1]

New York, June 22, 1785.

My Dear Brother:

I have received your letter of the 31st of May last, which, and one other, are the only letters I have received from you in many years. I am a little surprised you did not receive one which I wrote to you about six months ago.[2] The situation you describe yourself to be in gives me much pain, and nothing will make me happier than, as far as may be in my power, to contribute to your relief. I will cheerfully pay your draft upon me for fifty pounds sterling, whenever it shall appear. I wish it was in my power to desire you to enlarge the sum; but though my future prospects are of the most flattering kind my present engagements would render it inconvenient to me to advance you a larger sum. My affection for you, however, will not permit me to be inattentive to your welfare, and I hope time will prove to you that I feel all the sentiment of a brother. Let me only request of you to exert your industry for a year or two more where you are, and at the end of that time I promise myself to be able to [invite you to a more] [3] comfortable settlement [in this Country. Allow me only to give you one caution, which is to avoid if possible getting in debt. Are you *married* or *single?* If the *latter,* it is my wish for many reasons it may be agreeable to you to continue in that state.

But what has become of our dear father? [4] It is an age since I have heared] from him or of him, though I have written him several letters. Perhaps, alas! he is no more, and I shall not have the pleasing opportunity of contributing to render the close of his life more happy than the progress of it. My heart bleeds at the recollection of his misfortunes and embarrassments. Sometimes I flatter myself his brothers have extended their support to him, and that he now enjoys tranquillity and ease. At other times I fear he is suffering in indigence. I entreat you, if you can, to relieve me from my doubts, and let me know how or where he is, if alive, if dead, how and where he died. Should he be alive inform him of my inquiries, beg him to write to me, and tell him how ready I shall be to devote myself and all I have to his accommodation and happiness.

I do not advise your coming to this country at present, for the war has also put things out of order here, and people in your business find a subsistence difficult enough. My object will be, by-and-by, to get you settled on a farm.

Believe me always your affectionate friend and brother,

Alex. Hamilton.

[Mr. James Hamilton]

National Intelligencer, February 17, 1859; autograph fragment, MS Division, New York Public Library.

1. James Hamilton, H's older brother, was born in 1753. After the death of his mother in 1768, James was apprenticed to a carpenter on the island of St. Croix. Nothing is definitely known of the remainder of his life. Holger Utke Ramsing in his authoritative account of the parentage and boyhood of H states that James Hamilton died in 1786 ("Alexander Hamilton," *Personalhistorisk tidsskrift*, 225–70).

This letter is preceded in the *National Intelligencer* by the following paragraph: "A member of the family of the late General Alexander Hamilton has handed us a copy of the subjoined letter from that distinguished soldier and statesman to his brother, which it is thought will possess interest for our readers."

In the *Intelligencer* the letter is dated June 22, 1785. In Hamilton, *Intimate Life*, 6, and in Gertrude Atherton, ed., *A Few of Hamilton's Letters* (New York, 1903) 136, the letter is dated June 23, 1783. In Hamilton, *Reminiscences*, 2–3, and in Hamilton, *History*, VII, 842, the letter is dated June 23, 1785.

2. Neither of the two letters has been found.

3. Material within brackets taken from autograph fragment, MS Division, New York Public Library.

4. James Hamilton, H's father, who had gone to the island of St. Croix from the island of St. Kitts to collect a debt, returned to St. Kitts in 1765, leaving Rachel Fawcett Lavien and their two sons on St. Croix. Mitchell (*Hamilton*, 14) infers that James Hamilton lived on several of the southern islands before he moved to St. Vincent sometime before June, 1793.

To William Floyd [1]

[New York, July 7, 1785]

Received of William Floyd Esquire Fifty seven pound and ten shillings being the amount of a note of hand with Interest from him to John Carter alias John Church for Fifty pound New York Currency dated in Philadelphia sometime about the last of April in the year One thousand Seven hundred and Eighty three and which note has been mislaid in my hands. New York July 7th 1785

For John Church
Alex Hamilton

ADS, Mrs. J. T. Nichols, Garden City, New York. A copy of this document was obtained through the assistance of Mr. William Maxwell, New York City.

1. Floyd, who served with H in the Continental Congress in 1783, was at this time a member of the New York Senate.

From Jacob Hardenbergh [1]

Raritan [*New Jersey*] *July 14, 1785.* Hopes that his father will be given a new trial. Asks for Hamilton's assistance.

ALS, Hamilton Papers, Library of Congress.

1. Hardenbergh was the son of Johannes Hardenbergh of Ulster County, New York. See "Cash Book," March 1, 1782–1791, note 29.

To Richard Varick

[*New York*] *July 28, 1785.* Asks Varick to suggest names for a commission to examine witnesses in a case pending between John Wardrop and Alexander Macauley.

ALS, Estelle Doheny Collection in the Edward L. Doheny Memorial Library at St. John's Seminary, Camarillo, California.

To Angelica Church [1]

[New York, August 3, 1785]

You have been much better to me My Dear friend since you left America, than I have deserved, for you have written to me oftener than I have written to you. I will make no apology; for I am sure you will attribute it to any thing else rather than to a defect of pleasure in writing to you.

Mr. Van Schaik delivered me your last;[2] if he were not a man of merit (as he is) your patronage would be a conclusive title to my good will.

But now my Dear Sister let us talk a little of something else that interests us all much more nearly. You have I fear taken a final leave of America and of those that love you here. I saw you depart from Philadelphia with peculiar uneasiness, as if foreboding you were not to return. My apprehensions are confirmed and unless I see you in Europe I expect not to see you again.

This is the impression we all have; judge the bitterness it gives to those who love you with the *love of nature* and to me who feel an attachment for you not less lively.

I confess for my own part I see one great source of happiness snatched away. My affection for Church and yourself made me anticipate much enjoyment in your friendship and neighbourhood. But an ocean is now to separate us.

Let me entreat you both not precipitately to wed yourselves to a soil less propitious to you than will be that of America: You will not indeed want friends wherever you are on two accounts: One is You will have no need of them: another is that You have both too many qualities to engage friend ship. But go where you will you will find no *such* friends as those you have left behind.

Your Good and affectionate sister Betsey feels more than I can say on this subject. She sends you all a sisters love: She does not write now because I do but promises to be a more punctual correspondent. I remain as ever Your [3] Affectionate friend & Brother   A Hamilton

Augt. 3d. 1785

ALS, photostat in the Yale University Library from an original in the possession of Mrs. John F. Dunn, Denver.

1. John B. and Angelica Church came to America in June, 1785. They returned to England soon after that date.

2. Presumably Peter Van Shaack who, because of his Loyalist sympathies, was banished to England in 1778. Remaining in England for seven years, Van Shaack must have seen Angelica Church frequently after she and her husband established residence in London in 1784. The legislature of New York restored Van Shaack's citizenship in 1784, and in 1785 he returned to New York.

3. In MS, "you."

Power of Attorney from John B. Church

New York, August 3, 1785. Appoints Hamilton "attorney at law, my true and lawful attorney for me and in my name to my use to ask, demand, sue for, recover, and receive of and from all and every person and persons whatsoever, whom it doth shall or may concern, All and every such sum and sums of money, debts and demands whatsoever which now are due and owing and hereafter may grow due and owing unto me the said John Barker Church."

DS, Hamilton Papers, Library of Congress.

To Philip Schuyler

[New York] August 5, 1785. ". . . some time since . . . Hannah Brewer or rather her assignee John J. Skidmore . . . paid the £200 part of the purchase money of the farm in the possession of Doctor Perry. The deed is now wanting. If you will send that to me I will have the mortgage to you executed here."

ALS, Lloyd W. Smith Collection, Morristown National Historical Park, Morristown, New Jersey.

From Andrew P. Skene [1]

Montreal, August 10, 1785. Asks about the possibility of recovering property seized under the New York confiscation laws.

ALS, Hamilton Papers, Library of Congress.
 1. Philip Skene, the founder of Skenesborough, Vermont, and his son Andrew were Loyalists. They were both attainted and their lands confiscated. Early in the war Andrew P. Skene was captured and imprisoned in Connecticut.

Power of Attorney from Nathanael Greene to Jeremiah Wadsworth

[New York] August 16, 1785. On this date Hamilton witnessed a power of attorney from Greene to Wadsworth.

DS, signed by Nathanael Greene and witnessed by H and Dirck Ten Broeck. Connecticut State Library, Hartford.

From Walter Livingston [1]

New York, September 3, 1785. ". . . the House of De Lande and Fynje of Amsterdam have stopt Payment with a Considerable Sum in their hands belonging to the United States. I shall be glad of Your Opinion as Counsel what legal measures I can pursue for securing any Property belonging to that House, which may be in the Hands of Persons in this State."

ALS, Hamilton Papers, Library of Congress.
1. Livingston was a member of the Board of Treasury.

From Stephen De Lancey

Scarsdale [New York] September 12, 1785. Renews request made on May 27, 1785, for information on various legal actions taken to recover numerous debts.

ALS, Hamilton Papers, Library of Congress.

From Cleland Kinlock [1]

Belvoir near Charlottesville, Virginia, September 20, 1785. Discusses measures taken to pay John B. Church the amount of a bond given by the executors of Kinlock's father's estate.

ALS, Hamilton Papers, Library of Congress.
1. Cleland Kinlock was the brother of Francis Kinlock, a South Carolina planter and member of the Continental Congress.

From Peter Silvester [1]

September 24, 1785. Discusses pending litigation between Captain Phillips and Colonel Van Rensselaer concerning a debt contracted by Phillips in 1776.

ALS, Hamilton Papers, Library of Congress.
1. Silvester was a lawyer who practiced in the area which, in 1786, became Columbia County.

Certificate for Lieutenant Thomas Pool [1]

[New York, September 30, 1785]

I certify that I was privy to the Petitioners being employed by the Commander in Chief in the manner he mentions and that he made several trips to New York before he was taken up by the British. I further certify that from the accounts repeatedly received at Head Quarters of the treatment he experienced there is no reason to doubt he suffered every thing he could bear without loss of life.[2]

A. Hamilton

New York Sepr. 30th. 1785

ADS, Papers of the Continental Congress, National Archives.
1. Thomas Pool, a spy for the Americans during the Revolution, had been captured by the British and imprisoned for 235 days. He stated that during his imprisonment he underwent "tortures unknown even to the Bastile or Inquisition." He petitioned the Congress for compensation. H's certificate was written on the last page of Pool's petition.
Pool's petition is also accompanied by a certification from George Washington.
2. On report of the Secretary at War, Congress on September 7, 1786, granted Pool $1,097 "as a reward for personal and pecuniary injuries he sustained in the service of the United States" (JCC, XXXI, 639).

From John Adams [1]

Grosvenor Square London Oct. 19. 1785

Sir

At the Instance of Mr. Hartley [2] in behalf of his Friend Mr Francis Upton,[3] I advised Mr Upton to apply to some Councillor in New York and particularly to Mr Hamilton, whose Reputation was known to me although his Person was not.

Mr Hartley now requests for Mr Upton a Letter of Introduction. As a total Stranger but by Character, it would be very difficult to find a Pretence to excuse the Liberty I take in presenting Mr Upton to you, and recommending his Case to your Attention. but as we say at the Bar, where I wish I was, Valeat quantum valere potest.

With much Esteem I have the Honour to be Sir your most obedient and most humble Servant   John Adams

Mr. Hamilton

ALS, Hamilton Papers, Library of Congress.

1. John Adams, after serving as one of the American commissioners to negotiate a peace treaty with England, was appointed American envoy to the Court of St. James.

2. Presumably David Hartley, one of the British emissaries for the negotiation of peace with the United States.

3. Adams's letter was sent as an enclosure to a letter which Francis Upton wrote to H on December 6, 1785. Upton was the son of Clotworthy Upton, Lord Templeton. Lord Templeton had in 1764 "obtained the King's order in council for a grant of 20,000 acres of land in the province of New York . . . by Deed of the 3d. of April 1769 [he] conveyed the same in trust for the use of Francis Upton, Clotworthy Upton the younger and Sophia Upton and their heirs" (David Hartley to Thomas Jefferson, April 15, 1785, Thomas Jefferson Papers, Library of Congress). Francis Upton, who came of age on February 25, 1785, asked H to help him secure possession of this land. See Upton to H, December 6, 1785.

From John Lowell [1]

[*Boston, October 19, 1785.* On October 30, 1785, Hamilton wrote to Lowell: "Mr. Lowe has delivered me your letter of the 19th. Instant." *Letter not found.*]

1. Lowell, a judge of the Massachusetts Court of Appeals, was serving as a member of the New York-Massachusetts commission to settle the boundary dispute between those states.

[*Elegy on the Death of the Honorable Samuel Hardy, Esq.*] [1]

[New York, October 20, 1785]

The New-York Journal, or Weekly Register, October 20, 1785.

1. For a discussion of H's possible authorship of this poem, see Burnett, *Letters,* VIII, 239. According to a correspondent of Burnett, tradition ascribes the poem to H. There is no other evidence that he wrote it.

Samuel Hardy was a former member of Congress from Virginia.

To John Lansing, Junior

New York, October 22, 1785. Requests information concerning several cases in which Hamilton was serving as an attorney.

ALS, New-York Historical Society, New York City.

To Jeremiah Wadsworth

[New York, October 29, 1785]

Dear Sir

I have intended for some time to write to you on the subject of the bank of North America; but my absence from town and multiplied engagements have delayed my doing it. You of course know that the State of Pensylvania has repealed its act of incorporation.[1] What do you intend to do or what would you advise to be done for Mr Church? To sell unless at a great disadvantage is not practicable. To leave *so considerable a sum* in a Company of this kind not incorporated is too dangerous. To force it out of their hands is an uphill business. In this choice of difficulties I will submit to you what occurs to me.

It is believed the Republican party has prevailed at the last election, not in so decisive a manner however as to insure a decisive influence; but sufficiently in all probability to effect a revival of the act of Incorporation.[2] Should this happen, It will in some degree restore the credit of stock and make it easier to part with it, without any considerable loss.

I should think therefore it would be prudent to wait the result of the next meeting of their Legislature; if the Charter is not then revived, I should be of opinion to insist that measures may be taken to decide the Question whether the bank still remains an incorporated body by virtue of the original act of Congress or not.[3] The affirmative of this Question is strongly maintained by some lawyers of Pensylvania.[4] The mode of deciding it will be easy. It will be to get some person to refuse to pay a note to the bank, and to have an action instituted against him in behalf of the bank in their corporate capacity. If the Courts allow this action to be maintained it must be on the principle that the Bank still subsists a corporation in Pensylvania.

If the decision is in favour of the corporate existence of the bank, the proprietors will then know in what situation they are and may either continue such with greater safety or part with their interest with less disadvantage. If it is decided that the bank does not continue a corporation, you can then insist on your money being returned to you and may compel its being done. It seems to me essential you should ascertain upon what footing you stand.

Mr. Van Bukle [5] (who is a large Stockholder) has intimated to me that he will be glad to *cooperate* with us in whatever measures may be thought adviseable. I believe we can also acquire the aid of Marbois [6] representative. This will enable us to act with great efficacy in whatever plan it may be agreed to persue.

Mr. Church's wish is to get clear of the concern; but he would be unwilling to do it at too great a sacrifice.

Permit me to trouble you with a little matter of Mr Churchs in your state.[7] I mean the land he got of Walter Livingston.[8] Mr. Church wishes it to be sold upon any tolerable terms. If you can do it, I will send you a conveyance for which I have full power. Mr. Campfield (the Lawyer) [9] can give you information about it. I formerly wrote to him [10] but as you are near the spot I could wish you would give yourself the trouble to get rid of this useless property for Mr. Church. If not convenient to you be so good as to write to Mr. Campfield to do it and mention to him what terms of Credit may be proper to prevent its being given away, taking good security for payment: Mrs. Hamilton joins me in compliments to Your ladies. Believe me great warmth & sincerity   Dr Sir   Yr. friend & obed servt   A Hamilton

New York Oct 29. 1785

ALS, Connecticut Historical Society, Hartford.

1. The Pennsylvania Assembly repealed the charter of the Bank of North America on September 13, 1785.

2. The revocation of the bank's charter was the principal issue in the elections to the Pennsylvania Assembly in the fall of 1785. All but six of the supporters of the bank were returned, and there were nineteen new members who had campaigned primarily on the issue of restoring the institution. Robert

Morris, Thomas FitzSimons, and George Clymer at once took the lead in attempting to win back the charter.

3. The Bank of North America had been granted a charter by the state of Pennsylvania and the Continental Congress.

4. The most important lawyer of Pennsylvania who maintained "the affirmative of the question" was James Wilson. In the summer of 1785 Wilson published his *Considerations on the Bank of North America* (Philadelphia, 1785), in which he argued that Congress had the power to charter banks.

5. Pieter Johan Van Berckel, a burgomaster of Rotterdam, was appointed the first Dutch Minister to the United States in 1783.

6. The Marquis Barbé-Marbois, the French chargé d'affaires in the United States, appears on the list of the first subscribers to the Bank of North America as the purchaser of one share of stock. Through his agent, John Ross, he subscribed to an additional eight shares in 1784.

7. Jeremiah Wadsworth and H took the responsibility for liquidating John B. Church's property in the United States after Church's return to England in 1785.

8. Walter Livingston, a New York lawyer, was the son of Colonel Robert Livingston.

9. For information on Church's business affairs that were handled by John Canfield, see H to John B. Church, March 10, 1784.

10. See H to Canfield, August 3, 1783.

To Nicholas Low

[*New York, October 30, 1785.* "Since you were here I concluded to write a line in answer to Mr. Lowell [1] which I send you open to be forwarded in your letter to Mr Russell. Yr Obed. Ser., A. Hamilton." *Letter not found.*] [2]

ALS, sold by Thomas F. Madigan, December, 1935, Lot 107.
1. See H to John Lowell, October 30, 1785.
2. Extract taken from manuscript dealer's catalogue.

To John Lowell

New York, October 30, 1785. States that "Mr. Lowe has delivered me your letter [1] of the 19th. Instant." [2] Discusses the laws governing the attachment of property in New York State and the applicability of Massachusetts bankruptcy laws in New York.

ALS, Lloyd W. Smith Collection, Morristown National Historical Park, Morristown, New Jersey.
1. This letter was enclosed in H to Nicholas Low, October 30, 1785.
2. Letter not found.

To Neil Jamieson

[*New York*] *November 3, 1785.* Encloses a document relating to the case of *Samuel Griffin* adsm. *John Cottringer* and asks Jamieson to provide bail for Mr. Griffin.

Copy, Hamilton Papers, Library of Congress.

From John De Ponthieu Wilkes [1]

[New York] Nov 8th. 1785

Sir.

I received just now a Note from Mr. Atkinson [2] which you had written to him for Mr. Hearts [3] obligations to Mr. Mc.Cauley [4] and which I suppose was occasioned by my Message to you yesterday. I am very glad at any rate that the creditors are likely to obtain some settlement But I think at the same time that you have adopted a strange and injurious line of Conduct to me. It is now near six months since I first waited on you on that concern during which I have repeatedly called and left Messages for you requesting a settlement but you did not deign even any answer. I luckily saw you once prior to your going to Philadelphia when you promised me on your return that you would settle it but when you returned no notice was taken of me; you went out of Town again and still when you came back I received no news. I called after several days had elapsed and left word with one of your young Gentlemen that I requested you would see me on Mr. Mc.Cauleys business but without any effect; I wrote to you and sent my servant twice one day and on three successive days without even one line in answer although common civility demanded that, at last you were pleased to signify that you would shortly see me on the subject I waited four days more without hearing one word from you. The trustees and several of the Creditors kept calling on me and they must think I was in fault. I was not willing to assign so derogatory a reason to myself as that I could not obtain an answer from Colonel Hamilton, it would have appeared a very strange one. My Character for

Attention to my business was in Question, my Bread depends on my Character & it behoved me to clear it. I called again & not being able to see you, I desired my Compliments and that I requested an early answer as "I was suffering by your neglect." I desired the Gentleman to make use of those very words. I thought they would have aroused you to a sense of shame for having so long neglected me in a concern which would take so little time to determine and where I was acting as an Agent and neither demanded or wished the least favor. And I confess I felt particularly hurt that in a business where I am so singularly situated I should meet with less attention than is commonly given from one Gentleman to another in the same line of Profession however inferior the circle they move in. You are now Sir acquainted with my motives and if you persist in acting in the same manner you will add injury to injury and in my opinion inconsistently both as a Gentleman and a man of understanding and very much alter the favorable sentiments which I did and ever wished to entertain of your Character.

I am Sir with due respect Your most obedt. Servt.   John Wilkes

ALS, Hamilton Papers, Library of Congress.

1. Lodge (*HCLW*, IX, 406–12) states that this letter was written by Israel rather than by John Wilkes. See Hugh Seton to H, June 18, 1784, note 3.

For further information concerning this letter, see H to Seton, June 18, 1784, and January 1, 1785; Seton to H, February 2, 1785; H to Wilkes, November 8, 1785; and Wilkes to H, November 9, 1785.

2. Probably John or Francis Atkinson, New York City merchants.

3. Malcolm Hart.

4. Alexander Macauley. Letter not found.

To John De Ponthieu Wilkes

[New York] November 8, 1785.

Sir:

The message which you sent me yesterday, and your letter today,[1] were conceived in terms to which I am little accustomed. Were I to consult my feelings only upon the occasion, I should return an answer very different from that which I have, in justice to my own conduct, resolved upon. But in whatever light we are to view each other hereafter, and however harsh and indelicate I may think the method you have taken to obtain an explanation to be, I shall, for my own part, leave no room to suppose that I intentionally gave you any cause to complain. I shall, therefore, explicitly declare, that whatever inattention may have appeared towards you, was solely owing to the continual hurry in which my engagements, for a long time past, have kept me; and that, so far from its having been occasioned by any designed neglect, it was what, under the circumstances, might have happened to my best friend. Indeed, much of what you mention to have been done by you, I am a stranger to. The frequent callings, by yourself and by your servant, did not, that I recollect, come to my knowledge. It is possible some of them might have been mentioned to me, and, in the hurry of my mind, forgotten. Once, I remember, I saw your servant just as I was going out on some urgent business. I sent a verbal message, promising that I would see you; which I intended to do, as soon as I had made up my resolution on the business of the interview. When I received your note I was about sending you an answer in writing; but, upon inquiring for your servant, and finding him gone, I omitted it, with an intention to see you personally.

You say it is near six months since you first applied to me on the business in question. A great part of the time I gave you all the answer I could give you—-to wit, that I had written to Mr. Macaulay, and only waited his answer. About two months since, I received it. I have been the greater part of the time out of town on indispensable business. In the intervals I have been occupied about objects of immediate and absolute necessity, which could not have been delayed without letting my business run into utter confusion. Mr. Macaulay's concerns have been hanging upon my spirits. I have been promising myself, from day to day, to bring them to a conclusion, but more pressing objects have unavoidably postponed it. I thought the delay required some apology to Mr. Macaulay, but I never dreamt of having given occasion of offence to you.

I will not, however, deny, upon a review of what has passed, that there have been, through hurry and inadvertency on my part, appearances of neglect towards you; but between gentlemen and men of business, unfavorable conclusions ought not to be drawn before explanations are asked. Allowances ought to be made for the situations of parties; and the omissions of men, deeply involved in business, ought rather to be ascribed to that cause than to ill intentions.

Had you, in the first instance, expressed to me (in such a manner as respect for yourself and delicacy to me dictated) your sense of these appearances, I should have taken pains to satisfy you that nothing improper towards you was intended by me. But to make one of my clerks the instrument of communication, and the bearer to me of a harsh accusation, was ill-judged and ungenteel. To take it for granted that you had received an injury from me, without first giving me an opportunity of an explanation, and to couch your sense of it in terms so offensive as some of those used in your letter, is an additional instance of precipitation and rudeness. Inadvertencies susceptible of misapprehension, I may commit; but I am incapable of intending to wound or injure any man who has given me no cause for it; and I am incapable of doing any thing, sir, of which I need be ashamed. The intimation, on your part, is unmerited and unwarrantable. After thus having explained my own conduct to you, and given you my ideas of yours, it will depend on yourself how far I shall be indifferent, or not, to your future sentiments of my character. I shall only add, that tomorrow you shall receive from me my determination on the matter of business between us.

HCLW, IX, 406–12.
    1. See Wilkes to H, November 8, 1785.

From John Lowell [1]

Boston, November 9, 1785. States that there is no bankruptcy act in Massachusetts and sends information concerning the transfer of property by a citizen of Massachusetts to a New York creditor.

ALS, Hamilton Papers, Library of Congress.
    1. This letter is in reply to H to Lowell, October 30, 1785.

From John De Ponthieu Wilkes [1]

[New York] Novr. 9. 1785

Sir.

The moment I received yours I perceived the precipitancy of my own Conduct and was very sorry I had so far mistaken both our

Characters to act in the manner I have done. I flatter myself that the same Candor which has dictated yours will be exerted towards mine and that you will only view it as the act of a Man who conceived himself injured. As you have never experienced the cruel reverses of fortune you can scarcely judge how the least insinuation, to their prejudice will affect those persons who have, or how much more suspicious they are of the Behaviour of Mankind towards them.

The morning I left the message for you I had been called upon by one of the Creditors of Mr. Heart[2] who thought it very strange no dividend was made and He insinuated some party must be interested in the delay. It is the first money transaction I have engaged in since my release[3] I felt the insinuation as alluding to me and with a force which perhaps I should not, however, that moment I went to your Office. The next morning when I saw your Note[4] to Mr. Atkinson[5] and found myself totally set aside in a business where I had most undoubtedly been originally neglected I felt myself very much agitated and in that frame of Mind I wrote my last to you. So much I thought it necessary to add in explanation. I am convinced now I have been too hasty and I am sorry for it. It will put me on my Guard in future and I make no doubt prove beneficial to me Provided it has not been the means of hurting me in your Estimation which I am now more desirous than ever of obtaining.

I am Sir with respect your much obliged & most obedient Servant

John Wilkes

Col. Hamilton

ALS, Hamilton Papers, Library of Congress.

1. Lodge (*HCLW*, IX, 409) states that the writer of this letter was Israel Wilkes rather than John Wilkes. See Wilkes to H, November 8, 1785; and H to Wilkes, November 9, 1785.
2. Malcolm Hart.
3. See H to Hugh Seton, January 1, 1785.
4. Letter not found.
5. Probably John or Francis Atkinson, New York City merchants.

From Jeremiah Wadsworth

Hartford Novr 11th 1785

Dear Sir,

I received your favor of the 29th ulto. Thursday. I have been very uneasy about my stock in the Bank of North America and long before the repeal of the Pensilvania act of Incorporation, I had determined to take the first favorable opportunity to withdraw it. When I was last at New York it was pretty certain the state of Pensilvania would repeal their Act. I then wrote a letter to Mr Pettit [1] of which the inclosed is a Copy—and hoped that would have put me in possession of my money—but it failed and has I am told very much offended the president & directors of ye Bank [2]— and their *great Mr Francis* [3] the Cashier has been very busy I hear in trying to shew that I have acted inconsistently as he had read a letter to Chaloner [4] which I wrote at an earlier period—in which I gave it as my opinion that their assembly had proceded with "Violence & injustice." It seems Mr. F. has construed my letter into a censure of the conduct of the President & directors—and is exceedingly angry and so I believe are some of those who have heretofore been my friends. But I am perfectly willing they shoud think & act as they please if I can rescue my property from their grasp and I will come to New York before January and Co-opperate with You & such other friends as we can find in measures that may be most proper to obtain our wishes. Mr Arthur Lee (who has as Many Votes as any body can have according to the present System) [5] proposed to me to join in measures to withdraw our Stock & seemed to be exceedingly anxious & determined to withdraw his. Duer [6] expressed a desire to have us employ our Stock in a private Bank at New York and mentioned the brother in Law of Mr Constable [7] who is a large Stock holder as desireous to withdraw from Phila and join at New York. This was a Scheme I liked pretty well & gave some encouragement to it. but did not agree on any thing, but wished to have Mr Constables brother in Law pursue the same measures with us respecting the Bank of N.A. Mr Constable lately wrote me a letter of which I inclose you a Copy. I wrote him for answer that I could decide on Nothing before I arrived in New York.

I will endeaver to sell Churchs Land as soon as possible—but I have missed the best opportunity of doing it before ye Spring—as our General Assembly is over & Canfield gone home.[8] Mrs W & the Children join me in every good wish. Be assured that I am sincerely & affectionately   Your friend & Humle. Servant   Jere Wadsworth

PS.   Constable is perhaps so bound to Mr Morris [9] he dare not act against ye Bank of NA & Duer Livingston [10] &c. are anxious to have a Bank to play of[f] their Continental paper with. Think of all these things. I will come to you early in December.

ALS, Hamilton Papers, Library of Congress.
    1. Charles Pettit, a native of New Jersey, during the American Revolution was an aide to Governor William Livingston, and deputy quartermaster general from 1778 to 1781. After the war he settled in Philadelphia where he was an importing merchant. A member of the Pennsylvania legislature in 1784–1785, Pettit was elected in 1785 a delegate to the Continental Congress.
    2. The copy of the letter from Wadsworth to Pettit which was enclosed in this letter is not among the Hamilton Papers, Library of Congress. In it Wadsworth "reproached the directors for their conduct, expressed a belief that they had removed sums of money equal to the value of their stock by giving notes, and indicated he would be happy to find it possible to get his money back" (Platt, "Jeremiah Wadsworth," 152, note 2). Pettit apparently showed the letter to a member of the Pennsylvania Assembly who then showed it to other members.
    3. Tench Francis, as Wadsworth states, was cashier of the Bank of North America.
    4. John Chaloner, through whom all of Wadsworth's business in Philadelphia was conducted.
    5. Arthur Lee of Virginia, diplomat during the American Revolution and a member of the Continental Congress, was appointed a member of the Board of Treasury in July, 1785. In the second subscription to bank stock in 1784, Lee purchased nineteen shares (Lawrence Lewis, Jr., *A History of the Bank of North America* [Philadelphia, 1882], 144–47).
    6. William Duer.
    7. William Edgar was a native of the north of Ireland who had engaged in the western fur trade after he came to America. Assisted by a partnership with Alexander Macomb, another western trader, he acquired a fortune. The chief business of Macomb, Edgar, and Macomb was supplying the Indian Department of the British army. Settling in New York after the Revolution, Edgar married the sister-in-law of William Constable who was one of the most influential and affluent New York merchants. On behalf of Edgar, Constable subscribed to fifty-five shares of bank stock (Lewis, *A History of the Bank of North America*, 144).
    8. See H to Wadsworth, October 29, 1785.
    9. Constable was associated in business with Robert Morris and Gouverneur Morris. Robert Morris, perhaps the single most important person in determin-

ing the policies of the Bank of North America, had invested ten thousand pounds in the enterprise (Platt, "Jeremiah Wadsworth," 110).

10. Probably Walter Livingston, a close business associate of Duer.

To Theodorus Bailey [1]

[*New York, November 20, 1785.* On January 17, 1786, Bailey wrote to Hamilton: "An indisposition which has confined me the chief of the time since the receit of your favor of the 20th of november, has prevented me from giving it an earlier attention." *Letter not found.*]

1. Bailey, a major in the New York Militia, was practicing law in Pough-keepsie, New York.

To John B. Church

[*New York, November 24, 1785.* On April 5, 1786, Church wrote to Hamilton: "I am in your Debt and have to thank you for your Letters of the 24 Novr. 6 Decr. & 1st Feby." *Letter of November 24 not found.*]

To George Washington

[New York, November 25, 1785] [1]

Dr Sir

Major Fairly [2] is just setting out on a visit to You I believe on some business relating to the Cinninnati. The society of this state met some short time since and took into consideration the proposed alterations in the original frame of the Institution.[3] Some were strenuous for adhering to the old constitution a few for adopting the new and many for a middle line. This disagreement of opinion and the consideration that the different state societies pursuing different courses—some adopting the alterations entire others rejecting them in the same way—others adopting in part and rejecting in part—might beget confusion and defeat good purposes—induced a proposal which was unanimously agreed to, that a Committee should be appointed to prepare and lay before the society a circular letter expressive of the sense of the society on the different alterations proposed & recommending the giving powers to a General meeting of the Cinninati to make such alterations as might be thought adviseable to obviate objections and promote the Interests of the society.[4] I believe there will be no difficulty in agreeing to change the present mode of continuing the society; but it appears to be the wish of our members that some other mode may be defined and substituted & that it might not be left to the uncertainty of Legislative provision. We object too to putting the funds under legislative direction. Indeed it appears to us the Legislatures will not at present be inclined to give us any sanction.

I am of the Committee and I cannot but flatter myself that when the object is better digested & more fully explained it will meet your approbation.

The Poor *Baron*[5] is still soliciting Congress, and has every prospect of Indigence before him. He has his imprudencies; but upon the whole he has rendered valuable services; and his merits and the reputation of the Country alike demand that he should not be left to suffer want. If there could be any mode by which Your influence could be employed in his favour; by writing to Your friends in Congress or otherwise, The Baron and his friends would be under great obligations to you.

I have the honor to be with sincere esteem &c.   Your Obedt & hum serv   Alex Hamilton

November 25. 1785
General Washington

ALS, George Washington Papers, Library of Congress.
    1. In *JCHW*, I, 428, and *HCLW*, IX, 412, this letter is dated November 23, 1785.
    2. Major James Fairlie, a New Yorker, was aide-de-camp to Baron von Steuben from July, 1778, to the end of the American Revolution.
    3. The Society of the Cincinnati, formed in 1783 by Revolutionary War officers, restricted its membership to officers of the American army who had served honorably for three years. The general society was divided into state societies. George Washington was the first president general of the society.
    At its first general meeting, held in Philadelphia in May, 1784, fifteen amendments were offered to the plan for the society which had been drawn up a year earlier. The most important amendment was one abolishing hereditary succession, a principle which had occasioned frequent and bitter attacks on the society as an undemocratic, autocratic organization. The proposed alterations were submitted to the respective state societies for ratification. For the proposed amendments, see Schuyler, *Institution of the Society of the Cincinnati*, 31–33. Although there is no record of a meeting of the New York State

Society in 1785, the committee appointed to prepare a circular letter on the proposed amendments, to which H refers later in this letter, must have been appointed in that year.

4. The committee consisted of H, Richard Morris, David Brooks, Edward Dunscomb, and Robert Troup. Their report, dated July 6, 1786, was presented to the meeting of the New York State Society that was held on that date (Schuyler, *Institution of the Society of the Cincinnati*, 91).

5. For an account of Baron von Steuben's claims against the Continental Congress, see "Report on the Claim of Baron von Steuben," December 30, 1782.

From John Auldjo [1]

New York, November, 1785. "You have herewith the papers relating to the dispute with Mr. Rhinelander, but lest the business should still be treated with the same trifling attention it has hitherto had, I beg you to press for an explicit answer whether Mr. Rhinelander is seriously disposed to bring it to a hearing."

ALS, Hamilton Papers, Library of Congress.
   1. Auldjo was a partner of the house of Strachan McKenzie and Company of London.

To Helena Brasher

New York, December 6, 1785. "I am instructed by your brother Mr. Laurence Kortright [1] to make the following proposal to you; to wit—that if you will pay him the amount of his account for money and other articles supplied you druing your residence in the Jerseys in the course of the war and will deliver him up his bond for £200 to be paid you at the death of his mother, he will then give you a release of all claims on account of his father's personal estate."

ALS, The Andre deCoppet Collection, Princeton University Library.
   1. Lawrence Kortright was a New York City merchant.

To John B. Church

[*New York, December 6, 1785.* On April 5, 1786, Church wrote to Hamilton: "I am in your Debt and have to thank you for your Letters of the 24 Novr. 6 Decr. & 1st Feby." *Letter of December 6 not found.*]

From Francis Upton [1]

London, December 6, 1785. ". . . you will perceive that a considerable tract of land in the province of New York has been long since given in trust by My late Father for the use of myself Brother & Sister. As they are both Minors & Myself but just come of Age, it prevented our making a More early Application to take possession of these Lands; but I am now having the proper writings prepared . . . to invest me with full powers to Act by myself, or my Attorney, in such Manner as shall hereafter by you be advised; and as soon as they are so prepared I shall either immediately set out myself, or transmit you a proper Autjority to Act for me."

ALS, Hamilton Papers, Library of Congress; a duplicate of this letter dated December 6, 1785, which was enclosed in Upton to H, June 5, 1786, is also in the Hamilton Papers, Library of Congress.
1. See John Adams to H, October 19, 1785.

From Robert Howe [1]

December 8, 1785. "Mr. & Mrs. Wilson . . . are in very embarassed Circumstances. As I know you have the direction of Baron Polnitz's [2] House now Empty, if you could acommodate them with a few Rooms thro' the winter it would be of espestial service to them."

ALS, Hamilton Papers, Library of Congress.
1. Howe, who had been a major general during the Revolutionary War, resigned in 1783 and returned to his plantation in North Carolina.
2. Friedrich, Baron von Poellnitz, operated an experimental farm outside New York City. H managed both his business and personal affairs.

From George Washington

Mount Vernon Decr 11th. 1785

Dear Sir,

I have been favoured with your letter of the 25th. of November by Major Farlie.[1]

Sincerely do I wish that the several State Societies had, or would, adopt the alterations that were recommended by the General meeting in May 1784.[2] I then thought, and have had no cause since to change my opinion, that if the Society of the Cincinnati mean to live in peace with the rest of their fellow Citizens, they must subscribe to the alterations which were at that time adopted.

That the Jealousies of, and prejudices against this Society were carried to an unwarrantable length I will readily grant [3] —and that *less* than was done, *ought* to have removed the fears which had been imbibed, I am as clear in, as I am that it would not have done it; but it is a matter of little moment whether the alarm which siezed the public mind was the result of foresight—envy & jealousy —or a disordered imagination; the effect of perseverance would have been the same: wherein then would have been found an equivalent for the separation of Interests, which (from my best information, not from one state only but many) would inevitably have taken place?

The fears of the people are not yet removed, they only sleep, & a very little matter will set them afloat again. Had it not been for the predicament we stood in with respect to the foreign Officers [4] and the charitable part of the Institution [5] I should, on that occasion, as far as my voice would have gone have endeavoured to convince the narrow minded part of our Country men that the Amor Patri[ae] was much stronger in our breasts than theirs—and that our conduct through the whole of the business was actuated by nobler & more generous sentiments than were apprehended, by abolishing the Society at once, with a declaration of the causes, and the purity of its intention. But the latter may be interesting to many, and the former, is an insuperable bar to such a step.

I am sincerely concerned to find by your letter that the Baron is again in straighted circumstances. I am much disinclined to ask favors of Congress, but if I knew what the objects of his wishes are I should have much pleasure in rendering him any services in my power with such members of that body as I now and then corrispond with. I had flattered myself, from what was told me sometime ago, that Congress had made a final settlement with the Baron much to his satisfaction.

My Compliments and best wishes, in which Mrs. Washington joins me, are presented to Mrs. Hamilton.

I am Dear Sir   Yr. Most Obedt. Hble Servt   Go: Washington

P.S. When you see Genl. Schuyler and family I pray you to offer my best respects to them.

Alexr. Hamilton Esqr.

ALS, Hamilton Papers, Library of Congress; also LC, George Washington Papers, Library of Congress.
   1. In this letter to Washington H stated that Major James Fairlie was going to see the General on business relating to the Society of the Cincinnati.
   2. See H to Washington, November 25, 1785, note 3.
   3. Washington is referring to the attacks made on the Society of the Cincinnati. The attacks centered chiefly on the provision of the "Institution" of the society providing for hereditary succession. See H to Washington, November 25, 1785.
   4. Foreign officers who had served in America during the Revolution had been admitted to the society.
   5. The "Institution" of the society provided for the establishment of funds to assist the poor.

To Richard Varick

[*New York*] *December 20, 1785.* "In the cause of Macaulay v. Ludlow . . . I will thank you to take the suit to yourself and carry it on."

ALS, Pierpont Morgan Library, New York City.

From John B. Church

[*December 21, 1785.* On the back of a letter that Church wrote to Hamilton on April 5, 1786, Hamilton wrote: "Letters from J B Church December 21 April 5. 1786." *Letter of December 21 not found.*]

From Jacob Sarly [1]

[*New York*] *December 24, 1785.* Asks Hamilton "the date of the protest for non payment" of a bill of exchange.

ALS, Hamilton Papers, Library of Congress.
   1. Sarly was a member of the New York merchant firm known as Sarly and Barnewell.

From Robert R. Livingston

December 25, 1785. "I recd your notes[1] with Mr. Hoffmans[2] Letter. I have no objections to waving any formalities with respect to the return of the writ of error. I should be extremly sorry if any part of my letter strikes you disagreeably. The passage you allude to was inserted as well to contradict an assertion that I had treated Mr. Hoffmans memory with severity, as to express my resentment at the harsh things that have been publicly said of an ancestor whose memory I am bound to respect."

ALS, Hamilton Papers, Library of Congress.
   1. Letters not found.
   2. Nicholas Hoffman.

To John Sullivan[1]

[New York, December 25, 1785]

D Sir

Permit me to introduce to you Mr. Ducher[2] a French Gentleman who is appointed to reside as Vice Consul at Portsmouth in the State of New Hampshire. You will find him an intelligent speculative man. He came to this Country attracted by an affinity of principles and with a view to a philosophical retirement; but having been shipwrecked with a loss of *part of himself* and a much larger part of his property,[3] he has been obliged at least to suspend this plan. And his friends at Court, among the number of whom are the Chevalier De Chastelus[4] and the Marquis De la fayette have procured him his present appointment as introductory to something of greater importance. I have assured him that in your acquaintance he will find what an inquisitive sensible man wishes to find and that I flatter myself he can carry you no title to your civilities better than my recommendation, except his own merit.

I have the honor to be With the truest esteem & regard   Dr General   Yr Obed St   A Hamilton

New York
December 25. 1785

ALS, Mrs. Lewis E. Playford, Cassopolis, Michigan.
1. Sullivan was at this time president of New Hampshire.
2. Gaspard Joseph Amand Ducher.
3. Ducher's ship was wrecked on the coast of Long Island, New York. He suffered from exposure and had to have seven toes and a part of one heel amputated.
4. François Jean, Marquis de Chastellux, who had been a major-general in the French army during the American Revolution.

From William Leary [1]

New York, December 27, 1785. "Please . . . deliver all the papers . . . [respecting] my father to the bearer my Clark." [2]

ALS, Hamilton Papers, Library of Congress.
1. Leary owned a grocery store at 182 Water Street in New York City.
2. At the bottom of this letter, H wrote: "Delivered Bond Mortgage & Certificate of discharge according to the above."

1786

Pieter Johan Van Berckel, William Edgar,
Sampson Fleming, William Denning, and
Alexander Hamilton (for John Barker Church)
to Jeremiah Wadsworth [1]

[New York, January 3, 1786]

Instructions for Jeremiah Wadsworth Esquire
Sir

The step lately taken by the Legislature of Pensylvania in repeal-ing the act by which the government of that state had incorporated the Bank of North America has given rise to questions of a delicate and important nature.[2] We observe with regret that the very exist-ence of the Institution as a corporate body has by this proceeding been drawn into controversy: a circumstance which we consider in so serious a light as to render necessary the most speedy and effec-tual measures to decide the doubt.

Those who subscribed to the Bank of North America on the faith of the Pensylvania Charter might with great reason urge that so material a change in its situation is, at all events, with respect to them, a dissolution of the contract upon which their subscriptions were made; and that they have a right to reclaim their property. But not being disposed to agitate any questions injurious to the Institution, we are content to wave this right, so long as there remains any pros-pect of the bank being continued with safety and advantage. This prospect however we deem inseparable from its existence as a cor-poration; and if this cannot be maintained all hopes of security or utility in our apprehension fail.

Nothing will give us greater pleasure than to find that the Bank of North America has a solid foundation in the Charter of the United States; and that it will on experiment be considered in this light by the laws of that state in which from its position its operations would be carried on; but it appears to us essential that the experiment should be made without delay, in order that it may be ascertained in what light it will be considered by those laws. If these should pronounce that it is no corporation, no prudent alternative is left but to remove it to another state, where it will be protected by the laws, or to leave all those who wish to do it at liberty to withdraw their shares.

While on the one hand public as well as private considerations concur to restrain us from advising any measures incompatible with the Interest of the bank; on the other hand we cannot help feeling great anxiety to know what our *true situation* is; and to extricate ourselves from *one* (if such *it* is) in which we might hazard much more than we intended.

With these views and sentiments, we request you to represent us at the next meeting of the stockholders which is advertised for the ninth instant. There you will be pleased on our behalf to insist that a general resolution be taken to obtain in the most summary mode a judicial determination of this Question—Whether the laws of Pensylvania still acknowlege the bank of North America as a corporate body?—and if they do not, to return at a fixed period, to every proprietor who shall require it, the amount of his stock.

We forbear to recommend a removal to another state because we presume the other part of the alternative will be most agreeable to all parties.

This plan appears to us so intirely unexceptionable, founded on such evident propriety and even necessity, that we are persuaded the stockholders in general are too just and reasonable to refuse it their approbation.

The confidence we repose in your probity and judgment, as well as your own interest in the result, leave us no room to doubt, that you will execute this trust with as much prudence, as decision, and in a manner intirely consistent with your reputation and our own. We have the honor to be Sir Your obedt & humble servt

P. J. Van Berckel John Barker Church
William Edgar by Alex Hamilton his Atty
Sampson Fleming Wm. Denning

New York January 3d. 1786

LS, in writing of H, Connecticut State Library, Hartford; Df, in writing of
H, Hamilton Papers, Library of Congress; copy, Historical Society of Pennsylvania, Philadelphia.

1. The copy of this letter in the Stockholder's Minute Book of the Bank of
North America is preceded by the following statement, and is dated January
9, 1786: "At a meeting of the Stockholders this day, Jeremiah Wadsworth
Esqr. appeared, and produced a letter of instructions signed by five other
stockholders and dated at New York January 3d, 1786."

For information on Van Berckel, see H to Wadsworth, October 29, 1785,
note 5; for William Edgar's connection with the Bank of North America, see
Wadsworth to H, November 11, 1785, note 7. William Denning, a New York
merchant and a stockholder in the Bank of North America, was a commissioner
of the Board of Treasury. Sampson Fleming, a former British commissary who
had made a fortune trading at the western posts, settled in New York City at
the end of the Revolution. Fleming owned a total of sixty-three shares of bank
stock.

2. For information on the revocation of the charter of the Bank of North
America, see H to Wadsworth, October 29, 1785.

From Jeremiah Wadsworth

Philadelphia 9 Jan 178[6] [1]

Dear Sir

Previous to the meeting of the Stock Holders of the Bank, I had
several conf⟨erences⟩ with Mr R Morris and he softended down
much. He consented to our Propositions, & this day in a very great
meeting of the Stock Holders it was unanimously voted to have a
legal decision as soon as possible—agreeable to ye instructions I recd
from ye Gentlemen at N York.[2] Mr Wilson [3] then observed that
the other question was unnecessary as it followed of consequence
that each Stock Holder had a right to withdraw his Stock if the
decision was against the corporation.[4] I replied that as it had been
denied by others I wished ye question to be tried but if it was the
Unaniomous opinion of ye Stock Holders present that we had a
right [to] Withdraw if ye decision was against us I woud not urge
ye matter. Mr G Morris said it was his: but there was one stockholder present who differed from us. He woud second any Motion.
Mr R Morris declared it was his wish to finish ye Bank in its present
form if we were not a corporate Body by ye Laws of Pa & if ye
decision was against us he thot: every Stock Holder might withdraw
by right. Nobody objecting, I waved ye question. I then informed
ye Stock Holders that great alarms had been given respecting the

mode of discounts & that the Directors had been charged with Partiality, and as I saw Mr Wilson present who it was said had great discounts with out complying with ye usual forms, I thot it my duty & interest to thus publicly name him that he might give such explanations as he chose. (I had previously let him know my intention to do this & had his consent). He went into a detail of his schemes, disappointments and discounts which amounted to Near 100,000 dollrs. for which Mr Morris is responsible 10,000 and Other good men, ye remainder, to be paid if the Bank find it necessary one half in 30 the remainder in 60 days. For ye Security of these individuals he has given Mortgages on Lands for more than £ 100,-000. to Mr Nixon [5] who holds ym. in trust for those who are responsible to ye Bank for Mr Wilson. Mr President [6] made some *wise* Speeches & some *wiser* remarks—but as I came to do business & not altercate I did not treat them as the[y] deserved. I will soon be with you & relate every particular. I beg you present my Compliments to the Gentn & inform them we have obtained our wishes as nearly as coud be expected.

I am dr Sir Your very Hum set   Jere Wadsworth

ALS, Hamilton Papers, Library of Congress.
  1. Wadsworth mistakenly dated this letter January 9, 1785.
  2. For the instructions to Wadsworth by "the gentlemen at N. York," see H *et al.* to Wadsworth, January 3, 1786. Wadsworth submitted the instructions written by H to the stockholders. According to the minutes of the stockholders' meeting, Wadsworth "made the following motion, which being seconded by Mr. Gouverneur Morris, was committed to writing in these words: 'That it be an instruction to the Directors about to be chosen, to obtain as speedily as may be a legal decision of the following Question—Whether posterior to the first day of march next the president, Directors and company of the Bank of North America be a Corporation.' This motion being fully debated, and considered was unanimously agreed to" (Historical Society of Pennsylvania, Philadelphia).
  3. James Wilson.
  4. In this sentence Wadsworth is referring to the request made by H in the letter he drafted for the New York stockholders. This letter asked the Bank of North America to return to each stockholder the value of his stock if Pennsylvania refused to acknowledge the bank as a corporate body.
  5. John Nixon was a director of the Bank of North America. In 1792 he became its second president.
  6. Thomas Willing.

From Robert Milligan [1]

Philadelphia, January 15, 1786. Encloses documents necessary for instituting a suit to recover money owed by a client.

ALS, Hamilton Papers, Library of Congress.
1. Milligan was a Philadelphia attorney.

From Theodorus Bailey

Poughkeepsie [New York] January 17, 1786. Sends information concerning a litigation about which Hamilton had written to Bailey on November 20, 1785.[1]

ALS, Hamilton Papers, Library of Congress.
1. Letter not found.

From Ezekiel Forman

Philadelphia, January 21, 1786. Informs Hamilton of progress in various litigations in which Hamilton and Forman were concerned as attorneys.

ALS, Hamilton Papers, Library of Congress.

From Ezekiel Forman

[Philadelphia] January 22, 1786. Requests Hamilton's opinion on money due on "Middletons Bond."

ALS, Hamilton Papers, Library of Congress.

Inhabitants of the City of New York to the Legislature of New York State [1]

[New York, January–March, 1786]

To The Honorable The Legislature of the State of New York
The Petition of the Subscribers Inhabitants of the City of New York respectfully sheweth

That Your Petitioners anxious for the welfare of the community of which they are members have seen with peculiar regret the delay which has hitherto attended the adoption of the Revenue system recommended by Congress in their resolutions of the 2

That the anxiety which Your Petitioners have all along felt from motives of a more general nature is at the present junction increased by this particular consideration that the State of New York now stands almost alone, in a non compliance with a measure in which the sentiments and wishes of the Union at large appear to unite and by a further delay may render itself responsible for consequences too serious not to affect every considerate man.

That in the opinion of Your Memorialists all the considerations important to a state—all the motives of public honor faith reputation interest and safety conspire to urge a compliance with ⟨these resolutions.⟩ [3]

That Government without revenue cannot subsist. That the mode provided in the Confederation for supplying the treasury of the United States has in experiment been found inadequate.

That the system proposed will in all probability prove much more efficacious, and is in other respects as unexceptionable as the various circumstances and interests of these states will permit.

That any objection to it as a measure not warranted by the confederation is refuted by the thirteenth article which provides that alterations may be made if agreed to by Congress and confirmed by the Legislatures of each State; and the conduct of this state itself in adopting the proposed change of the Eighth article is a precedent in which we find the principle reduced to practice and affords a complete answer to every pretence of the Revenue system being unconstitutional.

That as to danger in vesting ⟨the United States with these funds, Your Memorialists⟩ consider their interests and liberties as not less safe in the hands of their fellow citizens delegated to represent them for one year in Congress than in the hands of their fellow citizens delegated to represent them for one year or four years in the Senate and Assembly of this state.

That Government implies trust; and every government must be trusted so far as is necessary to enable it to attain the ends for which it is instituted; without which insult and oppression from abroad confusion and convulsion at home.

ADf, Hamilton Papers, Library of Congress.

1. The exact date of this petition cannot be determined. It presumably was sent to the legislature between January and May, 1786, for it was written before the New York State legislature on May 4, 1786, passed the bill granting Congress, with important reservations, the impost requested by a congressional resolve of April 18, 1783. It probably was not drafted later than March of the same year. In the second paragraph of the petition it is stated that "New York now stands almost alone in a non compliance" with the congressional request for authority to levy an impost. The last state, save New York, to grant the impost was Georgia, which agreed to the measure late in March, 1786. Assuming that H would have known of Georgia's action, his draft of this petition must have been written before April.

2. Space left blank in MS.

After the refusal of the requisite number of states to grant Congress the impost requested by a congressional resolve of February 3, 1781, Congress, in March and April, 1783, debated plans for renewing the request. On April 18, 1783, resolutions were passed asking the states to grant Congress the power to levy specified duties on a list of imported goods and a five percent *ad valorem* duty on all other imported goods. Limited to a period of twenty-five years, the duties were to be applied to the interest and principal of debts contracted by the United States. Collectors of the duties were to be appointed by the states, but amenable to and removable by Congress.

By January, 1786, only two states, Georgia and New York, had failed to comply with the congressional resolution of April 18, 1783. The New York legislature had rejected, in both the 1784 and 1785 sessions, an act conforming to the congressional resolution. During its 1786 session, as in previous years, the legislature debated the advisability of compliance. At the end of the session a bill was passed which granted the impost to Congress but reserved to the state the exclusive power of collecting it. Collectors were made amenable not to Congress but to the state courts. An even more significant qualification of the request of Congress was the provision in the New York law which made the impost duties payable in the bills of credit of the state.

3. The words in broken brackets are from a JCH transcript.

To John B. Church

[*New York, February 1, 1786*. On April 5, 1786, Church wrote to Hamilton: "I am in your Debt and have to thank you for your Letters of the 24 Novr. 6 Decr. & 1st Feby." *Letter of February 1 not found.*]

To Robert Milligan

[*New York, February 4, 1786.* On February 18, 1786, Milligan wrote to Hamilton: "I am much obliged by your polite favour of the 4th. instant." *Letter not found.*]

From Robert Milligan

Philadelphia, February 18, 1786. "I am much obliged by your polite favour of the 4th. instant.[1] Not thinking myself authorized to transfer discretionary powers . . . in Mr. Lillys affair, I have wrote to him, signifying my inability to act for him further; and recommending . . . to send a special Agent for the purpose of securing his interests."

ALS, Hamilton Papers, Library of Congress.
  1. Letter not found.

From Isaac Gouverneur, Junior [1]

New York, February 24, 1786. ". . . I wish to have you my principal attorney for what I may have occasion to do in the law way."

ALS, Hamilton Papers, Library of Congress.
  1. Son of Isaac Gouverneur, prominent New York merchant.

To John Chaloner

[New York, March 1, 1786]

Dr Sir

I inclose you a letter to Mr. Wilcox[1] which after reading and noting the contents please to deliver to him.

There are three ships I think in which Mr. Church[2] is concerned ⅛ with Mr. Wilcox and others.[3] You will oblige him if you will endeavour to sell his interest for any thing short of giving them away. I have full power to convey & will do whenever you can find a pur⟨chaser⟩. Perhaps Mr. Wilcox will buy. You probably know the ships. Let me hear from you on the subject.

I am D Sir   Your obed & hum ser   Alex Hamilton
March 1. 1786

Let me hear from you; pray deliver the Inclosed as soon as it comes to hand.

ALS, Historical Society of Pennsylvania, Philadelphia.
  1. Letter not found. See John Wilcocks to H, March 5, 1786.
  2. John Wilcocks, a merchant of Philadelphia, had earlier been associated with affairs in which H was indirectly concerned. James Lytton of St. Croix, H's uncle, had appointed Wilcocks as one of the executors of estates he owned in North America.
  3. John B. Church returned to America in June, 1785, to settle his business affairs. His partnership with Jeremiah Wadsworth was dissolved in July, 1785, and he returned to England the following month. H was given the responsibility of terminating Church's affairs in the United States. Among the affairs of the company to be settled was the liquidation of the shipping ventures owned jointly by Wadsworth and Church.
  4. The ships in which Church had an interest are described in Wilcocks to H, March 5, 1786.

To John Wilcocks

[*New York, March 1, 1786.* On March 5, 1786, Wilcocks wrote to Hamilton: "I have your favor of the 1st." *Letter not found.*]

To Francis Upton

[*New York*] *March 2, 1786.* States that Upton's title to lands in New York is clear and advises Upton on measures to be taken to assure possession.[1]

ADfS, Lloyd W. Smith Collection, Morristown National Historical Park, Morristown, New Jersey.
  1. See Upton to H, December 6, 1785.

From John Wilcocks

Philada. March 5. 1786

Alexander Hamilton Esqr.
Sir

I have your favor of the 1st. handed me by Mr. Chaloner.[1] As

you have not full & clear information of what has pass'd between
Mr. Church, Mr. Moses, Mr. Wadsworth & Myself with Respect
to our Company Ships I shall briefly state the Matter.[2] The first
mentioned Gentleman was here I think in July with information
from Mr: Moses that he was ⅛ concerned & that I would make Him
acquainted with all their Business which I explicitly opened to him,
& his view with me was that I should become a Purchaser, give him
some certain Sum & take upon me all their Voyages & Negotiations.
From the diffused & uncertain state of their Funds I totally declined
this. He did not in any wise Instruct or leave me a Line of Directions
Respecting them. Mr. Moses & Mr. Low [3] also were fully acquainted
of every possible means being taken to effect a sale of the Tartar &
that it could not be done here; she was sent abroad limitted (as was
then thought & in proportion to her Outfit) low, all the freight
to be had taken for her, & Owners interested in her Cargo as light
as possible. In one particular Negotiation I offered her much lower
than Mr. Low affixed her Value in his Correspondence with me on
the Subject of her Sale, but she was of a war Construction & un-
suitable to every kind of Commerce, therefore all Endeavors were
in vain & as impossibilities were not to be expected no alternative
was left but such as took place. To acquaint me at this day that
what was transacted in August & September last year & then pass'd
to account is to be considered as mine is untimely & no Correspondence between Parties will warrant it, and with Regard to Mr. Wadsworth declaration against Adventures they will be found likewise
untimely. As to the St. Anne of which my last was the Subject as
she was under Charter on her present Voyage near fifteen Days
previous to the above mentioned Gentleman's arrival here & of
course the conversation to which you allude, probably this is different from the Representation you may have had of this Business. I
shall spare you the trouble of being more minute & pledge Myself
that on an investigation I shall be found right. I find it lately determined Mr. Church has ⅛ Interest in this Connexion but at times it
has been strongly asserted to the contrary. I shall be sorry he is detained in it against his & your Inclination & shall assist Mr. Chaloner
who you have appointed to sell the Vessels to effect it observing
that one eighth of a moiety of the St. Anne's Cargo must be disposed
of with that Vessel & this I expect he will accomplish without delay

that my proceedings may be on certainty & to prevent detention to the Vessel in Port for want of the concurrence of ⅛ Interest to the prejudice perhaps of the Others concerned. The best prospects have always been adopted for the owners Interest of those Vessels, the utmost done to get Rid of them both here & abroad (as 'twas my earnest desire to part with them) & that no alteration may hereafter take place I depend on Mr. Chaloners fulfiling your Directions speedily or concurring with me for the Employment of the Two Brothers & for which half a freight is offered to two Ports but the Owners depended on to supply the other half. I have made an offer to Mr. Chaloner which he will communicate, requesting your speedy answer. Respectfully I am Sir Your most Obed Servt.   John Wilcocks.

ALS, Hamilton Papers, Library of Congress.
  1. Letter not found. See H to John Chaloner, March 1, 1786.
  2. John B. Church, Isaac Moses, and Jeremiah Wadsworth. Wadsworth and Church in partnership had owned ships jointly with other traders. For a discussion of some of their shipping activities and their difficulties in terminating them, see Platt, "Jeremiah Wadsworth," 77ff.
  3. Nicholas Low, a New York merchant.

To John Chaloner [1]

[New York, March 10, 1786]

Duplicate
Dr Sir

On the subject of the Ships I am to request you will sell them on the best Terms you can.[2] I would mean one eighth of them absolutely as they now stand, without any consideration of expences incurred, for all these must come of course into a general account between the concerned. If Mr. Wilcox will give me as much as another so much the better. You may accommodate him as to the time of payment taking a note for the amount. Let me know what you conclude, to whom you sell. Finish the Matter and I will send a Bill of sale.

  Yrs with great regard   Alex Hamilton

March 10: 1786

LS, Historical Society of Pennsylvania, Philadelphia.
1. This letter was enclosed in H to Chaloner, March 16, 1786.
2. See H to Chaloner, March 1, 1786; and John Wilcocks to H, March 5, 1786.

To John Wilcocks [1]

[New York, March 10, 1786]

Sir

Your favour of the fith Inst. duly came to hand. I assure you Sir though the business does not concern myself it gives me pain that you should experience any inconvenience from a diversity in the views of those with whom you are Concerned in the Ships; [2] but you will be sensib⟨le⟩ as mere agent in a Case of this kind I could not with propriety do any thing to engage Mr. Church further than he may already consider himself as bound. The only thing I can do therefore is to desire Mr. Chaloner to Complete the Sale of Mr. Church's Share in the two Ships on the best terms he can.

I am with much esteem   Sir Your Obdt & humle Servant

Alexr. Hamilton

I have written to Mr. Wadsworth on the affair.

New York
March 10th 1786
John Wilcocks Esqr.

Copy, Historical Society of Pennsylvania, Philadelphia.
1. This letter was first enclosed in H to John Chaloner, March 10, 1786. The copy printed above was sent by H to Chaloner on March 16.
2. See H to Chaloner, March 1, 1786; Wilcocks to H, March 5, 1786; and H to Chaloner, March 10, 1786.

Memorial to Abolish the Slave Trade [1]

New York, March 13, 1786. On this date, H and other memorialists signed a petition to the New York legislature urging the end of the slave trade, "a commerce so repugnant to humanity, and so inconsistent with the liberality and justice which should distinguish a free and enlightened people."

The New-York Packet, March 13, 1786.

1. For information on H's membership in the Manumission Society, see "Attendance at a Meeting of the Society for Promoting the Manumission of Slaves," February 4, 1785.

Report on a Bond Due Columbia College

[*New York*] *March 14, 1786.* Reports with other members of a committee to the regents of the University of the State of New York [1] the circumstances of a supposed tender of money by Robert C. Livingston [2] to Columbia College.

ADS, Columbia University Libraries.
   1. At this time the regents of the University of the State of New York controlled Columbia College.
   2. Robert Cambridge Livingston was the fourth son of Robert Livingston, the third lord of Livingston Manor. He had insisted on paying the amount of a bond due Columbia College in "congress money," which the college refused to accept.

To John Chaloner

[New York, March 16, 1786]

March 16th.   The above [1] is copy of mine which went by a private hand inclosing the original of a letter to Mr. Wilcox of which the inclosed is a Copy.[2]

Yrs   A Hamilton

ALS, Historical Society of Pennsylvania, Philadelphia.
   1. H to Chaloner, March 10, 1786.
   2. H to John Wilcocks, March 10, 1786.

To Ezekiel Forman

New York, March 22, 1786. Encloses a bond and requests Forman to send "a receipt for it as a payment on account of the legacy in which you are interested."

Copy, in writing of Pierre Van Cortlandt, Jr., Hamilton Papers, Library of Congress.

To John Laurance

[*New York*] *March 23, 1786.* Plans to bring the cause of *Benjamin Paine, et al.* v. *Peter Mesier, Jr. and Jacob Van Voorhees* to trial at the next term of the Supreme Court.

Copy, Mr. Otto Madlener, Hubbard Woods, Illinois.

From John Wilcocks [1]

Philadelphia, March 24, 1786. Sends an account of the cargo of the *St. Anne* and a statement of the amount owed to John B. Church, owner of one-eighth of the cargo.

ALS, Hamilton Papers, Library of Congress.
  1. For an explanation of the account between Wilcocks and Church, see H to John Chaloner, March 1, 1786; Wilcocks to H, March 5, 1786; H to Chaloner, March 10, 1786; and H to Wilcocks, March 10, 1786.

To the Mayor and Corporation of the City of New York [1]

New York, March 28, 1786. Signs, with 136 other petitioners, a memorial asking that the "Mayor and Corporation of the City of New York" improve the street in front of the Coffee House, "the usual place of resort for your Memorialists and the merchants of this City." The memorialists complained that the street "for want of proper regulation and the great concourse of Carts is coverd with filth and is a great nuisance to your Memorialists and to all other persons frequenting that part of the City."

DS, Municipal Archives and Records Center, New York City
  1. On June 28, 1786, the committee to whom the petition was referred reported favorably. The Council "ordered that the Alderman and Assistant of the East Ward cause the above Report to be carried into execution" (*Minutes of the Common Council of the City of New York 1784–1831* [New York, 1917], I, 226–28).

To ———

[New York] April 3, 1786. "In your affair with Brothers Coste & Co. I have received a declaration. The business must be decided in Chancery. Send me a full detail of the facts upon which I can frame a bill."

ALS, Historical Society of Pennsylvania, Philadelphia.

From John B. Church

London April 5th 1786

My Dear Sir

I am in your Debt and have to thank you for your Letters of the 24 Novr. 6 Decr. & 1st Feby.[1] I left Directions at Sir Robt. Herries's[2] that in Case the Baron Polnitz[3] did not Pay the Bill you had drawn on him to send the Holder of it to me and that I would take it up for your Honor, as I have heard nothing from them since I hope it is Paid. Your last brought me a Bill of Lading for £782.10.8 Phila Curry. for which I thank you. I shall be very glad if you could succeed in getting my Money out of the Bank, for after the unwarrantable Lengths they have gone in assisting Wilson I do not think the Property can with Propriety be confided to their management.[4]

I think you have done the best with Respect to Moses's Matters and I am and shall be perfectly satisfied with whatever you think best to do in those Affairs.[5] With Respect to Kinloch[6] I wrote him that if he would Renew the Bond and Pay me the Interest annually and Punctually in London I had no Objection to let the Principal Remain ⟨some⟩ Years longer. You have the Copy of my Letters both to him and Bowman.[7] I have not Received a Line from either of them. I wish they could be forced to discharge their Debts to me. What has Troop done with Jacob Cuyler?[8] Is the Money yet Recover'd from him? As to the Land[9] I should be glad to have it disposed of as well and as soon as possible for as long as it Remains unsold it is a certain annual Loss of the Interest of the Money and

I have not the least Disposition to build, and I would sooner take £2000 for it than not get Rid of it if more cannot be obtained.

Mrs. Church is well; in about two Months she will give me another Boy or Girl; she joins in Love to Mrs. Hamilton and in wishing her well over her trying Time. Jack [10] is grown a fine Boy; he is now at a pleasant Villa which I have purchas'd on the Banks of the Thames three miles from Windsor where we shall soon Repair to pass the Summer. I am My Dear Sir   Your very affectionate Friend & Serv   J B Church

Alexr Hamilton Esqr.

ALS, Hamilton Papers, Library of Congress.
    1. Letters not found.
    2. Probably Sir Robert Herries, the founder of the banking firm of Herries, Farquhar and Company, London.
    3. Friedrich, Baron von Poellnitz, operated an experimental farm outside New York City. H managed both his business and personal affairs.
    4. For an account of James Wilson's relations with the Bank of North America, see Jeremiah Wadsworth to H, January 9, 1786.
    5. The bankruptcy of Isaac Moses, New York merchant, is described in H to Wadsworth, April 7, 1785; and Wadsworth to H, April 17, 1785.
    6. For an account of Church's business accounts with Francis and Cleland Kinlock, see H to Nathanael Greene, June 10, 1783; and Cleland Kinlock to H, September 20, 1785.
    7. Mr. Bowman was presumably the John Bowman about whom Hamilton had written to John Fitzgerald on June 10, 1783.
    8. Robert Troup, who at this time practiced law in New York City, presumably had been employed by Church to collect money from Jacob Cuyler. Like Church, Cuyler had been engaged during the Revolution in supplying the Continental Army.
    9. For information on the land Church wished to sell, see H to Church, March 10, 1784; and H to Wadsworth, October 29, 1785.
    10. The "Jack" mentioned was probably John B. Church, second son of John B. and Angelica Church. He was born in 1779 in Boston. At this time the Churches had two other children, Philip who was born in 1778, and Catherine who was born c. 1780.

To John Wilcocks [1]

[New York, April 5, 1786]

Sir,

I imagine you had not received my letter of the 10th. of March when yours of the 24th. was written. You must have perceived by that, that I do not consider myself at liberty to do any act recognising a concern of Mr. Church in the St. Annes last Cargo or in any other shipment of the same or any subsequent period in any of the vessels in Question

I have the honor to be   Sir Your Obed & hum ser   A Hamilton

New York
April 5 1786

ADfS, Hamilton Papers, Library of Congress.
    1. For information on the disposal of John B. Church's property, concerning which H was negotiating with Wilcocks, see H to John Chaloner, March 1, 1786; Wilcocks to H, March 5, 1786; H to Chaloner, March 10, 1786; H to Wilcocks, March 10, 1786; and Wilcocks to H, March 24, 1786.

From John Chaloner

Philada. April 10th, 1786

Dear Sir

Mr Wilcox has agreed to take the Vessels say two of them the one which saild lately from Cheasapeak and the one now here that daily expected from Lisbon he will not take.[1] He promised me his notes this day for two hundred pounds the sum he is to pay for the two Vessels. I shall propably receive them to morrow. He says he has considerable property on hand belonging to that concern.[2] I think it would be to the advantage of those interested therein to have a seperation it would in all propability facilitate the Sales.

I am Sir Your most Obdt Servant   John Chaloner

ALS, Hamilton Papers, Library of Congress.
    1. For H's role in the sale of ships to John Wilcocks, see H to Wilcocks, April 5, 1786, note 1.
    2. The "concern" to which Chaloner referred was probably the partnership of John B. Church, Isaac Moses, Jeremiah Wadsworth, and John Wilcocks, mentioned by Wilcocks to H, March 5, 1786.

To Richard Varick

[*New York, April 13, 1786.* The catalogue description of this letter states that Hamilton asked Varick if he would "meet a small number of friends this evening at the Tavern, formerly Capes—7 o'clock." *Letter not found.*]

ALS, sold at Parke-Bernet Galleries, May 17, 1948, Lot 214.

From John Chaloner

Philada. April 15. 1786

Dear Sir

Since my last I have concluded the negotiation with Mr. John Wilcox and have reced from him his note payble in nine months for two hundred pounds being in full for ⅛ of the two Ships St. Anne & Two Brothers.[1]

Our Assembly has rejected the application of the Citizens to establish the Bank.[2] The Stock holders therefore remain in that uncertain situation that you & Col Wadsworth apprehended prior to their last meeting in January; and are likely to continue in this State of Suspence for a considerable time.[3] The April Court at which the Question was to have been determined, is now nearly over and no action brot nor any thing done in the matter by the Directors save that of retain'g Council by the Bank;[4] Col Wadsworth when here apprehended (as does several Stockholders who were[5] present at the meeting) that the Bank were[6] to institute the suit, & employ Council on both sides to argue the matter, so that a speedy & amicable decision of the Question might be obtain at the expence of the Institution: this I am told is not so understood by the Directors. They mean only to employ Council on behalf of the Bank—nor can I learn that the Question will be brot forward, unless by an adverse suit, wch. is not likely to be brot by any Person here. I am clearly of opinion their object is delay: hopeing that another election may produce an Assembly more favourable to their measures than the present. Knowing Mr Church's Interest in this Institution I have thot proper to give you the above information and remain with Respect Sir   Your most obd hble Servt   John Chaloner

Alexr Hamilton Esqr

ALS, Hamilton Papers, Library of Congress.
   1. See Chaloner to H, April 10, 1786.
   2. For information on the revocation of the charter of the Bank of North America, see H to Jeremiah Wadsworth, October 29, 1785. In March, 1786, a committee of the Pennsylvania General Assembly, headed by George Clymer, issued a report on several petitions asking for the restitution of the charter of the Bank of North America. The committee reported that the bank had been the victim of "precipitancy, prejudice and partiality," and recommended that

the charter of the Bank be restored. On April 1, 1786, after a four-day acrimonious debate between the supporters of the bank and its enemies, the report of the committee was rejected by a vote of twenty-eight to forty-one. See Janet Wilson, "The Bank of North America, 1781–1787," *The Pennsylvania Magazine of History and Biography*, LXVI (January, 1942), 16–23.

3. See H *et al.* to Jeremiah Wadsworth, January 3, 1786. See also Wadsworth to H, January 9, 1786.

4. Wadsworth and other stockholders had asked for a "judicial determination of this Question—Whether the laws of Pensylvania still acknowlege the bank of North America as a corporate body?" See H *et al.*, to Wadsworth, January 3, 1786.

5. In MS, "where."

6. In MS, "where."

From Samuel Broome [1]

New Haven [Connecticut] April 18th. 1786

Alexander Hamilton Esqr

Sir

Mr James Jarvis [2] informed me a few weeks past that you was willing to take my Son Samuel P Broome into your office. It will be an additional favor if you will leave it optional in me untill next Fall to send him or not. My present Situation forbids a decision immediately.

I will thank you to inform me by letter at the return of my Son the bearer hereof the terms upon which you can admit him in Your office, and the term he must Continue with you. He is young (not yet Seventeen years old) therefore will want very Particular Care taken of him. This I am Sure will be Carefully attended to by you. I am   Sir   Your most obed servt   Sam Broome

ALS, Hamilton Papers, Library of Congress.

1. Broome was a merchant in New York City before the Revolution. A member of the New York Committee of One Hundred, which was organized in April, 1775, to govern the city, Broome in October of that year moved to New Haven, Connecticut, where he and Jeremiah Platt established the firm of Broome and Platt.

2. James Jarvis, a well-known speculator from New Haven. See Broome to H, August 13, 1788.

From Nathaniel Hazard [1]

New York 21st. April 1786

Sir

I took the Freedom a few days since to address you in Behalf of

a deserving Citizen and thank you for your friendly Interference.
I am not to beg it again in Favor of that unfortunate Corps to which
I belong. I claim it as your Friend Sir. You will doubtless startle
at this Expression, from a Man you are but barely acquainted with.
The friendliest Act an honest Man can wish to receive from another,
is to have his Character vindicated from false and unmerited Asper-
sions when absent. I have as much of the Milk of human Kindness
in me I hope as most Men, and ever wished the vanquished Adherents
to Britain might be treated with Humanity and Tenderness; and
that past Errors might be buried in Oblivion. I did not however
see the Necessity of granting to those, whose Temper and Biass must
as yet invitably be unfriendly to national measures, and partial to
british Interests; an immediate Participation of the important Rights
of Eligibility to Places of Trust; nor could I conceive that it pressed
itself. Drawing therefore (I hope with Sentiments of Candor and
Liberality) with many of those whose want of either Quality, lessens
themselves, and their Cause in the general Estimation; I have frequently expressed my disapprobation that a man of Science and
a brave officer, who had rendered important Services to the Country
before the war as a Man of Letters, and a very eminent ones during
its Continuance, both in the Cabinet of our Illustrious Chief and
in the Field, should be bitterly censured for Supporting Sentiments
different from theirs and mine, (on that one Occasion) which I
verily believed proceeded from an elevation of Sentiment, and too
generous a Spirit of Magnanimity, I had oftener Noticed in our
bravest and best officers than any other Class of Men. To return to
the Business of my Letter; We had a Bill before the Senate, the
main object of which was barely to have Commissioners appointed,
to enquire whether *any of us* and who had been *ruined*, and to report to the next Legislature as they should think fit; it barely
rubbed through.[2] Our humble Request is but to *be heard before
ruined*, and that we are dragged to Prison, by hungry british Agents
who are fast collecting from Philadelphia and other Quarters as
the Session of the Assembly draws to a Close, and hover like Cor-
morants over the devoted Carcasses of their captive Debtors. Some
of them are little illiberal insolent Upstarts, and Riders for their
manufacturing Masters, brutal and barbarous as the Savages that
tortured the unfortunate Colonel Crawford;[3] To goad and Sting

men of Feeling, who freely coin their Life Blood into Guineas to give them immediate and ample Satisfaction, was it in their Power is not Less Cruel. We would wish Sir, that such a man a Coll. Remsen,[4] once so independent, a worthy Citizen, ever humane, benevolent and public Spirited, may not have his House sold by execution, and his Family turned into the Streets; without even *a bare Inquiry* into his Situation and Demerits. Yet this probably will be the Case in the Assembly, unless General Schuylers [5] Connections in it, have right Ideas of the *humble and harmless Boon* we ask. I can in Confidence venture to tell you, it has been a moot Point with me, whether to apply to the present House or not. I am tired of supplications, and protested to the Committee of Merchants, my great aversion to signing another Petition. I prevailed on them to adopt my Plan of originating a bill in the Senate, as a Body of Men who at Least ought to possess more Information and Feeling than the other House.[6] General Schuyler had been uniformly understood by the Petitioning Merchants Committee, as so unfriendly to their Interests, that they thought it vain to apply to him. I have not the Honor to be personally known to him, but having known him as a public man and Friend to his Country, from those early Days when a Stripling, I used to attend the Debates of the Assembly, and hear him lash a Sett of callous impenetrable Wretches, who stood buff to wit, Satire and sound Reasoning, and eternally skulked behind the Question; I told the Committee it was impossible a man of his Rank Understanding & Patriotism, could be unfriendly to those who had suffered severely; and pressed such of them as had the Honor of being acquainted with the General, to converse with him on the Subject. It was done; and it has now even ceased to be *a wonder* that General Schuyler is as friendly to our Cause as others. I will make no apology on this Business, confident that *so far* as you conceive our request *is reasonable,* and *a Refusal* of it *would be cruel* It will give you Pleasure to have an opportunity of serving us by using your Influence in our Favor.

I am Sir   Respectfully your very huml. Servt.   Nathl. Hazard.

ALS, Hamilton Papers, Library of Congress.
1. Hazard was an ironmonger and a merchant of New York City. He was probably one of the signers of a petition sent by "Peter T. Curtenius, Thomas Hazard, and others, of the city of New-York, merchants, who were in exile

during the late war" to the New York legislature early in 1786 (New York Senate *Journal*, 1786, 17).

2. On April 23, 1785, in answer to a petition from New York merchants, the New York legislature passed a concurrent resolution recommending "to the British creditors of the memorialists . . . to forbear commencing suits against the said memorialists . . . for debts contracted previous to the ninth day of July, One Thousand Seven Hundred and Seventy-six, until the next meeting of the Legislature" (New York Senate *Journal*, 1785, 106). In January, 1786, the merchants again petitioned the New York Senate for relief from the demands of their British creditors. The Senate committed their memorial to a committee of the whole which reported on April 20. On that date the Senate passed "An Act for the relief of Peter T. Curtenius and others, merchants of the City of New-York," which provided for the appointment of commissioners to investigate the problem of debts due British merchants by New Yorkers as well as the debts owed New York merchants by citizens of other states. Although the Assembly considered the bill, it took no action during the 1786 session of the legislature.

3. Colonel William Crawford, a Virginian, while commanding an expedition against the Indians in 1782, was captured, tortured, and burned at the stake.

4. Henry Remsen, a prominent New York merchant, had left New York City during the Revolution and did not return until after the peace.

5. Philip Schuyler was in 1786 a member of the New York Senate.

6. See note 2.

To Nathaniel Hazard [1]

[New York, April 24, 1786]

Sir

Your letter of the 21st. was only delivered me this morning.[2] The good opinion of liberal men I hold in too high estimation not to be flatterd by that part of your letter which relates to me personally. The other part I have communicated to General Schuyler, and he assures me he will see all his friends this afternoon upon the subject; so that I have no doubt as far as his influence extends it will be employed in favour of the success of the Bill in the Assembly as it has already been in the Senate.

In taking this step however I would not be understood to declare any opinion concerning the principles of the Bill, with which I am not sufficiently acquainted to form a decided opinion. I have merely made your letter the occasion of Introducing the subject to General Schuyler; whose sentiments are as favorable to your wishes as you could desire.

I make this observation from that spirit of candour which I hope will always direct my conduct. I am aware that I have been represented as an enemy to the wishes of what you call your corps. If by this has been meant that I do not feel as much as any man, not immediately interested, for the distresses of those merchants who have been in a great measure the victims of the revolution, the supposition does not do Justice either to my head or my heart. But if it means that I have always viewed the mode of relieving them as a matter of peculiar delicacy and difficulty it is well founded.

I should have thought it unnecessary to enter into this explanation, were it not that I am held up as a candidate at the ensuing Election;[3] and I would not wish that the step I have taken in respect to your letter should be considered as implying more than it does: For I woud never wish to conciliate at the expence of candour. On the other hand, I confide in your liberality not to infer more than I intend from the explanation I have given; and hope you will believe me to be with great cordiality and esteem.

Dr Sir   Your Obedt Ser   Alex. Hamilton
April 24. 1786

Copy, Hamilton Papers, Library of Congress.
    1. As the letter is endorsed in H's writing "Letter to Mr. Hazard. April 22, 1786," it was probably retained as H's file copy.
    2. For information on the subject discussed by H in the first three paragraphs of this letter, see Hazard to H, April 21, 1786.
    3. H had been nominated as a candidate for the Assembly from the county and city of New York. In a list of nine candidates H received the fourth highest number of votes (*The New-York Packet*, May 1, 1786).

Appointment as Commissioner to the Annapolis Convention [1]

State of New York

In Senate [New York] May the 5th. 1786

Resolved (if the Honorable the Assembly concur herein) that Robert R. Livingston, James Duane, Egbert Benson, Alexander Hamilton, Leonard Gansevoort and Robert C. Livingston Esquires,[2] or any three of them, be Commissioners on the part of this State, to meet with such Commissioners, as are, or may be appointed by the other States in the Union; at such Time and place, as shall be agreed upon by the said Commissioners; to take into consideration the Trade and Commerce of the United States; to consider how far an uniform System in their Commercial Intercourse and Regulations, may be necessary to their common Interest and permanent Harmony; and to report to the several States, such an Act relative to this great Object, as when unanimously ratified by them, will enable the United States in Congress Assembled, to provide for the same; and that the said Commissioners or any three of them do make a report of their proceedings to the Legislature at their next Meeting.

Extract from the Journal
Abm. B. Bancker Clk

State of New York

In Assembly May 5th. 1786

Resolved that this House do concur with the Honorable the Senate in the said Resolution.

An Extract from the Journals
John McKesson, Clk

DS, in writings of Abraham B. Bancker and John McKesson, Papers of the Continental Congress, National Archives.

1. On March 16, 1786, Governor George Clinton submitted to the New York legislature a letter from the governor of Virginia, dated February 23, enclosing a copy of a resolution of that state "appointing Commissioners to meet with the Commissioners of the different States, for the purpose of framing such regulations of trade as may be judged necessary to promote the general interest." The Assembly resolved, the Senate concurring, that five commissioners be appointed to meet with commissioners of the other states "to take into consideration the trade and commerce of the United States." On May 5 the Assembly appointed H, Robert C. Livingston, and Gansevoort; the Senate added the names of Robert R. Livingston, Duane, and Benson (New York Assembly *Journal*, 1786, 83, 86, 149–50, 175; New York Senate *Journal*, 1786, 48–50, 102–03).

2. Robert R. Livingston was the chancellor of the State of New York. Duane was mayor of New York City. Benson was an associate judge of the Supreme Court of New York. Gansevoort of Albany County was later a member of the Assembly, a senator, a county and probate judge. Robert C. Livingston of New York City was later a member of the New York Assembly. Of the six nominees, only H and Benson attended the Annapolis Convention.

To John B. Church [1]

[New York, May 6, 1786]

By the last Packet I sent you the first of a set of bills of which the inclosed is second for £400 Sterling drawn by Constable Rucker &

Co: on Mr John Rucker.[2] I remitted you £782.10.8 Currency by the Roebuck packet. I have written you largely on other matters to which I have received no answer. This being term time I cannot inlarge but I shall write you fully in a short time. I am anxious to hear from you. I momently expect an addition to my family.[3] Betsy is well and joins me most Affectionately to Mrs: Church & your self. General Schuyler & Mrs: Schuyler are still with me and in good health.

Yrs: sincerely

New York May 6: 1786
John Barker Church Esqr:

Copy, Hamilton Papers, Library of Congress.
  1. As it is endorsed in the writing of H, this letter was probably retained as his file copy.
  2. William Constable and John Rucker organized the firm of Constable, Rucker and Company in 1784. John Rucker was a German with English commercial experience and with credit backing by I. L. and C. Le Couteulx, a French banking house.
  3. H's third child, Alexander, Jr., was born on May 16, 1786.

From Mrs. J. Campbell

[New York] May 8, 1786. Requests "the honor of seeing" Hamilton "in the course of this day."

ALS, Hamilton Papers, Library of Congress.

From Peter Pillet

Philadelphia, May 14, 1786. States that he has been "recommended by Mr. Jon. Chaloner of this City to put my interest into your hands." Describes a controversy which Pillet wishes Hamilton to settle.

ALS, Hamilton Papers, Library of Congress.

To Peter Pillet

[*New York, May 17, 1786.* The endorsement in Hamilton's writing on Pillet's letter of May 14, 1786, to Hamilton reads: "Letter from Mr. P. Pillet. Ansd. May 17. 1786." *Letter not found.*]

To Alexander Macaulay

New York, May 20, 1786. "I have at length concluded your affair with the Assignees of Heart [1] by agreeing to take the principal of your first demand . . . & to come in for any further demand you may have as any other Creditor."

ALS, Hamilton Papers, Library of Congress.
1. Malcolm Hart.

To Sempill and Company [1]

[New York, May 20, 1786]

Gentlemen

On the recommendation of Mr. Nicholas Cruger [2] of this City, I take the Liberty to commit to your care a small matter in which I am interested. I am informed that Mr John Hallwood a relation of mine who died some time since in St. Croix has by his will left me one fourth part of his Estate.[3] The amount I imagine is not very considerable; but whatever it may be I shall be glad to have it collected and remitted. Mr Hallwoods estate I believe consisted intirely in his share in his Grand fathers estate Mr James Lytton; whose affairs have been a long time in a dealing Court but one would hope are now ready for a final settlement. Doctor Hugh Knox can give you further information on the Subject.[4]

As I know money concerns in your Island rarely improve by delay, if things should not be in a train to admit of an immediate settlement, I shall be ready to effect this, to transfer my claim to any person who may incline to the purchase at a discount of five and twenty per Cent. This however I submit to your discretion and authorise you to do whatever you think for my interest. Inclosed I send you a Power of Attorney [5] which I presume you will find competent. Should it be in my power to render you any services here I shall with pleasure obey your commands.

I am with much consideratio⟨n⟩ Gentlemen Your Obedt. servant

New York May 20th. 1786
Messrs, Sempill & Co

[ENCLOSURE] [6]

Power of Attorney to John Sempill and William Amorey

[New York, May 18, 1786]

Know all Men by these presents, that I Alexander Hamilton of the City of New York, Counsellor at Law, have made, ordained, authorized, constituted and appointed, and by these presents do make, ordain, authorize, constitute and appoint John Sempill and William Amorey of the Island of St. Croix Merchants jointly and severally my true and lawfull Attornies, for me and in my Name, and to my Use to ask, demand, sue for, recover and receive of all and every person whomsoever in the said Island of St. Croix, all and every Sum and Sums of Money Debts, Legacies and Demands whatsoever which now are due, owing and coming unto me, and in default of payment thereof, to have use and take all lawfull ways and means in my Name or otherwise for the Recovery thereof, by Attachment, Arrest or otherwise, and to compound and agree for the same, and on Receipt thereof acquittances or other sufficient Discharges for the same for me and in my Name to make seal and deliver, and to do all lawfull Acts and Things whatsoever concerning the premises as fully in every Respect, as I myself might or could do if I was personally present, and an Attorney or Attornies under them or either of them to make for the purposes aforesaid, and at their pleasure to revoke, hereby ratifying allowing and confirming all and whatsoever my said Attornies or Attorney shall in my Name lawfully do or cause to be done in and about the premises by virtue of these presents—In Witness whereof I have hereunto set my Hand and Seal the eighteenth Day of May in the Year of our Lord one Thousand seven Hundred and eighty six.

Sealed and delivered in the presence
of Balthr. De Haert. Jo. Strong } Alexander Hamilton

To all to whom these presents shall come or may in any wise concern, I Balthazer De Haert Notary public, duly constituted and appointed by letters patent under the great Seal of the State of New
York, residing in the City of New York, do hereby certify, declare
and make Known, that on the Day of the date hereof, personally
appeared before me, Alexander Hamilton of the said City Esquire,
and sealed and delivered the within written Letter or Power of
Attorney as and for his Act and Deed, for the use and purposes
within mentioned in my presence, and in the presence of Joseph
Strong, who hath also subscribed his Name as a Witness thereto.
In Testimony whereof I have hereunto set my Hand and affixed my
Notarial Seal The eighteenth day of May in the year of our Lord
one Thousand seven Hundred & eighty six.

Balthr. De Haert Not: publ:

This done in the Presence of Jo. Strong

Copy, in writing of Pierre Van Cortlandt, Jr., Hamilton Papers, Library of
Congress.
1. The letter is endorsed in the writing of H, "Letter to Mess Sempill &
Co. St. Croix, as to a bequest from Mr. Halwood."
John Sempill and William Amorey were merchants on St. Croix.
2. H's mercantile apprenticeship was served with Nicholas Cruger's firm
on St. Croix.
3. John Hallwood was the son of the oldest daughter of James Lytton, H's
uncle-in-law. James Lytton, who died in 1769, willed two-sevenths of his
estate to his grandson. Hallwood, who was in school in Philadelphia, returned to St. Croix, probably in September, 1774, to claim his inheritance.
He remained there until 1780, when because of illness he returned to North
America. He died in 1781; legal notice of his estate was given on April 13,
1781 (Ramsing, "Alexander Hamilton," *Personalhistorisk tidsskrift*, 268).
4. Knox, a friend of the members of the Lytton family, had agreed to handle
the inheritance claims of Hallwood's widow who soon after her husband's
death had gone to Montgomery, Pennsylvania (*ibid.*, 254).
5. See the enclosure.
6. D, Panteprotokol f. St. Croix, libr. S (1785–88) fol. 267.

To John B. Church

[*New York, May 23, 1786.* On June 10, 1786, Hamilton wrote to
Church: "I have only time to inclose you a duplicate of my Letter
of the 23 of May." *Letter not found.*]

To Robert R. Livingston

[New York, May 23, 1786]

Dear Sir

We have talked over the Question. Who of the Commissioners are to go to the Southward? [1] And it seems to be decided that you and myself are to be of the number and that a *third* must be either Mr. R. C. Livingston or Mr Ganseevort, as they may arrange it between themselves.[2] I understand the meeting is to be sometime in September.

I remain with sincere esteem   Sir   Your obed & hum ser

A Hamilton

May 23d. 1786
The Honble R R Livingston Esquire

ALS, New-York Historical Society, New York City.
  1. For the appointment of New York commissioners to the Annapolis Convention, see "Appointment as Commissioners to the Annapolis Convention," May 5, 1786.
  2. The legislature appointed H, Robert R. Livingston, James Duane, Egbert Benson, Leonard Gansevoort, and Robert C. Livingston as the New York delegates to the Convention.

To Richard Varick

[*New York*] *May 24, 1786.* Encloses "a draft of the trust deed with the papers relating to it" and asks Varick to make the necessary amendments.

ALS, Columbia University Libraries.

From Marinus Willett [1]

[New York, May 24, 1786]

I do hereby Certify that on Casting up the Votes in the several Poll lists returned to me by the Inspectors of the General Election held in the several Wards of the City and County in April last it appears that Alexander Hamilton Esqr. was by plurality of Voices duly Elected one of the Representatives of the General Assembly for the City and County of New York.[2]

Given under my hand at New York this 24th. Day of May 1786.

M. Willett, Sheriff,

Alexr Hamilton Esqr
Present

LS, Hamilton Papers, Library of Congress.
1. Marinus Willett was appointed sheriff of New York County in February, 1784.
2. The other representatives elected from New York were Evert Bancker, Nicholas Bayard, David Brooks, William Denning, Robert C. Livingston, William Malcom, John Ray, and Richard Varick.

From William Donaldson [1]

New York, May 29, 1786. Seeks Hamilton's aid as an attorney in a controversy concerning the seizure of property by a landlord to whom Donaldson owed money for the rent of a house.

ALS, Hamilton Papers, Library of Congress.
1. Presumably William Donaldson, a brazier of 90 Queen Street, New York City.

From Lawrence and Morris [1]

[New York] Wednesday Morning 31st May 1786.

Dear Sir,

We are much concerned, that the matter has been so long delayed, respecting the return of the money, you have been so very obliging as to lend us. Every moment since the Receipt of your Note of the other day, we have been expecting to receive the money, from different Persons indebted to us in this City, under their most solemn assurances of payment, & it would have been more agreeable to us, as well as yourself, to have had the Cash, than to be troubled with the discounting a Note. Excuse us therefore my good Sir, that from the disappointments, which at present prevail, We are under the necessity of troubling you with the Note, but in the present situation of things, We cannot do better.

Accept our thanks for this instance of your politeness, and be assured, We shall be happy in any occasion of returning the Favor.

We are wth. great regard. Dear Sir   Your much obliged & Obedt.
servants.   Lawrence & Morris

the Discount We will seale   ⎫
seperately wth you when ascertained ⎰

A. Hamilton Esqr

LS, Hamilton Papers, Library of Congress.
1. According to *The New York Directory for 1786*, the firm of Thomas Lawrence and Jacob Morris was located at "83 Broadway, or at their store, corner Duke-street & Old-slip."

To Elizabeth Hamilton [1]

[May, 1786–April, 1788] [1]

Three or four days since I wrote to My angel by the Post, since which I have received a letter from her.[2] I am very unhappy to hear that my beloved is out of health. Heaven grant it may soon be restored. I entreat her to take care of herself & keep up her spirits. I cannot yet determine what will be our stay here and consequently I can make no determinations about my love; but I feel that it will be impossible for me to submit to a long separation however inconvenient it may be to incur the expence which will attend her coming here. I entreat you my charmer to let me hear from you as often as possible; for I stand in need of every consolation you can give for my absence from your dear bosom. Give my love to my darling Philip & kiss with all possible tenderness the other two. Adieu my dearest angel. Heaven bless you   A Hamilton

ALS, Mr. George Bowdoin, New York City.
1. This letter is undated. H mentions three children. Since the third child, Alexander, was born on May 16, 1786, and the fourth, James Alexander, was born on April 14, 1788, the inclusive date of May, 1786–April, 1788 has been given this letter.
2. Letter not found.

From Francis Upton

London, June 5, 1786. Sends duplicate of a letter addressed to Hamilton on December 6, 1785.

ALS, Hamilton Papers, Library of Congress.

To John B. Church

[New York, June 10, 1786]

My Dear friend,

Being to set out in few minutes on a Circuit I have only time to inclose you a duplicate of my Letter of the 23 of May [1] and of a Bill of Lading for a Sum of money by the last packett: the last I say; but I believe she has not yet set Sail. I have given direction to the Broker to make Insurance for you.

I have spoken to a friend to collect some more proper gold & Silver for you; which will be forwarded by the first Opportunity after my Return.

Yrs. unalterably   A Hamilton
New York June 10th. 1786

Copy, in writing of Pierre Van Cortlandt, Jr., Hamilton Papers, Library of Congress.
1. Letter not found.

To John Thomas [1]

[New York, June 22, 1786]

Sir

I think it necessary to apprise you that in my opinion you will not be safe in taking paper money [2] on Executions without the consent of the parties: and in those which I have sent to you that consent I believe can not be obtained This is a matter however which I mention to you in confidence for your own safety. I would not wish to have much said about it, till you should be under a necessity of explaining yourself lest it should injure the Credit of the paper on its first appearance, to which (whatever be my opinion of the measure itself since its has been adopted) I would not wish to be accessory.

I am Sir   Your obd. Servant.

New York June 22d: 1786
John Thomas Esquire
Sheriff of Westchester

Copy, Hamilton Papers, Library of Congress.
1. Thomas, the sheriff of Westchester County, before the Revolution was a
deputy to the Provincial Assembly and a county judge.
2. By a law passed on April 18, 1786, the New York legislature provided
for the issue of £200,000 in bills of credit.

From Broome and Platt [1]

New Haven [*Connecticut*] *June 30, 1786*. Authorizes Hamilton
to collect certain debts owed to the firm of Broome and Platt and
to advise "Our Saml Broome . . . whether there will be room in
your Office for his Son next Fall."

LS, Hamilton Papers, Library of Congress.
1. Samuel Broome and Jeremiah Platt established the firm of Broome and
Platt in New Haven in 1775. It was dissolved in November, 1786.

Oration before the New York State Society
of the Society of the Cincinnati

New York, July 4. 1786. According to the transactions of the New
York State Society, the meeting of the society was "opened by an
oration delivered by *Colonel* Hamilton."

John C. Schuyler, *Institution of the Society of the Cincinnati*, 89.

Report of a Committee of the New York State Society
of the Society of the Cincinnati [1]

[New York, July 6, 1786]

The Committee to whom were referred the proceedings of the
Society of the Cincinnati, at their last General Meeting,[2] beg leave
to report: that they have attentively considered the alterations proposed at that meeting to be made in the original Constitution of
the Society; and though they highly approve the motives which
dictated those alterations, they are of opinion it would be inexpedient to adopt them, and this chiefly on the two following accounts:

1st. Because the Institution, as proposed to be altered, would contain in itself no certain provision for the continuance of the Society beyond the heirs of the present members; this point (being left to the regulation of charters which may never be obtained, and which, in the opinion of this Committee, so far as affects this object,) ought never to be granted, since the dangers apprehended from the Institution could then only cease to be imaginary when it should secure the sanction of a legal establishment. The utmost the Society ought to wish or ask from the several legislatures, is to enable it to appoint trustees to hold its property, for the charitable purposes to which it is destined.[3]

2d. Because, by a fundamental article, it obliges the Society of each State to lend its funds to the State,[4] a provision which would be improper for two reasons: one, that in case the Society might be able to dispose of its funds to much greater advantage, the other, that the State might not always choose to borrow from the Society.

That while the Committee entertain this opinion with respect to the proposed alterations, they are at the same time equally of opinion, that some alterations in the original constitution will be proper, as well in deference to the sense of many of our fellow citizens, as in conformity to the true spirit of the Institution itself.

The alterations they have in view respect, principally, the duration or succession of the Society, and the distinction between Honorary and Regular Members. As to the first, the provision intended to be made appears to them to be expressed in terms not sufficiently explicit,[5] and as far as it may intend an hereditary succession, by right of primogeniture, is liable to this objection, that it refers to birth what ought to belong to merit only, a principle inconsistent with the genius of a Society founded on friendship and patriotism. As to the second, the distinction holds up an odious difference between men who have served their country in one way and those who have served it in another,[6] a difference ill-founded in itself, and improper in a Society where the character of Patriot ought to be an equal title to all its members.

The Committee, however, decline proposing any specific substitute for the parts of the original Constitution which appear to them exceptionable, as they are of opinion, any alterations necessary to be made, can only be digested in a General Meeting of the Society, specially authorised to agree upon and finally establish those alterations. With a view to this, they beg leave to recommend that a Circular Letter be written from the Society to the different State Societies,[7] suggesting the expediency of instructing and empowering their delegates at the next General Meeting, to concur in such alterations as may appear to that meeting proper, after a full communication of what shall be found to be the sense of the several societies.

> Rd. Morris,
> Alexander Hamilton,
> D. Brooks,
> E. Dunscomb,
> Rob. Troup.[8]

The Institution of the Society of the Cincinnati . . . Together with Some of the Proceedings of the General Society, and of the New-York Society (New York, 1851), 51–53.

1. Hamilton, *History*, III, 126, states that H "presented a report," implying that he was its author. In the *Institution of the Society of the Cincinnati*, cited above, the report is prefaced by the statement that "Col. HAMILTON presented the following report." In the edition of the transactions of the society prepared by John Schuyler in 1886 (*Institution of the Society of the Cincinnati*, 91), it is stated only that "this report was signed by Richard Morris, Alexander Hamilton, David Brooks, Edward Dunscomb and Robert Troup as the Committee." Although H doubtless presented the report, no proof of his authorship has been found.

2. For an account of the inauguration of the Society of the Cincinnati and the amendments to its original constitution proposed at the general meeting of 1784, see H to George Washington, November 25, 1785.

3. The amendment to which H refers reads, in part, ". . . the several State meetings shall, at suitable periods, make applications to their respective legislatures for grants of charters" (Schuyler, *Institution of the Society of the Cincinnati*, 32).

4. Section 12 of the revised "Institution" read: "The funds of each State meeting shall be loaned to the State by permission of the legislature; and the interest only, annually to be applied for the purposes of the Society" (Schuyler, *Institution of the Society of the Cincinnati*).

5. The original "Institution" of the society provided that the members form a "SOCIETY OF FRIENDS, to endure as long as they shall endure, or any of their eldest male posterity, and in failure thereof, the collateral branches, who may be judged worth of becoming its supporters and members" (Schuyler, *Institution of the Society of the Cincinnati*, 14). The amended "Institution" of the society stated that hereditary succession should be abolished.

6. The "Institution" of the society stated that ". . . as there are, and will at all times be, men in the respective States, eminent for their abilities and patriotism, whose views may be directed to the same laudable objects with those of the Cincinnati, it shall be a rule to admit such characters as Honorary Members of the Society, for their own lives only" (Schuyler, *Institution of the Society of the Cincinnati*, 17–18).

7. See "Circular Letter to the State Societies of the Cincinnati," November 1, 1786.
8. Richard Morris, chief justice of the State of New York, was made an honorary member of the society in 1786. David Brooks served as assistant clothier general for New York troops from 1780 to 1782. Edward Dunscomb was a captain during the Revolution. Robert Troup had served as aide-de-camp to Major General Horatio Gates.

From Philip Schuyler

[*Albany*] *July 11, 1786.* "A passage of thirty two hours brought me to my family. Mrs. Schuyler . . . altho mending is still not perfectly in health. Inclose you the mortgage which Mr. Loudon [1] is to assign to me. Pray as soon as you can send Mr. Renselaer [2] the papers I requested; his tenants seem at present in good humour and anxious for their lands."

ALS, Hamilton Papers, Library of Congress.
1. Presumably Samuel Loudon.
2. John Van Rensselaer.

To Thomas Wooldrige [1]

New York, July 20, 1786. Describes measures needed to satisfy the claims of Wooldrige's creditors.

ADfS, Hamilton Papers, Library of Congress.
1. Thomas Wooldrige, a former British subject, at this time was a resident of New York City and a member of the firms of Wooldrige and Kelly and of Kelly, Lot and Company, engaged in West Indian trade. In 1787 Wooldrige was imprisoned in New York City for debt.

From Robert Totten [1]

Stamford [*Connecticut*] *July 31, 1786.* "Be pleased to inform me what prospect you realy have of softening the present insolvent act of new York, and if you suppose my well known situation may have any claim to . . . indulgence with the representatives of the state of new York. I am determined not to venture myself into a goal and be at the caprice of a few of my creditors; every thing else I will submit to with cheerfulness and rectitude even to delivering my shirt if they should require it."

ALS, Hamilton Papers, Library of Congress.
1. Totten was a member of the Philadelphia firm of Stewart and Totten.

From Ebenezer Hazard [1]

New York, August 1, 1786. Requests Hamilton's opinion on questions concerning a government contract for carrying the mail.

LS, Papers of the Continental Congress, National Archives.
1. Hazard was Postmaster General of the United States. This letter was enclosed in a letter Hazard sent to Nathaniel Gorham, September 25, 1786.

From Alexander Macaulay

Yorktown, Virginia, August 1, 1786. Has "of this date drawed on you at Ten days sight for . . . One Hundred pounds currency of New York in favour of Colo. John Jameson." Requests Hamilton to pay this sum "out of the money arising from Harts [1] Debt."

ALS, Hamilton Papers, Library of Congress.
1. Malcolm Hart.

From Robert Harpur [1]

[August 2, 1786]

Sir,

At the Request of Genl. Schuyler, We have made a Copy of all the Poll Lists of the Counties of Albany and Montgomery, which copy was to be left with you to be forwarded to him.[2] The Secretary [3] estimated the Expences with which the Genl. was acquain[t]ed previous to the undertaking. And you was to be good enough to disburse the sum—being £10—which be pleased to deliver to the Bearer on your Receipt of the papers.

Your most obedt. servt. Robt Harpur, D secry

2 Augt. 1786

Recd. 2 Augt. 1786. of Col. Hamilton ten pounds, the fees of the Secretarys Office for copying all the Poll Lists of the Counties of Albany and Montgomery for and by order of Genl. Schuyler.

Robt Harpur, D. secry

DS, Hamilton Papers, Library of Congress.
1. Harpur was deputy secretary of the State of New York.
2. Philip Schuyler was a member of the New York Senate in 1786 and 1787.
3. Presumably the secretary of state, Lewis Allaire Scott.

To Bell and Woodmass

[*August 4, 1786*. Hamilton wrote to John B. Church: "I have written to Messrs. Bell and Woodmass by this opportunity." *Letter not found.*]

To John B. Church

Augt. 4. 1786

Dr Sir

The only letter I have received from you in a considerable time is one introducing Lt Col Hastings[1] to whom I have paid the attention which your recommendation will always give title to.

The following remittances made by me remain unacknowleged by you.

A bill of Exchange drawn by Constable & Rucker[2] for £400 Sterling

	Currency
Specie ℔ the Tankerville Packet	£1057.17.8
Ditto per the Carteret	1000

I take it for granted all is right. The specie has been insured here.

By a Ship I think of Murrays,[3] I sent you copies of two letters of which the Inclosed are duplicate copies.[4] By these you will perceive you have a right to call upon Mr. James Duff of Cadiz[5] and Messrs. Bell and Woodmass of London for ⅛ of what the Ship Tartar sold for. This you will recollect is one of the Ships in which Wadsworth and yourself were concerned with Isaac Moses & Co.[6]

I thought it better to secure the money in the hands of these Gentlemen than to let it pass into those of Mr. Wilcox [7] out of which it does not seem very easy to extract this kind of commodity. What you receive will of course be on the joint account of Wadsworth & yourself.

I have received for your account of Wadsworth and Shalor [8] 6500 dollars.

> say of Wadsworth 3500
> of Shalor 3000

Inclosed you have bill of Lading for the amount of 5000 dollars which is all I have been able conveniently to ship in the right Coin. There is a ship which will sail in about ten days by which I will send you the Residue and a further sum in my hands on your Account.

I have some hopes of shortly getting rid of your lot.

I have written to Messrs. Bell and Woodmass [9] by this opportunity and I enclose you duplicate of a letter which I wrote some time since to Mr. Duff.[10]

Betsey joins me in best affections to Mrs. Church & your self.
Adieu   A Hamilton

ADfS, Hamilton Papers, Library of Congress.

1. Presumably George Hastings, lieutenant colonel of the Third Regiment of the Foot Guards, British army. Letter not found.

2. William Constable and John Rucker, New York merchants, organized the firm of Constable, Rucker and Company in 1784.

3. John Murray, a New York merchant, was engaged in extensive shipping operations.

4. Letters not found.

5. James Duff was British consul at the port of Cadiz. In 1813 the title of baronet was conferred on him.

6. For information on the joint ownership of ships by Isaac Moses and Company, Jeremiah Wadsworth, and Church, see John Wilcocks to H, March 5, 1786.

7. John Wilcocks, like Isaac Moses, was involved in occasional joint ownership of ships with Wadsworth and Church. See Wilcocks to H, March 5, 1786.

8. Nathaniel Shaler, a New York merchant, was occasionally involved in business partnerships with Jeremiah Wadsworth.

9. Letter not found.

10. Letter not found.

From Samuel Broome

New Haven [Connecticut] August 18, 1786. Encloses "an order on The Honble. Nathan Miller Esquire a Delegate in Congress from the State of Rhode Island in your favor for £110.18."

ALS, Hamilton Papers, Library of Congress.

To Robert Totten

[New York, August 25, 1786. On the back of the letter that Totten wrote to Hamilton on July 31, 1786, Hamilton wrote: "Answered Aug. 25. 1786." *Letter not found.]*

Subscription to the Associated Manufacturing Iron Company

New York, August 26, 1786. On this date the "Original Articles of Agreement of the associated Manufacturing Iron Company" of the City and County of New York were filed in the Clerk's office. Hamilton's name appears on the list of subscribers as the purchaser of two shares.[1]

DS, Municipal Archives and Records Center, New York City.
1. The New York legislature by an act of April 28, 1786, granted the associates a charter. There is no evidence that the company ever began operations.

To Ebenezer Hazard [1]

New York, September 1, 1786. Answers questions concerning a government contract for carrying the mail which Hazard had sent to Hamilton on August 1, 1786.

Copy, Papers of the Continental Congress, National Archives.
1. Hazard enclosed H's answers in a letter to Nathaniel Gorham, September 25, 1786.

Alexander Hamilton and Egbert Benson to John Lansing, Junior

Newark [*New Jersey*] *September 1, 1786.* "We set out this afternoon on a journey to Anapolis in obedience to the appointment of the Legislature respecting the proposed commercial arrangements and are thus far on our journey.[1] This of course renders it impossible for either of us to be at the intended trials in which Mr. Rensselaaer is concerned."

ALS, in writing of H, New-York Historical Society, New York City.
1. See H to Richard Varick, September 1, 1786, note 1.

From Nathan Miller [1]

New York, September 1, 1786. Will pay a bill drawn on Miller by Samuel Broome in Hamilton's favor in about three weeks.

AL, Hamilton Papers, Library of Congress.
1. Miller was a delegate to Congress from Rhode Island. See Samuel Broome to H, August 18, 1786.

To Richard Varick

[New York, September 1, 1786]

Mrs. Hamilton insists on my dining with her to day as this is the day of departure[1] and you (who are not a prophane batchelor like Benson)[2] will know that in such a case implicit obedience on my part is proper. This deprives me of the pleasure of dining with you.

Yr. friend & serv   A Hamilton

Sepr. 1st 1786

ALS, Mr. William N. Dearborn, Nashville, Tennessee.
1. On this date H left to attend the Annapolis Convention to which he had been appointed a commissioner by the New York legislature on May 5, 1786. The Convention was scheduled to meet on the first Monday in September at Annapolis, both the place and the date having been chosen by the Virginia commissioners. Annapolis was selected, James Madison said, because "It was thought prudent to avoid the neighborhood of Congress and the large commercial towns, in order to disarm the adversaries to the object

of insinuations of influence from either of these quarters" (Madison to Thomas Jefferson, March 18, 1786, *Letters and Other Writings of James Madison* [Philadelphia, 1867], I, 225–26).

After stopping in Philadelphia, H reached Annapolis on or before September 8.

2. Egbert Benson.

To Elizabeth Hamilton

[Annapolis, September 8, 1786]

I wrote to you My beloved Betsey at Philadelphia; but through mistake brought off the letter with me; which I did not discover till my arrival here.[1] I was not very well on the first part of the journey; but my health has been improved by travelling and is now as good as I could wish. Happy, however I cannot be, absent from you and my darling little ones. I feel that nothing can ever compensate for the loss of the enjoyments I leave at home, or can ever put my heart at tolerable ease. In the bosom of my family alone must my happiness be sought, and in that of my Betsey is every thing that is charming to me. Would to heaven I were there! Does not your heart re-echo the wish?

In reality my attachments to home disqualify me for either business or pleasure abroad; and the prospect of a detention here for Eight or ten days perhaps a fortnight fills me with an anxiety which will best be conceived by my Betseys own impatience.

I am straitened for time & must conclude. I presume this will find you at Albany. Kiss my little ones a thousand times for me. Remember me affectionately to Your Parents, to Peggy,[2] to all. Think of me with as much tenderness as I do of you and we cannot fail to be always happy

Adieu My beloved   A Hamilton
Anapolis
Sepr. 8. 1786

ALS, Hamilton Papers, Library of Congress.

1. H had left New York on September 1 to attend the Annapolis Convention as a commissioner from New York. See H to Richard Varick, September 1, 1786.

The envelope of the letter states "To be forwarded by Mr. De Heart." Balthazar De Haert was H's law partner.

2. Margarita (Margaret) Van Rensselaer, Elizabeth's younger sister, who had married Stephen Van Rensselaer.

Thomas Cushing, Francis Dana, and Samuel Breck to Alexander Hamilton and Egbert Benson [1]

New York. Sept. 10. 1786

Gentlemen

Understanding on our arrival in this City last Fryday evening, that you had gone on for the Convention at Annapolis the week past, we take the Liberty to acquaint you and beg you to communicate to the Convention if it should be opened before we arrive there, that we shall set off from this Place to morrow to join them, as Commissioners from the State of Massachusetts, which we hope to do in the course of this week.[2] The Commissioners from Rhode Island were to sail from thence for this city on the 7th Instant; so that they may be expected soon after us.

With great Respect   Your most obed humble Servts

Thomas Cushing
Fra. Dana
Sam Breck

The Gentlemen
Commissioners for New York

LS, in writing of Samuel Breck, Hamilton Papers, Library of Congress.
1. Cushing, a leader of Massachusetts opposition to Great Britain in the decade before the Revolution, held many offices during and after the war. He was lieutenant governor of Massachusetts at the time of his appointment as a delegate to the Annapolis Convention. Dana, American Minister to Russia from 1781 to 1783, was appointed an associate justice of the Supreme Court of Massachusetts in 1785. Breck was a wealthy Boston merchant.
2. The Massachusetts delegates set out for Annapolis, but en route news reached them that the convention had broken up.

Annapolis Convention. Address of the Annapolis Convention [1]

[Annapolis, September 14, 1786] [2]

To the Honorable the Legislatures of Virginia, Delaware Pennsylvania, New Jersey, and New York.

The Commissioners from the said states, respectively assembled at Annapolis, humbly beg leave to report.

That, pursuant to their several appointments, they met, at Annapolis in the State of Maryland, on the eleventh day of September Instant, and having proceeded to a Communication of their powers;

DS, Papers of the Continental Congress, National Archives.

1. The only minutes of the Convention were taken by Egbert Benson. Dated September 11, 1786, Benson's minutes record that the Convention "Ordered that Mr. Benson, Mr. [Abraham] Clarke, Mr. [Tench] Coxe, Mr. [George] Read, and Mr. [Edmund] Randolph be a Committee to consider of and report the measures proper to be adopted by this Convention" (Benson's minutes are in Thomas A. Emmet, *Annapolis Convention held in 1786 with the Report of the Proceedings Represented to the States by President John Dickinson* [New York, 1891], extra-illustrated volume, New York Public Library). The report stated that it was "inexpedient for this Convention, in which so few States are represented, to proceed in the business committed to them" and recommended a future meeting of commissioners from all the states. A committee was appointed to prepare an address to the several states.

The authority for the attribution of the "Address of the Annapolis Convention" to H is James Madison. In his "Preface to Debates in the [Constitutional] Convention," written between 1830 and 1840, Madison, in discussing the reasons why a commercial convention issued a call for a convention to amend the Articles of Confederation, stated that the "commission of the N. Jersey Deputation, had extended its object to a general provision for the exigencies of the Union. A recommendation for this enlarged purpose was accordingly reported by a Come. to whom the subject had been referred. It was drafted by Col: H and finally agreed to unanimously" ("Notes of Debates in the Constitutional Convention," MS, James Madison Papers, Library of Congress). In a letter to Noah Webster, also written many years later, Madison again stated that "Mr. Hamilton was certainly the member who drafted the address" (Madison to Webster, October 12, 1804, Hunt, *Writings of Madison*, VII, 164–65).

The extent to which H's draft was altered by the other commissioners cannot be ascertained. John T. Morse (*The Life of Alexander Hamilton* [Boston, 1876], I, 167) states that H revised the draft because of the objections of Governor Edmund Randolph of Virginia.

2. When the commissioners met on Monday, September 11, 1786, only five states were represented. Subsequent meetings were held on September 13 and September 14. The report was agreed to September 14.

they found, that the States of New York, Pennsylvania and Virginia had, in substance, and nearly in the same terms, authorised their respective Commissioners "to meet such commissioners as were, or might be, appointed by the other States in the Union, at such time and place, as should be agreed upon by the said Commissioners to take into consideration the trade and Commerce of the United States, to consider how far an uniform system in their commercial intercourse and regulations might be necessary to their common interest and permanent harmony, and to report to the several States, such an Act, relative to this great object, as when unanimously ratified by them would enable the United States in Congress assembled effectually to provide for the same."

That the State of Delaware, had given similar powers to their Commissioners, with this difference only that the Act to be framed in virtue of those powers, is required to be reported "to the United States in Congress Assembled, to be agreed to by them, and confirmed by the Legislatures of every State."

That the State of New Jersey had enlarged the object of their Appointment, empowering their Commissioners, "to consider how far an uniform system in their commercial regulations and *other important matters*, might be necessary to the common interest and permanent harmony of the several States," and to report such an Act on the subject, as when ratified by them "would enable the United States in Congress Assembled, effectually to provide for the exigencies of the Union."

That appointments of Commissioners have also been made by the States of New Hampshire, Massachusetts, Rhode Island, and North Carolina, none of whom however have attended; but that no information has been received by your Commissioners of any appointments having been made by the States of Connecticut, Maryland, South Carolina, or Georgia.

That the express terms of the powers to your Commissioners supposing a deputation from all the States, and having for object the Trade and Commerce of the United States, Your Commissioners did not conceive it advisable to proceed on the business of their mission, under the Circumstance of so partial and defective a representation.

Deeply impressed however with the magnitude and importance

of the object confided to them on this occasion, your Commissioners cannot forbear to indulge an expression of their earnest and unanimous wish, that speedy measures may be taken, to effect a general meeting, of the States, in a future Convention, for the same and such other purposes, as the situation of public affairs, may be found to require.

If in expressing this wish, or in intimating any other sentiment, your Commissioners should seem to exceed the strict bounds of their appointment, they entertain a full confidence, that a conduct, dictated by an anxiety for the welfare, of the United States, will not fail to receive an indulgent construction.

In this persuasion your Commissioners submit an opinion, that the Idea of extending the powers of their Deputies, to other objects, than those of Commerce, which has been adopted by the State of New Jersey, was an improvement on the original plan, and will deserve to be incorporated into that of a future Convention; they are the more naturally led to this conclusion, as in the course of their reflections on the subject, they have been induced to think, that the power of regulating trade is of such comprehensive extent, and will enter so far into the general System of the foederal government, that to give it efficacy, and to obviate questions and doubts concerning its precise nature and limits, may require a correspondent adjustment of other parts of the Fœderal System.

That there are important defects in the system of the Fœderal Government is acknowledged by the Acts of all those States, which have concurred in the present Meeting; That the defects, upon a closer examination, may be found greater and more numerous, than even these acts imply, is at least so far probable, from the embarrassments which characterise the present State of our national affairs—foreign and domestic, as may reasonably be supposed to merit a deliberate and candid discussion, in some mode, which will unite the Sentiments and Councils of all the States. In the choice of the mode your Commissioners are of opinion, that a Convention of Deputies from the different States, for the special and sole purpose of entering into this investigation, and digesting a plan for supplying such defects as may be discovered to exist, will be entitled to a preference from consideration, which will occur, without being particularised.

Your Commissioners decline an enumeration of those national circumstances on which their opinion respecting the propriety of a future Convention with more enlarged powers, is founded; as it would be an useless intrusion of facts and observations, most of which have been frequently the subject of public discussion, and none of which can have escaped the penetration of those to whom they would in this instance be addressed. They are however of a nature so serious, as, in the view of your Commissioners to render the Situation of the United States delicate and critical, calling for an exertion of the united virtue and wisdom of all the members of the Confederacy.

Under this impression, Your Commissioners, with the most respectful deference, beg leave to suggest their unanimous conviction, that it may essentially tend to advance the interests of the union, if the States, by whom they have been respectively delegated, would themselves concur, and use their endeavours to procure the concurrence of the other States, in the appointment of Commissioners, to meet at Philadelphia on the second Monday in May next, to take into consideration the situation of the United States, to devise such further provisions as shall appear to them necessary to render the constitution of the Fœderal Government adequate to the exigencies of the Union; and to report such an Act for that purpose to the United States in Congress Assembled, as when agreed to, by them, and afterwards confirmed by the Legislatures of every State will effectually provide for the same.

Though your Commissioners could not with propriety address these observations and sentiments to any but the States they have the honor to Represent, they have nevertheless concluded from motives of respect, to transmit Copies of this report to the United States in Congress assembled, and to the executives of the other States.

By order of the Commissioners

Dated at Annapolis
September 14th. 1786 }

Resolved that the Chairman sign the aforegoing Report in behalf of the Commissioners

Then adjourned without day.

Egbt: Benson Alexander Hamilton	} New York
Abra: Clark Wm Chls Houston Js. Schureman	} New Jersey
Tench Coxe	Pennsylvania
Geo: Read John Dickinson Richard Bassett	} Delaware
Edmund Randolph Js. Madison Jr. St. George Tucker	} Virginia

To Robert Milligan

[*September 26, 1786.* On October 1, 1786, Milligan wrote to Hamilton: "I have your favour of the 26th Septr." *Letter not found.*]

From Robert Milligan

Philadelphia, October 1, 1786. "I have your favour of the 26th Septr.[1] Your objection to taking Mr Seixas's bond is conclusive; his base acknowlegement of the amount of our claim I cannot consent to accept. Let an amicable suit be instituted and judgment confessed by Mr Seixas for the balance, with stay till 1st October 1789."

ALS, Hamilton Papers, Library of Congress.
  1. Letter not found.

From Samuel Broome

New Haven [*Connecticut, October*] *2, 1786.* Requests Hamilton to collect the balance of a debt owed to Broome by Nathan Miller.

ALS, Hamilton Papers, Library of Congress.

To John Sitgreaves [1]

[*October 17, 1786.* On October 23, 1786, Sitgreaves wrote to Hamilton: "Your favor of the 17th. was handed me this morning." *Letter not found.*]

1. John Sitgreaves of North Carolina was a member of the Continental Congress in 1784 and 1785. From 1786 to 1789 he was a member of the state House of Commons.

From David Forman [1]

[*Auburn, Pennsylvania, October 18, 1786.* On November 7, 1786, Forman wrote to Hamilton: "I wrote you from Auburn (near Philada) on the 18th. ult." *Letter not found.*]

1. Brigadier General David Forman of New Jersey who became a judge of the Court of Common Pleas in Monmouth, New Jersey.

From John Sitgreaves

Philadelphia, October 23, 1786. "Your favor of the 17th. was handed me this morning.[1] Mr. Robert Bowne my Attorney . . . [will] call upon you for the One hundred and sixty Pounds received from Mr. Bostwick."

ALS, Hamilton Papers, Library of Congress.
  1. Letter not found.

From Alexander Macaulay

Alexandria, Virginia, October 24, 1786. Is detained at Alexandria. Asks Hamilton's assistance in settling various financial affairs in New York City.

ALS, Hamilton Papers, Library of Congress.

From Peter Van Schaack [1]

Kindorhook [New York] October 25, 1786. "I enclose you a Case for your Opinion, with a Fee. Tis a confused Business but I hope you will hit upon a clue to lead us through the Labyrinth. I have it also in Charge to retain you on Behalf of the Vandenberghs and Van Vechtens."

ALS, Hamilton Papers, Library of Congress.
    1. For information on Van Schaack, see H to Angelica Church, August 3, 1785, note 2.

From John Lansing, Junior

Albany, October 28, 1786. States that the sheriff of Montgomery County who "has been attached for a Contempt in proceeding to the Sale of Croghan's Land," wishes Hamilton "to take the necessary Steps to defend him."

ALS, Hamilton Papers, Library of Congress.

To William Wickham [1]

[*New York City*] *October 28, 1786.* "I shall in a very short time have an urgent call for a sum of money to make up which I shall be glad to receive the amount of my account for services in the controversy between Cheesecocks and Wawayanda,[2] or a considerable part of it."

ALS, Goshen Library and Historical Society, Goshen, New York.
    1. This letter is addressed to "The Agents for managing the Controversy on behalf of the proprietors of Wawayanda." The envelope was addressed to "William Wickham, Esquire."
    2. Chesecocks and Waywayanda were adjoining land patents in southern New York on the New Jersey border.

To John Chaloner

[New York, October 30, 1786]

Dr Sir

Inclosed I send you Mr. Church's Power of Atty to me to receive his bank dividends [1] &c. and a power from me to you to receive the *last* and the *next*.

I will be obliged to you to get the money & forward it by the first proper opportuni[t]y to this place.

Pray let me know how matters go on with the bank. What is intended? When is the next election of Directors? Can bank stock be sold at any rate & at what rate?

I remain Dr Sir   Yr Obed ser   A Hamilton
October 30. 1786

ALS, Historical Society of Pennsylvania, Philadelphia.
1. The dividends were from stock owned by John B. Church in the Bank of North America.

Circular Letter to the State Societies of the Cincinnati [1]

[New York, November 1, 1786]

Gentlemen

It is our duty to inform you, that we have been appointed by the New York State Society of the Cincinnati a Committee of correspondence, with instructions to frame and transmit to the other State Societies a circular letter, on several matters of importance to the Society of the Cincinnati in general.[2]

In pursuance of this trust, we send you an extract from the proceedings of our Society, began the fourth of July last and continued by adjournments to the twelveth of August following. This

LS, in writing of H, addressed to the president of the Society of the Cincinnati of Pennsylvania, Papers of the Society of the Cincinnati, Washington, D.C.; LS, in writing of H, addressed to the president of the Society of the Cincinnati of New Hampshire, Hamilton Papers, Library of Congress; LS, in writing of H, addressed to the president of the Society of the Cincinnati of Virginia, Yale University Library.

1. For the background of this letter and an explanation of the subjects discussed in it, see H to George Washington, November 25, 1785, and "Report of a Committee of the New York State Society of the Cincinnati," July 6, 1786.

2. According to the transactions of the New York State Society of the Cincinnati, this letter was presented on July 15, 1786, to the society by "The Committee on Correspondence, appointed to frame a Circular Letter to the other State Societies, composed of Alexander Hamilton, James Duane, and William Duer . . . through their chairman" (Schuyler, *Institution of the Society of the Cincinnati*, 93).

extract will itself explain the objects intended to be communicated by this letter, and will leave little to be added by us.[3]

Among other things comprised in it, you will find the Report of a Committee on the proceedings of the *General Society* of the Cincinnati, at their last meeting;[4] which report approved by our Society contains its dissent from the alterations proposed to be made in the Original Constitution, and assigns the principal reasons of that dissent. These reasons might be enforced by many additional considerations of weight; which, however, we shall omit, as we are persuaded your own reflections will supply them.

We cannot help thinking, that even those Societies, which have adopted the proposed alterations, will on a review of the matter, be struck with the objections Stated in the Report, and will chearfully concur in a plan for revising the business and digesting it into shape, that will be satisfactory to all the parts of the Institution.

At any rate, there appears to be an absolute necessity for such a revisal, if it were only to let in a mode of combining the views and sentiments of the respective Societies in some definitive result; without which, alterations agreed on every side to be proper, will either not be made at all, or made partially, and on principles dissimilar and subversive of the Uniformity of the Institution. This obvious idea will, we trust, demonstrate the Justness of the opinion— That it will be adviseable for each State Society to instruct and empower its delegates, at the next general meeting, to agree upon and finally establish all such alterations, in the Original constitution, as shall be thought, by a Majority expedient. The extension of the authority of the delegates to the final establishment of the alterations to be agreed upon is in our opinion indispensable. The prospect of an unanimous concurrence of all the particular Societies in any plan, which might be referred to their ultimate deliberations, would be remote; And the objects of the Society are too [5] simple and limited to require such a referrence.

Before we dismiss the Subject of the proposed alterations, we

3. For the proceedings of the society, see Schuyler, *Institution of the Society of the Cincinnati.*

4. The committee report, presented by H, is printed under date of July 6, 1786.

5. In MS, "two."

shall submit an observation on that part of them, which relates to the exclusion of the clause, by which it is made a fundamental principle of the Society: "To promote and cherish between the respective States that Union and national honor so essentially necessary, to their happiness and the future dignity of the American empire."

We flatter ourselves, we speak the sense of the Society of which we are members, as well as our own, in declaring, that we reverence the sentiment contained in that clause, too much to be willing to see it expunged. Nor can we believe that its continuance will on reflection, give umbrage to any whose views are not unfriendly to those principles which form the Basis of the Union and the only sure foundation of the tranquility and happiness of this Country. To such men it can never appear criminal, that a class of citizens who have had so conspicuous an Agency in the American Revolution as those who compose the Society of the Cincinnati should pledge themselves to each other, in a voluntary association, to support, by all means consistent with the laws, That noble Fabric of United Independence, which at so much hazard, and with so many sacrifices they have contributed to erect; a Fabric on the Solidity and duration of which the value of all they have done must depend! And America can never have cause to condemn, an Institution, calculated to give energy and extent to a sentiment, favorable to the preservation of that Union, by which she established her liberties, and to which she must owe her future peace, respectability and prosperity. Experience, we doubt not, will teach her, that the members of the Cincinnati, always actuated by the same virtuous and generous motives, which have hitherto directed their conduct, will pride themselves in being, thro every vicissitude of her future fate, the steady and faithful supporters of her Liberty, her Laws and her Government.

Permit us now Gentlemen to call your attention to two other resolutions contained in the extract, transmitted herewith, one relating to a limitation of the number of the members to be Elected in addition to those already elected in the Society of this State— The other relating to the right of the State Societies to Elect foreigners as Members of the Cincinnati; We believe the spirit of both these resolutions will appear to you prudent, and conducive, perhaps we might say essential, to the respectability of the Society. The first speaks for itself, and the last has the reasons for it detailed in a letter from Major L'Enfant included in the extract.[6] The opinion of our Society in this respect is founded on the particular terms of the clause of the constitution providing for the election of Honorary members, which seem inapplicable to any but *citizens* of the respective States eminent for abilities and "Patriotism."

But we presume, if there should be any difference of Opinion as to the *right* of electing Foreigners, there will be none as to the *expediency* of referring that matter exclusively to the general Society; who will no doubt be properly impressed with the necessity of circumspection, in admitting the claims of candidates of that description, and who will be less likely to be importuned with ill founded pretensions. The Society of this State will be happy to find, that the views of the Societies of the other States coincide with theirs, in the objects of this letter. Should this not be the case we at least persuade ourselves, they will be considered as the dictates of a pure zeal for the honor and interest of the Institution.

We are very respectfully Gentlemen　your obedt. and humble Servants　　　　　　　　　　　　　　　Alexander Hamilton

　　　　　　　　　　　　　　　　　　　　　　　Jas. Duane

　　　　　　　　　　　　　　　　　　　　　　　Wm. Duer

New York November 1st 1786
To the President of the Society of the Cincinnati of the State of Pensylvania

6. There is a letter from Major Pierre Charles L'Enfant in the transactions of the New York State Society for 1786. It discusses, however, the merits of the medal which L'Enfant was commissioned to design for the Society of the Cincinnati and not the reasons for allowing state societies to elect foreigners as members of the Cincinnati.

From David Forman

Middle Town Point [*New Jersey*] *November 7, 1786.* "I wrote you from Auburn (near Philada) on the 18th. ult." [1] Asks when "the Monies from Robt. Cocks would probably be Recd. &c."

ALS, Hamilton Papers, Library of Congress.
　1. Letter not found.

To Philip Schuyler

[*New York*] *November 20, 1786.* "I have received your letter. . . .[1] Your cause against Ten Eyck[2] was set down for hearing in October term; but the Chancellor[3] when last in town on account of his public engagements would not attend to my special business in his Court. If he is here in January term it will be brought on. . . . We have been Innoculating Angelica and Alexander.[4] The first as before has escaped without any appearance of Infection. The last has had a pretty good share of the disease but is now, I may say, well."

ALS, The Huntington Library, San Marino, California.
1. Schuyler to H, July 11, 1786.
2. Possibly Henry Ten Eyck.
3. Robert R. Livingston.
4. Angelica and Alexander were H's second and third children.

To John Chaloner

[New York, November 22, 1786]

Dr Sir

I received your letter[1] with the draft on Mr Ray[2] which I presented immediately. He would not accept it payable in specie. I did not protest because by your letter it appears to be an affair of accomodation and that you retain the money in your hands. Nor do I now return the draft because Mr. Ray tells me endeavours are making to turn paper into specie for the payment of it; if these do not succeed in a few days I will send it back to you.

I remain with great regard Yr Obed ser   A Hamilton
November 22d. 1786
J Chaloner

ALS, Historical Society of Pennsylvania, Philadelphia.
1. Letter not found.
2. Cornelius Ray was a New York City merchant.

To John Chaloner

[New York, December 1, 1786]

Dr Sir

I send you the bill drawn on Mr. Ray protested as you desire in your last.[1] You will be so good as to send forward the Specie by the first opportunity as the Packet sails in a short time.

Yr Obed serv   A Hamilton

Decr. 1st 1786

ALS, Historical Society of Pennsylvania.
    1. See H to John Chaloner, November 22, 1786.

From Francis Upton

London, December 6–7, 1786. Asks if Hamilton received Upton's "letters of December and June last." [1]

ALS, Hamilton Papers, Library of Congress.
    1. See Upton to H, December 6, 1785 and June 5, 1786.

From John Chaloner

Philada Decr, 13, 1786

Alexr Hamilton Esqr
Dr Sir

Yours of the 1st Inst covering Mr Whites Bill & Protest I reced the 10th Inst since which no Oppo has offerd by which I could send you the money.[1] I shall embrace the first. Did the money I sent you by Mr Lawry [2] come safe to hand? Our Assembly is now on the subject of the Bank & a proposition before them to restore the old Charter.[3] Mr Morris [4] is opposed to any alteration least it should faciltitate those who wish to take their money.[5]

I am with respt Dr Sir   Your most obdt Serv   John Chaloner

ALS, Hamilton Papers, Library of Congress.
    1. See H to Chaloner, November 22 and December 1, 1786. The bill

presented by H to Cornelius Ray was presumably drawn by Charles White, Chaloner's business partner.

2. Presumably Thomas Lowrey of Flemington, New Jersey, who through successful business ventures with Chaloner and Robert Morris during the Revolution was able to establish himself in business in Philadelphia in 1782.

3. The charter of the Bank of North America was repealed by the Pennsylvania legislature in September, 1785. The fight for recharter began immediately. Although a committee appointed by the legislature in March, 1786, reported that the charter had been repealed because of prejudice and ignorance, the Assembly adjourned in April, 1786, without rechartering the bank. In the election held in the autumn of 1786 supporters of the bank were encouraged by the election of a legislature friendly to the bank. As early as November, 1786, debate on the bank issue was revived in the legislature; and in December a committee, which had been appointed to consider a petition from the inhabitants of Philadelphia urging the restoration of the charter, recommended that the bank be rechartered.

4. Chaloner could have been referring to either Robert or Gouverneur Morris.

5. The committee appointed to report on the recharter of the bank recommended that the duration of the charter be limited and the capital stock restricted.

From John Chaloner

Philada Decemr. 16th. 1786.

Dear Sir,

Since my last the Assembly has adopted the Report of the Committee and have ordered a Bill to be brot in to Restore the Charter of the Bank restricting its duration and Capital;[1] the time and sum is not yet mentioned.[2] This displeasing a number of Stockholders has occasioned a petition to be preferd to the House praying that the Bank may be organized and put on a similar footing with respect to its regulations as the Bank of England—and particularly in the following particulars Viz Directors to be chosen by a Majority of Directors present each Stockholder to have One Vote—No person to be a Director without he holds four Shares—No person to Vote at Elections for directors without he has been an owner of Stock some given time so as to prevent the transfer of Stock for Election purposes. I have on my own account signed and promoted as much as is in my power this petition, and I believe if adopted it will so effectually remove the Jealousy and apprehension of Government as no longer to Cause the Bank to be an object of their Resentment; which was solely occasioned by the influence a few people had among the Stockholders to allways nominate and Elect the directors:

and by their Continuing to sit as Directors did in a great measure influence and Comand the Trade of the City and give a bias to all Elections for assembly or other purposes.

The Resentment of Government being removed, I doubt not but the Stock will Rise and come to par: whereas now it is below 10 ℔ Ct Discount. Wether this measure will succeed is very uncertain; I think it propable that it may. The Stockholders by call of the Directors on the 14th Inst are to meet on Monday the 8th of January to choose Directors. I have as yet met no oppo to send you the money which White's Bill was to have answered.[3] I shall embrace the first that I can with Confidence rely on. In the meantime I remain   Sir   Your most Obdt Servt   John Chaloner

LS, Hamilton Papers, Library of Congress; copy, Hamilton Papers, Library of Congress.

1. For the background of the recharter of the Bank of North America, see Chaloner to H, December 13, 1786. On December 13, the committee report recommending recharter was adopted, and a committee was appointed to prepare a recharter bill. The bill was reported on December 15 and debated until mid-March.

2. The bill that was finally passed provided that the corporate existence of the bank should be fourteen years and that its wealth should be limited to two million dollars.

3. See Chaloner to H, December 13, 1786.

From Jacob Hardenbergh

New Brunswick [*New Jersey*] *December 16, 1786.* Wishes to retain Hamilton as an attorney in an ejection suit against a tenant.

ALS, Hamilton Papers, Library of Congress.

From Thomas McKean [1]

Philadelphia, December 26, 1786. Requests Hamilton to collect a debt of £50 owed McKean by Richard Dowdle.

ALS, Hamilton Papers, Library of Congress.
1. McKean was chief justice of Pennsylvania.

To Stephen Lush [1]

[*New York, December 31, 1786.* The catalogue description of this letter states that Hamilton alluded "to the necessity of his attending the legislature of New York in January." *Letter not found.*]

ALS, sold at Anderson Galleries, January 10, 1908, Lot 105.
1. Stephen Lush of Troy, New York, had been active in the Revolution. After the war he entered into business in Albany and was elected a member of the state legislature in the seventeen-nineties.

To James Duane [1]

[*New York, 1786.*] Encloses draft of a certificate and asks Duane "to affix the seal of the Corporation" of the City of New York to the draft.

ALS, New-York Historical Society, New York City.
1. Duane was mayor of New York.

To Cornelius Hendrickson [1]

[*New York, 1786.*]"Mr. Laurence Kortright of this City has requested me to write to you concerning a suit in Chancery which has been depending between Mr Cornelius P. Lowe and himself [2] on a matter in which the estate of his brother to which You are an Executor is concerned; and in which suit Mr. B Livingston of this place and myself were employed as Council for Mr. Kortright. I send you herewith an exemplification of the Chancellor's decree by which you will see the principles upon which the affair has been decided." [3]

AL, Hamilton Papers, Library of Congress.
1. Hendrickson was a resident of St. Croix and the father-in-law of Cornelius Kortright, Lawrence Kortright's brother.
2. Lawrence Kortright and Cornelius P. Low were New York City merchants.
3. The last page of this letter is missing.

Notes on the History of North and South America

Introductory Note

These Notes, which Hamilton divided into two parts entitled "Notes on the History of North America" and "Notes on the History of South America," were prepared for a brief which he used in a case involving a land controversy between Massachusetts and New York. Some students of Hamilton have mistakenly assumed that these notes were prepared while Hamilton was a student in 1773 at the school maintained by Francis Barber in Elizabethtown, New Jersey. The basis of this error is undoubtedly the following note, in an unidentified handwriting, affixed to these Notes: "Early Geographical & Political Notices on U States by AH. exd. by F.B." For the brief for which these notes were in reality prepared, see Julius Goebel, Jr., ed., *The Legal Papers of Alexander Hamilton.*

The controversy between New York and Massachusetts involved western lands claimed by both states. As the Massachusetts claim was based on early charters, it was, in the words of a New York delegate to the Continental Congress, "a State Pretention which has laid dormant more than One Hundred and fifty Years" (Burnett, *Letters,* VII, 340, note 4). In 1783, Massachusetts's claim was reasserted. "We were not a little surprised," James Duane and Ezra L'Hommedieu wrote to George Clinton, "lately to hear the Delegates for the Massachusets seriously mention on the Floar of Congress The Claim of that State to the western Lands in the state of New York, and declare they had Instructions from their State on every Occasion to assert that Claim, and prevent any Act of Congress from passing which might be construed in favour of the Title of New York in preference to that of the Massachusets" (Burnett, *Letters,* VII, 340). In the spring of 1784, the Commonwealth of Massachusetts petitioned the Continental Congress to appoint a Federal court to decide the controversy. Congress assigned the first Monday in December, 1784, for the appearance of the agents of Massachusetts and New York "at the place in which Congress shall then be sitting" (*JCC,* XXVII, 547). The legislature of New York appointed James Duane, John Jay, Robert R. Livingston, Egbert Benson, and Walter Livingston agents for the state and authorized them to employ counsel (*Laws of the State of New York,* II, 5). On June 9, 1785, they named Hamilton and Samuel Jones "counsellors and solicitors on the part of this state" (see James Duane, John Jay, and Robert R. Livingston to Hamilton and Jones, June 9, 1785). Jones presumably refused the appointment (see Hamilton to Jones, June 9, 1785). Massachusetts appointed John Lowell, James Sullivan, Theophilus Parsons, and Rufus King, and in its May session the General Court empowered "the agents appointed by this government, to defend the territory on the West Side of Hudson's River, against the claims of the State of New York" (*Acts and Laws of the Commonwealth of Massachusetts, 1786–1787* [Boston, 1893], 53).

When the agents assembled at Trenton, where Congress was then sitting, they agreed on the men who should compose the Federal court. James Duane, one of the New York agents, wrote to Colonel Robert Livingston on January 6, 1785:

". . . we agreed on nine Gentlemen to be our Judges any five to form a quorum. Mr. Robt. Hanson Harrison, Chief Justice of Maryland (formerly Secretary to General Washington) was named by both parties. Mr. Tho. Johnson an eminent Lawyer lately Governour of Maryland, Mr. George Reade of Delaware, Mr. Isaac Smith one of the Judges and Mr. William Patterson late Attorney General both of New Jersey were nominated by us, and by Massachusetts Mr. John Rutledge late Governour of South Carolina, Mr. George Wythe Chancellor of Virginia and Mr. William Grason and Mr. James Monroe of the same State." (Burnett, *Letters*, VIII, 10, note 2.)

The first Tuesday in June, 1785, was agreed on for the opening of the court. It was soon evident, however, that no court could convene at such an early date, for it proved impossible to find five judges who would agree to hear the case. Harrison, Grayson, and Rutledge, for example, refused to serve and it was necessary to appoint judges in their places. (For acceptances, declinations, and new appointments, see *JCC*, XXVIII, 125n, 181, 181n, 182, 187n, 199, 211, 320, 351–52, 440–41; XXIX, 582, 707n, 776–77.) The convening of the court was therefore postponed until November 15, but, again because of the absence of a quorum, the hearing was deferred.

It became apparent, as the passing months proved it impossible to convene a court, that New York and Massachusetts must themselves decide the issue. In 1786, both states passed acts providing for the settlement of the controversy without recourse to the Federal courts. The Massachusetts agents proposed on September 7, 1786, that the agents of the two states meet at Newport, Hartford, or New Haven to settle the controversy; the New York agents selected Hartford and suggested November 6 as the date for the conference. The meeting finally convened on November 30. (See Burnett, *Letters*, VIII, 509, for references to the negotiations that took place between the agents.)

The conferees at Hartford agreed that New York should have "sovereignty and jurisdiction" of the disputed area and that Massachusetts should have "the right of preemption of the soil from the native Indians" (*JCC*, XXXIII, 623). The text of the agreement was, on motion of Nathan Dane, the Massachusetts delegate, printed in the *Journals of the Continental Congress* under date of October 8, 1787.

On January 13, 1787, Governor George Clinton announced to the New York legislature that the boundary dispute with Massachusetts had been settled "otherwise than by a Fœderal Court" by commissioners of New York (New York Assembly *Journal*, 1787, 6). The matter ceased to be of congressional concern after the adoption of a motion "that all further proceedings in and relative to the said federal court as also the commissions of the judges thereof cease and determine" (*JCC*, XXXIII, 619).

It is impossible to determine for how long Hamilton was the counsel for the New York commissioners. His bill to the state for "services in examining the controversy collecting testimony and drawing brief for the hearing" was submitted on November 18, 1788, and paid on April 14, 1789. He may have served as legal adviser from June, 1785 (see James Duane *et al.* to Hamilton and Samuel Jones, June 9, 1785), until the termination of the dispute December 16, 1786. It is more probable that he drew up his brief in the weeks or months following his commission as counsel from the New York agents, for when he was employed, the agents believed the dispute would be settled by a Federal court that would convene as soon as the requisite number of proposed judges had agreed to serve.

NOTES ON THE HISTORY OF NORTH AMERICA

[December, 1786]

North America

Purchase[1] Vol 5 Page 809 § 2 [2]
50. 60 [3]——

The Map of Sebastian Cabot cut by Clement Adam relateth that John Cabot a venetian and his son Sebastian set out from Bristol and discovering the land called it *Prima Vista* and the Island before it St Johns. But (says Purchase) Cabot discovered all along the Coast as far as Florida.

Idem 814. 815 § v

In 1607 Henry Hudson discovered those parts to the latitude of fourscore degrees.

La Hontan[4] Vol 1 P. 211—

Frederick Aschild a Dane was the first discoverer of North America.

The discoveries in South America appear to have extended North to about the 35 degree of North Latitude.

Robinsons H of A[5] 2d Volume
Book 4 P. 2—Cites Herrera
Dec 1 lib VI c 16—[6]

In the foregoing period North America had been discovered from the coast of Labrador to the confines of Florida; by the *English* and *Portuguese*.

AD, Hamilton Papers, Library of Congress.

1. Samuel Purchas, *Purchas his Pilgrimage or Relations of the World and the Religions Observed in all Ages and places Discovered, from the Creation unto this Present. Contayning a Theologicall and Geographicall Histoire of Asia, Africa, and America, with the Ilands adiacent* (4th ed.; London, Printed by William Stansby for Henrie Fetherstone, 1626). The first edition of this frequently reprinted work was in 1613. The fourth edition, 1626, appeared as a supplementary (or fifth) volume to Purchas's *Pilgrimes* which was published in 1625 (Samuel Purchas, *Purchas his Pilgrimes* . . . , 4 Vols. [London, Printed by W. Stansby, 1625]). Although it is not possible to determine which edition H used, his page references correspond to those of the fourth edition. All references to Purchas in the notes are to this edition.

2. This sign refers to parts or subdivisions of chapters. The reference here is to Book 8, Ch. 3, Part 2. H omitted the chapter number.

3. A reference to paragraph numbers.

4. Louis de Lom d'Arce Lahontan, *New Voyages to North-America*, 2 Vols. (London, Printed for H. Bonwicke, 1703).

5. The first edition of this book was William Robertson, *The History of America*, 2 Vols. (Dublin, 1777). H may have used a later edition than the 1777 as his page references do not always agree with this first edition.

6. H copied the citation given in Robertson. The full reference is Antonio de Herrera y Tordesillas, *Historia general de los hechos de los castellanos en los islas i tierra firme del mar oceano*, 8 Vols. (Madrid, 1726-27).

Humes history of Eng[7] Vol 3
                        Anno $\frac{1497}{1498}$
  Page 335–336

Henry 7 sent Sebastian Cabott (a *Venetian*) in quest of Discoveries who fell in with the main land of NA about the 60° & sailed Southwards without making any conquest or settlement.

Hume Idem—   Anno 1502

Elliot and other Merchants in Britain made a like attempt.

Princes Chronology[8] NE   Anno 1600
Page 2

About this period the French and English begin to be competitors for North America. First they send to Fish and Trade and then to settle.

Purchase vol 2. 1677 No 10—[9]

Cabott discovered as far South as the 38° of NL.

Purchases Pilgrim vol 4 ⎱
P. 1809 No. 10 & 20— ⎰

Marginal Note[10] Corteregalis a Portuguese in 1500 & 1501 made voyages to *these parts.*

Idem—1812

First possession was taken by Queen Eliz in 1584. In 1585 Sir Walter Raleigh settled a Colony.

Idem Vol 5 § 2–50 & ⎱
            60 ⎰

Hints at discoveries in North America by Gasper Corteregale a Portuguese Stephen Gomez[11] a Spaniard and Sebastian Cabot.

Canada & Acadia or *New France*

Prince NE Ch: P 2

The French direct their views to Canada and Acadia.

Idem P. 37   Anno 1613

Had made settlements about Sagadahock at Mount Mansel St Croix and Port Royal. Dislodged by the Government of South Virginia.

Idem P. 94—   Anno 1620

Besides the natives the nearest plantation to the Plimouth settlers was a French one at Port Royal who had another at Canada.

Idem 111—   Anno. 1621

King James gives Sir William Alexander a Patent for Nova Scotia, extending from *Cape Sables* to the bay of *St Mary*, thence N to the River St Croix thence N to Canada River so

7. David Hume, *The History of England from the Invasion of Julius Caesar to the Revolution in 1688.* It is not known which of the many editions of Hume's work H used.

8. Thomas Prince, *A Chronological History of New-England in the Form of Annals . . .* (Boston, 1736).

9. The page numbers given by H correspond to the four-volume 1625 edition. No. 10 refers to the paragraph number.

10. The reference to the marginal note should read Vol. 4, p. 1807, paragraphs 30 and 40.

11. The name is given in Purchas as "Gomes."

down the River to Gachepe thence SE to Cape Breton Islands thence round to Cape Sables again with all seas and Islands within six leagues of the Western Northern and Eastern parts & within 40 leagues to the Southward of cape Breton & Cape Sables to be called Nova Scotia.

2 Vol Collection of Voyages and Travels [12] page 796—

Novr. 8.
1603

Patent from King Henry the 4th. of France to Monsieur De Monts for inhabiting La Cadia Canada and other places in New France dated as ꝗ Margin to extend from the 40 to the 46 degree of Latitude.

797

1604
1605

French visit *Cape Sable Bay Francoise* The River Lequelle Port Royal at which last Place they dwelt three years.

802

Quare

Fortify themselves at the Island St Croix in 44 degrees.

813
815

Visit the River Kennebecke & Cape Malabar.

816..............

Return to Port Royal

821 May 11.   1606

Mr. De Poutrincourt sets out from France on a new voyage.

828_____

In August arrive at Port Royal.

838_____

Mr. De Poutrincourt after several excursions returns to Port Royal.

Purchases Pilgrim
4 vol P. 1807 No. 30. 40. 50.[13]_____

French establishments at Quebec: *Champlains* discovery of the St Laurence & the lakes from the Gulph upwards 1200 miles.

1809 No. 10. 20.[14]_____

Sir Samuel Argall in   [15] dispossessed the French at Port Royal: they surrendered <--->.[16]

Purchases Pilgrim Vol 4
Page 1872—

Map: by which New France is laid down NW of Canada River New England on the South East terminating about 40 leagues South of cape Cod without including Hudsons River.

12. *A Collection of Voyages and Travels, Consisting of Authentic Writers in our own Tongue, which have not before been collected in English*, 2 Vols. (London, Printed for and sold by Thomas Osborne, 1745). H's references are to Volume II.

13. H's reference is incorrect. The information is from Vol. 4, Ch. 19, p. 1809, paragraph 10.

14. The reference is incorrect. It should be Vol. 4, Ch. 19, p. 1808, paragraph 10.

15. Space left blank by H because Purchas gives no date. Argall's expedition was in 1613.

16. MS mutilated. Purchas (Vol. 4, Ch. 19, p. 1808) says, ". . . rendered themselves to Sir Samuel Argall . . . giving up the Patent they had from the French King to be cancelled."

Idem Vol. 3 P. 857

Idem Vol. 5   825 § 3

Idem—   826

Idem   828—

La hontan Voyages Vol 1 ⎫
Page 7 _____   ⎭

   8 _____

  11 _____
  12

  18 _____

  19 _____

  23 _____

  25 _____

  30 _____
  34—⎫
  80—⎭

  38.39—

  70—

  92.
  206—

Hondius' Map of New France, *Montreal* &c.

Champlain made a Voyage to Canada in *1603.*

In 1604 Monsieur De Monts in consequence of a Patent from Henry the 4th of France for the Country from 40 to the 46 degree, visited those parts that *trend* Westward from Cape Breton; fortified Port Royal. "One of the Ports he visited was called Lanalet from a French Captain who had made forty two voyages there."

Mentions Quebec and a Lake in Nova Franica *threescore leagues long.*

Speaks of their arrival at Quebec in 1684.

Speaks of soldiers of the Regiment of Carignan who had been inhabitants there 40 years.

Quebec lies in the latitude of 47°. 12^{m}.

Description of Quebec by which it appears to have been an ancient settlement.

Trois Rivieres a town in latitude 46°. French had peopled the *St Laurence* higher up.

Montreal then settled in 45°. of latitude. The banks of the St Laurence well peopled.

Speaks of Indian Villages on the South side of Lake Ontario or of *Frontenac.*

Fort Frontenac was then built. Charles 2d. instructed his *Governor of New York* to advise the Iroquois nations to live in peace with the French.

Progress to *Fort Frontenac.*

Missilimakenack was then a French post. Letter from thence dated May 26. 1688.

Speaks of the Governor of New York in transactions with the five nations.

Letter dated from Niagara Aug 2. 1687.

Fort St Joseph then in existence.

"Canada reaches from the 39 to the 65 degree of latitude that is from the South side of Lake Erie to the North side of Hudsons bay & from the 284 to the 336 degree of longitude viz from the River Mississippi to *Cape Rase* in the Island of New found land." "I mean (says he) the countries in which the French trade with the natives for beavers and in which they have *forts* magazines Missinaries and small settlements."

"Tis above a Century and a half since Canada was discovered. John Verasan was the first discoverer." About the beginning of last Century a Colony was sent over from Rouen who effected a settlement. The Colony computed to contain 180,000 souls. *Acadia* extends from the River Kennebecca to *L'isle Percee* near the mouth of St Laurence.

N England

Princes NE. Ch. P. 2		The English Claim South and North Virginia—Newfoundland and Bermudas—Virginia extending from *Florida* to the bay of Fundy, The Northern part took the name of New England in 1614.
Idem P. 17	Anno 1606 } April 10.	King James by Patent divides Virginia into two colonies. The Southern between 34 & 41 he gives to *London Company*. The Northern between 38 & 45° N he gives to Plymouth Company forbidding to plant within 100 miles of each other.
Idem *P. 21*	1607 } May 11 [17]	Plimouth Adventurers under George Popham as President and Rawly Gilbert as Admiral form a settlement at the Mouth of Sagadehock.
Idem P. 25	1608—	This Colony breaks up & returns to England.
Idem P. 33—	1611—	Voyage by Sir Edward Harlie & Nicholas Hobson towards the same Quarter. Have a little Quarrel with Indians who assault the Ship & take some of them. "*No more speeches of plantations*".
Idem P 39 & 40—	1614	Capt John Smith makes a voyage to N Virginia, ranges the Coast along from Penobscot to Sagadehock, Acocisco, Passataquack, Tragabigzanda. Called Cape Anne the Massachusettes Isles. Finds two French Ships who had been there six weeks. Sails to Accomack thence to Cape Cod, sails for England, arrives at London, makes a map of the Country and *first* calls it *New England*.
Idem P. 43	1615 } July—	Two ships sent to Fish at N England.
44 · · ·	1616	A few ships sail for New England to Fish.

17. Prince gives the date as May 31.

220—

45		This year Eight volunteer ships go to New England.
47···	1617	Smith undertakes a voyage to settle in N England which bv contrary winds is frustrated. He is appointed Admiral of New England for life.
54—	1618—	Two ships go to Fish in New England.
60—	1619	Sir F: Gorges sends Cap Thos. Dermer on a fishing voyage to N England.
Idem P. 63—	1619	Capt Dermer sails from Monahegan (an Island) near Sagadahock along the Coast to the mouth of James River: passes between Long Island and the main.
	1620—	This year 6 or 7 sail go to N E to fish.
Idem P. 67—		This Spring Dermer returns to New England. Discovers many goodly rivers and pleasant coasts and Islands 80 leagues E from Hudsons River to Cape Cod, *but arriving at New England again* writes a letter &c.
		N B. NE does not appear to have been then understood to extend further Southward than cape Cod. This was the Southern extent of Smiths coasting when he gave the name.
Idem 70—	1620 ⎱ July—⎰	King James gives a warrant to prepare "a new Patent of Incorporation" *for the Adventurers to North Virginia* between 40 & 48°. North, stiling them the *"Council for the Affairs of NE & their successors."*
Idem—72—	Novemb 9—	The first adventurers from Plymouth made land at Cape Cod, stand to the Southward to find some place of settlement about Hudsons River, meeting contrary winds they get into the *Cape harbour;* where or in the neighbourhood they make a landing; but their design and patent being for *Virginia* & not New England, they enter into a compact and association for their settlement & government.
Idem—73—		
	Decemr. 31—	fix their settlement at Plymouth, the first English town in all that Country. Form of the compact dated 11 Nov. 1620. They conceived themselves in a state of nature.
Page 84 & 85—		
Idem P. 94—		Besides the Natives the nearest plantation to them is a French *one at Port Royal* who had another at Canada.
95—		The only English settlements were at Virginia, Bermudas & Newfoundland. In this year Nov 3 unkown to and unsought by the adventurers a Patent

was signed for the Incorporation of the Adventurers to the Northern Colony of Virg between 40 & 48 degrees of N Latitude.

Prince NE Chro Page 101	1621	*Treaty of alliance* with Massasoit the Great Sagamore [18] of the Neighbouring Indians.
111...	do.	Nine Sachems subscribe an Instrument of Submission to King James (in the neighbourhood of Plymouth).
112...	do.	Visit Massachusettes bay, get a considerable quantity of beaver and return home. The Sachem of the *bay* (though not the Massachusettes Queen) [19] submits to King James on condition of protection.
114.	do.⎫ Nov. 9⎬	Receive a letter from Mr. Weston in which he writes "We (ie the Adventurers) *have procured you a charter the best we could better than your former and with less limitation.*"
118—	Ano 1622	Make another visit to Massachusettes trade and return.
119.	Idem June—	Arrive at Plymouth two ships with Adventurers to form a settlement at Massachusettes for which *Weston* had procured a Patent. They remain at Plymouth during the Summer, and then go to *Weymouth* in Massachusettes.
125—	1623—	The Governor with some Indians go to Manomet a town near 20 Miles S of Plimouth—stands on a Fresh River running into a bay which cannot be less than 60 Miles from thence. Twill bear a boat of 8 or ten tons. Hither the Dutch or French or both used to come. Tis about 8 Miles to the bay of Cape Cod. The Sachem of the Place with many others own themselves subject to King James.
131. 132	*Idem*	The Massachusettes settlement breaks up this year.
133	Id:	Capt J. Mason, Sir F Gorges and others having obtained patents from the New England Council for different tracts they send over persons to form a settlement, who settle 25 leagues NE from Plymouth near Smith's Isles at a place called Little

18. "Their Great Sagamore Massassoit, the Greatest King of the *Indians* bordering on us . . ." (Prince, *A Chronological History,* 101).

19. "The Squaw Sachem or Massachusetts Queen" (*ibid.,* 112).

Harbour West of Piscataqua River near the Mouth.

141. Idem Sep.   Capt Robert Gorges & others arrive at Massachusettes bay to form a plantation. Pitches upon the place Weston had abandonned, to Wit, Weymouth.

144. Anno 1624.   This Plantation breaks up. This Spring Mr. D Thompson who had begun a settlement at Piscataqua removes to Massachusettes bay & possesses a fruitful *Island* & *Neck* of land.

151.   Idem   A plantation is begun at Cape Anne under the Plymouth people.

152   (1625)   This year Capt Wollaston & others begin a settlement at braintree in Massachusettes.

162.   (1626)   Sometime in the fall Mr. Conant with the settlers at Cape Anne remove to Salem & there establish themselves.

Idem   170   (1627)   About this year a patent is procured for the Massachusettes colony.

                1623
171— March 19   The Council for New England sell to Sir Henry Roswell and four five others the tract comprehended in the Massachusettes Charter (prout the Charter). "By the Massachusettes colony Charter & records it seems the three former wholly sold their rights the three latter retaining theirs in equal partnership with the said associates." Names of Grantees: Sir Henry Rosswell Sir John Young, Thomas Southcoat John Hunphry John Endicott & Simon Whitcomb.

180—   1629⎱
     March 4⎰   King Charles grants a patent to the Massachusettes Colony to the above named & their associates. Note first the government is carried on in England.

192— Aug 29—   The Council of proprietors vote that the Patent & Government be transferred to Massachusettes.

        1630⎱
196— Jany 19.⎰   The Council for New England grant to William Bradford and others a patent for all the Country between Cohasset Rivulet on the North & Naragansett River towards the South &c. (prout the description).

Purchases Pilgrims Vol 4⎱
  Page 1830—[20] ⎰   There were disputes between the Virginia Company and New England adventurers decided in favour of the latter who obtained a *New patent.* "They were to have their grant agree-

20. The correct reference is to p. 1830–31.

Idem 1871...

Idem 1872.

Idem Vol 5 P 829⎱
　　　　　　830⎰ No. 50

Note He mentions
This present year *1616*

Collection of Voyages
and Travels 2 Vol

Douglass's Summary[21]
374

4 Purchase 1870

able to the liberty of the Virginia
Company the frame of their government excepted."
Charter to Sir William Alexander for
Nova Scotia.
Map in which New France is laid
down NW of Canada River, New
England SE terminating about 40
leagues South of Cape Cod without
including Hudsons River.
Speaking of North and South Virginia: "of the North (says he) our
method requires first mention. Ma-
wooshen was many years together
visited by our men extending between
43 & 45 degre[e]s &c."
These Northern parts (says he) are
lately called New England. "A map
1616　and discovery hereof was set forth
this last year by Capt John Smith. It
lieth between 41°. & 45ᵐ." He speaks
of Smiths Arguments for a New
Colony & expresses his hope of having
English colonies *renewed*.

P. 738　"In the year 1606 King James did
license a plantation there on condition
not to plant within an hundred miles
of each other."
In 1609 first settlement made on the
banks of *Saga de hoc* which lasted
only a year.
Shortly after a second settlemen[t]
was undertaken under Capt Hobson
which failed.
In 1614 & 15 a third and fourth voyage
was performed but neither with any
good success.
In 1620 the first successful settlement.
Originally, according to Capt Smiths
map approved of by the Court of
England New England extended from
twenty Miles east of Hudsons River
Northward &c.
The Indians affirm confidently that
New England is an Island and that the
Dutch or French pass through from
sea to sea between us and Virginia.

21. William Douglass, *A Summary, Historical and Political, of the First
Planting, Progressive Improvements, and Present State of the British Settlements in North-America*, 2 Vols. (Boston, 1755).

Woods New Eng Prospects [22] No. 1. 2. This book is No. 227 in the Pensyl library.[23] It was published in 1639 said to have been written in 1633. The author lived 4 years in the Country.

"The place whereon the English have built their colonies is judged by those who have best skill in discovery either to be an Island surrounded on the North Ride with the Spacious River Canada and on the South with Hudson's River or else a peninsula these two Rivers overlapping one another having their rise from the great lakes &c."

Pamphlet Intitled "Virginia richly valued" printed in 1650 by E Williams [24] No. 261 Phil Library.[25]

Same Ideas as to N England.

Virginia

Collection of Voyages
and Travels   P 740—

"Virginia is next adjoining Westerly to New Netherland."
It extends along the coast from 33 to 39 divided into two parts Northern & Southern.
Northern first settled in 1606 from 37 to 39.

Purchases Pilgrim Vol 3 P. 869
              Vol 5 Page 834 ⎫
              § 3 Part. 2.   ⎬

Hondius Map of Virginia and Florida. Virginia according to Capt Smiths account (whom Purchase speaks of as a discoverer of the Northern parts) extends between 34 & 44 degrees of North Latitude bounded on the East by the Great Ocean by Florida on the South on the North Nova Francia: Its Western limits unknown.
The Part planted in 1606 lies between 37 and 39.

Idem Page 853...

Title of Chap. 8 "Of the Countries situate *Westward from* FLORIDA and VIRGINIA towards the South Sea."

Idem 829 No. 40 & ⎱
     Marginal Note ⎰

Bartholomew Gosnold an Englishman discovered Northern parts of Virginia somewhere about 40°. 20ᵐ.

Idem 829 ⎱ No. 50—
     830 ⎰

Mentions Patent to Virginia from *30° to 45°* not to plant within 100 miles of each other.

---

22. William Wood, *New England's Prospect. Being a true, lively, and experimental description of the part of America, commonly called New England* (London, 1639).

23. This is a reference to the catalogue of the Library Company of Philadelphia (*The Charter Laws and Catalogue of Books of the Library Company of Philadelphia* [Philadelphia, Printed by Joseph Crukshank, 1770]).

24. Edward Williams, *Virginia: More especially the South part thereof, Richly and truly Valued* (London, Printed by T. H. for John Stephenson, 1650).

25. See note 23.

New York

Prince N E Chro: P 28	Anno 1609	This summer Henry Hudson an Englishman employed by the Dutch sails to Newfoundland and all along the Coast as far as the 33d degree of N L; now discovers Hudsons River (as supposed).
2 Vol Collection of Voyages & Travels Page 739		As [the bounds of] [26] New England *Westward,* and by the *South* ends with the Promontary Malabar so the Dutch Plantation begins here and extends itself most Westward & more Southward towards Virginia: was *first found out* in the year 1609 by Master Henry Hudson an Englishman employed by the States of the Low Countries, who after making the discovery returned to Amsterdam and was sent out the next year. Speaks of *Nassau* River by which he seems to mean Connecticut River.
	1611	

"On the North side of the Dutch Plantation springeth the River Machican called the Great North River" "There is yet another River bigger than the former called South River" described as the Dalaware.

Princes NE Chro: P 67	1620	This Spring Capt Dermer returns to New England meets with certain Hollanders who had a trade in Hudsons River *some years.*
Idem. 125.	1623	The Plymouth adventurers visit Manomet a town standing on a Fresh River 20 Miles South of Plymouth. Here the Dutch and French used to come.
Idem. 165.	(1627)	About mid march (say March 9. 1627) The Governor of the Dutch Plantation writes a letter of congratulation and offer of service to the Plymouth adventurers. This letter is dated from Fort Amsterdam at Manhattans— "The Dutch had traded in those Southern parts divers years before the *Plymouth adventurers* came; but began no plantation till four or five years after *their* coming." A letter of thanks and acceptance of friendship is returned.

26. Bracketed information is quoted from *A Collection of Voyages and Travels*, II, 739.

172   (1628)   A second communication takes place—letters and commodities. Trade is carried on for divers years between the Plymouth people & the *Dutch colony*.

La Hontan Vol 1 Page 210⎫
              211⎭

Henry Hudson having obtained a ship from the Dutch discovered New Holland which is now called New York.

NOTES ON THE HISTORY OF SOUTH AMERICA[27]

South America

Rob. H of A B 2d P 73—

Christopher Columbus, *a subject of Genoa*, the first discoverer of America.

Idem   P. 83–84–86

After Different applications to the Genoese, to the King of Portugal, England & various disappointments he at last undertakes the voyage in the service of Spain & in 1492 set out on his voyage.

95

102

Idem 111. 112—

Octr. 12. 1492 discovered land—the Island of San Salvador—& afterwards several other Islands.

Idem 132

Febr. 24. 1493. Returns to Europe & arrives at Lisbon. Goes to Spain. Communicates his success to the Court.

Idem 140—

Ferdinand King of Spain obtains from Pope Alexander 6 a grant of all the lands he had discovered or should discover to the Westward of an imaginary line drawn from pole to pole a hundred leagues to the Westward of the Azores. All to the Eastward was given to Portugal. Bull signed at Rome May 4. 1493.

Anno. 1493
Princes Chronology New Engd.
Part 1 P. 2—

Idem 141 Anno. 1493

Columbus set out on a second Voyage, November 22 arrives again at Hispaniola.

Idem 163 Anno. 1496

Returns again to Spain And

Idem 169. Anno 1498

Undertakes a third Voyage. And

Idem 170—

In the same year discovers the Continent of America.

Idem 183.   Anno 1499.

Alonso Di Ojeda a private adventurer made a voyage to the same part of the Coast of the Continent—*Paria*.

Idem 184. 185

Amerigo Vespucci who accompanied Ojeda in this voyage and wrote an account had the address to make him-

27. AD, Hamilton Papers, Library of Congress.
    The complete titles of the books cited by H are given in the notes to the "Notes on the History of North America."

self be considered as the Discoverer
of the Continent & gave a name to it—
America.

Idem 187—   Anno. 1500   The Portuguese discover the Coast of
the Brazil; Cabral the Discoverer by
accident.

Idem 196   1501   Roderigo De Bastidas discovers all
that part of the Continent from Cape
De Veda to the Gulf of Darien called
Tierra Firmé.

Page 235.   Anno. 1509   Settlement on the Continent attempted by Ojeda. Ferdinand erects
two governments, one extending from
Cape De Vela to the Gulf *of Darien,*
the other from that to *Cape Gracios
a Dios.*

Page 242   Anno 1511   Juan Ponce De Leon discovered Florida.

Idem 251.   Anno. 1513   Balboa discovers the South sea by
a march through the Isthmus of Dar-
ien.

Idem 298—   Anno 1518   Grijalva discovers New Spain.
Collection of Voyages & Travels 2d.   Visits made by French & Spainards to
Vol. P. 743—   Florida from 1512 to 1542.

INDEX

COMPILED BY JEAN G. COOKE